QUALITY AND PERFORMANCE EXCELLENCE

Management, Organization, and Strategy

QUALITY AND PERFORMANCE EXCELLENCE

Management, Organization, and Strategy

SIXTH EDITION

James R. Evans
University of Cincinnati

CENGAGE
Learning®

Andover • Melbourne • Mexico City • Stamford, CT • Toronto • Hong Kong • New Delhi • Seoul • Singapore • Tokyo

CENGAGE
Learning

Quality and Performance Excellence, 6e
James R. Evans

First India Edition 2012

ISBN-13: 978-81-315-1728-4
ISBN-10: 81-315-1728-4

Cengage Learning India Private Limited
418, F.I.E., Patparganj
Delhi 110092
India

Tel: 91-11-43641111
Fax: 91-11-43641100
Email: asia.infoindia@cengage.com

Cengage Learning is a leading provider of customized learning solutions with office locations around the globe, including Andover, Melbourne, Mexico City, Stamford CT, Toronto, Hong Kong, New Delhi, Seoul, Singapore, Tokyo. Locate your local office at:
www.cengage.com/global

Cengage Learning products are represented in Canada by Nelson Education, Ltd.

For product information, visit **www.cengage.co.in**

Printed in India

BRIEF CONTENTS

Preface xi

PART 1 Foundations of Quality and Performance Excellence 1

CHAPTER 1 Introduction to Quality and Performance Excellence 3

CHAPTER 2 Frameworks for Quality and Performance Excellence 45

CHAPTER 3 Tools and Techniques for Quality Design and Control 97

CHAPTER 4 Tools and Techniques for Quality Improvement 134

PART 2 Performance Excellence, Strategy, and Organization Theory 177

CHAPTER 5 Competitive Advantage and Strategic Management for Performance Excellence 179

CHAPTER 6 Quality in Customer-Supplier Relationships 230

CHAPTER 7 Designing Organizations for Performance Excellence 265

PART 3 Performance Excellence and Organizational Behavior 301

CHAPTER 8 Quality Teamwork 303

CHAPTER 9 Engagement, Empowerment, and Motivation 334

PART 4 | Leadership and Organizational Change 363

CHAPTER 10 Leadership for Performance Excellence 365

CHAPTER 11 Performance Excellence and Organizational Change 393

Index 427

Bibliography
(Available on the product website)

CONTENTS

Preface xi

PART 1 Foundations of Quality and Performance Excellence 1

CHAPTER 1 Introduction to Quality and Performance Excellence 3

Quality and Performance Excellence 5 / The Importance of Quality in Organizations 7 / A Brief History 10 / Quality in Organizations 14 / Principles and Practices of Total Quality and Performance Excellence 22 / TQ and Agency Theory 35 / TQ and Organizational Models 37 / Review and Discussion Questions 38 / Cases 40 / Endnotes 42

CHAPTER 2 Frameworks for Quality and Performance Excellence 45

Foundations of Performance Excellence 47 / The Malcolm Baldrige National Quality Award 58 / International Quality Award Programs 70 / ISO 9000:2000 75 / Six Sigma 80 / Comparing Baldrige, ISO 9000, and Six Sigma 87 / Review and Discussion Questions 89 / Cases 90 / Endnotes 95

CHAPTER 3 Tools and Techniques for Quality Design and Control 97

Designing Quality Goods and Services 99 / Designing Quality Processes 110 / Process Control 115 / Statistical Thinking and Process Control Tools 118 / Process Design and Control in Action 125 / Review and Discussion Questions 128 / Cases 129 / Endnotes 132

CHAPTER 4 Tools and Techniques for Quality Improvement 134

Process Improvement 136 / Improvement Processes 141 / Tools for Continuous Improvement 145 / Breakthrough Improvement 155 / Creativity and Innovation 160 / Process Improvement in Action 165 / Review and Discussion Questions 168 / Cases 170 / Endnotes 175

PART 2 Performance Excellence, Strategy, and Organization Theory 177

CHAPTER 5 Competitive Advantage and Strategic Management for Performance Excellence 179

Quality, Competitive Advantage, and the Bottom Line 181 / Sources of Competitive Advantage 185 / Quality and Differentiation Strategies 188 / Information and Knowledge for Competitive Advantage 199 / Strategic Planning for Performance Excellence 202 / Strategic Planning for Performance Excellence in Action 217 / TQ and Strategic Management Theory 223 / Review and Discussion Questions 225 / Cases 226 / Endnotes 228

CHAPTER 6 Quality in Customer-Supplier Relationships 230

Customer-Supplier Relationships and Performance Excellence 232 / Principles for Customer-Supplier Relationships 236 / Practices for Dealing with Customers 239 / Practices for Dealing with Suppliers 248 / Quality Customer-Supplier Relationships in Action 252 / Customer-Supplier Relations in Organization Theory 254 / Review and Discussion Questions 258 / Cases 259 / Endnotes 262

CHAPTER 7 Designing Organizations for Performance Excellence 265

Organizational Structure 267 / The Functional Structure 268 / Redesigning Organizations for Performance Excellence 270 / Organizational Design for Quality in Action 286 / Comparison to Organizational Design Theory 290 / Review and Discussion Questions 294 / Cases 295 / Endnotes 297

PART 3 Performance Excellence and Organizational Behavior 301

CHAPTER 8 Quality Teamwork 303

The Importance of Teams 305 / Types of Teams 306 / Cross-Functional Teamwork 313 / Effective Teamwork 314 / Teamwork in Action 324 / Comparison to Organizational Behavior Theories 327 / Review and Discussion Questions 328 / Cases 329 / Endnotes 332

CHAPTER 9 Engagement, Empowerment, and Motivation 334

Employee Engagement 336 / Empowerment 340 / Employee Engagement in Action 349 / Motivation 351 / Employee Engagement and Theories of Motivation 355 / Review and Discussion Questions 358 / Cases 359 / Endnotes 360

PART 4 Leadership and Organizational Change 363

CHAPTER 10 Leadership for Performance Excellence 365

Perspectives on Leadership 367 / The Roles of a Quality Leader 371 / Leadership for Performance Excellence in Action 374 / Leadership Systems 381 / Performance Excellence and Leadership Theory 382 / Review and Discussion Questions 388 / Cases 389 / Endnotes 391

CHAPTER 11 Performance Excellence and Organizational Change 393

The Importance of Change 395 / Cultural Change 397 / Sustaining Quality and Performance Excellence 406 / Organizational Change in Action 416 / Organizational Change and Organization Theory 418 / Review and Discussion Questions 422 / Cases 423 / Endnotes 424

Index 427

Bibliography
(Available on the product website)

PREFACE

The American Society for Quality (ASQ) monitors news items reported in the press (you can add the *ASQ Quality News Today* "app" to an iGoogle website). What types of stories do we find? Food safety and toy recalls, health care, the automotive industry, and various product glitches dominate. Indeed, quality—or lack of quality—is a vital issue in everyone's life. That's why this book is relevant and important for today's students and future business leaders, as well as those already in the workforce. Understanding the principles of quality and performance excellence is absolutely essential for new graduates to succeed in today's highly competitive business world.

It is difficult for students to learn about these principles on their own, because there are so many different approaches to the topic. Although these approaches are similar, each has its own jargon and acronyms, which makes trying to penetrate the subject for the first time a difficult experience. Furthermore, most books about quality are not written with the needs and experiences of students in mind.

This book has three objectives:

- to familiarize students with the basic principles and methods associated with total quality and performance excellence;
- to show students how these principles and methods have been put into effect in a variety of organizations; and
- to illustrate the relationship between basic principles and the popular theories and models studied in management courses.

The book presents the basic principles and tools associated with quality and performance excellence and provides many illustrations and end-of-chapter cases that can be used as the basis for class discussion. Many cases focus on large and small companies in manufacturing and service industries in North and South America, Europe, and Asia–Pacific.

This book is organized so that it can be used as a supplement to textbooks for courses in management, organization theory, organizational behavior, strategic management and/or operations. The book also can be used as a free-standing introduction to quality and performance excellence in an elective course. Students who have had the basic courses in management and organizational theory and behavior will be familiar with most of the various management theories used to place quality and performance excellence principles in perspective.

CHANGES IN THE SIXTH EDITION

I like to think that I practice what I preach—that is, I listen to my customers! Many of the changes in this edition were suggested by users of past editions, and I thank them for their comments. The biggest change in this edition is a reorganization of the chapters to provide a more logical approach to the subject by introducing tools early as a part of the foundation of TQ.

As with previous editions, this book has been revised to maintain its student-friendly style and keep up-to-date with recent evolutionary changes in the quality profession. Each chapter begins with a "Performance Excellence Profile," highlighting a recent Baldrige recipient whose practices have particular relevance to the material in that chapter. Throughout the book, key content areas have been updated to maintain currency and contemporary thinking. Numerous new boxed examples and cases have been added throughout to illustrate key ideas and themes and provide students with opportunities for critical thinking.

ORGANIZATION OF THE BOOK

Considerable flexibility is built into the book to meet the individual needs of instructors. After the first two chapters, all others can be sequenced in almost any order. Unlike most books on quality, this one is organized according to traditional management topics. This organization helps students to see the parallels between quality principles and management theories in areas such as organizational design and leadership. In many traditional management books, quality is often presented as new or different, which it clearly is not.

Many quality principles are based on management theories that are familiar to teachers and students. The organization of this book enables students to appreciate the ways in which quality and performance excellence really are different from those theories.

The book has four parts. Part I, Foundations of Quality and Performance Excellence, presents the core principles of total quality and performance excellence, and begins to explain how they relate to familiar management concepts. It also positions quality thinking within general business management frameworks and strategy, and it introduces tools used in process management.

Chapter 1 introduces the concepts of total quality and performance excellence and their applicability to manufacturing, services, health care, education, and not-for-profits; the evolution of quality principles; and the modern principles of total quality and its relationship with agency theory.

Chapter 2 describes three major frameworks for pursuing performance excellence in organizations: the Malcolm Baldrige National Quality Award, ISO 9000: 2000, and Six Sigma, focusing on the value of these approaches in building performance excellence and evaluating their similarities and differences. The philosophies of Deming, Juran, and Crosby serve to motivate and provide a foundation for these frameworks.

Chapter 3 introduces process management and summarizes the most important tools and techniques for designing quality goods and services and for controlling quality in manufacturing and service operations. These include topics such as quality function deployment, failure mode and effects analysis, poka-yoke, statistical thinking, and statistical process control. It also discusses the role of creativity and innovation in quality, statistical thinking, and the effective use of such tools as statistical process control.

Chapter 4 focuses on tools for quality and process improvement, including kaizen, the Deming Cycle, Six Sigma DMAIC, lean thinking, the Seven QC Tools, benchmarking and reengineering, and creativity and innovation concepts. The chapter presents several examples of process management in action.

Part II, Performance Excellence, Strategy, and Organization Theory, introduces the importance of quality and performance excellence from a strategic perspective, the idea of customer-supplier relationships, and the role of organizational design.

Chapter 5 addresses the role of quality and performance excellence in organizational strategy for achieving competitive advantage, the value of differentiating organizations from their competitors, and approaches for doing so. It also discusses quality-based strategic-planning processes and strategic work-design activities. An important aspect of strategic management is the use of a "balanced scorecard" of metrics and information for data-driven decisions. This topic is also addressed.

Chapter 6 discusses the importance of customers and suppliers in a high-performing organization. It presents principles of customer-supplier relationships, practices for dealing with customers and suppliers, and examples of customer-supplier relationships in action and how they relate to organization theory.

Chapter 7 focuses on designing organizations to support a focus on performance excellence. It explains how high-performing organizations must differ from traditional functional organizations, approaches to organizational design, examples of organizations that have successfully redesigned themselves with a quality focus, and comparisons with organizational design theory.

Part III, Performance Excellence and Organizational Behavior, discusses the themes of teamwork and empowerment, and relates quality to the topics of groups and motivation.

Chapter 8 focuses on teamwork. It highlights the importance of teams in a high-performance environment and describes the various types of teams commonly found in such organizations, including Six Sigma project teams. It also discusses what teams must do to work effectively from an organizational viewpoint, presents some examples of teamwork in action, and compares quality-based team concepts to organizational behavior theories.

Chapter 9 develops the important concepts of employee engagement, empowerment, and motivation. This chapter describes the scope and benefits of employee engagement, why empowerment is important in organizations, principles for successfully introducing and sustaining engagement and empowerment, and examples of organizations that have done so successfully. Motivation is discussed in the context of organizational practices that support quality efforts. These concepts also are discussed in the context of popular organizational theories of motivation.

Part IV, Leadership and Organizational Change, deals with practices for making performance excellence a part of today's modern organizations, focusing on leadership and the journey to performance excellence.

Chapter 10 is devoted to leadership, the roles of a quality leader, examples of leadership in action, and relationships with traditional theories of leadership.

Chapter 11 concludes the book with a discussion of organizational change and learning, organizational culture, and approaches for sustaining performance excellence initiatives for the long run. It also illustrates some examples of organizational change in action and how quality-focused change relates to organization theory.

The bibliography, available on the book's Web site, http://www.cengage.com/decisionsciences/evans provides a number of references for students who wish to deepen their understanding of various aspects of these topics.

Because the topics in this book are presented in different orders in different courses, we have made each chapter as free-standing as possible. In most cases, students should read Part I first as an introduction to the basic principles and frameworks. After that, the chapters can be covered in virtually any order, allowing the instructor a great deal of flexibility.

INSTRUCTOR RESOURCES

Instructors' resources for this new edition of *Quality and Performance Excellence* can be found online at http://www.cengage.com/decisionsciences/evans. Here you will find instructional tools, including the instructor's notes, PowerPoint slides, and the Test Bank.

ACKNOWLEDGMENTS

I wish to acknowledge my friend and colleague, Dr. James W. Dean, Jr., who was my coauthor of this book in its early editions and who was instrumental in defining its design and character, and for integrating the concepts of quality with traditional theories of management and organizations.

For previous editions, we are especially grateful to the many reviewers who provided comments and suggestions for improvement. They are:

Phyllis Alderdice, Jefferson Community College
Mohsen Attaran, California State University—Bakersfield
Victor Berardi, Kent State University
George Bertish, University of Central Florida
Dr. Joseph D. Bono, Barry University
Gary Bragar, Bloomfield College
Frank Carothers, Somerset Community College

Robert Carver, Stonehill College
Elia Chepaitis, Fairfield University
Tim Davis, Cleveland State University
Kevin Van Dewark, Humphreys College
Dean Elmuti, Eastern Illinois University
Elizabeth Evans, Concordia College
Lou Firenze, Northwood University
Mark Goudreau, Johnson & Wales University
Marjorie Hance, College of St. Catherine
Jodi Harrison, Northwood University
John Hironaka, California State University Sacramento
Jane Humble, Arizona State University
Santiago Ibarreche, University of Texas—El Paso
Yunus Kathawala, Eastern Illinois University
Kathleen Kerstetter, Davenport University
Dan Kipley, Azusa Pacific University
Dr. Kees Rietsema, Devry
Malcolm Keif, Cal Poly State University
Patrick Lee, Fairfield University
Roger McHaney, Kansas State University
Jalane Meloun, Barry University
Ellen Mink, Kentuckt Community and Technical College System
Connie Morrow, Somerset Community College
David Murphy, Madisonville Community College
Judi Neal, University of New Haven
Ken Paetsch, Cleveland State University
Dr. Michael Provitera, Barry University
Stanley Ross, Bridgewater State College
Mark Schuver, Purdue University
Kris Sperstad, Chippewa Valley Technical College
Matthew P. Stephens, Purdue University
Scott Stevens, Eastern Illinois University
Walter Tucker, Eastern Michigan University
Oya Tukel, Cleveland State University
Ryan Underdown, Lamar University
Thomas Velasco, Southern Illinois University
Larry Williamson, Pittsburgh State University
Nesa Wu, Eastern Michigan University

Finally, we greatly appreciate the help of our editors at Cengage Learning, Charles McCormick Jr. and Elizabeth Lowry, as well as our former editors at West Publishing Company and South-Western Publishing, Richard Fenton, Esther Craig, and Alice Denny.

I believe, like many business and academic leaders, that quality is an absolute essential not only for competitive success in business but also for meaningful work and integrity in many aspects of life. If this book helps students to contribute to the quality of their organizations' products and services and to understand the importance of quality in all their endeavors, then our efforts will have been worthwhile.

If you have any suggestions for improvement or perhaps a good story or case to contribute to the next edition, we would love to hear from you and acknowledge your contribution in the next edition. Please feel free to contact the author via e-mail at James.Evans@UC.edu.

James R. Evans

Foundations of Quality and Performance Excellence

PART 1

CHAPTER 1 Introduction to Quality and Performance Excellence 3

CHAPTER 2 Frameworks for Quality and Performance Excellence 45

CHAPTER 3 Tools and Techniques for Quality Design and Control 97

CHAPTER 4 Tools and Techniques for Quality Improvement 134

INTRODUCTION TO QUALITY AND PERFORMANCE EXCELLENCE

CHAPTER 1

Performance Excellence Profile: Poudre Valley Health System[1]

Poudre Valley Health System (PVHS) is a locally owned and private not-for-profit health care organization serving residents of northern Colorado, Nebraska, and Wyoming. In two acute care hospitals and a network of other facilities, PVHS offers a full spectrum of health care services, including emergency/urgent, intensive, medical/surgical, maternal/child, oncology, and orthopedic care. Founded in 1925 as the Poudre Valley Hospital (PVH) in Fort Collins, Colorado, the hospital expanded and diversified its services and has become PVHS—a regional medical hub with a service area covering 50,000 square miles. The focus areas of PVHS services include (1) Colorado's third largest cardiac center; (2) the only Level IIIa neonatal intensive care unit between Denver and Billings, Montana; (3) Level II and III trauma centers; and (4) a bariatric surgery Center of Excellence. The system's mission is to remain independent while providing innovative, comprehensive care of the highest quality, and exceeding customer expectations. Its vision is to provide world-class health care.

To meet its mission and attain its vision, senior leaders have built a culture that encourages high performance and satisfaction by engaging the workforce of 4,200 staff, 550 credentialed physicians, and 800 volunteers. Communication begins with new-employee orientation and continues with an open-door policy, a variety of paths for development, and many sharing opportunities. From design of new services to bedside care, PVHS uses interdisciplinary teams to meet patient needs. For example, a trauma resuscitation team of physicians, nurses, respiratory therapists, and radiology technologists is on call 24/7, and an interdisciplinary care team led by a trauma surgeon makes daily rounds to see trauma patients. These teams demonstrate "the best collaboration of nurses and doctors, relative to any trauma program in the United States," according to a recent survey team by the American College of Surgeons. In 2008, the system's overall staff voluntary turnover rate decreased to 8 percent, well below that of competitors, and reached the Healthcare Human Resources Administration's top 10 percent performance level. The system's overall employee satisfaction ranks in the 97th percentile nationally, and *Modern Healthcare* magazine named PVHS as one of "America's 100 Best Places to Work in Healthcare" in 2008.

Partnering relationships help PVHS focus on the future and turn competitors into allies. After first establishing relationships with physicians, PVHS expanded its partner base to include entities such as home health agencies, a long-term care provider, community health organizations, and a health plan administrator—a partnership that saves local employers $5 million each year. A partnership with a community hospital in Scottsbluff, Nebraska, led to the building of a new hospital. During the planning of this facility, PVHS listened closely to its customers, which led to improved emergency room layout, private patient rooms with spectacular mountain views and windows that open, healing gardens, and installation of family amenities such as showers and kitchens.

PVHS created a performance improvement system called the Global Path to Success (GPS)—a framework by which senior managers and staff integrate key processes. Using an innovative electronic Balanced Scorecard system, users can gauge progress on key measures relative to strategic objectives. If key performance measures are blue or green, PVHS is on track to accomplish the corresponding objectives. If key measures are yellow or red, an action plan—monitored by the appropriate senior manager—is developed to remedy the situation.

PVHS drives innovation by designing and testing innovative systems and technologies to meet health care needs. For example, PVHS was among the first health systems in the nation to use a robotic-assisted surgery system in four medical specialty areas and among the first 24 health systems in the world to integrate medical imaging systems across service lines. The Meditech Information System is a secure, user-friendly electronic network that ensures the flow of accurate, real-time information across the organization. To promote optimal patient experiences, PVHS uses the GetWell Network—an in-room, interactive patient education program that allows patients to obtain information about their care team, access the Internet and e-mail, communicate complaints and compliments, and order on-demand movies.

PVHS has received external verification of progress toward achieving its vision and goal. In 2007 and 2008, PVH was recognized as the nation's number one hospital for sustained nursing excellence by the American Nurses Association and the National Database of Nursing Quality Indicators (NDNQI). In RN hours per patient day, PVH has exceeded the NDNQI best quartile since 2005 and outperformed the American Nurses credentialing center's "magnet" hospitals' 90th percentile in 2008. For five consecutive years, PVH has been one of seven U.S. hospitals to be named a Thomson 100 Top Hospital (for superior outcomes, patient safety, and operational and financial performance). PVH and Medical Center of the Rockies (MCR) patient satisfaction scores surpass the national top 10 percent, according to the Center for Medicare and Medicaid Services. In 2008, PVHS received the Peak Performance Award—Colorado's highest award for performance excellence—making it the only organization to receive this honor twice.

In addition, the system's financial and market results validate its management approaches: In 2006, the average PVHS charge was $2,000 lower than that of its main competitor and $7,000 lower than the Denver metropolitan rate; and at 62.3 percent, market share in the system's primary service area is 42 percent higher than that of the closest competitor.

What does it take to create an excellent organization such as PVHS? The preceding profile provides some clues: a culture focused on quality, high performance, and meeting the needs of customers and stakeholders; a planning system that supports organizational goals, provides direction for improvement, and leads to innovation and "best practices"; and a commitment to supporting, developing, and engaging the workforce. In a nutshell, these represent the central themes of this book and apply to *all* organizations, whether they be health care, manufacturing, service, education, or government agencies.

In this chapter we will introduce you to the basic principles of quality and performance excellence. Specifically, we will:

- explain the concepts of quality and performance excellence;
- provide reasons why attention to these concepts should be a part of every organization's culture and management systems;
- provide a brief history of the "quality revolution";
- describe quality in manufacturing, service, health care, education, and government organizations;
- explain the fundamental principles and practices of quality and performance excellence; and
- discuss relationships of quality with organizational models in management theory.

QUALITY AND PERFORMANCE EXCELLENCE

People define quality in many ways. Some think of quality as superiority or excellence of a product or service, others view it as a lack of manufacturing or service defects, still others think of quality as related to product features or price. A study that asked managers of 86 firms in the eastern United States to define quality produced several dozen different responses, including:

1. perfection
2. consistency
3. eliminating waste
4. speed of delivery
5. compliance with policies and procedures
6. providing a good, usable product
7. doing it right the first time
8. delighting or pleasing customers
9. total customer service and satisfaction.[2]

Today, most managers agree that the main reason to pursue quality is to satisfy customers. The American National Standards Institute (ANSI) and the American Society for Quality (ASQ) define quality as "the totality of features and characteristics of a product or service that bears on its ability to satisfy given needs." The view of quality as the satisfaction of customer needs is often called *fitness for use*. In highly competitive markets, merely satisfying customer needs will not achieve success. To beat the competition, organizations often must *exceed* customer expectations. Thus, one of the most popular definitions of quality is *meeting or exceeding customer expectations*. This definition is reflected in the vision statement of Hollywood Casino Resort in Tunica, Mississippi: "Hollywood Casino Resort/Tunica is a place where guests feel invited and welcome. We provide the highest levels of personalized service and products for our guests, who always enjoy a fun-filled experience. Everyone at Hollywood Casino does the right thing right the first time, and puts the needs and wants of our guests in the forefront of every decision we make." Deer Valley Resort is another example of an organization dedicated to exceeding customer expectations (see box "At Deer Valley, Quality Is Not a Snow Job").

Customer-driven quality is fundamental to high-performing organizations. The president and CEO of Fujitsu Network Transmission Systems, a U.S. subsidiary of Fujitsu, Ltd., stated, "Our customers are intelligent; they expect us to continuously evolve to meet their ever-changing needs. They can't afford to have a thousand mediocre suppliers in today's competitive environment. They want a few exceptional ones."

Quality, however, should not be focused solely on the goods or services that an organization produces or provides. It should also be embedded in the management practices of the organization; in other words, quality should be an underlying value in how an organization is managed. If good management practices are designed and executed, then good results should follow. This leads to the concept of performance excellence. The term **performance excellence** refers to an integrated approach to organizational performance management that results in delivery of

At Deer Valley, Quality Is Not a Snow Job[3]

Deer Valley Resort in Park City, Utah, is viewed by many as the Ritz-Carlton of ski resorts, providing exceptional services and a superior ski vacation experience. The resort offers curbside ski valet service to take equipment from vehicles, parking lot attendants to ensure efficient parking, and a shuttle to transport guests from the lot to Snow Park Lodge. Guests walk to the slopes on heated pavers that prevent the pavement from freezing and assist in snow removal. The central gathering area by the base lifts is wide and level, allowing plenty of room to put on equipment and easy access to the lifts. At the end of the day, guests can store their skis without charge at each lodge. The resort limits the number of skiers on the mountain to reduce lines and congestion, and offers complimentary mountain tours for both expert and intermediate skiers. Everyone is committed to ensuring that each guest has a wonderful experience, from "mountain hosts" stationed at the top of the lifts to answer questions and provide directions, to the friendly workers at the cafeterias and restaurants, whose food is consistently rated number one by ski enthusiast magazines. "Our goal is to make each guest feel like a winner," says Bob Wheaton, vice president and general manager. "We go the extra mile on the mountain, in our ski school, and throughout our food-service operation because we want our guests to know they come first." It is no wonder why the resort is consistently rated one of the best in reader surveys of skiing enthusiast magazines.

ever-improving value to customers and stakeholders, contributing to organizational sustainability; improvement of overall organizational effectiveness and capabilities; and organizational and personal learning. Performance excellence is a characteristic of today's most outstanding organizations and is a requisite for providing high quality goods and services. All organizations—large and small, manufacturing and service, profit and not-for-profit—can benefit from incorporating these principles into their organizations.

THE IMPORTANCE OF QUALITY IN ORGANIZATIONS

Quality was THE buzzword among businesses—particularly manufacturing—during the 1980s and into the 1990s. Today, we generally do not hear much about quality except when things go wrong. Here is one example from the *Salt Lake Tribune*:

> One full-term infant died. Four healthy patients passed away unexpectedly after surgery. Another patient committed suicide. And dozens more left hospitals sick not from their illness, but from their stay: They fell down, were given the wrong drug and became infected from surgical equipment left inside their bodies. There were at least 89 of these most serious medical errors last year in Utah hospitals and surgical centers, up 56% from the 57 logged in 2007, according to a Utah Department of Health report ....[4]

Although many organizations don't talk about it as much, this example (as well as the many other recent global concerns over food and product safety, automobile recalls, software glitches, and the like) shows that quality remains a critical issue. H. James Harrington, one of the leading quality management consultants in the world and a columnist for *Quality Digest* magazine, observed

> From where I stand, CEOs around the world have lost much of their interest in quality.... we are more interested in reducing cost, removing waste, and reducing cycle time.... Maybe it's time we got back to basic quality measurements. We talk about getting to the root cause of problems. Well, I think we need to get to the root results of our actions by measuring the level of customer satisfaction improvement, the increase in mean time to failure, reducing percent defective during the first 90 days of usage, stopping product recalls, and lowering return rates—not dollars saved, inventory turns, or output per hour. We are trying to do everything for everybody, and as a result we are missing the real quality objective—better and better products and services.
>
> We need to take pride in what we do. When you go home at night and look in the mirror, will you able to smile and say, "I did my very best"? Too many of us stop short of being our best. We say, "That's good enough," never knowing how good we could be.... To make up for these sloppy work habits, we are using information technology to offset the lack of interest in the job and the lack of commitment to the organization.... What we need to do is get back to basics. The things that made us great in the first place are hard work, pride in accomplishment, technical education, and strong family values.[5]

Consumers today are intelligent enough to recognize quality issues that firms now face (see box "You Can Fool Some of the People Some of the Time ..."), and the organization that doesn't heed its customers is in for a rude awakening, or, at worst, a quick demise. This is why an understanding of quality is still vital to every employee in every organization. Joseph Juran, one of the most respected leaders of quality, suggested that the twentieth century would be defined by historians as the

You Can Fool Some of the People Some of the Time ...

Letters to the editor of *Business Week* show that quality is an important concern to consumers, and that quality guides their purchasing decisions: [Robert A.] Lutz and the other big hires will have to do more than spruce up GM's designs in order to regain market share. The new Cadillac CTS and other model changes will have very little effect unless GM buckles down to improve the quality of its products. As a longtime GM customer ... I have watched GM fall behind in product reliability and durability and just never quite get with it. Finally this year, I threw in the towel and reluctantly invested in a Lexus (September 17, 2001, p. 16). "Can the Nordstroms find the right style?" summarizes, in part, what my wife has been telling me for several years: The company has lost touch with its customer base. When a salesperson responded to an observation my wife made by telling her to write the company a letter—while telling her they had "100 letters on the same subject"—that tells you something (September 10, 2001, p. 22).

century of productivity. He also stated that the twenty-first century should be designated the century of quality. "We've made dependence on the quality of our technology a part of life."[6]

Stories of successful organizations generally end up in publications dedicated to quality professionals, which basically "preach to the choir." Here are just a few highlights of the results achieved by companies that have embraced quality and performance excellence as basic business principles but that have never made the pages of *Fortune* and *Business Week*.[7]

1. Among associates at Clarke American, overall satisfaction improved from 72 percent to 84 percent in five years. Rising associate satisfaction correlates with the 84 percent increase in revenue earned per associate. Annual growth in company revenues increased from a rate of 4.2 percent to 16 percent, compared to the industry's average annual growth rate of less than 1 percent over the five-year period.
2. Business satisfaction with the city of Coral Springs, Florida, has risen from 76 percent in 2004 to 97 percent in 2008; 90 percent of businesses would recommend the city to others, up from 82 percent in 2004. In 2006, *Money* magazine named Coral Springs as one of the Best Places to Live. In 2005, 2006, and 2007, the city was named as one of the 100 best communities for young people by America's Promise Alliance.
3. PRO-TEC Coating Company consistently achieves the quality expectations of its customers by delivering products with a defect rate of less than 0.12 percent and has scored better than its competition on product quality, on-time delivery, service, and product development. Its return on assets, a measure of long-term viability, has had a sustained upward trend since 2002.
4. Between 1999 and 2005, Sharp Healthcare gained more than four percentage points in market share, an unprecedented achievement in a mature health care marketplace. Sharp exceeds the national benchmark for first-year functional improvement following joint replacement, the result of a program that tracks parameters such as pain, function, deformity, and range of motion for 10 years following surgery.

5. In 2003, 2004, and 2005, North Mississippi Medical Center (NMMC) was recognized by Solucient, a leading source of information for the health care industry, as one of the top 100 performance-improvement leaders. NMMC is one of only four hospitals nationwide to be recognized for this distinction three years in a row. In 2006, physician overall satisfaction, measured by Press Ganey Associates, surpassed NMMC's benchmark by 8 to 9 percent, with overall satisfaction and ease of practice scores at 99 percent and leadership score at 98 percent.
6. The operating margin at Premier, Inc. grew from 35 percent in 2003 to 50 percent in 2006 and exceeded that of Premier's largest competitor in all years, while operating expenses have remained well below those of that competitor. Between 2003 and 2006, operating income per employee grew from $144,000 to $225,000.
7. Sales at MESA Products, Inc. have increased 93 percent since 2000, growing total revenues from $14 million to $27 million in 2006, and return on equity improved from −5 percent in 1999 to more than 25 percent in 2005 and presently exceeds that of industry competitors by 20 percent.
8. Drop-out rates, a measure of student satisfaction for students at Jenks Public Schools in Oklahoma, have decreased steadily from 6.3 percent in 1999 to 1.2 percent at the close of the 2004 school year.

Many more statistics like these can be cited, and considerable empirical evidence exists that firms implementing effective quality and performance excellence approaches improve their business results on measures of income, sales growth, cost control, and growth in employment and total assets (see box "Research Validates TQ Practices"). Nevertheless, scores of companies have either failed to take the first step in a performance excellence journey, or have let initial successes fade away because of lack of commitment and sustainability.

RESEARCH VALIDATES TQ PRACTICES[8]

Kevin Hendricks and Vinod Singhal published one of the most celebrated studies based on objective data and rigorous statistical analysis in 1997, showing that when implemented effectively, total quality management approaches improve financial performance. Using a sample of about 600 publicly traded companies that received quality awards and recognition, the researchers tracked the percent change in operating income and a variety of measures that might affect operating income: percent change in sales, total assets, number of employees, return on sales, and return on assets. These results were compared to a set of control firms that were similar in size to the award recipients and in the same industry. The analysis revealed significant differences between the sample and the control group. Specifically, the growth in operating income averaged 91 percent versus 43 percent for the control group. Award recipients also experienced a 69 percent jump in sales (compared to 32 percent for the control group), a 79 percent increase in total assets (compared to 37 percent), a 23 percent increase in the number of employees (compared to 7 percent), an 8 percent improvement in return on sales (compared to 0 percent), and a 9 percent improvement in return on assets (compared to 6 percent). Small companies actually outperformed large companies, and over a five-year period, the portfolio of award recipients beat the S&P 500 index by 34 percent.

A BRIEF HISTORY

To understand the importance of quality in business today, we need to review some history. Before the Industrial Revolution, skilled craftspeople served both as manufacturers and inspectors, building quality into their products through their considerable pride in their workmanship. Customers expected quality, and craftspeople understood it.

The Industrial Revolution changed everything. Thomas Jefferson brought Honore Le Blanc's concept of interchangeable parts to America. Eli Whitney mistakenly believed that this idea would be easy to carry out. The government awarded him a contract in 1798 to supply 10,000 muskets in two years. He designed special machine tools and trained unskilled workmen to make parts according to a standard design, measure them, and compare them to a model. Unfortunately, Whitney grossly underestimated the effect of variation in the production process and its impact on quality. It took more than 10 years to complete the project, perhaps the first example of cost-overrun in government contracts! This same obstacle—variation—continues to plague American managers to this day.

Frederick W. Taylor's concept of "scientific management" greatly influenced the nature of quality in manufacturing organizations. By focusing on production efficiency and decomposing jobs into small work tasks, the modern assembly line destroyed the holistic nature of manufacturing. To ensure that products were manufactured correctly, independent "quality control" departments assumed the tasks of inspection. Thus, the separation of good from bad product became the chief means of ensuring quality.

Statistical approaches to quality control had their origins at Western Electric when the inspection department was transferred to Bell Telephone Laboratories in the 1920s. The pioneers of quality control—Walter Shewhart, Harold Dodge, George Edwards, and others—developed new theories and methods of inspection to improve and maintain quality. Control charts, sampling techniques, and economic analysis tools laid the foundation for modern quality assurance activity and influenced the thinking of two of their colleagues, W. Edwards Deming and Joseph M. Juran, both of whom also worked at Western Electric in the first half of the twentieth century.

Deming and Juran introduced statistical quality control to Japanese workers after World War II as part of General MacArthur's rebuilding program. Although this was not much different than what was being done in America, there was one vital difference. They convinced top Japanese managers that quality improvement would open new world markets and was necessary for the survival of their nation. The managers believed in, and fully supported, the concept of quality improvement. The Japanese were in an ideal position to embrace this philosophy. Their country was devastated from the war, and they had few natural resources with which to compete, except their people. During the next 20 years, while the Japanese were improving quality at an unprecedented rate, quality levels in the West remained stagnant. Western manufacturers had little need to focus on quality. America had a virtual monopoly in manufacturing, and the postwar economy was hungry for nearly any kind of consumer good. Top managers focused their efforts on marketing, production quantity, and financial performance.

During the late 1970s and early 1980s, many businesses in the United States lost significant market share to other global competitors, Japan in particular. By 1987 *Business Week* posed a stern warning to American management: "Quality. Remember it? American manufacturing has slumped a long way from the glory days of the 1950s and '60s when 'Made in U.S.A.' proudly stood for the best that industry could turn out.... While the Japanese were developing remarkably higher standards for a whole host of products, from consumer electronics to cars and machine tools, many U.S. managers were smugly dozing at the switch. Now, aside from aerospace and agriculture, there are few markets left where the U.S. carries its own weight in international trade. For American industry, the message is simple. Get better or get beat."[9]

The "quality revolution" in America can be traced to 1980, when NBC aired a documentary titled "If Japan Can ... Why Can't We?" This program introduced the 80-year-old Deming, who was virtually unknown in the United States, to corporate executives across America. Ford Motor Company was among the first to invite Deming to help transform its operations. Within a few years, Ford's earnings were the highest for any company in automotive history, despite a 7 percent drop in U.S. car and truck industry sales, higher capital spending, and increased marketing costs. In 1992, the media celebrated the fact that the Ford Taurus outsold the Honda Accord to become the leader in domestic sales. Former Ford CEO Donald Petersen stated: "The work of Dr. Deming has definitely helped change Ford's corporate leadership.... Dr. Deming has influenced my thinking in a variety of ways. What stands out is that he helped me crystallize my ideas concerning the value of teamwork, process improvement, and the pervasive power of the concept of continuous improvement." Ironically, by the turn of the new century, Ford's quality had dropped to last place among American car companies, demonstrating that sustaining quality efforts is indeed a difficult challenge.

America woke up to the importance of quality during the 1980s as most major companies embarked on extensive quality improvement campaigns. In 1984, the U.S. government designated October as National Quality Month. In 1987—some 34 years after Japan established the Deming Prize—Congress established the Malcolm Baldrige National Quality Award, spawning a remarkable interest in quality among American businesses. By the end of the decade, Florida Power and Light had become the first non-Japanese company to win Japan's coveted Deming Prize for quality. After the publicity that quality received from the manufacturing sector, the quality movement shifted to services. Companies such as FedEx and The Ritz-Carlton Hotel Company demonstrated clearly that quality principles can be applied effectively in the service sector.

During the 1990s, health care, government, and education began to pay increased attention to quality. As more public and government attention focused on the nation's health care system, its providers turned toward quality as a means of achieving better performance and lower costs.[10] One hospital, for example, lowered its rate of postsurgical infections to less than one fifth of the acceptable national norms through the use of quality tools. In 1993, Vice President Al Gore spearheaded the National Performance Review, an initiative driven by the need to improve quality, which made 384 recommendations and indicated 1,214 specific actions that the federal government should take to improve operations and reduce costs. In 1991, a consortium of professional associations, business associations, and individual businesses and universities incorporated a nonprofit group called the National Education Quality Initiative to improve educational processes through quality principles. Many local school systems, colleges, and universities made considerable progress.

Although quality initiatives focused initially on reducing defects and errors in products and services through the use of measurement, statistics, and other problem-solving tools, organizations began to recognize that lasting improvement could not be accomplished without significant attention to the quality of the management practices used on a daily basis. Managers began to realize that the approaches they use to listen to customers and develop long-term relationships, map out strategy, measure performance and analyze data, reward and train employees, design and deliver products and services, and act as leaders in their organizations are the true enablers of quality, customer satisfaction, and business results. In other words, they recognized that the "quality of management" is as important as the "management of quality." Many began to use the term **Big Q** to contrast the difference between managing for quality in all organizational processes and focusing solely on manufacturing quality (**Little Q**). As organizations began to integrate quality principles into their management systems, the notion of *total quality management*, or *TQM*, became popular. Quality took on a new meaning of organization-wide performance excellence rather than a narrow engineering- or production-based technical discipline and permeated every aspect of running an organization.

Today, the term TQM has virtually disappeared from business vernacular; however, the underlying principles of quality management are recognized as the foundation of high-performance management systems and an important factor for competitive success. Perhaps it is unfortunate that a three-letter acronym was chosen to represent such a powerful management concept. It is equally unfortunate that people generalize the demise of faddish terminology to the concepts themselves. Many organizations have integrated quality principles so tightly with daily work activities that they no longer view quality as something special. In contrast, many other organizations have barely begun.

Reasons for failure of quality initiatives are rooted in organizational approaches and systems, many of which this book addresses. As a former editor of *Quality Digest* put it: "No, TQM isn't dead. TQM failures just prove that bad management is still alive and kicking." The most successful organizations have found that the fundamental principles of total quality are essential to effective management practice, and continue to represent a sound approach for achieving business success. The real challenge today is to ensure that managers do not lose sight of the basic principles on which quality management and performance excellence are based. The global marketplace and domestic and international competition has made organizations around the world realize that their survival depends on high quality.[11]

Many countries, such as Korea, India, and China are mounting national efforts to increase quality awareness, including conferences, seminars, radio shows, school essay contests, and pamphlet distribution. Spain and Brazil are encouraging the publication of quality books in their native language to make them more accessible. These trends will only increase the level of global competition. Many other factors are changing how organizations view quality (see the box "What Will Influence the Future of Quality?") As Tom Engibous, president and chief executive officer of

Texas Instruments, commented on the present and future importance of quality in 1997: "Quality will have to be everywhere, integrated into all aspects of a winning organization." This is what performance excellence is all about.

What Will Influence the Future of Quality?

In 2008, the American Society for Quality identified seven key forces that will influence the future of quality:[12]

1. *Globalization*: Globalization is driving global supplier networks and the need to manage global quality platforms. Organizations are no longer bound by location and space. Likewise, entirely new consumer markets are being created—often by the Internet, which creates opportunity and concern. Globalization will influence trade policy and trading partners in new, unimagined ways.
2. *Social responsibility (SR)*: As organizations begin to realize that social responsibility is not only the moral thing to do but that it's also good for business, the world will continue to embrace SR philosophies and practices at an increasing rate. Consumers are demanding more knowledge of organizational practices, and corporate reputation will play a greater role in consumer buying choices. Organizations that seek to improve their practices will need to know the concepts, techniques, and tools of quality management in order to deliver on their goals. Issues such as ethics, transparency, social behavior, and the environment coincide with the broader considerations of SR and formulate what some have called a "triple bottom line" impact that encompasses people, planet, and profits.
3. *New dimensions of quality*: A new collection of quality-related competencies will be required if quality is to remain relevant in a rapidly changing world. Organizations are looking for leadership in innovation—the ability to develop new ideas and manage change. This necessitates the commingling of quality issues and innovation. The new model must function within the systems of organizations—not just be focused on products and services. Organizations must master change and these emerging capabilities or give way to smaller, newer, and more agile competitors.
4. *Aging population*: The world's population is getting older, and with that trend comes both problems and their solutions. By 2025, the majority of the population will be aged 60 or older. This aging population will push economies and organizations to respond to the resulting market needs. Older workers will leave the workforce, and organizations will be charged with replacing their skills. This, in turn, may cause traditional retirement to be redefined, as organizations seek to tap into the skills of those who have officially left the workforce.
5. *Health care*: A byproduct of the other forces on this list, globalization and the aging population have heightened the need and expectation for quality health care. Quality management can play an important role in health care by taking waste out of the system so that more people can benefit from it. On the positive side, advancements in biotechnology and nanotechnology will result in cures for diseases and prolonged lives. This will require increased focus on quality in the waste-free development of these technologies. Quality control can also help to ensure operational efficiencies in health care delivery.
6. *Environmental concerns*: The world has come to understand that much of the environmental damage that has been done cannot be reversed and that increasing consumption will put even more strain on finite resources. Quality control provides the concepts, tools, techniques, and standards to foster change.

(continued)

7. *Twenty-first century technology*: Technology's impact is difficult to forecast and will most certainly surprise us in terms of how it affects current models that we think we understand. Some believe technology will deliver solutions to energy, food, and water shortages and the need for clean air. Information technology and advances in genetics, biotechnology, and nanotechnology will change everyday life and drive our future state. A new, innovative definition of quality is required for this innovative age.

QUALITY IN ORGANIZATIONS

Managers of manufacturing and service functions deal with different types of quality issues; the following sections provide a brief overview of these issues. Although the details of quality management differ between manufacturing and service industries, the customer-driven definition eliminates these artificial distinctions and provides a unifying perspective.

QUALITY IN MANUFACTURING

Well-developed quality systems have existed in manufacturing for some time. However, these systems focused primarily on technical issues such as equipment reliability, inspection, defect measurement, and process control. The transition to a customer-driven organization has caused fundamental changes in manufacturing practices, changes that are particularly evident in areas such as product design, human resource management, and supplier relations. Product design activities, for example, now closely integrate marketing, engineering, and manufacturing operations. Human resource practices concentrate on empowering workers to collect and analyze data, make critical operations decisions, and take responsibility for continuous improvements, thereby moving the responsibility for quality from the quality control department onto the factory floor. Suppliers have become partners in product design and manufacturing efforts. Many of these efforts were stimulated by the automobile industry, which forced their network of suppliers to improve quality.

Manufactured products have several quality dimensions including the following:[13]

1. *Performance*: a product's primary operating characteristics.
2. *Features*: the "bells and whistles" of a product.
3. *Reliability*: the probability of a product's surviving over a specified period of time under stated conditions of use.
4. *Conformance*: the degree to which physical and performance characteristics of a product match preestablished standards.
5. *Durability*: the amount of use one gets from a product before it physically deteriorates or until replacement is preferable.
6. *Serviceability*: the ability to repair a product quickly and easily.
7. *Aesthetics*: how a product looks, feels, sounds, tastes, or smells.
8. *Perceived quality*: subjective assessment resulting from image, advertising, or brand names.

Most of these dimensions revolve around the design of the product. In designing the initial Lexus automobile for instance, Toyota bought several competitors' cars—including Mercedes, Jaguar, and BMW—and put them through grueling test track runs before taking them apart.[14] The chief engineer decided that he could match Mercedes on performance and reliability, as well as on luxury and status features. He developed 11 performance goals. The final design had a drag coefficient smaller than any other luxury car (resulting in higher aerodynamic performance), a lighter weight, a more fuel-efficient engine, and a lower noise level. Sturdier materials were used for seat edges to maintain their appearance longer. The engine was designed with more torque than German models to give the car the quick start that Americans prefer. Ford's director of North American interior design called the instrument cluster "a work of art."

Quality control in manufacturing is usually based on conformance, specifically *conformance to specifications*. Specifications are targets and tolerances determined by designers of products and services. Targets are the ideal values for which production strives; tolerances are acceptable deviations from these ideal values. For example, a computer chip manufacturer might specify that the distance between pins on a computer chip should be 0.095 ± 0.005 inches. The value 0.095 is the target, and $\pm$ 0.005 is the tolerance. Thus, any pin distance between 0.090 and 0.100 would be acceptable. A lack of defects has constituted quality in manufacturing for many years. Many studies comparing domestic and foreign products focus on statistical measures of defects. However, the lack of defects alone will not satisfy or exceed customer expectations. Many top managers have stated that good quality of conformance is simply the "entry into the game." A better way to achieve distinction and delight customers is through improved product design. Thus, manufacturers are turning their attention toward improved design for achieving their quality and business goals.

Quality in Services

Service can be defined as "any primary or complementary activity that does not directly produce a physical product—that is, the non-goods part of the transaction between buyer (customer) and seller (provider)."[15] A service might be as simple as handling a complaint or as complex as approving a home mortgage. Service organizations include hotels; health, legal, engineering, and other professional services; educational institutions; financial services; retailers; transportation; and public utilities.

Today services account for nearly 80 percent of the U.S. workforce. The importance of quality in services cannot be underestimated, as statistics from a variety of studies reveal:[16]

- The average company never hears from more than 90 percent of its unhappy customers. For every complaint it receives, the company has at least 25 customers with problems, about one fourth of which are serious.
- Of the customers who make a complaint, more than half will do business again with that organization if their complaint is resolved. If the customer feels that the complaint was resolved quickly, this figure jumps to about 95 percent.

- The average customer who has had a problem will tell nine or ten others about it. Customers who have had complaints resolved satisfactorily will tell only about five others.
- It costs six times more to get a new customer than to keep a current customer.

So why do many companies treat customers as commodities? In Japan the notion of customer is equated with "honored guest." Service clearly should be at the forefront of a firm's priorities.

The service sector began to recognize the importance of quality several years after manufacturing had done so. This can be attributed to the fact that service industries had not confronted the same aggressive foreign competition that faced manufacturing. Another factor is the high turnover rate in service industry jobs, which typically pay less than manufacturing jobs. Constantly changing personnel makes establishing a culture for continuous improvement more difficult.

The production of services differs from manufacturing in many ways, and these differences have important implications for managing quality. The most critical differences are:

1. Customer needs and performance standards are often difficult to identify and measure, primarily because the customers define what they are, and each customer is different.
2. The production of services typically requires a higher degree of customization than does manufacturing. Doctors, lawyers, insurance salespeople, and food-service employees must tailor their services to individual customers. In manufacturing, the goal is uniformity.
3. The output of many service systems is intangible, whereas manufacturing produces tangible, visible products. Manufacturing quality can be assessed against firm design specifications, but service quality can only be assessed against customers' subjective, nebulous expectations and past experiences. Manufactured goods can be recalled or replaced by the manufacturer, but poor service can only be followed up by apologies and reparations.
4. Services are produced and consumed simultaneously, whereas manufactured goods are produced prior to consumption. In addition, many services must be performed at the convenience of the customer. Therefore, services cannot be stored, inventoried, or inspected prior to delivery as manufactured goods are. Much more attention therefore must be paid to training and building quality into the service as a means of quality assurance.
5. Customers often are involved in the service process and present while it is being performed, whereas manufacturing is performed away from the customer. For example, customers of a quick-service restaurant place their own orders, carry their food to the table, and are expected to clear the table when they have finished eating.
6. Services are generally labor intensive, whereas manufacturing is more capital intensive. The quality of human interaction is a vital factor for services that involve human contact. For example, the quality of hospital care depends heavily on interactions among the patients, nurses, doctors, and other medical staff. Hence, the behavior and morale of service employees is critical in delivering a quality service experience.

7. Many service organizations must handle very large numbers of customer transactions. For example, on a given business day, FedEx and UPS handle millions of shipments across the globe every day, and banks process similar volumes of transactions. Such large volumes increase the opportunity for error.

These differences made it difficult for many service organizations to fully understand and apply total quality principles when it was the rage in manufacturing, although many have caught up admirably.

Many service organizations have well-developed quality assurance systems. However, they often tend to be based on manufacturing analogies and tend to be more product-oriented than service-oriented. Many of the key dimensions of product quality apply to services. For instance, "on time arrival" for an airline is a measure of service performance; frequent flyer awards and "business class" sections represent features. A typical hotel's quality assurance system focuses on technical specifications such as properly made-up rooms (see box "Knock Three Times"). However, service organizations have special requirements that manufacturing systems cannot fulfill. The most important dimensions of service quality include the following:[17]

- *Time*: How much time must a customer wait?
- *Timeliness*: Will a service be performed when promised?
- *Completeness*: Are all items in the order included?
- *Courtesy*: Do frontline employees greet each customer cheerfully?
- *Consistency*: Are services delivered in the same fashion for every customer, and every time for the same customer?
- *Accessibility and convenience*: Is the service easy to obtain?
- *Accuracy*: Is the service performed right the first time?
- *Responsiveness*: Can service personnel react quickly and resolve unexpected problems?

Knock Three Times[18]

Marriott has become infamous for its obsessively detailed standard operating procedures (SOPs), which result in hotels that travelers either love for their consistent good quality or hate for their bland uniformity. "This is a company that has more controls, more systems, and more procedural manuals than anyone—except the government," says one industry veteran. "And they actually comply with them." Housekeepers work with a 114-point checklist. One SOP: Server knocks three times. After knocking, the associate should immediately identify him- or herself in a clear voice, saying, "Room Service!" The guest's name is never mentioned outside the door.

Although people love to make fun of such procedures, they are a serious part of Marriott's business, and SOPs are designed to protect the brand. Recently, Marriott has removed some of the rigid guidelines for owners of hotels it manages, empowering them to make some of their own decisions on details.

Service organizations must look beyond product orientation and pay significant attention to customer transactions and employee behavior. Several points that service organizations should consider are as follows:[19]

- The quality characteristics that a firm should control may not be the obvious ones. Customer perceptions are critical, although it may be difficult to define what the customer wants. For example, speed of service is an important quality characteristic, yet perceptions of speed may differ significantly among different service organizations and customers. Marketing and consumer research can play a significant role.
- Behavior is a quality characteristic. The quality of human interaction is vital in every transaction that involves human contact. For example, banks have found that the friendliness of tellers is a principal factor in retaining depositors.
- Image is a major factor in shaping customer expectations of a service and in setting standards by which customers evaluate that service. A breakdown in image can be as harmful as a breakdown in delivery of the service itself. Top management is responsible for shaping and guiding the image that the firm projects.
- Establishing and measuring service levels may be difficult. Service standards, particularly those relating to human behavior, are often set judgmentally and are hard to measure. In manufacturing, it is easy to quantify output, scrap, and rework. Customer attitudes and employee competence are not as easily measured.
- Quality control activity may be required at times or in places where supervision and control personnel are not present. Often work must be performed at the convenience of the customer. This calls for more training of employees and self-management.

These issues suggest that the approach to managing quality in services differs from that used in manufacturing. However, manufacturing can be seen as a set of interrelated services, not only between the company and the ultimate consumer but also within the organization. Manufacturing is a customer of product design; assembly is a customer of manufacturing; sales is a customer of packaging and distribution. If quality is meeting and exceeding customer expectations, then manufacturing takes on a new meaning, far beyond product orientation. Total quality provides the umbrella under which everyone in the organization can strive to create customer satisfaction.

Quality in Health Care, Education, Government, and Not-for-Profits

One service industry that faces continuing pressure to improve quality—and one with the fastest-growing interest in quality—is health care. Quality has been a focus for the industry for some time. In 1910, Ernest Codman, M.D., proposed the "end result system of hospital standardization." Under this system, a hospital would track every patient it treated long enough to determine whether the treatment was effective. If the treatment was not effective, the hospital would then attempt to determine why, so that similar cases could be treated successfully in the future. The American College of Surgeons (ACS) developed Minimum Standards for Hospitals in 1917 and began inspections the following year. The Joint Commission on Accreditation of Healthcare Organizations (JCAHO)—the principal accreditation agency for health care—was created in 1951 through a collaboration of ACS and several other agencies to provide voluntary accreditation. Its mission is "to continuously improve the safety and quality of care provided to the public through the provision of health care accreditation and related services that support performance improvement in health care organizations." By 1970, accreditation standards were recast to represent optimal achievable levels of quality, rather than minimum essential levels of quality. JCAHO issued new standards in 1992 requiring all hospital CEOs to educate themselves on CQI (continuous quality improvement—the term used in the health care profession to denote quality initiatives) methods.[20] The new standards emphasize performance improvement concepts and incorporate quality improvement principles more fully in areas such as surgical case review, blood usage evaluation, and drug usage evaluation.

Other organizations, such as the Institute for Healthcare Improvement (IHI), have emerged to support quality improvement in health care. IHI's goals are improved health status, better clinical outcomes, reduced costs that do not compromise quality, greater access to care, an easier-to-use health care system, and improved satisfaction to patients and communities. IHI focuses on fostering collaboration, rather than competition, among health care organizations, and promotes the use of quality control tools that have proven to be beneficial in manufacturing. One early pilot project driven by IHI at 37 intensive care units resulted in huge drops in pneumonia and other complications, shorter patient stays, and cost reductions of up to 30 percent.

In 1990, SSM Health Care became one of the first health care organizations in the United States to implement CQI throughout its entire system. Five years later, after visiting manufacturing recipients of the Malcolm Baldrige National Quality Award and learning about their practices, SSM instituted a new leadership plan, improved strategic and financial planning processes, a new conference to share best practices among its hospitals, and an improved CQI model that permits rapid identification and correction of potential problems. In 2002, SSM became the first health care recipient of the Baldrige Award. Although many health care organizations notice measurable improvements from their quality initiatives, they primarily occur in the areas of cost reduction and increased efficiency. A difficult challenge that most face is getting physicians involved in the quality process. Many are requiring their participation on teams and steering committees, creating a liaison role between management and physicians, using physicians as champions, and targeting training.[21] Today, health care is the fastest growing adopter of quality management principles.

Education represents one of the most interesting and challenging areas for quality improvement (see the box "Quality is Elementary"). Attacks on the quality of education in the United States, from kindergarten through the 12th grade (K–12) and at colleges and universities provided a rallying cry for education reform during the last decade.[22] Jenks Public Schools is one of the more innovative school districts that applies the principles of TQ in managing its organization. Jenks Public

Quality is Elementary[23]

In the 1980s, several teachers and the principal at Frederick C. Carder Elementary School in Corning, New York identified a key area where they felt their students needed improvement—reading. They observed that students did not read much beyond what was required in the classroom. Students were handing in homework with numerous errors, and teachers were convinced that the kids could correct them themselves but that they simply didn't see the importance of doing it right the first time. The Carder faculty then developed a student-focused reading plan in which students signed contracts to read books they chose, give book reports, and record each book they finished. It was the teachers' responsibility to let their students know what level of work was expected of them: best work the first time. Students learned to ask themselves, "Is this my best work?" When it was, their efforts were displayed on the walls of the school and students were recognized for "Koalaty" work (using a koala bear mascot!). This approach became known as "Koalaty Kid," and students eagerly strove to become "Koalaty Kids"—to read more, do their best work the first time, and treat others with courtesy and respect.

Two quality professionals visited the school and immediately saw the parallels to total quality: critical issues had been identified, a plan for improvement was developed and implemented, clear expectations were communicated, a measurement system was put in place, and a consistent system of recognition and reward reinforced student success. Through their efforts and professional sponsorship, more than 800 U.S. schools and many overseas adopted similar initiatives. The real magic of Koalaty Kid is when students realize that using quality tools isn't magic at all. The students can explain how to use a quality tool and can chart their progress. They actually understand the patterns that they have and can say, "I did this, and this improved." Elementary school kids aren't always consciously aware that they're using quality tools. As one former teacher who helped schools implement the program observed, "I don't know if they'd ever use the words 'quality tools,' but they understand when to use a flowchart and they understand how a cause-and-effect diagram or a Pareto chart can help them. When I walk into a school and hear a first-grader or a fifth-grader explain to me how they've improved, it's awesome."

Schools (JPS) is the 11th largest public school district in Oklahoma. JPS has established four "pillars"—Strong Quality Leadership, Continuous Improvement, Customer Focus, and Systems/Process Focus—that serve as a foundation for the school district. Through the district's Strategic Planning Process, JPS senior leaders create a focus on the future, set organizational vision, values, goals, and strategic objectives, and ensure that site and department goals and action plans support the district's goals, strategic objectives, core values, mission, and vision.

JPS sets an expectation for performance excellence that supports its Pillar of Continuous Improvement. Continuous improvement is evaluated using four processes: the Performance Appraisal Review Process; the Comprehensive Local Education Plan (CLEP) in which sites include a Plan, Do, Study, Act (PDSA) component; the Performance Measurement System; and surveys and committee evaluations. JPS's key learning-centered system is determined by its mission of preparing all learners for productive, responsible citizenship in an ever-changing world and the Comprehensive Local Education Plan mandates of the state, which include continuous improvement cycles. JPS has adopted a team-based learning approach that has resulted in multiple awards and recognition of its students, faculty, and staff for a variety of achievements of its academic programs and services. Two classroom teachers were selected as Oklahoma Teachers of the Year; both received the Presidential Award for Excellence in Mathematics and Science Teaching, and a JPS teacher received the Milken Family Foundation Educator Award. JPS's system addresses students' education, well-being, and success by organizing curriculum and decision making around the entire period of a child's education, through the use of research-based instructional strategies and differentiation of instruction, by providing performance data to support instructional decision making and to keep parents informed, and by addressing safety, communication, teamwork, and educational experiences to develop character and citizenship. JPS is among the top 1 percent of schools in Oklahoma, and the dropout rates—a measure of satisfaction—have decreased steadily from 6.3 percent in 1999 to 1 percent by 2004 while faculty turnover has also decreased from 15 percent to 6 percent.[24]

Federal, state, and local government agencies have gained momentum in developing their own performance excellence programs and processes. For example, the Presidential Award for Management Excellence—the President's Quality Award (PQA)—is the highest award given to executive branch agencies for management excellence. The award was established in 1988 to recognize excellence in quality and productivity. In Massachusetts, a Quality Improvement Council was formed to oversee and facilitate a broad quality program. State quality award programs provide a basis for many state and local agencies to learn about quality and pursue performance excellence in the same manner as private business. In the state of Ohio, for instance, the Ohio Department of Transportation (ODOT) has implemented extensive quality improvement efforts that have earned multiple districts the state's highest award recognition for performance excellence from the Ohio Partnership for Excellence.

Not-for-profits, unlike their business counterparts, are not driven by the bottom line (although tight budgets can certainly be a driving factor in pursuing quality and performance excellence) and their managers often lack the business acumen and technical expertise needed to make an organizational transformation. Little literature exists on how to apply quality principles to not-for-profits, and employees use a "language" different from business, making it challenging for them to translate business concepts into meaningful applications. Among the key challenges that not-for-profits face are overcoming the fear of change, changing the mindset that not-for-profits are different and cannot effectively apply quality principles, identifying a vision and customers, understanding work processes, dealing with limited resources, and understanding relationships with government and large corporations.[25]

Nevertheless, numerous not-for-profit organizations are adopting quality principles because of their impact on the public and society—their major customers and stakeholders. The United Way of America, for example, began recognizing United Way organizations for quality achievements in 1994. The American Red Cross, for example, launched a multiyear, multimillion-dollar quality effort to enhance organizational effectiveness and improve its process of collecting, testing, and distributing blood. Their focus is to drive any variability, deviation, or error down to zero using initiatives such as the following:

- New technologies to reduce the potential for human error
- Restructuring and increasing the level of quality assurance staff
- Creating a more streamlined and comprehensive training system
- Reengineering the core manufacturing processes to make them more efficient and simplified so as to reduce and prevent errors
- Investing in facilities to enable more efficient and effective adoption of new technology[26]

PRINCIPLES AND PRACTICES OF TOTAL QUALITY AND PERFORMANCE EXCELLENCE

The philosophies of Deming, Juran, and Crosby addresssed management deficiencies of their times and laid the foundation for the principles of modern quality management that have transcended time. A definition of *total quality* was endorsed in 1992 by the chairs and CEOs of nine major U.S. corporations in cooperation with deans of business and engineering departments of major universities, and recognized consultants:

> Total Quality (TQ) is a people-focused management system that aims at continual increase in customer satisfaction at continually lower real cost. TQ is a total system approach (not a separate area or program) and an integral part of high-level strategy; it works horizontally across functions and departments, involves all employees, top to bottom, and extends backward and forward to include the supply chain and the customer chain. TQ stresses learning and adaptation to continual change as keys to organizational success.[27]

The term "Total Quality" is primarily a carryover from the heyday of the quality revolution. Some people continue to use the term today; some don't, preferring instead to use the more general term "performance excellence." Throughout this book we will use both terms somewhat interchangeably. However, don't let jargon get in the way of the basic principles that provide the foundation for organizational success!

In a classic research article, James W. Dean, Jr. and David E. Bowen characterize total quality by its *principles*, *practices*, and *techniques*.[28] Principles are the foundation of the philosophy, practices are activities by which the principles are implemented, and techniques are tools and approaches that help managers and employees make the practices effective. All must work together.

The principles of TQ involve some very basic management concepts: (1) customer and stakeholder focus; (2) a process orientation supported by continuous improvement and learning; (3) employee engagement and teamwork; (4) management by fact; (5) a strategic focus on quality as a source of competitive advantage; and (6) visionary leadership that views performance excellence as an integrated system. In the following sections we will briefly explain these principles and list key associated practices. Chapter 2 will present a variety of tools and techniques for performance excellence. In the remaining chapters we will elaborate on these concepts and also focus on the changes in organization design, work processes, and culture that must be made to support these principles, practices, and techniques.

Customer and Stakeholder Focus

The customer is the judge of quality. Jack Taylor, founder of Enterprise Rent-A-Car, the largest and most prosperous rental car company in the U.S., perhaps summarized the importance of a customer focus best: If you take care of your customers and employees, the bottom line will take care of itself. From a total quality perspective, all strategic decisions a company makes are "customer-driven." Organizations need to build relationships with customers so they will continue to use their goods and services and actively advocate for and recommend them; in other words, build *customer engagement*. Focusing on the customer also requires an understanding of customer needs, both current and future; effective strategies for listening to and learning from customers; and measuring their satisfaction, dissatisfaction, and level of engagement. A company close to its customer knows what the customer wants, how the customer uses its products, and anticipates needs that the customer may not even be able to express. It also continually develops new techniques to obtain customer feedback. Customer needs—particularly differences among key customer groups—must be linked closely to an organization's strategic planning, product design, process improvement, and workforce training activities. Banks, which traditionally have been rather customer-unfriendly—charging customers to speak to real people, for checking accounts, and for ATM access—have made some dramatic changes (see box "Banks Are Discovering that Customers Are People").

TQ views everyone inside the enterprise as a customer of an internal or external supplier and a supplier of an external or internal customer. Internal customers—the recipients of any work output, such as the next department in a manufacturing process or the order-picker who receives instructions from an order entry clerk—are as important in assuring quality as are external customers who purchase the product. Failure to meet the needs of internal customers will likely affect external customers. Employees must view themselves as customers of some employees and suppliers to others. Employees who view themselves as both customers of and suppliers to other employees understand how their work links to the final product. After all, the

Banks Are Discovering that Customers Are People[29]

Washington Mutual, known as "WaMu (recently acquired by Chase)," is leading the charge (no pun intended) and changing traditional banking practices to become more customer focused. In doing so, it has vaulted to become the seventh-largest financial institution in the U.S. and the number two home loan lender, increasing its assets by 18,000 percent since 1990. Being located in the same city as the Starbucks chain (Seattle), WaMu has drawn upon Starbucks' customer-friendly practices to make its operations more attuned to today's customer; for example, by hiring khaki-clad employees with retail experience and playing hip music in its "stores"—its term for its branches. Everyone works on commission, from the branch manager on down; a beginning teller can earn up to $50,000 in his or her first year. WaMu was named one of *Fortune*'s best places to work. Other banks are following suit; Bank One sent hundreds of employees out into the streets of Chicago to invite potential customers to visit the bank.

responsibility of any supplier is to understand and meet customer requirements in the most efficient and effective manner possible.

Customer focus extends beyond the consumer and internal relationships, however. Society represents an important customer of every organization. A world-class company, by definition, is an exemplary corporate citizen. Business ethics, public health and safety measures, concern for the environment, and sharing quality-related information in the company's business and geographic communities are required. In addition, company support—within reasonable limits of its resources—of national, industry, trade, and community activities and the sharing of nonproprietary quality-related information demonstrate far-reaching benefits.

Some of the more effective customer-focused practices for performance excellence are to:

- Identify the most important customer groups and markets, considering competitors and other potential customers, and to segment the customer base to better meet differing needs.
- Understand both near-term and longer-term customer needs and expectations (the "voice of the customer") and employ systematic processes for listening and learning from customers, potential customers, and customers of competitors to obtain actionable information about products and customer support.
- Understand the linkages between the voice of the customer and design, production, and delivery processes; use voice-of-the-customer information to identify and innovate product offerings and customer support processes to meet and exceed customer requirements and expectations, to expand relationships, and to identify and attract new customers and markets.
- Create an organizational culture and manage customer relationships to ensure a consistently positive customer experience and contribute to customer engagement, the ability to meet and exceed customer expectations, and to acquire new customers.
- Develop effective complaint management processes to ensure that customers receive prompt resolution of their concerns and which lead to recovery of customer confidence, enhance customer satisfaction and engagement, and enable aggregation and analysis of customer complaints to facilitate improvement.
- Measure customer satisfaction, engagement, and dissatisfaction, compare the results relative to competitors and industry benchmarks, and use the information to evaluate and improve organizational processes.

Process Orientation

The traditional way of viewing an organization is by surveying the vertical dimension—by keeping an eye on an organization chart. However, work gets done (or fails to get done) horizontally or cross-functionally, not hierarchically. One can no longer view an enterprise as a collection of separate, highly specialized individual performers and units loosely linked by a functional hierarchy.

A **process** is a sequence of activities that is intended to achieve some result. According to AT&T, a process is how work creates value for customers.[30] We typically think of processes in the context of production: the collection of activities and operations involved in transforming *inputs* (physical facilities, materials, capital, equipment, people, and energy) into *outputs* (products and services). Common types of production processes include machining, mixing, assembly, filling orders, or approving loans. However, nearly every major activity within an organization involves a process that crosses traditional organizational boundaries. For example, an order fulfillment process might involve a salesperson placing the order; a marketing representative entering it on the company's computer system; a credit check by finance; picking, packaging, and shipping by distribution and logistics personnel; invoicing by finance; and installation by field service engineers. This is illustrated in Figure 1.1.

TQ views the enterprise as a system of interdependent processes, linked laterally over time through a network of collaborating (internal and external) suppliers and customers. Each process is connected to the enterprise's mission and purpose through a hierarchy of micro- and macro-processes. Every process contains sub-processes and is also contained within a higher process. This structure of processes is repeated throughout the hierarchy. A process perspective links all necessary activities together and increases one's understanding of the entire system, rather than focusing on only a small part. Many of the greatest opportunities for improving organizational performance lie in the organizational interfaces—those spaces between the boxes on an organization chart.

Good practices that support a process focus include those that:

- Identify vital work processes that relate to an organization's core competencies and that deliver customer value, profitability, organizational success, and sustainability.
- Determine key work-process requirements, incorporating input from customers, suppliers, partners, and collaborators.

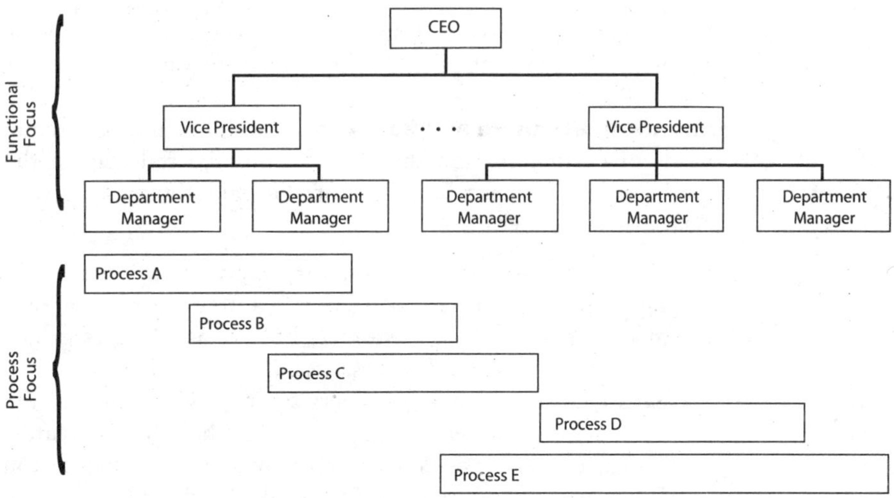

FIGURE 1.1 | PROCESS VERSUS FUNCTION

Source: James R. Evans and William M. Lindsay, *Managing for Quality and Performance Excellence*, 8th ed. South-Western Cengage Learning, 2011.

- Design and innovate work processes to meet all requirements, incorporating new technology, organizational knowledge, cycle time, productivity, cost control, and other efficiency and effectiveness factors.
- Minimize overall costs associated with inspections, tests, and process or performance audits; seek to prevent defects and service errors; and rework and minimize warranty costs or customers' productivity losses, as appropriate.
- Implement work processes and control their day-to-day operation to ensure that they meet design requirements, using appropriate performance measures along with customer, supplier, partner, and collaborator input as needed.
- Improve work processes to achieve better performance, reduce variability, improve products and services, and keep processes current with business needs and directions, as well as share improvements with other organizational units and processes to drive organizational learning and innovation.

The president of a former Texas Instruments division had a sign in his office that said "If you don't change the process, why would you expect the results to change?" Thus, management's job is to provide the leadership for continuous improvement and learning. Continuous improvement should be a part of the management of all systems and processes. "Continuous improvement" refers to both incremental and "breakthrough" improvement. Improvement and learning need to be embedded in the way an organization operates. This means they should be a regular part of daily work, seek to eliminate problems at their source, and be driven by opportunities to do better as well as by problems that need to be corrected.

Improvements may be of several types:

- enhancing value to the customer through new and improved products and services;
- improving productivity and operational performance through better work processes and reductions in errors, defects, and waste;
- improving flexibility, responsiveness, and cycle time performance; and
- improving organizational management processes through learning.

Improving Products and Services Careful research is required to determine the needs of customers, and those needs must be reflected in the design of products and services. A Japanese professor, Noriaki Kano, suggests that three classes of customer needs exist:

- *Dissatisfiers*—those needs that are expected in a product or service, such as a radio, heater, and required safety features in an automobile. Such items generally are not stated by customers but are assumed as given. If they are not present, the customer is dissatisfied.
- *Satisfiers*—needs that customers say they want, such as air conditioning or a compact disc player in a car. Fulfilling these needs creates satisfaction.
- *Delighters/exciters*—new or innovative features that customers do not expect. When first introduced, antilock brakes and air bags were examples of exciters. Newer concepts still under development, such as collision avoidance systems, offer other examples. The presence of such unexpected features, if valued, leads to high perceptions of quality.

The importance of this classification is realizing that although satisfiers are relatively easy to determine through routine marketing research, special effort is required to elicit customer perceptions about dissatisfiers and delighters/exciters. Over time, delighters/exciters become satisfiers as customers become used to them (as is the case today with antilock brakes and air bags), and eventually satisfiers become dissatisfiers (customers are dissatisfied if they are not provided). Therefore, companies must innovate continually and study customer perceptions to ensure that their needs are being met.

Improving Work Processes Quality excellence derives from well-designed and well-executed work processes and administrative systems that stress prevention. Improvements in the work processes may lead to major reductions in scrap and defects and, hence, to lower costs.

Improving Flexibility, Responsiveness, and Cycle Time Success in globally competitive markets requires a capacity for rapid change and flexibility. Electronic commerce, for instance, requires more rapid, flexible, and customized responses than traditional market outlets. **Flexibility** refers to the ability to adapt quickly and effectively to changing requirements. This might mean rapid changeover from one product to another, rapid response to changing demands, or the ability to produce a wide range of customized services. Flexibility might demand special strategies such as modular designs, sharing components, sharing manufacturing lines, and specialized training for employees. It also involves outsourcing decisions, agreements with key suppliers, and innovative partnering arrangements.

One important business metric that complements flexibility is cycle time. **Cycle time** refers to the time it takes to accomplish one cycle of a process—for instance, the time a customer orders a product to the time that it is delivered, or the time to introduce a new product. Reductions in cycle time serve two purposes. First, they speed up work processes so that customer response is improved. Second, reductions in cycle time can only be accomplished by streamlining and simplifying processes to eliminate non–value-added steps such as rework. This forces improvements in quality by reducing the potential for mistakes and errors. By reducing non–value-added steps, costs are reduced as well. Thus, cycle time reductions often drive simultaneous improvements in organization, quality, cost, and productivity. Significant reductions in cycle time cannot be achieved simply by focusing on individual subprocesses; cross-functional processes must be examined all across the organization. This forces the company to understand work at the organizational level and to engage in cooperative behaviors. **Agility** is a term that is commonly used to characterize flexibility and short cycle times.

Learning refers to understanding why changes are successful through feedback between practices and results, and leads to new goals and approaches. A learning cycle has four stages:

1. planning,
2. execution of plans,
3. assessment of progress, and
4. revision of plans based upon assessment findings.

EMPLOYEE ENGAGEMENT AND TEAMWORK

A company's success depends increasingly on the knowledge, skills, and motivation of its workforce. Employee motivation and success depend increasingly on having opportunities to learn and to practice new skills. These can be fostered by employee engagement, and teamwork. The traditional view of motivation is often summarized by McGregor's Theory X model of motivation: workers dislike work and require close supervision and control. TQ organizations support the premise of Theory Y: workers are self-motivated, seek responsibility, and exhibit a high degree of imagination and creativity at work. TQ managers provide leadership rather than overt intervention in the processes of their subordinates, who are viewed as process managers rather than functional specialists.

Much evidence exists that supports the role of good human resource practices in organizational performance. For example, one study of call centers found that quit rates were lower and sales growth was higher in firms that emphasized high skills, employee participation in decision making and in teams, and human resource incentives such as better pay and job security.[31]

Employee engagement simply means that workers have a strong emotional bond to their organization, are actively involved in and committed to their work, feel that their jobs are important, know that their opinions and ideas have value, and often go beyond their immediate job responsibilities for the good of the organization. Engagement is often manifest by *empowerment*, which simply means that people have the authority to make decisions based on what they feel is right, have control over their work, take risks and learn from mistakes, and promote change. For example, employees can make decisions that satisfy customers without a lot of bureaucratic hassles, and barriers between levels are removed. Empowerment requires, as the management philosophy of Wainwright Industries states, *a sincere belief and trust in people*. A survey by Annandale, Virginia-based Mastery-Works Inc. concluded that employees leave their organizations because of trust, observing that, "Lack of trust was an issue with almost every person who had left an organization."[32]

Many studies have shown that high levels of workforce engagement have a significant, positive impact on organizational performance. Research has indicated that engagement is characterized by performing meaningful work; having organizational direction, performance accountability, and an efficient work environment; and having a safe, trusting, and cooperative environment. In many nonprofit organizations, employees and volunteers are drawn to and derive meaning from their work because the work is aligned with their personal values. Thus, key practices that support this principle include those that:

- Understand the key factors that drive workforce engagement, satisfaction, and motivation.
- Design and manage work and jobs to promote effective communication, cooperation, skill sharing, empowerment, innovation, and the ability to benefit from diverse ideas and thinking of employees and to develop an organizational culture conducive to high performance and motivation.
- Create an environment that ensures and improves workplace health, safety, and security and supports the workforce via policies, services, and benefits.

- Develop a performance management system based on compensation, recognition, reward, and incentives that supports high performance work and workforce engagement.
- Assess workforce engagement and satisfaction and use results for improvement of workplace practices.
- Assess workforce capability and capacity needs and use the results to capitalize on core competencies, address strategic challenges, recruit and retain skilled and competent people, and accomplish the work of the organization.
- Make appropriate investments in development and learning, both for the workforce and the organization's leaders.
- Manage career progression for the entire workforce and succession planning for management and leadership positions.

The design of work and jobs in today's organizational environment often involves teams. A TQ philosophy encourages and facilitates teamwork and team development across the entire enterprise. Competitive behavior—one person against another or one group against another—is contrary to the principles of TQ. Effective reward systems recognize individual as well as team contributions and reinforce cooperation. The areas for teamwork and collaboration are broad, particularly in education, training, and meaningful involvement of employees in the improvement of processes that they affect and that affect their work. Teamwork can be viewed in three ways:

1. *Vertical*—teamwork between top management and lower-level employees.
2. *Horizontal*—teamwork within work groups and across functional lines (often called cross-functional teams).
3. *Interorganizational*—partnerships with suppliers and customers.

Vertical Teamwork Everyone must participate in quality improvement efforts. The person in any organization who best understands his or her job and how it can be improved is the one performing it. Vertical teamwork is the sharing of responsibility among organizational levels through empowerment. This often represents a profound shift in the philosophy of senior management, because the traditional philosophy is that the workforce should be "managed" to conform to existing business systems. Many organizations empower their people to act on ideas for improvement without prior approval.

Companies can encourage participation by recognizing team and individual accomplishments; sharing success stories throughout the organization; encouraging risk taking by removing the fear of failure; encouraging the formation of employee-involvement teams, implementing suggestion systems that act rapidly, provide feedback, and reward implemented suggestions; and by providing financial and technical support to employees to develop their ideas.

Employees need training in skills related to performing their work and to understanding and solving quality-related problems. Frontline workers need the skills to listen to customers; manufacturing workers need specific skills in developing technologies; and all employees need to understand how to use measurements to drive continuous improvement. Training brings all employees to a common understanding of goals and objectives and the means to attain them. Training usually begins with awareness of quality management principles and is followed by specific skills in quality improvement. Training should be reinforced through on-the-job applications of learning, involvement, and empowerment.

Horizontal Teamwork Problem solving and process improvement are best performed by cross-functional work teams. For example, a product development team might consist of designers, manufacturing personnel, suppliers, salespeople, and customers. Texas Instruments Defense Systems & Electronics Group (since acquired by Raytheon) employed corporation teams to work on corporate-level goals, employee effectiveness teams to prevent potential problems in specific work areas, and department action teams to solve departmental problems. Graniterock Company, with fewer than 400 employees, has about 100 functioning teams, ranging from 10 corporate quality teams to project teams, purchasing teams, task forces, and function teams composed of people who do the same job at different locations.

Interorganizational Partnerships Partnerships must be created both internally and externally. Companies should seek to build partnerships that serve mutual and larger community interests. Partnerships might include those that promote labor-management cooperation such as agreements with unions that entail employee development, cross-training, or new work organizations. Rather than dictating specifications for purchased parts, a company might develop specifications jointly with suppliers to take advantage of the suppliers' manufacturing capabilities. Internal partnerships might also involve creating network relationships among company units to improve flexibility, responsiveness, and knowledge sharing. External partnerships might be with suppliers, customers, or educational organizations. Partnerships permit the blending of a company's core competencies with complementary strengths and capabilities of partners.

Suppliers, in particular, are important partners who need vital information, product designs, performance feedback and assistance, and so on. The aim of the partnership is innovation, reduction in variation of critical characteristics of supplied materials, lower costs, and better quality. The aim may be enhanced by reducing the number of suppliers and establishing long-term relationships.

Management by Fact

Measurements provide critical data and information about key processes, outputs, and results. When supported by sound analytical approaches that project trends and infer cause-and-effect relationships, measurements provide an objective foundation for learning, leading to better customer, operational, and financial performance. Organizations need good performance measures to:

- lead the entire organization in a particular direction; that is, to drive strategies and organizational change;
- manage the resources needed to travel in this direction by evaluating the effectiveness of action plans; and
- operate the processes that make the organization work and continuously improve.[33]

Data and information support analysis at all organizational levels. The types of information and how it is disseminated and aligned with organizational levels are equally vital to success. At the work level, data provide real-time information to identify reasons for variation, determine root causes, and take corrective action as needed. This might require lean communication channels consisting of bulletins, computerized quality reports, and digital readouts of part dimensions to provide immediate information on what is happening and how things are progressing. At the process level, operational performance data such as yields, cycle times, and productivity measures help managers determine whether they are doing the right job, whether they are using resources effectively, and whether they are improving. Information at this level generally is aggregated; for example, daily or weekly scrap reports, customer complaint data obtained from customer service representatives, or monthly sales and cost figures faxed in from field offices. At the organization level, quality and operational performance data from all areas of the firm, along with relevant financial, market, human resource, and supplier data, form the basis for strategic planning and decision making. Such information is highly aggregated and obtained from many different sources throughout the organization.

A comprehensive set of measures and indicators tied to customer and company performance requirements provides a clear basis for aligning all activities of the company with its goals. A company should select performance measures and indicators that best represent the factors that lead to improved customer, operational, and financial performance. These typically include:

- customer satisfaction,
- product and service performance,
- financial and market performance,
- workforce performance,
- process performance, and
- leadership performance.

One of the many issues facing organizations today is how to manage, use, evaluate, and share their ever-increasing organizational knowledge. Leading organizations benefit from the knowledge assets of their workforce, customers, suppliers, collaborators, and partners, who together drive organizational learning and improve performance. The focus of an organization's knowledge management is on the knowledge that people need to do their work; improve processes, products, and services; keep current with changing business needs and directions; and develop innovative solutions that add value for the customer and the organization.

Some key practices for managing data, information, and organizational knowledge are to:

- Select, collect, align, and integrate data and information for tracking daily operations and overall organizational performance, including progress relative to strategic objectives and action plans, and using data and information to support organizational decision making and innovation.
- Select and ensure the effective use of comparative data and information.
- Review organizational performance and capabilities using effective methods of analysis to assess organizational success, competitive performance, and

progress relative to strategic objectives and action plans, and use these reviews to assess the organization's ability to respond rapidly to changing organizational needs and challenges.

- Translate organizational review findings into priorities for continuous and breakthrough improvement and into opportunities for innovation, and deploy them to work group and functional-level operations to support for decision making.
- Make needed data and information available and accessible to the workforce, suppliers, partners, collaborators, and customers, as needed.
- Ensure that hardware and software are reliable, secure, and user-friendly, and that information systems support the continued availability of data and information in the event of an emergency.
- Ensure that organizational data, information, and knowledge are accurate, reliable, timely, secure, and confidential.
- Manage organizational knowledge to accomplish the collection and transfer of workforce knowledge; knowledge from and to customers and other stakeholders; rapid identification, sharing, and implementation of best practices; and the assembly and transfer of relevant knowledge for use in strategic planning.
- Keep performance measurement systems, hardware, and software current with business needs and directions, and changes in the organizational or external environment.

STRATEGIC FOCUS

Achieving quality and market leadership requires a strong future orientation and a willingness to make long-term commitments to key stakeholders—customers, employees, suppliers, stockholders, the public, and the community. The success of market penetration by Japanese manufacturers evolved over several decades. A focus on quality as a driver of strategic business planning is characteristic of TQ organizations; in others we usually see an emphasis on finance and marketing. Strategic business planning should be the driver for quality and performance excellence throughout the organization. Measures such as customer satisfaction, defect rates, and process cycle times receive as much attention in the strategic plan as financial and marketing objectives.

Long-term organizational sustainability and competitiveness are key strategic issues that need to be integral parts of an organization's overall planning. A strategic focus on performance excellence addresses strategic and action planning, deployment of plans, how adequate resources are ensured to accomplish the plans, how plans are changed if circumstances require a change, and how accomplishments are measured and sustained. While many organizations are increasingly adept at strategic planning, plan execution is still a significant challenge. This is especially true given market demands to be agile and to be prepared for unexpected change, such as volatile economic conditions or disruptive technologies that can upset an otherwise fast-paced but more predictable marketplace.

Some key practices that support a strategic focus on performance excellence are to:

- Understand the organization's operating environment and its key relationships with customers, suppliers, partners, and stakeholders.
- Understand the competitive environment, the principal factors that determine success, the organization's core competencies, and the strategic challenges—business, operational, and human resource-related—associated with organizational sustainability.
- Gather and analyze relevant data and information pertaining to such factors as the organizations strengths, weaknesses, opportunities, and threats; emerging trends in technology, markets, customer preferences, competitions, and the regulatory environment; long-term organizational sustainability; and the ability to execute strategic plans.
- Develop and refine a systematic approach for conducting strategic planning and setting strategic objectives, including identifying blind spots, leveraging strengths, and addressing challenges over appropriate time horizons.
- Develop and align short-term action plans with long-term strategic objectives, ensure adequate resources and the ability to sustain outcomes, assess financial and other risks associated with the plans, and communicate them throughout the organization.
- Derive the human resource plans required to accomplish longer-term strategic objectives and shorter-term action plans that address the potential impacts on the workforce and potential changes to workforce capability and capacity needs.
- Identify key measures or indicators for tracking progress on action plans, ensure that the measurement system reinforces organizational alignment, and project performance of these key measures compared with competitors or comparable organizations to identify gaps and opportunities.
- Determine the organization's core competencies, and understand how they relate to the mission, competitive environment, and strategic objectives.
- View the work performed within the organization as a system, and make rational decisions about the mix of internal and external work processes that can best achieve the organization's mission.

Visionary Leadership

Leadership for quality is the responsibility of top management. Senior leadership must set directions; create a customer orientation, clear quality values, and high expectations that address the needs of all stakeholders; and build them into the way the company operates. Senior leaders need to commit to the development of the entire workforce and should encourage participation, learning, innovation, and creativity throughout the organization. Reinforcement of the values and expectations requires the substantial personal commitment and involvement of senior management. Through their personal roles in planning, reviewing company quality performance, and recognizing employees for quality achievement, the senior leaders serve as role models, reinforcing the values and encouraging leadership throughout the organization.

If commitment to quality is not a priority, any initiative is doomed to failure. Lip service to quality improvement is the kiss of death. The CEO of Motorola, one of the first Baldrige recipients, listed quality as the first agenda item at every top management meeting. He frequently left after quality was discussed, sending the message that once quality was taken care of, financial and other matters would take care of themselves. When The Ritz-Carlton Hotel Company opens a new facility, the CEO works alongside the housekeeping and kitchen staffs making beds and washing dishes. Imagine the message these actions send to the workers! Many companies have a corporate quality council made up of top executives and managers, which sets quality policy and reviews performance goals within the company. Quality should be a major factor in strategic planning and competitive analysis processes.

Many of the management principles and practices required in a TQ environment may be contrary to long-standing practice. Top managers, ideally starting with the CEO, must be the organization's performance excellence leaders. The CEO should be the focal point providing broad perspectives and vision, encouragement, and recognition. The leader must be determined to establish improvement initiatives and committed to sustain TQ activities through daily actions in order to overcome employees' inevitable resistance to change.

Unfortunately, many organizations do not have the commitment and leadership of their top managers. This does not mean that these organizations cannot develop a quality focus. Improved quality can be fostered through the strong leadership of middle managers and the workforce. In many cases, this is where quality begins. Leadership provides people with opportunities for personal growth and development. People are able to take pride and joy in learning and accomplishment, and the ability of the enterprise to succeed is enhanced. People are active contributors, valued for their creativity and intelligence. Every person is a process manager presiding over the transformation of inputs to outputs of greater value to the enterprise and to the ultimate customer. In the long run, however, an organization cannot sustain quality initiatives without strong leadership at the top.

Key practices for leaders include:

- Setting organizational vision and values and deploying them through the organization's leadership system to the workforce, to key suppliers and partners, and to customers and other stakeholders as appropriate.
- Demonstrating a commitment to organizational values through personal actions.
- Promoting an organizational environment that fosters, requires, and leads to legal and ethical behavior.
- Creating a sustainable organization.
- Creating an environment for organizational performance improvement, the accomplishment of the organization's mission and strategic objectives, innovation, competitive or role-model performance leadership, and for organizational agility.
- Creating an environment for organizational and workforce learning.

- Personally participating in succession planning and the development of future organizational leaders.
- Communicating with and engaging the entire workforce.
- Encouraging frank, two-way communication throughout the organization.
- Communicating key decisions.
- Taking an active role in reward and recognition programs to reinforce high performance and a customer and business focus.
- Creating a focus on action to accomplish the organization's objectives, improve performance, and attain the organization's vision.
- Reviewing performance measures to inform the workforce on needed actions.
- Creating and balancing value for customers and other stakeholders in their organizational performance expectations.
- Evaluating their own performance and using the results to improve their personal leadership effectiveness and that of the organization's leadership system.
- Contributing to supporting and strengthening key communities such as charitable organizations, education, and others.

The principles of TQ are embodied in the business philosophy of many leading companies (see box "Bringing TQ to Life at KARLEE" for an example of a company that exemplifies these principles). Interestingly, some research has suggested that the six TQ principles don't exert the same influence on organizational performance.[34] One study of 1,200 Australian and New Zealand manufacturers found that although TQ principles and practices clearly drive performance, leadership, customer focus, and workforce management practices were the strongest significant predictors of performance, and that managers should seek to leverage these as much as possible.

Our purpose in this book is to provide a solid link between concepts of total quality and the traditional management areas of organization theory, organizational behavior, and strategy. When any company begins to think of how to improve, it will be led to the various approaches that are united under the TQ concept. Today, performance excellence is a matter of survival.

TQ AND AGENCY THEORY[35]

One model in organizational theory that has received considerable attention is agency theory. Agency theory is based on the concept of an agency relationship, in which one party (the principal) engages another party (the agent) to perform work. Agency theory makes the assumption that individuals in agency relationships are utility maximizers and will always take actions to enhance their self-interests. As a consequence, when authority is delegated to agents on behalf of the principal, agents may use this power to promote their own well-being, at the expense of the principal. Monitoring is a central issue in agency theory, because it is a primary mechanism used by both parties to maintain and govern the relationship.

Agency theory provides a stark contrast to TQ. TQ views the management system as one based on social and human values, whereas agency theory is based on an economic perspective that removes people from the equation. Whereas agency theory propounds the belief that people are self-interested and opportunistic and

Bringing TQ to Life at KARLEE[36]

KARLEE is a contract manufacturer of precision sheet metal and machined components for telecommunications, semiconductor, and medical equipment industries, located in Garland, Texas. Some of the ways it exemplifies the principles of TQ are described below.

Customer Focus. KARLEE made a strategic decision to carefully select customers that support its values—particularly a systematic approach to business and performance management, desire for long-term partnerships, and global leadership. Management and Team Leaders work with each customer to establish current requirements and future needs, and each customer is assigned a three-person Customer Service team that is on call 24 hours a day for day-to-day production issues.

Process Orientation. Processes such as prototype development, scheduling, production setup, fabrication, assembly, and delivery require process owners to be responsible for maintaining the process to customer requirements. A Quality Assurance team member works with manufacturing teams to create process documentation.

Continuous Improvement and Learning. Teams use a structured approach to evaluate and improve their processes, documenting them and presenting a status report of improvements to senior leaders and the KARLEE Steering Committee. Teams benchmark competitors, "best practice" companies, and customers to learn from others.

Empowerment and Teamwork. Production and delivery processes are designed around cell manufacturing. Teams are responsible for knowing their customer's requirements and producing according to those requirements. Teams are empowered to change targets recommended during strategic planning if they believe it will help them achieve higher performance, as well as to schedule work, manage inventory, and design the layout of their work areas.

Management by Fact. Teams analyze defect data, customer-reported problems, and control charts generated during production to identify problems and opportunities for improvement. Every business goal and project has defined methods for measurement, and senior leaders meet weekly to review company performance and ensure alignment with directions and plans.

Leadership and Strategic Planning. Senior Executive Leaders (SELs) and the KARLEE Leadership Committee (KLC) set the strategic direction of the company, and communicate and reinforce values and expectations through performance reviews, participation in improvement or strategic projects, regular interactions with customers and team members, and recognition of team member achievements.

All this has contributed to an annual average increase in sales growth of 35 percent from 1995 to 2000, and high levels of customer and employee satisfaction, and quality and operational performance.

that their rights are conditional and proportional to the value they add to the organization, TQ suggests that people are also motivated by interests other than self, and that people have an innate right to be respected. Agency theory assumes an inherent conflict of goals between agents and principals, and that agent goals are aligned with principal goals through formal contracts. In TQ, everyone in the organization shares common goals and a continuous improvement philosophy, and goals are aligned through adoption of TQ practices and culture. Sharing information to achieve these goals is fundamental to TQ, whereas agency theory suggests that information may be concealed to advance self-interests. TQ takes a long-term perspective based on continuous improvement, whereas agency theory focuses on short-term achievement of the contract between the principal and agent. In TQ, risk taking is necessary in order to innovate, whereas agency theory assumes that risks are to be minimized and shared between the two parties.

Finally, TQ leaders provide a quality vision and play a strategic role in the organization; leaders in agency theory develop control mechanisms and engage in monitoring. TQ proponents argue that it is a superior strategy because a quality culture can be sustained and is less costly in the long term. Agency theory advocates suggest that high performance may be achieved by appropriately structuring agents' contracts and aligning their interests. As we shall see in Chapter 5, some elements of agency theory are evident in strategy implementation approaches within a TQ environment. Both theories have shaped the activities of scholars and practitioners, and research has yet to arrive at a definitive conclusion. However, it is difficult to argue with the results that firms choosing a clear TQ path have achieved.

TQ AND ORGANIZATIONAL MODELS[37]

Although TQ is a new way of thinking about the management of organizations, it is not a totally new paradigm. When compared with well-known organizational models, it can be seen as capturing many aspects of these established models and amplifying them by providing a useful methodology. Three major organizational models that management theorists have studied are the mechanistic, organismic, and cultural models of organizations. The mechanistic model, described by classical management theorists, views an organization as a tool or a machine designed solely to create profits for its owners. Work is reduced to elementary tasks with a focus on efficiency, conformity, and compliance. Although both the mechanistic model and TQ assume that the organization exists to achieve a specific performance goal, TQ has a broader definition of quality. It takes more of an open-systems perspective, which views managers as leaders and visionaries rather than as individuals who plan, organize, direct, and control. It broadens employees' roles; uses a horizontal, rather than vertical, work organization; and focuses on continuous improvement rather than stability. Narrow-minded managers and those who criticize TQ often view it in a mechanistic sense and do not see the broader implications.

The organismic model views organizational systems as living organisms that depend on their environments for resources and adjust the behavior of their parts to maintain the properties of the whole within acceptable limits. This model assumes that systems goals, such as the need to survive, displace performance goals, such as profit. TQ is similar in that survival in competitive environments is often the primary motivation for adopting it. Customer satisfaction as a definition of quality is compatible with this notion. In the organismic model, organizations are not autonomous entities. This is consistent with the notion of partnership development espoused by TQ: vision replaces fear as a motivator and driver of management actions; employees work for shared beliefs and values; horizontal communication becomes as important as vertical communication and direction in stressing coordination and organizational rationality; and the organization must adapt to a broad array of external forces. It is evident that TQ shares many similarities with this organizational model. This helps explain why many practitioners have viewed TQ as something new, whereas many academics recognize its roots in systems theory that was popular decades ago.

The cultural model views an organization as a collection of cooperative agreements entered into by individuals with free will. The organization's culture and social environment are enacted or socially constructed by organization members. From the perspective of this model, the goal of an organization is to serve the diverse needs of all whom it affects—its stakeholders—a view often expressed by TQ philosophers. Because of the multiplicity of stakeholders, quality has many meanings, although some degree of consensus regarding the organization's values and purposes is needed. Although TQ generally assumes that organizations must adapt to the expectations of customers, more recent views of building partnerships and sharing of best practices (even with competitors) is consistent with the cultural model. In the cultural model, managers take on a more distinctive leadership role, relinquishing control and sharing power in order to meet the needs of the many individuals in the organization; employees have greater voice in establishing organizational goals; all structural decisions are value-based and have clear implications with regard to individual autonomy (political rationality); and learning needs are driven not by adaptation to environmental forces but in response to individual needs. Many of these attributes are characteristic of recent trends in the evolution of TQ themes in high-performing organizations.

In summary, TQ appears to have evolved from reactionary influences against the mechanistic model of management and embraced many of the characteristics of the organismic model. Recent trends, however, suggest that ideas from the cultural model are influencing the maturity of TQ in modern organizations. This will become more evident as we discuss the Malcolm Baldrige Criteria for Performance Excellence in the next chapter.

Review and Discussion Questions

1. Describe how the specific practices of Poudre Valley Health System in the opening Performance Excellence Profile support the principles of performance excellence.
2. Explain why quality became the most important issue facing American business in the 1980s. In addition to economic competition from Japan, what other factors may have contributed to the importance that quality has assumed?
3. Cite several examples in your own experience in which your expectations were met, exceeded, or not met in purchasing goods or services. How did you regard the company after your experience?
4. How might the definition of quality apply to your college or university? Provide examples of who some customers are and how their expectations can be met or exceeded.
5. What implications do you think the forces that will influence the future of quality (see the box "What Will Influence the Future of Quality" in the chapter) will have on management practice?
6. Think of a product with which you are familiar. Describe the eight "multiple quality dimensions" (e.g, performance, features, and so on) for this product that are listed in this chapter.
7. What might the eight "multiple quality dimensions" mean for a college or university? For a classroom?
8. Explain the differences between manufacturing and service organizations and their implications for quality.
9. Describe the key elements of total quality.
10. How might you apply the concepts of TQ to your personal life? Consider your relations with others and your daily activities such as being a student, belonging to a fraternity or professional organization, and so on.

11. Why is a customer focus a critical element of a high-performing organization?
12. Make a list of your personal "customers." What steps might you take to understand their needs and build customer engagement?
13. Cite an example in which you did not purchase a product or service because it lacked "dissatisfiers" as defined in the chapter. Cite another example in which you received some "exciters/delighters" that you did not expect.
14. In what ways might the lack of top management leadership in a quality effort hinder or destroy it?
15. Explain the various areas within an organization in which continuous improvement and learning may take place.
16. Why is measurement important in an organization pursuing performance excellence?
17. Examine some process with which you are familiar. Make a list of ways that the process can be measured and improved. What difficulties might you face in implementing these ideas?
18. Describe the three ways of viewing teamwork.
19. Describe some possible ways in which vertical, horizontal, and interorganizational teamwork can be applied at a college or university.
20. What is employee engagement? How does it differ from empowerment? How might an employee really know that he or she is truly empowered? How might an organization know that employees are truly engaged?
21. Have you ever felt restricted in your work because of a lack of empowerment? Can you cite any experiences in which you noticed a lack of empowerment in a person who was serving you? Why is this such a difficult concept to implement in organizations?
22. How does TQ differ from agency theory?
23. Explain the mechanistic, organismic, and cultural models of organizations, and how TQ is similar to or different from them.
24. Investigate recent quality initiatives in either health care or education. What have these organizations learned from business? What unique issues do they face with respect to quality? How are they trying to overcome them?
25. Discuss the implications of the following statements with respect to introducing TQ principles in a college classroom.[38] Do you agree with them? How do they reflect TQ principles? What changes in traditional learning approaches would they require for both students and instructors?
    a. Embracing a customer focus doesn't mean giving students all As and abandoning standards.
    b. If students fail, the system has failed.
    c. Faculty members are customers of those who teach prerequisites.
    d. Treating students as customers means allowing students to choose not to come to class.
    e. Completing the syllabus is not a measure of success.
    f. New and tenured instructors should visit each other's classrooms.
    g. Eliminate performance appraisals based on classroom evaluations.
    h. No matter how good the test, luck will be involved.
26. Today, both manufacturing and service depend greatly on information technology and the Internet. What would be some ways of evaluating the quality of a Web site?

CASES

U.S. Water Resource Agency—Flagstaff District[39]:

The Flagstaff District (FD) is one of 41 districts within the U.S. Water Resource Agency (USWRA—an Agency in the Department of Renewable Resources—DoRR) charged with the responsibility to develop, protect, and administer water resources within the United States. The Flagstaff District provides six major product lines of goods and services: (1) the development of new infrastructure and projects; (2) management of the operation and maintenance of existing infrastructure; (3) the performance of reimbursable work for others; (4) administration of regulatory requirements; (5) provision of emergency response and recovery; and (6) the delivery of defense, environmental, and restoration programs.

The Flagstaff District's purpose, vision, mission, and values are

Purpose—To be effective stewards of the public trust.

Vision—The Flagstaff District embraces the Agency's vision as its own. This vision can be summed up in terms of our commitment to protect and promote our nation's water resources to be second to none.

Mission—To ensure and protect water resources for economic and recreation benefit to the nation, partner states, and local governments. FD's principal mission areas include

- development and management of projects and programs to provide for inland navigation, flood-damage reduction, environmental protection, recreation, water supply, and other public benefits
- protection of the region's waterways and wetlands
- support for emergency preparedness, natural-disaster relief, and recovery work worldwide
- provision of a broad range of engineering and technical support for other organizations

Values—The district achieves its mission by means of five core values that serve as the foundation of the organization's overall operations and the behavior of every employee.

- Honor and respect
- Selfless service and courage
- Integrity
- Sharing knowledge
- Working safely

Field employees operate 24 multi-purpose dam projects and six lock-and-dam complexes, an equipment-repair station, and a fleet of maintenance vessels. Field offices are connected to the District Office by a radio network and wide area network, or WAN. Computer-Aided Design (CAD) is used in all design projects, as well as Global Positioning System techniques and, most recently, tele-engineering. Tele-engineering is a critically important advance in state-of-the-art engineering practices in that many projects support international efforts, such as mapping the hydrology of Iraq in just two weeks using a simultaneous combination of U.S.-based and on-site engineering capabilities.

One of the hardest concepts to translate from the private sector into the public sector is that of "competition." In many cases, the services provided to the public by an agency of the federal government can be obtained from only that government agency. Historically, this has led to the unfortunate perception that government service providers are "the only game in town," lessening the concern for, or need to understand, customer needs, desires, or drivers of satisfaction. In recent years, however, nothing could be further from reality. This realization has served to strengthen the USWRA commitment to providing exceptional value for its customers and continuously improving every aspect of its business. As a government agency, FD "competes" in three major ways: (1) with private companies for projects or portions of projects; (2) with other districts for reimbursable work; and (3) through outsourcing studies that determine whether work will continue to be accomplished by government employees or will be contracted to private companies.

Discussion Questions

1. As a public not-for-profit agency, Flagstaff District has which customers?
2. How might the district define quality? How could it use this definition to evaluate its success in "competing" with other entities?

The Reservation Nightmare[40]

H. James Harrington, a noted quality consultant, related the following story in *Quality Digest* magazine:

I called to make a flight reservation just an hour ago. The telephone rang five times before a recorded voice answered. "Thank you for calling ABC Travel Services," it said. "To ensure the highest level of customer service, this call may be recorded for future analysis." Next, I was asked to select from one of the following three choices: "If the trip is related to company business, press 1. Personal business, press 2. Group travel, press 3." I pressed 1.

I was then asked to select from the following four choices: "If this is a trip within the United States, press 1. International, press 2. Scheduled training, press 3. Related to a conference, press 4." Because I was going to Canada, I pressed 2.

Now two minutes into my telephone call, I was instructed to be sure that I had my customer identification card available. A few seconds passed and a very sweet voice came on, saying, "All international operators are busy, but please hold because you are a very important customer." The voice was then replaced by music. About two minutes later, another recorded message said, "Our operators are still busy, but please hold and the first available operator will take care of you." More music. Then yet another message: "Our operators are still busy, but please hold. Your business is important to us." More bad music. Finally the sweet voice returned, stating, "To speed up your service, enter your 19-digit customer service number." I frantically searched for their card, hoping that I could find it before I was cut off. I was lucky; I found it and entered the number in time. The same sweet voice came back to me, saying, "To confirm your customer service number, enter the last four digits of your social security number." I pushed the four numbers on the keypad.

The voice said: "Thank you. An operator will be with you shortly. If your call is an emergency, you can call 1-800-CAL-HELP, or push all of the buttons on the telephone at the same time. Otherwise, please hold, as you are a very important customer." This time, in place of music, I heard a commercial about the service that the company provides.

At last, a real person answered the telephone and asked, "Can I help you?" I replied, "Yes, oh yes." He answered, "Please give me your 19-digit customer service number, followed by the last four digits of your social security number so I can verify who you are." (I thought I gave these numbers in the first place to speed up service. Why did I have to rattle them off again?)

I was now convinced that he would call me Mr. 5523-3675-0714-1313-040. But, to my surprise, he said: "Yes, Mr. Harrington. Where do you want to go and when?" I explained that I wanted to go to Montreal the following Monday morning. He replied: "I only handle domestic reservations. Our international desk has a new telephone number: 1-800-1WE-GOTU. I'll transfer you." A few clicks later a message came on, saying: "All of our international operators are busy. Please hold and your call will be answered in the order it was received. Do not hang up or redial, as it will only delay our response to your call. Please continue to hold, as your business is important to us."

Discussion Questions

1. Summarize the service failures associated with this experience.
2. What might the travel agency have done to guarantee a better service experience for Mr. Harrington? How do your suggestions relate to the TQ principles?

Santa Cruz Guitar Company[41]

Santa Cruz Guitar Company (SCGC) is a small-scale manufacturing operation producing fewer than 800 instruments a year. The company does not have a formal quality department, nor has it consciously tried to apply the principles of TQM. Nevertheless, a tour of its facilities and operations suggest that many of the principles of TQM are evident.

Although modern computer numerical controlled (CNC) equipment is used to manufacture minor parts of the guitar, the secret of SCGC's success lies in the small staff of 14 craftspeople, known as luthiers, who apply care and attention to detail while hand-crafting the major components of each instrument. The shop floor is divided into six workstations at which the guitars are progressively assembled as they move from station to station. Experienced luthiers, who are empowered to make their own quality decisions, staff each station. The guitar does not move to the next station until the luthier and another more senior luthier are satisfied with the quality of the work. The manufacturing department inspects what it produces. The company recruits only those who desire to work in a team environment and have a passion for guitar making.

There are seven major steps in the process of making a guitar:

1. Selecting and drying the wood: The guitar-making process starts with the selection of the highest grades of tonewoods. The wood is treated in an evaporative dehumidifying kiln that slowly and carefully removes bound cellular moisture from the wood. The target moisture level is 3%, but when exposed to the temperature/humidity conditions of the shop floor, the moisture content stabilizes at 6%. The shop floor is kept at a constant 47% humidity, which is optimum for maintaining the equilibrium of moisture conditions.
2. Rough-cutting the wood: Once dried, the wood is worked down to rough usable forms using traditional woodworking tools. However, SCGC uses a CNC machine for creating the necks.
3. Bending the sides: To create the desired shapes, the guitar sides are first dipped into water for 10 minutes to condition the wood and then placed under gradual hand pressure on a hot bending template. At that point, the tension in the wood has been relaxed, and the wood eventually takes the shape of the template. This process is best performed by human hands because sides that are shaped by machines have a tendency to spring back when they are being forced into molds.
4. Cutting the top and back: The top and back of the guitars are then cut to shape, and braces are applied to each surface. The thicknesses of the top and braces have the most influence on the final sound of the guitar. As the luthier shaves off ribbons of wood from the top and braces, he or she will tap the top to hear the tone that results from each series of shavings until the tone is perfect. Since the true sound of the instruments will not be fully realized until they are assembled, the luthiers write down what they did while building the top. After final assembly, if a guitar produces a sound so special it knocks the player's socks off, the luthier who built the top will immediately be notified and asked to check his notes to see how this was accomplished so the sound can be duplicated in the future.
5. Cutting the neck: About 60 percent of the SCGC guitar necks are cut on the CNC machine. It is the only major part that is not hand-made. It is critical that the dimensions of the neck be consistent, and the CNC machine does that better than human hands. The 40 percent of necks that are hand-made are done that way because of a customer's specifications.

   Ebony fret boards, which are inlaid with mother-of-pearl, are then glued to the necks.
6. Applying the finish: The guitar body is finished with 12 protective layers of a specially formulated lacquer composed primarily of nitrocellulose and plasticizers to preserve the wood surfaces. But the lacquer is thin enough that the sound is not dampened.
7. Completing final assembly and setup: The neck is fitted to the body using a dovetail joint and then glued in place. Then the bridge is glued to the body. In the next step, called the setup, the saddle and nut, which suspend the strings over the instrument and are made from bovine bones, are installed. Finally, the strings are placed on the guitar, and it is played for the first time. A technician then adjusts the neck or string height to optimize the feel and playability of the instrument.

   SCGC has a web page where guitar owners can have questions about their guitars answered. At SCGC, workers are encouraged to further enhance their skills either by taking external courses or by a practice that allows them to build two instruments a year for personal use. These opportunities allow the craftspeople to explore new techniques in guitar building and become familiar with the entire guitar building process. SCGC workers are even encouraged to go out on their own to open a luthier business someday.

Based on this tour of SCGC, can you identify how the operations and quality practices reflect the principles of TQ?

Endnotes

1. Baldrige National Quality Program 2008 Award Recipient Profile, National Institute of Standards and Technology, U.S. Department of Commerce.
2. Nabil Tamimi and Rose Sebastianelli, "How Firms Define and Measure Quality," *Production and Inventory Management Journal*, Vol. 37, No. 3, Third Quarter 1996, pp. 34–39.
3. Courtesy of Deer Valley Resort. Interesting summaries of Deer Valley's customer-focused approaches can be found in ski magazines.

4. *Salt Lake Tribune*, "Utah Hospitals Log Nearly 90 Major Mistakes," June 30, 2009; cited in *ASQ Quality News Today*, www.asq.org/qualitynews.
5. H. James Harrington, "Are We Going Astray? *Quality Digest*, Feb 2008; "The Decline of U.S. Dominance – Part 1" *Quality Digest*, April, 2008; "The Decline of U.S. Dominance – Part 2" *Quality Digest*, May 2008, all available at www.qualitydigest.com.
6. Thomas A. Stewart, "A Conversation with Joseph Juran," *Fortune*, January 11, 1999, 168–169.
7. Results of selected Baldrige Award recipients. Others may be found by reading the recipient profiles on the Baldrige Web site, www.baldrige.nist.gov.
8. Kevin B. Hendricks and Vinod R. Singhal, "Does Implementing an Effective TQM Program Actually Improve Operating Performance? Empirical Evidence from Firms That Have Won Quality Awards," *Management Science*, Vol. 43, No. 9, September 1997.
9. "The Push for Quality," *Business Week*, June 8, 1987, p. 131.
10. "Reinventing Health Care," *Fortune*, July 12, 1993, advertisement section.
11. Lori L. Silverman with Annabeth L. Propst, "Quality Today: Recognizing the Critical SHIFT," *Quality Progress*, February 1999, pp. 53–60.
12. Seiche Sanders, "What's Up? ASQ's futures study offers insights into where quality is headed," *Quality Progress*, October 2008, 42–49.
13. David A. Garvin, "What Does 'Product Quality' Really Mean?" *Sloan Management Review*, Vol. 26, No. 1, 1984, pp. 25–43.
14. "A New Era for Auto Quality," *Business Week*, October 2, 1990, pp. 84–96.
15. D.A Collier, "The Customer Service and Quality Challenge," *The Service Industries Journal*, Vol. 7, No. 1, January 1987, p. 79.
16. Karl Albrecht and Ronald E. Zemke, *Service America*, Homewood, Ill.: Dow Jones-Irwin, 1985.
17. A. Parasuraman, V. A. Zeithaml, and L. L. Berry, "SERVQUAL: A Multiple-Item Scale for Measuring Consumer Perceptions of Service Quality," *Journal of Retailing*, Vol. 64, No. 1, Spring 1988, pp. 12–40.
18. Eryn Brown, "Heartbreak Hotel?" *Fortune*, November 26, 2001, pp. 161–165.
19. Carol A. King, "Service Quality Assurance Is Different," *Quality Progress*, Vol. 18, No. 6, June 1985, pp. 14–18.
20. "New JCAHO Standards Emphasize Continuous Quality Improvement," *Hospitals*, August 5, 1991, 41–44.
21. Nada R. Sanders, "Health Care Organizations Can Learn from the Experiences of Others," *Quality Progress*, February 1997, 47–49.
22. See, for example, Christina Del Valle, "Readin', Writin', and Reform," *Business Week/Quality Special Issue*, October 25, 1991, 140–142; Myron Tribus, "Quality Management in Education," *Journal for Quality and Participation* (January–February 1993), 12–21. See also Christopher W. L. and Paula E. Morrison, "Students Aren't Learning Quality Principles in Business Schools," *Quality Progress* 25, No. 1, January 1992, 25–27; John A. Byrne, "Is Research in the Ivory Tower 'Fuzzy, Irrelevant, and Pretentious'?" *Business Week*, October 29, 1990, 62–66.
23. Kennedy Smith, "Koalaty Kid: A student-focused initiative to improve the quality of education," *Quality Digest*, August 2002. http://www.qualitydigest.com/aug02/articles/07_article.shtml
24. Baldrige Award Recipient Profiles, National Institute of Standards and Technology, U.S. Department of Commerce.
25. Madhav N. Sinha "Helping Those Who Help Others," *Quality Progress*, July 1997; and Renee Oosterhoff Cox, "Quality in Nonprofits: No Longer Uncharted Territory," *Quality Progress*, October 1999, 57–61.
26. Kennedy Smith, "American Red Cross Undergoes Quality Transfusion," *Quality Digest*, March 2003, 6–7.
27. Procter & Gamble, "Report to the Total Quality Leadership Steering Committee and Working Councils," Cincinnati, Ohio, 1992.
28. James W. Dean, Jr. and David E. Bowen "Management Theory and Total Quality: Improving Research and Practice Through Theory Development," *Academy of Management Review*, 19, 3, 392–418, 1994.
29. Based on Scott M. Paton, "A Change for the Better," First Word Editorial, *Quality Digest*, December 2003, p. 4.
30. AT&T Corporate Quality Office, "*AT&T's Total Quality Approach*," 1992, p. 6.
31. Rosemary Batt, "Managing Customer Services: Human Resource Practices, Quit Rates, and Sales

Growth," *Academy of Management Journal*, Vol. 45, No. 3, 587–597, 2002.

32. "It's My Manager, Stupid," *Across the Board*, January 2000, p. 9.
33. Kicab Casteñeda-Mendez, "Performance Measurement in Health Care," *Quality Digest*, May 1999, pp. 33–36.
34. Danny Samson and Mile Terziovski, "The relationship between total quality management practices and operational performance," *Journal of Operations Management* 17, 1999, pp. 393–409.
35. See S. S. Masterson, J. D. Olian, and E. R. Schnell, "Belief versus practice in management theory: Total quality management and Agency Theory," in D. Fedor and S. Ghosh (eds.), *Advances in the Management of Organizational Quality* (Vol. 2), JAI Press, 1997, pp. 169–209.
36. Adapted from KARLEE 2000 Malcolm Baldrige Application Summary, National Institute of Standards and Technology, U.S. Department of Commerce.
37. Based on Barbara A. Spencer, "Models of Organization and Total Quality Management: A Comparison and Critical Evaluation," *Academy of Management Review*, Vol. 19, No. 3, 1994, pp. 446–471.
38. Adapted from Ronald E. Turner, "TQM in the College Classroom," *Quality Progress*, Vol. 28, No.10, October 1995, pp. 105–108.
39. Adapted from Baldrige National Quality Program, 2006 Flagstaff Case Study. This is a fictional agency and was used for training purposes for the not-for-profit Baldrige Award process.
40. H. James Harrington, "Looking for a Little Service," *Quality Digest*, May 2000.
41. Adapted from Luke T. Foo, "Good Vibrations: Ingrained quality practices mirror Deming's 14 Points," *Quality Progress*, February 2008, 25–30

FRAMEWORKS FOR QUALITY AND PERFORMANCE EXCELLENCE

CHAPTER 2

Performance Excellence Profile: City of Coral Springs[1]

Chartered in 1963, Coral Springs is located in Broward County in southern Florida. During the 1980s, the city was one of the fastest growing in the nation and now is home to about 132,000 people, making it the 13th largest city in the state. With an annual budget of $135 million, the city of Coral Springs has a council-manager form of government with the city commission serving as the board of directors and the city manager as chief executive officer, with input from citizens and businesses. The city has a workforce of about 770 full-time employees and about 300 part-time and temporary employees as well as a large pool of more than 800 people who volunteer as needed for emergencies, special events, or other activities. The city delivers a broad array of products and services, including police patrol, crime investigation, fire prevention and suppression, emergency medical services, parks maintenance, and economic development.

In 1993, the City of Coral Springs began its journey to becoming a high-performing "municipal corporation," a city government following a corporate management model. And, much like a business, Coral Springs is customer focused and data driven. The city's organizational culture is reflected in its four core values: customer focus—demonstrate a passion for customer service; leadership—establish an inspiring vision that creates a government that works better and costs less; empowered employees—empower the people closest to the customer to continuously improve the organization's quality and services; and continuous improvement—commit every day, in every way, to getting better and better.

The city relies heavily on input from its two key customer groups, residents and businesses, and on data analysis to develop priorities and make strategic and business decisions. Included are results from neighborhood "Slice of the Springs" meetings; 27 advisory committees and boards composed of residents and business people; customer surveys; trends in demographics; information on local, state, and national economic conditions; an overview of technological developments; and an analysis of current strengths, weaknesses, and opportunities. The city's strategic plan, which is reviewed and updated annually, represents a shared vision for the future of the community and spells out its priorities: customer-involved government; financial health and economic development; excellence in education; neighborhood and environmental vitality; youth development and family values; strength in diversity; and traffic, mobility and connectivity.

With citizen involvement, a low crime rate, and an abundance of parks and cultural and community activities, the city is achieving its mission "to be the nation's premier community in which to live, work, and raise a family." A number of mechanisms make it as convenient as possible for customers to get information on services, conduct business, and communicate with city officials and employees. They include the city's Web site, podcasts and streaming video, e-mail, the CityHelpDesk (automated comment and complaint system), and the City Hall in the Mall, which offers services such as paying cable and water bills and applying for a passport and permits. The city has taken a leadership role in minimizing adverse impacts on the environment, including using environmentally safe cleaning products and bio-diesel fuel to run all of its large trucks. To protect native plants and animals, the city has purchased and placed in trust 66 acres of environmentally sensitive land. In 1995, Coral Springs became a model in Broward County by establishing a Multi-Cultural Advisory Committee to promote appreciation, acceptance, and respect for the city's diverse cultural community.

A motivated, empowered, and high-performing workforce is vital to Coral Springs achieving its mission and priorities, and the city strives to retain its top-notch staff through job security, competitive pay and benefits, a safe and positive work environment, and recognition. The city's flat organizational structure, training, and recognition encourage employees to be innovative in addressing customer concerns and make on-the-spot improvements. Teams of employees from across the organization work together to solve problems and review processes, promoting cooperation and driving organizational innovation. The city actively identifies and develops its future leaders through training; participation in meetings, workshops, and other events; and mentoring by senior managers.

Its performance excellence practices are validated by exceptional results. Coral Springs has attained a AAA credit rating from all three of the nation's largest bond rating agencies. The city has received the Government Financial Officers Association's Distinguished Budget award for well over a decade. The strategic planning process has been cited by a number of organizations, including the American Productivity and Quality Center, as a "best practice." Business satisfaction has risen from 76 percent in 2004 to 97 percent in 2008; 90 percent of businesses would recommend the city to others, up from 82 percent in 2004. The crime rate has decreased by nearly half over a 10-year period. For the past 10 years, more than 90 percent of employees have been satisfied with their jobs and are willing to recommend the city as a place to work, outperforming a comparison group of federal government employees.

Using a business model to run a city is highly unusual; even more so is one that is grounded in performance excellence practices. Yet the City of Coral Springs' approaches have yielded outstanding results, culminating in being one of the first two recipients of the Malcolm Baldrige National Quality Award in the nonprofit category. Although awards justifiably recognize only a select few, the award or certification criteria provide frameworks for managing from which every organization can benefit. The two frameworks that have had the most impact on quality management practices worldwide are the U.S. Malcolm Baldrige National Quality Award and the international ISO 9000 certification process. Recently, the concept of Six Sigma has evolved into a unique framework for managing quality and performance excellence. All of these frameworks evolved from the philosophies of three key individuals, W. Edwards Deming, Joseph M. Juran, and Philip B. Crosby. This chapter introduces you to their philosophies and describes the frameworks for managing and improving quality in organizations.

The objectives of this chapter are to:

- describe the philosophies of Deming, Juran, and Crosby, which provide a basis for modern approaches to achieving quality and performance excellence;
- to provide an overview of the Malcolm Baldrige National Quality Award and other related award programs, ISO 9000, and Six Sigma as frameworks for quality and performance excellence; and
- to understand the differences in scope, purpose, and philosophy of these frameworks, so as to make informed choices when deciding to pursue an approach to organizational excellence.

FOUNDATIONS OF PERFORMANCE EXCELLENCE

W. Edwards Deming, Joseph M. Juran, and Philip B. Crosby are regarded as true "management gurus" in the quality revolution. Their insights on measuring, managing, and improving quality have greatly influenced the practices that organizations use today. In this section we review their thinking as the foundation for modern concepts of performance excellence.

THE DEMING PHILOSOPHY[2]

Deming was trained as a statistician and worked for Western Electric during its pioneering era of statistical quality control development in the 1920s and 1930s. During World War II he taught quality control courses as part of the national defense effort. Although Deming taught many engineers in the United States, he was not able to reach upper management. After the war, Deming was invited to Japan to teach statistical quality control concepts. Top managers there were eager to learn, and he addressed 21 top executives who collectively represented 80 percent of the country's capital. They embraced Deming's message and transformed their industries. By the mid-1970s, the quality of Japanese products exceeded that of Western manufacturers, and Japanese companies had made significant penetration into Western markets. Deming received Japan's highest honor, the Royal Order of the Sacred Treasure. The former chairman of NEC Electronics once said, "There is not a day I don't think about what Dr. Deming meant to us."

Deming was virtually unknown in the United States until 1980, when NBC aired a documentary entitled "If Japan Can ... Why Can't We?" This program made Deming a household name among corporate executives, and companies such as Ford invited him to assist them in revolutionizing their quality approaches. Deming worked with passion until his death in December 1993 at the age of 93, knowing he had little time left to make a difference in his home country. When asked how he would like to be remembered, Deming replied, "I probably won't even be remembered." Then after a long pause, he added, "Well, maybe ... as someone who spent his life trying to keep America from committing suicide."[3]

Unlike other management gurus and consultants, Deming never defined or described quality precisely. In his last book, he stated, "A product or a service possesses quality if it helps somebody and enjoys a good and sustainable market."[4] Deming stressed that higher quality leads to higher productivity, which in turn leads to long-term competitive strength. The Deming "chain reaction," shown in Figure 2.1, summarizes this view.

The Deming philosophy of quality and management is complex; indeed, several books have been written in an effort to explain and interpret it. Deming summarized his philosophy in what he called "A System of Profound Knowledge," which consists of four parts: (1) appreciation for a system, (2) understanding process variation, (3) theory of knowledge, and (4) psychology.

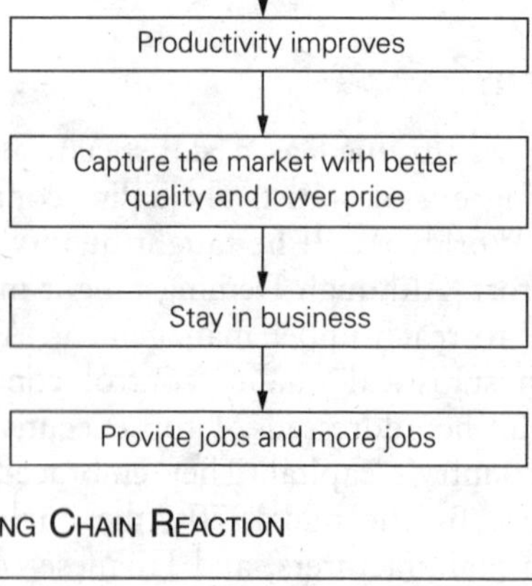

FIGURE 2.1 | THE DEMING CHAIN REACTION

Systems A system is a set of functions or activities within an organization that work together to achieve organizational goals. A system must have an aim, a purpose to which it continually strives. Deming believed that the aim of any system is for everybody—stockholders, employees, customers, community, the environment—to gain over the long term. Stockholders can realize financial benefits, employees can have opportunities for training and education, customers can receive products and services that meet their needs and create satisfaction, the community can benefit from business leadership, and the environment can benefit from socially responsible management.

For example, a McDonald's restaurant can be viewed as a system. It consists of the order-taker/cashier subsystem, grill and food preparation subsystem, drive-through subsystem, and so on. The components of any system must work together for the system to be effective. If the order-taker places the wrong order or the grill breaks down, customers will not get what they want. To run any system, managers must understand the interrelationships among all subsystems and the people that work in them (would a McDonald's operate successfully without a store manager?).

Deming emphasized that management's job is to optimize the system. By making decisions that are best for only a small part of the system (often encouraged by competition), we suboptimize. Suboptimization will prevent a system from achieving its goal. For example, a common practice is to purchase materials or services at the lowest bid. Inexpensive materials may be of such inferior quality that they will cause excessive costs in adjustment and repair during manufacture and assembly. Although the purchasing department's track record might look good, the overall system will suffer.

This concept applies to managing people also. Pitting individuals or departments against each other for resources is self-destructive. The individuals or departments will perform to maximize their expected gain, not that of the firm as a whole. Systems require cooperation.

Variation Just as no two snowflakes are exactly alike, no two outputs from any production process are exactly alike. A production process contains many sources of variation. Different lots of material will vary in strength, thickness, or moisture content, for example. Cutting tools will have inherent variation in strength and composition. During manufacturing, tools will experience wear, machine vibrations will cause changes in settings, and electrical fluctuations will cause variations in power. Operators may not position parts on fixtures consistently. The complex interaction of all these variations in materials, tools, machines, operators, and the environment cannot be understood. Variation due to any individual source appears random; however, their combined effect is stable and can usually be predicted statistically. Factors that are present as a natural part of a process are called **common causes of variation.**

Common causes generally account for about 80 to 90 percent of the observed variation in a production process. The remaining 10 to 20 percent result from **special causes of variation**, often called **assignable causes**. Special causes arise from external sources that are not inherent in the process. A bad batch of material purchased from a supplier, a poorly trained operator, excessive tool wear, or miscalibration of measuring instruments are examples of special causes. Special causes result in unnatural variations that disrupt the random pattern of common causes. Hence, they are generally easy to detect using statistical methods, and it is usually economical to remove them.

A system governed only by common causes is stable and its performance can be predicted. Special causes disrupt the predictable pattern. (Think of your commute to work or school—what happens when a snowstorm or accident occurs?) Unfortunately, managers either overreact to common cause variation or ignore special causes when they do occur. If they try to "fix" a common cause, they will actually increase the variation in the system. If they ignore special causes, they miss the opportunity to improve.

In Deming's view, variation is the chief culprit of poor quality. In mechanical assemblies, for example, variations from specifications for part dimensions lead to inconsistent performance and premature wear and failure. Likewise, inconsistencies in service frustrate customers and damage a firm's image.

Variation also increases the cost of doing business. An example was published in the Japanese newspaper *Asahi* comparing the cost and quality of Sony televisions at plants in Japan and San Diego.[5] The color density of all the units produced at the San Diego plant was within specifications, although the density of some of those shipped from the Japanese plant was not (see Figure 2.2). However, the average loss per unit at the San Diego plant was $0.89 greater than that of the Japanese plant. This was because units out of specification at the San Diego plant were adjusted within the plant, adding cost to the process. Furthermore, a unit adjusted to just within specifications was more likely to generate customer complaints than a unit that was closer to the original target value, therefore incurring higher field service costs. Figure 2.2 shows that fewer U.S.-produced sets met the target value for color density. The distribution of quality in the Japanese plant was more uniform around the target value, and even though some units were out of specification, the total cost was less.

By minimizing variation, everyone benefits. The producer benefits by having less need for inspection, less scrap and rework, and higher productivity. The consumer is assured that all products have similar quality characteristics; this is especially important when the consumer is another firm using large quantities of the product in its own manufacturing or service operations. The only way to reduce common cause variation is to change the technology of the process—the machines,

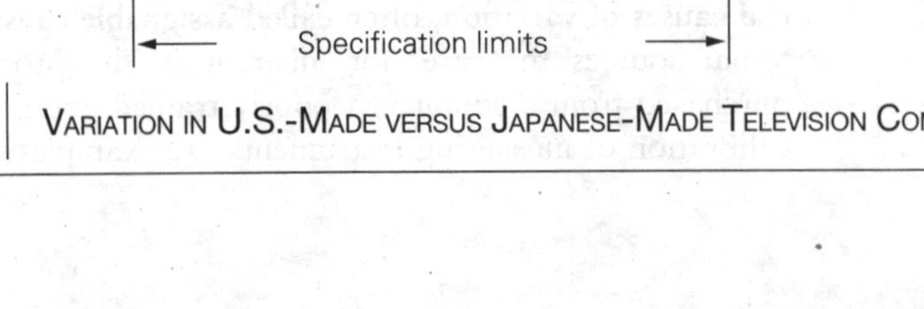

FIGURE 2.2 VARIATION IN U.S.-MADE VERSUS JAPANESE-MADE TELEVISION COMPONENTS

people, materials, methods, or measurement system. Only management can make these decisions; pressuring workers to perform at higher quality levels will only result in frustration. However, special cause variation can be identified by workers through the use of control charts, which were introduced in Chapter 2. This requires training and management support.

Theory of Knowledge The third part of Profound Knowledge is called the "theory of knowledge," which is a branch of philosophy concerned with the nature and scope of knowledge, its presuppositions and bases, and the general reliability of claims to knowledge. Deming was influenced greatly by Clarence Irving Lewis.[6] Lewis stated, "There is no knowledge without interpretation. If interpretation, which represents an activity of the mind, is always subject to the check of further experience, how is knowledge possible at all? ... An argument from past to future at best is probable only, and even this probability must rest upon principles which are themselves more than probable."

What this basically means is that management decisions should be driven by facts, data, and justifiable theories, not solely by opinions. Experience cannot be tested or validated, but good theories supported by data can establish a cause-and-effect relationship that can be used for prediction. Theory explains why things happen. For example, many companies have jumped on the latest fads advocated by popular business consultants, only to find that they result in failure. This often happens because they simply did not understand the context and assumptions required to make them work successfully.

Psychology People design products and processes, serve customers, and achieve results. Psychology helps us to understand people, interactions between people and circumstances, interactions between leaders and employees, and the drivers of behavior. No leader can manage well without understanding these factors and incorporating them in key decisions. More important, people inherit the right to enjoy work. Psychology helps us to nurture and preserve people's positive innate attributes.

Little in Deming's system of Profound Knowledge is original. The concept of common and special causes of variation was developed by Walter Shewhart in the 1920s; behavioral theories to which Deming subscribed were developed in the 1960s; systems theory was refined by management scientists from the 1950s through the 1970s; and scientists in all fields have long understood the relationships among prediction, observation, and theory. Deming's contribution was in tying together some basic concepts. He recognized the synergy among these diverse subjects and developed them into a theory of management.

Peter Scholtes, a noted consultant, makes some salient observations about the failure to understand the components of Profound Knowledge:[7]

1. When people don't understand systems:
    - they see events as individual incidents rather than the net result of many interactions and interdependent forces;
    - they see the symptoms but not the deep causes of problems;
    - they don't understand how an intervention in one part of [an organization] can cause havoc in another place or at another time;

- they blame individuals for problems even when those individuals have little or no ability to control the events around them; and
- they don't understand the ancient African saying, "It takes a whole village to raise a child."

2. When people don't understand variation:
   - they don't see trends that are occurring;
   - they see trends where there are none;
   - they don't know when expectations are realistic;
   - they don't understand past performance so they can't predict future performance;
   - they don't know the difference between prediction, forecasting, and guesswork; and
   - they give others credit or blame when those people are simply either lucky or unlucky. This usually occurs because people tend to attribute everything to human effort, heroics, frailty, error, or deliberate sabotage, no matter what the systemic cause; and they are less likely to distinguish between fact and opinion.
3. When people don't understand psychology:
   - they don't understand motivation or why people do what they do;
   - they resort to carrots and sticks and other forms of induced motivation that have no positive effect and impair the relationship between the motivator and the one being motivated;
   - they don't understand the process of change and the resistance to it;
   - they revert to coercive and paternalistic approaches when dealing with people; and
   - they create cynicism, demoralization, demotivation, guilt, resentment, burnout, craziness, and turnover.
4. When people don't understand the theory of knowledge:
   - they don't know how to plan and accomplish learning and improvement;
   - they don't understand the difference between improvement and change; and
   - problems will remain unsolved, despite their best efforts.

Deming espoused a transformation in management with his "14 Points for Management " It is important to realize that the 14 Points date back several decades to when many organizations were ruled by autocratic managers who were driven by short-term profits and who had little regard for engaging the workforce or interest in quality improvement. Although management practices today are vastly different from when Deming first began to preach his philosophy, the 14 Points still convey important insights for managers. Failure to heed them might only lead to repeating the mistakes of the past.

1. *Management Commitment*—Making a commitment to drive improvement within an organization is still difficult for managers. Even when managers have conducted a thorough assessment of their organization and know what they need to change, many do not effectively follow up on opportunities.[8] Reasons range from denial ("We can't be that bad!") to excuses ("We have

a lot of irons on the fire right now."). Effective leadership begins with commitment. We will revisit this issue in Part IV of this book.

2. *Learn the New Philosophy*—Deming recognized that historical methods of management built on early twentieth-century principles of Frederick Taylor, such as quota-driven production, work measurement, and adversarial work relationships, simply don't work. Although leadership begins with commitment, it also requires new ways of thinking. Today, many companies have adopted the principles of total quality that we will study as an essential part of their business strategy (see Chapter 5). However, people change jobs and organizations generally have a short memory—both need to continually renew themselves to learn new approaches and relearn many older ones. Today's "new philosophies" include the Baldrige framework and Six Sigma, which we study later in this chapter.
3. *Understand Inspection*—In the mid-twentieth century, inspection had been the principal means for quality control; companies employed dozens or even hundreds of people who inspected for quality on a full-time basis and added little value to the product. Deming suggested that inspection should be used judiciously as an information-gathering tool for improvement. Today, this new role of inspection has been integrated into the quality management practices of most companies. However, few managers truly how variation affects their processes and inspection practices. Through better understanding, managers can eliminate unnecessary inspection, thus reducing non–value-added costs, or perform critical inspection tasks that avoid more expensive downstream repairs.
4. *End Price Tag Decisions*—Purchasing decisions traditionally have been driven by cost through competitive bidding, not by quality. Costs due to inferior materials and components increase costs in later stages of production and can far exceed the "savings" realized through competitive bidding. Deming promoted the recognition of purchasing departments as "internal suppliers" to production, and urged businesses to establish long-term relationships with a few suppliers, leading to loyalty and enhanced opportunities for improvement. Today's emphasis on supply chain management (SCM) reflects the achievement of Point 4. SCM focuses heavily on a system's view of the supply chain with the objective of minimizing total supply chain costs and developing stronger partnerships with suppliers. These ideas will be addressed in Chapter 6.
5. *Improve Constantly*—Traditionally, continuous improvement was not a common business practice; today it is recognized as a necessary means for survival in a highly competitive and global business environment. Improvements are necessary in both design and operations. Improved design of goods and services comes from understanding customer needs and continual market surveys and other sources of feedback, and from understanding the manufacturing and service delivery process. Improvements in operations are achieved by reducing the causes and impacts of variation, and engaging all employees to innovate and seek ways of doing their jobs more efficiently and effectively. The tools for improvement are constantly evolving, and organizations need to ensure that their employees understand and apply them effectively, which requires training, the focus of the next Point. Improvement is a theme that runs throughout this book.

6. *Institute Training*—People are an organization's most valuable resource; they want to do a good job, but they often do not know how. Not only does training result in improvements in product and service quality and organizational performance, but it adds to worker morale, and demonstrates to workers that the company is dedicated to helping them and investing in their future. Training must transcend such basic job skills as running a machine or following the script when talking to customers. Training should include tools for identifying, diagnosing, analyzing, and solving quality and performance problems. Today, many companies have excellent training programs for technology related to direct production but still fail to enrich the ancillary skills of their workforce. Here is where some of the most lucrative opportunities exist to make an impact on key business results.
7. *Institute Leadership*—The job of management is leadership and guidance, not supervision and work direction. Supervisors should be coaches, not policemen, and supervision should provide the link between management and the workforce. Leadership can help to eliminate fear and encourage teamwork. Leadership was, is, and will continue to be a challenging issue in every organization, particularly as new generations of managers replace those who have learned to lead. Thus, this Point of Deming's will always be relevant to organizations.
8. *Drive Out Fear*—Fear in work manifests in many ways: fear of reprisal, fear of failure, fear of the unknown, fear of change. Fear encourages short-term, selfish thinking, not long-term improvement for the benefit of all. Fear is a cultural issue for all organizations. Creating a culture without fear is a slow process but can be destroyed in an instant with a transition of leadership and a change in corporate policies. Therefore, today's managers need to continue to be sensitive to the impact that fear can have on their organizations. Positive motivation will be studied in Chapter 9.
9. *Optimize Team Efforts*—Barriers between individuals and departments lead to poor quality, because "customers" do not receive what they need from their "suppliers." This is often the result of internal competition for raises or performance ratings. Teamwork helps to break down barriers between internal customers and suppliers. The focus should be on meeting customer needs and improving processes. Teamwork is an important means of achieving a company's goals, and we discuss this further in Chapter 8.
10. *Eliminate Exhortations*—Motivation can be better achieved through trust and leadership than slogans. Slogans calling for improved quality usually assume that poor quality results from a lack of motivation. Workers cannot improve solely through motivational methods when the system in which they work constrains their performance. On the contrary, they will become frustrated and their performance will decrease further. Improvement stems from better organizational design and use of data-driven processes (see Chapters 3 and 4).
11. *Eliminate Quotas and MBO (Management by Objective)*—Numerical quotas encourage short-rather than long-term behavior, particularly if rewards or performance appraisals are tied to meeting quotas. Deming acknowledged that goals are useful, but numerical goals set for others without incorporating a method to reach the goal generate frustration and resentment. Furthermore, variation in the system year-to-year or quarter-to-quarter—a 5 percent increase

or a 6 percent decrease, for example—makes comparisons meaningless. Management must understand the reasons for variation or poor performance and provide the means to improve, rather than focus on short-term goals.

12. *Remove Barriers to Pride in Workmanship*—Some organizations view workers as a "commodity." Factory workers are given monotonous tasks; provided with inferior machines, tools, or materials; told to run defective items to meet sales pressures; and report to supervisors who know nothing about the job. This attitude has given way to increased levels of empowerment, providing workers with a sense of ownership of their work processes and higher self-esteem. This will be explored further in Chapter 9.
13. *Institute Education*—"Training" in Point 6 refers to job skills; education refers to self-development. Firms have a responsibility to develop the value and self-worth of the individual. Investing in people is a powerful motivation method. Today, many companies understand that elevating the general knowledge base of their workforce—outside of specific job skills—returns many benefits. However, others still view this task as a cost that can be easily cut when financial tradeoffs must be made.
14. *Take Action*—Any cultural change begins with top management and includes everyone. Changing an organizational culture generally meets with skepticism and resistance that many firms find difficult to deal with, particularly when many of the traditional management practices Deming felt must be eliminated are deeply ingrained in the organization's culture. We address this further in Chapter 11.

Deming's principles continue to live in many organizations today (see box "Louisville Slugger Hits a Home Run with Deming").

Louisville Slugger Hits a Home Run with Deming[9]

Hillerich & Bradsby Co. (H&B) has been making the Louisville Slugger brand of baseball bat for more than 115 years. In the mid-1980s, the company faced significant challenges from market changes and competition. CEO Jack Hillerich attended a four-day Deming seminar, which provided the basis for the company's current quality efforts. Returning from the seminar, Hillerich decided to see what changes that Deming advocated were possible in an old company with an old union and a history of labor-management problems. Hillerich persuaded union officials to attend another Deming seminar with five senior managers.

Following the seminar, a core group of union and management people developed a strategy to change the company. They talked about building trust and changing the system "to make it something you want to work in." Employees were interested, but skeptical. To demonstrate their commitment, managers examined Deming's 14 Points, and picked several they believed they could make progress on through actions that would demonstrate a serious intention to change. One of the first changes was the elimination of work quotas that were tied to hourly salaries and a schedule of warnings and penalties for failures to meet quotas. Instead, a team-based approach was initiated. Although a few workers took advantage of the change, overall productivity actually improved as rework decreased because workers were taking pride in their work to produce things the right way first. H&B also eliminated performance appraisals and commission-based pay in sales. The company also has focused its efforts on training and education, resulting in an openness for change and capacity for teamwork. Today, the Deming philosophy is still the core of H&B's guiding principles.

The Juran Philosophy

Joseph M. Juran joined Western Electric in the 1920s during its pioneering days in the development of statistical methods for quality. He spent much of his time as a corporate industrial engineer. In 1951 Juran wrote, edited, and published one of the most comprehensive books on quality, the *Quality Control Handbook*, which has been revised many times. Juran taught quality principles to the Japanese in the 1950s just after Deming and was a principal force in their quality reorganization.

Juran takes a more pragmatic approach to change than Deming, advocating approaches that are designed to fit into a company's current strategic business planning with minimal risk of rejection. Juran views the pursuit of quality on two levels: (1) the mission of the firm as a whole is to achieve high product quality; and (2) the mission of each individual department in the firm is to achieve high production quality. Senior management must play an active and enthusiastic leadership role in the quality management process.

Juran contends that employees at different levels of an organization speak in different "languages." (Deming believed statistics should be the common language.) Top management speaks in the language of dollars, workers speak in the language of things, and middle management must be able to speak both languages and translate between dollars and things. Thus, to get top management's attention, quality issues must be cast in the language they understand—dollars. Juran advocates the accounting and analysis of quality costs to focus attention on quality problems.

At the operational level, Juran focuses on increasing conformance to specifications through elimination of defects, supported extensively by statistical tools for analysis. Juran defines quality as "fitness for use." This is broken down into four categories: quality of design, quality of conformance, availability, and field service. Quality of design focuses on market research, the product concept, and design specifications. Quality of conformance includes technology, manpower, and management. Availability focuses on reliability, maintainability, and logistical support. Field service quality comprises promptness, competence, and integrity.

Juran's prescriptions focus on three major aspects of quality called the Quality Trilogy (a registered trademark of the Juran Institute): quality planning: the process for preparing to meet quality goals; quality control: the process for meeting quality goals during operations; and quality improvement: the process for breaking through to unprecedented levels of performance.

Quality planning begins with identifying customers, both external and internal, determining their needs, and developing product features that respond to customer needs. Quality control involves determining what to control, establishing units of measurement so that data may be objectively evaluated, establishing standards of performance, measuring actual performance, interpreting the difference between actual performance and the standard, and taking action on the difference. Quality improvement is best achieved by identifying specific projects for improvement, getting the right people involved, diagnosing causes of poor performance, developing remedies for the causes, proving that the remedies will be effective, and providing control to hold improvements.

Dr. Juran continued to actively promote quality and write books until he passed away in 2008 at the age of 103. A tribute to his life and work can be found in the April 2008 issue of *Quality Progress* magazine, published by the American Society for Quality.

THE CROSBY PHILOSOPHY

Philip B. Crosby, who passed away in 2001, was corporate vice president for quality at International Telephone and Telegraph (ITT) for 14 years after working his way up from line inspector. After leaving ITT, he established Philip Crosby Associates in 1979 to develop and offer training programs. He also was the author of several popular books. His first book, *Quality Is Free*, sold about one million copies, and is credited with bringing quality to the attention of top American executives.

The essence of Crosby's quality philosophy is embodied in what he calls the Absolutes of Quality Management and the Basic Elements of Improvement. Crosby's Absolutes of Quality Management are as follows:

- *Quality means conformance to requirements not elegance.* Crosby dispels the myth that quality is simply a feeling of "excellence." Requirements must be clearly stated so that they cannot be misunderstood. Requirements are communication devices and are ironclad. Once a task is done, one can take measurements to determine conformance to requirements. The nonconformance detected is the absence of quality. Quality problems become nonconformance problems—that is, variation in output. Setting requirements is the responsibility of management.
- *There is no such thing as a quality problem.* Problems must be identified by the individuals or departments that cause them. There are accounting problems, manufacturing problems, design problems, front-desk problems, and so on. Quality originates in functional departments, not in the quality department, and the burden of responsibility for such problems lies with the functional departments. The quality department should measure conformance, report results, and lead the drive to develop a positive attitude toward quality improvement. This is similar to Deming's Point 3.
- *There is no such thing as the economics of quality: it is always cheaper to do the job right the first time.* Crosby supports the premise that "economics of quality" has no meaning. Quality is free. What costs money are all the actions that involve not doing jobs right the first time. The Deming Chain Reaction provides a similar message.
- *The only performance measurement is the cost of quality.* The cost of quality is the expense of nonconformance. Crosby notes that most companies spend 15 to 20 percent of their sales dollars on quality costs. A company with a well-run quality management program can achieve a cost of quality that is less than 2.5 percent of sales, primarily in the prevention and appraisal categories. Crosby's program calls for measuring and publicizing the cost of poor quality. Quality cost data are useful in calling problems to management's attention, selecting opportunities for corrective action, and tracking quality improvement over time. Such data provide visible proof of improvement and recognition of achievement. Juran also supports this theme.
- *The only performance standard is Zero Defects.* According to Crosby:

> Zero Defects is a performance standard. It is the standard of the craftsperson regardless of his or her assignment.... The theme of ZD is do it right the first time. That means concentrating on preventing defects rather than just finding and fixing them.
>
> People are conditioned to believe that error is inevitable; thus they not only accept error, they anticipate it. It does not bother us to make a few errors in our work.... To err is human. We all have our own standards in business or academic

> life—our own points at which errors begin to bother us. It is good to get an A in school, but it may be okay to pass with a C.
>
> We do not maintain these standards, however, when it comes to our personal life. If we did, we should expect to be shortchanged every now and then when we cash our paycheck; we should expect hospital nurses to drop a constant percentage of newborn babies.... We as individuals do not tolerate these things.
>
> We have a dual standard: one for ourselves and one for our work. Most human error is caused by lack of attention rather than lack of knowledge. Lack of attention is created when we assume that error is inevitable. If we consider this condition carefully and pledge ourselves to make a constant conscious effort to do our jobs right the first time, we will take a giant step toward eliminating the waste of rework, scrap, and repair that increases cost and reduces individual opportunity.[10]

Juran and Deming, by contrast, would argue that it is pointless, if not hypocritical, to exhort a line worker to produce perfection, because the overwhelming majority of imperfections are due to poorly designed manufacturing systems beyond the worker's control.

Crosby's Basic Elements of Improvement included *determination*—commitment by the organizational leadership—*education*, and *implementation*. Unlike Juran and Deming, Crosby's program was primarily behavioral. He placed more emphasis on management and organizational processes for changing corporate culture and attitudes than on the use of statistical techniques. Like Juran and unlike Deming, his approach fits well within existing organizational structures.

THE MALCOLM BALDRIGE NATIONAL QUALITY AWARD

The Malcolm Baldrige National Quality Award (MBNQA) has been one of the most powerful catalysts of total quality in the United States and, indeed, throughout the world. More important, the award's *Criteria for Performance Excellence* establish a framework for understanding and integrating principles of performance excellence in any organization. In this section we present an overview of the MBNQA, its criteria, and the award process.

HISTORY AND PURPOSE

Recognizing that U.S. productivity was declining, President Reagan signed legislation mandating a national study/conference on productivity in October 1982. The American Productivity and Quality Center (formerly the American Productivity Center) sponsored seven computer networking conferences in 1983 to prepare for an upcoming White House Conference on Productivity. The final report on these conferences recommended that "a National Quality Award, similar to the Deming Prize in Japan, be awarded annually to those firms that successfully challenge and meet the award requirements. These requirements and the accompanying examination process should be very similar to the Deming Prize system to be effective." The Baldrige Award was signed into law (Public Law 100-107) on August 20, 1987. The award is named after President Reagan's Secretary of Commerce who was killed in an accident shortly before the Senate acted on the legislation. Malcolm Baldrige was highly regarded by world leaders, having played a major role in carrying out the administration's trade policy, resolving technology transfer differences with China and India, and holding the first Cabinet-level talks with the Soviet Union in seven years, which paved the way for increased access for U.S. firms in the Soviet market.

The purposes of the award are to:

- help stimulate American companies to improve quality and productivity for the pride of recognition while obtaining a competitive edge through increased profits;
- recognize the achievements of those companies that improve the quality of their goods and services and provide an example to others;
- establish guidelines and criteria that can be used by business, industrial, governmental, and other enterprises in evaluating their own quality improvement efforts; and
- provide specific guidance for other American enterprises that wish to learn how to manage for high quality by making available detailed information on how winning enterprises were able to change their cultures and achieve eminence.

The Baldrige Award recognizes U.S. companies that excel in quality management practice and performance. The Baldrige Award does not exist simply to recognize product excellence, nor does it exist for the purpose of "winning." Its principal focus is on promoting high-performance management practices that lead to customer satisfaction and business results. Up to three companies can receive an award in each of the categories of manufacturing, small business, service, nonprofit health care, and nonprofit education. Health care and education award categories were established in 1999 and the nonprofit categories in 2007. Table 2.1 shows the recipients through 2008.

TABLE 2.1 | MALCOLM BALDRIGE AWARD RECIPIENTS THROUGH 2008

Manufacturing

Motorola, Inc. (1988)

Westinghouse Commercial Nuclear Fuel Division (1988)

Xerox Corp. Business Products and Systems (1989)

Milliken & Co. (1989)

Cadillac Motor Car Division (1990)

IBM Rochester (1990)

Solectron Corp. (1991)

Zytec Corp. (now part of Artesyn Technologies) (1991)

AT&T Network Systems (now Lucent Technologies, Inc. Optical Networking Group) (1992)

Texas Instruments Defense Systems & Electronics Group (now part of Raytheon Systems Co.) (1992)

Eastman Chemical Co. (1993)

Armstrong World Industries Building Products Operations (1995)

Corning Telecommunications Products Division (1995)

Continued

TABLE 2.1 MALCOLM BALDRIGE AWARD RECIPIENTS THROUGH 2008 *CONTINUED*

ADAC Laboratories (1996)
3M Dental Products Division (1997)
Solectron Corp. (1997)
Boeing Airlift and Tanker Programs (1998)
Solar Turbines, Inc. (1998)
STMicroelectronics, Inc.–Region Americas (1999)
Dana Corporation–Spicer Driveshaft Division (now Torque Traction Technologies, Inc.) (2000)
KARLEE Company (2000)
Clarke American Checks, Inc. (2001)
Motorola, Inc. Commercial, Government and Industrial Solutions Sector (2002)
Medrad, Inc. (2003)
The Bama Companies, Inc. (2004)
Sunny Fresh Foods, Inc. (2005)
Cargill Corn Milling North America (2008)
Honeywell Federal Manufacturing & Technologies (2009)

Small Business

Globe Metallurgical, Inc. (1988)
Wallace Co., Inc. (1990)
Marlow Industries (1991)
Granite Rock Co. (1992)
Ames Rubber Corp. (1993)
Wainwright Industries, Inc. (1994)
Custom Research Inc. (1996)
Trident Precision Manufacturing, Inc. (1996)
Texas Nameplate Company, Inc. (1998)
Sunny Fresh Foods (1999)
Los Alamos National Bank (2000)
Stoner, Inc. (2003)
Texas Nameplate Company, Inc. (2004)
Park Place Lexus (2005)
MESA Products, Inc. (2006)
PRO-TEC Coating Company (2007)
MidwayUSA (2009)

Service

Federal Express (FedEx) (1990)
AT&T Universal Card Services (now part of Citigroup) (1992)

Continued

TABLE 2.1 | MALCOLM BALDRIGE AWARD RECIPIENTS THROUGH 2008 *CONTINUED*

The Ritz-Carlton Hotel Co. (now part of Marriott International) (1992)
AT&T Consumer Communication Services (now the Consumer Markets Division of AT&T) (1994)
Verizon Information Services (formerly GTE Directories, Inc.) (1994)
Dana Commercial Credit Corp. (1996)
Merrill Lynch Credit Corp. (1997)
Xerox Business Services (1997)
BI (1999)
The Ritz-Carlton Hotel Company, L.L.C. (1999)
Operations Management International, Inc. (2000)
Pal's Sudden Service (2001)
Branch-Smith Printing Division (2002)
Boeing Aerospace Support (2003)
Caterpillar Financial Services (2003)
DynMcDermott Petroleum Operations (2005)
Premier Inc. (2006)

Education

Chugach School District (2001)
Pearl River School District (2001)
University of Wisconsin–Stout (2001)
Community Consolidated School District #15, Palatine, IL (2003)
Robert W. Monfort College of Business (2004)
Richland College (2005)
Jenks Public Schools (2005)
Iredell-Statesville Schools (2008)

Health Care

SSM Health Care (2002)
Baptist Hospital, Inc., Pensacola, FL (2003)
Saint Luke's Hospital of Kansas City (2003)
Robert Wood Johnson University Hospital Hamilton (2004)
Bronson Methodist Hospital (2005)
North Mississippi Medical Center (2006)
Mercy Health System (2007)
Sharp HealthCare (2007)
Poudre Valley Health System (2008)
AtlantiCare (2009)
Heartland Health (2009)

Nonprofit

City of Coral Springs (2007)
U.S. Army Armament Research, Development and Engineering Center (2007)
VA Cooperative Studies Program Clinical Research Pharmacy Coordinating Center (2009)

The award has evolved into a comprehensive National Quality Program, administered through the National Institute of Standards and Technology in Gaithersburg, Maryland, of which the Baldrige Award is only one part. The National Quality Program is a public-private partnership, funded primarily through a private foundation. The program's Web site at http://www.baldrige.nist.gov provides current information about the award, the performance criteria, award recipients, and a variety of other information.

The Criteria for Performance Excellence

The award examination is based upon a rigorous set of criteria, called the *Criteria for Performance Excellence*, designed to encourage companies to enhance their competitiveness through an aligned approach to organizational performance management that results in:

1. Delivery of ever-improving value to customers, contributing to marketplace success
2. Improvement of overall company performance and capabilities
3. Organizational and personal learning

The criteria consist of a hierarchical set of *categories, items,* and *areas to address*. The seven categories are

1. *Leadership*: This category examines how an organization's senior leaders personal actions guide and sustain the organization. Also examined are an organization's governance system and how the organization fulfills its ethical, legal, and societal responsibilities, and supports its key communities.
2. *Strategic Planning*: This category examines how an organization develops strategic objectives and action plans. Also examined is how the chosen objectives and plans are deployed and changed if circumstances require, and how progress is measured.
3. *Customer Focus*: This category examines how an organization engages its customers for long-term marketplace success and builds a customer-focused culture. Also examined is how the organization listens to the voice of its customers and uses this information to improve and identify opportunities for innovation.
4. *Measurement, Analysis, and Knowledge Management*: This category examines how an organization selects, gathers, analyzes, manages, and improves its data, information, and knowledge assets, and how it manages its information technology. Also examined is how the organization reviews and uses reviews to improve its performance.
5. *Workforce Focus*: This category examines how an organization engages, manages, and develops its workforce to utilize its full potential in alignment with the organization's overall mission, strategy, and action plans. Also examined is the organization's ability to assess workforce capability and capacity needs and to build a workforce environment conducive to high performance.
6. *Process Management*: This category examines how an organization designs its work systems and how it designs, manages, and improves its key processes for implementing those work systems to deliver customer value and achieve organizational success and sustainability. It also examines an organization's readiness for emergencies.

7. *Results*: This category examines an organization's performance and improvement in key business areas—product outcomes, customer-focused outcomes, financial and market outcomes, workforce-focused outcomes, process-effectiveness outcomes, and leadership outcomes. Performance levels are examined relative to those of competitors and other organizations providing similar products and services.

We encourage you to read the entire document for clarifying notes and explanations. Also, slightly different versions of the criteria are written for education and health care, primarily to conform to unique language and practices in these sectors. Because the criteria are updated every other year, we suggest that you obtain the current version. The criteria can be downloaded from the Baldrige Web site http://www.baldrige.nist.gov.

The seven categories form an *integrated management system*, as illustrated in Figure 2.3. The umbrella over the seven categories reflects the focus that organizations must have on customers through their strategy and action plans for all key decisions. Leadership, Strategic Planning, and Customer Focus represent the "leadership triad," and suggest the importance of integrating these three functions. Workforce Focus and Process Management represent how the work in an organization is accomplished and leads to Business Results. These functions are linked to the leadership triad. Finally, Measurement, Analysis, and Knowledge Management supports the entire framework by providing the foundation for a fact-based system for improvement.

Each category consists of several *items* (numbered 1.1, 1.2, 2.1, etc.) or major requirements on which businesses should focus. Each item, in turn, consists of a small number of *areas to address* (e.g., 6.1a, 6.1b) that seek specific information on *approaches* used to ensure and improve competitive performance, the *deployment* of

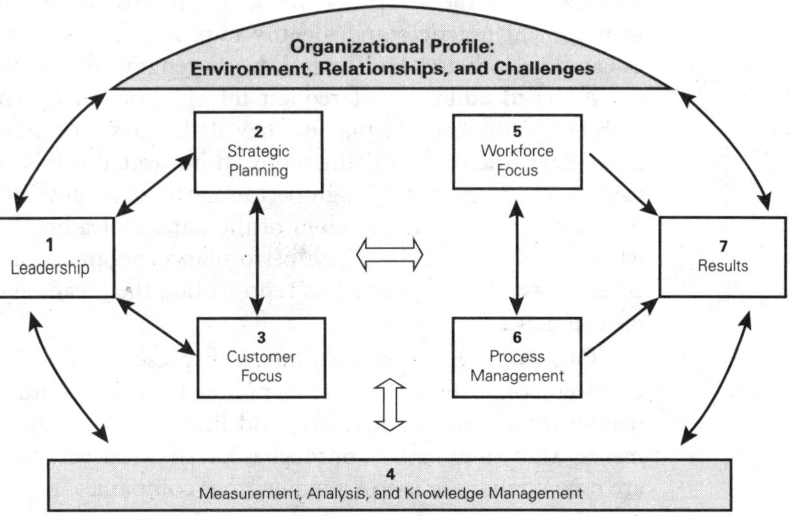

FIGURE 2.3 MALCOLM BALDRIGE NATIONAL QUALITY AWARD CRITERIA FRAMEWORK

these approaches, or *results* obtained from such deployment. For example, the Leadership Category consists of the two items with a total of five areas to address:

1.1 Senior Leadership
  a. Vision, Values, and Mission
  b. Communication and Organizational Performance
1.2 Governance and Societal Responsibilities
  a. Organizational Governance
  b. Legal and Ethical Behavior
  c. Societal Responsibilities and Support of Key Communities

The Vision, Values, and Mission area to address (1.1a) asks organizations to answer the following questions:

1. How do senior leaders set organizational vision and values? How do senior leaders deploy your organization's vision and values through your leadership system, to the workforce, to key suppliers and partners, and to customers and other stakeholders, as appropriate? How do senior leaders' personal actions reflect a commitment to the organization's values?
2. How do senior leaders promote an environment that fosters, requires, and results in legal and ethical behavior?
3. How do senior leaders create a sustainable organization? How do senior leaders create an environment for organizational performance improvement, the accomplishment of your mission and strategic objectives, innovation, competitive or role-model performance leadership, and organizational agility? How do they create an environment for organizational and workforce learning? How do they develop and enhance their personal leadership skills? How do they personally participate in succession planning and the development of future organizational leaders?

Applicants for the award as well as organizations that simply wish to assess their management practices and identify improvement opportunities use these questions as catalysts to better understand their strengths and weaknesses.

Areas to address that request information on approach or deployment begin with the word "how"; that is, they define a set of actionable management practices. Thus, the criteria define both an integrated infrastructure and a set of fundamental practices for a high-performance management system. These practices represent the collective wisdom of the nation's leading business experts and reflect what a truly world-class high-performance organization must do to succeed. The criteria have been described as representing the "leading edge of validated management practice."

One thing the criteria do not do is prescribe specific quality tools, techniques, technologies, systems, or starting points. Companies are encouraged to develop and demonstrate creative, adaptive, and flexible approaches to meeting basic requirements. Many innovative approaches have been developed by Baldrige recipients and are now commonly used by many other companies.

THE BALDRIGE AWARD EVALUATION PROCESS

The Baldrige evaluation process is rigorous. In the first stage, each application is thoroughly reviewed by up to seven or more examiners chosen from among leading quality professionals in business, academia, health care, and government (all of whom are volunteers). Examiners evaluate the applicant's response to each examination item, listing major "strengths" and "opportunities for improvement" relative to the criteria. Strengths demonstrate an effective and positive response to the criteria. Opportunities for improvement do not prescribe specific practices or examiners' opinions on what the company should be doing but, rather, deficiencies in responding to the criteria. To help examiners understand the context of the organization, applicants are required to provide an *Organizational Profile*, which is basically a snapshot of the organization that describes the organizational environment; key relationships with customers, suppliers, and other partners; types of employees and technologies used; the competitive environment; key strategic challenges it faces; and its system for performance improvement. The Organizational Profile helps the organization focus on key performance requirements and results, and helps examiners to understand the organization and what it considers important.

Based on the comments, a percentage score from 0 to 100 in increments of 5 percent is given to each item. Detailed scoring guidelines can be found in the criteria document. Each examination item is evaluated on approach/deployment or results. *Approach* refers to the methods the company uses to achieve the requirements addressed in each category. The factors used to evaluate approaches include:

- the appropriateness of the methods to the requirements;
- the effectiveness of methods, namely, the degree to which the approach is systematic, integrated, and consistently applied; the degree to which the approach embodies effective evaluation/improvement cycles; and the degree to which the approach is based upon reliable information and data;
- alignment with organizational needs; and
- evidence of innovation.

Deployment refers to the extent to which the approaches are applied to all requirements of the item. The factors used to evaluate deployment include:

- use of the approach in addressing item requirements relevant to the organization; and
- use of the approach by all appropriate work units.

Results refers to the outcomes and effects in achieving the purposes given in the item. The factors used to evaluate results include:

- current performance levels;
- performance relative to appropriate comparisons and/or benchmarks;
- rate, breadth, and importance of performance improvements; and
- linkage of results measures to important customer, market, process, and action plan performance requirements identified in the approach/deployment items and the organizational profile.

Scores for each examination item are computed by multiplying the examiner's score by the maximum point value that can be earned, with a total possible score of 1,000. The examiners' comments and scores are then discussed among the team of examiners who reviewed the examination to smooth out differences and variations in comments. This is called the consensus stage during which the group arrives at consensus comments and scores for each item. A national panel of judges then reviews the scores and selects the highest-scoring applicants for site visits.

At this point, six or seven examiners visit the company for up to a week to verify information contained in the written application and resolve issues that are unclear. The judges use the site visit reports to recommend award recipients. All information is kept strictly confidential, and examiners are bound by conflict-of-interest rules and a code of conduct.

All applicants receive a feedback report that critically evaluates the company's strengths and areas for improvement relative to the award criteria. The feedback report, frequently 30 or more pages in length, contains the evaluation team's response to the written application. It includes a distribution of numerical scores of all applicants and a scoring summary of the individual applicant. This feedback is one of the most valuable aspects of applying for the award. We should note that the typical score for recipients is in the 650–750 range. This indicates that although their practices and results are indeed outstanding, they still have opportunities for improvement. As a former Xerox CEO once said, quality is a race without a finish line.

Criteria Evolution

As the important management practices of any organization should be, the specific award criteria are evaluated and improved each year. Over the years, the criteria have been streamlined and simplified to make them more relevant and useful to organizations of all types and size, improve the linkage between process and results, and make the criteria more generic and user friendly. Most significantly, the word *quality* was judiciously dropped in the mid-1990s. For example, prior to 1994, the Strategic Planning category was titled "Strategic Quality Planning." The change to "Strategic Planning" signifies that quality should be a part of business planning, not a separate issue. Throughout the document, the term *performance* has been substituted for quality as a conscious attempt to recognize that the principles of total quality are the foundation for a company's entire management system, not just the quality system. As Dr. Curt Reimann, former director and architect of the Baldrige Award Program, noted, "The things you do to win a Baldrige Award are exactly the things you'd do to win in the marketplace. Our strategy is to have the Baldrige Award criteria be a useful daily tool that simulates real competition."

To this end, the most significant changes in the criteria reflect the maturity of business practices and total quality approaches. The criteria evolved from a primary emphasis on product and service quality assurance to a broad focus on performance excellence in a global marketplace. In addition, criteria updates are designed to address emerging and relevant issues facing business. In 2003, for example, the criteria strengthened its emphasis on organizational governance and ethics in the wake of the Enron, WorldCom, and Arthur Andersen scandals that occurred the year before. In 2005, Baldrige introduced the concept of **sustainability**—which refers to an organization's ability to address current business needs and to have the agility and strategic management to prepare successfully for the future, and to prepare for real-time or short-term emergencies—into the criteria. Recently, concepts of workforce and customer engagement have also been integrated within the criteria.

Impacts of the Baldrige Program

The Baldrige Award criteria form a model for business excellence in any organization—manufacturing or service, large or small (see box "Baldrige Pays Off for Texas Instruments"). An economic evaluation study of the Baldrige program by the U.S. Department of Commerce concluded that a conservative estimate of the present value of the net social benefits associated with the program was $24.65 billion in constant 2000 dollars. This return was achieved by a $119 million investment in total social costs associated with the program, a 207:1 ratio. More importantly, the program changed the way in which many organizations around the world manage their operations, and helped significantly to bring the principles of TQ into the daily culture of these organizations. The true benefactors are the customers and other stakeholders, who received better products and services. Jim Collins (author of *Good to Great: Why Some Companies Make the Leap ... and Others Don't*) endorsed Baldrige with the following statement: "I see the Baldrige process as a powerful set of mechanisms for disciplined people engaged in disciplined thought and taking disciplined action to create great organizations that produce exceptional results."

A large number of organizations are using the award criteria to evaluate their own quality programs, set up and implement quality initiatives, communicate better with suppliers and partners, and for education and training, even if they have no intention to apply for the award. For example, although the legal profession in general has not adopted quality management practices, the Trial Division of Nationwide Insurance, which operates 56 law offices in 20 states, uses the Baldrige model as a key component of its business plan. Senior leaders introduced it to the company's managing trial attorneys and encouraged individual offices to apply for local or state Baldrige-based awards.

Many small businesses (defined by the Baldrige program as those with 500 or fewer employees) believe that the Baldrige criteria are too difficult to apply to their organizations because they cannot afford to implement the same types of practices as large companies. However, an organization's practices need not be formal or complex. For example, the ability to obtain customer and market knowledge through independent third-party surveys, extensive interviews, and focus groups, which are common practices among large companies, may be limited by the resources of a small business. What is important, however, is whether the company is using appropriate mechanisms to gather information and use it to improve customer focus and satisfaction. Similarly, large corporations frequently have sophisticated computer/information systems for data management, whereas small businesses may perform data and information management with a combination of manual methods and personal computers. Also, systems for employee involvement and process management may rely

Baldrige Pays Off for Texas Instruments[11]

Texas Instruments (TI) Defense Systems & Electronics Group (acquired by Raytheon Corporation in 1997) faced a critical issue that many businesses struggle with: Is the payoff of greater competitive advantage worth the effort of achieving total quality, specifically competing for the Baldrige Award? Their answer is a definite yes.

TI understands firsthand that the real benefit of applying for the Baldrige Award lies in adopting its quality criteria. The application itself is the single most powerful catalyst for the kinds of organizational and cultural changes that companies must make to compete.

TI's commitment to quality and productivity improvement dates back to the 1950s. But, like most corporations, most of its efforts were aimed at improving manufacturing and product quality. In the early 1980s, a total quality initiative was formalized across the entire corporation. Some business units made tremendous progress; the semiconductor operation in Japan won the Deming Prize in 1985.

When the Baldrige Award criteria appeared, TI used them to provide focus and coherence to the activities across the corporation. Using the criteria, they were able to tackle a part of total quality that previously had been unreachable: implementing quality efforts in staff, support, and nonmanufacturing areas. In 1989, TI asked every business unit to prepare a mock award application as a way of measuring its progress. This task represented a radical change for some operations because, until that time, most staff functions were not required to measure their processes or their results.

The Defense Systems & Electronics Group's self-assessment revealed that they were a long way from applying for and winning the Baldrige Award. But the group aggressively adopted the criteria as a blueprint for improving its business.

Many executives did not believe that the criteria could be applied to defense contractors. Similarly, many executives today question whether small businesses can realistically meet the Baldrige Award criteria. TI discovered that all companies have one thing in common: customers. Focusing on customers to make the company more competitive gives meaning to the award.

The Baldrige Award application process changed almost everything within the Defense Systems & Electronics Group. Before applying, the group had no way of systematically measuring how well it understood its customers' concerns, captured customers' feedback, or made improvements in interacting with customers. Mountains of data were being collected, but most of the data measured internal criteria, not customer satisfaction. The structured, hierarchical management environment made it difficult to adopt ideas from outside sources.

The Baldrige Award process provided a way to make the customer the centerpiece of daily activities. It led to much better communication with customers and employees and accelerated progress toward less hierarchical, more functional work teams. It changed the management process from an individual activity to a team effort, leading to better decisions. Finally, it introduced two radical new ideas: benchmarking and stretch goals. Changing the culture was not easy and did not happen quickly. It took teamwork, consensus building, and buy-in. At TI, it took about five years of dedicated pulling in the same direction to begin seeing measurable results.

heavily on informal verbal communication and less on formal written documentation. Thus, the size or nature of a business does not affect the appropriateness of the criteria but, rather, the context in which the criteria are applied.

The incorporation of education and health care as categories in the award program in 1999 was a reflection of the growing interest in these sectors. Many school districts are now using the criteria. One large Chicago-area hospital applied for the Baldrige-based Lincoln Award for Excellence and prepared for its accreditation visit by the Joint Commission on Accreditation of Healthcare Organizations (JCAHO) at the same time, recognizing the synergy and overlap of Baldrige principles and JCAHO standards.

Most states have developed award programs similar to the Baldrige Award. State award programs generally are designed to promote an awareness of productivity and quality, foster an information exchange, encourage firms to adopt quality and productivity improvement strategies, recognize firms that have instituted successful strategies, provide role models for other businesses in the state, encourage new industry to locate in the state, and establish a quality-of-life culture that will benefit all residents of the state.[12]

Each state is unique, however, and thus the specific objectives will vary. For instance, the primary objectives of Minnesota's quality award are to encourage all Minnesota organizations to examine their current state of quality and to become more involved in the movement toward continuous quality improvement, as well as to recognize outstanding quality achievements in the state. Missouri, by contrast, has as its objectives to educate all Missourians in quality improvement, to foster the pursuit of quality in all aspects of Missouri life, and to recognize quality leadership. Ohio's program is focused on developing organizations early in their performance excellence journey as well as recognizing outstanding organizations. Information about state award programs can be found at the Baldrige Web site cited earlier in this section.

The Baldrige Criteria and the Deming Philosophy

It is no secret that W. Edwards Deming was not an advocate of the Baldrige Award.[13] (Joseph Juran, however, was highly influential in its development.) The competitive nature of the award is fundamentally at odds with Deming's teachings. However, many of Deming's principles are reflected directly or in spirit within the criteria. In fact, one firm, Zytec, implemented its total quality system around Deming's 14 Points *and* received a Baldrige Award. Specific portions of the Baldrige criteria that support each of Deming's 14 Points are summarized here.

1. *Statement of Purpose.* Strategy development requires a mission and vision. Commitment to aims and purposes by senior leaders is specifically addressed in the Leadership category and in enhancing customer satisfaction and relationships.
2. *Learn the New Philosophy.* Communication of values, expectations, customer focus, and learning is a key area of the Organizational Leadership item.
3. *Understand Inspection.* The Process Management category addresses the development of appropriate measurement plans. The Criteria also seek evidence of how a company aims to minimize the costs associated with inspection.
4. *End Price Tag Decisions.* This is implicitly addressed throughout the Process Management category and in the Criteria's emphasis on overall performance and linkages among processes and results.

5. *Improve Constantly*. Continuous improvement and learning is a core value of Baldrige. The criteria specifically ask how the company evaluates and improves its processes.
6. *Institute Training*. The Human Resource Focus category recognizes the importance of training and employee development in meeting performance objectives.
7. *Teach and Institute Leadership*. Category 1 is devoted exclusively to leadership, and it is recognized as the principal driver of the management system in Figure 2.1.
8. *Drive Out Fear and Innovate*. The Human Resource Focus, Customer and Market Focus, and Strategic Planning categories focus on work design, empowerment, and implementation issues that support this point.
9. *Optimize the Efforts of Teams and Staff*. The Criteria have a significant focus on teamwork and customer knowledge in product/process design and process management, as well as in the Human Resource Focus category.
10. *Eliminate Exhortations*. While not directly addressed, the focus on employee engagement as the driver of high performance makes this a moot point.
11. *Eliminate Quotas and MBO; Institute Improvement; and Understand Processes*. The Leadership and Strategy Deployment items, as well as the Measurement, Analysis and Knowledge Management and Process Management categories deal with fact-based management and understanding processes.
12. *Remove Barriers*. The Leadership and Human Resource Focus categories, as well as the Customer Satisfaction and Relationships item support this goal.
13. *Encourage Education*. This is addressed directly in the Workforce Focus category.
14. *Take Action*. This role of leadership is addressed directly in the Leadership category.

The consistencies among Deming's 14 Points and the Baldrige criteria attest to the universal nature of quality management principles.

INTERNATIONAL QUALITY AWARD PROGRAMS

Numerous countries and regions of the world have established awards and award criteria. Many other award programs are similar in nature to the Baldrige criteria.

The Deming Prize

The Deming Application Prize was instituted in 1951 by the Union of Japanese Scientists and Engineers (JUSE) in recognition and appreciation of W. Edwards Deming's achievements in statistical quality control and his friendship with the Japanese people. The Deming Prize has several categories, including prizes for individuals, factories, and small companies, and the Deming application prize, which is an annual award presented to a company or a division of a company that has achieved distinctive performance improvements through the application of Companywide Quality Control (CWQC). As defined by JUSE, CWQC is a system of activities to assure that quality products and services required by customers are economically designed, produced, and supplied while respecting the principle of customer-orientation and the overall public well-being. These quality assurance activities involve market research, research and development, design, purchasing, production, inspection and sales, as well as all other related activities inside and outside the company. Through everyone in the company understanding both statistical concepts and methods, through their application to all the aspects of quality assurance, and through repeating the cycle of rational planning, implementation, evaluation, and action, CWQC aims to accomplish business objectives.[14]

The judging criteria consist of a checklist of 10 major categories: policies, the organization and its operations, education and dissemination, information gathering, communication and its utilization, analysis, standardization, control/management, quality assurance, effects, and future plans. Each major category is divided into subcategories, or "checking points." For example, the policy category includes policies pursued for management, quality, and quality control; methods for establishing policies; appropriateness and consistency of policies; utilization of statistical methods; communication and dissemination of policies; checks of policies and the status of their achievement; and the relationship between policies and long- and short-term plans. Each category is weighted equally.

Hundreds of companies apply for the award each year. After an initial application accepted as eligible for the process, the company must submit a detailed description of its quality practices. Based on review of the written descriptions, only a few companies believed to be successful in CWQC are selected for a site visit. The site visit consists of a company presentation, in-depth questioning by examiners, and an executive session with top managers. Examiners visit plants and are free to ask any worker any question.

For example, at Florida Power and Light (see box "Electric Quality"), examiners asked questions of specific individuals such as "What are your main accountabilities?" "What are the important priority issues for the corporation?" "What indicators do you have for your performance? For your target?" "How are you doing today compared to your target?" They request examples of inadequate performance. Documentation must be made available immediately. The preparation is extensive and sometimes frustrating.

The Deming Prize is awarded to all companies that meet the prescribed standard. However, the small number of awards given each year is an indication of the difficulty of achieving the standard. The objectives are to ensure that a company has so thoroughly deployed a quality process that it will continue to improve long after a prize is awarded. The application process has no "losers." For companies that do not qualify, the examination process is automatically extended up to two times over three years.

ELECTRIC QUALITY[15]

Florida Power and Light (FPL) is one of the largest electric utilities in the United States. During the 1970s the company was forced to increase utility rates repeatedly because of increasing costs, slower sales growth, and stricter federal and state regulations. The company had become bureaucratic and inflexible. In 1981, Marshall McDonald, then chairman of the board, realized that the company had been concerned with keeping defects under control rather than improving quality. Because of his concern for quality, McDonald introduced quality improvement teams at FPL. Management knew this was a step in the right direction, but such teams alone would not bring about the change needed for the company to survive. McDonald tried to convince other executives that a total quality improvement process was needed, but all the experts that FPL talked to were in manufacturing, while FPL was primarily a service company. In 1983, while in Japan, McDonald met a president of Kansai Electric Power Company, a Deming Prize recipient, who told him about their total quality efforts. Company officials began to visit Kansai regularly, and with their help, FPL began its quality improvement program (QIP) in 1983.

Its quality efforts included empowering each department to develop improvement plans, standardizing work routines, removing waste from them, promoting the concept of internal customers, and enabling better practice to be replicated from one location to another. FPL revamped a centralized suggestion system it had been using for many years. Only about 600 suggestions had been submitted annually and it usually took six months for evaluation. A new decentralized system was proposed with simplified procedures to improve the response time. Employees participated in the implementation of their own suggestions. In 1988, 9,000 suggestions were submitted; in 1989 this number increased to 25,000. As a result of these efforts, the average length of service interruptions dropped from about 75 minutes in 1983 to about 47 minutes in 1989; the number of complaints per 1,000 customers fell to one third of the 1983 level; safety has improved; and the price of electricity has stabilized. In 1989, FPL became the first non-Japanese company to win the Deming Prize.

EUROPEAN EXCELLENCE AWARD

In October 1991, the European Foundation for Quality Management (EFQM) in partnership with the European Commission and the European Organization for Quality announced the creation of the European Quality Award (now called the European Excellence Award). The award was designed to increase awareness throughout the European Community, and businesses in particular, of the growing importance of quality to their competitiveness in the increasingly global market and to their standards of life. The award is based on the following premise: *Excellent results with respect to Performance, Customers, People, and Society are achieved through Leadership driving Policy and Strategy, that is, delivered through People, Partnerships and Resources, and Processes.* EFQM has three recognition levels. The EFQM Excellence Award is the highest form of recognition, similar to Baldrige. Two additional recognition levels have been added: (1) Recognized for Excellence, designed for organizations that are well along the journey to excellence, and (2) Committed to Excellence, for organizations that are at the beginning of the journey.

The award process is similar to the Deming Prize and Baldrige Award. The assessment is based on customer satisfaction, business results, processes, leadership, people satisfaction, resources, people management, policy and strategy, and impact on society. Like Baldrige, results—including customer satisfaction, people (employee) satisfaction, and impact on society—constitute a high percentage of the total score. These are driven by "enablers"—the means by which an organization approaches its business responsibilities.

The categories are roughly equivalent to those in Baldrige. However, the results criteria of people satisfaction, customer satisfaction, impact on society, and business results are somewhat different.[16] The impact on society results category focuses on the perceptions of the company by the community at large and the company's approach to the quality of life, the environment, and the preservation of global resources. The European criteria places greater emphasis on this category than is placed on the public responsibility item in the Baldrige criteria.

Canadian Awards for Business Excellence

Canada's National Quality Institute (NQI) recognizes Canada's foremost achievers of excellence through the prestigious Canada Awards for Excellence. NQI is a nonprofit organization designed to stimulate and support quality-driven innovation within all Canadian enterprises and institutions, including business, government, education, and health care. The Canadian Awards for Business Excellence quality criteria are similar in structure to the Baldrige Award criteria, with some key differences. The major categories and items within each category are:

1. *Leadership*: strategic direction, leadership involvement, and outcomes.
2. *Customer Focus*: voice of the customer, management of customer relationships, measurement, and outcomes.
3. *Planning for Improvement*: development and content of improvement plan, assessment, and outcomes.
4. *People Focus*: human resource planning, participatory environment, continuous learning environment, employee satisfaction, and outcomes.
5. *Process Optimization*: process definition, process control, process improvement, and outcomes.
6. *Supplier Focus*: partnering and outcomes.

These categories seek similar information as the Baldrige Award criteria. For example, the People Focus category examines the development of human resource planning and implementation and operation of a strategy for achieving excellence through people. It also examines the organization's efforts to foster and support an environment that encourages and enables people to reach their full potential.

Australian Business Awards

The Australian Quality Awards (now called the Australian Business Awards) were developed independently from the Baldrige Awards in 1988. The awards are administered by the Australian Quality Awards Foundation, a subsidiary of the

Australian Quality Council. The Australian Business Excellence Prize is the preeminent award available for businesses in Australia. Only two organizations have achieved this level of excellence since the Awards' inception in 1988. In addition to the Australian Business Excellence Prize, four levels of awards are given:

1. The Foundation in Business Excellence Level—provides encouragement recognition for progress toward business excellence.
2. The Bronze Award Level—Bronze Award recipients demonstrate Approach and Deployment that are well defined, planned, subject to review, and show evidence of improvement over time.
3. The Silver Award Level—organizations at this level demonstrate not only performance against the framework at Bronze level but also a philosophy of management that reflects the principles that underpin it and other frameworks around the globe.
4. The Gold Award Level—organizations at this level meet Silver recognition, are able to demonstrate superior performance in at least five of the categories in the framework, and must have scored at least 50 percent on each item.

The assessment criteria address leadership, strategy and planning, information and knowledge, people, customer focus, processes, products and services, and business results. In this model, leadership and customer focus are the drivers of the management system and enablers of performance. Strategy, policy and planning, information and analysis, and people are the key internal components of the management system. Quality of process, product, and service is focused on how work is done to achieve the required results and obtain improvement. Business results are the outcome of the management system—a results category.

As with Baldrige, the framework emphasizes the holistic and interconnected nature of the management process. The criteria are benchmarked with the Baldrige criteria and the European Business Excellence Model. One of the distinctive aspects of Australia's program is solid union support.

Quality Awards in China[17]

In 2001, the China Association for Quality (CAQ) introduced the National Quality Award, which it recently renamed the Performance Excellence Award. To facilitate the emerging economy of China, the Chinese government has issued new quality standards that became effective on Jan. 1, 2005 and are designed to encourage China's thriving business sector to strive for better quality. The award criteria are based on components of the Malcolm Baldrige National Quality Award and are geared toward China's unique business environment—especially in improving business credibility, brand-building strategy, and sustainable development. The Chinese government used representatives of the Shanghai Academy of Quality Management to help write the country's new quality standard, and invited Baldrige Award winners to Shanghai to report on their processes. At the same time, they held many seminars to study Baldrige criteria, learning to adapt those concepts to Chinese quality policy. Seventeen businesses were awarded the Chinese National Quality Award during the first three years.

Among them, Baosteel and Shanghai Dazhong Taxi won the World Class Organization Award and the Asia-Pacific Quality Award, in 2002 and 2004, respectively.

In 2004 Shenzhen became the first city to launch a local quality award, called the Mayor's Cup Quality Award. It is operated by the Shenzhen Bureau of Quality and Technical Supervision. The vice mayor leads an evaluation committee of local experts, which uses many of the Baldrige criteria, including international best practices, social factors and governmental strategic initiatives issued by Shenzhen government leaders.

At the end of 2006, more than 55 organizations had applied for the award, and six firms had won, including Huawei in 2004, one of the first winners. The 3 million RMB ($387,000 U.S.) prize is the highest among quality awards in China and has encouraged many organizations to participate and share best practices. Other cities and provinces, including Shanghai and Ningbo, have now set up local governmental quality awards to promote quality management systems and share experiences in various industries.

Baldrige and National Culture

It is interesting to observe that although many countries adopt much of the Baldrige criteria, many of them have made changes to the criteria or scoring system, as we saw with the European Quality Award framework. As another example, China issued a new quality standard in 2005—The Chinese National Quality Award Criteria—using components of the Baldrige criteria, but which is geared toward China's unique business environment, and focused on improving business credibility, brand-building strategy, and sustainable development. International cultural differences can help to understand and explain these differences. A recent study found support for the notion that the Baldrige award is better suited to some national cultures than with others.[18] Receptiveness to change differs greatly among cultures, suggesting the need for countries to adapt their quality award programs to local conditions to ensure their effective implementation. Perhaps surprisingly, Baldrige is a better fit to the national culture of Japan than it is to the U.S. Some of the reasons for this are that the Baldrige framework was initially influenced heavily by Japanese quality management practices, and that changes to the criteria over the years are focused on changing U.S. management culture, not reflecting its current practice. These results provide even more validation of Deming's observation related to the Theory of Knowledge, that best practices cannot be copied blindly, but must be understood and adapted intelligently. This is an important lesson for managing in today's global environment.

ISO 9000:2000

As quality became a major focus of businesses throughout the world, various organizations developed standards and guidelines. Terms such as *quality management, quality control, quality system*, and *quality assurance* acquired different, and sometimes conflicting, meanings from country to country, within a country, and even within an industry.[19] As the European Community moved toward the European free trade agreement, which went into effect at the end of 1992, quality management became a key strategic objective.

To standardize quality requirements for European countries within the common market and those wishing to do business with those countries, a specialized agency for standardization, the International Organization for Standardization, founded in 1946 and composed of representatives from the national standards bodies of 91 nations, adopted a series of written quality standards in 1987, which were revised in 1994, and again (significantly) in 2000. The most recent version is called the *ISO 9000:2000* family of standards.

The standards have been adopted in the United States by the American National Standards Institute (ANSI) with the endorsement and cooperation of the American Society for Quality (ASQ). The standards are recognized by about 100 countries, including Japan. In some foreign markets, companies will not buy from noncertified suppliers. Thus, meeting these standards is becoming a requirement for international competitiveness. The standards are intended to apply to all types of businesses, including electronics and chemicals, and to services such as health care, banking, and transportation.

ISO 9000 defines *quality system standards*, based on the premise that certain generic characteristics of management practices can be standardized, and that a well-designed, well-implemented, and carefully managed quality system provides confidence that the outputs will meet customer expectations and requirements. The standards were created to meet five objectives:

1. Achieve, maintain, and seek to continuously improve product quality (including services) in relationship to requirements.
2. Improve the quality of operations to continually meet customers' and stakeholders' stated and implied needs.
3. Provide confidence to internal management and other employees that quality requirements are being fulfilled and that improvement is taking place.
4. Provide confidence to customers and other stakeholders that quality requirements are being achieved in the delivered product.
5. Provide confidence that quality system requirements are fulfilled.

Structure of the ISO 9000 Standards

The ISO 9000:2000 standards focus on developing, documenting, and implementing procedures to ensure consistency of operations and performance in production and service delivery processes, with the aim of continual improvement, and supported by fundamental principles of total quality. The standards consist of three documents:

- ISO 9000—Fundamentals and vocabulary
- ISO 9001—Requirements
- ISO 9004—Guidance for performance improvement

ISO 9000 provides definitions of key terms. ISO 9001 provides a set of minimum requirements for a quality management system, and is intended to demonstrate compliance with recognized quality principles to customers and for third-party certification. An example of one of the requirements is, "The supplier's management with executive responsibility shall define and document its policy for quality, including objectives for quality and commitment to quality. The quality policy shall be relevant to the supplier's organizational goals and the expectations and needs of its customers. The supplier shall ensure that this policy is understood, implemented, and maintained at all levels of the organization." Thus, the requirements state precisely what the organization needs to do. The requirements are organized into four major sections: Management Responsibility; Resource Management; Product Realization; and Measurement, Analysis, and Improvement.[20] Finally, ISO 9004 focuses on improving the quality management system beyond these minimum requirements.

The standards are intended to apply to all types of businesses, including electronics and chemicals, and to services such as health care, banking, and transportation. For example, in July 2000, the B2B (business-to-business) firm, bestroute.com, became the first e-commerce distributorship to achieve ISO registration. Interpreting the standards to e-business required some unique strategies to ensure compliance. The company focused on the key concept of the standard that is common to any industry: customer service. The company developed and documented processes for all aspects of bestroute.com's customer service—from call routing to return processing to phone etiquette. As the customer service manager observed, "In the end, the processes we established, implemented and are keeping on top of in order to comply with the standard are the very same things we needed to do to keep customers happy."[21]

Factors Leading to ISO 9000:2000

The original ISO 9000:1994 series standards consisted of 20 fundamental elements of a basic quality system that included such things as management responsibility, design control, purchasing, product identification and traceability, process control, inspection and testing, corrective and preventive action, internal quality audits, training, and statistical techniques. The original standards and the 1994 revision met with considerable controversy.[22] The standards required only that the organization have a documented, verifiable process in place to ensure that it consistently produces what it says it will produce. A company could comply with the standards and still produce a poor-quality product—as long as it does so consistently! Dissatisfaction with ISO 9000 resulted in the European Union calling for deemphasizing ISO 9000 registration, citing the fact that companies are more concerned with "passing a test" than on focusing their energies on quality processes.

The deficiencies in the old ISO 9000 standards led to a joint effort 1994 by the big three automobile manufacturers—Ford, Chrysler, and General Motors—as well as several truck manufacturers, to develop QS-9000, an interpretation and extension of ISO 9000 for automotive suppliers. The goal was to develop fundamental quality systems that provide for continuous improvement, emphasizing defect prevention and the reduction of variation and waste in the supply chain. QS-9000 is based on ISO 9000 and includes all ISO requirements. However, QS-9000 went well beyond ISO 9000 standards by including additional requirements such as continuous improvement, manufacturing capability, and production part approval processes.

ISO 9000:2000 is a response to the widespread dissatisfaction that resulted from the old standards. The new standards have a completely new structure, based on eight principles—"comprehensive and fundamental rules or beliefs for leading and operating an organization" that reflect the basic principles of total quality that we introduced in Chapter 1. These eight principles, shown in Table 2.2, were voted on, and overwhelmingly approved, at a conference in 1997 attended by 36 representatives of countries that have delegates in the TC 176 technical committee, charged with the responsibility of revising the ISO 9000 standards.[23]

With this underlying philosophy, the ISO 9000:2000 revision aligns much closer to the spirit of TQ. For example,

- Organizations now need a process to determine customer needs and expectations, translate them into internal requirements, and measure customer satisfaction and dissatisfaction.

TABLE 2.2 | ISO 9000:2000 QUALITY MANAGEMENT PRINCIPLES

Principle 1: Customer Focus
Organizations depend on their customers and therefore should understand current and future customer needs, should meet customer requirements, and strive to exceed customer expectations.

Principle 2: Leadership
Leaders establish unity of purpose and direction of the organization. They should create and maintain the internal environment in which people can become fully involved in achieving the organization's objectives.

Principle 3: Involvement of People
People at all levels are the essence of an organization and their full involvement enables their abilities to be used for the organization's benefit.

Principle 4: Process Approach
A desired result is achieved more efficiently when activities and related resources are managed as a process.

Principle 5: System Approach to Management
Identifying, understanding, and managing interrelated processes as a system contributes to the organization's effectiveness and efficiency in achieving its objectives.

Principle 6: Continual Improvement
Continual improvement of the organization's overall performance should be a permanent objective of the organization.

Principle 7: Factual Approach to Decision Making
Effective decisions are based on the analysis of data and information.

Principle 8: Mutually Beneficial Supplier Relationships
An organization and its suppliers are interdependent and a mutually beneficial relationship enhances the ability of both to create value.

Source: The terms and definitions taken from the quality management principles of ISO 9000 are reproduced with the permission of the International Organization for Standardization, ISO. They can be obtained from any ISO member and from the Web site of the ISO Central Secretariat at the following address: http://www.iso.org. Copyright remains with ISO.

- Managers must communicate the importance of meeting customer and regulatory requirements, integrate ISO 9000 into business plans, set measurable objectives, and conduct management reviews. No longer can top management delegate the program to people lower in the organization.
- Organizations now must view work as a process and manage a system of interrelated processes. This is significantly different from the "document what you do" requirements of earlier versions.
- Analysis now needs to be done to provide information about customer satisfaction and dissatisfaction, products, and processes with the focus on improvement.
- Training effectiveness must be evaluated and personnel made aware of the importance of their activities in meeting quality objectives.
- In the previous standards, organizations were required to perform corrective and preventive action, but now must have a planned process for improvement.

In 2008, an amendment to the ISO 9001 standards was released, designed to clarify some of the language and concepts and improve compatibility with ISO 14001:2004, the popular environmental standard. The result, ISO 9001:2008, does not introduce any additional requirements nor does it change the intent of ISO 9001:2000, but simply represents a fine-tuning of the standard. It is intended to clarify legal standards, outsourcing, internal audits, the concept of competence, design and development processes, monitoring and measuring processes, and controlling nonconforming products.

Implementation and Registration

Implementing ISO 9000 is not an easy task.[24] The ISO 9000 standards originally were intended to be advisory in nature and to be used for two-party contractual situations (between a customer and supplier) and for internal auditing. However, they quickly evolved into criteria for companies who wished to "certify" their quality management or achieve "registration" through a third-party auditor, usually a laboratory or some other accreditation agency (called a registrar). This process began in the United Kingdom. Rather than a supplier being audited for compliance to the standards by each customer, the registrar certifies the company, and this certification is accepted by all of the supplier's customers.

The registration process includes document review by the registrar of the quality system documents or quality manual; preassessment, which identifies potential noncompliance in the quality system or in the documentation; assessment by a team of two or three auditors of the quality system and its documentation; and surveillance, or periodic reaudits to verify conformity with the practices and systems registered. During the assessment, auditors might ask such questions as (using *management responsibility* as an example): Does a documented policy on quality exist? Have management objectives for quality been defined? Have the policy and objectives been transmitted and explained to all levels of the organization? Have job descriptions for people who manage or perform work effecting quality been documented? Are descriptions of functions that affect quality available? Has management designated a person or group with the authority to prevent nonconformities in products, identify and record quality problems, and recommend solutions? What means are used to verify the solutions?[25]

Recertification is required every three years. Individual sites—not entire companies—must achieve registration individually. All costs are borne by the applicant, so the process can be quite expensive. A registration audit may cost anywhere from \$10,000 to over \$40,000, whereas the internal cost for documentation and training may exceed \$100,000. Hundreds of thousands of organizations around the world have received registration.

BENEFITS OF ISO 9000:2000

ISO 9000 provides a set of good basic practices for initiating a quality system, and is an excellent starting point for companies with no formal quality assurance program. In fact, it provides detailed guidance on process and product control. Thus, for companies in the early stages of developing a quality program, the standards enforce the discipline of control that is necessary before they can seriously pursue continuous improvement. The requirements of periodic audits reinforce the stated quality system until it becomes ingrained in the company.

Many diverse organizations have realized significant benefits from ISO 9000 (see box "Using ISO 9000 at Sears"). At DuPont, for example, ISO 9000 has been credited with increasing on-time delivery from 70 to 90 percent, decreasing cycle time from 15 days to 1.5 days, increasing first-pass yields from 72 to 92 percent, and reducing the number of test procedures by one-third. Sun Microsystems' Milpitas plant was certified in 1992, and managers believe that it has helped deliver improved quality and service to customers.[26] The first home builder to achieve registration, Michigan-based Delcor Homes, reduced its rate for correctable defects from 27.4 to 1.7 in two years and improved its building experience approval rating from the mid-60s to the mid-90s on a 100-point scale.[27] Thus, using ISO 9000 as a basis for a quality system can improve productivity, decrease costs, and increase customer satisfaction.

In addition to such anecdotal evidence, formal research has demonstrated the impact of ISO 9000. One study tracked financial performance from 1987 to 1997 of all publicly traded ISO 9000 certified manufacturing firms in the United States and tested whether ISO 9000 certification leads to productivity improvements, market benefits, and improved financial performance.[28] The research ruled out the hypothesis that ISO 9000 has no causal effect on performance but is simply adopted by firms that are better managed. The evidence supports the view that careful design and implementation of consistent and documented quality management systems can contribute significantly to superior financial performance.

SIX SIGMA

Six Sigma can be best described as a business improvement approach that seeks to find and eliminate causes of defects and errors in manufacturing and service processes by focusing on outputs that are critical to customers and a clear financial

Using ISO 9000 at Sears[29]

Sears, Roebuck and Co., a wholly owned subsidiary of Sears Holdings Corp., is one of the largest retailers in North America. After an eight-year effort, the company registered its product repair centers' and in-home service's quality management systems (QMS) to ISO 9001. Once the repair centers were registered, Sears turned to the in-home service side of its business. About 10,000 Sears' technicians repair one of every five appliances in America. By the end of 2005, Sears had 383 locations under the scope of its ISO 9001 registration, including all six in-home regions. Recognizing that ISO 9001 provides a framework for large organizations to implement a consistent, cohesive program across geographic lines and throughout a multifaceted business, Sears sought registration to enhance its organizational process compliance. The company wanted a consistent process for improving customer satisfaction and enhancing service capabilities. ISO 9001 implementation played a large role in assisting with process standardization across the company. ISO 9001 is often associated with the manufacturing industry, and one major hurdle Sears had to overcome was communicating the value of a QMS within a retail and service environment.

Using, ISO 9001 as a basis for continual improvements, Sears has made dramatic improvements in calibrating the tools used for repairs and service calls. Although the company had calibrated some of its tools prior to implementing ISO 9001, the standard requires 100-percent tool calibration for safety purposes. Another significant benefit of ISO 9001 involves the company's handling of refrigerant. Sears works with Freon and other hazardous materials, which could pose a serious environmental violation if not handled properly. As part of its ISO 9001 efforts, Sears improved its existing hazardous materials program by implementing a comprehensive program on refrigerant handling. The standard also helped Sears' efficiency in completing repairs. For instance, in the Chattanooga, Tennessee, carry-in facility, the average daily completion rate for repairing lawn mowers or other items doubled from four or five to eight or nine per repairpersons as a result of ISO 9001 implementation. Sears' district office in Houston has improved its technician recall rate because of the QMS. The recall rate is the percentage of times service technicians must return to customers' homes for a second time within 30 days. Before the SST, the recall rate in Houston was about 12 percent. In 2004, Houston service technicians made more than a quarter of a million service calls, with a 9.3 percent recall rate. In 2005, the rate dropped to 7.9 percent.

return for the organization. Six Sigma has garnered a significant amount of credibility over the last decade because of its acceptance at such major firms as Allied Signal (now part of Honeywell) and General Electric; however, it is not as new a concept as it seems. This concept is facilitated through use of basic and advanced quality improvement and control tools by teams whose members are trained to provide fact-based decision-making information.

The origin of the term *six sigma* came from a statistical measure that equates to 3.4 or fewer errors or defects per million opportunities. *Six Sigma* relates to the broader philosophy and improvement approach. An ultimate "stretch" goal of all organizations that adopt a Six Sigma philosophy is to have all critical processes, regardless of functional area, at a six sigma level of capability.

Evolution of Six Sigma

Motorola pioneered the concept of Six Sigma as an approach to measuring product and service quality. The late Bill Smith, a reliability engineer at Motorola, is credited with originating the concept during the mid-1980s and selling it to Motorola's CEO, Robert Galvin. Smith noted that system failure rates were substantially higher than predicted by final product test, and suggested several causes, including higher system complexity that resulted in more opportunities for failure, and a fundamental flaw in traditional quality thinking. He concluded that a much higher level of internal quality was required and convinced Galvin of its importance. As a result, Motorola set the following goals in 1987:

> Improve product and services quality ten times by 1989 and at least one hundred fold by 1991. Achieve six-sigma capability by 1992. With a deep sense of urgency, spread dedication to quality to every facet of the corporation, and achieve a culture of continual improvement to assure total customer satisfaction. There is only one ultimate goal: zero defects—in everything we do.[30]

The core philosophy of Six Sigma is based on some key concepts:[31]

1. Think in terms of key business processes and customer requirements with a clear focus on overall strategic objectives.
2. Focus on corporate sponsors responsible for championing projects, support team activities, help to overcome resistance to change, and obtain resources.
3. Emphasize such quantifiable measures as defects per million opportunities (dpmo) that can be applied to all parts of an organization: manufacturing, engineering, administrative, software, and so on.
4. Ensure that appropriate metrics are identified early in the process and that they focus on business results, thereby providing incentives and accountability.
5. Provide extensive training followed by project team deployment to improve profitability, reduce non–value-added activities, and achieve cycle time reduction.
6. Create highly qualified process improvement experts ("green belts," "black belts," and "master black belts") who can apply improvement tools and lead teams.
7. Set stretch objectives for improvement.

The recognized benchmark for Six Sigma implementation is General Electric (GE). The efforts by General Electric in particular, driven by former CEO Jack Welch, brought significant media attention to the concept and made Six Sigma a popular approach to quality improvement. In the mid-1990s, quality emerged as a concern of many employees at GE. Jack Welch invited Larry Bossidy, then CEO of Allied Signal, who had phenomenal success with Six Sigma, to talk about it at a Corporate Executive Council meeting. The meeting caught the attention of GE managers and, as Welch stated, "I went nuts about Six Sigma and launched it," calling it the most ambitious task the company had ever taken on.[32] To ensure success, GE changed its incentive compensation plan so that 60 percent of the bonus was based on financials and 40 percent on Six Sigma, and provided stock option grants to employees in Six Sigma training. In their first year, they trained 30,000 employees at a cost of $200 million and got back about $150 million in savings. From 1996 to 1997, GE increased the number of Six Sigma projects from 3,000 to 6,000 and achieved $320 million in productivity gains and profits. By 1998, the company had generated $750 million in Six Sigma savings over and above their investment, and would receive $1.5 billion in savings the next year.

GE had many early success stories. GE Capital, for example, fielded about 300,000 calls each year from mortgage customers who had to use voicemail or call back 24 percent of the time because employees were busy or unavailable. A Six Sigma team analyzed one branch that had a near-perfect percentage of answered calls and applied their learning of their best practices to the other 41 branches, resulting in a 99.9 percent chance of customers' getting a representative on the first try. A team at GE Plastics improved the quality of a product used in CD-ROMs and audio CDs from a 3.8 sigma level to a 5.7 level and captured a significant amount of new business from Sony.[33] GE credits Six Sigma with a 10-fold increase in the life of CT scanner X-ray tubes, a 400 percent improvement in return on investment in its industrial diamond business, a 62 percent reduction in turnaround time at railcar repair shops, and $400 million in savings in its plastics business.[34]

One of the key learnings GE discovered was that Six Sigma is not only for engineers. Welch observed the following:[35]

- Plant managers can use Six Sigma to reduce waste, improve product consistency, solve equipment problems, or create capacity.
- Human resource managers need it to reduce the cycle time for hiring employees.
- Regional sales managers can use it to improve forecast reliability, pricing strategies, or pricing variation.
- For that matter, plumbers, car mechanics, and gardeners can use it to better understand their customers' needs and tailor their service offerings to meet customers' wants.

After many years of implementation, Six Sigma has become a vital part of GE's company culture. In fact, as GE continues to acquire new companies, integrating Six Sigma into different business cultures is a significant challenge. Six Sigma is a priority in acquisitions and addressed early in the acquisition process.

Many other organizations such as Texas Instruments, Allied Signal (which merged with Honeywell), Boeing, 3M, Home Depot, Caterpillar, IBM, Xerox, Citibank, Raytheon, and the U.S. Air Force Air Combat Command have developed quality improvement approaches designed around the Six Sigma concept and also report significant results. Between 1995 and the first quarter of 1997, Allied Signal reported cost savings exceeding $800 million from its Six Sigma initiative. Citibank groups reduced internal callbacks by 80 percent, credit processing time by 50 percent, and cycle times of processing statements from 28 days to 15 days.[36]

Six Sigma as a Quality Framework

Six Sigma provides a blueprint for implementation of a total quality system (see box "Six Sigma Integration at Samsung"). In many ways, Six Sigma is the realization of many fundamental concepts of "total quality management," notably, the integration of human and process elements of improvement.[37] Human issues include management leadership, a sense of urgency, focus on results and customers, team processes, and culture change; process issues include the use of process management techniques, analysis of variation and statistical methods, a disciplined problem-solving approach, and management by fact. However, it is more than simply a repackaging of older quality approaches and traditional concepts of "total quality" (see box: Six Sigma: Reincarnation of TQM?") Some of the contrasting features include:

- TQ is based largely on worker empowerment and teams; Six Sigma is owned by business leader champions.
- TQ activities generally occur within a function, process, or individual workplace; Six Sigma projects are truly cross-functional.
- TQ training is generally limited to simple improvement tools and concepts; Six Sigma focuses on a more rigorous and advanced set of statistical methods and a structured problem-solving methodology, DMAIC—define, measure, analyze, improve, and control—which will be discussed in detail in Chapter 6.
- TQ is focused on improvement with little financial accountability; Six Sigma requires a verifiable return on investment and focus on the bottom line. In

Six Sigma: Reincarnation of TQM?[38]

A research team studied the Six Sigma quality management procedures and literature to investigate whether Six Sigma is simply a repackaging of traditional TQM methods or whether it provides a new approach to improving quality and organizational excellence. The research team identified three new practices that are critical for implementing Six Sigma: providing a Six Sigma role structure within the organization's human resource management system, instituting the structured improvement procedure as a formal paradigm of conducting improvement projects, and emphasizing using quantitative objective metrics in quality improvement. Using a formal research model and a sample of 226 U.S. manufacturing plants, they concluded that the three Six Sigma practices are distinct from traditional quality management practices, but that they complement the traditional quality management practices in improving performance. The results suggest some important areas that managers need to consider when they implement the Six Sigma practices. Top management support directly affects the implementation of Six Sigma role structure and Six Sigma focus on metrics, which suggests that for successful adoption of Six Sigma, it is critical that top management accepts the concept of Six Sigma and is willing to allocate resources to adapt the organizational structure, policies, and processes for Six Sigma. Middle managers may complement traditional workforce management practices with the Six Sigma role structure to augment their organization's ability in developing employees for continuous improvement. Finally, it is important to emphasize using the Six Sigma structured improvement procedure and performance metrics to motivate and guide improvement activities in product design and process management with the supply of timely and accurate quality information.

addition, Six Sigma has elevated the importance of statistics and statistical thinking in quality improvement. Six Sigma's focus on measurable bottom-line results, a disciplined statistical approach to problem solving, rapid project completion, and organizational infrastructure make it a powerful methodology for improvement.

SIX SIGMA IN SERVICE ORGANIZATIONS

Because Six Sigma was developed in the manufacturing sector, and most publicity has revolved around companies such as Motorola and GE, many people in the service sector think that Six Sigma does not apply to their organizations. Nothing can be further from the truth.[39] All Six Sigma projects have three key characteristics:

1. a problem to be solved;
2. a process in which the problem exists; and
3. one or more measures that quantify the gap to be closed and can be used to monitor progress.

These characteristics are present in all business processes; thus, Six Sigma can easily be applied to a wide variety of transactional, administrative, and service areas. In fact, it is generally agreed that 50 percent or more of the total savings opportunity in an organization lies outside of manufacturing. Within the service sector, Six Sigma is beginning to be called *transactional Six Sigma*. However, although Six Sigma applies equally well in service areas, it is true that services have some unique characteristics relative to manufacturing processes. First, the culture is usually less scientific and service employees typically do not think in terms of processes, measurements, and data. The processes are often invisible, complex, and not well defined or well documented. Also, the work typically requires considerable human intervention, such as customer interaction, underwriting or approval decisions, or manual report generation. These differences make opportunities difficult to identify, and projects difficult to define. Finally, similar service activities are often done in different ways. If you have three people doing the same job, perhaps in three different locations, it is unlikely that they will do the job in the same way.

Because service processes are largely people-driven, measurements are often nonexistent or ill-defined, because many believe that defects cannot be measured. Therefore, one must create measurement systems before collecting any data. Applying Six Sigma to services requires examination of four key measures of the performance:

1. Accuracy, as measured by correct financial figures, completeness of information, or freedom from data errors
2. Cycle time, which is a measure of how long it takes to do something, such as pay an invoice
3. Cost, that is, the internal cost of process activities (in many cases, cost is largely determined by the accuracy and/or cycle time of the process; the longer it takes, and the more mistakes that have to be fixed, the higher the cost)
4. Customer satisfaction, which is typically the primary measure of success

Fortunately, important similarities can be shown between manufacturing and nonmanufacturing processes. First, both types of processes have "hidden factories," those places where the defective "product" is sent to be reworked or scrapped (revised, corrected, or discarded in nonmanufacturing terms). Find the hidden factory and you also find opportunities to improve the process. Performing manual account reconciliation in accounting, revising budgets repeatedly until management will accept them, and making repeat sales calls to customers because all the information requested by the customer was not available are all examples of the hidden factory.

Consider how a janitorial service company might use DMAIC. In the Define stage, a key question would be to define what a defect represents. One might first create a flowchart of the cleaning process, specifying what activities are performed. One example of a defect might be leaving streaks on windows, because it is a source of customer dissatisfaction, a CTQ (critical to quality). In the Measure stage, not only would the firm want to collect data on the frequency of defects, but also information about what products and tools employees use. The Analyze stage might include evaluating differences among employees to determine why some appear better at cleaning than others. Developing a standard operating procedure might be the focus of the Improve stage. Finally, Control might entail teaching employees the correct technique and measuring improvement over time.

In one application at CNH Capital, Six Sigma tools were applied to decrease asset management cycle time in posting repossessions to a bid list and remarketing Web site.[40] Cycle time was reduced 75 percent, from 40 days to 10 days, resulting in significant ongoing dollar savings. A facility management company had a high level of "days sales outstanding." Initially, it tried to fix this issue by reducing the term of days in its billing cycle, which, however, upset customers. Using Six Sigma, it found that a large percentage of accounts with high days sales outstanding received invoices having numerous errors. After understanding the source of the errors and making process changes, the invoice process improved and days sales outstanding were reduced. At DuPont, a Six Sigma project was applied to improve cycle time for an employee's application for long-term disability benefits.[41] Some examples of financial applications of Six Sigma include the following:[42]

- Reduce the average and variation of days outstanding of accounts receivable.
- Close the books faster.
- Improve the accuracy and speed of the audit process.
- Reduce variation in cash flow.
- Improve the accuracy of journal entries (most businesses have a 3–4 percent error rate).
- Improve accuracy and cycle time of standard financial reports.

Other applications of Six Sigma in service organizations include a large insurance company that reduced its defect rate by more than 70 percent, increasing customer satisfaction dramatically, and saving over $250,000 in the first five months of the project; a financial services company that reconfigured its Web site to better reflect the questions being asked at its call center, reducing costs and improving the quality of customer service as customers were more easily able to access account information on the Web; and a facility management company that discovered that a large percentage of accounts with high days sales outstanding received error-ridden invoices from the company—by preventing these errors, days sales outstanding were reduced.[43]

COMPARING BALDRIGE, ISO 9000, AND SIX SIGMA

We examined three major frameworks for quality management systems: the Baldrige Criteria for Performance Excellence, ISO 9000, and Six Sigma. Although each of these frameworks are process-focused, data-based, and management-led, each offers a different emphasis in helping organizations improve performance and increase customer satisfaction. For example, Baldrige focuses on performance excellence for the entire organization in an overall management framework, identifying and tracking important organizational results; ISO focuses on product and service conformity for guaranteeing equity in the marketplace and concentrates on fixing quality system problems and product and service nonconformities; and Six Sigma concentrates on measuring product quality and driving process improvement and cost savings throughout the organization.

Although the 2000 revision of ISO 9000 incorporated many of the Baldrige criteria's original principles, it still is not a comprehensive business performance framework. Nevertheless, it is an excellent way to begin a quality journey. ISO 9000 provides a set of good basic practices for initiating a quality system, and is an excellent starting point for companies with no formal quality assurance program. In fact, it provides more detailed guidance on process and product control than Baldrige, and provides systematic approaches to many of the Baldrige criteria requirements in the Process Management category. Thus, for companies in the early stages of developing a quality program, the standards enforce the discipline of control that is necessary before they can seriously pursue continuous improvement. The requirements of periodic audits reinforce the stated quality system until it becomes ingrained in the company.

Implementing Six Sigma fulfills in part many of the elements of ISO 9000:2000, including the Quality Management System, Resource Management, Product Realization, and Measurement, Analysis, and Improvement sections of the standards.[44] For instance, Six Sigma helps to demonstrate management commitment through periodic review of Six Sigma plans and projects, providing champions to sponsor projects, providing training resources, and communicating progress and achievements.

A critical question is whether an organization using Baldrige will be more successful if it also uses Six Sigma, and vice versa. If one views Six Sigma as only a small part of the Process Management category, one might believe that the impact would be marginal. However, let us examine the role of Six Sigma in each of the seven Baldrige categories. Six Sigma enhances the ability of leadership to focus on the critical factors that make a business successful and select appropriate strategies and action plans. Therefore, Six Sigma can strengthen management practices in Leadership and Strategic Planning. Understanding customer requirements and linking them to processes and delivery systems is a principal focus of Baldrige. By focusing on critical to quality (CTQ) customer requirements—one of the important concepts in Six Sigma, organizations gain better knowledge about customer requirements, a key component of the Customer Focus category.

Six Sigma methodology is driven by a management-by-fact methodology. This basis can improve an organization's ability to meet the requirements in the Measurement, Analysis, and Knowledge Management category. The role of people in championing projects and providing the technical and application-specific knowledge is vital. Six Sigma can improve work systems, training, and the work environment—all critical components of the Workforce Focus Baldrige category. With Six Sigma, process management is not a by-product, but it is one of the primary organizational goals. The DMAIC methodology provides a structured approach to Category 6, Process Management. Finally, Six Sigma's focus on business results leads organizations to track and monitor appropriate metrics.

Building On Quality Frameworks[45]

With about 100 employees, Veridian Homes builds single-family and condominium homes each year in Madison, Wisconsin, and the surrounding area. Using best quality practices to increase customer focus and satisfaction, it has improved productivity while reducing impact on the environment by using such frameworks as the National Housing Quality Award (NHQA), the Baldrige Award criteria, builder certification, and Six Sigma. The NHQA program is based on the Baldrige award, and provides applicants expert evaluation and feedback on their organizations' quality management practices. Unlike the Baldrige award, however, the NHQA process includes a third-party survey of the applicants' customers on their satisfaction with their homes and the home-building process. Self-assessments are conducted annually using Baldrige Express, an employee survey based on the Baldrige criteria. Employees rate the company on each criterion and provide detailed comments on strengths and weaknesses, which are summarized for management. Veridian uses this analysis to drive its annual strategic planning process (SPP).

In 2004, Veridian Homes earned NAHBRC builder certification status for quality and safety management systems. The certification, based on ISO 9000, is third-party audited and includes Veridian's construction, sales, and customer relations departments. Since earning certification, the land development, purchasing, estimating, and design departments have been incorporated into the certification. Veridian's quality initiatives have resulted in several performance improvements, including:

- Model homes sold cycle times reduced from 32 to 15 days
- Drafting time on models reduced by more than an hour
- Estimating time on model homes reduced by 32%
- Material variance (difference between ordered and required, perhaps due to damage on site) down by 20 percent for lumber, 24 percent for siding and 38 percent for trim
- Paperwork processing reduced by 208 hours per year, with a total estimated savings across Veridian of $200,000 through performance increases by implementing a production scheduler software system called Builder MT
- Person hours down by 200 per year through escrow and warranty process improvements
- Defects cut in half by using ten defect reduction teams in cooperation with trade partners

Review and Discussion Questions

1. Summarize the Deming management philosophy. Why has it been controversial?
2. Explain the 14 Points in the context of the four categories of Profound Knowledge.
3. Why doesn't the Deming Chain Reaction terminate with "Increased Profits"? Would this contradict the basis of Deming's philosophy?
4. Provide an example of a system with which you are familiar and define its purpose. Examine the interactions within the system and whether the system is managed for optimization.
5. Describe a process with which you are familiar. List some factors that contribute to common cause variation. Cite some examples of special causes of variation in this process.
6. How does the theory of knowledge apply to education? What might this mean for improving the quality of education?
7. Explain the implications of not understanding the components of Profound Knowledge as suggested by Peter Scholtes.
8. Extract three or four key themes in Deming's 14 Points. How might the 14 Points be grouped in a logical fashion?
9. What implications might the 14 Points have for college education? What specific proposals might you suggest as a means of implementing the 14 Points at your school?
10. Discuss the interrelationships among Deming's 14 Points. How do they support each other? Why must they be viewed as a whole rather than separately?
11. The following themes form the basis for Deming's philosophy. Classify the 14 Points into these categories and discuss the commonalties within each category.
    a. Organizational purpose and mission
    b. Quantitative goals
    c. Revolution of management philosophy
    d. Elimination of seat-of-the-pants decisions
    e. Cooperation building
    f. Improvement of manager-worker relations
12. Summarize Juran's philosophy. How is it similar to and different from Deming's?
13. What is Juran's Quality Trilogy? Is it any different from management approaches in other functional areas of business, such as finance?
14. What implications might Juran's Quality Trilogy have for colleges and universities? Would most faculty and administrators agree that the emphasis has been on quality control rather than planning and improvement?
15. How could you apply Juran's Quality Trilogy to improve your personal approach to study and learning?
16. Summarize the Crosby philosophy. How does it differ from Deming and Juran?
17. Which quality philosophy—Deming, Juran, or Crosby—do you personally feel more comfortable with? Why?
18. Summarize the framework of the Baldrige Award. What are its key philosophical underpinnings?
19. Describe the key issues addressed in each of the seven categories of the Criteria for Performance Excellence.
20. What might be some "best practices" evident in the Performance Excellence Profile of Baptist Hospital? How do these practices align with the first six categories of the Baldrige Award Criteria for Performance Excellence?
21. How do the Baldrige criteria support Deming's 14 Points?
22. Explain the differences among the Baldrige, European, Canadian, and Australian Quality Awards.
23. Prepare a list of specific actions that a high-scoring company in the Baldrige Award process might take in each of the seven categories. How difficult do you think it is for a company to score well in all the categories?
24. Create a matrix diagram in which each row is a category of the Baldrige Award criteria and four columns correspond to a level of

organizational maturity with respect to quality:
- traditional management practices;
- growing awareness of the importance of quality;
- development of a solid quality management system; and
- outstanding, world-class management practice.

In each cell of the matrix, list two to five characteristics that you would expect to see for a company in each of the four situations above for that criteria category. How might this matrix be used as a self-assessment tool to provide directions for improvement?

25. Discuss the implications of the Baldrige criteria for e-commerce. What are the specific challenges that e-commerce companies face within each category of the criteria?
26. Explain the benefits of and controversy surrounding ISO 9000. Can ISO 9000 lead an organization to world-class quality?
27. Map the elements of ISO 9000:2000 against the Baldrige criteria. How are they similar? How are they different?
28. Search the Web for detailed information about ISO 9000 requirements. Although the language of the standard appears to be primarily for manufacturing, try to rewrite some of the requirements in language that would provide a framework for a typical public school system to use the standard.
29. Describe the evolution of Six Sigma. What impact has it had on General Electric? What differences must be addressed in applying Six Sigma in service organizations?
30. What are the similarities and differences among Six Sigma, ISO 9000, and the Baldrige approaches?
31. What philosophical changes might be required to implement a Six Sigma process in a hospital, government agency, or not-for-profit organization? Are they likely to be easy or difficult?
32. How might the principles of Six Sigma be used to improve a quality process in a school or university? What elements of the Six Sigma philosophy might be difficult to obtain support for in the educational environment? Why?
33. Find a company that has implemented a Six Sigma process. What changes have they made in the organization in order to develop their Six Sigma approach?

CASES

The Technical Support Clerk

Melissa Claire works as a technical support representative at a call center for a major computer manufacturer. Her duties include answering the telephone, answering technical questions, troubleshooting customer problems, and providing other general information and guidance to customers. Her supervisor told her to be courteous and not to rush callers. However, the supervisor also told her that she must process at least five calls per hour because of the volume of calls that typically comes in and the limited staff available. Melissa comes home each day frustrated because she cannot always find the information that she needs in the database, and she becomes stressed whenever she is told to "speed it up."

Discussion Questions

1. What is Melissa's job as opposed to her job description? What might Deming say about this situation?
2. Drawing upon Deming's principles, outline a plan to improve this situation.

Nightingale College of Nursing[46]

Central Texas University's (CTU's) Nightingale College of Nursing (NCON) was established in 1954 as an autonomous, degree-recommending unit, with a primary mission to provide undergraduate and graduate nursing education. NCON began as the Riverview School of Nursing, a diploma program established in 1914 and nationally accredited in 1950. Today NCON offers nursing education on three Texas campuses: the main campus is located in Freedom, and two satellite campuses are in San Antonio and Dallas. The Commission on Collegiate Nursing Education (CCNE) accredits the baccalaureate and graduate degree nursing programs, while the Southern Association of Colleges and Schools (SACS) accredits the entire university. NCON is approved by the Texas Higher Education Coordinating Board (THECB) and is a member of the Council of Baccalaureate and Higher Degree Programs of the American Nursing League (ANL) and the American Association of Colleges of Nursing (AACN). The College of Nursing is one of four academic units of CTU; the others are the College of Professional Studies, College of Health Sciences, and College of Arts and Sciences.

A summary of the organizational environment, relationships, and challenges that impact NCON's performance excellence approaches is given below. These are the key factors that would be described in the Baldrige Organizational Profile.

Organizational Environment

- College of Nursing, part of larger university
- Three campuses, including primary (Freedom) and two satellites (San Antonio, Dallas)
- Degree programs for BSN, MSN, DNP, plus RN-to-BSN program
- Classes offered on campus, accelerated, and online
- Multiple student assistance programs, including financial assistance, traineeships, graduate teaching, and research assistantships
- Key characteristics of organizational culture: Commitment to excellence in teaching and preparing nurses to deliver high-quality patient care; creativity, knowledge, and skills of faculty, staff members, and students are greatest strengths
- Core competencies: High-quality nursing instruction, effective use of instructional technology, and leading-edge distance education in nursing
- Mission: To prepare nurses by fostering curiosity to learn through engaging students of all ages and ethnic groups in scholarship or inquiry and practice and dissemination; serving the health care needs and issues of the people of Texas, the nation, and the world through collaborative practice, professional leadership, and integration of health promotion and disease prevention for the sake of patient care; and promoting lifelong learning and healthy communities in a time of rapid technological and societal change and commitment to the advancement of the nursing profession
- Vision: Be an exemplar of excellence among nursing schools through academic achievement, research and creativity, innovation, collaboration, and commitment to fiscal accountability
- Values: Collaboration, compassion, quest for knowledge, competence, and integrity
- 118 faculty and staff members include 97 full-time and part-time faculty members, plus 60 adjunct and loaned hospital faculty members, all nonunion
- All but two faculty members hold a doctorate; 96% are female; 79.7% are Caucasian, 11.3% are African American, 7% are Hispanic, 2% are Asian; the average age is 51
- Facilities housed in building on main university campus, built in 1920, renovated in 1977; shared facilities on satellite campuses with College of Health Sciences
- Simulation and Clinical Learning Center at San Antonio satellite
- Pilot site for parent university's new technologies; Golden Fleece is data warehouse for campus transactions, student records, financial data, and HR information
- Classroom Resource Exchange (CRE) designed to provide access to Golden Fleece to facilitate communication; to be an operational tool for student outcomes and portfolios; to be a faculty development resource; and to provide an action plan tool to develop, deploy, and monitor goals
- Regulatory environment: Parent university policies and procedures (under THECB mandates); federal regulations for higher education institutions (OSHA, ADA, FERPA); standards and accreditation (SACS and CCNE); state board (TBN) approves nursing programs
- Nursing accreditation agency (CCNE) requires mission-driven assessment on a ten-year cycle

Organizational Relationships

- Parent is governed by a Board of Regents (BR)—with nine voting members and one nonvoting student appointed by the Texas governor. BR meets quarterly to set/review budget and academic framework and provide oversight of financial, physical, and personnel affairs
- Parent structured in five divisions, each headed by a VP; VP of Academic Affairs is the Provost, and all college deans report to this position

- Parent supplies a $10.5 million budget; applicant supplements this with $1 million in grants and clinic revenues; new or innovative projects can garner additional university funding support
- Dean, three associate deans, and assistant to the dean form the Dean's Council that provides day-to-day oversight; dean represents applicant on university-wide councils
- Nursing Professional Administrative Council (NPAC) is applicant's primary strategy group
- Key faculty committees support key processes: Admissions, Curriculum, Faculty Development, Evaluation and Assessment
- Texas is the primary market area, though college draws from other regions as well
- 2,493 students in 2008 (5.5% increase): 1,914 undergraduates, 436 master's level, and 143 doctoral students
- Students are 90% female, 50% Caucasian, 24% African American, 14% Hispanic, 10% Asian, and about 2% other ethnicities
- Student markets segmented as prospective and enrolled; enrolled students further segmented by participation (transfer, distance, minority, international, graduate)
- Five key stakeholder groups (in addition to students): BR, feeder schools, employers and graduate schools, alumni/donors, and the community
- Key suppliers valued on timeliness and reliability as well as value/price; services integrated where possible to reduce costs
- Practicum sites are key partners—partners serve on an advisory council for the college
- Key partners internal to university: Admissions, Development, Information Technology, Undergraduate Studies, Library, Student Life
- Key student requirements: *All students:* Excellent instruction, flexible scheduling, placement, instructional support, advising, accessible faculty, and technology. *Transfer students:* Orientation, assessment of capabilities, and articulation of courses. *Distance students:* IT support; ability to ask questions and receive prompt answers. *Minority students:* Respect for diversity, sense of identity, and inclusion. *International students:* Assistance with visa status, orientation, sense of identity, and inclusion. *Graduate students:* Flexible scheduling
- Key stakeholder requirements: *Board of Regents:* Communication about current and future campus needs, meet state demand for nurses and nursing faculty, sound fiscal management, increased enrollments, and maintain accreditation. *Feeder schools:* Opportunities for input, regular communications about campus events, continuing education opportunities, knowledge of current and future admissions requirements, and articulation agreements. *Community:* Support for community projects; educational resources and expertise.
- *Employers and graduate schools:* High-quality, clinically competent pool of graduates; meet changing needs. *Alumni/donors:* Positive image and reputation; continued communication, including updates; employment opportunities; and support for lifelong learning

Competitive Environment

- Largest nursing school in the state (graduates the largest number of nurses); numerous competitors, especially in large urban areas
- Increasing competition from "fast-track" and online programs
- Success critically dependent on reputation, high-quality academic programs, moderate tuition rates, and agility to respond to needs of employers and students
- Collaborates with other programs where needed for specialty offerings
- Numerous comparative sources available for academic and operational metrics
- Increasing competition for qualified faculty members

Strategic Context

- Strategic challenges: Grow enrollment while differentiating the college, maintain financial viability and integrate technology, increase capacity to meet workforce needs (e.g., aging nursing faculty), and increase enrollment of males and male/female minorities and retention and graduation of minority students
- Strategic advantages: Reputation of its BSN programs, responsiveness to changing market, fiscal strength, use of technology in education delivery, and supportive alumni base

Performance Improvement System

- Baldrige process provides focus on continual organizational refinement of processes
- Regular oversight and review by university and accreditation boards
- LIGHT Scorecard of Key Performance Indicators (KPIs)

- Focus on student/stakeholder requirements, improving performance, and effective strategic planning
- Roundtable Review Process and Learn, Analysis, Design, Development, Implement, Evaluate (LADDIE) models to design and improve systems and processes
- Multiple learning/listening posts to gather input from faculty, staff members, and students
- Self-study on each degree program every five years

Discussion Questions

In examining the scope of the first six categories (excluding results) in the 2009-10 Baldrige Education criteria (which you can access at the Baldrige Web site), list the most relevant factors that would affect NCON's management practices. For example, in considering the Process Management category, you might note that one of their strategic challenges is to grow enrollment while differentiating the college, and to maintain financial viability and integrate technology. Therefore, you might expect to see that a key process would be student recruitment and retention. You might also note that their core competencies are high-quality nursing instruction, effective use of instructional technology, and leading-edge distance education in nursing. Thus, you might expect to see some key work processes that relate to and capitalize on these core competencies. Therefore, in your listing of the most relevant factors for the Process Management category, the first two factors might be the following:

- Grow enrollment while differentiating college, maintain financial viability and integrate technology, increase capacity to meet workforce needs (e.g., aging nursing faculty), and increase enrollment of males and male/female minorities and retention and graduation of minority students
- Core competencies: High-quality nursing instruction, effective use of instructional technology, and leading-edge distance education in nursing

Complete this list for each category and briefly justify why these factors would be important to the design of NCON's performance excellence approaches to achieving high quality and excellent business results.

TecSmart Electronics

TecSmart Electronics designs, manufactures, and repairs electronic power supplies for a variety of original equipment manufacturers in the computer, medical, and office products fields. The company's focus is summed up in three simple words: quality, service, and value. The top management team started its quality journey in the mid-1980s, basing it on Deming's 14 Points. They established a Deming Steering Committee to guide the process and champion each of the 14 Points, and trained most of the employees by sending them to Deming seminars. Although the Deming philosophy provided the foundation to carry the company into the twenty-first century, the current CEO decided to pursue a Baldrige focus and began a process of self-assessment against the criteria to identify opportunities for improvement.

As a first preparatory step, the executive team spent a day off-site to think about its management practices and create an initial list of its strengths, which are summarized here.

- Senior leaders set company objectives and guide cross-functional teams to review and develop individual plans for presentation to employees. Each department manager develops a supporting objective for each company objective, and nearly every employee works on a team to support these objectives.
- Senior leaders participate in quarterly communication meetings with all employees to discuss company issues and answer questions. All employees receive full financial information from their managers each month.
- Senior leaders teach courses in TecSmart University on change management, customer service, quality, and leadership; meet with customers, suppliers, and benchmarking partners; and are actively engaged in professional and community organizations.
- The company collects operational data in every department and evaluates its information requirements in monthly senior staff meetings and cross-functional task team meetings.
- TecSmart sets Six Sigma goals for most of its processes and converted process measurements to parts per million on all product lines.
- All employees are trained in a five-step problem-solving process based on defining problems, collecting data, analyzing the cause of the problem, developing a solution, and implementing change.
- Inputs to the strategic planning process include customer feedback, market research, and

benchmarking information from customers, suppliers, competitors, and industry leaders. Team analyses are evaluated at an off-site planning meeting by all managers, resulting in long-range strategic planning documents, which are discussed with the rest of the workforce as well as major suppliers for feasibility. Once agreed upon, department teams develop detailed action plans with measurable goals. The CEO reviews progress every month.

- TecSmart uses more than a dozen different processes to gather customer information, and validates the information by consolidation and cross-referencing.
- All employees receive customer relationship training. Customer service employees help define service standards, which are tracked on a routine basis.
- All complaints are handled by the vice president of sales and resolved within two days. The vice president is responsible for ensuring that any process that generated a complaint is improved.
- Customer satisfaction data is acquired from sales representatives, executive phone calls and visits, and satisfaction surveys. These data are reviewed and compared by the executive team during the strategic planning process.
- TecSmart uses self-managed work groups in which employees make most day-to-day decisions while managers focus on coaching and process improvement. Hourly workers can make process changes with the agreement of only one other person, and salespeople are authorized to travel whenever they feel it necessary for customer service.
- The average employee receives 72 hours of internal quality/service-related training, and quality training is mandatory for all salespeople, engineers, office staff, and managers.
- Employees are surveyed each year to gauge how effectively the company implemented Deming's 14 Points, rating each on a scale of 1 to 10.
- Cross-functional teams guide product development, which includes four interim reviews by executive management. Meetings are held with customers to identify needs and requirements and to review progress at the end of each phase of the development process.
- New product introduction teams work with design engineers and customers to ensure that design requirements are met during manufacturing and testing. All processes are formally documented, using statistical process control to monitor variation and provide a basis for corrective action. Statistical methods are used to optimize processes.
- Quality is assessed through internal audits, employee opinion surveys, and customer feedback.
- Suppliers are involved in early stages of a product development program. Quality requirements for suppliers have been identified, and certified suppliers' materials are exempt from incoming inspection.

Discussion Questions

1. Discuss how the practices that TecSmart identified support Deming's 14 Points.
2. How do these practices support the Baldrige criteria? Specifically, identify which of the questions in the criteria each of these practices address.
3. What are some of the obvious opportunities for improvement relative to the Baldrige criteria? What actions would you recommend that TecSmart do to improve its pursuit of performance excellence using the Baldrige criteria?

Can Six Sigma Work in Health Care?

Colin David is the CEO of a Southwest Louisiana Regional Medical Center (SLRMC), a small nonprofit hospital with 150 beds and 825 employees, offering a wide range of outpatient and inpatient services. Colin had just returned from a health care conference during which one of the keynote speakers—from the financial services industry—discussed the philosophy and benefits of Six Sigma and urged health care organizations to consider moving toward a Six Sigma framework. Colin was quite excited. However, he knew that changing the culture in a hospital was indeed difficult. He felt that if he could accomplish that, SLRMC could truly become a nationally recognized leader in the industry. In discussing the concept, the executive management team was also excited at the possibilities. They identified four key areas where they thought that Six Sigma could lead to significant benefits: patient services, quality assessment, financial management, and human resources. As time was running short for the meeting, the team concluded with one major action item: the directors in charge of each of these four areas were to develop a set of strategic Six Sigma projects that would form the basis for the initiative. However, after the meeting broke up, Colin realized that in their initial euphoria over the potential of Six Sigma, they had not thought of how to introduce it to the hospital staff and physicians, or how to manage the initiative. Colin decided that it would be best to call in a consultant to help. Because *you* were highly recommended, you have a meeting scheduled with Colin in one week.

Discussion Questions

1. What would be your agenda for this meeting?
2. What questions would you need answered before proposing a Six Sigma implementation plan?
3. How would you design an infrastructure to support Six Sigma at SLRMC?

Santa Cruz Guitar Company Revisited

Read the Santa Cruz Guitar Company Case in Chapter 1. Explain how Deming's 14 Points are reflected in its management practices and procedures.

Endnotes

1. Baldrige National Quality Program 2005 Award-Recipient Profile, National Institute of Standards and Technology, U.S. Department of Commerce.
2. W. Edwards Deming, *Out of the Crisis*, Cambridge, Mass.: MIT Center for Advanced Engineering Study, 1986.
3. John Hillkirk, "World-Famous Quality Expert Dead at 93," *USA Today*, December 21, 1993.
4. W. Edwards Deming, *The New Economics for Industry, Government, Education*, Cambridge, Mass.: MIT Center for Advanced Engineering Study, 1993.
5. April 17, 1979; cited in L. P. Sullivan, "Reducing Variability: A New Approach to Quality," *Quality Progress*, Vol. 17, No. 7, July 1984, pp. 15–21.
6. Clarence Irving Lewis, *Mind and the World*, Mineola, N.Y.: Dover, 1929.
7. Peter R. Scholtes, "Communities as Systems," *Quality Progress*, July 1997, pp. 49–53.
8. Matthew W. Ford and James R. Evans, "Managing Organizational Self-Assessment: Follow-Up and Its Influence Factors," working paper, Department of Management & Marketing, Northern Kentucky University, 2003.
9. Adapted from March Laree Jacques, "Big League Quality," *Quality Progress*, August 2001, pp. 27–34.
10. Philip B. Crosby, *Quality Is Free*, New York: McGraw-Hill, 1979, pp. 200–201.
11. Adapted from Jerry R. Junkins, "Insights of a Baldrige Award Winner," *Quality Progress*, Vol. 27, No. 3, March 1994, pp. 57–58.
12. Paul M. Bobrowski and John H. Bantham, "State Quality Initiatives: Mini-Baldrige to Baldrige Plus," *National Productivity Review*, Vol. 13, No. 3, Summer 1994, pp. 423–438.
13. Letter from W. Edwards Deming, *Harvard Business Review*, January–February 1992, p. 134.
14. JUSE, The Deming Prize Guide for Oversea Companies, TOKYO, 1992, p. 5.
15. Brad Stratton, "A Beacon for the World," *Quality Progress*, May 1990, pp. 60–65; Al Henderson and Target Staff, "For Florida Power and Light After the Deming Prize: The "Music Builds ... and Builds ... and Builds," *Target*, Summer 1990, pp. 10–21.
16. B. Nakkai and J. Neves, "The Deming, Baldrige, and European Quality Awards," *Quality Progress*, April 1994, pp. 24–29.
17. "China Issues New Quality Standard," *Quality Digest*, December 2004, http://www.qualitydigest.com/dec04/news.shtml#3, accessed 4/08/06. See also Jack Pompeo "Living Inside China's Quality Revolution" *Quality Progress*, August 2007, 30–35
18. Barbara B. Flynn and Brooke Saladin, "Relevance of Baldrige Constructs in an International Context: A Study of National Culture," *Journal of Operations Management*, 24, 5, September 2006, pp. 583–603.
19. Michael J. Timbers, "ISO 9000 and Europe's Attempts to Mandate Quality," *Journal of European Business*, March/April 1992, pp. 14–25.
20. http://www.bsi.org.uk/iso-tc176-sc2/. "Transition Planning Guidance for *ISO/DIS 9001:2000*," ISO/TC 176/SC 2/N 474, December 1999.
21. Richard C. Randall, "Quality in the Dot.Com World," *Quality Progress*, February 2001, 86–87.
22. Amy Zuckerman, "ISO/QS-9000 Registration Issues Heating Up Worldwide," *The Quality Observer*, June 1997, pp. 21–23.

23. Amy Zuckerman and Rosalind McClymont, "Tracking the Ongoing ISO 9000 Revisions," *Business Standards*, Vol. 2, No. 2, March/April 2000, pp. 13–15; Jack West with Charles A. Cianfrani and Joseph J. Tsiakals, "A Breeze or a Breakthough? Conforming to ISO 9000:2000," *Quality Progress*, March 2000, pp. 41–44. See also by West et al., "Quality Management Principles: Foundation of ISO 9000:2000 Family, Part 5," *Quality Progress*, February 2000, pp. 113–116; and "Quality Management Principles: Foundation of ISO 9000:2000 Family, Part 6," *Quality Progress*, March 2000, pp. 79–81.
24. Implementation guidelines are suggested by the case study by Steven E. Webster, "ISO 9000 Certification, A Success Story at Nu Visions Manufacturing," *IIE Solutions*, April 1997, pp. 18–21.
25. AT&T Corporate Quality Office, *Using ISO 9000 to Improve Business Processes*, July 1994.
26. "ISO 9000 Update," *Fortune*, September 30, 1996, p. 134[J].
27. "Home Builder Constructs Quality with ISO 9000," *Quality Digest*, February 2000, p. 13.
28. Charles J. Corbett, María J. Montes-Sancho, David A. Kirsch, "The Financial Impact of ISO 9000 Certification in the United States: An Empirical Analysis," *Management Science*, Vol. 51, No. 7, July 2005, pp. 1046–1059.
29. Pam Parry, "Sears Delivers a Better QMS," *Quality Digest*, January 10, 2007
30. "Origin of Six Sigma: Designing for Performance Excellence," *Quality Digest*, May 2000, 30; and Mikel Harry and Richard Schroeder, *Six Sigma*, New York: Currency, 2000, 9–11.
31. A composite of ideas suggested by Stanley A. Marash, "Six Sigma: Business Results Through Innovation," *ASQ's 54th Annual Quality Congress Proceedings*, 2000, 627–630; and Dick Smith and Jerry Blakeslee, *Strategic Six Sigma: Best Practices from the Executive Suite*, New York: Wiley, 2002.
32. Jack Welch, *Jack: Straight from the Gut*, New York: Warner Books, 2001, 329–330.
33. Welch, Jack, 333–334.
34. "GE Reports Record Earnings with Six Sigma," *Quality Digest*, December 1999, 14.
35. See note 34.
36. Rochelle Rucker, "Six Sigma at Citibank," *Quality Digest*, December 1999, 28–32.
37. Ronald D. Snee, "Guest Editorial: Impact of Six Sigma on Quality Engineering," *Quality Engineering*, 12, No. 3, 2000, ix–xiv.
38. Xingxing Zu, Lawrence D. Fredendal, and Thomas J. Douglas, "The evolving theory of quality management: the role of Six Sigma," *Journal of Operations Management*, 26, 2008, pp. 630–650. See also Roger G. Schroeder, Kevin Linderman, Charles Liedtke, and Adrian S. Choo, "Six Sigma: Definition and underlying theory," *Journal of Operations Management*, 26, 2008, pp. 536–554 for a comprehensive evaluation of the differences between Six Sigma and traditional quality management approaches.12
39. This discussion of the adaptability of Six Sigma to services is adapted from Soren Bisgaard, Roger W. Hoerl, and Ronald D. Snee, "Improving Business Processes With Six Sigma," *Proceedings of ASQ's 56th Annual Quality Congress*, 2002 (CD-ROM), and Kennedy Smith, "Six Sigma for the Service Sector," *Quality Digest*, May 2003, 23–28.
40. Elizabeth Keim, LouAnn Fox, and Julie S. Mazza, "Service Quality Six Sigma Case Studies," *Proceedings of the 54th Annual Quality Congress of the American Society for Quality*, 2000 (CD-ROM).
41. Lisa Palser, "Cycle Time Improvement for a Human Resources Process," *ASQ's 54th Annual Quality Congress Proceedings*, 2000 (CD-ROM).
42. Roger Hoerl, "An Inside Look at Six Sigma at GE," *Six Sigma Forum Magazine*, 1, No. 3, May 2002, 35–44.
43. Kennedy Smith, "Six Sigma for the Service Sector," *Quality Digest*, May 2003, 23–27.
44. Ronald D. Snee and Roger W. Hoerl, *Leading Six Sigma*, Upper Saddle River, N.J.: Prentice Hall, 2002.
45. Denis Leonard, "Building Quality at Veridian Homes," *Quality Progress*, October 2006, 49–54
46. Based on 2008 Malcolm Baldrige National Quality Award examiner training case study. U.S. Department of Commerce, 2008.

Tools and Techniques for Quality Design and Control

CHAPTER 3

Performance Excellence Profile: Texas Nameplate Company, Inc.[1]

The smallest business ever to receive a Baldrige Award, Texas Nameplate Company, Inc. (TNC), is also the only small business to receive the Baldrige Award twice, first in 1998 and again in 2004. Located in Dallas, Texas, TNC is a privately held, family business that produces custom nameplates in small and frequent orders primarily for small businesses nationwide and abroad. These identification tags and labels display important equipment usage and safety information for products ranging from high-pressure valves and oil field equipment to computers.

Relationships with customers are key to TNC's success. The company uses a variety of formal and informal approaches to build and maintain relationships, including a guarantee to deliver material on time and free of defects—or to supply them free of charge. A variety of communication and customer access mechanisms helps these relationships grow and thrive. They include face-to-face contact with employees at all levels, a database of customer interactions, and a voicemail system that ties into the company's e-mail system to track customer requests and concerns. Complaints are aggregated in a database and resolved by a Corrective Action Team.

TNC's senior leaders, a group that includes nearly half the staff, are engaged in all aspects of TNC's strategy development and deployment approaches. All employees participate in monthly meetings and all managers and supervisors in weekly or biweekly meetings to review organizational performance, share ideas, and identify opportunities for improvement. Semiannually, senior leaders conduct Management Reviews. TNC has been recertified under ISO (International Organization for Standardization) 9001:2000 for its Quality Management System.

Effective use of innovative, systematic processes and new technology is helping TNC achieve its goal to be "better, not bigger." The company developed an intranet, called The New Hotrod™, which tracks workflow and displays real-time production information throughout the plant. Two other intranet programs—Real-Time Dashboard™ and Pipeline Dashboard™—collect and organize the production data. The New Hotrod™ provides Web pages that display information and enable employees to monitor production and search an extensive database of production and customer information.

More than 80 percent of TNC's workforce has been cross-trained to perform multiple tasks across departments. Employees regularly check real-time information on workflow tracked through the intranet and displayed on a centrally controlled Smart TV. They respond to changes in workflow by promptly rotating to areas that need assistance. The New Hotrod™ also provides a forum for employee discussions and suggestions. Employees are encouraged to develop and maintain personal Web pages, an activity that expands their computer skills and earns them recognition. Technology and training have led to dramatic improvements in production. Between 1998 and 2004, the incidence of product nonconformity with specifications, as a percentage of sales, dropped from 1.4 percent to about 0.5 percent, significantly lower than the Industry Week median (2 percent). In that same period, TNC reduced its quote response time from 6 hours to less than 2 hours, and it trimmed the length of its production cycle from 14 days to under 8 days.

TNC improved its fiscal processes as well. Better management of aged receivables has reduced the percentage of unpaid accounts (90 days or older) from 7 percent in 2002 to less than 4 percent in 2004. And, to better guide its product pricing policy, the company developed its Simon™ Pricing System, which enables the sales staff to adjust pricing based on both an individual customer's needs and the pricing policies of TNC's competitors. Everyone in the company is valued, trusted, and counted on for the success of the organization. Continuous, open, two-way communication between senior leaders and employees at all levels has created an environment in which employees are highly motivated and empowered.

Organizations like TNC cannot succeed in producing high quality goods and services without effectively designing, controlling, and improving all of its organizational processes. Joseph Juran characterized quality management using the "Quality Trilogy": *planning*, *control*, and *improvement*. Planning involves the design of the goods and services that customers want, as well as the processes that create and deliver them. Control is focused on maintaining target levels of performance. Improvement is simply making goods, services, and processes better. He observed that most managers devote too much attention to control and too little to planning and improvement—which may be the most important activities for meeting and exceeding customer expectations and gaining competitive advantage.

Process management involves design, control, and improvement—the key activities necessary to achieve a high level of performance in key value creation and support processes, identifying opportunities for improving quality and operational performance, and, ultimately, customer satisfaction. Good process management helps to prevent defects and errors and eliminate waste and redundancy and thereby leads to better quality and improved company performance through shorter cycle times, improved flexibility, and faster customer response. AT&T, for example, bases its process management philosophy on the following principles:

- Process quality improvement focuses on the end-to-end process.
- The mind-set of quality is one of prevention and continuous improvement.
- Everyone manages a process at some level and is simultaneously a customer and a supplier.
- Customer needs drive process quality improvement.
- Corrective action focuses on removing the root cause of the problem rather than on treating its symptoms.
- Process simplification reduces opportunities for errors and rework.
- Process quality improvement results from a disciplined and structured application of the quality management principles.[2]

Tools and techniques provide the means for objectively evaluating process performance activities and effectively designing, controlling, and improving them. Quality practitioners have adapted a variety of tools and techniques from other disciplines, such as statistics, operations research, and creative problem solving, to help design, improve, and control processes. These tools provide a means by which problems and issues can be viewed objectively, data can be used as a basis for fact-driven decisions, and managers can deal with variation in a logical fashion. This chapter, along with the next chapter, provides an overview of the essential tools and techniques used to support process management activities. (The online bibliography of this book provides supplementary reading on these and others.) In this chapter we focus on process design and contol; Chapter 4 is devoted to process improvement.

The objectives of this chapter are to:

- describe approaches to designing products and services to achieve better customer satisfaction;
- illustrate the application of a variety of tools for process improvement, including those used in Six Sigma and Lean Six Sigma;
- discuss the importance of creativity and innovation for quality improvement and the management environment that fosters these characteristics; and
- describe principles of statistical thinking as a basis for effective management and to introduce statistical process control.

DESIGNING QUALITY GOODS AND SERVICES

Despite remarkable advances in manufacturing and service technology, businesses and consumers are still plagued by product failures or service upsets. Consumers don't receive the quality they expect. Thousands of people die from medical errors each year. Software applications that control most modern products are prone to failure.[3] Most of these problems result fundamentally from poor design or inadequate design processes.

Companies today face incredible pressures to continually improve the quality of their products while simultaneously reducing costs to meet ever-increasing legal and environmental requirements and to shorten product life cycles to meet changing consumer needs and remain competitive. The ability to achieve these goals depends on a large extent on product design (by which we also imply *redesign*). Better designs not only reduce costs but also improve quality. For example, simpler designs have fewer components, which mean fewer points of failure and less chance of assembly error.[4] Although we tend to equate product design with manufactured goods, it is important to realize that design processes apply to services as well. For example, in the late 1980s, Citibank designed a new mortgage approval procedure that reduced turnaround times from 45 days to less than 15; FedEx has consistently developed new variations of its package delivery services.[5]

Customers' needs and expectations drive the planning process for goods and services. Marketing plays a key role in identifying customer expectations. Once they are identified, managers must translate them into specific product and service specifications that manufacturing and service delivery processes must meet. In some cases, the product or service that customers receive is quite different from what they expect. It is management's responsibility to minimize such gaps. Organizations can use several tools and approaches to help them focus on their external and internal customers.

Most companies have some type of structured product design and development process. Design for Six Sigma (DFSS) is an emerging discipline that represents a set of tools and methodologies used in the product development process for ensuring that goods and services will meet customer needs and achieve performance objectives and that the processes used to make and deliver them achieve Six Sigma capability. DFSS consists of four principal activities:[6]

1. *Concept development*, in which product functionality is determined based upon customer requirements, technological capabilities, and economic realities.
2. *Design development*, which focuses on product and process performance issues necessary to fulfill the product and service requirements in manufacturing or delivery.
3. *Design optimization*, which seeks to minimize the impact of variation in production and use, creating a "robust" design.
4. *Design verification*, which ensures that the capability of the production system meets the appropriate level of performance.

These activities are often incorporated into a process known as DMADV, which stands for Define, Measure, Analyze, Design, and Verify. Some organizations customize this approach. Caterpillar, for example, uses a process they call DMEDI (Define, Measure, Explore, Design, Implement):

1. *Define Opportunities*: Understand the purpose of the process to be developed by goal statements, generation plans, and resource identification.
2. *Measure Customer Needs*: Understand the outputs required of the new process by examining customer needs and competitive analysis.
3. *Explore Design Concepts*: Use creative techniques to develop alternative concepts and evaluate those ideas by validating customer requirements.

4. *Develop Detailed Design*: Turn the concept into reality by the use of process and product designs, pilot programs, and testing.
5. *Implement Detailed Design*: Fully deploy the new process and assess its value against the desired outcome.

Two important tools used for product design are concept engineering and quality function deployment.

Concept Engineering

Concept engineering (CE) emerged from a consortium of companies that included Polaroid and Bose along with researchers at MIT and is promoted and taught by the Center for Quality of Management (http://www.cqm.org). CE is a focused process for discovering customer requirements and using them to select superior product or service concepts that meet those requirements. Although similar to QFD in many respects, it puts the voice of the customer into a broader context and employs numerous other techniques to ensure effective processing of qualitative data.

Five major steps comprise the process:

1. *Understanding the customer's environment.* This step involves first project planning activities such as team selection, identifying fit with business strategy, and gaining team consensus on the project focus. It also includes collecting the voice of the customer to understand the customer's environment—physical, psychological, competitive, and so on.
2. *Converting understanding into requirements.* In this step, teams analyze the customer transcripts to translate the voice of the customer into more specific requirements. Essentially, this step focuses on identifying the technical requirements in the context of QFD, selecting the most significant requirements, and "scrubbing" the requirements to refine them into clear and insightful statements.
3. *Operationalizing what has been learned.* This step involves determining how to measure how well a customer requirement is met. For example, a requirement developed for a project at Polaroid was "Document photographer delivers document photo quickly while the customer waits." The principal requirement is about throughput time, so the concept of "quickly" needs to be operationalized and measured.[7] Once potential metrics are defined, they are evaluated to reduce the number of metrics that need to be used while ensuring that they cover all key requirements. This evaluation usually requires some sort of customer questionnaire to identify the importance of the requirements and prioritize them.
4. *Concept generation.* This step focuses on generating ideas for solutions that will potentially meet customers' needs. One unique approach is to brainstorm ideas that might resolve each individual customer requirement, select the best ones, and then classify them under the more traditional functional product characteristics. This approach helps to develop a "market in" rather than a "product out" orientation. Creative thinking techniques are applied here to increase the number and diversity of potential ideas.

5. *Concept selection.* Finally, the potential ideas are evaluated with respect to meeting requirements, tradeoffs are assessed, and prototyping may begin. The process ends with reflection on the final concept to test whether the decision "feels right" based on all the knowledge acquired.

Concept engineering leaves a strong audit trail back to the voice of the customer. This evidence makes it difficult for skeptics to challenge the results and easier to convert them. The process helps to build consensus and gives the team confidence in selling the concept to management. It takes a lot of discipline and patience, but the end result is well worth the effort. See box "The Perfect Supplier" for an example of CE in action.

Quality Function Deployment

Quality function deployment (QFD) is a methodology used to ensure that customers' requirements are met throughout the product design process and in the design and operation of production systems. QFD is both a philosophy and a set of

The Perfect Supplier

Bose Corporation, a leader in high-end audio products, used concept engineering to improve its European delivery system, at the same time decreasing overhead cost to the company.[8] The delivery system included every activity from the time a dealer realizes that he or she needs a product from Bose until the product is delivered. In personal visits to dealers in France, Germany, Holland, Spain, Belgium, and the United Kingdom, Bose developed an interview guide that addressed the following:

1. How do you describe the perfect supplier?
2. Please describe your process of ordering.
3. Where does customer service fit into your business?
4. General questions about your impressions of Bose.

In processing the qualitative data obtained from the interviews, Bose focused on the question, "What scenes or images come to mind when you visualize a supplier's delivery system?" From an analysis of more than 100 customer requirements, 24 were selected as key requirements for a world-class delivery system. This analysis led the team to the conclusion that supplier reliability and system efficiency build confidence and create trusting relationships. Next, these requirements were stated in measurable terms and questionnaires were developed to ensure that the requirements truly reflected the opinions of the dealers. For example, a requirement might be "Have a simple and swift return policy for faulty or damaged products." This requirement might then be measured by the amount of information required to process a product return.

The team spent nearly three days generating potential solutions for each customer requirement. As they discussed the strengths of each idea, new ideas often emerged, even from seemingly bizarre ideas. The four strongest ideas were chosen, and the team wrote a story or scenario with specific changes that needed to be made to the delivery system as a way of presenting the solution; this form of presentation would enable those outside of the team to understand how the new systems would work in delighting the customer. Although the process was quite tedious, the team members agreed that it was an excellent approach for arriving at an effective solution and turned them "into believers."

planning and communication tools that focuses on customer requirements in coordinating the design, manufacturing, and marketing of goods. A major benefit of QFD is improved communications and teamwork among all constituencies in the production process—marketing and design, design and manufacturing, and purchasing and suppliers. QFD allows companies to simulate the effects of new design ideas and concepts. This allows them to bring new products into the market sooner and to gain competitive advantage.

QFD originated in 1972 at Mitsubishi's Kobe shipyard site. Toyota began to develop the concept shortly thereafter, and it has been used since 1977. The initial results were impressive: Between January 1977 and October 1979, for example, Toyota realized a 20 percent reduction in startup costs on the launch of a new van. By 1982, startup costs had fallen 38 percent from the 1977 baseline, and by 1984 they were reduced by 61 percent. In addition, development time fell by one third and quality improved.

In the United States, the 1992 Cadillac was planned and designed entirely with QFD. The concept has been publicized and developed in the United States by the American Supplier Institute, Inc., a nonprofit organization, and by GOAL/QPC, a consulting firm in Massachusetts. Today QFD is successfully used by manufacturers of electronics, appliances, clothing, and construction equipment, and by firms such as General Motors, Ford, Mazda, Motorola, Xerox, Kodak, IBM, Procter & Gamble, Hewlett-Packard, and AT&T.

The focus of QFD is translating customer requirements into the appropriate technical requirements for each stage of product development and production. The customers' requirements—expressed in their own terms—are appropriately called *the voice of the customer*. These are the collection of customer needs, including all satisfiers, delighters/exciters, and dissatisfiers—the "whats" that customers want from a product. For example, a consumer might ask that a dishwashing liquid be "long lasting" and "clean effectively" or that an MP3 player have "good sound quality." Sometimes these requirements are referred to as *customer attributes*. Under QFD, all operations of a company are driven by the voice of the customer, rather than by top management edicts or design engineers' opinions.

Technical features are the translation of the voice of the customer into technical language. They are the "hows" that determine the means by which customer attributes are met. For example, a dishwashing detergent loosens grease and soil from dishes. The soil becomes trapped in the suds so that dishes can be removed from the water without picking up grease. Eventually the suds become saturated with soil and break down. Thus, a technical feature of a dishwashing liquid would be the weight of greasy soil that the suds generated by a fixed amount of dishwashing liquid can absorb before breaking down. Another might be the size of the soap bubble (which, incidentally, has been found to be a key attribute of customers' perception of cleaning effectiveness!).

A set of matrices is used to relate the voice of the customer to technical features and production planning and control requirements. The basic planning document is called the customer requirement planning matrix. Because of its structure (Figure 3.1), it is often referred to as the **House of Quality**. The House of Quality relates customer attributes to technical features to ensure that any engineering decision has a basis in meeting a customer need.

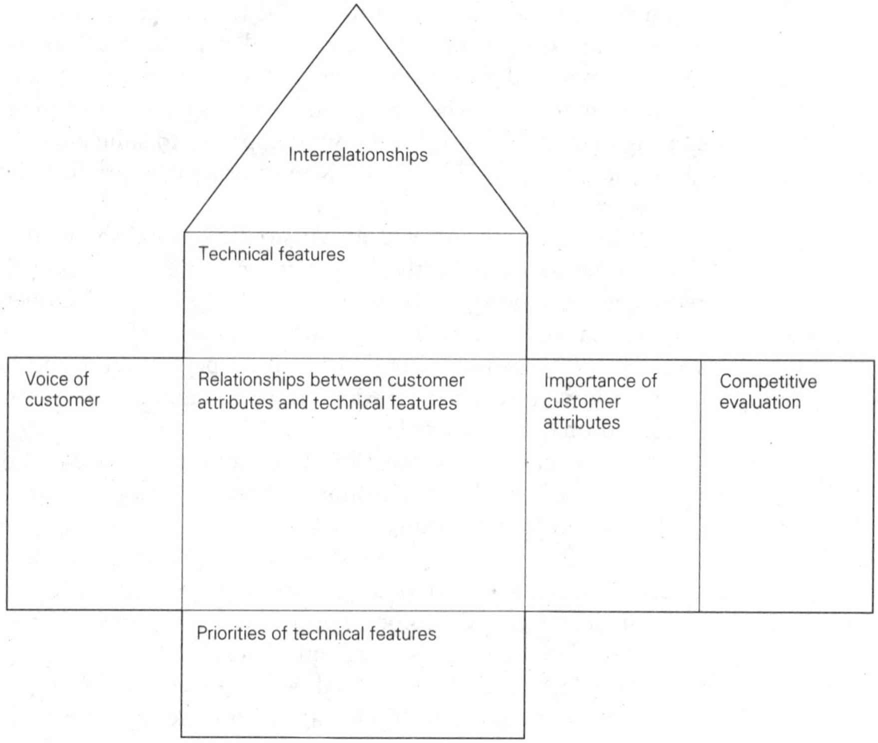

FIGURE 3.1 | THE HOUSE OF QUALITY

Building the House of Quality requires six basic steps:

1. Identify customer attributes.
2. Identify technical features.
3. Relate the customer attributes to the technical features.
4. Evaluate competing products.
5. Evaluate technical features and develop targets.
6. Determine which technical features to deploy in the production process.

The first step is identifying customer attributes. In applying QFD, it is important to use the customer's own words so as not to have customer needs misinterpreted by designers and engineers. Recall that not all customers are end users. For a manufacturer, customers might include government regulators, wholesalers, and retailers. Thus, many classes of customer needs may exist.

The second step is listing the technical features that are necessary to meet customer requirements. These technical features are design attributes expressed in the language of the designer and engineer. They form the basis for subsequent design, manufacturing, and service process activities. They must be measurable, because the output will be controlled and compared to objective targets.

The roof of the House of Quality shows the interrelationships between any pair of technical features. Various symbols are used to denote these relationships.

A typical scheme is to use the symbol • to denote a very strong relationship, ○ for a strong relationship, and Δ to denote a weak relationship. These notations help determine the effects of changing one product characteristic and enable planners to assess the tradeoffs between characteristics. This process enables designers to focus on features collectively rather than individually.

Next, a relationship matrix between the customer attributes and the technical features is developed. Customer attributes are listed down the left column, and technical features are written across the top. In the matrix itself, a symbol is used to indicate the degree of relationship in a manner similar to that used in the roof of the house. The purpose of the relationship matrix is to show whether the final technical features adequately address the customer attributes. This assessment may be based on expert experience, customer responses, or controlled experiments.

Technical features can affect several customer attributes. The lack of a strong relationship between a customer attribute and any of the technical features suggests that the attributes are not being addressed and that the final product will have difficulty meeting customer needs. Similarly, if a technical feature does not affect any customer attribute, it may be redundant or the designers may have missed an important customer attribute.

The next step is adding market evaluation and key selling points. This step includes rating the importance of each customer attribute and evaluating existing products on each of the attributes. Customer importance ratings represent the areas of greatest interest and highest expectations to the customer.

Competitive evaluation helps highlight the absolute strengths and weaknesses of competing products. This step enables designers to seek opportunities for improvement. It also links QFD to a company's strategic vision and allows priorities to be set in the design process. For example, focusing on an attribute that receives a low evaluation on all competitors' products can help to gain a competitive advantage. Such attributes become key selling points and help establish promotion strategies.

Next comes the evaluation of the technical features of competitive products and the development of targets. This is usually accomplished through in-house testing and translated into measurable terms. These evaluations are compared with the competitive evaluation of customer attributes to find inconsistencies. If a competing product best satisfies a customer attribute, but the evaluation of the related technical feature indicates otherwise, then either the measures used are faulty or the product has an image difference (either positive toward the competitor or negative toward the product) that affects customer perceptions. Targets for each technical feature are set on the basis of customer importance ratings and existing product strengths and weaknesses.

The final step in building the House of Quality is selecting technical features to be deployed in the remainder of the process. This means identifying the characteristics that have a strong relationship to customer needs, have poor competitive performance, or are strong selling points. These characteristics need to be deployed—or translated into the language of each function—in the design and production process so that proper actions and controls are taken to maintain the voice of the customer. Characteristics that are not identified as critical do not need such rigorous attention.

A simple example of a House of Quality is shown in Figure 3.2 for the hypothetical case of a quick-service franchise that wishes to improve its hamburger. The voice of the customer consists of four attributes. The hamburger should:

- be tasty,
- be healthy,
- be visually appealing, and
- provide good value.

The technical features that can be designed into the product are price, size, calories, sodium content, and fat content. The symbols in the matrix show the relationships between each customer attribute and technical feature. For example, taste bears a strong relationship to sodium content, a moderate relationship to fat content, and a weak relationship to caloric content. In the roof of the house, price and size are seen to be strongly related (as size increases, the price must increase). The competitive evaluation shows that competitors are currently weak on nutrition and value; these can become key selling points in a marketing plan if the franchise can capitalize on them.

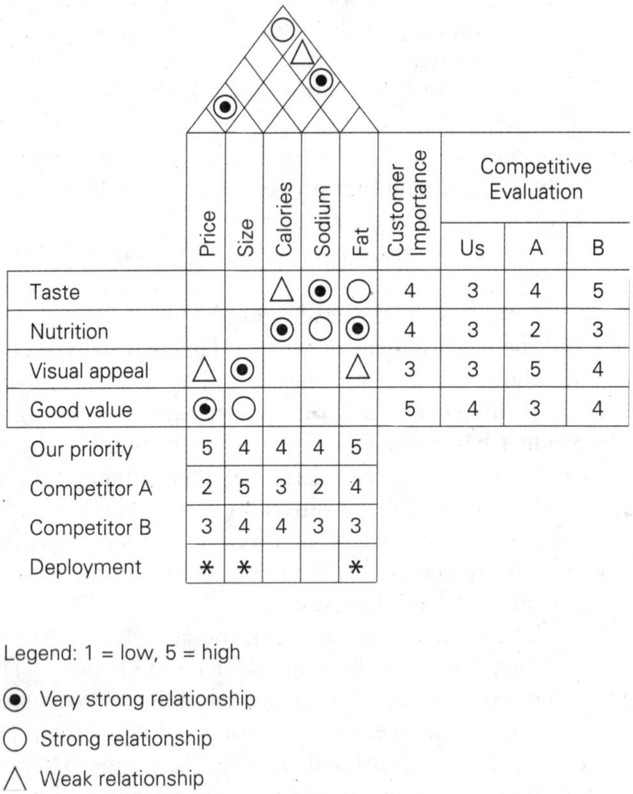

FIGURE 3.2 HOUSE OF QUALITY EXAMPLE

Finally, at the bottom of the house, are targets for the technical features based on an analysis of customer importance ratings and competitive ratings. The features assigned asterisks will be deployed in subsequent design and production activities.

The House of Quality provides marketing with an important tool to understand customer needs and gives top management strategic direction. However, it is only the first stage in the QFD process. The voice of the customer must be carried throughout the production process. Three other houses of quality are used to deploy the voice of the customer to component parts characteristics, process planning, and production planning. These are:

1. *technical features deployment matrix*, which translates technical features of the final product into design requirements for critical components;
2. *process plan and quality control charts*, which translate component features into critical process and product parameters and control points for each; and
3. *operating instructions*, which identify operations to be performed by plant personnel to assure that important process and product parameters are achieved.

Most of the QFD activities represented by the first two houses of quality are performed by people in the product development and engineering functions. At the next stage, the planning activities begin to involve supervisors and production-line operators. This represents the transition from planning to execution. If a product component parameter is critical and is created or affected during the process, it becomes a control point. This tells the company what to monitor and inspect and forms the basis for a quality control plan for achieving those critical characteristics that are crucial to achieving customer satisfaction. The last house relates the control points to specific requirements for quality assurance activity. This includes specifying control methods, sample sizes, and so on, to achieve the necessary level of quality.

The success of QFD depends on effective communication and cooperation among all major functions that contribute to getting a product to market. The designer's objective is to create a product that meets the desired functional requirements. The manufacturing engineer's objective is to produce the designed product efficiently. The salesperson's goal is to sell the product, and that of finance personnel is to make a profit. Purchasing must ensure that purchased parts meet quality requirements. Packaging and distribution personnel must ensure that the product reaches the customer in good operating condition. Because all these functions have a stake in the product, they must all work together. Building cross-functional teams to accomplish product development is often called **concurrent engineering**.

Design Failure Mode and Effects Analysis

The purpose of **design failure mode and effects analysis** (DFMEA) is to identify all the ways in which a failure can occur, to estimate the effect and seriousness of the failure, and to recommend corrective design actions. A DFMEA usually consists of specifying the following information for each design element or function:

- *Failure modes*—ways in which each element or function can fail. This information generally takes some research and imagination. One way to start is with known failures that have occurred in the past. Documents such as quality and reliability reports, test results, and warranty reports provide useful information.

- *Effect of the failure on the customer*—such as dissatisfaction, potential injury or other safety issue, downtime, repair requirements, and so on. Maintenance records, customer complaints, and warranty reports provide good sources of information. Consideration should be given to failures on the function of the end product, manufacturability in the next process, what the customer sees or experiences, and product safety.
- *Severity, likelihood of occurrence, and detection rating*. Severity might be measured on a scale of 1 to 10, where a "1" indicates that the failure is so minor that the customer probably would not notice it, and a "10" might mean that the customer might be endangered. The frequency of occurrence based on service history or field performance provides an indication of the significance of the failure. Based on severity and likelihood, a risk priority can be assigned to identify critical failure modes that must be addressed.
- *Potential causes of failure*. Often failure is the result of poor design. Design deficiencies can cause errors either in the field or in manufacturing and assembly. Identification of causes might require experimentation and rigorous analysis.
- *Corrective actions or controls*. These controls might include design changes, mistake proofing, better user instructions, management responsibilities, and target completion dates.

Using DFMEA will not only improve product functionality and safety but also reduce external failure costs—particularly warranty costs—as well as decrease manufacturing and service delivery problems. It also can provide a defense against frivolous lawsuits. DFMEA should be conducted early in the design process to save costs and reduce cycle times, and provide a knowledge base to improve subsequent design efforts. This approach also can be used for processes to identify hazardous conditions that may endanger a worker or operational problems that can disrupt a production process and result in scrap, downtime, or other non–value-added costs.

Design for Service Quality

Services are quite different from manufactured goods. First, the outputs of service processes are not as well defined. Services are intangible and represent an interaction between the customer and service provider; they cannot be inventoried, moved, or inspected as can manufactured goods. Second, most service processes involve a greater interaction with the customer, often making it more difficult to identify needs and expectations. By contrast, customers often cannot define their needs for service until after they have some point of reference or comparison. Fast-food restaurants, for example, have carefully designed their processes to improve quality of service and speed.[9] New hands-free intercom systems, better microphones that reduce ambient kitchen noise, and screens that display a customer's order are all focused on these requirements. Timers at Wendy's count every segment of the order completion process to help managers identify problem areas. Kitchen workers wear headsets to hear orders as they are placed. McDonald's eliminated many items from its menu to simplify kitchen operations and developed new menu boards showing more pictures to keep ordering simple. It also reduced the number of possible keypad options on registers and installed newly automated drink dispensers and French-fry bins.

Service processes often involve both internal and external activities, a factor that complicates quality design. In a bank, for example, poor service can result from the way that tellers treat customers and also from poor quality of computers and communications equipment beyond the control of the tellers. Internal activities are primarily concerned with efficiency (quality of conformance), whereas external activities—with direct customer interaction—require attention to effectiveness (quality of design). All too often, workers involved in internal operations do not understand how their performance affects the customers they do not see. The success of the process depends on everyone—workers involved in internal as well as external activities—understanding that they add value to the customer.

Services have three basic components: physical facilities, processes, and procedures; employees' behavior; and employees' professional judgment.[10] Designing a service essentially involves determining an effective balance of these components. The goal is to provide a service whose elements are internally consistent and directed at meeting the needs of a specific target market segment. Too much or too little emphasis on one component will lead to problems and poor customer perceptions. For example, too much emphasis on procedures might result in timely and efficient service, but might also suggest insensitivity and apathy toward the customer. Too much emphasis on behavior might provide a friendly and personable environment at the expense of slow, inconsistent, or chaotic service. Too much emphasis on professional judgment might lead to good solutions to customer problems but also to slow, inconsistent, or insensitive service.

A useful approach to designing effective services is first to recognize that services differ in the degree of customer contact and interaction, the degree of labor intensity, and the degree of customization. For example, a railroad is low in all three dimensions. On the other hand, an interior design service would be high in all three dimensions. A fast-food restaurant would be high in customer contact and labor intensity, but low in customization. Services low in all three dimensions of this classification are more similar to manufacturing organizations. The emphasis on quality should be focused on the physical facilities and procedures; behavior and professional judgment are relatively unimportant.

As contact and interaction between the customer and the service system increases, two factors must be taken into account. In services low in labor intensity, the customer's impression of physical facilities, processes, and procedures is important. Service organizations must exercise special care in choosing and maintaining reliable and easy-to-use equipment. With higher levels of contact and interaction, appropriate staff behavior becomes increasingly important. As labor intensity increases, variations between individuals become more important; however, the elements of personal behavior and professional judgment will remain relatively unimportant as long as the degrees of customization and contact and interaction remain low. As customization increases, professional judgment becomes a bigger factor in the customer's perception of service quality. In services that are high in all three dimensions, facilities, behavior, and professional judgment must be equally balanced.

Bringing Factory Design to Customer Service[11]

Dell's focus on cost efficiency has long been a core strategy. The direct sales model of selling computers to consumers via phone and the Internet eliminates the costs of shipping to stores and tracking inventory. However, some of Dell's cost-cutting efforts have alienated its customers. Dell, for instance, staffs some customer service call centers with fewer than 500 workers. A center that small is almost guaranteed to be frequently overwhelmed. Richard L. "Dick" Hunter, Dell's new head of customer service, thinks the solution is to treat the call center like a factory. For example, workers in the company's call centers will have a colored flag to raise when they run into trouble helping a customer. When the flag goes up, a supervisor will come running to help out. Currently, many call center reps are trained to solve only one type of problem—say, a hardware glitch on a Dimension desktop. That explains why it's so common for the agent who answers a call to have to transfer it to a person with the right expertise. Hunter estimates that almost 45 percent of calls to Dell require at least one transfer. Just as each Dell factory worker is trained to assemble different types of computer models, Hunter plans to train the phone reps in fixing more types of machines to increase the likelihood that the first person who answers a call will be able to help. As another example, Dell long ago found the optimal size for its factories. Now, Hunter intends to do the same for call centers. He plans to expand small centers to house 1,000 to 3,000 reps. That should boost the chances that any caller's problem can be solved by someone within the building. In addition, Dell will install large monitors to let workers see the number of callers who are on hold.

The box "Bringing Factory Improvement Ideas to Customer Service" provides an interesting perspective on applying traditional manufacturing process concepts to services.

DESIGNING QUALITY PROCESSES

The design of the processes that produce and deliver goods and services—to both external and internal customers—can have a significant impact on cost (and hence profitability), flexibility (the ability to produce the right types and amounts of products as customer demand or preferences change), and quality. See box "90,000 DVDs and No Shelves" for an example of an innovative process design that centers on efficiency and rapid customer service.

The design of a process begins with the process owner. A process owner might be an individual, a team, a department, or some cross-functional group. A basic approach to process design is suggested by Motorola:

1. *Identify the product or service*: What work do I do?
2. *Identify the customer*: Who is the work for?
3. *Identify the supplier*: What do I need and from whom do I get it?
4. *Identify the process*: What steps or tasks are performed? What are the inputs and outputs for each step?
5. *Mistake-proof the process*: How can I eliminate or simplify tasks and prevent defects and errors?
6. *Develop measurements and controls, and improvement goals*: How do I evaluate the process? How can I improve further?

90,000 DVDs and No Shelves[12]

Netflix turned the DVD rental industry on its ear by offering an all-DVD library of more than 15,000 titles sent through the mail, with no due dates and no late fees. In 2003, Netflix had over one million customers. Netflix's Worcester, Massachusetts, hub is a former shoe warehouse that stocks around 90,000 DVDs, and yet has no shelves. Each morning at 8:00, the U.S. Postal Service (cheaper and quicker than the alternatives, incredibly) drops off "pumpkin carts," orange bins with thousands of returned DVDs from all over New England. Instead of cataloging titles at fixed shelf locations and retrieving them to satisfy a customer order, operators scan the returned discs, collecting data, which computers at Netflix's San Jose headquarters match to new orders. After lunch, the Worcester operators rescan every disc in their inventory; with each scan, they act on instructions from San Jose to "Ship Disc," if a customer wants the film, or "Scan Tomorrow," if not. The Scan Tomorrows move faster, set aside by the handful. Ship Discs get an envelope and a pair of stickers. Outgoing discs pass through the Omega, a 40-foot-long machine that can organize more than 20,000 outgoing rentals an hour into bins specified by zip codes. Presorting saves Netflix six to seven cents per DVD, as well as providing faster shipping times to customers.

Steps 1 through 3 address such questions as "What is the purpose of the process?" "How does the process create customer satisfaction?" and "What are the essential inputs and outputs of the process?" Step 4 focuses on the actual process design by defining the specific tasks performed in transforming the inputs to outputs. Step 5 focuses on making the process efficient and capable of delivering high quality. Step 6 ensures that the process will be monitored and controlled to the level of required performance. This monitoring involves gathering in-process measurements and/or customer feedback on a regular basis and using this information to control and improve the process.

A good process design focuses on the prevention of poor quality by ensuring that goods and services meet both external and internal customer requirements, and that the process is capable of achieving the requisite level of performance. Standardized processes establish consistency of output. For example, in producing a new, very small CD player, Sony had to develop entirely new manufacturing processes, because no process in existence was able to make this product as small and as accurate as the design required. FedEx developed a wireless data collection system that employs laser scanners to manage millions of packages daily through its six main hubs, improving not only customer service, but saving labor costs as well.[13] However, standardized processes may not be able to meet the needs of different customer segments. Today, many companies such as Dell use a strategy of **mass customization**—providing personalized, custom-designed products to meet individual customer preferences at prices comparable to mass-produced items. Mass customization requires significant changes to traditional processes that focus on either customized, crafted products, or mass-produced, standardized products.[14] These include flexible manufacturing technologies, just-in-time systems, information technology, and an emphasis on cycle time reduction.

A process design should include a step-by-step process map, or flowchart (see the next chapter for details about developing and using flowcharts), along with standard operating procedures and work instructions. Many companies use ISO 9000 as a basis for defining and documenting key processes. Branch-Smith Printing, for example, created more than 40 process maps as part of the process of converting to ISO 9000. Corning Telecommunications Products Division (TPD) identified and documented more than 800 processes in all areas of its business, of which 50 were designated as "core business processes" that merit special emphasis in continuous improvement efforts. Each core process is owned and managed by a key business leader.

Design for Agility

Agility is an important factor in being competitive. **Agility** is a term that is commonly used to characterize flexibility and short cycle times. Agility is crucial to such customer-focused strategies as mass customization, which requires rapid response and flexibility to changing consumer demand (see box "Leveraging Fashion Fads"). Enablers of agility include close relationships with customers to understand their emerging needs and requirements, empowering employees as decision makers, effective manufacturing and information technology, close supplier and partner relationships, and breakthrough improvement. One important metric of agility is cycle time—the time it takes to accomplish one cycle of a process (e.g., the time from when a customer orders a product to the time that it is delivered, or the time to introduce a new product). Significant reductions in cycle time cannot be achieved simply by focusing on individual subprocesses; cross-functional processes must be examined all across the organization. Through these activities, the company comes to understand work at the organizational level and to engage in cooperative behaviors.

Poka-Yoke (Mistake-Proofing)

Poka-yoke is an approach for mistake-proofing processes using automatic devices or methods to avoid simple human error. The poka-yoke concept was developed and refined by the late Shigeo Shingo, a Japanese manufacturing engineer who developed the Toyota production system. The idea is to avoid repetitive tasks or actions that depend on vigilance or memory in order to free workers' time and minds to pursue more creative and value-adding activities.

Leveraging Fashion Fads[15]

One example of agility is the Stockholm-based fashion retailer, Hennes & Mauritz (H&M). While traditional clothing retailers design their products at least six months in advance of the selling season, H&M can rush items into stores in as little as three weeks. By monitoring consumer trends and identifying hot-selling items, its designers immediately start to sketch new styles, which are then developed by pattern makers, often using employees as live models. Designs are sent electronically to factories in Europe and Asia that can handle the jobs quickly, and in less than two months, most H&M stores will have the new styles in stock. One of the company's enablers is empowered employees who can dream up and produce new fashions without formal approval.

Poka-yoke is focused on two aspects: prediction, or recognizing that a defect is about to occur and providing a warning; and detection, or recognizing that a defect has occurred and stopping the process. Many applications of poka-yoke are deceptively simple, yet creative. Usually, they are inexpensive to implement. Some examples:

- Many machines have limit switches connected to warning lights that tell the operator when parts are positioned improperly on the machine.
- A device on a drill counts the number of holes drilled in a workpiece; a buzzer sounds if the workpiece is removed before the correct number of holes has been drilled.
- Passwords or e-mail addresses are often required to be entered twice for verification.
- Pills roll down an incline; broken ones can't and are easily eliminated.

Poka-yoke techniques are also applied to the design of consumer products to prevent inadvertent user errors or safety hazards. For example, most cars will provide an audible signal if the door is opened with the key in the ignition, preventing one from leaving or locking it inside. Power lawnmowers have a safety bar on the handle that must be engaged in order to start the engine. Computer software such as Microsoft Word will automatically check for any unsaved files before closing down. A proxy ballot for an investment fund will not fit into the return envelope unless a small strip is detached. The strip asks the respondent to check whether the ballot is signed and dated.

Richard B. Chase and Douglas M. Stewart suggest that the same concepts can be applied to services.[16] The major differences are that service mistake-proofing must account for the customers' activities as well as those of the producer, and mistake-proof methods must be set up for interactions conducted directly or by phone, mail, or other technologies, such as ATM. Chase and Stewart classify service poka-yokes by the type of error they are designed to prevent: server errors and customer errors. Server errors result from the *task, treatment*, or *tangibles* of the service. Customer errors occur during *preparation, the service encounter*, or during *resolution.*

Task errors include doing work incorrectly, in the wrong order, or too slowly, as well as doing work not requested. Some examples of poka-yoke devices for task errors are computer prompts, color-coded cash register keys, measuring tools such as McDonald's French-fry scoop, and signaling devices. Hospitals use trays for surgical instruments that have indentations for each instrument, preventing the surgeon from leaving one of them in the patient.

Treatment errors arise in the contact between the server and the customer, such as lack of courteous behavior, and failure to acknowledge, listen, or react appropriately to the customer. A bank encourages eye contact by requiring tellers to record the customer's eye color on a checklist as they start the transaction. To promote friendliness at a fast-food restaurant, trainers provide the four specific cues for when to smile: when greeting the customer, when taking the order, when telling about the dessert special, and when giving the customer change. They encourage employees to observe whether the customer smiled back, a natural reinforcer for smiling.

Tangible errors are those in physical elements of the service, such as unclean facilities, dirty uniforms, inappropriate temperature, and document errors. Hotels wrap paper strips around towels to help the housekeeping staff identify clean linen and that which should be replaced. Spell-checkers in word processing software help eliminate misspellings (provided they are used!).

Customer errors in preparation arise when customers do not bring necessary materials to the encounter, do not understand their role in the service transaction, or do not engage the correct service. Digital Equipment provides a flowchart to specify how to place a service call. By guiding the customers through three yes-or-no questions, the flowchart prompts them to have the necessary information before calling.

Customer errors during an encounter can be because of inattention, misunderstanding, or simply a memory lapse, and include failure to remember steps in the process or to follow instructions. Poka-yoke examples include height bars at amusement rides that indicate rider size requirements, beepers that signal customers to remove cards from ATM machines, and airplane lavatory doors that must be locked to turn on the lights. Some cashiers at restaurants fold back the top edge of credit card receipts, holding together the restaurant's copies while revealing the customer's copy.

Customer errors at the resolution stage of a service encounter include failure to signal service inadequacies, learn from experience, adjust expectations, and execute appropriate postencounter actions. Hotels might enclose a small gift certificate to encourage guests to provide feedback. Strategically placed tray-return stands and trash receptacles remind customers to return trays in fast-food facilities.

Mistake-proofing a service process requires identifying when and where failures generally occur (see box "Mistake-Proofing the U.S. Election Process"). Once a

Mistake-Proofing the U.S. Election Process[17]

The controversy surrounding the 2000 U.S. presidential election is well known. A difference of roughly 500 votes out of 5.8 million cast in Florida is smaller than the predictable number of errors for miscounted votes, miscast votes, incorrectly rejected ballots, and other vote-casting and vote-counting errors caused by systems and processes (people, equipment, methods, materials, and environment). Several issues affect the quality of the results.

- The prescored punch cards commonly used for ballots require that voters punch the cards in a way that meets machine specifications. The stylus used to punch out the chad (the little piece that gets punched out of the ballot card) could be inadequate in terms of shape or sharpness. The die that prescores the cards during manufacturing wears down over time. Cards may be too thick or thin. Cards exposed to too much humidity may not be counted properly in machines.
- Process errors can occur in several places. The voter may not have actually cast a vote, or the voter may not have been able to vote for the candidate of choice because of confusing ballot design. The ballot may not have been counted correctly. Manual recounts may not record the voter's intent correctly.
- Lack of uniform standards among voting jurisdictions make it difficult to predict process error rates accurately.

Reducing such errors will require a systematic approach to problem solving built on quality principles and mistake-proofing ideas. Although such thinking has been successful in many organizations, it has not become a part of the public policy dialog nor has it been institutionalized as part of any national debate.

failure is identified, the source must be found. The final step is to prevent the mistake from occurring through source inspection, self-inspection, or sequential checks.

PROCESS CONTROL

Control is the activity of ensuring conformance to the requirements and taking corrective action when necessary to correct problems and maintain stable performance. Lack of control can not only cause customer dissatisfaction, but can result in serious consequences, not only for the business, but for customers as well (see box "Poor Control Can Leave a Bitter Taste"). Not recognizing when contamination occurs in a bottling process, for instance, signifies a lack of control.

Any control system has three components: (1) a standard or goal, (2) a means of measuring accomplishment, and (3) comparison of actual results with the standard, along with feedback to form the basis for corrective action. Goals and standards are defined during planning and design processes. They establish what is supposed to be accomplished. These goals and standards are reflected by measurable quality characteristics, such as dimensions of machined parts, numbers of defectives, customer complaints, or waiting times. For example, golf balls must meet five standards to be considered as conforming to the Rules of Golf: minimum size, maximum weight, spherical symmetry, maximum initial velocity, and overall distance. Methods for measuring these quality characteristics may be automated or performed manually by the workforce. Golf balls are measured for size by trying to drop them through a metal ring—a conforming ball sticks to the ring while a nonconforming ball falls through; digital scales measure weight to one-thousandth of a gram; and initial velocity is measured in a special machine by finding the time

Poor Control Can Leave a Bitter Taste

An international study by Landor & Associates, an independent design and image firm, showed conclusively that Coca-Cola is the number one brand in the minds of soft-drink consumers around the world, and affirmed that the company is totally committed to quality. Coca-Cola has stated, "Our commitment to quality is something for which we will never lose our taste."[18] However, in early June, 1999, quite a few people in Europe did when almost 100 Belgian children fell ill after drinking Coca-Cola. This incident caused the Belgian Health Ministry to require Coca-Cola to recall millions of cans of product in Belgium and to cease product distribution. Later, France and the Netherlands also halted distribution of Coke products as the contamination scare spread. It was quickly determined that contaminated carbon dioxide had been used during the carbonation process at the Antwerp bottling facility. According to the official statement from Coca-Cola, "Independent laboratory testing showed that the cause of the off-taste in the bottled products was carbon dioxide. That carbon dioxide was replaced and all bottles with off-taste have been removed from the market. The issue affects the taste of the soft drinks only.... The second issue involves an external odor on some canned products. In the case of the Belgian distribution system, a substance used in wood treatment has caused an offensive odor on the outside bottom of the can. Independent analysis determined that the product is safe. The Company, in conjunction with its bottling partner in Belgium, is taking all necessary steps to eliminate this offensive odor."[19] After two weeks, the company was allowed to begin producing and distributing products in the three countries.

it takes a ball struck at 98 mph to break a ballistic screen at the end of a tube exactly 6.28 feet away.[20]

Short-term corrective action generally should be taken by process owners who are responsible for doing the work. In many organizations, such as The Ritz-Carlton Hotel Company, this extends to everyone. The company has a policy by which the first person who detects a problem is empowered to break away from routine duties, investigate and correct the problem immediately, document the incident, and then return to their routine. Long-term corrective action is the responsibility of management. For an interesting application of quality control in the government, see box "QC in the CIA."

The responsibility for control can be determined by checking the three components of control systems. Process owners must have the means of knowing what is expected (the standard or goal) through clear instructions and specifications; they must have the means of determining their actual performance, typically through inspection and measurement; and they must have a means of making corrections if they discover a variance between what is expected of them and their actual performance. If any of these criteria is not met, then the process is the responsibility of management, not the process owner. Both Juran and Deming made this important distinction. If process owners are held accountable for or expected to act on problems beyond their control, they become frustrated and end up playing games with management. Juran and Deming stated that the majority of quality problems are management-controllable.

Process control requires a good measurement system to track quality and operational performance. Measurement provides the ability to capture important quality and performance indicators to reveal patterns about process performance. Each measurement should aim for a standard or target that is driven by customer requirements. Meeting these two conditions ensures that sufficient data can be collected to reveal useful information for evaluation and control, as well as learning that leads to improvement and maturity. For example, the key measures used by SSM Health Care to monitor their processes are shown in Table 3.1. Daily, weekly,

QC IN THE CIA[21]

The *Los Angeles Times* reported that the CIA's internal investigative branch will begin using new checks and controls designed to give targets of in-house probes greater ability to defend themselves. Among the changes is the creation of two positions to oversee the work of the CIA's inspector general, including a "quality control officer" charged with monitoring the inspector's handling of evidence and testimony. That officer would be required to "attest, among other things, that reports include all exculpatory and relevant mitigating information." CIA officials who were targets of investigations in recent years have complained that their accounts and explanations were not given adequate weight in reports issued by the Inspector General's office. Other changes include the installation of new equipment for recording inspector general interviews with employees and the creation of a Web site that would advise employees on how to obtain legal representation and allow them to examine draft reports of investigations. The Inspector General had also committed to reducing the time it takes to complete an investigation. Employees have complained that certain Helgerson probes dragged on for years, leaving targeted workers in a state of investigative limbo.

TABLE 3.1 PROCESSES, REQUIREMENTS, AND MEASURES USED BY SSM HEALTH CARE

Process	Key Requirements	Key Measures
Admit		
Admitting/ Registration	Timeliness	• Time to admit patients to the setting of care • Timeliness in admitting/registration rate on patient satisfaction survey questions
Assess		
Patient assessment	Timeliness	• % of histories and physicals charted within 24 hrs or prior to surgery • Pain assessed at appropriate intervals, per hospital policy
Clinical laboratory and radiology services	Accuracy & Timeliness	• Quality control results/Repeat rates • Turnaround time • Response rate on medical staff satisfaction survey
Care Delivery/Treatment		
Provision of clinical care	Nurse responsiveness Pain management Successful clinical outcomes	• Response rate on patient satisfaction and medical staff survey questions • Wait time for pain medications • % CHF patients received med instructions/ weighing • % Ischemic heart patients discharged on proven therapies • Unplanned readmits/Returns to ER or Operating Room • Mortality
Pharmacy/ Medication use	Accuracy	• Use of dangerous abbreviations in medication orders • Med error rate or adverse drug events resulting from med errors
Surgical services/ Anesthesia	Professional skill, competence/ communication	• Clear documentation of informed surgical and anesthesia consent • Perioperative mortality • Surgical site infection rates
Discharge		
Case management	Appropriate utilization	• Average length of stay (ALOS) • Payment denials • Unplanned readmits
Discharge from setting of care	Assistance and clear directions	• Discharge instructions documented and provided to patient • Response rate on patient satisfaction survey

Source: Courtesy of SSM Health Care.

monthly, and quarterly performance assessments provide the opportunity to review and manage these measures and identify ways of preventing potential errors before they affect the patient.

Many companies use various automated and visual control systems. For example, DaimlerChrysler manufactures the PT Cruiser at the company's Toluca Assembly Plant in Mexico. To ensure quality, the Toluca plant verifies parts, processes, fit, and finish every step of the way, from stamping and body to paint and final assembly. The control practices include visual management through quality alert systems, which are designed to call immediate attention to abnormal conditions. The system provides visual and audible signals for each station for tooling, production, maintenance, and material flow.[22] Others use statistical process control, which is based on analyzing data patterns statistically; this will be described further in the next section. Graniterock for instance, was the first in the construction materials industry to apply statistical process control in the management of production of aggregates, concrete, and asphalt products.

STATISTICAL THINKING AND PROCESS CONTROL TOOLS

Statistical thinking is at the heart of the Deming philosophy and is the basis for good management. **Statistical thinking** is a philosophy of learning and action based on the principles that:

1. all work occurs in a system of interconnected processes,
2. variation exists in all processes, and
3. understanding and reducing variation are keys to success.[23]

Statistical thinking is more than simply applying statistical methods. Statistical thinking focuses on understanding and reducing variation, not merely quantifying it. Nevertheless, statistical methods are important to be a good statistical thinker.

By viewing work as a process, we can apply management-by-fact and various quality tools to establish consistent, predictable processes, study them, and improve them. By viewing processes as interconnected components of a system, we avoid suboptimization—one of the key principles of Deming's Profound Knowledge. When managers make decisions in isolation, they often fail to see chains of events that might occur throughout the company because of their decisions. A typical example is designing a product without consideration of the capability of processes to manufacture it or the support systems required to service it in the field.

Recognizing and understanding variation is the essence of statistical thinking. We discussed principles of variation within the context of Deming's Profound Knowledge in Chapter 2, particularly the differences between common and special causes of variation. Some of the operational problems created by excessive variation include the following:[24]

- *Variation increases unpredictability:* If we don't understand the variation in a system, we cannot predict its future performance.
- *Variation reduces capacity utilization:* If a process has little variability, then managers can increase the load on the process because they do not have to incorporate slack into their production plans.

- *Variation contributes to a "bullwhip" effect:* This well-known phenomenon occurs in supply chains; when small changes in demand occur, the variation in production and inventory levels becomes increasingly amplified upstream at distribution centers, factories, and suppliers, resulting in unnecessary costs and difficulties in managing material flow.
- *Variation makes it difficult to find root causes:* Process variation makes it difficult to determine whether problems are due to external factors such as raw materials or reside within the processes themselves.
- *Variation makes it difficult to detect potential problems early:* Unusual variation is a signal that problems exist; if a process has little inherent variation, then it is easier to detect when a problem actually does occur.

Although variation exists everywhere, many business decisions do not often account for it. How often do managers make decisions based on a single data point or two, seeing trends when they don't exist, or manipulating financial figures they cannot truly control (see box "The VP's Dilemma")? The lack of broad and sustained use of statistical thinking in many organizations is due to two reasons.[25] First, statisticians historically have functioned as problem solvers in manufacturing, research, and development, and thereby focused on individual clients rather than on organizations. Second, statisticians have focused primarily on technical aspects of statistics rather than emphasizing the focus on process variation that will lead to bottom-line results. Statistical thinking is fundamental to good process management. Understanding processes provides the context for determining the effects of variation and the proper type of managerial action to be taken. This variation is

THE VP'S DILEMMA[26]

Brian Joiner, a noted quality management consultant, relates the following case:

Ed was a regional VP for a service company that had facilities around the world. He was determined that the facilities in his region would get the highest customer satisfaction ratings in the company. If he noticed that a facility had a major drop in satisfaction ratings in one month or had "below average" ratings for three months in a row, he would call the manager and ask what had happened—and make it clear that next month's rating had better improve. And most of the time, it did! As the average satisfaction score dropped from 65 to 60 between February and March, Ed's memo to his managers read:

> Bad news! We dropped five points! We should all focus on improving these scores right away! I realize that our usage rates have increased faster than anticipated, so you've really got to hustle to give our customers great service. I know you can do it!

Joiner observed, Do I look at data this way? This month versus last month? This month versus the same month last year? Do I sometimes look at the latest data point? The last two data points? I couldn't understand why people would only want to look at two data points. Finally, it became clear to me. With any two data points, it's easy to compute a trend: "Things are down 2 percent this month from last month. This month is 30 percent above the same month last year." Unfortunately, we learn nothing of importance by comparing two results when they both come from a stable process ... and most data of importance to management are from stable processes.

quantified through statistical analysis of process data and requires understanding the sources, magnitude, and nature of the variation.

Senior management needs to champion the use of statistical thinking by defining the strategy and goals of the approach, clearly and consistently communicating the benefits and results, providing the necessary resources, coaching others, and recognizing and rewarding the desired behavior. To help managers work in this fashion, many organizations are using Six Sigma initiatives to create core groups of highly trained professionals who are skilled in statistical thinking and can help others to use it effectively. This requires an environment conducive to learning new behaviors and concepts.

Statistical Process Control

Statistical process control (SPC) is a methodology for monitoring a process to identify special causes of variation and signaling the need to take corrective action when it is appropriate. As such, it provides a rational basis for applying statistical thinking to controlling processes. When special causes are present, the process is deemed to be *out of control.* If the variation in the process is due to common causes alone, the process is said to be *in statistical control.* Basically, statistical control means that both the process average and variance are constant over time.

SPC is a proven technique for improving quality and productivity. Many customers require their suppliers to provide evidence of statistical process control. Thus, SPC provides a means by which a firm may demonstrate its quality capability, an activity necessary for survival in today's highly competitive markets. In addition,

SPC Can Be Motivating[27]

Managers of TQM organizations are often confronted with the dilemma of how to motivate frontline organization members toward continuous improvement and highest quality of output without fundamentally changing the motivational structure of their work. Research consistent with sociotechnical systems theory has shown how crucial it is to specify and align both technical and social effects of any intervention so as to maximize the probability of successful implementation and continued sustainability. One research study has shown that the effective implementation and practice of SPC can provide process operators with greater intrinsic rewards and allow them to achieve higher levels of motivation and job satisfaction by making the work that process operators perform more motivating. Realizing that the deployment of SPC can lead to unintentional improvements in intrinsic rewards can also explain why attempts at deploying and sustaining SPC might fail. Deploying SPC in production environments staffed by process operators who do not desire enriched jobs would, very likely, backfire and lead to disgruntled employees. Likewise, when process operators perceive that their jobs have become enriched due to greater skills, more immediate feedback, greater control, etc., they may expect to be recognized and compensated accordingly. Failure to do so might lead to perceptions of exploitation and feelings of inequity vis-a-vis other employees whose jobs have not changed and who are governed by the same compensation scheme.

research has suggested that it can motivate the workforce (see box "SPC Can Be Motivating"). Because SPC requires processes to show measurable variation, it is ineffective for quality levels approaching six sigma. However, SPC is quite effective for companies in the early stages of quality efforts.

Walter Shewhart was the first to distinguish between common causes and special causes in process variation. He developed the control chart to identify the effects of special causes. A control chart displays the state of control of a process (Figure 3.3). Time is measured on the horizontal axis, and the value of a variable on the vertical axis. A central horizontal line usually corresponds to the average value of the quality characteristic being measured. Two other horizontal lines represent the upper (UCL) and lower (LCL) control limits, chosen so that there is a high probability that sample values will fall within these limits if the process is under control—that is, affected only by common causes of variation. If points fall outside of the control limits or if unusual patterns such as shifts up or down, trends up or down, cycles, and so forth exist, special causes may be present.

Although control charts were first developed and used in a manufacturing context, they are easily applied to service organizations. Table 3.2 lists just a few of the many potential applications of control charts for services. The key is in defining the appropriate quality measures to monitor. Most service processes can be improved through the appropriate application of control charts. Consider the following example. The Joint Commission Accreditation of Health Care Organizations (JCAHO) monitors and evaluates health care providers according to strict standards and guidelines. Improvement in the quality of care is a principal concern. Hospitals are required to identify and monitor important quality indicators that

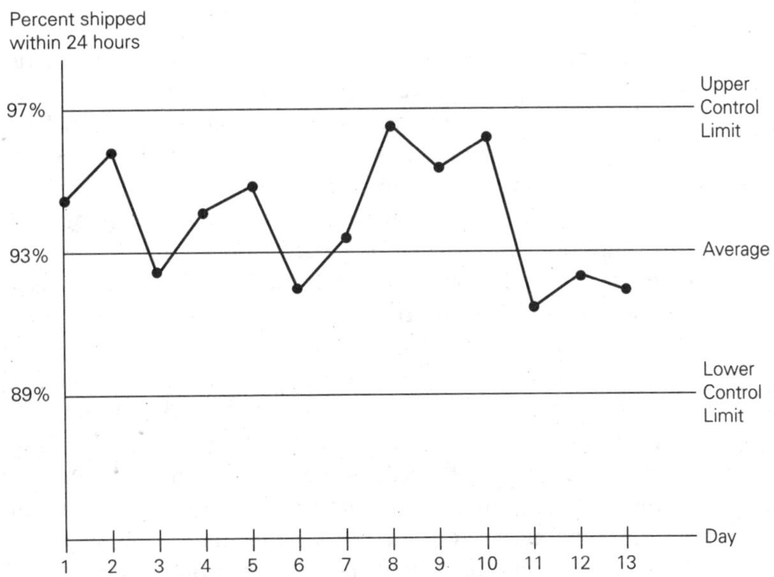

FIGURE 3.3 | EXAMPLE OF A CONTROL CHART

TABLE 3.2 APPLICATIONS OF CONTROL CHARTS IN SERVICE ORGANIZATIONS

Organization	Quality Measure
Hospital	Lab test accuracy Insurance claim accuracy On-time delivery of meals and medication
Bank	Check-processing accuracy
Insurance company	Claims-processing response time Billing accuracy
Post Office	Sorting accuracy Time of delivery Percentage of express mail delivered on time
Ambulance	Response time
Police Department	Incidence of crime in a precinct Number of traffic citations
Hotel	Proportion of rooms satisfactorily cleaned Checkout time Number of complaints received
Transportation	Proportion of freight cars correctly routed Dollar amount of damage per claim
Auto service	Percentage of time work completed as promised Number of parts out of stock

affect patient care and establish "thresholds for evaluation" (TFEs), which are levels at which special investigation of problems should occur. TFEs provide a means of focusing attention on nonrandom errors (that is, special causes of variation). A logical way to set TFEs is through control charts. For instance, a hospital collects monthly data on the number of infections after surgeries. These data are shown in Table 3.3. Hospital administrators are concerned about whether the high percentages of infections (such as 1.76 percent in month 12) are caused by factors other than randomness. A control chart constructed from these data is shown in Figure 3.4. (Note that if the control limits are removed, it becomes a simple run chart.) The average percentage of infections is 55/7995 = 0.688 percent.

Using formulas described in more advanced books, the upper control limit is computed to be 2.35 percent. None of the data points fall above the upper control limit, indicating that the variation each month is due purely to chance and that the process is stable. To reduce the infection rate, management would have to attack the common causes in the process. The upper control limit would be a logical TFE to use, because any value beyond this limit is unlikely to occur by chance. Management can continue to use this chart to monitor future data.

TABLE 3.3 MONTHLY DATA ON INFECTIONS AFTER SURGERY

Month	Surgeries	Infections	Percent
1	208	1	0.48
2	225	3	1.33
3	201	3	1.49
4	236	1	0.42
5	220	3	1.36
6	244	1	0.41
7	247	1	0.40
8	245	1	0.41
9	250	1	0.40
10	227	0	0.00
11	234	2	0.85
12	227	4	1.76
13	213	2	0.94
14	212	1	0.47
15	193	2	1.04
16	182	0	0.00
17	140	1	0.71
18	230	1	0.43
19	187	1	0.53
20	252	2	0.79
21	201	1	0.50
22	226	0	0.00
23	222	2	0.90
24	212	2	0.94
25	219	1	0.46
26	223	2	0.90
27	191	1	0.52
28	222	0	0.00
29	231	3	1.30
30	239	1	0.42
31	217	2	0.92
32	241	1	0.41
33	220	3	1.36
34	278	1	0.36
35	255	3	1.18
36	225	1	0.44
	7,995	55	

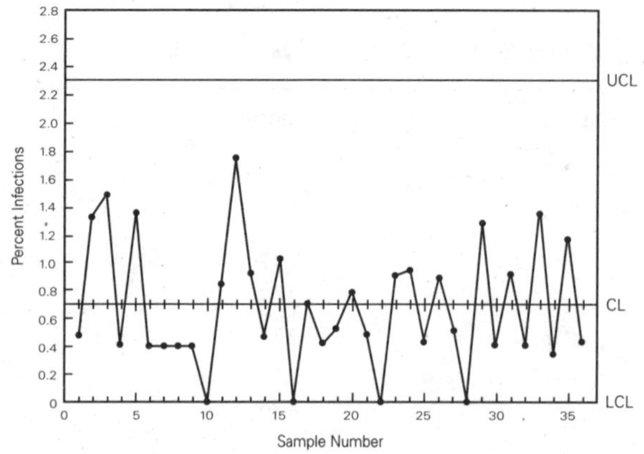

FIGURE 3.4 CONTROL CHART FOR SURGERY INFECTIONS

PROCESS CONTROL IN SERVICES

Many people think that process control applies only to manufacturing. This assumption could not be further from the truth. The approach used by The Ritz-Carlton Hotel Company to control quality is proactive because of their intensive personalized service environment.[28] Systems for collecting and using quality-related measures are widely deployed and used extensively throughout the organization. Each hotel tracks service quality indicators on a daily basis. The Ritz-Carlton recognizes that many customer requirements are sensory, and thus, difficult to measure. However, by selecting, training, and certifying employees in their knowledge of The Ritz-Carlton Gold Standards of service, they are able to assess their work through appropriate sensory measurements—taste, sight, smell, sound, and touch—and take appropriate actions.

The company uses three types of control processes to deliver quality:

1. Self-control of the individual employee based on their spontaneous and learned behavior.
2. Basic control mechanism, which is carried out by every member of the workforce.
3. Critical success factor control for critical processes. Process teams use customer and organizational requirement measurements to determine quality, speed, and cost performance. These measurements are compared against benchmarks and customer satisfaction data to determine corrective action and resource allocation.

In addition, The Ritz-Carlton conducts both self-audits and outside audits. Self-audits are carried out internally at all levels, from one individual or function to an entire hotel. Process walk-throughs occur daily in hotels while senior leaders assess field operations during formal reviews at various intervals. Outside audits are performed by independent travel and hospitality rating organizations. All audits must be documented, and any findings must be submitted to the senior leader of the unit being audited. They are responsible for action and for assessing the implementation and effectiveness of recommended corrective actions.

PROCESS DESIGN AND CONTROL IN ACTION

Many organizations have made substantial improvements by applying process management principles. In this section, we present some examples. In addition to these, some formal research studies provide evidence of the impact of process management on quality and the bottom line (see box "Process Management Drives Performance").

CHUGACH SCHOOL DISTRICT[29]

The Chugach School District (CSD) is located in Southcentral Alaska and includes most of the Prince William Sound coastline and islands. With less than 20 full-time faculty, CSD serves students scattered throughout 22,000 square miles of isolated and remote areas. Some village and school sites are 100 percent Aleut (Native Alaskan), while other sites include heterogeneous groups. The Chugach School District is fairly representative of "Bush Alaska" in regard to the obstacles standing in the way of educational excellence, including high unemployment and poverty, and various social problems in the communities served. Students receive educational services in one of three small villages, accessible by small aircraft, or from itinerant teachers who regularly visit wilderness homes in the Valdez and Fairbanks regions through the Extension School Program.

A comprehensive restructuring effort was initiated in 1994. Using input from schools, communities and businesses, CSD realigned its curriculum to create ten performance-based standards: mathematics, science, technology, reading, writing, social sciences, service learning, career development, cultural awareness and expression, and personal/social/health development. Individual Learning Plans (ILP), Student Assessment Binders (SAB), Student Learning Profiles (SLP), and Student Lifeskills Portfolios support and document consistent progress toward proficiency in all standards. CSD developed performance standards continuums for all content areas.

The success of CSD's educational programs and services lies in the design and delivery of their educational processes and continuous improvement efforts as seen

PROCESS MANAGEMENT DRIVES PERFORMANCE[30]

Through a study of quality practices in 418 manufacturing plants from multiple industries, researchers demonstrated that both design and process management efforts have an equal positive impact on internal quality outcomes such as scrap, rework, defects, and performance, and external quality outcomes such as complaints, warranty, litigation, and market share. One interesting result was that although design efforts influence customer-based quality perceptions through visible product changes, they influence these external quality outcomes primarily through their contribution to efficient production of high performance quality products; that is, internal quality. However, firms need not always strive for visible breakthrough improvements in product features. These efforts need to be balanced with on-going efficiency and production cost improvement. These findings indicate that, to attain superior quality outcomes, firms need to balance their design and process management efforts and persevere with long-term implementation of these efforts.

in Figure 3.5. The processes maintain a focus on students with student input garnered from beginning to end. The design process integrates customer requirements from all stakeholders to secure a powerful shared vision, which can be supported by all. Action plans drove the design of this process. The process is simple, efficient, effective and includes evaluation and refinement segments to continually improve each step of the process, as well as the process itself.

A key process is the Chugach Instructional Model (CIM), which has been continuously improved and now encompasses clear and effective teaching methods. The CIM is summarized in Figure 3.6. This instructional methodology aims to create

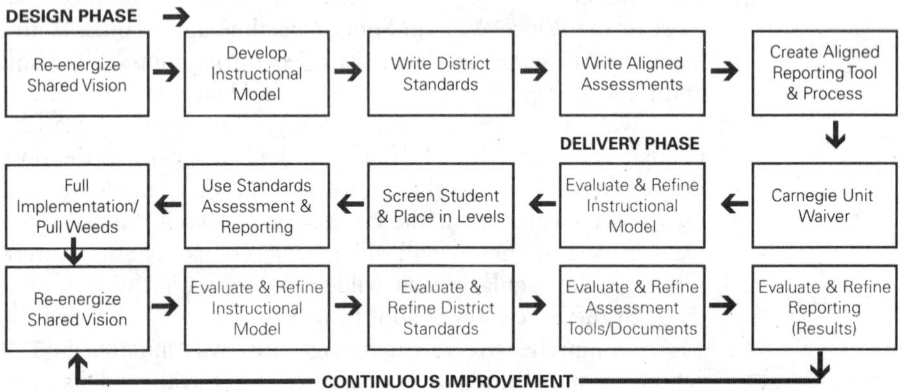

FIGURE 3.5 | CSD EDUCATIONAL DESIGN AND DELIVERY PROCESSES

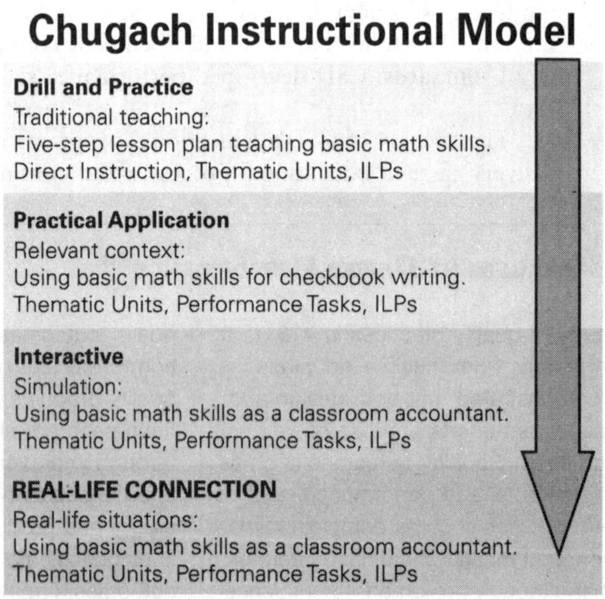

FIGURE 3.6 | CHUGACH INSTRUCTIONAL MODEL

Source: Chugach School District.

real-life learning situations in all content areas. Chugach has developed a process for creating thematic units, which allow teachers to design contextual units relevant to students. The Chugach staff participates in this process every April to plan for the following year. Thematic units directly support the purpose of the CIM, which is to help teachers make a connection with students' performance levels and the theme being developed. Thematic units teach relationships among disciplines. By its nature and definition it is expansive, respecting no walls with names like math, science, social studies, and art. Thematic units, put simply, take and nurture the natural propensity of humans to make connections between disciplines.

The Student Learning Profile has been developed to help teachers anticipate the whole child and facilitate learning, not just the intellectual system. It helps students to understand themselves as learners with unique patterns. CSD anticipated this revolutionary approach as a need by CSD after years of trial and error and stakeholder input. Each student's intellectual, emotional, and volitional development patterns are identified and used to better focus instruction for each student. Cognitive, emotional, and values information gained through testing is at the teachers' and students' fingertips to focus instruction and learning.

A unique feature of CSD is the lack of grade levels. One student may work in Level V math for a year while another student the same age masters the same level in four months and moves on to level VI. Developmental levels are the levels at which students are working, based on what is known about how children and youth develop, learn, and demonstrate their learning at various ages. The students' performance levels coincide with the developmental levels of the Chugach developmental report card. The levels permit students to work at their own rate continually. An Individual Learning Plan is a custom-designed document written and used by students, teachers, and parents to meet the educational needs of the individual student. Goals are identified and tied to standards focusing on student-driven performance, implementation, and accountability. The ILP anticipates individual differences and allows every child in the system to design their education by setting goals. Students create and achieve ILP goals throughout the year.

These processes have had remarkable results. National percentile scores on the California Achievement Test in reading increased from 28.44 to 71.1 between 1995 and 1999; in language from 26.46 to 71.9; in math from 53.6 to 78.1; and in spelling from 22 to 65. Chugach was the only school district in the United States to be awarded the New American High School Award, a national award earned by top performing high schools, and, in addition, was one of the first education sector winners of the Malcolm Baldrige National Quality Award in 2001.

THE WALT DISNEY COMPANY

One unusual example is provided by the Walt Disney Company.[31] The opening of Euro Disneyland in 1992 near Marne la Vallee, France, brought to four the number of parks operated around the world by the Walt Disney Company. Disneyland, the original, opened in 1955 in Anaheim, California. Disney World, in Orlando, Florida, opened in 1971 and was expanded in 1982 to include Epcot Center and later MGM Studios Theme Park. Tokyo Disneyland, Disney's first overseas park, opened in 1983.

Disney faced a difficult challenge in bringing its American style of fun to the French people, who are often ambivalent at best about American cultural imperialism. The opening of Euro Disney was not without problems, as Disney faced labor disputes over its personal appearance policies, such as no facial hair, and substantial difficulties with getting construction work done on time and under budget. The company anticipated and tried to defuse any cross-cultural difficulties through an exchange of hundreds of European and American managers.

One major advantage possessed by Disney in establishing its European park was its ability to learn from its past successes, as well as its past mistakes. When the original park was opened in Anaheim, it was quickly surrounded by hotels and restaurants that competed with Disney's own. This mistake was not repeated either in Orlando, where Disney bought 28,000 acres (much of which is still unused), or in France.

Disney built six hotels for the opening of Euro Disney, far more than would be immediately needed. Why? The company had dragged its heels in building hotels in Florida, allowing competitors to become established.

Almost unbelievably, the plans for Euro Disney (which is also known as Disneyland Paris) call for an additional 4,000 hotel rooms, a retail and industrial park, and even 8,000 private homes. When one thinks of continuous improvement, processes that are repeated every hour, day, or week come to mind. However, Disney has applied continuous improvement to the process of park design, which it has practiced only about every 10 years!

Review and Discussion Questions

1. Texas Nameplate Company, highlighted in the Performance Excellence Profile, is a small company with fewer than 50 employees and a high level of ethnic diversity. What challenges would such a firm face in implementing process design and control tools? How might it overcome these challenges?
2. What is process management? What are the three types of activities that it comprises?
3. Explain the rationale behind AT&T's process management principles. How are each of these important in designing, controlling, and improving a process?
4. Identify some of the key processes associated with the following business activities for a typical company: sales and marketing, supply chain management, managing information technology, and managing human resources. What factors might influence the design of these processes?
5. Explain the four principal activities of Design for Six Sigma (DFSS).
6. Explain concept engineering. Why is it an important tool for assuring quality in product and process design activities?
7. Explain the benefits of the quality function deployment approach. How does it help organizations to design better products and services?
8. Using whatever "market research" techniques you feel are appropriate, define a set of customer attributes for (a) purchasing books at your college bookstore, (b) a hotel room used for business, and (c) a college registration process. How might QFD be used to design these services? Define a set of "hows" and try to construct the relationship matrix for the House of Quality for each of these examples.
9. What is design failure mode and effects analysis (DFMEA)? Provide a simple example illustrating the concept.

10. How does the design of a service process differ from designing a manufactured good? Explain the factors that one must consider for a good service design.
11. Describe Motorola's approach to process design. How does this approach help to ensure high quality and performance?
12. What is mass customization? Why does mass customization present process design challenges?
13. Why is agility important in process design?
14. Identify several sources of errors in your personal life. Develop some mistake-proofing ideas for eliminating them.
15. How might poka-yoke be applied to the U.S. election system based on the information described in the example in this chapter? You might wish to do some additional research on the subject or find out how your local election process is performed.
16. Search the Internet for John Grout's Poka-Yoke Web site. Read several of the interesting articles available there and write a report on the information you discover.
17. At a university library, many activities take place. Some of these are
    - processing request forms from patrons for copying of journal articles;
    - reshelving books that readers have left on desks (books are picked up, placed on carts, sorted, and reshelved); and
    - locating missing books.

    For these activities, identify potential problems that might arise and what the library might do to "mistake-proof" its activities to provide better service.
18. Explain how a control system works. Provide some examples in your everyday life.
19. Provide some examples of standardized processes with which you are familiar. How are they controlled?
20. What is statistical thinking? How might the traditional teaching of statistics be improved by incorporating this notion? Draw your response from your own experiences in learning statistics.
21. Describe the operational problems that are created by excessive variation.
22. Explain the concept of statistical process control. How does it support the Deming philosophy discussed in Chapter 2?
23. List some applications of control charts in service organizations that differ from those in Table 3.2.

CASES

Customer Service Processes at Orbitz[32]

Scott Paton, an editor-at-large for *Quality Digest*, related the following customer service experience with Orbitz, a leading online travel Web site:

I use Orbitz four or five times a month to book travel for me or the trainers who work with Paton Press. I've always been impressed with the site's low fares and easy-to-navigate interface. Despite having purchased hundreds of airline tickets through the site, I never had an occasion to call customer service until recently. (I guess that in itself says something about the quality of the service I've received.)

While reviewing my last American Express statement, I noticed two charges for the same amount and the same itinerary. I knew that this was a mistake because I had only purchased one ticket. I logged onto the Orbitz site and looked at my past trips. I saw that there was only one booked itinerary for that person for that week. Orbitz had made a mistake.

I knew I would have to call the company to get the error corrected, and I began to experience that uneasy feeling I get whenever I have to call customer service. Where would my call get routed? Would they believe me? Had I made a $335 error?

I began the process by going to the Orbitz home page. I was impressed. At the top of the page in large, easy-to-read type was a tab that said "Customer Service." Probably a link to a "Frequently Asked Questions" database, I thought. To my surprise, when I clicked on the tab, there were three options: an FAQ database, an e-mail link, and a toll-free number to call for help. The customer service department is open 7 days a week, 24 hours a day. This is impressive, especially when traveling. Okay. This was looking good, but how would my call be answered?

I dialed the number and was immediately connected to the Orbitz voicemail system, which asked for my home phone number. Apparently, this let them know where I was calling from. After entering my phone number, I was led through a surprisingly quick and easy voicemail navigation system that divides calls by type of inquiry. I generally hate these kinds of voicemail systems, but Orbitz's system was painless. I was through it in a matter of seconds.

When I selected "Help," my call was answered within a minute. A pleasant woman asked how she could help me. I explained that upon reviewing my American Express statement it appeared as though I had been double-charged. Her first reaction was to apologize.

"I'm sorry you had a problem," she said. "Let's see what we can do to resolve it for you."

She asked me for some information and then asked me to hold while she checked on the problem. When she came back on the line after about two minutes, she apologized for leaving me on hold. The Orbitz system had indeed double-charged me. She explained that Orbitz would refund my money and that it might take 30 to 60 days to show up on my American Express card statement, depending on when my statement was issued. She again apologized and asked if there was anything else she could do and if I was satisfied with the problem resolution.

About one week later, I received a letter from Orbitz apologizing for the problem with an explanation for what had occurred. The letter also included a $50 discount coupon toward my next Orbitz purchase.

Discussion Questions

1. What aspects of Orbitz's service processes led to Mr. Paton's favorable service experience?
2. Generalize the lessons learned from this example to other organizations. What challenges might organizations encounter in designing quality customer service processes?

Scott's Fitness Center

Figure 3.7 shows a partially completed House of Quality for a proposed fitness center.

1. Examine the relationships in the roof of the House of Quality. Explain why they do or do not make sense. How would this assessment help in the design activity?
2. Complete the matrix in the body of the House of Quality. That is, examine each pair of customer and technical requirements and determine whether there is a very strong relationship, strong relationship, weak relationship, or no relationship, and fill in the appropriate symbols in the matrix.
3. Suppose that the most important customer requirements identified through surveys and focus groups are "Has programs I want," "Family activities available," "Equipment available when desired," "Easy to sign up for programs," and "Value for your money." "Staff available when needed" was ranked low, while the remaining were ranked moderate in importance.

Based on this information, identify the most important technical requirements that should be addressed in subsequent design activities.

Southwest Regional Hospital

Stuart Kendall just returned from an annual medical conference. Stuart is director of Southwest Regional Hospital. At the conference, he heard that over 50,000 people die each year from medical errors, and of those, medication errors account for about 7,000 deaths a year. Medication errors can also lead to disabilities, lawsuits, and millions of dollars spent on longer hospital stays and medical treatments. Dr. Kendall knew that SWRH had to be more proactive in preventing medication errors. After pulling together a team to map the process, he hired you to analyze it and make some recommendations to help prevent errors and mistakes. Discuss possible sources of errors, the types of individuals responsible (e.g., physicians, nurses, pharmacists, other), and poka-yokes that might be used to mitigate these errors.

The HMO Pharmacy Crisis[33]

John Dover just completed an intensive course, "Statistical Thinking for Continuous Improvement," that was offered to all employees of a large health maintenance organization (HMO). There was no time to celebrate,

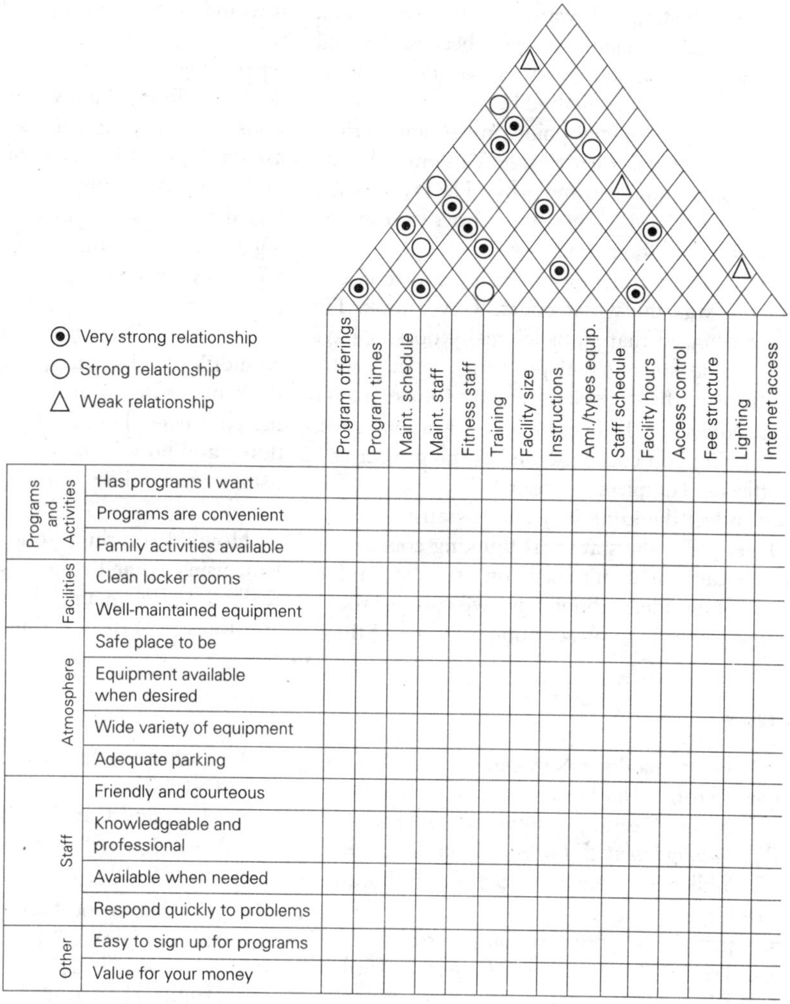

FIGURE 3.7 | HOUSE OF QUALITY FOR SCOTT'S FITNESS CENTER

however, because he was already under a lot of pressure. Dover worked as a pharmacy assistant in the HMO's pharmacy, and his manager, Juan de Pacotilla, was about to be fired. Pacotilla's dismissal appeared imminent because of numerous complaints—and even a few lawsuits—over inaccurate prescriptions.

Pacotilla now was asking Dover for his assistance in trying to resolve the problem. "John, I really need your help," said Pacotilla. "If I can't show some major improvement or at least a solid plan by next month, I'm history." "I'll be glad to help," replied Dover, "but what can I do? I'm just a pharmacy assistant." "Your job title isn't important. I think you're just the person who can get this done," said Pacotilla. "I realize that I've been too far removed from day-to-day operations in the pharmacy, but you work there every day. You're in a much better position to find out how to fix the problem. Just tell me what to do, and I'll do it." "But what about the statistical consultant you hired to analyze the data on inaccurate prescriptions?" asked Dover.

"To be honest, I'm really disappointed with that guy. He has spent two weeks trying to come up with a new modeling approach to predict weekly inaccurate prescriptions. I tried to explain to him that I don't want to predict the mistakes, I want to eliminate them. I don't think I got through, however, because he said we need a month of additional data to verify the model before he can apply a new method he just read about in a journal to identify 'change points in the time series,' whatever that means. But get this, he will only identify the change points and send me a list. He says it's my job to figure out what they mean and how to respond. I don't know much about statistics."

"The only thing I remember from my course in college is that it was the worst course I ever took. I'm becoming convinced that statistics really doesn't have much to offer in solving real problems. Since you've just gone through the statistical thinking course, maybe you can see something I can't. I realize it's a long shot, but I was hoping you could use this as the project you need to officially complete the course."

"I used to feel the same way about statistics, too," replied Dover. "But the statistical thinking course was interesting because it didn't focus on crunching numbers. I have some ideas about how we can approach making improvements in prescription accuracy. I think it would be a great project. But we might not be able to solve this problem ourselves. As you know, there is a lot of finger pointing going on. Pharmacists blame the doctors' sloppy handwriting and incomplete instructions for the problem. Doctors blame the pharmacy assistants, who do most of the computer entry of the prescriptions, claiming that they are incompetent. Pharmacy assistants blame the pharmacists for assuming too much about their knowledge of medical terminology, brand names, known drug interactions, and so on."

"It sounds like there's no hope," said Pacotilla. "I wouldn't say that at all," replied Dover. "It's just that there might be no quick fix we can do by ourselves in the pharmacy. Let me explain what I'm thinking about doing and how I would propose attacking the problem using what I just learned in the statistical thinking course."

How do you think John should approach this problem, using what he has just learned? Assume that he really did pick up a solid understanding of the concepts and tools of statistical thinking in the course.

Endnotes

1. 2005 Malcolm Baldrige National Quality Award Recipient Profile, U.S Department of Commerce.
2. AT&T Quality Steering Committee, *Process Quality Management & Improvement Guidelines*, AT&T Publication Center, AT&T Bell Laboratories (1987).
3. Peter Svensson, "It's not just computers: Gadgets crash," *The Cincinnati Enquirer*, April 3, 2003, A3.
4. Steven H. Wildstrom, "Price Wars Power Up Quality," *BusinessWeek*, September 18, 1995, 26.
5. Philip A. Himmelfarb, "Fast New-Product Development at Service Sector Companies," *Quality Digest*, April 1996, 41–44.
6. C. M. Creveling, J. L. Slutsky, and D. Antis, Jr., *Design for Six Sigma in Technology and Product Development* (Upper Saddle River, NJ, Prentice Hall, 2003).
7. Christina Hepner Brodie, "A Polaroid Notebook: Concept Engineering," *Center for Quality of Management Journal* Vol. 3, No. 2 (1994), pp. 7–14.
8. Laura Horton and David Boger, "How Bose Corporation Applied Concept Engineering to a Service," *Center for Quality of Management Journal* 3, no. 2 (1994), 52–59.
9. Sarah Anne Wright, "Putting Fast-Food to the Test," *The Cincinnati Enquirer*, July 9, 2000, F1, 2; and David Grainger, "Can McDonald's Cook Again?" *Fortune*, April 14, 2003, pp. 120–129.
10. John Haywood-Farmer, "A Conceptual Model of Service Quality," *International Journal of Operations and Production Management* Vol. 8, No. 6 (1988), pp. 19–29.
11. Dell: Facing Up to Past Mistakes, *Business Week*, June 19, 2006, pp. 35–36.
12. Lucas Conley, "90,000 DVDs. No Shelves," *Fast Company*, September 2003, p. 38.
13. Kelly Scott, "How Federal Express Delivers Customer Service," *APICS—The Performance Advantage*, November 1999, pp. 44–46.
14. Rebecca Duray and Glenn W. Milligan, "Improving Customers Satisfaction Through Mass Customization," *Quality Progress*, August 1999, pp. 60–66.
15. "It's the Latest Thing—Really," *Business Week*, March 27, 2006, pp. 70–71.
16. Excerpts reprinted from Richard B. Chase and Douglas M. Stewart, "Make Your Service Fail-Safe," *Sloan Management Review*, Vol. 35, No. 3, Spring 1994. Copyright 1994 by the Sloan Management Review Association. All rights reserved.

17. Howard R. Schussler, "Can Quality Concepts and Tools Fix the U.S. Election Process?" *Quality Progress*, April 2001, pp. 46–50.
18. "Coca-Cola: A Taste for Quality," The Coca-Cola Company, Atlanta, Georgia.
19. http://www.thecoca-colacompany.com/news/NewsDetail.asp?NewsDate=6/15/99.
20. "Testing for Conformity: An Inside Job," *Golf Journal*, May 1998, pp. 20–25.
21. "Quality Control Comes to the CIA," *Los Angeles Times*, February 4, 2008. Cited by the American Society for Quality, http://www.asq.org/quality-news/qnt/execute/displaySetup?newsID=3011
22. "DaimlerChrysler's Quality Practices Pay Off for PT Cruiser," News and Analysis, http://www.metrologyworld.com (accessed March 23, 2000).
23. Adapted from Galen Britz, Don Emerling, Lynne Hare, Roger Hoerl, and Janice Shade, "How to Teach Others to Apply Statistical Thinking," *Quality Progress*, June 1997, pp. 67–79.
24. Steven A. Melnyk and R. T. Christensen, "Variance is Evil," *APICS The Performance Advantage*, June 2002, 19.
25. Ronald D. Snee, "Getting Better Business Results: Using Statistical Thinking and Methods to Shape the Bottom Line," *Quality Progress*, June 1998, pp. 102–106.
26. Adapted from Brian L. Joiner, *Fourth Generation Management*, New York: McGraw-Hill, 1994, p. 129.
27. Manus Rungtusanatham "Beyond improved quality: the motivational effects of statistical process control," *Journal of Operations Management* 19, 2001, pp. 653–673
28. Adapted from The Ritz-Carlton Hotel Company, Application Summaries for the Malcolm Baldrige National Quality Award, 1992 and 1999.
29. Chugach School District.
30. Sanjay L. Ahire and Paul Dreyfus, "The impact of design management and process management on quality: an empirical investigation," *Journal of Operations Management* 18, 2000, pp. 549–575
31. Based on Cheri Henderson, "Monsieur Mickey," *TQM Magazine*, September/October 1992, pp. 220–224.
32. Scott M. Paton, "Stellar Customer Service," *Quality Digest*, June 2006, p. 64.
33. Adapted from Galen Britz, Don Emerling, Lynne Hare, Roger Hoerl, and Janice Shade, "How to Teach Others to Apply Statistical Thinking," *Quality Progress*, June 1997, pp. 67–79. © 1997 American Society for Quality, Reprinted with permission.

CHAPTER 4

TOOLS AND TECHNIQUES FOR QUALITY IMPROVEMENT

Performance Excellence Profile: Iredell-Statesville Schools[1]

Iredell-Statesville Schools (I-SS) is a K–12 public school system located in southwestern North Carolina within a diverse community and economy. To meet the needs of its 20,900 students, I-SS offers a variety of educational programs delivered in heterogeneously grouped classrooms, two at-risk behavior schools, and virtual curriculum and early college settings. The system also offers before- and after-school programs, short-term alternative site placement programs, and dual enrollment courses in partnership with a local community college. I-SS, which segments its 3,416 employees as certified, classified, and administrative staff, considers them to be "knowledge assets in achieving organizational learning and improvement."

With a new vision to "improve student learning by igniting a passion for learning," I-SS senior leaders are moving the district from a "focus on teaching" to a "focus on learning." The superintendent of schools and the Senior Leadership Team use the I-SS Performance Excellence Model as the management approach to share and accomplish the district's vision. Their strategic plan is linked to the North Carolina State Board of Education Strategic Priorities: high student performance; healthy, safe, orderly, and caring schools; quality teachers, administrators, and staff; strong family-community-business support; and effective-efficient operations. These five priority goal areas are aligned with division-, department-, and school-improvement plans to provide clear direction for the system.

To fulfill its mission of realizing high student performance and long-term student success, I-SS uses its Model to Raise Achievement and Close Gaps (RACG). In the classroom, five key learning questions form the basis for action by focusing discussion and analysis on what students should know and be able to do: (1) "What do students need to know?" (2) "How will they learn it?" (3) "How will we know they have learned it?" (4) "What will we do if they have not learned it?" and (5) "What will we do if they already know it?" When student performance does not meet targets, the gap is addressed through the systematic use of a Plan, Do, Study, Act (PDSA) cycle to identify and implement improvements. Best practices are shared throughout the district, departments, and schools. To support RACG, both administrative and site-based teams receive extensive analysis of student achievement data in midyear and end-of-year organizational reviews. The system's results illustrate the impact of its focused efforts to improve student achievement. For example:

- I-SS has achieved 94 percent of its Adequate Yearly Progress goals and outperforms peer districts and the state in this measure, which is required by the No Child Left Behind (NCLB) Act.
- Cohort graduation rates (the percentage of ninth-grade students who graduate from high school four years later) increased steadily from 64 percent in 2002–2003 to 80.7 percent in 2007–2008.
- In five years, the system's composite SAT scores have improved by over 60 points to 1056, with its current performance level ranking seventh in the state.
- I-SS closed the EOG reading proficiency gap between African-American children and all students from 23 percent to 12.3 percent.

As one approach to building healthy, safe, orderly, and caring schools, an I-SS committee in 2003–2004 identified alternative schools, alternative learning processes, and student attendance as high priorities for improvement that could impact dropout rates. As a result of a district PDSA on alternative learning programs, the structure of alternative learning processes changed significantly. Several innovative programs were added, including an out-of-school suspension-reporting center, an in-school credit recovery program, an attendance recovery program, virtual courses, virtual credit recovery courses, summer credit recovery programs, and Day Treatment and Community Classrooms provided by a strategic partnership. A Differentiated Diploma Program was targeted at preventing juniors and seniors from dropping out of school.

Effective training and mentoring approaches ensure that the system has quality teachers, administrators, and staff to increase student achievement and close gaps. Professional Learning Communities provide classroom teachers with face-to-face and virtual opportunities to improve student learning and share best practices across grade levels and departments. Instructional Facilitators support these communities by providing ongoing professional development through coaching, modeling, and mentoring. Throughout I-SS, teaching assistants are trained alongside teachers and staff. Beyond the classroom, a Leadership Academy trains administrators in the Performance Excellence Model.

I-SS depends on strong family, community, and business support from active partners—including suppliers, community organizations, parents, and volunteers—to achieve its goals. They participate on school and district improvement teams, advisory committees, and specific task forces, working side by side with staff on school initiatives. I-SS volunteers contributed nearly 147,000 hours serving in roles such as mentors, tutors, lunch buddies, and clerical/classroom support for staff. I-SS partners with a community college and another school district to offer students dual-enrollment opportunities in an early college setting. I-SS is working with the Statesville City Council and the Blumenthal Center for Performing Arts to establish a performance and fine arts magnet school and with the Boys and Girls Club to provide after-school enrichment activities for at-risk students. A strategy to involve key partners in obtaining grants to impact strategic goals has resulted in more than $8 million in grants being awarded in just three years.

In the previous chapter we introduced process management and focused on tools and techniques used for designing and controlling products and processes. Improvement is the third element of process management. The profile on Iredell-Statesville schools shows the power of using systematic approaches to improvement. Continuous improvement is essential to total quality. The TQ ideal is not to make a big splash by improving a system, only to mindlessly operate in the same "new and improved" manner for years to come. TQ-oriented organizations relentlessly improve their processes, products, and services, as well as their people (through training) day-by-day and month-by-month, over years and even decades. A good illustration is Dell. Although it has had some of the highest quality ratings in the PC industry, CEO Michael Dell became obsessed with finding ways to reduce machine failure rates. He concluded that failures were related to the number of times a hard drive was handled during assembly, and insisted that the number of "touches" be reduced from an existing level of more than 30 per drive. Production lines were revamped and the number was reduced to fewer than 15. Soon after, the reject rate of hard drives fell by 40 percent and the overall failure rated dropped by 20 percent.[2]

Because of its importance in every organization, we devote a full chapter here to describe the most important tools and techniques that organizations use. Specifically, we will

- explain the philosophy and approaches to continuous improvement;
- describe systematic improvement processes used by many organizations;
- illustrate the application of a variety of tools for process improvement, including those used in Six Sigma and Lean Six Sigma; and
- discuss breakthrough improvement and the importance of creativity and innovation.

PROCESS IMPROVEMENT

The distinction between control and improvement is illustrated in Figure 4.1. Any process performance measure naturally fluctuates around some average level. Abnormal conditions cause an unusual deviation from this pattern. Removing the causes of such abnormal conditions and maintaining level performance is the essence of control. Improvement means changing the performance to a new level. To be able to improve a process, it must be (1) repeatable and (2) measurable. Repeatability means that the process must recur over time. The cycle may be long, as with product development processes or patent applications; or it may be short, as with a manufacturing operation or an order entry process. In other words, you need the ability to learn from both successes and failures. Many organizations use a variety of approaches (see box "Keeping That Touch of Elegance"), including formal problem-solving methodologies to identify potential improvements, analyze data, and implement solutions.

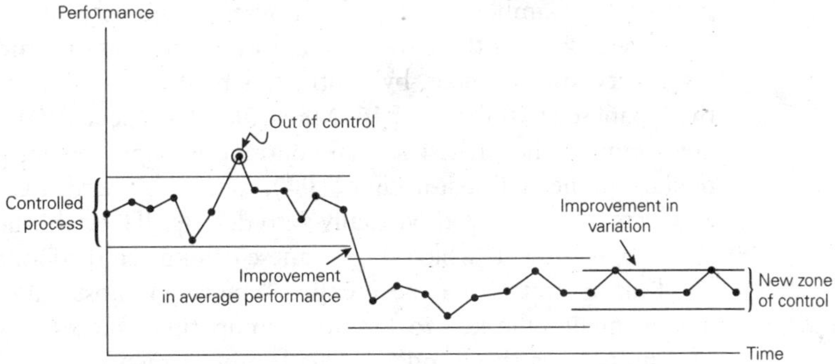

FIGURE 4.1 CONTROL VERSUS IMPROVEMENT

KEEPING THAT TOUCH OF ELEGANCE

The Ritz-Carlton has eight mechanisms devoted solely to the improvement of process, product, and service quality:

1. New hotel startup improvement process: a cross-functional team from the entire company that works together to identify and correct problem areas.
2. Comprehensive performance evaluation process: the work area team mechanism that empowers people who perform a job to develop the job procedures and performance standards.
3. Quality network: a mechanism of peer approval through which an individual employee can advance a good idea.
4. Standing problem-solving team: a standing work area team that addresses any problem it chooses.
5. Quality improvement team: special teams assembled to solve an assigned problem identified by an individual employee or leaders.
6. Strategic quality planning: annual work area teams that identify their missions, primary supplier objectives and action plans, internal objectives and action plans, and progress reviews.
7. Streamlining process: the annual hotel evaluation of processes, products, or services that are no longer valuable to the customer.
8. Process improvement: the team mechanism for corporate leaders, managers, and employees to improve the most critical processes.

THE KAIZEN PHILOSOPHY

The concept of continuous improvement dates back many years. One of the earliest examples in the United States was at National Cash Register Company (NCR). After a shipment of defective cash registers was returned in 1894, the company's founder discovered unpleasant and unsafe working conditions. He made many changes, including better lighting, new safety devices, ventilation, lounges, and lockers. The company offered extensive evening classes to improve employees' education and skills, and instituted a program for soliciting suggestions from factory workers. Workers received cash prizes and other recognitions for their best ideas; by the 1940s the company was receiving an average of 3,000 suggestions each year. Over the years, many other companies such as Lincoln Electric and

Procter & Gamble developed innovative and effective improvement approaches. However, many of these focused almost exclusively on productivity and cost. A focus on quality improvement, by contrast, is relatively recent, stimulated by the success of the Japanese. Toshiba in 1946, Matsushita Electric in 1950, and Toyota in 1951 initiated some of the earliest formal continuous improvement programs. Toyota, in particular, pioneered just-in-time (JIT), which showed that companies could make products efficiently with virtually zero defects. JIT established a philosophy of continuous improvement, which the Japanese call **kaizen** (pronounced ki-zen).

Kaizen strategy has been called "the single most important concept in Japanese management—the key to Japanese competitive success." It is the cumulative effect of hundreds or thousands of small improvements that creates dramatic change in performance. In the kaizen approach as practiced in Japan, financial investment is minimal; everyone participates in the process; and improvements result from the know-how and experience of workers. At Nissan Motor Co., Ltd., for instance, any suggestion that saves at least 0.6 seconds in a production process is seriously considered by management. This is not to say that large improvement breakthroughs do not occur; they certainly do, especially in the early phases of TQ. To use football as a metaphor, the successful practice of TQ is not reflected in the glamour of the occasional "long bomb," it consists of grinding out improvements "one yard at a time."

Consider the chart in Figure 4.2, which shows the result of attempts by a foundry to reduce its production of scrap (products rejected because of poor quality) over three years. Several points about continuous improvement are illustrated by this chart.

- The average amount of scrap declined each year, from approximately 9.5 in the first year to 6.5 in the second year and to 3.5 in the third year.

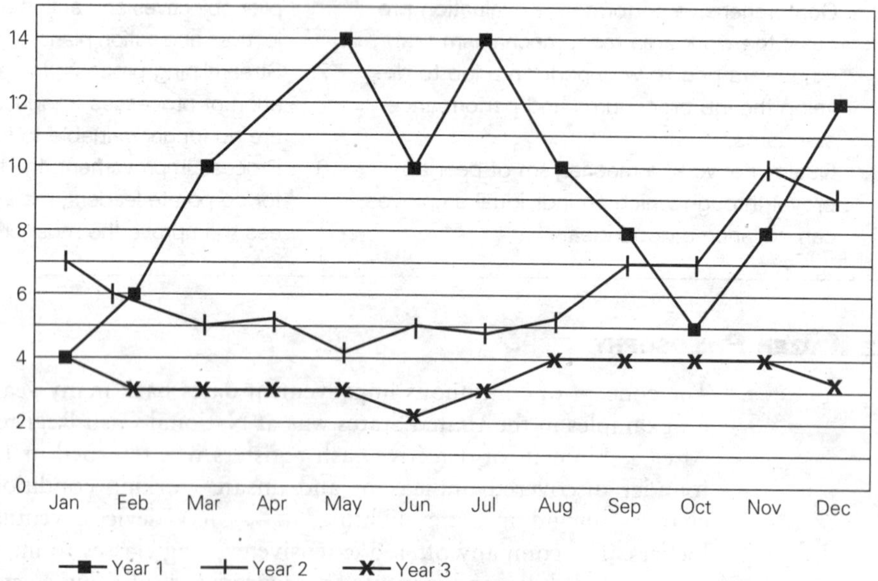

FIGURE 4.2 | SCRAP REDUCTIONS IN A FOUNDRY OVER THREE YEARS

- Not only the level but also the variation from month to month declined each year. Compare the wild variation in the first year to the relative stability of the third.
- Even when quality efforts had not been undertaken, the company occasionally got lucky and produced good quality. It took the foundry two years to produce a month as good as the first month of the first year.

Obviously, the first-year first-month was a fluke, as scrap was 50 percent higher the next month! The philosophy of continuous improvement was captured very well by the quality manager who said, "We're nowhere near where we ought to be, but we're getting better. And we're going to be better tomorrow."

The kaizen philosophy has been widely adopted and is used by many firms in the United States and around the world. For example, at ENBI Corporation, a New York manufacturer of precision metal shafts and roller assemblies for the printer, copier, and fax machine markets, kaizen projects have resulted in a 48 percent increase in productivity, a 30 percent reduction in cycle time, and a 73 percent reduction in inventory.[3] Kaizen has been successfully applied in the Mercedes-Benz truck factory in Brazil, resulting in reductions of 30 percent in manufacturing space, 45 percent in inventory, 70 percent in lead time, and 70 percent in setup time over a three-year period. Sixteen employees have full-time responsibility for kaizen activities.[4]

Continuous improvement efforts can be directed at a number of different types of improvement. For example, changes could result in work being done more easily, more accurately, faster, at lower cost, more safely, and in a way that provides greater customer satisfaction.[5] Thinking about continuous improvement in this way makes it clear how many opportunities for improvement exist in almost any system. How many operations are there that couldn't be improved on even one of these dimensions? Persistence is important in pursuing continuous improvement. Not only will small changes in operations take some time to add up to any serious improvement but also they are often disruptive when first implemented.

According to the late Japanese manufacturing expert, Shigeo Shingo:[6]

> Since improvement ... demands new procedures, a certain amount of difficulty will be encountered.... Initially, new methods will be difficult. Old procedures, however, are easy just because they are familiar.... As long as it is unfamiliar, even an improved procedure will be more difficult and will take more time than the old procedure.... Thus, no improvement shows its true worth right away ... 99 percent of all improvement plans would vanish without a trace if they were to be abandoned after only a brief trial.

Like the cultural change that motivates it, continuous improvement is difficult to sustain. Perhaps the "if it's not broke, don't fix it" mentality is too deeply embedded in our culture. In any case, many organizations that wish to embrace continuous improvement have not been able to do so successfully.

The most important ingredient for continuous improvement is one we have already discussed: an appropriate organizational culture (see box "No Lawyer Jokes Here"). If everyone in the organization understands and believes in the importance of continuous improvement, the rest is a question of technique. If not, no techniques will do the job.

No Lawyer Jokes Here[7]

Implementing a continuous improvement process in most law firm cultures can be difficult. This is partly because lawyers' compensation is directly linked to the number of hours they bill; many don't see themselves as being able to devote time to a quality initiative, even though, in the long run, such a program would likely streamline their processes and give them more time. In a culture with many individual habits and idiosyncrasies, standardizing processes and procedures can be difficult, if not impossible.

Nevertheless, some firms have made remarkable progress. The 130-lawyer firm of Mays & Valentine in Richmond, Virginia, set up quality improvement teams. A short survey was mailed to clients to find out where the firm stood with its external customers. At the same time, an internal survey was administered to the entire firm to determine whether the firm's culture was receptive to the TQ philosophy. The firm's executive committee carefully selected the mission and objectives for each team. Based on the survey results, they chose areas for improvement as attorney responsiveness and accessibility to clients, the firm's copying operations, and the use of alternative billing methods. Some of the changes that resulted included new standards for responsiveness to clients, which were made firm policy; a new branch office telephone system; outsourcing copy center operations to Xerox; and new measurements for administrative systems such as computer performance, turnover rate, central fax operations, speed of billing, complaints, and collection rates.

Not only has service improved, but employees are more satisfied because they are asked for their input and encouraged to suggest ways to improve effectiveness.

Given the large number of possible areas in an organization that could be improved, setting priorities is crucial, and there are several ways to do this. Many organizations rely on customer input and feedback to help set their priorities.[8] For example, if late deliveries are the most common customer complaint, continuous improvement efforts should be directed at reducing delivery times. Often customers cannot see inside the organization to identify the root causes of problems, so some additional sorting out is generally necessary.

The time-honored tradition of the suggestion system has taken on a new life under TQ to serve this purpose. At Portman Equipment Company, an employee who sees an improvement opportunity fills out a Proposal for Change form, which initiates the formation of a team to attack the issue.[9] At Wainwright Industries, employees fill out a short form describing their idea (which may be as simple as repairing a frayed extension cord before an accident occurs), and obtain a supervisor's approval. The employee's name is entered in a weekly drawing (a safety idea counts as three entries, and all members of a team idea receive an entry); the winner receives a gift certificate for whatever they want. The process is run entirely by employees without management involvement; they even set the program's annual budget.

Kaizen Blitz

Many organizations apply kaizen thinking within a compressed time frame to solve an urgent problem. A **kaizen blitz** is an intense and rapid improvement process in which a team or a department throws all its resources into an improvement project over a short time period, as opposed to traditional kaizen applications, which are performed on a part-time basis. Blitz teams are generally comprised of employees from all areas involved in the process who understand it and can implement changes on the spot. Improvement is immediate, exciting, and satisfying for all those involved in the process. Some examples of using kaizen blitz at Magnivision include the following:[10]

- The molded lens department ran two shifts per day, using 13 employees, and after 40 percent rework, yielded 1,300 pieces per day. The production line was unbalanced and work piled up between stations, which added to quality problems as the work-in-process was often damaged. After a three-day blitz, the team reduced the production to one shift of six employees and a balanced line, reducing rework to 10 percent and increasing yield to 3,500 per day, saving more than $179,000.
- In Retail Services, a blitz team investigated problems that continually plagued employees, and discovered that many were related to the software system. Some of the same customer information had to be entered in multiple screens, sometimes the system took a long time to process information, and sometimes it was difficult to find specific information quickly. Neither the programmers nor the engineers were aware of these problems. By getting everyone together, some solutions were easily determined. Estimated savings were $125,000.

IMPROVEMENT PROCESSES

Managers need systematic approaches to drive continuous improvement programs. Some organizations follow some standard and popular approaches, while others develop unique approaches to meet their own needs and cultures. These approaches are routinely taught in employee training programs and form the basis for disciplined problem-solving efforts. For example, Eastman Chemical uses seven steps for accelerated continuous improvement.

1. *Focus and pinpoint.* "Focus" is about getting everyone on the same page with regard to goals; "pinpoint" is about specifying in measurable terms what is expected.
2. *Communicate.* Communication is done company-wide by publicizing key result areas, the vision, and the mission statement so that employees can answer the questions: What is being improved? Why is it important to the customer, to the company, and to me? What has the management team committed to do to help? And what, specifically, is the company asking me to do?
3. *Translate and link.* Teams translate the company-wide objectives into their own language and environment.
4. *Create a management action plan.* Management creates a plan with specific actions to reach a goal, including metrics to measure success. Each team member is asked to know what tasks need to be done, why they are important, and what the team's role is in getting them done.
5. *Improve processes.* Teams use a six-step problem-solving process.

6. *Measure progress and provide feedback.* Eastman is adamant about the importance of unambiguous, visual feedback to employees and appropriate measures of performance. Eastman's rules include:
   - Feedback should be visual, frequent, simple, and specific.
   - The baseline performance should be shown for comparison.
   - The past, current period, and future goals should be posted.
   - The best-ever score should be posted.
   - A chart should be immediately understandable.
   - A good scorecard allows comments and annotations.
7. *Reinforce behaviors and celebrate results.* Eastman reinforces that learning leads to positive results by encouraging teams at celebrations to answer the questions: What did you do? Why did it work? Why is it important for the customer, the company, and the team? How did the team accomplish its achievement?

Much of Eastman's approach deals with organizational and cultural issues. However, the real work is done in Step 5. Eastman points out that its formula cannot be blindly followed by others but must be adapted to the specific corporate culture. Nevertheless, the human principles are universal.

A structured improvement approach, which describes a logical, data-driven process for solving problems, generally includes four key steps:

1. redefining and analyzing the perceived problem,
2. generating ideas,
3. evaluating ideas and selecting a workable solution, and
4. implementing the solution.

In redefining and analyzing a problem, information is collected and organized, the data and underlying assumptions are analyzed, and the problem is reexamined from new perspectives. At this stage, the goal of the problem solver is to collect facts and achieve a useful problem definition. The purpose of generating ideas is to develop novel solutions. After ideas have been generated, they are evaluated and the best one is identified and selected. Finally, the solution must be put to work, for example, by making changes to processes or procedures. We discuss some of the more popular approaches.

THE DEMING CYCLE

One of the earliest approaches focused on quality improvement that can be learned and applied by everyone in an organization is the Deming Cycle. This methodology was originally called the "Shewhart Cycle" after Walter Shewhart, its founder, but was renamed for Deming by the Japanese in 1950. The **Deming Cycle** is based on the premise that improvement comes from the application of knowledge.[11] Knowledge of engineering, management, or operations may make a process easier, more accurate, faster, less costly, safer, or better suited to customer needs. Three fundamental questions to consider are

1. What are we trying to accomplish?
2. What changes can we make that will result in improvement?
3. How will we know that a change is an improvement?

The Deming Cycle is composed of four stages: Plan, Do, Study, Act (Figure 4.3). Sometimes it is called the PDSA cycle. The Plan stage consists of studying the current situation, gathering data, and planning for improvement. In the Do stage, the plan is implemented on a trial basis in a laboratory, pilot production process, or with a small group of customers. The Study stage is designed to determine whether the trial plan is working correctly and to see whether any further problems or opportunities can be found. The last stage, Act, is the implementation of the final plan to ensure that the improvements will be standardized and practiced

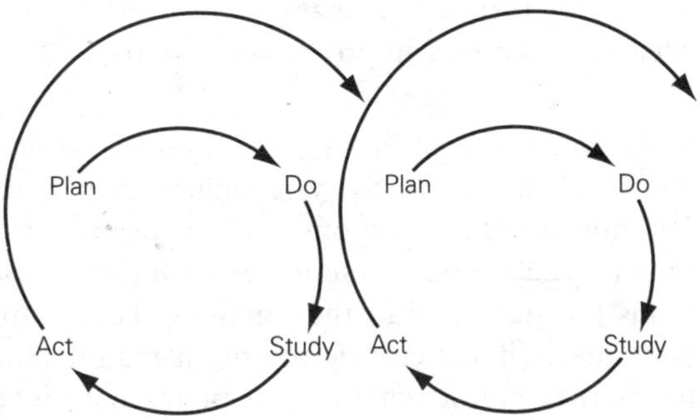

FIGURE 4.3 | THE DEMING CYCLE

CRYING OUT FOR THE DEMING CYCLE[12]

Kevin Dooley and his wife applied the Deming Cycle and various quality tools to help stop their infant daughter from crying whenever her diaper was changed, which, as any new parent or older sibling knows, can break your heart or drive you crazy.

Their first cycle involved creating an experiment to determine the percentage of time crying while on the diaper changing table (Plan); collecting data on 15 diaper changes and plotting them on a run chart (Do); observing that the data appeared to be random (Study); and focusing on the steps involved in the changing process (Act). The second cycle involved developing a flowchart to document the steps in changing a diaper (Plan); constructing the chart (Do); studying the process (which did not appear complex or incorrect—Study); and deciding to seek other causes (Act).

Cycles 3, 4, and 5 involved developing a cause-and-effect diagram, collecting data to test the hypothesis that the type of outfit worn caused her to cry more (studied with a Pareto diagram), and looking for correlations between the time crying and the time since last changing. In cycle 6, the Dooleys collected data to determine whether she cried less when being changed by her mother. Histograms confirmed a difference between the parents! Cycle 7 was to observe what Kevin's wife did differently (Plan); make a list of key differences (Do); study the differences—his wife had captured the baby's attention better—and develop some attention-getting strategies (Act).

The last cycle implemented these, and data indeed confirmed an improvement! We're sure the Dooleys can't wait to apply the Deming Cycle when it's time to teach their daughter to drive....

continuously. This leads back to the Plan stage for further diagnosis and improvement (see box "Crying Out for the Deming Cycle").

As Figure 4.3 suggests, this cycle is never ending. That is, it is focused on continuous improvement, so the improved standards serve as a springboard for further improvements. This distinguishes it from more traditional problem-solving approaches and is one of the essential elements of the Deming philosophy.

Six Sigma DMAIC Methodology

Six Sigma uses a systematic improvement approach known as DMAIC—Define, Measure, Analyze, Improve, and Control.

1. Define After a Six Sigma project is selected, the first step is to clearly define the problem. This activity is significantly different from project selection. Project selection generally responds to symptoms of a problem and usually results in a rather vague problem statement. One must describe the problem in operational terms that facilitate further analysis. For example, a firm might have a history of poor reliability of electric motors it manufactures, resulting in a Six Sigma project to improve motor reliability. A preliminary investigation of warranty and field service repair data might suggest that the source of most problems was brush wear, and more specifically, suggest a problem with brush hardness variability. Thus, the problem might be defined as "reduce the variability of brush hardness." This process of drilling down to a more specific problem statement is sometimes called **project scoping**.

A good problem statement also should identify customers and the CTQs—critical to quality characteristics—that have the most impact on product or service performance, describe the current level of performance or the nature of errors or customer complaints, identify the relevant performance metrics, benchmark best performance standards, calculate the cost/ revenue implications of the project, and quantify the expected level of performance from a successful Six Sigma effort. The Define phase should also address such project management issues as what will need to be done, by whom, and when.

2. Measure This phase of the DMAIC process focuses on how to measure the internal processes that impact CTQs. It requires an understanding of the causal relationships between process performance and customer value. However, once they are understood, procedures for gathering facts—collecting good data, observation, and careful listening—must be defined and implemented. Data from existing production processes and practices often provide important information, as does feedback from supervisors, workers, customers, and field service employees.

3. Analyze A major flaw in many problem-solving approaches is a lack of emphasis on rigorous analysis. Too often, we want to jump to a solution without fully understanding the nature of the problem and identifying the source of the problem. The Analyze phase of DMAIC focuses on *why* defects, errors, or excessive variation occur.

After potential variables are identified, experiments are conducted to verify them. These experiments generally consist of formulating some hypothesis to investigate, collecting data, analyzing the data, and reaching a reasonable and statistically supportable conclusion. Statistical thinking and analysis plays a critical role in this phase. It is one of the reasons why statistics is an important part of Six Sigma training (and one that engineering and many business curricula often ignore). Other experiments might employ computer simulation techniques.

4. Improve Once the root cause of a problem is understood, the analyst or team needs to generate ideas for removing or resolving the problem and improve the performance measures and CTQs. This idea-gathering phase is a highly creative activity, because many solutions are not obvious. One of the difficulties in this task is the natural instinct to prejudge ideas before thoroughly evaluating them. Most people have a natural fear of proposing a "silly" idea or looking foolish. However, such ideas may actually form the basis for a creative and useful solution. Effective problem solvers must learn to defer judgment and develop the ability to generate a large number of ideas at this stage of the process, whether practical or not. After a set of ideas have been proposed, it is necessary to evaluate them and select the most promising. This process includes confirming that the proposed solution will positively impact the key process variables and the CTQs, and identifying the maximum acceptable ranges of these variables.

Problem solutions often entail technical or organizational changes. Often some sort of decision or scoring model is used to assess possible solutions against important criteria such as cost, time, quality improvement potential, resources required, effects on supervisors and workers, and barriers to implementation such as resistance to change or organizational culture. To implement a solution effectively, responsibility must be assigned to a person or a group who will follow through on what must be done, where it will be done, when it will be done, and how it will be done.

5. Control The Control phase focuses on how to maintain the improvements, which includes putting tools in place to ensure that the key variables remain within the maximum acceptable ranges under the modified process. These improvements might include establishing the new standards and procedures, training the workforce, and instituting controls to make sure that improvements do not die over time. Controls might be as simple as using checklists or periodic status reviews to ensure that proper procedures are followed, or employing statistical process control charts to monitor the performance of key measures. These topics are discussed in Chapter 7.

The box "Using DMAIC at American Express" shows an example of the DMAIC process.

TOOLS FOR CONTINUOUS IMPROVEMENT

No matter which improvement approach is followed, many tools have been created or adapted from other disciplines (such as operations research and industrial engineering) to facilitate the process. In this section, we describe the most common ones used in quality improvement applications.

USING DMAIC AT AMERICAN EXPRESS[13]

American Express used Six Sigma to improve the number of customers who received renewal cards. (In this example, data have been masked to protect confidentiality.) A brief description of how DMAIC was applied follows.

Define and Measure: On average in 1999, American Express received 1,000 returned renewal cards each month. Of these renewals, 65 percent were due to the fact that the card members changed their addresses and did not tell the company. The U.S. Post Office calls these forwardable addresses. American Express does not currently notify a card member when they receive a returned plastic card.

Analyze: Analysis of the data noted significant differences in the causes of returned plastics between product types. Optima, the revolving card product, had the highest incidence of defects, but was not significantly different from other card types in the percentage of defects. Renewals had by far the highest defect rate among the three areas of replacement, renewal, and new accounts. After additional testing, returns with forwardable addresses were overwhelmingly the largest percentage and quantity of returns.

Improve: An experimental pilot study was run on all renewal files issued, comparing records against the National Change of Address database. As a result, they were able to reduce the dpmo (defects per million opportunities) rate by 44.5 percent, from 13,500 to 6,036 defects per million opportunities. This action enabled over 1,200 card members who would not have automatically received their credit cards to receive them, increasing revenue and customer satisfaction.

Control: American Express began tracking the proportion of returns over time as a means of monitoring the new process to ensure that it remains in control.

THE SEVEN QC TOOLS

Seven simple statistically based tools are used extensively to gather and analyze data. Like the seven management and planning tools, these tools—flowcharts, check sheets, histograms, Pareto diagrams, cause-and-effect diagrams, scatter diagrams, and control charts—are visual in nature and simple enough for anyone to understand. Historically, these tools preceded the seven management and planning tools and often are called the "seven QC (quality control) tools," which is a bit of a misnomer as they deal primarily with improvement. The seven management and planning tools (discussed in the next chapter) have been referred to as the "new seven."

Flowcharts A flowchart (or **process map**) is a picture of a process that shows the sequence of steps performed. Figure 4.4 is an example. Flowcharts are best developed by the people involved in the process—employees, supervisors, managers, and customers. A facilitator often is used to provide objectivity, to ask the right questions, and to resolve conflicts. The facilitator can guide the discussion through questions such as "What happens next?," "Who makes the decision at this point?," and "What operation is performed here?" Often the group does not agree on the answers to these questions, due to misconceptions about the process or a lack of awareness of the "big picture."

Flowcharts help the people involved in the process to understand it better. For example, employees realize how they fit into a process—that is, who their suppliers

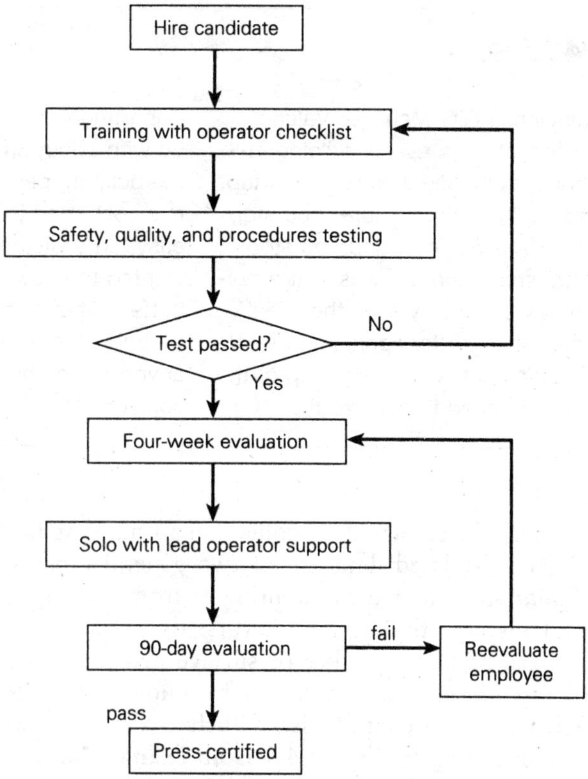

FIGURE 4.4 | EXAMPLE OF A FLOWCHART FOR TRAINING NEW PRINTING PRESS OPERATORS

and customers are. By helping to develop a flowchart, workers begin to feel a sense of ownership in the process and become more willing to work on improving it. Using flowcharts to train employees on standard procedures leads to more consistent performance.

Once a flowchart is constructed, it can be used to identify quality problems as well as areas for improvement. Questions such as "How does this operation affect the customer?," "Can we improve or eliminate this operation?," or "Should we control a critical quality characteristic at this point?" help to identify such opportunities. Flowcharts help people to visualize simple but important changes that could be made in a process (see box "One Stop, 473 Steps").

Check Sheets These tools aid in data collection. When designing a process to collect data, one must first ask basic questions such as:

- What question are we trying to answer?
- What type of data will we need to answer the question?
- Where can we find the data?
- Who can provide the data?
- How can we collect the data with minimum effort and minimum chance of error?

ONE STOP, 473 STEPS

When former Cincinnati City Manager Valerie Lemmie started her job, she asked building inspectors whether the city had a "one-stop shop" for building permits. They said, "Sure. You stop here once, you stop there once, and you stop there once." What she found out was that a permit stops 473 times on its way from the initial application to the printer! After spending a week at City Hall and taking notes on every step of the process, a consultant hired to analyze the Department of Buildings and Inspections ended up with about 30 feet of flowcharts that depicted the building permit process. Although Ms. Lemmie conceded that improvement wouldn't be easy, an assistant noted that a lot of people wanted to know how they could do their jobs better. "They know everything that's wrong with it probably more than anyone else. And more than anyone else, they need to be part of the solution."[14]

Check sheets are data collection forms that facilitate the interpretation of data. Quality-related data are of two general types—attribute and variable. *Attribute data* are obtained by counting or from some type of visual inspection: the number of invoices that contain errors, the number of parts that conform to specifications, and the number of surface defects on an automobile panel, for example. *Variable data* are collected by numerical measurement on a continuous scale. Dimensional characteristics such as distance, weight, volume, and time are common examples. Figure 4.5 is an example of a check sheet for discrete data (that is, obtained by counting), and Figure 4.6 shows a check sheet for continuous measurements.

Histograms Variation in a process always exists and generally displays a pattern that can be captured in a histogram. A histogram is a graphical representation of the variation in a set of data. It shows the frequency or number of observations of a particular value or within a specified group.

Histograms provide clues about the characteristics of the population from which a sample is taken. Using a histogram, the shape of the distribution can be

Type	Week 1	Week 2	Week 3	Week 4
Lost baggage	𝍷		𝍷𝍷	𝍷
Baggage delay	𝍸 𝍷	𝍷𝍷𝍷𝍷	𝍸 𝍷𝍷𝍷	𝍸
Missed connection	𝍷𝍷	𝍷	𝍷𝍷𝍷	𝍷
Poor cabin service	𝍷𝍷𝍷	𝍸	𝍷𝍷𝍷	𝍷𝍷𝍷
Ticketing error	𝍷			𝍷

FIGURE 4.5 EXAMPLE OF A CHECK SHEET FOR DISCRETE DATA: AIRLINE COMPLAINTS

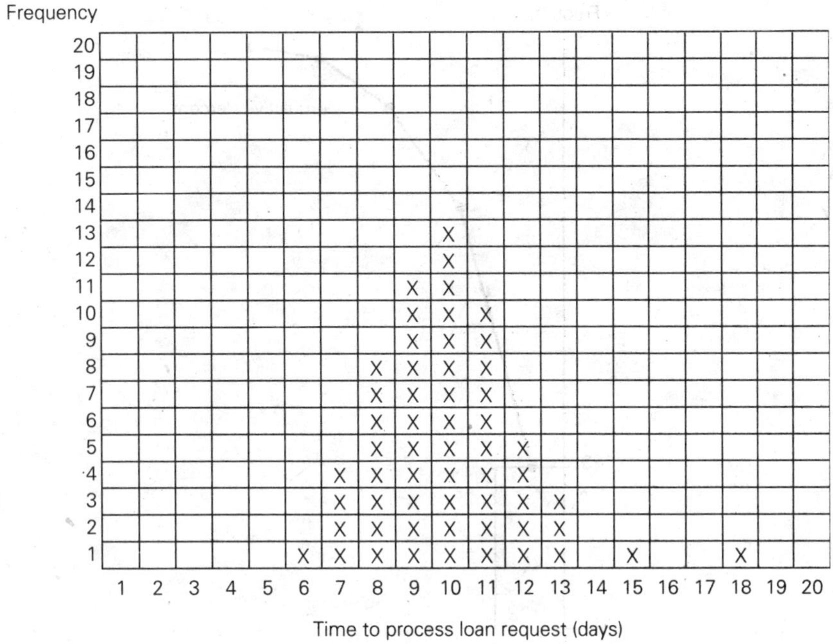

FIGURE 4.6 | EXAMPLE OF A CHECK SHEET FOR CONTINUOUS DATA

seen clearly, and inferences can be made about the population. Patterns can be seen that would be difficult to see in an ordinary table of numbers. The check sheet in Figure 4.6 was designed to provide the visual appeal of a histogram as the data are tallied. It is easy to see how the output of the process varies and what proportion of output falls outside of any specification limits.

Pareto Diagrams Pareto analysis is a technique for prioritizing types or sources of problems. Pareto analysis separates the "vital few" from the "trivial many" and provides help in selecting directions for improvement. It is often used to analyze the attribute data collected in check sheets. In a Pareto distribution, the characteristics are ordered from largest frequency to smallest. For example, if the data in Figure 4.5 is placed in order of decreasing frequency, the result is:

1. Baggage delay
2. Poor cabin service
3. Missed connection
4. Lost baggage
5. Ticketing error

A Pareto diagram is a histogram of these data, as shown in Figure 4.7.

A cumulative frequency curve is usually drawn on the histogram, as shown. Such pictures clearly show the relative magnitude of defects and can be used to identify the most promising opportunities for improvement. They also can show the results of improvement projects over time.

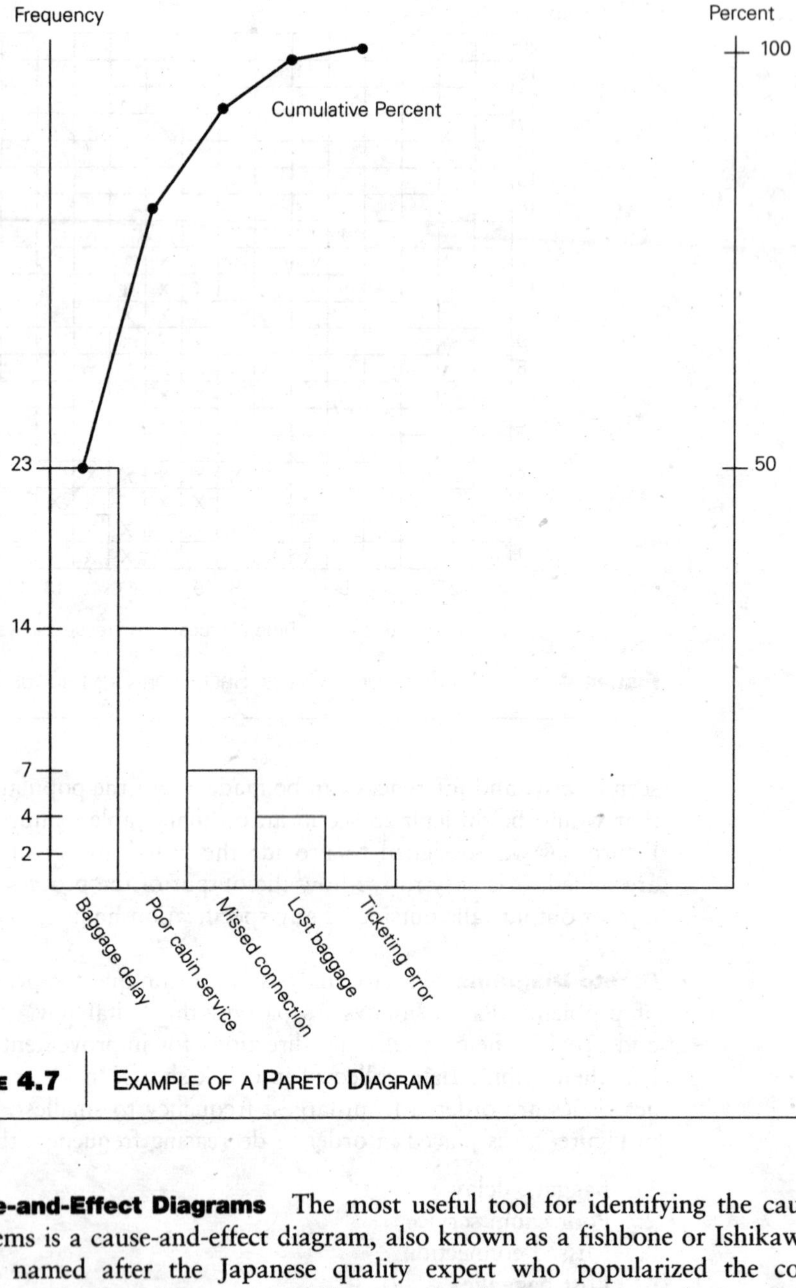

FIGURE 4.7 | EXAMPLE OF A PARETO DIAGRAM

Cause-and-Effect Diagrams The most useful tool for identifying the causes of problems is a cause-and-effect diagram, also known as a fishbone or Ishikawa diagram, named after the Japanese quality expert who popularized the concept. A cause-and-effect diagram is simply a graphical representation of an outline that presents a chain of causes and effects.

An example is shown in Figure 4.8. At the end of the horizontal line is the problem to be addressed. Each branch pointing into the main stem represents a possible cause. Branches pointing to the causes are contributors to these causes. The diagram is used to identity the most likely causes of a problem so that further data collection and analysis can be carried out.

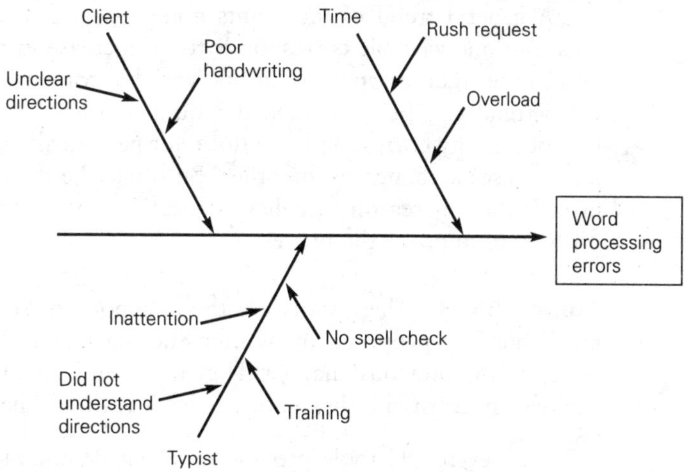

FIGURE 4.8 EXAMPLE OF A CAUSE-AND-EFFECT DIAGRAM

Cause-and-effect diagrams are usually constructed in a brainstorming setting so that everyone can contribute their ideas. Usually, small groups drawn from operations or management work with an experienced facilitator. The facilitator guides the discussion to focus attention on the problem and its causes, on facts, not opinions. This method requires significant interaction among group members. The facilitator must listen carefully to the participants and capture the important ideas.

Scatter Diagrams Scatter diagrams illustrate relationships between hypothesized causes and effects, such as the percentage of an ingredient in an alloy and the hardness of the alloy, or the number of employee errors and overtime worked (Figure 4.9). Typically, these are obtained from cause-and-effect diagrams.

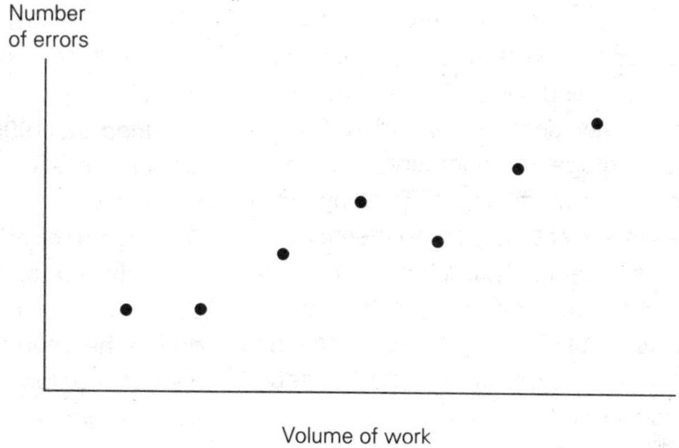

FIGURE 4.9 EXAMPLE OF A SCATTER DIAGRAM

A general trend of the points going up and to the right indicates that an increase in one variable corresponds to an increase in the other. If the trend is down and to the right, an increase in one variable corresponds to a decrease in the other. If no trend can be seen, then it would appear that the variables are not related. Of course, any correspondence does not necessarily imply that a change in one variable causes a change in the other. Both may be the result of something else. However, if there is reason to believe causation, the scatter diagram may provide clues on how to improve the process.

Control Chart These tools are the backbone of statistical process control (SPC), and were first proposed by Walter Shewhart in 1924. Control charts were introduced in the previous chapter. They are useful for identifying improvement opportunities and verifying that improvements really do have the desired effect.

The seven QC tools provide excellent communication vehicles both vertically and horizontally across organizational boundaries (see box "Shooting for Quality").

Lean Thinking

Waste is the enemy of effective processes. Reducing waste of any kind encompasses both TQ and JIT practices and is a central theme in Japanese manufacturing management. Poor processes waste time, money, material, effort, and customer goodwill. Improving processes to reduce waste involves the concept of lean thinking. Lean is often used to refer to approaches initially developed by the Toyota Motor Corporation that focus on the elimination of waste in all forms, including defects requiring rework, unnecessary processing steps, unnecessary movement of materials

Shooting for Quality[15]

Timothy Clark observed that in basketball games, his son Andrew's free-throw percentage averaged between 45 and 50 percent. Andrew's process was simple: Go to the free-throw line, bounce the ball four times, aim, and shoot. To confirm these observations, Andrew shot five sets of 10 free throws with an average of 42 percent, showing little variation among the five sets. Timothy developed a cause-and-effect diagram to identify the principal causes. After analyzing the diagram and observing his son's process, he believed that the main causes were not standing in the same place on the free-throw line every time and having an inconsistent focal point.

They developed a new process in which Andrew stood at the center of the line and focused on the middle of the front part of the rim. The new process resulted in a 36 percent improvement in practice. Toward the end of the 1994 season, he improved his average to 69 percent in the last three games.

During the 1995 season, Andrew averaged 60 percent. A control chart showed that the process was quite stable. In the summer of 1995, Andrew attended a basketball camp where he was advised to change his shooting technique. This process reduced his shooting percentage during the 1996 season to 50 percent. However, his father helped him to reinstall his old process, and his percentage returned to its former level, also improving his confidence.

or people, waiting time, excess inventory, and overproduction. A simple way of defining it is "getting more done with less."[16] It involves identifying and eliminating non–value-added activities throughout the entire value chain to achieve faster customer response, reduced inventories, higher quality, and better human resources. As one article about Toyota observed, to see the Toyota production system in action is to "behold a thing of beauty."

Lean is facilitated by a focus on measurement and continuous improvement, cross-trained workers, flexible and increasingly automated equipment, efficient machine layout, rapid setup and changeover, just-in-time delivery and scheduling, realistic work standards, worker empowerment to perform inspections and take corrective action, supplier partnerships, and preventive maintenance. Some of the benefits claimed by proponents of lean production include the following:

- At least 60 percent reduction in cycle times
- 40 percent improvement in space utilization
- 25 percent greater throughput
- 50 percent reduction in work-in-process and finished goods inventories
- 50 percent improvement in quality
- 20 percent improvements in working capital and worker productivity

However, as one industry expert observed, it takes "an incredible amount of detailed planning, discipline, hard work, and painstaking attention to detail." Surveys have noted that mid-sized and large companies are likely to be familiar with lean principles and have systems in place; however, few small manufacturing shops have much familiarity with the principles. Thus, considerable opportunity exists for this important economic sector.

Some of the general principles of lean include:[17]

1. *Reducing handoffs.* Every time a process is handed from one person or group to another, errors can occur (think of passing the baton in a relay race). Time is often wasted as one group waits for the other to finish or needs to consult with the first group before continuing.
2. *Eliminating steps.* The best way to save time on a step is not to do it at all. If the step does not add value to the product or service or make the product more attractive to customers, stop doing it. In manufacturing organizations, moving, storing, and inspecting products rarely add value and should be eliminated wherever possible.
3. *Performing steps in parallel rather than in sequence.* Unless one operation cannot be done until another is finished, why not do them both at once? Many organizations operate like two people doing the dishes, where one washes all the dishes that will fit in the drainer, then calls the other to dry them. When the drying is done, the dryer calls the washer back in and leaves again. Stupid? Yes, but that's the way they've always done it.
4. *Involving key people early.* The point of this is to avoid having to do things over as a result of key people not having given their input until the process is under way. For years, manufacturing companies have had their engineers design entire products before consulting the manufacturing engineers who built them. The manufacturing engineers would then suggest a number of changes

that the designers would reluctantly incorporate into their designs. Many firms have changed this process to allow early involvement of manufacturing.[18] This is one of the most common forms of process reengineering and is consistent with the TQ principle, "Do it right the first time!"

Lean thinking also uses a variety of tools:

- *The 5S's*. The 5S's are derived from Japanese terms: *seiri* (sort), *seiton* (set in order), *seiso* (shine), *seiketsu* (standardize), and *shitsuke* (sustain). They define a system for workplace organization and standardization. Sort refers to ensuring that each item in a workplace is in its proper place or identified as unnecessary and removed. Set in order means to arrange materials and equipment so that they are easy to find and use. Shine refers to a clean work area. Not only is this important for safety but, as a work area is cleaned, maintenance problems such as oil leaks can be identified before they cause problems. Standardize means to formalize procedures and practices to create consistency and ensure that all steps are performed correctly. Finally, sustain means to keep the process going through training, communication, and organizational structures.
- *Visual controls*. Visual controls are indicators for tools, parts, and production activities that are placed in plain sight of all workers so that everyone can understand the status of the system at a glance. Thus, if a machine goes down, or a part is defective or delayed, immediate action can be taken.
- *Efficient layout and standardized work*. The layout of equipment and processes is designed according to the best operational sequence, by physically linking and arranging machines and process steps most efficiently, often in a cellular arrangement. Standardizing the individual tasks by clearly specifying the proper method reduces wasted human movement and energy.
- *Pull production*. In this system (also described as *kanban* or *just-in-time*), upstream suppliers do not produce until the downstream customer signals a need for parts.
- *Single minute exchange of dies (SMED)*. SMED refers to rapid changeover of tooling and fixtures in machine shops so that multiple products in smaller batches can be run on the same equipment. Reducing setup time adds value to the operation and facilitates smoother production flow.
- *Total productive maintenance*. Total productive maintenance is designed to ensure that equipment is operational and available when needed.
- *Source inspection*. Inspection and control by process operators guarantees that product passed on to the next production stage conforms to specifications.

Lean thinking can easily be applied to nonmanufacturing environments. Pure service firms such as banks, hospitals, and restaurants have benefited from lean principles. For example, banks require quick response and efficiency to operate on low margins, making many of their processes, such as check sorting and mortgage approval, natural candidates for lean enterprise solutions.[19] Handling of paper checks and credit card slips, for instance, involves a physical process not unlike an assembly line. The faster a bank moves checks through its system, the sooner it can collect its funds and the better its returns on invested capital.

Six Sigma is a useful and complementary approach to lean production. For example, a cycle time reduction project might involve aspects of both. Lean tools might be applied to streamline an order entry process. This application leads to the discovery that significant rework occurs because of incorrect addresses, customer numbers, or shipping charges and results in high variation of processing time. Six Sigma tools might then be used to drill down to the root cause of the problems and identify a solution. Because of these similarities, many industry training programs and consultants have begun to focus on "Lean Six Sigma," drawing upon the best practices of both approaches. Both are driven by customer requirements, focus on real dollar savings, have the ability to make significant financial impacts on the organization, and can be used in non-manufacturing environments.

However, some differences clearly exist between lean thinking and Six Sigma. First, they attack different types of problems. Lean approaches address visible problems in processes, for example, inventory, material flow, and safety. Six Sigma is more concerned with less visible problems, for example, variation in performance. Another difference is that lean approaches are more intuitive and easier to apply by anybody in the workplace, whereas many Six Sigma tools require advanced training and expertise of Black Belt or Master Black Belt specialists, or consultant equivalents. For example, the concept of the 5S's is easier to grasp than statistical methods. Thus, organizations might be well advised to start with basic lean principles and evolve toward more sophisticated Six Sigma approaches.

BREAKTHROUGH IMPROVEMENT

Breakthrough improvement refers to discontinuous change, as opposed to the gradual, continuous improvement philosophy of kaizen. Breakthrough improvements result from innovative and creative thinking; often these are motivated by **stretch goals**, or **breakthrough objectives**. Stretch goals force an organization to think in a radically different way, and to encourage major improvements as well as incremental ones. When a goal of 10 percent improvement is set, managers or engineers can usually meet it with some minor improvements. However, when the goal is 1,000 percent improvement, employees must be creative and think "out of the box." The seemingly impossible is often achieved, yielding dramatic improvements and boosting morale.

Two approaches for breakthrough improvement that help companies achieve breakthrough improvement are benchmarking and reengineering.

BENCHMARKING

Benchmarking is the search for best practices that will lead to superior performance. Benchmarking helps a company learn its strengths and weaknesses—and those of other leading organizations—and incorporate the best practices into its own operations. The term **best practices** refers to approaches that produce exceptional results, are usually innovative in terms of the use of technology or human resources, and are recognized by customers or industry experts. Through benchmarking, a company discovers its strengths and weaknesses and those of other industrial leaders and learns how to incorporate the best practices into its own operations. Benchmarking can provide motivation by helping employees to see what

Making Pharmacies Lean[20]

Metro Health Hospital in Grand Rapids, Michigan, has successfully applied lean principles in its pharmacy services. The Metro pharmacy started with a modest goal of reducing the lead time for getting the first dose of a medication to a patient. The lead time was measured from the time an order arrived at the pharmacy to its delivery on the appropriate hospital floor. Using lean, the Metro pharmacy carefully laid out all the process steps involved in getting the first dose of the correct medication to the right patient. The pharmacy found that it had a 14-stage process with some unnecessary steps, resulting in a total lead time of 166 minutes. During the evaluation process, the pharmacy calculated that it took technicians an average of 1.5 minutes to locate a product. For a pharmacy operating around the clock and delivering more than 100,000 doses a month, time wasted in searching was costly to the organization. In fact, technicians were spending 77.4 percent of their time locating products; when a pharmacist needed a technician for clinical activities, the technician was usually off searching for a drug.

The lean teams outlined several non-value-added steps in the process, only one of which was out of the pharmacy's control (i.e., the time it took to transport the ordered medication, once filled, to the appropriate floor). Standardization was a key component of the redesign, especially with the process flow as it moved through the department. As a part of the standardization process, the pharmacy implemented two new counters: a "check" counter and a "to-go" counter. They put in a simple color system in which red indicated the check counter and green indicated the to-go counter. They decreased the number of distractions by implementing a "safe zone," where a pharmacist could check medications without being disturbed. Product no longer sits on the counter without a pharmacist knowing it's there, nor are there redundant steps between the delivery baskets and delivery carts. After the checkpoint, the medication automatically goes in the "to-go" area delivery bin. Overall, the pharmacy at Metro realized a 33 percent reduction in time to get medications to patients and reduced the number of process steps from 14 to 9 simply by removing non–value-added steps. Patients have experienced a 40 percent reduction in pharmacy-related medication errors, and the severity of those errors has decreased.

others can accomplish. For example, to meet a stretch target of reducing the time to build new 747 and 767 airplanes at Boeing from 18 months (in 1992) to 8 months, teams studied the world's best producers of everything from computers to ships. By 1996, the time had been reduced to 10 months.[21]

Modern benchmarking was initiated by Xerox, an eventual winner of the Malcolm Baldrige National Quality Award. Xerox initially studied its direct competitors and discovered that:

- its unit manufacturing cost equaled the Japanese selling price in the United States,
- the number of production suppliers was nine times that of the best companies,
- assembly-line rejects were ten times higher,
- product lead times were twice as long, and
- defects per hundred machines were seven times higher.

These results helped Xerox to understand the amount of change that would be required and to set realistic targets to guide its planning efforts.

Two major types of benchmarking are competitive and generic. *Competitive benchmarking* usually focuses on the products and manufacturing of a company's competitors, as Xerox initially did. *Generic benchmarking* evaluates processes or business functions against the best companies, regardless of their industry. Xerox recognized the potential for improving all business processes and realized that better practices in service companies and other types of manufacturing firms could be adapted to its operations. For example, the warehousing and distribution practices of L.L. Bean were adopted by Xerox. Thus, benchmarking should not be aimed solely at direct competitors (see box "Smart Bombs and Pink Cadillacs").

In order to be effective, benchmarking must be applied to all facets of a business. For example, Motorola encourages everyone in the organization to ask "Who is the best person in my own field and how might I use some of their techniques and characteristics to improve my own performance in order to be the best (executive, machine operator, chef, purchasing agent, and so on) in my 'class'"?

The benchmarking process can be described as follows:

1. *Determine which functions to benchmark.* These should have a significant impact on business performance and key dimensions of competitiveness. If fast response is an important dimension of competitive advantage, then processes that might be benchmarked would include order processing, purchasing, production planning, and product distribution. There also should be an indication that the potential for improvement exists.
2. *Identify key performance indicators to measure.* These should have a direct link to customer needs and expectations. Typical performance indicators are quality, performance, and delivery.
3. *Identify the best-in-class companies.* For specific business functions, benchmarking might be limited to the same industry: a bank in one state might

SMART BOMBS AND PINK CADILLACS

Although Xerox is credited with developing modern approaches to benchmarking, the concept of benchmarking is not new.[22] In the early 1800s, Francis Lowell, a New England industrialist, traveled to England to study manufacturing techniques of the best British mill factories. Henry Ford created the assembly line after taking a tour of a Chicago slaughterhouse and watching carcasses, hung on hooks mounted on a monorail, move from one work station to another. Toyota's just-in-time production system was influenced by replenishment practices of U.S. supermarkets.

Convex Computer Corporation sent its facilities manager to Disney World to see what they could learn about facilities management. And Texas Instrument's former Defense Systems and Electronics Group, makers of "smart bombs" and other advanced weapon systems, studied the kitting (order preparation) practices of six companies, including Mary Kay Cosmetics (a pink Cadillac being a reward to their top salespeople), and designed a process that captured the best practices of each of them, cutting kitting cycle time in half.

benchmark the check-processing operations of a bank in another state. For generic business functions, it is best to look outside one's own industry: a university financial aid office might benchmark a bank's loan operation, for example. Selecting companies requires knowledge of which firms are superior performers in the key areas. Such information can be obtained from published reports and articles, industry experts, trade magazines, professional associations, former employees, or customers and suppliers.

4. *Measure the performance of the best-in-class companies and compare the results to your own performance.* Such information might be found in published sources or might require site visits and in-depth interviews.
5. *Define and take actions to meet or exceed the best performance.* This usually requires changing organizational systems. Simply trying to emulate the best is like shooting at a moving target—their processes will continually improve. Therefore, attempts should be made to exceed the performance of the best.

Briefly, benchmarking is the search for best practices in any company, in any industry, anywhere in the world, and reengineering is the radical redesign of business processes to achieve significant improvements in performance. As an example of benchmarking, when Graniterock could not find any company that was measuring on-time delivery of concrete, it talked with Domino's Pizza, a worldwide leader in on-time delivery of a rapidly perishable product (a characteristic shared with freshly mixed concrete) to acquire new ideas for measuring and improving its processes. By observing how a NASCAR pit crew worked, General Mills was able to cut the time it took workers to change a production line from one Betty Crocker product to another from 4.5 hours to 12 minutes. It also looked at how Stealth bomber pilots and maintenance crews cooperated and improved its own teamwork, cutting production costs by 25 percent at one plant.[23]

To illustrate the concept of reengineering, Intel Corporation previously used a 91-step process costing thousands of dollars to purchase ballpoint pens—the same process used to purchase forklift trucks! The improved process was reduced to eight steps. In rethinking its purpose as a customer-driven, retail service company rather than a manufacturing company, Taco Bell eliminated the kitchen from its restaurants. Meat and beans are cooked outside the restaurant at central commissaries and reheated. Other food items such as diced tomatoes, onions, and olives are prepared off-site. This innovation saved about 11 million hours of work and $7 million per year over the entire chain.[24]

REENGINEERING

Reengineering (also known as process redesign) is focused on "breakthrough" improvement to dramatically improve the quality and speed of work and to reduce its cost by fundamentally changing the processes by which work gets done (see box "Reengineering for Cycle Time Reduction at Procter & Gamble").

Reengineering involves asking basic questions about business processes: "Why do we do it?" and "Why is it done this way?" Such questioning often uncovers obsolete, erroneous, or inappropriate assumptions. Reengineering is often used when the improvements needed are so great that incremental changes to operations will

Reengineering for Cycle Time Reduction at Procter & Gamble

One example of a reengineering effort to reduce cycle time was carried out by Procter & Gamble's over-the-counter (OTC) clinical division, which conducts clinical studies that involve testing drugs, health care products, or treatments in humans.[25] Such testing follows rigorous design, conduct, analysis, and summary of the data collected. P&G had at least four different ways to perform a clinical study and needed to find the best way to meet its research and development needs. They chose to focus on cycle time reduction. Their approach built on fundamental TQ principles: focusing on the customer, fact-based decisions, continual improvement, empowerment, the right leadership structure, and an understanding of work processes. The team found that final reports took months to prepare. Only by mapping the existing process did they fully understand the causes of long production times and the amount of rework and recycling during review and signoff. By restructuring the activities from sequential to parallel work and identifying critical measurements to monitor the process, they were able to reduce the time to less than four weeks.

not get the job done. Ten percent improvements can be created by tinkering, but 50 percent improvements call for process redesign. The goal is to achieve quantum leaps in performance. For example, IBM Credit Corporation cut the process of financing IBM computers, software, and services from seven days to four hours by rethinking the process. Originally, the process was designed to handle difficult applications and required four highly trained specialists and a series of handoffs. The actual work took only about 1.5 hours; the rest of the time was spent in transit or delay. By questioning the assumption that every application was unique and difficult to process, IBM Credit Corporation was able to replace the specialists by a single individual supported by a user-friendly computer system that provided access to all the data and tools that the specialists would use.

The irony of reengineering is that, once the new process is in place, people often feel that the new way of operating is so much better, they should have thought of it long ago. Another common reaction is "Why did we ever do it like that in the first place?" The answer is often, "That's the way we've always done it." GE Chairman Jack Welch has compared his company to a 100-year-old attic, which has collected a lot of useless junk over the years.

Process redesign (called *Work-Out* in GE jargon) is the process of cleaning all the junk out of the attic.[26] Often the old ways of doing things were a function of administrative, rather than customer-centered, thinking. In one plant, a product was boxed and wrapped to be sent from one side of the plant to the other, only to be unwrapped and unboxed. Why? Because the two parts of the plant were separate profit centers, and the first had to "sell" the product to the second!

If a process is driven by an administrative logic such as cost accounting or functional specialization, it is ripe for reengineering.[27] The importance of process redesign to quality improvement can be seen in Figure 4.10, based on the work of Professor Asbjorn Aune of Norway.[28] Process is what connects customer expectations to the products or services they receive. It is what ensures (or fails to ensure) that products meet or exceed customer expectations.

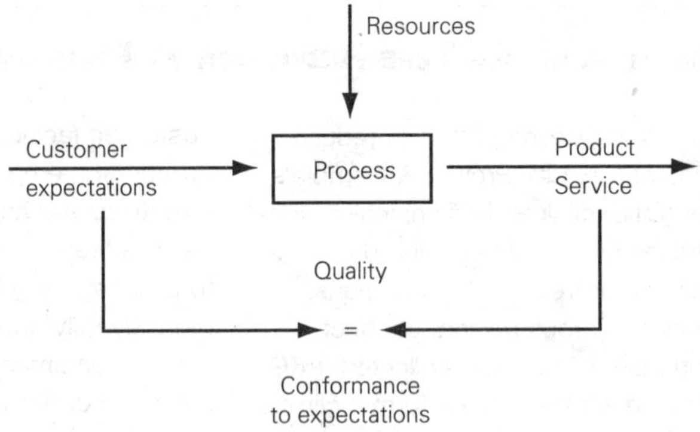

FIGURE 4.10 THE KEY ROLE OF PROCESS

ORGANIZATIONAL ISSUES IN PROCESS IMPROVEMENT[29]

Process improvement is a difficult activity to perform in many organizations, yet it represents one of the most common types of organizational change. Success rates, however, are far from satisfactory. The organizational literature addresses the factors that facilitate or inhibit successful implementation. For example, one research study identified two factors critical to the long-term success of reengineering initiatives:

1. *Breadth*: the extent to which the process maps onto the dimensions of the business, from a single activity in one function to spanning the entire business unit; and
2. *Depth*: how many of the "depth levers"—structure, skills, IT systems, roles, measurements/incentives, and shared values—are manipulated.

Others have investigated resistance to change, top management support, diversity of human resources involved, methodological rigor, and the pay-offs associated with these efforts. Interestingly, some data suggest that success is more likely when sponsorship is strong; when mid-level managers, rather than top executives, sponsor the projects; and when fact-based measurements drive the efforts (failed projects were often described qualitatively). In Chapter 11, we shall discuss organizational change further.

CREATIVITY AND INNOVATION

Creativity is the ability to discover useful new relationships or ideas; *innovation* refers to the practical implementation of such ideas. Research studies have suggested that the achievement of business excellence requires a change-oriented environment where creativity of employees is nurtured, developed, and sustained.[30] Creativity and innovation are fundamental to improving both products and processes and need to be understood, developed, and supported within any organization.

From the perspective of total quality, creativity and innovation are needed to better respond to customer needs, particularly the "exciters/delighters" that customers cannot articulate, and to develop the products and services that will position an organization strategically ahead of its competitors. They also are needed to support continuous improvement efforts, for example the poka-yoke devices and methods discussed in the previous chapter. Finally, an environment that fosters creativity and innovation can motivate employees more than any extrinsic reward—"joy in work" as Deming used to say (see box "Creativity in the Heartland").

In Japanese, the word *creativity* has a literal translation as *dangerous opportunity*. In the Toyota production system, which has become the benchmark for world-class efficiency, a key concept is *soikufu*—creative thinking or inventive ideas, which means capitalizing on worker suggestions. The chairman of Toyota once observed: "One of the features of Japanese workers is that they use their

CREATIVITY IN THE HEARTLAND

In 1994, three companies received the Malcolm Baldrige National Quality Award: AT&T Consumer Communications Services (CCS), GTE Directories Corporation, and Wainwright Industries. AT&T CCS (the long-distance provider) and GTE Directories (which publishes and sells advertising for telephone directories and was since acquired by Verizon) are large, innovative firms with sophisticated technologies and human resource development activities that support empowered teams and foster an atmosphere of creativity throughout their organizations. Both companies also offer a wide variety of training and education courses, including courses devoted specifically to creativity and innovation. It is not surprising that they have achieved remarkable results in product and service quality, customer satisfaction, and in various operational and financial measures.

Wainwright Industries, headquartered in rural St. Peters, Missouri, is considerably different from CCS and GTE. Wainwright is a small, family-owned business that manufactures stamped and machined parts for the automotive and other industries. Since initiating continuous improvement processes in 1991, Wainwright has seen continual, and sometimes dramatic, improvements in customer satisfaction, defect and scrap rates, work-related accidents, manufacturing cycle times, and quality costs. At the same time, market share, productivity gains, and profit margins have all increased.

Innovation is a way of life at Wainwright. Each associate averages more than one implemented improvement per week! That's over 50 each year, in an industry that averages at most one suggestion per employee per year in the United States. Wainwright does not have the comparable resources available to large corporations like AT&T or GTE. The company spends a relatively high proportion of its budget on training, some of which is outsourced, yet no formal creativity training is offered. What the company does have is a culture that exudes a spirit of creativity and innovation. The plant has a folksy, Midwestern atmosphere.

Everyone—up to the chairman of the board—wears a company uniform with his or her first name stitched on it. The human resources function is called "The People Zone." The training director is known simply as "The Training Guy." And a stuffed duck is the company's mascot and symbol of quality leadership.

Wainwright is an excellent example of how creativity, integrated within a traditional American company, can lead to exceptional improvements in quality and business performance. More important, when visitors tour the plant, they see clearly the spirit and enthusiasm exuded by Wainwright associates. The associates are having fun! Improving quality—and work itself—should be fun, and people have fun when they are creative.

brains as well as their hands. Our workers provide 1.5 million suggestions a year, and 95 percent of them are put to practical use. There is an almost tangible concern for improvement in the air at Toyota."[31]

Creativity is often motivated by an individual's or group's need to invent solutions from limited resources. The Japanese have shown remarkable creativity in developing solutions to manufacturing quality problems. This is no wonder, given the limited natural resources in Japan and the Japanese culture focused on eliminating waste and conserving every precious resource available. The largest source of creativity in any organization are the frontline employees. They gather a wealth of data and information about their work every day. To tap into their knowledge, companies must make creativity a key part of their culture and think of improvement as everybody's job. This requires companies to empower their employees to allow them to put their ideas to work. We will address this further in Chapter 9.

Innovation and creativity are important aspects of the Malcolm Baldrige National Quality Award Criteria for Performance Excellence. Mechanisms used to encourage innovation and creativity include:

1. The nonprescriptive nature of the criteria, which encourages innovative approaches and breakthrough thinking toward meeting the purpose of the specific items in the criteria. This channels activities toward purpose, not toward following procedures.
2. Customer-driven quality, which places major emphasis on the positive side of quality, and stresses enhancement, new services, and customer relationship management. Enhancing the positive side of quality relies heavily on creativity, usually more so than steps to reduce errors and defects, which tend to rely more on well-defined techniques.
3. Continuous improvement and cycles of learning, which are stressed as integral parts of the activities of all work units. This encourages analysis and problem solving everywhere within the company.
4. Strong emphasis on cycle time reduction in all company operations, which encourages companies to analyze work processes, work organizations, and the value-added contributions of all process steps. This fosters change, innovation, and creative thinking in how work is organized and conducted.
5. Focus on future requirements of customers, which encourages companies to seek innovative and creative ways to serve needs.

Many examples of creativity and innovation are seen in firms that have received the Baldrige Award. Among the many examples are:

- The benchmarking process, pioneered by Xerox.
- The "run the business-change the business" paradigm of classifying organizational measurements, first introduced by Clarke-American Checks, and later adopted by many other Baldrige users.
- Wainwright Industries' practice of reenacting and videotaping workplace accidents for study and prevention.

Research has shown that people can be taught and learn to be more creative. Organizations need to understand how creative thinking tools can help to improve organizational performance and quality.

CREATIVITY AND ORGANIZATIONAL SYSTEMS

Warren Bennis, a recognized expert on leadership, noted: "There are two ways of being creative. One can sing and dance. Or one can create an environment in which singers and dancers flourish." While the tools discussed in this chapter all help to promote creative thinking, they cannot be applied effectively in a noncreative environment. Because management designs the organizational systems, management is responsible for developing a climate conducive to creativity and innovation. The organizational literature contains many different recommendations for fostering creativity. Some of these are[32]

- *Remove or reduce obstacles to creativity within an organization.* These obstacles include the various environmental blocks such as autocratic bosses, distractions (constant meetings or phone calls), and lack of management support. In addition, creative people should be relieved of routine duties and administrative chores.
- *Match jobs to individuals' creative abilities.* Some people work best alone; others work better in groups. Some work well in 9-to-5 time frames; others require flex time. Managers need to be tolerant of individual idiosyncrasies, nonconformity of dress codes, frequent coffee breaks, and so on.
- *Tolerate failures and establish direction.* Creative people need an atmosphere that allows radical ideas without being harshly judged. Seemingly silly ideas often turn into the best products. However, appropriate direction must be given, and realistic goals and objectives must be set to maintain a sense of urgency. (See box "Learning from Failure" for some examples).
- *Improve motivation to increase productivity and solve problems creatively.* Creative accomplishments should be recognized publicly, to peers, superiors, and upper management. Such recognition increases both self-esteem and motivation.
- *Enhance the self-esteem and build the confidence of organization members.* Creative individuals are at their best when their minds are challenged—not their security or ego. Job security, adequate wages, and job satisfaction enhance an individual's self-confidence and security.
- *Improve communication so that ideas can be better shared.* This is certainly true within an organization. Creative individuals also have the need to communicate with peers outside the organization; such activities should be encouraged. Creative people need a sounding board for their ideas and continuous feedback from their efforts.
- *Place highly creative people in special jobs and provide training to take advantage of their creativity.* Establish career paths and financial rewards so as not to disadvantage creative people who are not part of the line organization.

If you examine carefully the underlying principles of Deming's 14 Points, you see many similarities with attitudes and organizational structures that support creativity. This is particularly true in the elimination of fear, the removal of barriers that inhibit joy in work, elimination of numbers driven and short-term goal-driven management, a focus on continuous improvement, leadership, and continual training and education. Fear, in particular, is a creativity killer. The head of a corporate legal office commented that "when someone tries to use fear to motivate

Learning from Failure[33]

Ever heard of Choglit? How about OK Soda or Surge? Long after "New Coke" became nearly synonymous with innovation failure, these products joined Coca-Cola Co.'s graveyard of beverage busts. Given that history, failure hardly seems like a subject Coca-Cola Chairman and CEO E. Neville Isdell would want to trot out in front of investors. But Isdell did just that, deliberately airing the topic at Coke's annual meeting in April. "You will see some failures," he told the crowd. "As we take more risks, this is something we must accept as part of the regeneration process." Isdell wants Coke to take bigger risks, and, to do that, he knows he needs to convince employees and shareholders that he will tolerate the failures that will inevitably result. Intelligent failures—those that happen early and inexpensively and that contribute new insights about customers—should be more than just tolerable. They should be encouraged.

"Getting good" at failure, however, doesn't mean creating anarchy out of organization. It means leaders who create an environment safe for taking risks and who share stories of their own mistakes. As an example, Virgin Atlantic Airways Ltd. made a $67 million investment in 2000 to create new sleeper seats, called "J2000s," that reclined at an angle for the airline's "upper-class" section. Although sleeper seats had long existed in first class, airlines had not yet adopted them for business class. Virgin was the first to announce it would be offering "a bed in business." Within a year, however, Virgin's idea was one-upped by its chief competitor, British Airways PLC (BAB), which rolled out a truly flat bed. While customers were initially enthusiastic about the J2000 seats, some complained about sliding and discomfort. In the end, it was wildly unsuccessful. But Virgin took another risk, committing $127 million to an overhaul of the airline's upper-class seats years before the traditional product life cycle would have ended. The new version, launched in 2003, has been a solid success. The new design allows flight attendants to flip over the back and seat cushions to make the bed, allowing for different foam consistencies for sitting and sleeping.

me, I get all tied up. I get less creative and less willing to take chances, and you've got to take risks to do good work." A midlevel manager observed, "Where there is a lot of fear of screwing up, people don't change behaviors or work systems. Creativity is inhibited. People work one day at a time, rather than looking to the future."[34] Generally, the cultures of most organizations do not support the conditions that lead to creative behavior. Cultural change, education, and training are necessary to develop a creative climate.

Leadership, in particular, can have a significant influence on creativity.[35] Researchers have noted that personality, cognitive style orientation, and level of intrinsic motivation are core characteristics for employee creativity. Cognitive style is the natural orientation or preferred means of problem solving. An individual with an innovative cognitive style will seek and integrate diverse information, redefine posed problems, and generate novel ideas. Those with adaptive cognitive styles will tend to use data within a well-established domain, accept problems as defined, and generate ideas consistent with accepted convention. When people enjoy creativity-related tasks, their level of creative output is high. Researchers have discovered that creativity does not appear to be enhanced for employees working with supervisors having similar cognitive styles. In particular, those with innovative cognitive styles receive little benefit from working with supervisors who also exhibit creative tendencies, probably because they already possess the skills, confidence, and values to be creative. However, it appears that when employees work with supervisors who possess a similar intrinsic motivation, creative performance is enhanced.

Researchers also have found that when employees with a low intrinsic motivation for creativity are assigned to high intrinsic motivation supervisors, they produced lower creative output, perhaps because such supervisors may unintentionally intimidate or suppress creativity of these employees.

These findings have practical implications for selecting, assigning, and training employees. Managers must consider individuals' motivation to be creative. Identifying and assigning employees with the appropriate motivational orientation for jobs involving creative tasks is likely to enhance innovation.

Placing a supervisor with a true appreciation for creative work among employees with the motivation to create is also useful. The ability and willingness of supervisors to create positive experiences conducive to creativity may provide a powerful and effective means by which organizational creativity can be enhanced. We will discuss issues of leadership and motivation further in later chapters.

PROCESS IMPROVEMENT IN ACTION

In this section we provide some examples of organizations that have used the tools and techniques described in this chapter to improve their processes.

GENERAL ELECTRIC[36]

Jack Welch, former CEO of General Electric for over 20 years, has been recognized as one of the greatest corporate leaders of the twentieth century. In his first letter to GE shareholders in 1981, he noted that "This commitment to the utmost in quality and personal excellence is our surest path to continued business success. Quality is our best assurance of customer allegiance. It is our strongest defense against foreign competition and the only path to sustained growth and earnings." Mr. Welch's approach to business improvement has gone through three cycles of learning:

1. In the first cycle (early 1980s to late 1980s), he focused GE on the elimination of variety in its portfolio of businesses by reducing the nonperforming business units as judged by market performance. The elimination of unprofitable businesses permitted a better use of working capital. However, only so much gain can result from trimming the organization or eliminating bureaucracy. This led to the next phase of learning.
2. During the late 1980s to mid-1990s, he focused the company on simplifying and eliminating non–value-added activities through creative efforts of teams using Work-Outs and the Change Action Process (later renamed the Change Acceleration Process). Work-Out is a tool for involving all people from all ranks, levels, and functions of the organization for problem solving and improvement. Work-Out demolished the artificial barriers and walls within the organization and fostered the idea of "boundaryless learning."

3. Throughout his learning journey, Welch had challenged his people to keep looking for creative ways to apply new learning from any source to improve the business. In 1995, Welch discovered Six Sigma and studied its implementation at both Motorola and Allied Signal. This phase of discovery focused on the elimination of variation from already lean business operations to drive gains in productivity and financial performance with a better focus on the customer.

Welch's process for continuous learning led to the discovery that business must simplify first, then automate best practice that has been designed for robust performance in the face of variation in business conditions. As Welch noted, "It is this passion for learning and sharing that forms the basis for the unrelenting optimism with which we view the future, and for the conviction that our greatest days lie ahead."

Froedtert Hospital[37]

Medication administration and laboratory processing/results reporting are examples of complex systems in health care that are known to be error prone. At Froedtert Hospital in Milwaukee, Wisconsin, errors with IV medication drips and laboratory processing and results reporting were well documented. Additionally, errors in ordering, transporting, analyzing, and reporting clinical laboratory tests were known to be a significant source of error at the hospital. A consortium was created by four Milwaukee-based organizations committed to the development of an approach to use Six Sigma to reduce errors and improve patient safety.

The design employed the classic Six Sigma DMAIC process. A multidisciplinary group of physicians, nurses, pharmacists, and administrators identified medication delivery by continuous IV infusions as a process subject to substantial error. Continuous IV infusions are used in many clinical settings and errors can severely impact patient well-being. Team members developed a process map (flowchart) to delineate each step in the procedure for continuous IV medication infusion: (1) physician order, (2) order review, (3) pharmacist order entry, (4) dose preparation, (5) dose dispensing, (6) infusion rate calculation, (7) IV pump setup, (8) pump programming, and (9) pump monitoring. Each of the steps was analyzed to identify possible points of failure and effects of failures based on frequency of occurrence, detectability, and severity. The analysis confirmed that IV rate calculations and IV pump setup were the two most error-prone steps in the IV infusion process, and initial efforts to determine the causes and reduce errors focused on these two steps. Specific interventions included implementation of standardized physician order sheets, a policy requiring preparation of all IV medications in a standard concentration, and use of color-coded labels when nonstandard concentrations were in use. Thirty days after implementation, measurable improvement was evident. Level 1 discrepancies fell from 47.4 percent to 14 percent. Level 2 discrepancies fell from 21.1 percent to 11.8 percent and level 3 discrepancies fell from 15.8 percent to 2.9 percent.

Using Six Sigma methods and statistical tools, the team also examined the hospital's clinical laboratory process. Key elements in the acquisition, laboratory analysis, and reporting of patient specimens were identified. The steps included (1) physician order, (2) order entry, (3) matching the order to the patient, (4) collecting the specimen, (5) labeling the specimen, (6) transporting the specimen, (7) analyzing the specimen, (8) reporting the results, and (9) entering the results into the patient's chart. Each of these steps is subject to error. Applying Six Sigma analysis, the most critical steps leading to errors were: order entry by the unit clerical staff, transportation of the specimens to the lab, and analysis of specimens in the lab. A laboratory error reduction task force was established that included members from administration, lab, nursing, clerical staff, information systems, and quality management. The task force used various Six Sigma tools to analyze the clinical laboratory problem in depth and prioritize the steps in the laboratory analysis in terms of their vulnerability to error.

BOEING[38]

The Boeing C-17 On-Board Inert Gas Generating System (OBIGGS) II improvement project team completely redesigned a system that prevents fuel tanks from exploding if struck by enemy gunfire. This project resulted in one of the strongest systems on the C-17. The group was one of three teams to earn a silver medal in the 2007 International Team Excellence Competition sponsored by ASQ's Team and Workplace Excellence Forum.

Although the previous system, OBIGGS I, successfully protected the fuel tanks, it required frequent maintenance. The low system reliability caused high repair costs, many labor hours, and airplanes that were not mission capable. The team realized that improving the OBIGGS reliability would have more impact on the airplane's reliability than almost any other system.

The team included more than 200 Boeing employees, 150 suppliers, and 50 Air Force members. The team used data, quality tools, and quality concepts, including a Pareto analysis and brainstorming, to first select the project and then to determine the root causes of the problem.

Stakeholders were closely involved in the entire process, especially in identifying the root causes and project selection, because the project was customer funded. Stakeholders included engineering groups, support systems groups, and Air Force customers and suppliers.

One of the most important tools the team used was maintenance data from the Air Force that provided the best source for identifying component failures, because the records were generated by pilots and maintenance crews at the time of failure. From these records, Boeing also created a tool to capture the time required to maintain each of the aircraft systems.

From there, the team established a list of possible root causes of the need for frequent maintenance. Team members discussed which components had inherent design weaknesses, where maintenance malpractices were occurring, why some components would fail again shortly after being repaired, and why some troubleshooting procedures were lacking. The team also used suppliers' repair databases to obtain detailed information about the specific cause of each failure. Lastly, the team used failure modes effects analysis (FMEA) during the search for the final root cause.

Team members found that not only were the system's components failing far too often but that it also took too long to initialize the system and placed unnecessary stress on other systems. The system's drain on maintenance—both in time and money—was significant. The team discovered it was generally successful in fixing the original root causes of the component failures. However, team members also found that when the parts lasted longer, new failure modes appeared and prevented the breakthrough reliability improvement expected. The team found that even after implementing multiple component design changes, the system was not achieving the reliability improvement expected. Additionally, they realized that because the system was so complex, the reliability goal it was shooting for would always be perceived as being too low and the Air Force would always be unhappy with its performance. Furthermore, after conducting a FMEA of the entire OBIGGS I using detailed analysis results, the team concluded there were far too many failure modes, leading to the conclusion that OBIGGS I was just too complex to fix! As a result, they decided to completely redesign the system.

The team used a variety of quality tools to develop a possible solution for the redesign, including brainstorming and benchmarking suppliers. Team members analyzed four possible solutions and defined the architecture and required performance for each. A quality function deployment (QFD) analysis defined the relationship between each design criterion and the system requirements. A trade study to select the final solution was conducted following the standard Boeing systems engineering practice for optimizing a balanced tradeoff of requirements among various engineering design alternatives.

After several planes with OBIGGS II were delivered, a new reliability evaluation verified that reliability targets were met. Both the tangible and intangible results greatly exceeded everyone's expectations for the system. The redesign

- Increased system reliability by 7,400%.
- Reduced initialization time by a factor of 11.
- Reduced weight by 517 pounds, allowing for increased cargo capacity.
- Achieved 20 percent system savings and 3:1 life-cycle cost savings.
- Improved customer satisfaction and strengthened stakeholder relationships.
- Caused Boeing to become the industry leader in inerting system design.
- Incorporated an open architecture design that reduced the cost of future improvements.
- Achieved an aggressive financial improvement by reducing logistic and production costs and earning excellent ratings from customers.

Review and Discussion Questions

1. What are the key features of Iredell-Statesville Schools that support continuous improvement?
2. Why must processes be repeatable and measurable in order to improve them?
3. How could you improve your process for studying for an exam? Getting to class on time? Cleaning your room or apartment?
4. The kaizen philosophy seeks to encourage suggestions, not to find excuses for failing to improve. Typical excuses are "If it's not broken, don't fix it," "I'm too busy to work on it," and "It's not in the budget." Think of at least five other excuses people give for why they don't try to improve.
5. How does kaizen differ from kaizen blitz?
6. What is the Deming Cycle? Explain the activities that make up each step.
7. Identify a problem in your work or school activities. Outline a plan for using the Deming Cycle to improve it.

8. How might a professor use the Deming Cycle to improve his or her teaching performance?
9. Explain the Six Sigma DMAIC methodology. How is it similar to or different from the Deming Cycle?
10. Explain how the Deming Cycle and DMAIC relate to the four key steps of any structured improvement approach described in this chapter.
11. Explain the purpose and uses of each of the "seven QC tools."
12. Select a process that you do routinely (for example, washing your car, preparing for an exam, cooking a meal) and draw a flowchart of it. Describe how the flowchart helps you to understand and improve the process.
13. A flowchart for a fast-food drive-through window is shown in Figure 4.11. Discuss the important quality characteristics inherent in this process and suggest possible improvements.
14. Design a check sheet to help a high school student who is getting poor grades on a math quiz determine the source of his or her difficulty.
15. Develop cause-and-effect diagrams for (a) a poor exam grade, (b) no job offers, (c) too many speeding tickets, and (d) being late for work or school.
16. What is lean thinking? Describe some of the popular tools used in lean applications.
17. Explain how Six Sigma can complement lean thinking.
18. Give some examples of breakthrough improvement. How can the notion motivate workers? What must management do to ensure success?
19. Explain the concepts of benchmarking and best practices. How might these be used by students to improve learning?
20. Discuss how a college or university might apply benchmarking to improving its operations. You might solicit views from academic

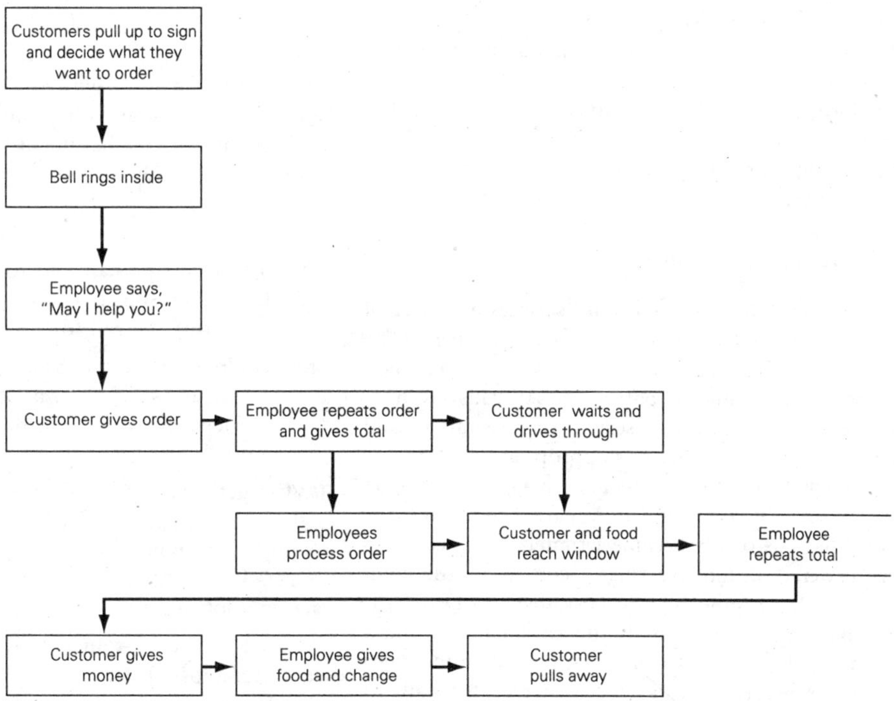

FIGURE 4.11 FLOWCHART OF A FAST-FOOD DRIVE-THROUGH PROCESS

administrators and from business people. (You might find some differences of opinion!)

21. What is reengineering? How can benchmarking support reengineering efforts?
22. Explain how creativity is embodied in the various tools and approaches described in this chapter.
23. In his book, *Weird Ideas That Work* (New York: Free Press, 2002), Robert I. Sutton suggests 11½ practices for promoting, managing, and sustaining innovation. These include:
    - hiring "slow learners" (of the organizational code);
    - hiring people who make you uncomfortable, even those you dislike;
    - encouraging people to ignore and defy superiors and peers;
    - finding some happy people and getting them to fight;
    - thinking of some ridiculous or impractical things to do, then planning to do them; and
    - forgetting the past, especially your company's successes.

    Why do you think these practices work? (If you have few ideas, you should probably read the book!)
24. Propose some reasons to support the findings that successful process improvement changes are more likely when sponsorship is strong; when mid-level managers, rather than top executives, sponsor the projects; and when fact-based measurements drive the efforts.

CASES

Can You Improve This Mess?

Read the State University Experience case in Chapter 7. As a consultant to this institution, outline a plan to improve the design of the student experience. Draw upon ideas presented in this chapter, such as Motorola's approach to process design and the Six Sigma DMAIC methodology. Present your findings in a neatly organized report.

Welz Business Machines[39]

Welz Business Machines sells and services a variety of copiers, computers, and other office equipment. The company receives many calls daily for service, sales, accounting, and other departments. All calls are handled centrally by customer service representatives and routed to other individuals as appropriate.

A number of customers had complained about long waits when calling for service. A market research study found that customers became irritated if the call was not answered within five rings. Scott Welz, the company president, authorized the customer service department manager, Tim, to study this problem and find a method to shorten the call-waiting time. Tim met with the service representatives who answered the calls to attempt to determine the reasons for long waiting times. The following conversation ensued:

TIM: This is a serious problem. How a customer phone inquiry is answered is the first impression the customer receives from us. As you know, this company was founded on efficient and friendly service to all our customers. It's obvious why customers have to wait: You're on the phone with another customer. Can you think of any reasons that might keep you on the phone for an unnecessarily long time?

ROBIN: I've noticed quite often that the person to whom I need to route the call is not present. It takes time to transfer the call and to see whether it is answered. If the person is not there, I end up apologizing and transferring the call to another extension.

TIM: You're right, Robin. Sales personnel often are out of the office on sales calls, away on trips to preview new products, or away from their desks for a variety of reasons. What else might cause this problem?

RAVI: I get irritated at customers who spend a great deal of time complaining about a problem that I cannot do anything about except refer to someone else. Of course, I listen and sympathize with them, but this eats up a lot of time.

LAMARR: Some customers call so often, they think we're long-lost friends and strike up a personal conversation.

TIM: That's not always a bad thing, you realize.

LAMARR: Sure, but it delays my answering other calls.

NANCY: It's not always the customer's fault. During lunch, we're not all available to answer the phone.

RAVI: Right after we open at 9 a.m., we get a rush of calls. I think that many of the delays are caused by these peak periods.

ROBIN: I've noticed the same thing between 4 and 5 p.m.

TIM: I've had a few comments from department managers who received calls that didn't fall in their areas of responsibility and had to be transferred again.

MARK: But that doesn't cause delays at our end.

NANCY: That's right, Mark, but I just realized that sometimes I simply don't understand what the customer's problem really is. I spend a lot of time trying to get him or her to explain it better. Often, I have to route it to someone because other calls are waiting.

RAVI: Perhaps we need to have more knowledge of our products.

TIM: Well, I think we've covered most of the major reasons why many customers have to wait. It seems to me that we have four major reasons: the phones are short-staffed, the receiving party is not present, the customer dominates the conversation, and you may not understand the customer's problem. Next we need to collect some information about these possible causes. I will set up a data collection sheet that you can use to track some of these things. Mark, would you help me on this?

Over the next two weeks, the staff collected data on the frequency of reasons why some callers had to wait. The results are summarized as follows:

Reason	Total number
Operators short-staffed	172
Receiving party not present	73
Customer dominates conversation	19
Lack of operator understanding	61
Other reasons	10

Discussion Questions

1. From the conversation between Tim and his staff, draw a cause-and-effect diagram.
2. Perform a Pareto analysis of the data collected.
3. What actions might the company take to improve the situation?

National Furniture

National Furniture is a large retail design and furniture store. The store often orders special merchandise at the request of its customers. However, the store recently experienced problems with the on-time delivery of these special orders. Sometimes the orders were never received, resulting in irate customers.

The process of fulfilling a special order begins with the sales associate who records the customer information and obtains approval from a manager to process the order. The sales associate puts the order form in a bin for the office manager to fax to the special order department at the regional office. When the office manager faxes the special order forms from the bin, she files them in a notebook.

If a problem arises with the order, the manager receives notification, and contacts the sales associate who took the order to decide what needs to be done next. Typical problems that are often observed include sales associates not filling out the order form completely or entering a request date that is impossible to fulfill. Sometimes the sales associate does not put the form in the proper bin, so the form never gets faxed. Other times, sales associates are asked to obtain more information from the customer, but fail to call the customer back, or do not inform the office associate to refax the form after getting additional information from the customer.

At the regional office, the special order department receives the fax from the store, reviews it, and informs the store if additional information is needed. When all the information is complete, they process the order. Sometimes they lose or misplace the form after it arrives on the fax machine, order the wrong merchandise, or fail to notify the store when additional information is needed or when the merchandise should be expected to arrive.

Discussion Questions

1. Develop a process map for special orders. What steps might you suggest to improve this process?
2. Construct a cause-and-effect diagram for identifying reasons why special orders are not received on time.
3. Discuss the relationship between the process map and the cause-and-effect diagram. How can they be used together to attack this problem?

LT, Inc.[40]

LT, Inc. started as a small, family-owned company. For a long time, owners managed most of the operations, including billing, and customers were happy. Over time, the company grew steadily and acquired plants in the United States and many other countries. Most of its operations were departmentalized, and the accounting systems varied among the many companies LT acquired. While LT successfully dealt with most of the problems caused by rapid growth, it remained unable to get a grip on billing errors. The customer service and billing departments were often flooded with complaints about erroneous bills.

The billing process at LT evolved over time, resulting in a lack of consistency among billing personnel. Customer order taking and billing procedures were confusing, inadequate, and obsolete. Not all billing clerks had the same level of knowledge and training. A lack of documentation added to the confusion and aggravated the situation. Billing personnel followed the policies and procedures they thought were reasonable and did things the way they felt was right.

To get a handle on its billing problem, LT appointed a Six Sigma team composed of employees with various interdisciplinary backgrounds and expertise. The team discussed the problem, researched Six Sigma and lean tools and techniques, learned from other companies, and consulted with experts in the field.

The first thing the team did was study the billing process and prepare a flow chart (see Figure 4.12). The team then reviewed how billing errors were resolved. Most scenarios followed a similar path: A customer calls to inquire about a bill and listens to a prerecorded message with menu options. The customer listens to several options that don't describe his or her particular problem and gets frustrated when the system only deals with select inquiries. After several minutes, the customer finally gets to speak to a customer service representative, but only after being put on hold or bounced from one representative to another, forcing the customer to repeat the problem several times. Finally, the customer is assured that the problem will be corrected, only to have the next month bring the same bill, the same error, the same complaint, the same aggravation and, in the end, the company's loss of an annoyed customer.

A further study revealed many different types of billing errors:

- Bills with wrong prices and charges
- Bills sent to the wrong customer

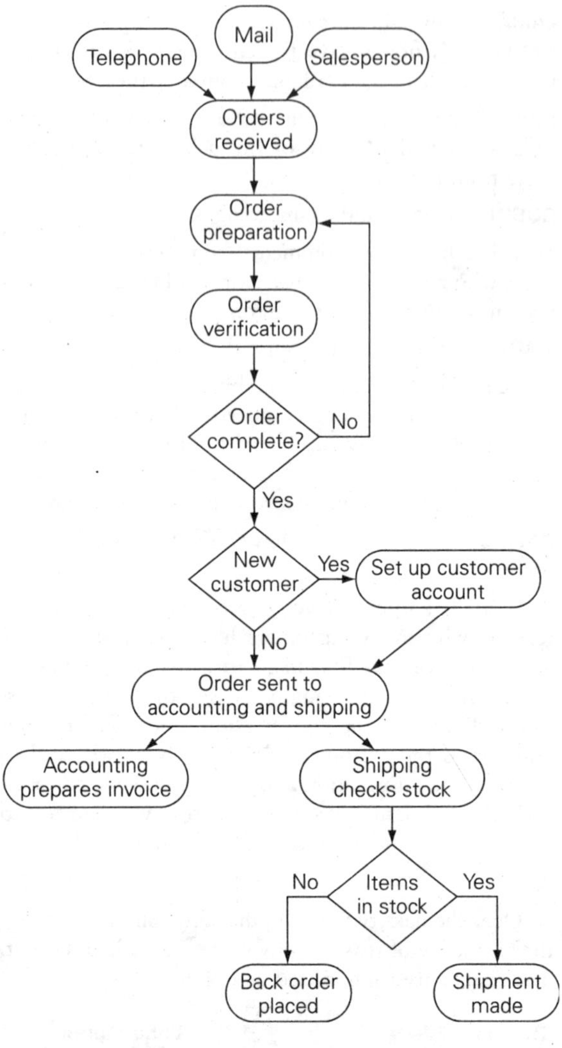

FIGURE 4.12 | FLOWCHART OF LT BILLING PROCESS

- Bills sent to the wrong address
- Double billing and late billing
- Billing for unordered goods
- Billing for returned goods
- Billing before the goods were shipped

A Pareto analysis showed that 70 percent of the errors were due to an incorrect amount on the bill or billing for unordered goods. Using cause-and-effect diagrams, the Six Sigma team brainstormed potential causes and explored them in depth (see Figure 4.13).

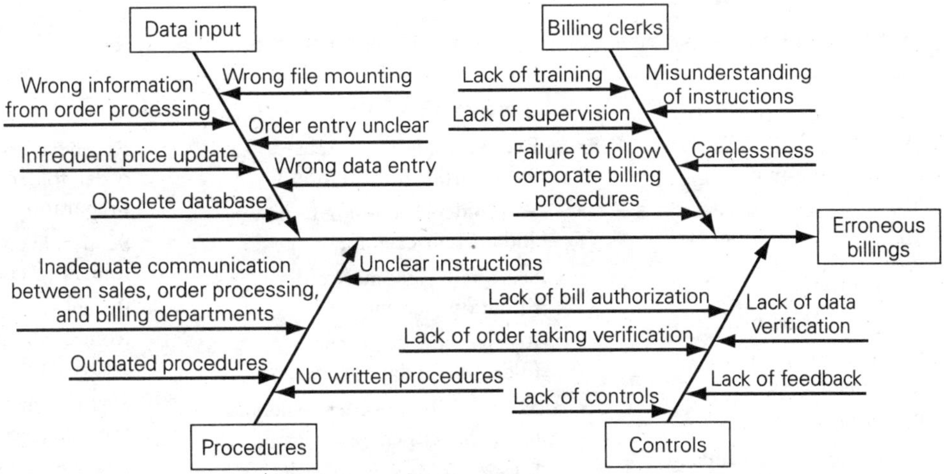

FIGURE 4.13 | CAUSE-AND-EFFECT DIAGRAM FOR BILLING ERRORS

To gain a better understanding of the sources of communication errors, the team members decided to walk through the billing activities. Customer orders arrived via mail, fax, and phone. At each step, they were batched and queued for processing. The main steps included order taking (folders made for each customer); order preparation (current and new customers sorted, information added); and order pricing, shipping, and billing. Table 4.1 provides a detailed description of the activities.

Using the information provided, outline specific steps that you would recommend to improve the process. Include a list of performance metrics that you would recommend that the company monitor to track the efficiency and effectiveness of the process. Summarize your results in a formal report to the company's management.

TABLE 4.1 | DATA AND ACTIVITIES INCLUDED IN THE BILLING PROCESS

Customer

- Orders via mail, fax, phone, and e-mail.
- Average daily orders: 200/day.

Central mailroom

- Receive outside mail.
- Sort according to departments.
- Put in boxes.
- Deliver to departments.
- Stamp postage and send outgoing mail.

Older taking

- Receive orders from customers and central mailroom.
- Open customer mail orders.
- Record customer phone orders on paper.
- Sort all orders by customer name and stamp date.
- Prepare folders with customer order information.
- More batch of customer orders to order preparation once a day.

Credit check

- Check customer credit once a week.
- Add credit status to folders.
- Sort customers according to acceptable and not acceptable credit.
- Batch and move the sorted folders to billing.

Order preparation

- Receive folders with customer order information.
- Sort folders according to new and current customers.
- Send new customer folders to data processing.
- Receive new customer folders from data processing.
- Move customer order folders to order verification.
- Receive folders from order verification.
- Make two copies of customer order folders.
- Send one copy of the order to shipping and one copy to billing.

Data processing

- Receive new customer folders from order taking.
- Batch the folders, assign a customer number and create customer record.
- Add new customer number and other information to customer folders.
- Batch customer folders to order preparation once a day.

Order verification

- Receive customer order folders from order preparation.
- Check stock availability.
- Make price estimates.
- Add price estimates to customer order folder.
- Move the folders to order preparation once a day.

Billing

- Receive copy of customer order folders from order preparation.
- Send new customer folders to credit check.
- Receive customer folders from credit check with credit status.
- Sort the customer folders according to acceptable and not acceptable credit.
- Send the customer folders with not acceptable status back to order takers.
- Send the acceptable customer folders to sales tax department.
- Receive customer folders from sales tax.
- Calculate the total amount (purchases, taxes) to bill.
- Enter all the necessary data into computer and print invoices twice a month.
- Address envelopes, fold, insert invoices, and close. Move the envelopes to central mailroom twice a day.

Shipping

- Receive customer order folders from order preparation.
- Pick and pack the items in the order.
- Print and paste address labels on the boxes.
- Ship the packages twice a day.

Endnotes

1. 2008 Malcolm Baldrige National Quality Award Recipient Profile, U.S. Department of Commerce.
2. Andrew E. Serwer, "Michael Dell Turns the PC World Inside Out," *Fortune*, September 8, 1997, pp. 76–86.
3. Lea A. P. Tonkin, "Kaizen Blitz[SM] 5: Bottleneck-Bashing Comes to Rochester, NY," *Target*, Vol. 12, No. 4, September/October 1996, pp. 41–43.
4. Mark Oakeson, "Makes Dollars & Sense for Mercedes-Benz in Brazil," *IIE Solutions*, April 1997, pp. 32–35
5. Based on Chapter 14 in Alan Robinson (ed.), *Continuous Improvement in Operations: A Systematic Approach to Waste Reduction*, Cambridge, Mass.: Productivity Press, 1991.
6. S. Shingo, *The Sayings of Shigeo Shingo: Key Strategies for Plant Improvement*, Cambridge, Mass.: Productivity Press, 1987, p. 152.
7. Adapted from Nancy Blodgett, "Law Firm Pioneers Explore New Territory," *Quality Progress*, April 1996, pp. 90–94.
8. See Chapter 6 for a discussion of various ways to get ideas from customers.
9. Interview by former co-author James W. Dean, Jr. with Richard Buck, vice president for Quality, Portman Equipment.
10. Eleanor Chilson, "Kaizen Blitzes at Magnivision: $809,270 Cost Savings," *Quality Management Forum* Vol. 29, No. 1, Winter 2003.
11. Gerald Langley, Kevin Nolan, and Thomas Nolan, "The Foundation of Improvement," Sixth Annual International Deming User's Group Conference, Cincinnati, Ohio, August, 1992.
12. Adapted from Kevin Dooley, "Use PDSA for Crying Out Loud," *Quality Progress*, October 1997, pp. 60–63.
13. Chris Bott, Elizabeth Keim, Sai Kim, and Lisa Palser, "Service Quality Six Sigma Case Studies," *ASQ's 54th Annual Congress Proceedings*, 2000, pp. 225–231.
14. Gregory Korte, "473 Steps," *The Cincinnati Enquirer*, October 30, 2002, A1, A10.
15. Timothy Clark and Andrew Clark, "Continuous Improvement on the Free-Throw Line," *Quality Progress*, October 1997, pp. 78–80.
16. Gary Conner, "Benefiting from Six Sigma," *Manufacturing Engineering* Vol. 130, No. 2, February 2003.
17. These principles are based on Richard C. Whiteley, *The Customer-Driven Company: Moving from Talk to Action*, Reading, Mass.: Addison-Wesley, 1991.
18. See J. W. Dean, Jr., and G. I. Susman, "Organizing for Manufacturable Design," *Harvard Business Review*, January–February 1989.
19. Anthony R. Goland, John Hall and Devereaux A Clifford, "First National Toyota," *The McKinsey Quarterly*, No. 4, 1998, pp. 58–66.
20. Patricia Houghton, "Improving Pharmacy Service," *Quality Digest*, October 18, 2007.
21. Shawn Tully, "Why to Go for Stretch Targets," *Fortune*, November 14, 1994, pp. 45–58.
22. Pallavi Gogoi, "Thinking Outside the Cereal Box," *Business Week*, July 28, 2003, pp. 74–75.
23. Michael Hammer and James Champy, *Reengineering the Corporation*, New York: HarperBusiness, 1993, pp. 177–178.
24. Christopher E. Bogan and Michael J. English, "Benchmarking for Best Practices: Winning Through Innovative Adaptation," *Quality Digest*, August 1994, pp. 52–62.
25. David A. McCamey, Robert W. Bogs, and Linda M. Bayuk, "More, Better, Faster From Total Quality Effort," *Quality Progress*, August 1999, pp. 43–50.
26. N. Tichy and R. Charan, "Speed, Simplicity, and Self-Confidence: An Interview with Jack Welch," in J. Gabarro (ed.), *Managing People and Organizations*, Boston, Mass.: Harvard Business School Publications, 1992.
27. Robinson, *Continuous Improvement*.
28. Reprinted from "Total Quality Management: Time for a Theory?" Paper presented at the EOQ Conference in Prague, 1991, by Asbjorn Aune.
29. Martin Smith, "Business Process Design: Correlates of Success and Failure," *Quality Management Journal*, 10, 2, 2003, pp. 38–49.
30. See, for example, Jacob Eskildsen, Jens Dahlgaard, and Anders Norgaard, "The Impact of Creativity and Learning on Business Excellence," *Total Quality Management*, Vol. 10, Issue 4/5, July 1999, pp. S523–S530.
31. Masaaki Imai, *Kaizen: The Key to Japan's Competitive Success*, New York: McGraw-Hill, 1986, p. 15.
32. Mark R. Edwards and J. Ruth Sproull, "Creativity: Productivity Gold Mine?" *Journal of Creative Behavior*, Vol. 18, No. 3, 1984, pp. 175–184; and Michael K. Badawy, "How to Prevent Creativity

Mismanagement," *Research Management*, Vol. 29, No. 4, 1986, p. 28.

33. Jena McGregor, "How Failure Breeds Success, *Business Week*, July 10, 2006, pp. 42–48.
34. Kathleen D. Ryan and Daniel K. Oestreich, *Driving Fear Out of the Workplace*, San Francisco: Jossey-Bass, Inc., 1991, pp. 63, 64.
35. Pamela Tierney, Steven Farmer, and George Graen, "An Examination of Leadership and Employee Creativity: The Relevance of Traits and Relationships," *Personnel Psychology*, Vol. 52, No. 3, Autumn 1999, pp. 591–620.
36. Gregory H. Watson, "Cycles of Learning: Observations of Jack Welch," *Six Sigma Forum Magazine*, Vol. 1, No. 1, November 2001, pp. 13–17.
37. Adapted from Cathy Buck, "Application of Six Sigma to Reduce Medical Errors," *Proceedings of the 55th Annual Quality Congress of the American Society for Quality*, 2001 (CD-ROM).
38. Nicole Adrian, Quality Tools, Teamwork Lead to a Boeing System Redesign, *Quality Progress*, November 2007, pp. 43–48
39. This case was developed from a classic example published in "The Quest for Higher Quality: The Deming Prize and Quality Control" by RICOH of America, Inc.
40. Adapted from Lakshmi U. Tatikonda, "A Less Costly Billing Process," *Quality Progress*, January 2008, pp. 31–39.

Performance Excellence, Strategy, and Organization Theory

PART 2

CHAPTER 5 Competitive Advantage and Strategic Management for Performance Excellence 179

CHAPTER 6 Quality in Customer-Supplier Relationships 230

CHAPTER 7 Designing Organizations for Performance Excellence 265

Competitive Advantage and Strategic Management for Performance Excellence

CHAPTER **5**

Performance Excellence Profile: Premier, Inc.[1]

Serving 1,700 hospitals and more than 43,000 other health care sites, Premier Inc. is the largest health care alliance in the United States dedicated to improving patient outcomes while safely reducing the cost of care. Premier's three business units provide the following services: group purchasing and supply chain management, insurance and risk management, and informatics and performance improvement tools.

Premier's "Big Hairy Audacious Goal" is for its member hospitals to deliver the best, most cost-effective care in the nation and for the alliance to have a major influence on reshaping health care. To that end, the alliance has focused its business units on disciplines where outstanding opportunities exist to drive measurable improvement and performance breakthroughs. The success of this strategy is evident:

- Hospitals that make up the Premier alliance have validated more than $2.5 billion in savings over the past three years achieved through cooperative purchasing and participation in Premier's other services.
- Premier's customer satisfaction levels of over 90 percent significantly exceed industry benchmarks.
- Premier is partnering with the Centers for Medicare and Medicaid Services (CMS) in a voluntary national demonstration project aimed at improving the quality of inpatient health care. Through the Premier Hospital Quality Incentive Demonstration, CMS is rewarding top performing hospitals for high quality care by increasing their payments for Medicare patients. The results show that participating hospitals have shown dramatic improvements in quality and performance.

- Operating margin grew from 35 percent in 2003 to 50 percent in 2006 and exceeded that of Premier's largest competitor in all years, while operating expenses have remained well below those of that competitor.

Premier has taken a leadership role in promoting best practices in ethical conduct, transparency, and accountability within its own organization and throughout the industry. In 1998, Premier instituted a Corporate Values Program and an employee Values Conference at which employees and senior leaders together discuss Premier's Core Values—focusing on people, integrity, passion for performance, and innovation. Premier also has taken a leadership role in product safety and environmental concerns. In 1999, Premier founded and maintains the Premier Safety Institute to provide information, resources and tools to promote safety—not just among member hospitals, but throughout the health care industry. Premier's Environmentally Preferable Purchasing program provides information and resources about products and services that are environmentally friendly.

The hospital purchasing market is mature, with virtually 100 percent of hospitals aligned with at least one Group Purchasing Organization (GPO). Thus, retaining current members is key to maintaining the scale of membership required to attract competitive group contract terms. Overall retention of hospital members increased from 94 percent in 2002 to approximately 97 percent in 2006 and annual survey results show satisfaction levels above industry benchmarks. The company's customers, who are also its owners, work closely with Premier and its employees to achieve their mutual goals. All of Premier's owners and other customers have ready access to the company's information, staff, resources and services, particularly through Premier's field staff and its customer solution centers.

Premier's core value of "focus on people" embodies the company's commitment to providing a safe, positive work environment and opportunities for career growth. Learning and development practices are designed to enable Premier's employees to meet the customer's requirements now and in the future, and cover new hire orientation, diversity, ethical business practices, management and leadership development, process management and improvement process, specific business unit skills, and employee, workplace and environmental safety.

Competitive advantage denotes a firm's ability to achieve market superiority over its competitors. In the long run, a sustainable competitive advantage provides above-average performance, as exemplified by Premier, Inc. in the profile above. A firm has many options in defining its long-term goals and objectives, the customers it wants to serve, the products and services it produces and delivers, and the design of the production and service system to meet these objectives. Creating a sustainable competitive advantage depends on developing and executing a good strategy. **Strategy** is the pattern of decisions that determines and reveals a company's goals, policies, and plans to meet the needs of its stakeholders. **Strategic planning** is the process by which the members of an organization envision its future and develop the necessary procedures and operations to carry out that vision.

This chapter focuses on how total quality contributes to competitive advantage and discusses the role of quality and performance excellence in an organization's business strategy. This chapter will:

- examine the relationship between quality and profitability;
- discuss cost leadership, differentiation, and people as principal sources of competitive advantage, and their relationship to quality;
- describe the importance of quality in meeting customer expectations in product design, service, flexibility and variety, innovation, and rapid response;
- discuss the role of information in strategic planning and quality-focused decisions; and
- describe the role of quality in strategy formulation and implementation.

QUALITY, COMPETITIVE ADVANTAGE, AND THE BOTTOM LINE

A strong competitive advantage has six characteristics,[2] each of which relates closely to, and is supported by, a focus on quality and performance excellence.

1. A strong competitive advantage is driven by customer wants and needs. A company provides value to its customers that competitors do not. Customer wants and needs form the basis for all quality initiatives. Six Sigma projects, for example, revolve around improving CTQs—"critical to quality" characteristics that are vital to customers.
2. A strong competitive advantage makes a significant contribution to the success of the business. There is considerable evidence that performance excellence approaches positively affects the bottom line. Baldrige recipients have typically outperformed their industries as a whole, and Six Sigma projects must be justified financially.
3. A strong competitive advantage matches the organization's unique resources with the opportunities in the environment. No two companies have the same resources; a good strategy uses them effectively. The principles of TQ pay particular attention to an organization's human resources and process designs in executing a business strategy.
4. A strong competitive advantage is durable and lasting and difficult for competitors to copy. A superior research and development department, for example, can consistently develop new products or processes to remain ahead of competitors. A performance excellence culture takes years to develop but, once in place, is difficult to diffuse because it has become so ingrained in the attitudes and thinking processes of all employees—workers and managers alike.
5. A strong competitive advantage provides a basis for further improvement. A performance excellence culture is constantly focusing on improvement and learning, and exploits the myriad of tools and techniques available to implement improvements. Six Sigma projects are vital for continually improving designs and processes.

IT'S NOT ROCKET SCIENCE

The role of quality in achieving competitive advantage was demonstrated by several research studies back in the 1980s. PIMS Associates, Inc., a subsidiary of the Strategic Planning Institute, maintains a database of 1,200 companies and studies the impact of product quality on corporate performance.[3] PIMS researchers determined that:

- Product quality is the most important determinant of business profitability.
- Businesses offering premium quality products and services usually have large market shares and were early entrants into their markets.
- Quality is positively and significantly related to a higher return on investment for almost all kinds of products and market situations. PIMS studies have shown that firms with products of superior quality can more than triple return on sales over products perceived as having inferior quality.
- A strategy of quality improvement usually leads to increased market share, but at a cost, in terms of reduced short-run profitability.
- High-quality producers can usually charge premium prices.

General Systems Company, a prominent quality management consulting firm, also found that firms with total quality systems in place consistently exceed industry norms for return on investment. This is attributed to three factors:

1. An effective quality system reduces the direct costs associated with poor quality.
2. Improvements in quality tend to lead to increases in productivity.
3. The combination of improved quality and increased productivity leads to an increase in market share.

6. A strong competitive advantage provides direction and motivation to the entire organization. Quality-focused initiatives marshal the collective talents of everyone. The GE experience in deploying Six Sigma throughout the company, for example, aligns everyone on working toward common goals. When supported by incentives and rewards, such initiatives can motivate everyone.

We may conclude that a focus on quality and performance excellence can be an important means of developing, gaining, and sustaining competitive advantage (see box "It's Not Rocket Science"); nevertheless, many organizations fail to recognize this.

The relationships between quality and the bottom line are summarized in Figure 5.1. The value of a product in the marketplace is influenced by the quality of its design. Improvements in performance, features, and reliability will differentiate the product from its competitors, improve a firm's quality reputation, and improve the perceived value of the product. This allows the company to command higher prices and achieve an increased market share. This, in turn, leads to increased revenues that offset the added costs of improved design.

Improved conformance in production leads to lower manufacturing and service costs through savings in rework, scrap, and warranty expenses. This viewpoint was popularized by Philip Crosby in his book *Quality Is Free*.[4] As Crosby states:

> Quality is not only free, it is an honest-to-everything profit maker. Every penny you don't spend on doing things wrong, over, or instead of, becomes half a penny right on

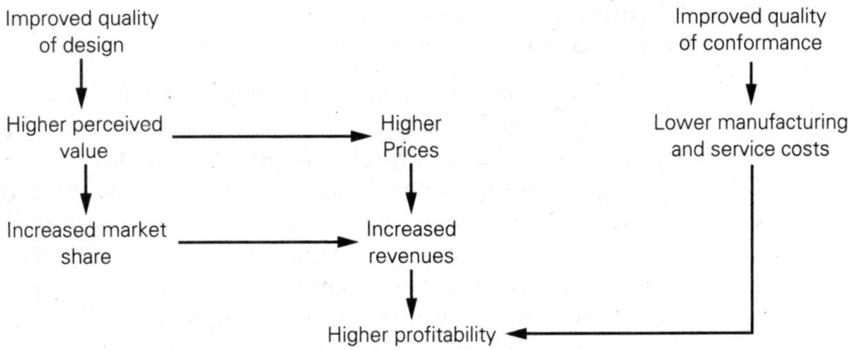

FIGURE 5.1 | QUALITY AND PROFITABILITY

> the bottom line. In these days of "who knows what is going to happen to our business tomorrow," there aren't many ways left to make a profit improvement. If you concentrate on making quality certain, you can probably increase your profit by an amount equal to 5 percent to 10 percent of your sales. That is a lot of money for free.

The net effect of improved quality of design and conformance is increased profits.

Today, most consumers make their purchasing decisions on *value*. Value can be defined as quality relative to price. When organizations provide less perceived value than their competitors, they lose market share. High conformance quality alone does not provide sufficient value to attract customers. Thirty years ago it would have; today it is simply the "entry into the game." For example, while the quality of domestic automobiles as measured by defect rates has steadily improved, increasing consumer demands on dimensions of quality beyond low levels of manufacturing defects has raised the bar for all automobile manufacturers. Domestic defect rates have fallen more than 80 percent since 1980, and current J.D. Power & Associates surveys of initial quality show significant improvements in today's automobiles. Many of today's complaints revolved around things that a carmaker builds flawlessly but aren't quite what a consumer wants. Technical failures have given way to failures to satisfy the customer. As a result, U.S. companies have been aggressively pursuing new and innovative model designs, even recruiting European designers.[5] No longer can firms focus their quality efforts solely on defect elimination. Thus, firms must focus their efforts at both improving the quality of design and service as well as reducing defects and their associated costs to create customer value. Both Deming and Juran stressed the need for never-ending cycles of market research, improved product development and design, production, and sales.

Baldrige Award finalists and recipients have demonstrated that quality leads to competitive advantage and improved business performance. A General Accounting Office study of Baldrige finalists in the first two years of the award program explored four measurable areas of a company's operations that could demonstrate the impact of TQ practices on corporate performance:[6]

1. employee relations,
2. operating procedures,

3. customer satisfaction, and
4. financial performance.

In employee relations, significant improvements were realized in employee satisfaction, attendance, turnover, safety and health, and suggestions received. In operating procedures, favorable results were realized in reliability, timeliness of delivery, order-processing times, errors and defects, product lead time, inventory turnover, cost of quality, and overall cost savings. Overall customer satisfaction also improved, as customer complaints fell and customer retention rose. In the financial performance area, market share, sales per employee, return on assets, and return on sales all showed positive improvement for most companies.

The GAO developed a general framework for describing Total Quality Management and its effect on competitiveness (see Figure 5.2.). The solid line shows how TQ processes lead to improved competitiveness, beginning with leadership dedicated to improving products and services, as well as quality systems. Improvements in these areas lead to customer satisfaction and benefits to the organization, both of which improve competitiveness. The dotted lines show the information feedback necessary for continuous improvement. The arrows in the boxes show the expected direction of the performance indicators.

Although the GAO study is somewhat dated, the conclusions remain valid today. A more recent survey of almost 1,000 executives conducted by Zenger Miller Achieve noted similar benefits from quality initiatives, including increased employee

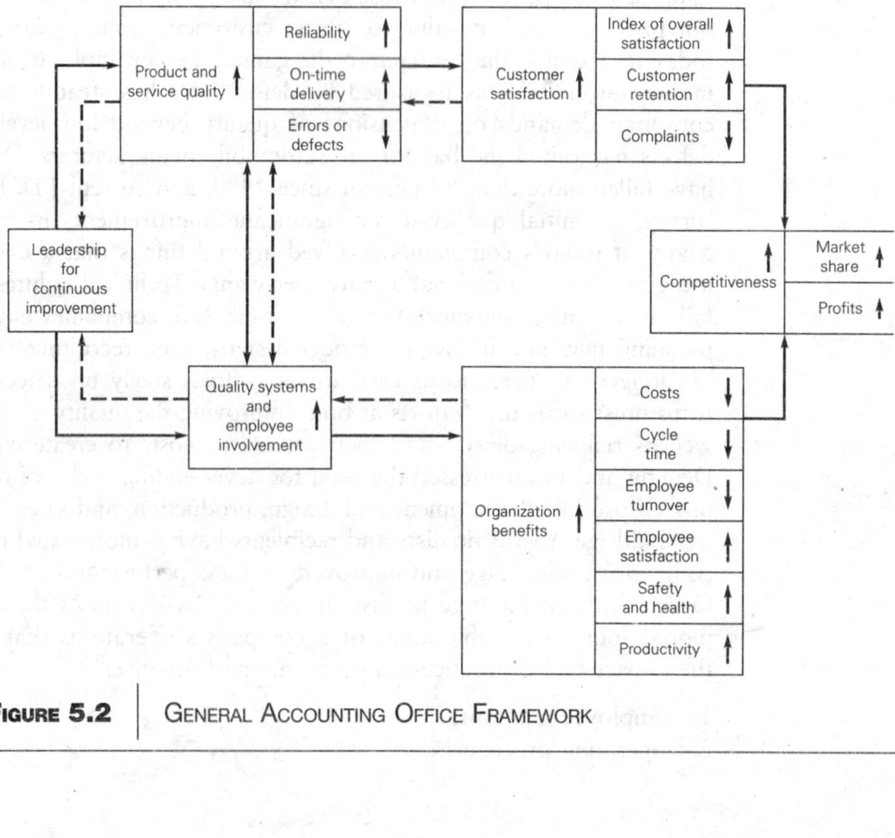

FIGURE 5.2 GENERAL ACCOUNTING OFFICE FRAMEWORK

participation, improved product and service quality, improved customer satisfaction, improved productivity, and improved employee skills.[7]

SOURCES OF COMPETITIVE ADVANTAGE

The classic literature on competitive strategy suggests that a firm can possess two basic types of competitive advantage: low cost and differentiation.[8] For example, Marriott's Fairfield Inn was designed to appeal to business travelers who wanted clean, comfortable rooms at inexpensive prices. Within this market, they are focused on cost leadership. By contrast, The Ritz-Carlton hotels focus on differentiation (exceptional personal attention, twice-a-day housekeeping service, and special amenities such as bathrobes and rooms with bay windows) and can command premium prices. Figure 5.1 supports this premise by showing how cost reduction and improved design affect profitability. Modern thinking has added a third source of competitive advantage—an organization's people.[9]

Cost Leadership

Many firms gain competitive advantage by establishing themselves as the low-cost leader in an industry. These firms produce high volumes of mature products and achieve their competitive advantage through low prices. Such firms often enter markets that were established by other firms. They emphasize achieving economies of scale and finding cost advantages from all sources.

A cost leader can achieve above-average performance if it can command prices at or near the industry average. However, it cannot do so with an inferior product (see box "You Can't Fool All the People All the Time"). The product must be perceived as comparable with competitors or the firm will be forced to discount prices well below competitors' prices to gain sales. This can cancel any benefits that result from cost advantage.

Low cost can result from high productivity and high capacity utilization. More important, improvements in quality lead to improvements in productivity, which in turn lead to lower costs. Lower costs result from innovations in product design and process technology that reduce the costs of production and from efficiencies gained through meticulous attention to operations. This approach has been exploited by many Japanese firms. Japanese companies adopted many product innovations and process technologies that were developed in the United States. They refined the designs and manufacturing processes to produce high-quality products at low costs, resulting in higher market shares. Thus, a strategy of continuous improvement is essential to achieve a low-cost competitive advantage.

To achieve cost leadership for high-volume products, companies use a variety of approaches:[10]

- Early manufacturing involvement in the design of the product both for make-versus-buy decisions and for assurance that the production processes can achieve required tolerances.
- Product design to take advantage of automated equipment by minimizing the number of parts, eliminating fasteners, making parts symmetric whenever possible, avoiding rigid and stiff parts, and using one-sided assembly designs.

You Can't Fool All of the People All of the Time

The problems with focusing on costs at the expense of quality are illustrated by the case of the Schlitz Brewing Company.[11] In the early 1970s, Schlitz, the second-largest brewer in the United States, began a cost-cutting campaign. It included reducing the quality of ingredients in their beers by switching to corn syrup and hop pellets and shortening the brewing cycle by 50 percent.

In the short term, it achieved higher returns on sales and assets than Anheuser-Busch (and the acclaim of Wall Street analysts). *Forbes* magazine stated, "Does it pay to build quality into a product if most customers don't notice? Schlitz seems to have a more successful answer." But customers do recognize inferior products. Soon after, market share and profits fell rapidly.

By 1980 Schlitz's sales had declined 40 percent, the stock price fell from $69 to $5, and the company was eventually sold.

- Limited product models and customization in distribution centers rather than in the factory.
- A manufacturing system designed for a fixed sequence of operations. Every effort is made to ensure zero defects at the time of shipment. Work-in-process inventory is reduced as much as possible, and multiskilled, focused teams of employees are used.

Six Sigma can be an important way for organizations to build and sustain low-cost leadership, because they identify sources of problems and opportunities for process and design improvements that have clear financial justifications and impact on the bottom line. Moreover, Six Sigma creates the organizational infrastructure for continually focusing on cost reduction in all manufacturing and service operations.

Differentiation

To achieve differentiation, a firm must be unique in its industry along some dimensions that are widely valued by customers. It selects one or more attributes that customers perceive as important and positions itself uniquely to meet those needs. For instance, Dell's direct business model was the first of its kind in the computer industry and differentiated the company from its competitors.

Often, a firm with a differentiation strategy can command premium prices and achieve higher profits. Juran cites an example of a power tool manufacturer that improved reliability well beyond that of competitors.[12] Field data showing that the differences in reliability resulted in significantly lower operating costs were publicized, and the company was able to secure a premium price.

However, a firm that uses differentiation as its source of competitive advantage must make its products or systems difficult to copy. Often this involves culture, habits, and sunk costs. For example, why doesn't every company copy Dell's superior direct business model? Dell's approaches are hardly a secret; and Michael Dell even wrote a book about it. Competitors have copied its Web site with stunning precision, but they face far greater difficulty copying the supporting activities—purchasing, scheduling, and logistics—that Dell has built around its direct model over several decades. Competitors are burdened by long-standing relationships with suppliers and distributors and by a different culture.[13]

PEOPLE

The importance of people in building and sustaining a TQ organization is illustrated by the following anecdote about Toyota. Toyota's Georgetown, Kentucky, plant has been a three-time winner of the J. D. Power Gold Plant Quality Award. When asked about the "secret" behind the superior Toyota paint finishes, one manager replied, "We've got nothing, technology-wise, that anyone else can't have. There's no secret Toyota Quality Machine out there. The quality machine is the workforce—the team members on the paint line, the suppliers, the engineers—everybody who has a hand in production here takes the attitude that we're making world-class vehicles."[14] The human resource is the *only* one that competitors cannot copy, and the *only* one that can synergize—that is, produce output whose value is greater than the sum of its parts. Apple hires only people who are passionate about what they do; and Genentech screens out people who ask too many questions about titles and options, because they only want people who are driven to serve customers.[15]

The competitive advantage resulting from an organization's people can drive low cost and differentiation. For example, over several decades, Southwest Airlines has been the most profitable U.S. carrier. It has fewer employees per aircraft and flies more passengers per employee. Much of its cost advantage comes from its very productive, motivated, and unionized workforce.[16]

Is its competitive advantage low cost, or is it the people? Southwest Airlines has one of the most distinct competitive advantages in the airline industry. Herb Kelleher, former CEO, once stated, "It's the intangibles that are the hardest things for competitors to imitate. You can get on an airplane. You can get ticket-counter space, you can get baggage conveyors. But it is our esprit de corps—the culture, the spirit—that is truly our most valuable competitive asset." Similar comments can be made about The Ritz-Carlton Hotel Company, a two-time Baldrige recipient. One of the author's personal observations about Baldrige recipients is the fact that employees genuinely like to work for their organizations and are highly satisfied with their jobs. Many Baldrige recipients have been cited on *Fortune* magazine's list of "best companies to work for."

Providing a work environment that fosters cooperation, initiative, and innovation; educating and training the workforce; and enhancing the factors that affect well-being, satisfaction, and motivation are very difficult for competitors to copy. This is a significantly different philosophy from the work environment that came into being during the Industrial Revolution. Prior to the Industrial Revolution, skilled craftspeople had a major stake in the quality of their products because their families' livelihoods depended on the sale of those products. The departure from the craftsmanship concept was promulgated by Frederick W. Taylor. Taylor concluded that a factory should be managed on a scientific basis. So he focused on work methods design, the establishment of standards for daily work, selection and training of workers, and piecework incentives. Taylor separated planning from execution, concluding that foremen and workers of those days lacked the education necessary to plan their work. The foreman's role was to ensure that the workforce met productivity standards. Other pioneers of scientific management, such as Frank and Lillian Gilbreth and Henry Gantt, further refined the Taylor system through motion study, methods improvement, ergonomics, scheduling, and wage incentive systems.

The Taylor system dramatically improved productivity and was principally responsible for the industrial growth of the twentieth century. However, it also changed many manufacturing jobs into a series of mundane and mindless tasks. Without a systems perspective and a focus on the customer, the responsibility for quality shifted from workers to inspectors, and as a result, quality eroded. The Taylor philosophy also contributed to the development of labor unions and established an adversarial relationship between labor and management that has yet to be completely overcome. Perhaps the most significant failure of the Taylor system was that it failed to make use of an organization's most important asset—the knowledge and creativity of the workforce. As executives at The Ritz-Carlton Hotel Company have stated, human beings don't serve a function, they have a purpose, and the role of the human resources function is to unleash the power of the workforce to achieve the goals of the organization.[17]

QUALITY AND DIFFERENTIATION STRATEGIES

Competitive advantage is gained from meeting or exceeding customer expectations—the fundamental definition of quality. A business may concentrate on any of several quality-related dimensions in order to differentiate itself from its competition. These key dimensions are

- superior product and service design,
- outstanding service,
- high agility,
- continuous innovation, and
- rapid response.

Traditional management strategists advocated focusing on a single dimension.

However, as consumers become more demanding, firms can no longer compete along only one dimension. Pursuing a strategy of performance excellence helps improve all of these dimensions. In fact, a careful review of the Baldrige Award criteria will show that these dimensions are prominent throughout the criteria. The following sections discuss these approaches to differentiation and the role of quality in each.

COMPETING ON SUPERIOR PRODUCT DESIGN

Among the most important strategic decisions a firm makes are the selection and development of new products (we focus on manufactured goods in this section). These decisions determine the growth, profitability, and future direction of the firm. Significant competitive advantage can be achieved by having products of superior design. In addition, products that are appealing, reliable, easy to operate, and economical to service give the consumer a perception of quality. One need only look at the evolution of computers and the continual change that is occurring in this industry to appreciate the value of good design.

The quality of a product's design is influenced by several dimensions, which we first introduced in Chapter 1:[18]

Performance—the primary operating characteristics of the product: the horsepower of an engine or the sound quality of a stereo amplifier.

Features—the "bells and whistles" of a product: antilock brakes or a navigation system in an automobile or surround-sound options in an amplifier.

Reliability—the probability of a product's surviving over a specified period of time under stated conditions of use: the ability of a car to start consistently in all types of weather and the lack of failure of electronic components.

Durability—the amount of use one gets from a product before it physically deteriorates or until replacement is preferable: the number of miles one would expect from an automobile with normal maintenance.

Aesthetics—how a product looks, feels, sounds, tastes, or smells: the sleekness of an automobile's exterior and the black "high-tech" look of modern stereo components, for example.

The product design function that traditionally was concerned solely with technical aspects of the product must now be concerned with manufacturing and marketing issues. Product designers must match the right products with the continually changing variety of customer needs. This requires great flexibility. At the same time, costs must be minimized, which demands attention to the manufacturing process during the design stage.

The Role of Quality in Product Design

A firm must focus on the key product dimensions that reflect specific customer needs. If these expectations are not identified correctly or are misinterpreted, the final product will not be perceived to be of high quality by customers. Innovative marketing efforts are needed to ensure that the needs are properly identified (see box "Quirky, Funky, Independent, Maverick").

The Malcolm Baldrige Award criteria emphasize the importance of systematic processes to design and improve products and the processes that create them. For example, the award application requires evidence of how customer requirements are identified and used for purposes of product planning. For many firms, product design is regarded as a key value creation process. From this perspective, these firms need good processes to translate customer needs into product requirements; select key process performance characteristics based on customer requirements; address quality requirements early in the design process; and coordinate and integrate designs with production and delivery systems.

A focus on quality in product design requires significant investment in engineering to ensure that designs meet customer expectations. Quality engineering is

Quirky, Funky, Independent, Maverick[19]

That's how the designers of the Honda Element describe it, meeting the challenge to design a totally new product that could coexist with both the current Civic model and appeal to both young Gen Y males and the new Gen X family that did not want to buy into mainstream vehicles or sell out to convention. Executives gave the design team carte blanche to understand how these potential customers were using their cars. The design team engaged in "immersion research," going to fraternity houses and hanging out with surfers and mountain bikers to understand their lifestyles. Honda designers incorporated several themes into the car—"hobby space," "campground friendly," and "road-trip friendly." The car was designed to fit two mountain bikes or a 10-foot surfboard. It can sleep two people comfortably. The car has spill-proof material on seats and a wipeable flat floor.

concerned with the plans, procedures, and methods for the design and evaluation of quality in goods and services. Useful techniques of quality engineering include:

- *concurrent engineering*, in which engineering and production personnel jointly develop product designs that are both functional and easy to manufacture, thus reducing opportunities for poor quality;
- *value analysis*, in which the function of every component of a product is analyzed to determine how it might be accomplished in the most economical fashion;
- *design reviews*, in which managers assess how well the design relates to customer requirements and how it might be improved prior to releasing it to production; and
- *experimental design*, in which formal statistical experiments are applied to determine the best combinations of product and process parameters for high quality and low cost. All of these efforts involve a high level of teamwork.

Competing on Service

With the vast majority of the U.S. economy being service-based, the quality of service is a major factor in consumer perception and business success. Until rather recently, manufacturing companies viewed service as secondary in importance to manufacturing itself. However, next to the quality of the product itself, service is perhaps the greatest key to achieving competitive success (see box "Customer Service: Not a New Frontier at Alaska Airlines"). This may be because, as the average level of product quality increases, consumers turn to service as the primary means of differentiating among competing firms. For example, one of the biggest sources of dissatisfaction for computer manufacturers is the lack of adequate service after the sale.

The importance of service was recognized in the early 1980s because of the book *In Search of Excellence* by Tom Peters and Bob Waterman.[20] One of their key themes was that excellent companies share an obsession with service. How important is it? A 1985 Gallup poll on the quality of American products and services found that the vast majority of consumers believe that quality is determined by employee behavior, attitudes, and competence. They also believe—to an even greater degree—that poor service quality is due to the same set of factors. These attitudes hold true even today.

Good service translates into dollars. Banking studies have found that 10 percent of customers leave each year,[21] and 21 percent of those leave because of poor service. Each customer contributes $121 per year in profit, and the cost to acquire a new customer is $150. If a bank has a base of 200,000 customers, this means that 4,200 will leave because of poor service. The arithmetic shows that the combined lost profit and replacement effort costs are more than $1 million per year. Similar studies in other industries have found a high correlation between customer retention and profitability.

We discussed many aspects of services and how they differ from manufacturing in Chapter 1. However, managing intangible quality characteristics is more difficult, as they usually depend on employee behavior and system performance. Thus, two key components of service system quality are *employees* and *information technology*. Customers evaluate a service primarily by the quality of the human contact. A *Wall Street Journal* survey found that Americans' biggest complaints about service employees are of delivery people or salespeople who fail to show up when you have stayed home at a scheduled time waiting for them; salespeople who are poorly informed; and salesclerks who talk on the phone when waiting on you, who say "It's not my department," who talk down to you, or who cannot describe how a product works.

Customer Service: Not a New Frontier at Alaska Airlines

At many airports, the passenger check-in area often resembles a mob scene. Passengers queue up in long lines, customers waiting for agents block self-serve kiosks, and finished passengers must push through the crowd again. The process often takes 25–30 minutes. But at Alaska Airlines, employees roam a spacious hall, directing customers toward kiosks. Lines aren't more than three-people deep, and travelers are on their way to security in eight minutes or less.

Moving customers from frustration to relief—in a fraction of the time—has been at the focus of Alaska Airlines' Airport of the Future project. The carrier has spent more than a decade designing a better way to get customers through airport check-in. Alaska's embrace of the future came out of necessity. By the mid-1990s, it was running out of space to handle its Seattle passengers. A new terminal would have cost around $500 million. Alaska tried self-serve kiosks, but technology alone wasn't the answer. Kiosks were pushed against the ticket counter, which only slowed the flow of passengers. The airline assembled a team of employees from across the company and visited theme parks, hospitals, and retailers to see what it could learn. Similar to Disneyland, Alaska placed "lobby coordinators" out front to help educate travelers. The bag-drop stations are further back and arranged so that passengers can see security. Other airlines' agents lose precious time hauling bags and walking the length of the ticket counter to reach customers. Alaska agents stand at a station with baggage conveyor belts on each side, assisting one passenger while a second traveler places luggage on the free belt. With just a slight turn, the agent can assist the next customer. The project has significantly reduced customer wait times and increased agent productivity.[22]

Researchers repeatedly have demonstrated that when service employee job satisfaction is high, customer satisfaction is high, and that when job satisfaction is low, customer satisfaction is low.[23] Many service companies act on the motto, "If we take care of our employees, they will take care of our customers." At FedEx, for instance, the company credo is stated simply as *People, Service, Profits*. All potential decisions in the company are evaluated on their effects on the employees (people), on their customers (service), and the company's financial performance (profits), in that order. In many companies, unfortunately, the frontline employees—salesclerks, receptionists, delivery personnel, and so on, who have the most contact with customers—receive the lowest pay, minimal training, little decision-making authority, and little responsibility (empowerment).

Information technology is essential in modern service organizations because of the high volumes of information they must process and because customers demand service at ever-increasing speeds. Intelligent use of information technology not only leads to improved quality and productivity but also to competitive advantage. This is particularly true when technology is used to better serve the customer and to make it easier for customers to do business with the company. Every service industry is exploiting information technology to improve customer service. Restaurants, for example, use hand-held order-entry computer terminals to speed up the ordering process. An order is instantaneously transmitted to the kitchen or bar, where it is displayed and the guest check is printed. In addition to saving time, such systems improve accuracy by standardizing the order-taking, billing, and inventory procedures and reducing the need for handwriting. Credit authorizations, which once took several minutes by telephone, are now accomplished in seconds through computerized authorization systems.

Another important aspect of service is complaint resolution (an important criterion in the Baldrige Award). Research has shown that about 80 to 95 percent of unhappy customers (depending on the amount of loss) will purchase from a company again if their complaints are resolved quickly. This drops to around 20 to 45 percent if complaints are not resolved. Furthermore, of the majority of unhappy customers that do not complain at all, only about 10 to 40 percent will become repeat customers.

THE ROLE OF QUALITY IN SERVICE

For services, research shows that five key dimensions of service quality contribute to customer perceptions:

Reliability—The ability to provide what was promised, dependably and accurately. Examples include customer service representatives responding in the promised time, following customer instructions, providing error-free invoices and statements, and making repairs correctly the first time.

Assurance—The knowledge and courtesy of employees, and their ability to convey trust and confidence. Examples include the ability to answer questions, having the capabilities to do the necessary work, monitoring credit card transactions to avoid possible fraud, and being polite and pleasant during customer transactions.

Tangibles—The physical facilities and equipment, and the appearance of personnel. Tangibles include attractive facilities, appropriately dressed employees, and well-designed forms that are easy to read and interpret.

Empathy—The degree of caring and individual attention provided to customers. Some examples might be the willingness to schedule deliveries at the customer's convenience, explaining technical jargon in a layperson's language, and recognizing regular customers by name.

Responsiveness—The willingness to help customers and provide prompt service. Examples include acting quickly to resolve problems, promptly crediting returned merchandise, and rapidly replacing defective products.

Understanding these features and proactively designing them into services and service delivery processes is an important aspect of a TQ organization.

Companies that have consistently provided superior service—such as IBM, FedEx, Nordstrom, and many others—have certain elements in common:[24]

1. They establish service goals that support business and product-line objectives.
2. They identify and define customer expectations for service quality and responsiveness.
3. They translate customer expectations into clear, deliverable, service features.
4. They set up efficient, responsive, and integrated service delivery systems and organizations.
5. They monitor and control service quality and performance.
6. They provide quick but cost-effective response to customers' needs.

These ideas are embodied in the Malcolm Baldrige Award criteria in the Customer Focus category. The criteria look at how an organization builds relationships to acquire and satisfy customers and to develop repeat business and positive referrals. Included in the criteria requirements are how organizations determine key customer contact requirements, what access mechanisms are available for customers to seek information, conduct business, and make complaints, and how customer contact requirements are deployed along the entire response chain. The criteria also address an organization's complaint management process, and how it ensures prompt and effective problem resolution.

Competing on Agility

Success in globally competitive markets requires a capacity for flexibility and rapid change of product variety; this is called **agility**. **Flexibility** means adapting successfully to changing environmental conditions and process requirements. Flexibility might demand special strategies such as modular designs, sharing components, sharing manufacturing lines, and specialized training for employees. It also involves outsourcing decisions, agreements with key suppliers, and innovative partnering arrangements. **Variety** refers to the ability to produce a wide range of products and options. Companies that can change product lines more rapidly in the face of changing consumer demands and exploit new technologies can gain a competitive advantage in certain markets. E-business, for example, requires and enables more rapid, flexible, and customized responses.

To better understand these issues, we review some key concepts. Basically, there are three types of products: custom products, option-oriented products, and standard products.[25]

Custom products, generally made in small quantities, are designed to meet customers' specifications precisely. Two examples are a wedding gown or a machine tool designed to perform a specific, complex task. The production cost is relatively high and the assurance of quality requires careful attention at every step in the manufacturing process. Because custom products can only be produced on demand, the customer must wait for the product to be made.

Option-oriented products are unique configurations of subassemblies that are designed to fit together. The customer participates in choosing the options to be assembled. A good example is a personal computer system in which the customer defines the types of disk drives, wireless card, memory configurations, and so forth. The subassemblies are made in relatively large quantities; therefore, costs are reduced, and quality is easier to achieve because of repetition. Because the manufacturer cannot anticipate all of the configurations a customer may desire, the customer sometimes must wait while the product is assembled to the desired configuration.

Standard products are made in larger quantities. Examples include radios, TVs, appliances, and most consumer goods found in department stores. The customer has no options to choose from, and quality is easiest to achieve because the product is made the same way every time. Because the manufacturer makes standard products in anticipation of customer demands, the customer will not have to wait for the product unless it is out of stock.

Standard products offer many advantages in terms of manufacturing efficiency, quality, and dependability. Mass production on fixed assembly lines yields high levels of productivity. Thus, standard products are the basis for cost leadership. With fewer different parts to purchase, make, and assemble, quality is generally improved because there is less chance for error. Schedules are more predictable, so dependability is improved. Standard products also simplify purchasing and customer service. Orders of components are more consistent, and shipments can be scheduled more frequently, resulting in lower inventories.

Marketing personnel are concerned with sales and how to respond correctly and successfully in the market. They prefer products to be customized to the individual needs of customers. Custom and option-oriented products can be produced to meet customer expectations, whereas standard products offer little flexibility in meeting changing customer needs. Customer expectations can be incorporated only in the design stages. However, this leads to manufacturing efficiencies. This inherent conflict between manufacturing and marketing must be addressed from a strategic perspective.

In the quick-service restaurant industry, similar strategic choices are made. McDonald's, for example, produces a standard product and achieves an advantage in terms of service delivery. Burger King and Wendy's, by contrast, produce option-oriented products. Although their selection may be greater, these companies sacrifice speed of service. Neither the standard nor the option-oriented approach is necessarily better; each firm must decide what tradeoffs must be made with each approach and select the approach that best provides competitive advantage.

Many products begin as custom products and, over time, become standard products. For instance, Henry Ford was one of the first to standardize production of the automobile. Later, however, consumers demanded more variety of options, and the American automobile evolved into the classic option-oriented product. Customers can now choose from dozens of colors, seat types, engines, transmissions, tires, and other options. Many German and Japanese automobile manufacturers have chosen a strategy that limits the number of options. Few options exist, and some are installed by the dealer rather than the manufacturer. This strategy provides a distinct cost advantage and enables the factory to achieve higher levels of productivity. Flexibility is achieved by offering several model variations of the same car and frequent design changes. The Japanese can produce as many as seven models on a single production line. (Most U.S. manufacturers' production lines are dedicated to a single model.)

Many firms use flexibility and variety as a competitive weapon. Many firms are focusing their strategies on flexibility and variety—more and better product features, factories that can change product lines quickly, expanded customer service, and continually improving new products. For instance, Toshiba's computer factory assembles 9 different word processors on the same production line and 20 varieties of laptop computers on another.[26] The flexible lines guard against running short of a hot model or overproducing one whose sales have slowed. Nissan describes its strategy as "five anys": to make anything in any volume anywhere at any time by anybody. Nissan's high-tech Intelligent Body Assembly System can weld and inspect body parts for any kind of car, all in 46 seconds. As U.S. automakers think about dropping entire car lines, Nissan is gearing up to fill market niches with more models.

From the perspective of gaining competitive advantage, the value of flexibility and variety was illustrated by the "Honda-Yamaha war" in 1981. Honda, whose supremacy in motorcycles was being challenged by Yamaha, responded by introducing 113 new or revamped models in 18 months. Yamaha could only manage 37 model changes and finally announced that it was content to be number two.

The Role of Quality in Agility

To be agile, an organization needs both effective processes and the ability to modify those processes as business conditions change. For example, it requires the ability to continually monitor and sense changing customer needs and expectations, change designs as necessary, and rapidly roll out new processes and products. Drawing on the principles of TQ, a customer-focused organization and a process orientation are necessary prerequisites for agility.

Equally important is the ability of different functions and groups of employees to work together as teams in designing and operating the type of production systems that require continuous change and improvement. In fact, the Baldrige criteria seek evidence on how companies organize and manage work and jobs to achieve "the agility to keep current with business needs" in the Human Resource Focus category. Good supplier relations, a key issue in total quality, are also critical as designs and volumes change.

Competing on Innovation

Many firms focus on research and development as a core component of their strategy. Such firms are on the leading edge of product technology, and their ability to innovate and introduce new products is a critical success factor. Innovation has become the most important factor in satisfying demanding consumers in today's technological world. One need only look at the iPod and iPhone to realize the importance of innovation in the marketplace.

Product performance, not price, is the major selling feature. When competition enters the market and profit margins fall, these companies often drop out of the market while continuing to introduce innovative new products. These companies focus on outstanding product research, design, and development; high product quality; and the ability to modify production facilities to produce new products frequently.

As global competition increases, the ability to innovate has become almost essential for remaining competitive. Many years ago, National Cash Register (NCR), for example, clung to outdated mechanical technologies for a long time, while competitors developed innovative new electronic systems. The lack of innovation nearly destroyed the company. Today, leading companies do not wait for customers to change; they use innovation to create new customer needs and desires. At 3M, for example, every division is expected to derive 25 percent of its sales each year from products that did not exist five years earlier. This forces managers to think seriously about innovation. Being innovative also requires being close to customers. As 3M's CEO once stated:

> We're fighting hard to get our customers into our hallways and our customers into our labs. With some customers, we've loaned them a full-time employee for a couple of years to help them use Six Sigma tools to improve their operations. This is not about getting a fast sale, but we do get something valuable: a much better understanding of our customer's needs.[27]

Such a spirit not only will result in new products but also will help managers to create better processes that improve quality.

The Role of Quality in Innovation

Managing for Innovation is one of the Core Values and Concepts in the Malcolm Baldrige Award criteria. The criteria state that Innovation should lead an organization to new dimensions of performance. Innovation is no longer strictly the purview of research and development departments; innovation is important for all aspects of a business and all processes. Organizations should be led and managed so that innovation becomes part of the culture and is integrated into daily work.

The award criteria encourage innovation through several means:

- The criteria are nonprescriptive. They encourage creativity and breakthrough thinking because they channel activities toward the organization's purpose and are not focused on following specific procedures.
- Customer-driven quality emphasizes the "positive side of quality"—enhancement, new services, and customer relationship management. Success with the positive

side of quality depends heavily on creativity, more so than on steps to reduce errors and defects that rely on well-defined techniques.

- Workforce focus stresses employee involvement, development, and recognition, and encourages creative approaches to improving employee effectiveness, empowerment, and contributions.
- Continuous improvement and learning are integral parts of the activities of all workgroups. This requires analysis and problem solving everywhere within the company. Emphasis on continuous improvement encourages change, innovation, and creative thinking in how work is organized and conducted.
- The focus on future requirements of customers encourages companies to seek innovative and creative ways to serve their patrons.

Competing on Time

In today's fast-paced society, people hate to wait. Time has come to be recognized as one of the most important sources of competitive advantage. **Cycle time** refers to the time it takes to accomplish one cycle of a process (e.g., the time from when a customer orders a product to the time that it is delivered, or the time to introduce a new product). Reductions in cycle time serve two purposes. First, they speed up work processes so that customer response is improved. Second, reductions in cycle time can only be accomplished by streamlining and simplifying processes to eliminate non–value-added steps such as rework. This approach forces improvements in quality by reducing the potential for mistakes and errors. By reducing non-value-added steps, costs are reduced as well. Thus, cycle time reductions often drive simultaneous improvements in organization, quality, cost, and productivity.

The total time required by a company to deliver a finished product that satisfies customers' needs is referred to as the product lead time. This includes time spent on design, engineering, purchasing, manufacturing, testing, packaging, and shipping. Short product lead times offer many advantages. First, they allow companies to introduce new products and penetrate new markets more rapidly (see box "Sending Old Designs Down the Drain"). Being the first to market a new product allows a firm to charge a higher price, at least until competitive products are offered. For example, when first introduced, Motorola's pocket-sized cellular telephone was 50 percent smaller than any competing Japanese product and sold for twice the price; and the Mazda Miata sold for up to $5,000 above sticker price. Second, every month saved in development time can save a large company millions of dollars in expenses. Third, short lead times reduce the need to forecast long-term sales, allow more accurate production plans to be developed, and reduce inventory. Short lead times increase the flexibility of a company to respond to changing customer needs.

The Role of Quality in Time Competitiveness

The Malcolm Baldrige Award criteria emphasize the importance of reducing cycle times in all business processes, particularly the design-to-introduction or innovation cycle time. Success in competitive markets increasingly demands shorter cycles for

Sending Old Designs Down the Drain[28]

Moen Inc. makes faucets for bathrooms and kitchens. In the mid-1990s, as plumbing fixtures became fashion necessities of new homes and remodeling projects, the company needed to provide a much larger set of styles in silver, platinum, and copper, instead of its current product line designed in the 1960s and 1970s. Moen revitalized its product design approach using the Web, collaborating with suppliers in the design process. Previously, engineers would spend six to eight weeks coming up with a new design, burning it onto CDs, and mailing them to suppliers in 14 countries that make the hundreds of parts that go into a faucet. The suppliers would return the CDs with changes and suggestions that needed to be reconciled with each other. Redesign activities and tool design and production might extend this process to up to 24 weeks.

With the Web-based approach, a new faucet goes from drawing board to store shelf in 16 months, down from an average of two years. The time savings allows Moen's engineers to work on three times as many projects, and introduce from 5 to 15 new faucet lines each year. This helped boost sales by 17 percent from 1998 to 2001, higher than the industry average of 9 percent over the same period, and moved Moen from number 12 in market share to a tie for number three with rival Delta Faucet Co.

new or improved product and service introduction. Also, faster and more flexible response to customers is a more critical requirement of business management (see box "Domino's Pizza Changed the Rules").

Significant reductions in cycle time cannot be achieved simply by focusing on individual subprocesses; cross-functional processes must be examined all across the organization. Through these activities, the company comes to understand work at the organizational level and to engage in cooperative behaviors. Major improvements in response time often require work organizations, processes, and paths to be simplified and shortened. To accomplish this, more attention needs to be paid to time performance. This can be done by making response time a key indicator for work unit improvement processes. Simplified processes reduce opportunities for errors, leading to improved quality. Improvements in response time often result from increased understanding of internal customer-supplier relationships and

Domino's Pizza Changed the Rules[29]

Tom Monaghan, founder of Domino's Pizza, determined that customers ordering home-delivered pizza wanted their pizzas quickly because they were usually hungry when they ordered. He also understood that people anticipated having their pizzas delivered anywhere from 20 minutes to 2 hours after placing their orders. This wide variation in delivery was acceptable because people had been conditioned to accept that there were no other options available. Because fast, consistent delivery was not an option, customers placed their pizza orders based only on taste and price.

Monaghan changed all that by promising fast and consistent delivery—30 minutes or less—or the order would be free. Domino's exceeded customers expectations. Today, this "delighter/exciter" has become a satisfier, and consistently fast delivery is often the first criterion in the pizza-ordering decision process.

teamwork. Cutting response time requires a significant commitment from all employees and leadership from top management. Such efforts must involve the entire organization and often require organizational redesign.

INFORMATION AND KNOWLEDGE FOR COMPETITIVE ADVANTAGE

Managing information and knowledge can require a significant commitment of resources as the sources of information grow dramatically each year. Information from internal operations, from the Internet, and from business-to-business (B2B) and business-to-consumer (B2C) communications challenges organizational abilities to provide the information that people need to do their work, keep current, and improve.

Understanding the impact of business decisions on results and benchmarking results against competitors and industry leaders has taken on increased importance in recent years. A supply of consistent, accurate, and timely information across all functional areas of business provides real-time information for evaluation and improvement of processes, products, and services to meet business objectives and rapidly changing customer needs—in short, to create and sustain a competitive advantage (see box "The Data Will Set You Free"). This requires a systematic and effective system for measuring performance and managing knowledge assets.

Organizations need performance measures for three reasons:

- to lead the entire organization in a particular direction; that is, to drive strategies and organizational change;
- to manage the resources needed to travel in this direction by evaluating the effectiveness of action plans; and
- to operate the processes that make the organization work and continuously improve.[31]

"THE DATA WILL SET YOU FREE"[30]

In the early 1990s, Boeing's assembly lines were morasses of inefficiency. A manual numbering system dating back to World War II bomber days was used to keep track of an airplane's four million parts and 170 miles of wiring; changing a part on a 737's landing gear meant renumbering 464 pages of drawings. Factory floors were covered with huge tubs of spare parts worth millions of dollars. In an attempt to grab market share from rival Airbus, the company discounted planes deeply and was buried by an onslaught of orders. The attempt to double production rates, coupled with implementation of a new production control system, resulted in Boeing being forced to shut down its 737 and 747 lines for 27 days in October 1997, leading to a $178 million loss and a shakeup of top management. Much of the blame was focused on Boeing's financial practices and lack of real-time data. With a new CFO and finance team, the company created a "control panel" of vital measures such as material costs, inventory turns, overtime, and defects using a color-coded spreadsheet. For the first time, Boeing was able to generate a series of bar charts showing which of its programs were creating value and which were destroying it. The results were eye-opening; not only did they help improve operations, but they also helped formulate a growth plan. As one manager noted, "The data will set you free."

A survey conducted by William Schiemann & Associates found that measurement-managed companies are more likely to be in the top third of their industry financially, complete organizational changes more successfully, reach clear agreement on strategy among senior managers, enjoy favorable levels of cooperation and teamwork among management, undertake greater self-monitoring of performance by employees, and have a greater willingness by employees to take risks.[32]

Many managers and quality professionals view measurement activities only in terms of outputs from the production system. This is a mistake because a broad base of measurements, tied together by strong information systems, can help to align a company's operations with its strategic directions.

Most businesses have traditionally relied on organizational performance data based almost solely on financial or factory productivity considerations, such as return on investment, earnings per share, direct labor efficiency, and machine utilization.[33] Unfortunately, many of these indicators are inaccurate and stress quantity over quality.[34] They reward the wrong behavior; lack predictive power; do not capture key business changes until it is too late; reflect functions, not cross-functional processes; and give inadequate consideration to difficult-to-quantify resources such as intellectual capital.[35] Today, many organizations create a "balanced scorecard" of measures that provide a comprehensive view of business performance.

The term **balanced scorecard** was coined by Robert Kaplan and David Norton of the Harvard Business School in response to the limitations of traditional accounting measures. Its purpose is "to translate strategy into measures that uniquely communicate your vision to the organization." Their version of the balanced scorecard consists of four perspectives:

- *Financial Perspective*: Measures the ultimate results that the business provides to its shareholders. This includes profitability, revenue growth, return on investment, economic value added (EVA), and shareholder value.
- *Internal Perspective*: Focuses attention on the performance of the key internal processes that drive the business. This includes such measures as quality levels, productivity, cycle time, and cost.
- *Customer Perspective*: Focuses on customer needs and satisfaction as well as market share. This includes service levels, satisfaction ratings, and repeat business.
- *Innovation and Learning Perspective*: Directs attention to the basis of a future success—the organization's people and infrastructure. Key measures might include intellectual assets, employee satisfaction, market innovation, and skills development.

A good balanced scorecard contains both leading and lagging measures and indicators. *Lagging measures* (outcomes) tell what has happened; *leading measures* (performance drivers) predict what will happen. For example, customer survey results about recent transactions might be a leading indicator for customer retention (a lagging indicator); employee satisfaction might be a leading indicator for turnover, and so on. These measures and indicators should also establish cause-and-effect relationships across perspectives. Clarke American structures its performance measurements along two unique dimensions: how they are used—to either *change the business* or *run the business*—and whether they are predictive (*leading*) or diagnostic (*lagging*). "Change the business" measures are those most critical to the achievement of strategic objectives and evaluate organizational performance, such as total order cycle time and implemented ideas. "Run the business" measures are those used for daily operations and include measures of accuracy, responsiveness, and timeliness for deliveries.

Kaplan and Norton's balanced scorecard is only one version of performance measurement systems that have emerged as companies recognize the need for a broad set of performance measures that provide a comprehensive view of business performance. Raytheon's version defines Customer, Shareholder, Process, and People perspectives. The Malcolm Baldrige Criteria for Performance Excellence Results category groups performance measures into six sets:

- Product and service outcomes
- Customer-focused outcomes
- Financial and market outcomes
- Human resource outcomes
- Organizational effectiveness outcomes
- Leadership and social responsibility outcomes

These performance indicators span the entire business operation, from suppliers to customers, and from frontline workers to top levels of management.

Wainwright Industries, for example, aligns the company's business objectives with customers' critical success factors: price, minimal line defects, delivery, and partnership. This alignment process prompted the development of five key strategic indicator categories: safety, internal customer satisfaction, external customer satisfaction, defect rate, and business performance. Within each category, Wainwright developed specific indicators and goals. For instance, for external customer satisfaction, they measure a satisfaction index and monthly complaints; for business performance, they track sales, capital expenditure, and market share for drawn housings.

Comparative information includes comparisons relative to direct competitors as well as best-practices benchmarking, either inside or outside of one's industry. Such information allows organizations to know where they stand relative to competitors and other leading companies, provides the impetus for breakthrough improvement, and helps them understand their own processes before they compare performance levels. For example, Corning Telecommunications Products Division (TPD) uses a Competitive Analysis Process to gather publicly available data to analyze competitors' intentions and capabilities, including manufacturing capacity, cost, and cost of incremental capacity, and determines product capability and quality through direct evaluation of competitors' products.

Companies need to ask the key question: How do overall improvements in product and service quality and operational performance relate to changes in company financial performance and customer satisfaction? Leading companies employ

Understanding the Drivers of Business Success[36]

IBM's AS/400 Division in Rochester, Minnesota, recipient of the 1990 Malcolm Baldrige National Quality Award, initiated a study to determine whether any relationships existed among a variety of measurements, such as market share, overall customer satisfaction, employee morale, job satisfaction, warranty costs, inventory costs, product scrap, and productivity. Using 10 years of data, the researchers identified a strong correlation among market share, customer satisfaction, productivity, warranty cost, and employee satisfaction. By developing a statistical model relating these variables, IBM learned that to improve employee satisfaction, a manager must focus on improving job satisfaction, satisfaction with management, and satisfaction with having the right skills for the job. This will positively impact productivity, market share, and customer satisfaction. Improving employee satisfaction will also directly impact productivity and customer satisfaction and will decrease warranty costs. Decreasing warranty costs will directly impact customer satisfaction and market share.

Improving customer satisfaction also will directly impact market share. These relationships provide empirical evidence to support the conventional wisdom of TQ that we noted in many chapters of this book: that improving the human element in organizations positively impacts customers as well as business success.

a variety of statistical tools and structured approaches for analyzing data and turning it into useful information. Fuji-Xerox, a Japanese subsidiary of Xerox, uses a variety of statistical techniques such as regression and analysis of variance to develop mathematical models relating such factors as copy quality, machine malfunctions, and maintenance time to customer satisfaction results. Such approaches can provide an indication of important cause-and-effect relationships (for another perspective, see box "Understanding the Drivers of Business Success").

STRATEGIC PLANNING FOR PERFORMANCE EXCELLENCE

In the executive suite at Best Buy's Minneapolis headquarters is a mock "retail hospital"—including a row of beds in which effigies of retailers like Kmart and Woolworth lie with their corporate logos propped up on pillows and their awful financial results displayed on bedside charts. A sign nearby reads:[37]

This Is Where Companies Go When Their Strategies Get Sick

One of the critical aspects of any organization that requires the attention of senior leadership is strategic planning. Through strategic planning, leaders mold an organization's future and manage change by focusing on an ideal vision of what the organization should and could be three, five, or more years in the future. The objective of strategic planning is to build a posture that is so strong in selective ways that the organization can achieve its goals despite unforeseeable external forces.

The role of quality in strategic planning can be viewed in two ways: first, how quality and performance excellence are reflected in an organization's strategy, and, second, how TQ concepts and practices can improve the strategic planning process.

Quality and Performance Excellence as a Strategic Focus

Effective strategies develop around a few key concepts and thrusts that provide focus. The essence of strategy is to build a posture that is so strong in selective ways that the organization can achieve its goals despite unforeseeable external forces that may arise. The traditional focus of business strategies has been finance and marketing, which parallel two of the principal sources of competitive advantage—cost and differentiation—discussed earlier in this chapter. Performance excellence leads to improvements in both areas, and therefore, can be viewed as a strategy in itself, particularly when one considers the importance of meeting customer wants and needs. Many firms have recognized that a strategy driven by quality can lead to significant market advantages. Today, it is relatively common to see quality principles integrated into most strategic business plans; that is, for many organizations, quality has become a basic operating philosophy that provides the foundation for effective management.

The integration of quality into strategic business planning is the result of a natural evolution. For most new companies—or those that have enjoyed a reasonable measure of success—quality often takes a back seat to increasing sales, expanding capacity, or boosting production, and strategic planning usually focuses exclusively on financial and marketing strategies. As a company begins to face increasing competition, cost-cutting objectives take precedence. Some departments or individuals may champion quality initiatives, but quality is not integrated in the company's strategic business plan. However, in the face of market crises and rising consumer expectations, quality begins to take on increasing importance and becomes an integral part of the overall strategic plan and is viewed as a central operating strategy.

Quality in the Process of Strategic Planning

Strategic planning helps leadership mold an organization's future and manage change by focusing on an ideal vision of what the organization should and could be 10 to 20 years in the future and developing objectives and action plans both in the short and longer term to achieve that vision.

Many organizations do a poor job of strategic planning simply because they do not view it as a business process. This is where quality principles can have a significant impact and help establish a better performance excellence system. The role of strategic planning, in addition to creating viable directions and specific objectives, is to align work processes with the company strategic directions, thereby ensuring that improvement and learning reinforce company priorities. Using a systematic process helps to optimize the use of resources, ensure the availability of trained employees, and ensure bridging between short-term and longer-term requirements that may entail capital expenditures or supplier development, for example.

In viewing strategic planning as a process, an organization needs to:

- plan for the long term, and understand the key influences, risks, challenges, and other requirements that might affect the organization's future opportunities and directions. This is to help ensure that short-term action plans are aligned with the organization's longer-term strategic directions.

- project the future competitive environment to help detect and reduce competitive threats, shorten reaction time, and identify opportunities.
- develop action plans and deploy resources—particularly human resources—to achieve alignment and consistency, and provide a basis for setting and communicating priorities for ongoing improvement activities.
- ensure that deployment will be effective—that a measurement system enables tracking of action plan achievement in all areas.

Strategic planning consists of two principal activities: *development* and *implementation*. Strategy development consists of defining the mission of the organization—the concept of the business and the vision of where it is headed; setting objectives—translating the mission into specific performance objectives; and defining a strategy—determining specific actions to achieve the performance objectives. Implementation focuses on executing the strategy effectively and efficiently, as well as on evaluating performance and making corrective adjustments when necessary.

Strategy Development

The organization's leaders first must explore and agree upon the mission, vision, and guiding principles of the organization; these form the foundation for the strategic plan. The **mission** of a firm defines its reason for existence. For example, the mission of Premier, Inc. is *To improve the health of communities.* A firm's mission guides the development of strategies by different groups within the firm. It establishes the context within which daily operating decisions are made, and it sets limits on available strategic options. In addition, it helps to make tradeoffs among the various performance measures and between short- and long-term goals.

The **vision** describes where the organization is headed and what it intends to be. (See Chapter 9 for a discussion of vision from a leadership perspective.) Premier's vision is stated as its "Big Hairy Audacious Goal"—*Premier's Owners will be the leading healthcare systems in their markets, and, with them, Premier will be a major influence in reshaping healthcare.* It is brief and memorable, inspiring and challenging, appeals to all stakeholders, and describes an ideal state.

The **values**, or **guiding principles** direct the journey to a vision by defining attitudes and policies for all employees that are reinforced through conscious and subconscious behavior at all levels of the organization. For Premier, the core values are

> ***Integrity** of the individual and the enterprise.*
>
> ***A passion for performance** and a bias for action, creating real value for all stakeholders, and leading the pace.*
>
> ***Innovation**: Seeking breakthrough opportunities, taking risks, and initiating meaningful change.*
>
> ***Focus on people**: Showing concern and respect for all with whom we work, building collaborative relationships with the community, our customers, co-workers, and business associates.*

Not all companies clearly separate their mission, vision, and values.

The mission, vision, and guiding principles serve as the foundation for strategic planning. Top management and others who lead, especially the CEO, must articulate them. They also have to be transmitted, practiced, and reinforced through symbolic and real action before they become "real" to the employees and the people, groups, and organizations in the external environment that do business with the firm. It does not matter what you call them; what is important is that a company can articulate them and more importantly, commit to them.

Although an organization's mission, vision, and values rarely change (although they might be tweaked to reflect changing business directions), the environment in which the organization exists usually does. Thus, strategy development requires an assessment of the organizational environment, addressing such factors as customer and market requirements, expectations, and opportunities; technological and other innovations that might affect products or operations; changes in the global or national economy; partner and supply chain needs; and so on. Of critical importance to any organization is an assessment of its **strategic challenges**, those pressures that exert a decisive influence on an organization's likelihood of future success (see box "Strategic Challenges in Health Care"). Strategic challenges frequently are driven by factors that influence an organization's future competitive position relative to other providers of similar products or services. These might include operational costs (e.g., materials, labor, or geographic location); expanding or decreasing markets; mergers or acquisitions both by the organization and by its competitors; economic conditions, including fluctuating demand and local and global economic

Strategic Challenges In Health Care[38]

Like most health care organizations today, North Mississippi Medical Center (NMMC) faces strategic challenges such as shortages of health care providers and unique challenges in their community such as a high poverty level, poor health status, and lack of health care insurance. Their most significant strategic challenges are organized by their five critical success factors:

PEOPLE – Maintain and enhance our employees' satisfaction, skills and engagement. Recruit and retain skilled staff. Develop staff and physician leaders.

SERVICE – Increase our patients' and physicians' satisfaction. Enhance our patient-customer loyalty.

QUALITY – Provide high level, evidence-based, quality care and maintain patient safety.

FINANCIAL – Generate the financial resources necessary to support the organization in an environment of reimbursement pressures and increasing charity care.

GROWTH – Continue to expand in areas consistent with our Mission.

Identifying and balancing these critical success factors and challenges is core to how NMMC organizes, aligns, and links their meetings, analyses, challenges, goals, performance indicators, and action plans. During their planning process, they identify two types of goals for each critical success factor:

- RUN-THE-BUSINESS goals, which improve or maintain established functions, address long-standing challenges, and utilize key process indicators; and
- GROW-THE-BUSINESS goals, which stretch the organization with a new service, a monumental improvement in an existing service, or address a new challenge.

downturns; the cyclical nature of the industry; the introduction of new or substitute products or services; rapid technological changes; or new competitors entering the market. In addition, an organization may face challenges related to the recruitment, hiring, and retention of a qualified workforce. Understanding these issues is often facilitated using SWOT (strengths, weaknesses, opportunities, threats) analyses and forms the basis for formulating key strategic objectives.

Strategy development leads to clear definitions of strategies, objectives, and action plans. **Strategies** are broad statements that set the direction for the organization to take in realizing its mission and vision. A strategy might be directed toward becoming a preferred supplier, a low-cost producer, a market innovator, or a high-end or customized service provider. **Strategic objectives** are what an organization must change or improve to remain or become competitive. They are typically focused externally and relate to customer, market, product, service, or technological opportunities and challenges. Strategic objectives set an organization's long-term direction and guide resource allocation decisions. For example, a strategic objective for a supplier in a highly competitive industry might be to develop and maintain a price leadership position. Specific **action plans** derive from strategy and clearly describe the things that need to be done, human resource plans and support, performance measures and indicators, and resource deployment. This process is summarized in Figure 5.3.

Quality and Strategy Development The principles of total quality can help improve an organization's strategic planning process and therefore lead to better strategies. Effective strategic planning depends upon a clear understanding of customer and market needs and expectations, as well as the competitive environment

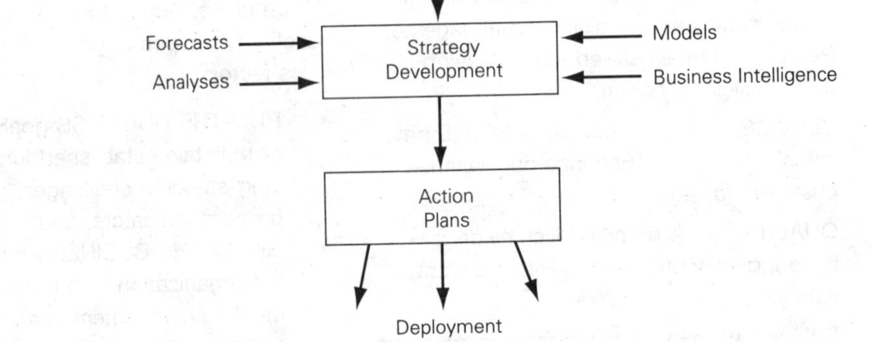

FIGURE 5.3 STRATEGIC PLANNING PROCESS

and internal capabilities. The Ritz-Carlton, for instance, evaluates all action plans on how effectively they address customer requirements. A key goal is to become the first hospitality company with 100 percent customer retention; all plans must address this goal.

The focus on teamwork creates an expectation that everyone in the organization play a role in the formulation of the strategy. Top management, employees, and even customers or suppliers actively participate in the planning process in many organizations. At Solar Turbines, Inc., for example, the strategy development process involves people from all parts of its worldwide organization, customers, and suppliers. Sales, marketing, service, engineering, and manufacturing people in functional and cross-functional teams perform information gathering, analysis, and conclusions. This information is carried forward to the leadership system committees and the Operations Council where it is integrated and synthesized into strategies and critical success factor goals. It is not unusual for customers and suppliers to be involved in strategic planning efforts because of their importance in the supply chain. Customers and suppliers may offer vital advice to an organization as it plans for the future.

The focus on measurement and objective reasoning introduces a reality check in determining the effectiveness of strategy and performance in meeting goals and objectives. The notion of continuous improvement leads organizations to understand how to improve their strategic planning process (see box "Searching for Strategy"). The aspects of this process that could be improved are the forecasting of future demand, assessment of internal capabilities, and integration of internal

Searching for Strategy[39]

Xerox, Ford, Microsoft, Motorola, Hewlett-Packard, and other companies have used an approach called the Search Conference method to facilitate their strategic planning processes. A Search Conference is a participative event that enables a large group to collectively create a plan that its members will implement. Typically, 20 to 40 people from an organization work progressively for two or three days on planning tasks in large group plenary sessions.

They develop long-term strategic visions, achievable goals, and concrete action plans. All of the work is conducted in self-managed teams that are responsible for the entire planning process. Even after the conference, those who created the plan are responsible for its implementation. This democratic approach gives those employees most affected by the change more control over direction setting and policy deployment.

Senior management cannot manipulate a Search Conference agenda to steer participants in some predetermined direction. Furthermore, everything that is discussed is public information. The intended result is to produce a committed group of knowledgeable people who have a deep understanding of the challenges confronting their organization, agreement about the ideals the strategy is supposed to serve, action plans that are aligned with those ideals, a social mechanism for participation, and a process for engaging the whole system in the strategy implementation. As one Xerox vice president reflected, "We used the output from the Search Conference teams in our annual planning process to develop our business strategy for the next three years. Our culture has engineered a big shift; we've moved the [unit's] members from being highly dependent on top-down planning to acting like entrepreneurs."

and external perspectives into the planning process. One way of doing this is by studying effective processes used by others and adapting new ideas into their own organizations.

Strategy Implementation

Top management requires a method to ensure that their plans and strategies are successfully executed (the term "deployed" is frequently used) within the organization. The Japanese deploy strategy through a process known as **hoshin planning,** or policy deployment. **Hoshin** means policy or policy deployment. Policy deployment is a systems approach to managing change in critical business processes. It emphasizes organization-wide planning and setting of priorities, providing resources to meet objectives, and measuring performance as a basis for improving performance. Policy deployment is essentially a TQ-based approach to executing a strategy. King describes it eloquently:[40]

> Imagine an organization that knows what customers will want five to ten years from now and exactly what they will do to meet and exceed all expectations. Imagine a planning system that has integrated [Plan, Do, Study, Act] language and activity based on clear, long-term thinking, a realistic measurement system with a focus on process and results, identification of what's important, alignment of groups, decisions by people who have the necessary information, planning integrated with daily activity, good vertical communication, cross-functional communication, and everyone planning for himself or herself, and the buy-in that results. That is hoshin planning.

With policy deployment, top management is responsible for developing and communicating a vision, then building organization-wide commitment to its achievement.[41] This vision is deployed through the development and execution of annual policy statements (plans). All levels of employees actively participate in generating a strategy and action plans to attain the vision.

At each level, progressively more detailed and concrete means to accomplish the annual plans are determined. The plans are hierarchical, cascading downward from top management's plans. There should be a clear link to common goals and activities throughout the organizational hierarchy. Policy deployment provides frequent evaluation and modification based on feedback from regularly scheduled audits of the process. Plans and actions are developed based on analysis of the root causes of a problem, rather than only on the symptoms.

Planning has a high degree of detail, including the anticipation of possible problems during implementation. The emphasis is on the improvement of the process, as opposed to a results-only orientation.

Policy deployment starts with the senior managers of the company. The senior managers establish the vision and core objectives of the company. An example of an objective might be "to improve delivery," which supports the long-term vision of "to be the industry leader in customer satisfaction." Middle management negotiates with senior management regarding the goals that will achieve the objectives. Goals specify numerically the degree of change that is expected. These should be challenging, but people should feel that they are attainable.

Strategies specify the means to achieve the goals. They include more specific actions to be taken. Middle managers are responsible for managing the resources to accomplish the goals. Middle management then negotiates with the implementation teams regarding the performance measures that are used to indicate progress toward accomplishing the strategies.

Measures are specific checkpoints to ensure the effectiveness of individual elements of the strategy. The implementation teams are empowered to manage the actions and schedule their activities. Senior management then uses a review process to understand both the progress of the implementation teams and the success of their planning system. The Seven Management and Planning Tools described in Chapter 4 are used extensively in the process.

Linking Human Resource Plans and Business Strategy

Whenever an organization seeks to do something different, people are invariably impacted. Thus, it is important to consider organizational change and plan for necessary human resource changes that may be needed. These changes might include new training initiatives, work reorganization, or compensation and incentive approaches. For example, to address a national nursing shortage, Baptist Hospital's strategy for nurse recruitment and retention required numerous human resource changes, such as revamping the clinical ladder program, pay adjustments to recruit graduate nurses, increasing the number of scholarships to nursing students, and involving experienced nurses to speak to high school students to raise interest in the field. Motorola's Commercial, Government, and Industrial Solutions Sector ties the following human resource plans into its strategic planning process: breakthrough changes in work design, team member development, education, and training; compensation, recognition, and benefits; and human resources needs such as identification and recruitment. When GE decided to adopt a Six Sigma framework for the organization, it was necessary to train 12,000 black-belt leaders to implement the plan. Incentives for project champions in upper management were restructured to account for 40 percent of their bonuses.

Strategic human resource plans often include one or more of the following:

- Redesign of the work organization to increase empowerment and decision-making or team-based participation
- Initiatives for promoting greater labor/management cooperation, such as union partnerships
- Initiatives to foster knowledge sharing and organizational learning
- Partnerships with educational institutions to help ensure the future supply of well-prepared employees

Whatever the choices, it is vital that they support the organization's overall strategy. For example, suppose that a firm identifies its critical success factors as customer satisfaction, employee satisfaction, market growth, and world-class performance. Each critical success factor will have one or more strategic objectives defined through the firm's strategic planning process. Because successful accomplishment of these strategic objectives will depend on execution by the firm's workforce, it is important that key

TABLE 5.1 ALIGNMENT OF HUMAN RESOURCE PLANS WITH CRITICAL SUCCESS FACTORS AND STRATEGIC OBJECTIVES

Critical Success Factor and Strategic Objectives	Human Resource Plans
Customer Satisfaction	
Strengthen customer relationships by improving responsiveness	Implement new training program for front line staff
Employee Satisfaction	
Encourage employee development and career planning to capitalize on workforce diversity	Develop, implement, and deliver online training courses Require leadership rotation in team projects
Market Growth	
Pursue new and expanded market opportunities	Actively participate on marketing teams to determine HR requirements Develop a hiring plan for new product development and marketing initiatives
World Class Performance	
Improve process quality	Support Six Sigma training initiatives
Reduce costs to world-class benchmark levels	Develop lean expertise throughout the workforce

human resource plans, such as enhancing skills, knowledge, and motivation, be identified to support these strategic objectives. Some examples are shown in Table 5.1.

THE SEVEN MANAGEMENT AND PLANNING TOOLS

The "seven management and planning tools" had their roots in post–World War II operations research developments in the United States, but were refined in Japan. They were popularized in the United States by the consulting firm GOAL/QPC and have been used by a number of firms since 1984 to improve their quality planning efforts. These tools can be used to address problems typically faced by managers who are called upon to structure unstructured ideas, organize and control large, complex projects, and to more effectively develop strategy. We will illustrate them in the context of strategic planning for a hypothetical high-technology consumer electronics company, MicroTech. MicroTech's mission is

> to design and manufacture miniature electronics products utilizing radio frequency technologies, digital signal-processing technologies, and state-of-the-art surface mount manufacturing techniques.

AFFINITY DIAGRAMS

The affinity diagram is a tool for organizing a large number of ideas, opinions, and facts relating to a broad problem or subject area. In developing a vision statement, for example, senior management might conduct a brainstorming session to develop a list of ideas to incorporate into the vision. This list might include

low product maintenance
satisfied employees features
courteous order entry
low price innovation
quick delivery
growth in shareholder value
teamwork
responsive technical support
personal employee growth
low production costs
innovative product
high return on investment
constant technology
high quality
motivated employees
unique products
small, lightweight designs

Once a large number of ideas have been generated, they can be grouped according to their "affinity," or relationship, to each other. An affinity diagram for the preceding list is shown in Figure 5.4.

INTERRELATIONSHIP DIGRAPH

An interrelationship digraph identifies and explores causal relationships among related concepts or ideas. It shows that every idea can be logically linked with more than one other idea at a time, and allows for "lateral thinking" rather than "linear thinking." This technique is often used after the affinity diagram has clarified issues and problems. Figure 5.5 shows an example of how the key strategic factors for MicroTech relate to one another. The elements having the most net outward-pointing arrows (number out minus number in) represent the primary drivers of

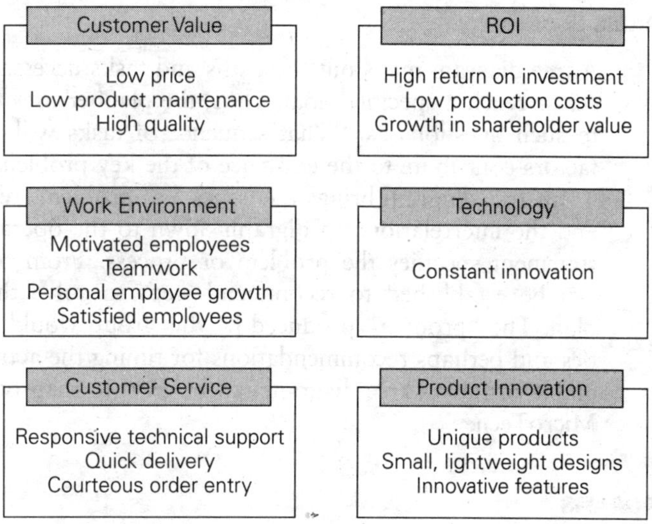

FIGURE 5.4 | AFFINITY DIAGRAM FOR MICROTECH

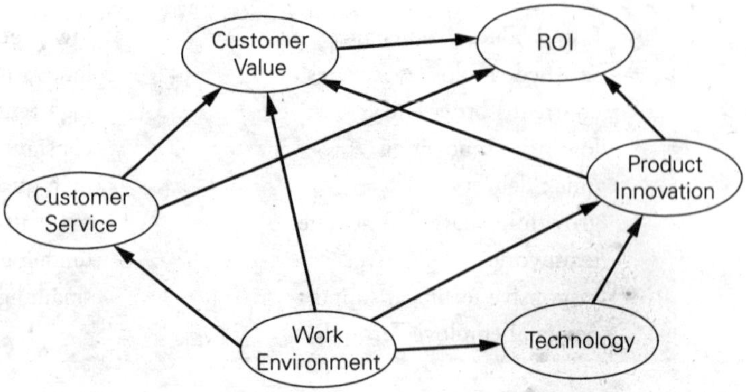

FIGURE 5.5 | INTERRELATIONSHIP DIGRAPH OF MICROTECH'S STRATEGIC FACTORS

the company's vision: in this case, work environment and customer service. As a result, MicroTech might develop the following vision statement:

> We will provide exceptional value to our customers in terms of cost-effective products and services of the highest quality, leading to superior value to our shareholders. We will provide a supportive work environment that promotes personal growth and the pursuit of excellence and allows each employee to achieve his or her full potential. We are committed to advancing the state of the art in electronics miniaturization and related technologies and to developing market opportunities that are built upon our unique technical expertise.

TREE DIAGRAMS

A tree diagram maps out the paths and tasks necessary to complete a specific project or reach a specified goal. Thus, the planner uses this technique to seek answers to such questions as "What sequence of tasks will address the issue?" or "What factors contribute to the existence of the key problem?"

A tree diagram brings the issues and problems revealed by the affinity diagram and the interrelationship digraph down to the operational planning stage. A clear statement specifies the problem or process. From this general statement, a team can be established to recommend steps to solve the problem or implement the plan. The "product" produced by this group would be a tree diagram with activities and perhaps recommendations for timing the activities. Figure 5.6 shows an example of how a tree diagram can be used to map out key goals and strategies for MicroTech.

MATRIX DIAGRAMS

Matrix diagrams are "spreadsheets" that graphically display relationships between ideas, activities, or other dimensions in such a way as to provide logical connecting points between each item. A matrix diagram is one of the most versatile tools in quality planning and was used in quality function deployment in Chapter 3. One example

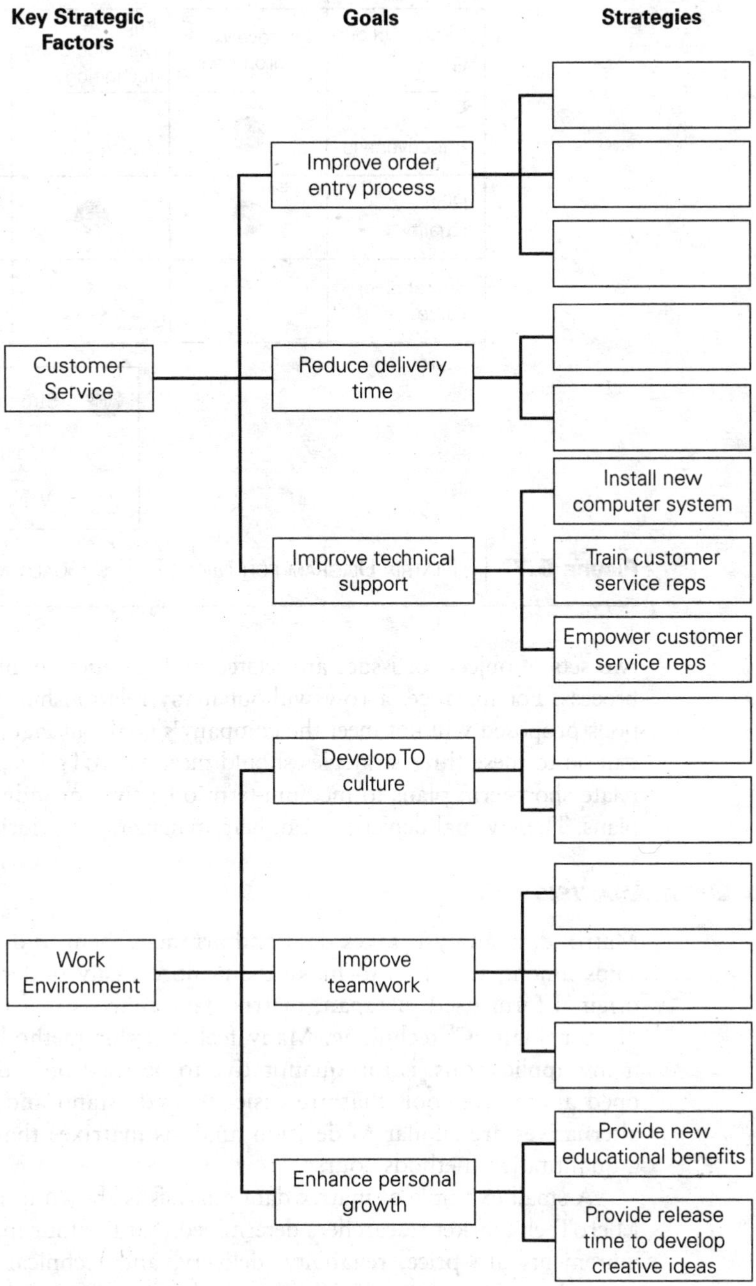

FIGURE 5.6 TREE DIAGRAM OF MICROTECH GOALS AND STRATEGIES

is shown in Figure 5.7. Here, we have listed the three principal goals articulated in MicroTech's vision statement along the rows and the key strategies down the columns. Typically, symbols such as •, ○, and Δ are used to denote strong, medium, and weak relationships, respectively. Matrix diagrams provide a picture of how well

Goals \ Actions	Improve Work Environment	Improve Manufacturing Technology	Develop New Products
Cost Effectiveness	●	○	
High Quality	●	●	
Shareholder Value		△	●

● = Strong relationship
○ = Medium relationship
△ = Weak relationship

FIGURE 5.7 | MATRIX DIAGRAM FOR MICROTECH'S GOALS AND STRATEGIES

two sets of objects or issues are related and can identify missing pieces in the thought process. For instance, a row without many relationships might indicate that the actions proposed will not meet the company's goals. In Figure 4, we see that focused attention to these three strategies should meet MicroTech's goals. Other matrices might relate short-term plans to medium-term objectives or individual actions to short-term plans. These visual depictions can help managers set priorities on plans and actions.

MATRIX DATA ANALYSIS

Matrix data analysis takes data and arranges them to display quantitative relationships among variables to make them more easily understood and analyzed. In its original form used in Japan, matrix data analysis is a rigorous, statistically based "factor analysis" technique. Many feel that this method, although worthwhile for many applications, is too quantitative to be used on a daily basis and have developed alternative tools that are easier to understand and implement. Some of these alternatives are similar to decision analysis matrixes that you may have studied in a quantitative methods course.

A small example of matrix data analysis is shown in Figure 5.8. In this example, MicroTech market researchers determined that the four most important consumer requirements are price, reliability, delivery, and technical support. Through market research, an importance weighting was developed for each. They also determined numerical ratings for the company and their best competitor. Such an analysis provides information as to which actions the company should deploy to better meet key customer requirements. For example, in Figure 5.9, reliability is the highest in importance, and MicroTech has a narrow lead over its best competitor; thus, they should continue to strive for improving product reliability. Also, technical support is of relatively high importance, but MicroTech is perceived to be inferior to its best competitor in this category. Thus, improving the quality of support services should be a major objective.

Requirement	Importance Weight	Best Competitor Evaluation	MicroTech Evaluation	Difference*
Price	.2	6	8	+2
Reliability	.4	7	8	+1
Delivery	.1	8	5	−3
Technical support	.3	7	5	−2

*MicroTech Evaluation-Best Competitor Evaluation

FIGURE 5.8 | MATRIX DATA ANALYSIS OF CUSTOMER REQUIREMENTS FOR MICROTECH

PROCESS DECISION PROGRAM CHARTS

A process decision program chart (PDPC) is a method for mapping out every conceivable event and contingency that can occur when moving from a problem statement to possible solutions. A PDPC takes each branch of a tree diagram, anticipates possible problems, and provides countermeasures that will (1) prevent the deviation from occurring, or (2) be in place if the deviation does occur. Figure 5.9 shows one example for implementing a strategy to educate and train all employees to use a new computer system.

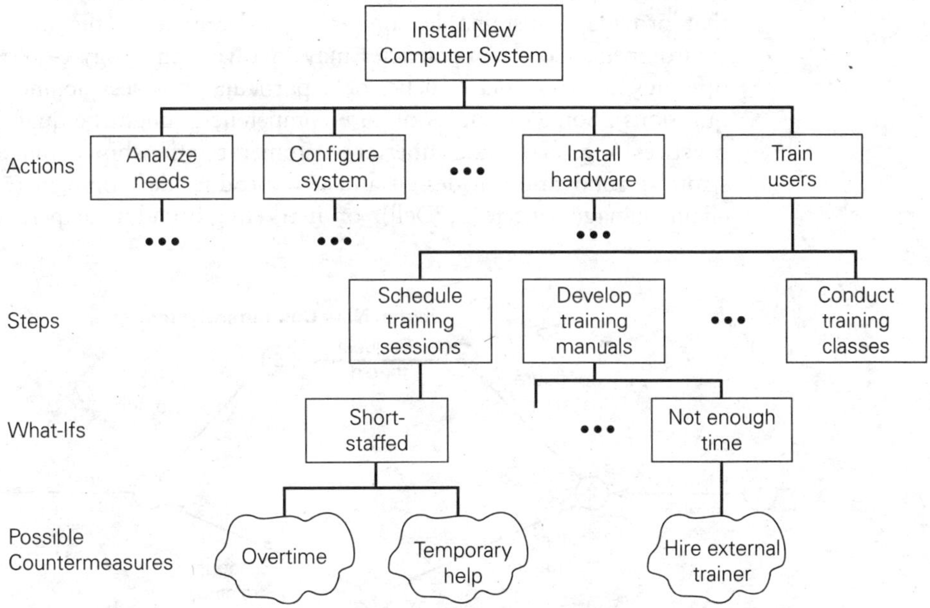

FIGURE 5.9 | A PROCESS DECISION PROGRAM CHART

Arrow Diagrams

For years, construction planners have used arrow diagrams to sequence and schedule project tasks. Arrow diagramming has also been taught extensively in quantitative methods, operations management, and other business and engineering courses in the United States for a number of years. Unfortunately, its use has generally been confined to technical experts. Adding arrow diagramming to the "quality toolbox" has made it more widely available to general managers and other nontechnical personnel. Figure 5.10 shows an example. Time estimates can easily be added to each activity in order to schedule and control the project.

Core Competencies and Strategic Work System Design

Work systems, which refers to how the work of an organization is accomplished, coordinate the internal work processes and the external resources necessary to develop, produce, and deliver products and services to customers and to succeed in marketplace. Work systems involve the workforce, key suppliers and partners, contractors, collaborators, and other components of the supply chain needed to produce and deliver products, services, and business and support processes. For example, Henry Ford's early factories did everything from steel-making to final assembly; today's automobile companies are characterized by complex networks of suppliers that are much more decentralized. Decisions about work systems are strategic. These decisions involve protecting and capitalizing on core competencies and deciding what should be procured or produced outside the organization in order to be efficient and sustainable in the marketplace.

Core competencies refers to an organization's areas of greatest expertise that provide a sustainable competitive advantage in the marketplace or service environment. Core competencies may involve technology expertise, unique service offerings, a marketplace niche, or a particular business acumen (e.g., business acquisitions). Some examples of core competencies might be quality and productivity practices (e.g., Toyota), superior customer relationship management (e.g., Nordstrom's), innovation in design and new product development (e.g., Apple), supply chain management (e.g., Dell), or marketing/branding expertise (e.g., Procter &

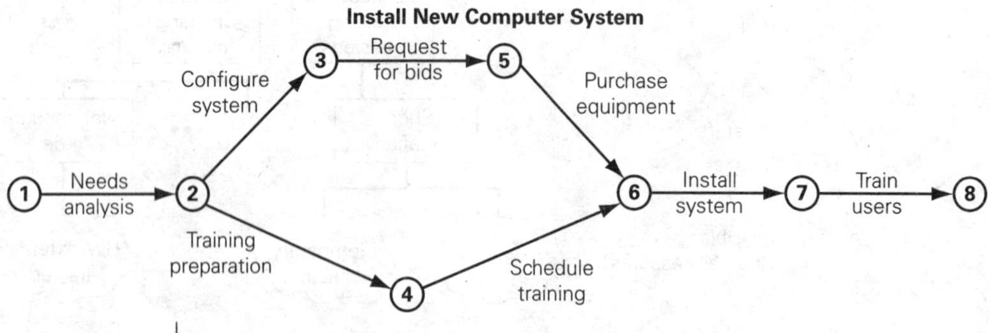

Figure 5.10 An Arrow Diagram for Project Planning

Gamble). An organization needs to understand its core competencies and how they support the organization's mission, enable it to compete against its competitors, and help drive strategic objectives and action plans.

Some contemporary theories suggest that business activities that do not make up an organization's core competency should be outsourced. **Outsourcing** is the practice of transferring the operations of a business function to an outside supplier. Many organizations have done this; for example, manufacturing or assembly, information technology operations, human resource management, and customer service telephone support operations. Much outsourcing is done through offshoring, in which the outsourced function is relegated to foreign shores. The opposite of outsourcing is **vertical integration**, by which certain business functions are acquired and consolidated within a firm. For example, a firm may purchase a key supplier to strengthen its value chain. The decision to outsource or vertically integrate should be examined relative to all factors that can affect organizational performance. In many cases, the decision is based solely on costs without considering the impact on other business priorities such as quality and customer satisfaction or risks associated with protecting intellectual property. For instance, the toy industry recently faced serious issues with toxic chemicals found in toys manufactured in China; Dell had moved a customer call center to India to lower costs, but later closed that center and moved it back to the United States because of dissatisfaction with the level of technical support that customers were receiving. Because outsourcing can have significant impacts on an organization's work system effectiveness, it must be dealt with strategically.

STRATEGIC PLANNING FOR PERFORMANCE EXCELLENCE IN ACTION

In this section we provide some examples that illustrate the themes we have discussed about strategic planning and its link to total quality.

Plan for Excellence at Bronson Methodist Hospital[42]

The culture of Bronson Methodist Hospital (BMH), a Baldrige recipient, is built upon a focus and passion for excellence. The hospital's purpose and reason for existence is stated in its mission to "Provide excellent healthcare services." This statement reflects what BMH does and why it exists. The values promoted by BMH are simple:

We believe in, and our actions will reflect:

- *Care and respect for all people*
- *Teamwork*
- *Stewardship of resources*
- *Commitment to our community*
- *The pursuit of excellence*

These corporate values are enhanced by a Philosophy of Nursing Excellence and Commitment to Patient Care Excellence:

Philosophy of Nursing Excellence

- *Respect*
- *Compassion*

- *Expertise*
- *Impact*
- *Pride*

Commitment to Patient Care Excellence

- *Healing with our knowledge*
- *Caring with our hearts*
- *Working together for Bronson patients and families*

The mission, values, commitment to patient care excellence, and philosophy of nursing excellence provide the foundation that supports the organizational strategy, which is illustrated in the vision: *Bronson will be a national leader in health care quality*, and the three corporate strategies: Clinical Excellence (CE), Customer and Service Excellence (CASE), and Corporate Effectiveness (CORE). These elements, comprising the Plan for Excellence (PFE) form the culture and guide decision making.

Annually, the Executive Team (ET) and Board of Directors (BOD) engage in the strategic planning process, referred to as the Strategic Management Model (SMM). Leaders and physicians participate in several steps of the SMM process and provide input into planning through membership on organizational teams (strategic oversight teams, Clinical Practice Council, service line teams, etc.). The planning cycle kicks off in the spring with the Business Development Division preparing the strategic input document using a variety of input sources. A day-long quarterly strategic planning (QSP) retreat, which includes the ET and key directors, is held to review the strategic input document along with a summary of the previous years' performance. At this time, improvements to the leadership system and SMM are identified for the upcoming annual cycle of planning. Key health care services and delivery processes are determined. At the QSP retreat, the elements of the PFE, including the mission, vision, and values, as well the organization's long term goals, are reviewed and revised, if warranted. Using a SWOT analysis, the ET develops key strategic and budget assumptions that are tested at a series of planning meetings with leaders and physicians. The ET assigns responsibility to the appropriate strategic oversight team (SOT). Three SOTs are aligned to support each of the corporate strategies. Each SOT is chaired by an ET member; other team members include physicians as well as leaders from key operational and support departments.

The SOTs develop preliminary short-term objectives. At the summer QSP retreat, the SOTs present these objectives for approval and begin tactic development. During the summer, the strategic assumptions are revisited with the BOD at the annual strategic planning retreat. This review enables the BOD to validate the strategic challenges based on current information and provides the necessary foundation for the organization to prepare for strategic plan and budget approval later in the year. During the summer, Human Resources (HR) and Finance use the SOT tactics and leader input to formulate the HR staffing, education, and budget plans. The SOTs finalize tactics and the scorecard measures in the fall. The strategies, LT goals, ST strategic objectives, organizational scorecard, budget, HR staffing, and education plans are approved by the ET at the fall QSP retreat and by the

BOD at a monthly meeting in late fall. Deployment of the strategic plan begins in the winter.

In between each QSP retreat, the ET meets to review organizational performance and progress in achieving the strategic objectives. Regular updates at the weekly ET and monthly or biweekly SOT meetings, support the continuous planning process and ensure that the most current information is integrated into the SMM. A systematic review of organizational performance, review of the Quarterly System Indicator Report (QSIR), along with regular environmental scanning, mitigates the potential for blind spots caused by factors that may have changed since the initial development of strategic objectives and tactics. The Business Development Division maintains a compilation of competitive events in the marketplace. This information assists in identifying possible market trends that could impact BMH. The ET establishes planning horizons based on the analysis of market dynamics. Market analysis and intelligence resources indicate that one year is currently appropriate for short-term plans to remain responsive to market forces and synchronized with the budget cycle. The long-term planning horizon, three to five years, is determined by evaluating constraints, such as the time to introduce new services, the optimum life cycle of existing services, as well as market intelligence related to competitive strategies and plans. This approach enables BMH to be responsive to changing factors in the marketplace while maintaining stability of the LT strategic focus. The SMM results in the development of ST strategic objectives and LT goals that support achievement of the vision. During the SMM, consideration is given to the necessary action plans that must be completed to make progress in each corporate strategy. Through the integration of operational, clinical, financial, and HR perspectives, the enhanced SMM facilitates the allocation of adequate resources to complete the action plans in support of the short-term strategic objectives and long-term goals.

Strategic Planning at Branch-Smith Printing Division[43]

Branch-Smith, Inc., is a fourth-generation, family business founded by Aaron Smith in 1910. The Branch-Smith Printing Division in Ft. Worth, Texas, has only 70 full-time employees and specializes in creating multipage, bound materials with services ranging from design to mailing for specialty customers. The company produces publications, magazines, catalogs, directories, and books, as well as some general commercial printing, typically in quantities generally less than 20,000. It offers a complete array of turnkey services to customers, including design, image scanning, electronic and conventional prepress work, printing, binding, and mailing/delivery.

Within the Printing Division, the context of the business is set through its Vision Statement: "Market Leading Business Results through an Expert Team providing Turnkey Solutions to Customer Partners." This vision expresses the desire to produce strong and sustainable results through balanced performance improvement. It creates success for long-term customers and rewards for its employees who bring solutions to bear on its opportunities. The mission is stated as: "The mission of the Branch-Smith Printing Division is to provide expert solutions for publishers." This purpose guides Branch-Smith Printing in meeting customers' needs on its own terms. Publishers work with Branch-Smith because the company focuses on serving publishers' niche requirements for printing as well as offering the vertically integrated value-added services that result in lower costs, reduced cycle times, and on-time delivery. An important component of the solution is easy accessibility for the customer, and timely and appropriate information. It is also expressed in its Quality Policy, which states: "Branch-Smith Printing will seek to continuously improve results for all stakeholders through the application of its Innovating Excellence Process."

The printing industry is very competitive with numerous companies seeking market share. Branch-Smith Printing stands out among competitors based on its approach for identifying and serving a specific niche, focusing on development of long-term relationships, partnering with suppliers, and involvement in standard defining industry associations. To ensure a competitive position, it focuses on serving a select market niche that most other printers have difficulty serving well. Many competitors focus on attracting jobs with greater quantity outputs because of the limitations of their equipment. They charge much higher prices for the shorter runs, thus giving Branch-Smith an advantage in this market. Its equipment and technologies are directed to cost-effectively serve this niche through sheet-fed press versus the popular web printing. This technology allows for faster changeovers from one type of print to another and process automation offers cost savings.

Although Branch-Smith is a small family business, it engages in a formal planning process annually with monthly updates during management reviews. The process is built around a continuous learning cycle that begins with lessons learned from previous years to determine and implement improvements. The strategic planning process (SPP) is a key tool the company uses to visualize the ideal future and create strategies and plans to achieve it, and to incorporate improvement opportunities into prioritized action plans. Strategic planning occurs formally each year with updates and tracking conducted monthly during management reviews. Ongoing updates throughout the year allow the company to correct direction or to proactively respond to risks and opportunities.

Figure 5.11 represents the full strategic planning, deployment, and review process. A month prior to strategic planning, assignments are made to PLT members to research information needed for strategic decision making. The assignment list includes 28 specific areas for understanding organizational and supplier/partner

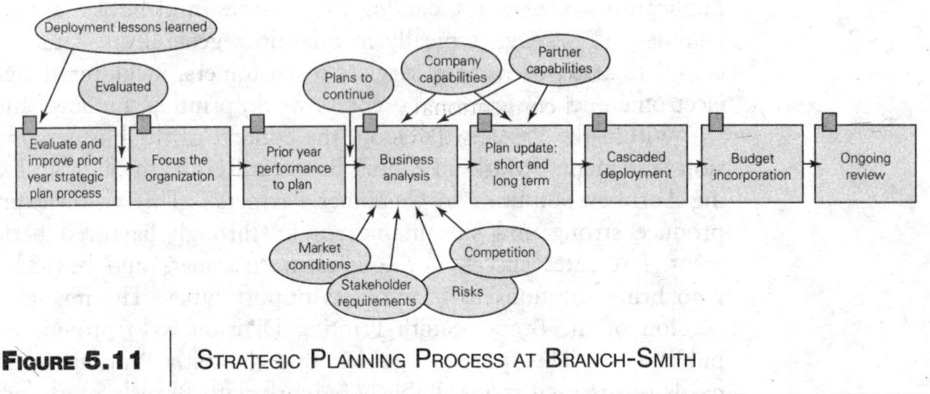

FIGURE 5.11 STRATEGIC PLANNING PROCESS AT BRANCH-SMITH

capabilities, market conditions, stakeholder input and requirements, competitive information, industry issues, and risks. Branch-Smith gathers information through a customer survey, lost revenues, and complaints to identify customer needs and their importance, trends and directions of the printing industry, and market requirements from industry association networking.

Involvement in professional associations provides industry knowledge and benchmarks concerning customer needs and competitor actions, including emerging tools and competitors. Trade magazines and discussions with key suppliers provide additional input about customer needs, competitor directions, and supplier capabilities. Trends and directions in technology and other environmental changes are also identified through involvement with trade associations and external benchmarking groups, and through general understanding of the business climate gained through newspapers, journals, and periodicals.

One important source of information for strategic planning regarding human resource needs and capability is an annual employee survey. Human resource and operational capabilities are identified through review of aggregate measures of performance and productivity, which are enhanced with feedback from scheduled ISO audits that identify processes in need of improvement. Primary inputs on process efficiency and capability come from in-process productivity measures, revenue lost due to complaints, and other measures, which include spoilage cost, frequency, and reason. These measures are recorded daily through electronic, shop-floor data collection.

Strategic partnerships with key suppliers help to gather information about availability of materials and supplier growth plans to help determine their capability to meet Branch-Smith's changing needs. Finally, part of the annual operational review involves understanding suppliers' current financial position and trends in profitability and utilization, which is compared to external economic conditions to identify areas of potential risk and opportunity over the short and longer term.

The formal planning activity is conducted during the fall of each year by the Print Leadership Team (PLT) through a series of meetings on- and off-site. Step 1 of Figure 5.11 ensures that lessons learned and improvement cycles are built into the SPP. The PLT analyzes the effectiveness of the overall planning and deployment process to determine and implement improvements. The effectiveness of the leadership system is also evaluated and areas for improvement for the coming year are determined. These improvements are documented as potential actions for the strategic plan. In Step 2, the company reviews its vision, mission, and values to ensure they still reflect the current environment. Next, management reviews and revises objectives, which are intended to communicate to employees and all stakeholders what the company expects to accomplish in the next three to five years.

In Step 3, the company conducts an operational review to analyze the results of the organization's key performance measures for the prior year. It then reviews and incorporates information into the plan from annual Baldrige-based self-evaluation or from external review feedback. This analysis provides an understanding of key strengths and weaknesses for the SWOT (strengths, weaknesses, opportunities, and threats) analysis in Step 5. Step 4 involves a business analysis to evaluate the external environment to forecast changing trends and gain market requirements. PLT members bring forward defined inputs, including literature and studies for scanning the environment and identifying new opportunities for products, services, competitive advantage, marketing, and technology approaches. From the review of this information, the PLT develops a list of potential opportunities and threats for each environmental element. In Step 5, a SWOT analysis is conducted based upon the issues identified in Steps 1, 3, and 4. SWOT elements are used to identify and prioritize key areas to address.

Based upon the SWOT review, the PLT develops short- and longer-term strategies and actions to move the company toward its vision and objectives. It adds in action plans that are still in process from the prior year to allow them to also be prioritized, sets appropriate measures and goals for objectives and strategies, and sorts and prioritizes the action plans. Action plans are assigned to PLT members to develop (or update) steps, timelines, resources, costs, and measures of success. These plans are then entered into the Quality Improvement Database (QID) for review and tracking. A final balancing meeting is held to review the plan as a whole and make needed adjustments to timing of plans and financial and human resource requirements to balance the plan to resource constraints. In Step 6, the company creates documents and methods to support deployment of the plan.

Results of strategic planning are first communicated to employees through a deployment meeting. Leaders, with their departmental teams or other appropriate members, then discuss the plans during follow-up sessions. Teams and individuals update goals and mission statements for their departments that support the division plans, thus aligning actions, measures, and goals throughout the organization. Other stakeholders receive a variety of communications to detail plans and strategies for informational and planning purposes. For example, a supplier appreciation luncheon is held to provide a more direct opportunity to present plans to key supplier partners and receive feedback on plans and needs. In Step 7, financial resource requirements to accomplish the action plans are rationalized into short- and longer-term budget projections. Then, in Step 8, ongoing tracking of action plans is conducted through monthly management review of overall progress to plans and key measures. Throughout the year as needed, the strategic plan is updated with new or modified action plans to reflect the changes to the environment.

Strategic Work System Design for the City of Coral Springs, Florida[44]

The City of Coral Springs, Florida (see the opening Performance Excellence Profile in Chapter 2) bases its work system design on four principles that support City values and encourage innovation. They are customer focus, empowerment, continuous improvement, and team-based operations. These design features are covered in new-employee orientation because employees at all levels are involved in design. Customer focus encourages innovation, while government systems traditionally focus on documenting regulatory compliance; empowerment encourages minimal layers of bureaucracy; continuous improvement promotes innovation; and diversity in teams stimulates creativity. The City bases decisions to operate a process with internal resources on two criteria: whether the process is a key work process and whether an external resource can do it cheaper while sustaining quality standards. Key work processes are central to public trust and therefore are operated with internal resources. The City needs to directly manage these areas to monitor the quality of outputs on a daily basis and to have the agility needed to adapt to changing customer requirements and civic emergencies. Occasionally, processes that are not fundamental to local government are subject to an RFP (request for proposal) process to determine if City staff can perform the function better and at a lower cost than the private sector. Fleet maintenance, operation of the Tennis Center, and Water Billing are examples of functions assessed through an RFP process. External resources are used for the operation of the Center for the Arts because Professional Facilities Management can take advantage of economies of scale (they run several facilities in Florida) to get better prices on shows; Waste Management provides trash removal and recycling services for many South Florida municipalities; Charter School USA uses one management staff for several facilities and specializes in customer-driven education.

TQ AND STRATEGIC MANAGEMENT THEORY[45]

The TQ perspective, as reflected in the Baldrige criteria, suggests several requirements for effective strategic planning:

- A definable approach for developing company strategy. The approach should consider factors related to the market environment, the competitive environment, risk, human resource capabilities, company capabilities, and supplier/partner capabilities.
- A clear company strategy with action plans derived from it, and human resource plans related to the action plans. Differences between short- and longer-range plans should be recognized and understood.
- An approach for implementing action plans. The approach should consider how the critical requirements for implementing action plans—including human resource plans, key processes, performance measures, and resources—will be aligned and deployed.
- An approach for monitoring company performance relative to the strategic plan.
- Projections of strategy-related changes in key indicators of company performance. These projections should include relevant comparisons to competitors or other benchmarks, and the assumptions used in the projections.

Strategic planning and deployment have been issues of management research for many years, and the conceptual literature in strategic management generally supports these requirements. For example, strategy as a deliberate, definable undertaking has constituted an essential element of classical strategic management frameworks developed by strategy scholars. These classic frameworks portray the strategist as scanning the external environment for opportunities and threats, assessing the firm's internal resources and capabilities for strengths and weaknesses, and determining a strategic plan that exploits external-internal matches in the context of the firm's objectives. However, the general usefulness of strategy making to enhance performance has not been rigorously affirmed. Henry Mintzberg, for instance, suggests that an organization's realized strategy is a product of its planned, intended strategies and unplanned, emergent strategies, which are not a result of formal, top-down planning mechanisms. Many successful strategies can emerge without prior planning, often in response to unseen circumstances.

Three of the six factors that TQ perspectives suggest should comprise strategy development—market environment, competitive environment, and company capabilities—pervade most classic work in strategy formulation. However, the other three factors—financial and societal risk, human resource capabilities, and supplier/partner capabilities—gain only indirect support from the strategy literature. The criteria's specification of human resource capabilities and supplier/partner capabilities appears somewhat redundant, as these factors are asset classes that can be appropriately filed under the "internal capabilities" factor.

The strategy literature sometimes refers to strategic plans as *strategic content*. The Baldrige criteria provide little detail as to what a strategy or an action plan should contain, or the form it should take. Such a nonprescriptive stance fits the literature robustly, because strategy scholars have proposed many purposes and forms of strategy. A common notion among organization and strategy theorists has been that strategy must be broken down into plans for action for effective implementation. The specification for differentiating between short- and longer-term plans garners little direct literature support, although the notion can be indirectly linked to the general concept of dividing strategic goals into doable pieces.

Structure for implementing strategy, in the form of human resource plans, key processes, performance measures, and resources, must be aligned and deployed. Alignment, which is defined by the Baldrige criteria as "consistency of plans, processes, information, resource decisions, actions, results, analysis, and learning to support key organization-wide goals," requires a common understanding of purposes and goals and use of complementary measures and information for planning, tracking, analysis, and improvement at three levels: the organizational level, the key process level, and the work unit level. Aligning strategies to competitive challenges, resources to action plans, and action plans to measurements constitutes some of the most important activities that an organization must address. A well-aligned organization has its processes focused on achieving a shared vision and strategy.

Aligning the organization is a challenging task that is accomplished through a sound strategy and effective deployment. The most damaging alignment problem to which many TQ failures have been attributed is the lack of alignment between expectations that arise from TQ change processes and reward systems. In one survey, an overwhelming percentage (65.8 percent) of managers surveyed ranked the number one barrier to TQ as "Management's compensation is not linked to achieving quality goals."[46] The role of managerial systems, particularly those connected to middle management, in strategy implementation has been examined by several strategy researchers.

Although the TQ perspective requires only specification of how performance will be tracked, it addresses only indirectly the issue of control. Nevertheless, control has been a fundamental concept in management, dating back to Anthony's classic framework, and the literature is replete with studies on managerial control systems. The most compelling support of employing performance measures in strategic management, perhaps, relates to the managerial control notion that measurements provide objective information for managers to judge how well the organization is performing in comparison to strategic targets, and to signal the need for corrective action.

Stating the assumptions behind strategic projections has some grounding in systems theory and some strategy development literature. Inclusion of competitive comparisons and other benchmarks in performance projections can be indirectly related to the requirement for industry and competitive scanning as part of strategy.

Review and Discussion Questions

1. What might be some advantages and disadvantages of setting a BHAG (big, hairy, audacious goal), like Premier does in the opening Performance Excellence profile, in terms of facilitating or hindering strategic planning?
2. Explain how a total quality perspective can support the six characteristics of competitive advantage introduced at the beginning of the chapter.
3. Discuss the three basic types of competitive advantage. Can a company achieve all of them?
4. List 10 firms or businesses that you have read about or have personal experience with. Describe their sources of competitive advantage and how you believe that quality supports (or does not support) their strategy.
5. Prepare a report (using sources such as business periodicals, personal interviews, and so on) profiling a company that competes on each of the major dimensions of differentiation discussed in the chapter. What aspects of its total quality approach support its strategic focus?
6. Think of a product or service you have purchased recently. What aspects of the product or service design made it attractive?
7. What is the importance of total quality to achieving competitive advantage?
8. Explain how quality affects profitability.
9. Discuss the key quality dimensions of differentiation strategies.
10. Explain the differences among custom, option-oriented, and standard products.
11. How might the dimensions of product design (performance, features, reliability, durability, and aesthetics) discussed in this chapter be applied to services?
12. Describe one good and one bad service experience that you encountered. How did this change your perceptions of the company?
13. How is agility a source of competitive advantage? What relationships does agility have with quality?
14. What is the role of quality in innovation?
15. How might the principles of competitive advantage that we discussed be applied to the management of your college or university? How about a fraternity or student professional organization? What types of results measurements would be appropriate?
16. What is a strategy? What elements does a formal strategy contain?
17. What factors have led companies to pursue a strategy based on quality?
18. Research some of the background of recent Baldrige recipients. How do they integrate quality into their business strategies? Discuss different approaches that these firms use.
19. Discuss the process of strategy formulation. How can TQ improve this process?
20. Interview managers at some local companies to determine whether their businesses have well-defined missions, visions, and guiding principles. If they do, how are these translated into strategy? If not, what steps should they take?
21. What is hoshin planning, or policy deployment? Explain how this approach is used in organizations.
22. What are core competencies, and why is it important to consider them in strategic work systems design?
23. Does your university or college have a mission and strategy? How might policy deployment be used in a university setting?

CASES

The Bama Companies, Inc.[47]

The Bama Companies, Inc., is a privately held corporation that began in the Texas kitchen of Cornillia Alabama ("Bama") Marshall in 1927 and has grown into a leading developer and manufacturer of frozen, ready-to-use food products served worldwide by quick-service and casual dining restaurant chains such as McDonald's and Pizza Hut. From four production facilities in Tulsa, Oklahoma, and two in Beijing, China, Bama's 1,100 employees generate over $200 million a year in revenues. The company's three main product categories—hand-held pies, biscuits, and pizza crust—account for 92 percent of revenues.

In an industry dominated by companies several times its own size, Bama's agility, its unique approach to product innovation, and its System View pricing strategy—it has not raised prices for its hand-held pies and biscuits since 1996—give it tremendous leverage in the marketplace. Continuity has enabled the third-generation company to remain firmly rooted in its original guiding principles: keep your eyes on quality and remember that people make a company. Yet the way that Bama applies these principles in today's competitive business environment is anything but traditional. The company's stated vision is to "Create and Deliver Loyalty, Prosperity, and Fun for All, While Becoming a Billion Dollar Company." Bama sees itself and its mission as, "People Helping People Be Successful."

In its endless quest for improvement, Bama uses a battery of advanced strategies and tools, including the Bama Quality Management System, based on the quality improvement philosophies of W. Edwards Deming and the company's own performance excellence model. The Bama Excellence System provides a framework for all decision making. A Principle Centered Bama Culture, based on tenets developed by Stephen Covey, provides a context for creating and measuring excellence. Using Six Sigma methodologies since 2000, Bama has dramatically improved processes throughout the company. Total savings from Six Sigma improvements equates to over $17 million since 2001.

In 1999, Bama utilized a strategic planning process called Prometheus to develop a company Future Picture—a high-level view of the company as it wants to be in 2010. The future that Bama envisions includes: billion-dollar sales, recognition of the company's world-class quality, being first-choice supplier in all its target markets, and providing employees and other stakeholders with unparalleled personal and financial opportunities. To help achieve these goals, but maintain its small company culture, the company focuses on five strategic outcomes: 1) People—Create & Deliver Loyalty, Prosperity and Fun, 2) Learning and Innovation, 3) Continuous Improvement, 4) Be Customer's First Choice, 5) Value Added Growth. Bama uses its Centers of Gravity (short-term action plans) and a Balanced Scorecard to assess progress toward meeting these outcomes. The plans and scorecard support the company's decision-making process at all levels and are posted throughout its facilities allowing all employees to see at a glance how their unit is performing against goals. The senior management team reviews the information at weekly and monthly meetings.

Building long-term relationships with suppliers and customers also helps Bama stay at the top of its game. Most of its key suppliers have been partners for 10 years or more, two have worked with the Bama Companies for three decades. Relationships with customers are just as enduring. The McDonald's system has been a Bama customer for 37 years and Pizza Hut for 11 years. Through these long-term relationships, Bama understands its customers, its customers' markets and what its customers need to succeed. The company has tailored its services to meet customer requirements in critical areas such as assured supply, precision manufacturing, and value pricing. Since 2001, Bama has achieved 98 percent on-time delivery of products to customers, with 99 percent of orders completely filled on the initial shipment. Customer satisfaction for the company's major national accounts has increased from 75 percent in 2001 to 100 percent in 2004, considerably higher than the food manufacturing benchmark of 85 percent.

Bama is committed to the success of everyone associated with its business—customers, employees, and the community. The company's People Assurance System (PAS) ensures that each employee is well trained, fully informed, and empowered, and centers on helping all employees develop their potential and achieve personal success. Bama encourages employees to seek a college education by providing tuition reimbursement. Satisfaction and loyalty of its people is key, and the company shares its success with employees when certain financial measures are met. Since 2001, profit sharing payments have averaged around $3,000 per year for each employee. A promote-from-within philosophy offers every qualified employee opportunities for advancement and the opportunity to be considered for job openings. This commitment to employees is paying off. Bama's 14 percent employee turnover rate is well below the average rate in the Tulsa area at 20 percent.

Discussion Questions

1. How are the vision and mission statements of The Bama Companies reflected in its management processes?
2. What factors appear to lead to Bama's ability to compete with much larger competitors?

Clifton Metal Works

Clifton Metal Works (CMW) was founded in the mid-1940s by Donald Chalmer in a 3,000-square-foot building with nine people as a small family business to produce custom-machined parts. In the 1960s, as business grew, the company expanded its facilities and its capability to develop its own tooling patterns, eventually moving into a 40,000-square-foot building.

However, as technology advanced, small family businesses like CMW met stiff competition. To survive, the company knew it had to listen more to its customers. From surveys and focus groups, the firm discovered that customers were not happy with the quality of the products they had been receiving. In 1985, CMW made a commitment to quality by hiring a quality assurance manager, Paul Levitt. Driven by the Deming philosophy, the company developed a variety of quality approaches and eventually became ISO 9000 certified in 1998. CMW made some substantial improvements in the quality of its products, particularly reducing scrap and reject rates. Paul worked closely with the factory workers directly responsible for the products, asking them what they needed to get the job done and ensuring management commitment to provide the necessary resources. For example, CMW invested in computer-based statistical process control technology, which enabled workers to monitor their processes and adjust them as needed. The success of this project led the company to empower employees to control many other aspects of the system.

Business remained steady, but after hearing presentations from some Baldrige recipients, Chalmer realized that a lot more could be done. In 2005, he hired a senior executive for performance excellence, James Hubbard. Hubbard saw an opportunity to change the company's culture and introduce many Baldrige principles he had learned in his previous job at a manufacturing firm that had applied the Baldrige criteria for many years. One of the first things he did was to review the current mission statement, which had remained relatively untouched since 1985:

Our mission at CMW is to improve the return on investment. We can accomplish this by changing attitudes and incorporating a quality/team environment. This will improve the quality of our products, enhance our productivity (which in turn will allow us to quote competitive prices), and elevate our service and response level to our customers. There are several factors which make positive change imperative.

The standards for competitive levels of quality and service are becoming more demanding. The emergence of the "World Market" has brought on new challenges. We are in a low-growth, mature market. In order for CMW to improve return on investment, we must develop a strategy to improve quality and responsiveness in all areas of the company. We need to have all employees recognize the importance of product quality and service and move toward more favorable pricing. We need to change thinking throughout the organization to get employees involved, to encourage teamwork, to develop a more flexible workforce and adaptable organization. We need to instill pride in the workplace and the product.

We believe that we can best achieve the desired future state by study of and adherence to the teachings of W. Edwards Deming.

Hubbard did not feel that this mission statement provided a clear and vivid direction, especially in the twenty-first century. Consequently, he set up a planning retreat for senior management (including Chalmer) to develop a new strategic vision.

Discussion Questions

1. Comment on the current mission statement. Does it provide the strategic direction necessary for success for this company?
2. How can the mission statement be improved? Suggest a better statement of mission, vision, and guiding principles.

Endnotes

1. 2006 Malcolm Baldrige National Quality Award Recipient Profile, National Institute of Standards and Technology, U.S. Department of Commerce.
2. S. C. Wheelwright, "Competing through Manufacturing," in Ray Wild (ed.), International Handbook of Production and Operations Management, London: Cassell Educational, Ltd., 1989, pp. 15–32.
3. *The PIMS Letter on Business Strategy*, The Strategic Planning Institute, No. 4, Cambridge, Mass., 1986.
4. Philip Crosby, *Quality Is Free*, New York: McGraw-Hill, 1979.
5. Kathleen Kerwin, "When Flawless Isn't Enough," *Business Week*, December 8, 2003, pp. 80–82. The quote on Lexus appeared in a column by Carol Traeger, "Lexus IS 300 loses luster," *The Cincinnati Enquirer*, July 31, 2004, pp. G1, G2.
6. U.S. General Accounting Office, "Management Practices: U.S. Companies Improve Performance through Quality Effort," GA/NSIAD-91-190, May 1991.
7. "Progress on the Quality Road," *Incentive*, April 1995, p. 7.
8. Michael E. Porter, *Competitive Advantage: Creating and Sustaining Superior Performance*, New York: Free Press, 1985.
9. See, for example, J. Pfeffer and J. F. Veiga, "Putting People First for Organizational Success," *Academy of Management Executive*, Vol. 13, No. 2, 1999, p. 37; J. Pfeffer, *Competitive Advantage through People*, Boston, MA: Harvard Business School Press, 1994; C. A. O'Reilly III and J. Pfeffer, *Hidden Value: How Great Companies Achieve Extraordinary Results with Ordinary People*, Boston, MA: Harvard Business School Press, 2000.
10. H. Lee Hales, "Time Has Come for Long-Range Planning of Facilities Strategies in Electronic Industries," *Industrial Engineering*, April 1985.
11. Bradley T. Gale, "Quality Comes First When Hatching Power Brands," *Planning Review*, July/August 1992, pp. 4–9, 48.
12. J. M. Juran, *Juran on Quality by Design*, New York: The Free Press, 1992, p. 181.
13. Larry Selden and Geoffrey Colvin, "Will Your E-Business Leave You Quick or Dead?" *Fortune*, May 28, 2001, pp. 112–124.
14. Robin Yale Bergstrom, "People, Process, Paint," *Production*, April 1995, pp. 48–51.
15. Betsy Morris, "The New Rules," *Fortune*, July 24, 2006, 70–87.
16. Jeffrey Pfeffer, *Competitive Advantage through People*, Boston, MA: Harvard Business School Press, 1994.
17. Town Hall discussion at the Quest for Excellence Conference, Washington, D.C., March 2000.
18. David A. Garvin, "What Does Product Quality Really Mean?" *Sloan Management Review*, Vol. 26, No. 1, 1984, pp. 25–43.
19. "Fast Talk: Hard Drive," Profile of Tim Benner, Honda Motor Company, Co-designer, Honda Element, *Fast Company*, May 2003, p. 62.
20. Tom Peters and Bob Waterman, *In Search of Excellence*, New York: Harper & Row, 1982.
21. F. F. Reichheld and W. E. Sasser, Jr. "Zero Defections: Quality Comes to Services," *Harvard Business Review*, September–October, 1990.
22. Dave Demerjian, "Hustle & Flow," Fast Company, March 2008, 60–62
23. Ron Zemke, "Auditing Customer Service: Look Inside as Well as Out," *Employee Relations Today*, Vol. 16, Autumn 1989, pp. 197–203.
24. Jeffrey Margolies, "When Good Service Isn't Good Enough," *The Price Waterhouse Review*, Vol. 32, No. 3, New York: Price Waterhouse, 1988, pp. 22–31.
25. Charles A. Horne, "Product Strategy and Competitive Advantage," *P&IM Review with APICS News*, Vol. 7, No. 12, December 1987, pp. 38–41.
26. Thomas A. Stewart, "Brace for Japan's Hot New Strategy," *Fortune*, September 21, 1992, pp. 62–73.
27. *Fortune* special insert: CEOs on Innovation (undated).
28. Faith Keenan, Opening the Spigot, *BusinessWeek* e.biz, June 4, 2001, pp. EB17–20.
29. Joan Uhlenberg, "Redefining Customer Expectations," *Quality*, September 1992, pp. 34–35.
30. Jerry Useem, "Boeing Versus Boeing," *Fortune*, October 2, 2000, 148–160.
31. Kicab Casteñeda-Méndez, "Performance Measurement in Health Care," *Quality Digest*, May 1999, pp. 33–36.
32. Laura Struebing, "Measuring for Excellence," *Quality Progress*, December 1996, 25–28.

33. Robert S. Kaplan and David P. Norton, "The Balanced Scorecard—Measures That Drive Performance," *Harvard Business Review*, January/February 1992, pp. 71–79.
34. Ernest C. Huge, "Measuring and Rewarding Performance," in Ernst & Young Quality Consulting Group, Total Quality: An Executive's Guide for the 1990s, Homewood, Ill.: Irwin, 1990.
35. *New Corporate Performance Measures, A Research Report*, Report Number 1118-95-RR, New York: The Conference Board, 1995.
36. Steven H. Hoisington and Tse-Hsi Huang, "Customer Satisfaction and Market Share: An Empirical Case Study of IBM's AS/400 Division," in Earl Naumann and Steven H. Hoisington, *Customer Centered Six Sigma*, Milwaukee, Wisc.: ASQ Quality Press, 2001.
37. Matthew Boyle, "Best Buy's Giant Gamble," *Fortune*, April 3, 2006, 69–75.
38. 2007 North Mississippi Medical Center Malcolm Baldrige Application Summary.
39. Ronald E. Purser and Steven Cabana, "Involve Employees at Every Level of Strategic Planning," *Quality Progress*, May 1997, pp. 66–71.
40. Bob King, *Hoshin Planning: The Developmental Approach*, Methuen, Mass.: GOAL/QPC, 1989, pp. 2–3.
41. The Ernst & Young Quality Improvement Consulting Group, *Total Quality: An Executive's Guide for the 1990s*, Homewood, Ill.: Dow Jones-Irwin, 1990.
42. Bronson Methodist Hospital, 2005 Malcolm Baldrige National Quality Award Application Summary.
43. Branch-Smith Printing, Application Summary, 2002. Courtesy of David Branch, President.
44. Adapted from City of Coral Springs, Florida, Application for the 2007 Malcolm Baldrige National Quality Award.
45. Based on Ford and Evans, op. cit.
46. Nabil Tamimi and Rose Sebastianelli, "The Barriers to Total Quality Management," *Quality Progress*, June 1998, pp. 57–60.
47. Adapted from 2005 Malcolm Baldrige National Quality Award Recipient Profile, National Institute of Standards and Technology, U.S. Department of Commerce.

CHAPTER 6

Quality in Customer-Supplier Relationships

Performance Excellence Profile: Mercy Health System[1]

In 1989, Mercy Hospital was a single stand-alone community hospital primarily serving Janesville, Wisconsin. Today, Mercy Health System (MHS) is a fully integrated health care system with three hospitals and a network of 64 facilities consisting of 39 multi-specialty outpatient centers located in six counties throughout southern Wisconsin and northern Illinois. Mercy has a unique W2 Physician Partnership Model with 285 primary and specialty physicians. To further its mission of providing "exceptional health care services, resulting in healing in the broadest sense," MHS has created a culture of high quality care, customer focus, partner cooperation, innovation, and cost consciousness. The entire organization is aligned around these cultural elements and its values, which are: Healing in its broadest sense, Patients come first, Treat each other like family, and Strive for excellence. Every MHS partner is committed to exceeding patient expectations by making quality care a top priority. Best-practice benchmarks are used to measure clinical care and ensure continuous improvement and patient safety. At MHS, an engaged, empowered workforce and advanced medical and information technology are key to high quality patient care.

MHS focuses on patient and customer satisfaction, timely resolution of problems, and expanding and improving services. Continuous benchmarking, tracking of quality indicators, and surveying patients and customers help MHS ensure excellence in patient care. MHS's "Take the L.E.A.D" program—Listen to the customer; Empathize with the customer; Accept the customer's perspective; Apologize, Acknowledge concern, and take Action to recover; and Direct the customer to the person able to recover the situation—is used to turn negative experiences into positive ones. The Mercy Health Mall is a one-stop superstore offering a number of services, including acupuncture, massage therapy, a vision center, a pharmacy, durable medical equipment and supplies, an urgent care clinic, a cardiac rehabilitation and fitness center, outpatient diabetic treatment, an entire array of health products, and more. A system-wide, secure electronic network gives authorized partners at all sites access to patient health information, including visit history, diagnostic and medication orders, test results, and images.

A basic belief at MHS is that engaged, empowered, and valued partners, including 285 W2 physician partners, are vital to providing exceptional health care services. At the time they are hired, partners are asked to commit to achieving the MHS mission, participate in performance improvement efforts, and create a personal and professional growth and development plan. MHS's leaders live by a "servant leadership" philosophy: When leaders provide excellent service to partners, partners provide excellent service to patients. MHS encourages and entices partners to identify innovative ideas for growing revenue and decreasing expenses and waste, as well as increasing productivity and effectiveness.

Evidence of success in achieving its mission includes:

- MHS is the leader in market share for inpatient services and outpatient surgery in its Wisconsin service area. In 2006, about 84 percent of hospital customers and about 90 percent of multi-specialty outpatient center customers would recommend MHS to others, a key indicator of customer loyalty and a reflection of overall satisfaction.
- Effectiveness in resolving patient and customer concerns has risen from about 90 percent in 2002 to 94 percent in 2007.
- Staff turnover at MHS has declined from 13.5 percent in 2002 to 7.5 percent in 2007.

Mercy Health System illustrates the importance of successful relationships between an organization (a "supplier") and its customers. As we noted in Chapter 1, customer focus is one of the basic principles of TQ. In Japanese, the word *okyakusama* means both "customer" and "honorable guest." World-class organizations are obsessed with meeting and exceeding customer expectations. Many companies such as Disney and Nissan Motor Co.'s Infiniti division were built on the notion of satisfying the customer. Don Peppers and Martha Rogers sum up the importance of customers eloquently:

> The only value your company will ever create is the value that comes from customers—the ones you have now and the ones you will have in the future. Businesses succeed by getting, keeping, and growing customers. Customers are the only reason you build factories, hire employees, schedule meetings, lay fiber-optic lines, or engage in any business activity. Without customers, you don't have a business.[2]

In recent years, there has been a lot of emphasis in business on supply chain management. Businesses have recognized that supply chain management is crucial for effective operations and meeting customer needs. A supply chain includes the materials and other inputs purchased from suppliers, their use in the production of goods and services, and distribution and service to customers. Quality should start with the customer and extend back through the supply chain to the sources of procurement. Many businesses traditionally have kept suppliers at arm's length, but the quality of output can be no better than the quality of the input. In 1982,

IBM purchased some parts from a Japanese manufacturer. According to the specifications, IBM would accept 300 defective parts per million of the product. The response from Japan raised a lot of questions and gave IBM the opportunity to change its perspective on quality and relationships with suppliers. The Japanese commented, "We have a hard time understanding North American business practices. But the 3 defective parts per 10,000 have been included and are wrapped separately. Hope this pleases."[3]

Deming emphasized the importance of using customer research to improve inputs, processes, and outputs. This chapter will:

- demonstrate the importance of customer-supplier relationships to achieving performance excellence;
- identify the principles and practices of quality customer-supplier relationships;
- give examples of effective partnerships between customers and suppliers; and
- compare a quality-focused approach to customers and suppliers to conventional organizational theories.

CUSTOMER-SUPPLIER RELATIONSHIPS AND PERFORMANCE EXCELLENCE

From the TQ perspective, every company is part of a long chain (actually many long chains) of customers and suppliers.[4] Each company is a customer to its suppliers and a supplier to its customers, so it does not make sense to think of a company as only one or the other (Figure 6.1). One implication of this concept is that your customer's customers are, in a sense, your customers as well. Sometimes a company must focus on both its immediate customers and those next in the chain. Procter & Gamble, for example, works hard to satisfy the needs of both the people who use their products and the retail establishments that sell them. Companies should try to establish the same kinds of productive relationships with its suppliers that it has with its customers.

Many companies work closely with suppliers that share common values. This close relationship improves supplier capabilities by teaching them quality-related tools and approaches. Although many companies have formal supplier certification programs in which they rate their suppliers, some companies ask suppliers to rate them as customers. Motorola uses a 15-member council of suppliers that rates

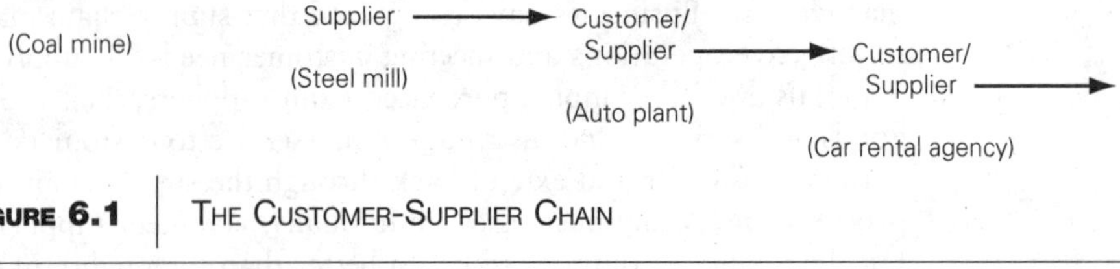

FIGURE 6.1 | THE CUSTOMER-SUPPLIER CHAIN

Motorola's practices and offers suggestions for improving, for example, the accuracy of production schedules or design layouts that Motorola provides.[5] Some typical questions that companies might ask of their suppliers are:[6]

- What expectations do you have that are not being met?
- What type of technical assistance would you like from us?
- What type of feedback would you like from us?
- What benefits are you looking for in a partnership?

Better two-way communication can improve both products and relationships. By developing partnerships, customers and suppliers can build relationships that will help them satisfy their shared customers further along the customer-supplier chain. This is why we have written one chapter on customer-supplier relationships, rather than separate chapters on customers and suppliers. The idea of creating mutually beneficial relationships with both customers and suppliers is a major departure from the traditional approach to customer and supplier relationships (CSRs). As one book on quality put it, "The historical picture of customer-supplier relationships has been one of self-interested adversaries negotiating against each other to maximize their slice of the pie at the expense of the other."[7] The authors go on to say that the focus of CSRs under TQ is on expanding the pie rather than on arguing over its division.

The Importance of Customers

The importance of customers has evolved over the years, from a view of the customer as a buyer to increase profitability, to a view of the customer as an active partner and the focus of all quality activities. Customer satisfaction translates directly into increased profits. However, while satisfaction is important, modern firms need to look further. Achieving strong profitability and market share requires *loyal* customers—those who stay with a company and make positive referrals. Satisfaction and loyalty are very different concepts.

To quote Patrick Mehne, the former chief quality officer at The Ritz-Carlton Hotel Company: "Satisfaction is an attitude; loyalty is a behavior." Customers who are merely satisfied may often purchase from competitors because of convenience, promotions, or other factors. Loyal customers place a priority on doing business with a particular organization, and will often go out of their way or pay a premium to stay with the company. Loyal customers spend more, are willing to pay higher prices, refer new clients, and are less costly to do business with. For instance, although Home Depot customers spend only about $38 each visit, they shop 30 times annually and spend more than $25,000 throughout a lifetime.[8] Carl Sewell, owner of Sewell Cadillac in Dallas, calculated that the average lifetime value of a loyal customer for his dealership was $332,000.[9] Statistics also show that the typical company gets 65 percent of its business from existing customers, and it costs at least five times more to find a new customer than to keep an existing one happy.[10]

Poor-quality products and services, by contrast, lead to customer dissatisfaction in the form of complaints, returns, and unfavorable word-of-mouth publicity (see box "'United Breaks Guitars' Goes Viral"). Dissatisfied customers purchase

"United Breaks Guitars" Goes Viral

Canadian musician Dave Carroll and other members of his band, Sons of Maxwell, were changing planes at Chicago's O'Hare airport on March 31, 2008 when another passenger looked out the window and exclaimed, "My God, they're throwing guitars out there!" Guess whose? When the band arrived in Omaha, Carroll discovered that his $3,500 Taylor guitar had been damaged. For nearly a year, he spent countless hours arguing with United Airlines agents in Chicago and India for compensation; the airline refused to deal with him because he had not filed a claim within 24 hours of the flight. So he decided to write some songs about the saga. "United Breaks Guitars" was posted on YouTube on July 6, 2009, had over 150,000 hits in the first two days, and has had millions of views since. In addition, his experience was chronicled in hundreds of news articles across the world and on the Internet. Not long after, a spokesperson for United stated, "This has struck a chord with us, and we've contacted him directly to make it right." By that time, Carroll said he was no longer looking for compensation but would rather see the money go to a charity of their choice. United subsequently made a $3,000 donation to the Thelonious Monk Institute of Jazz.

from competitors. One study found that customers are five times more likely to switch because of perceived service problems than for price concerns or product quality issues.[11] Studies have also shown that dissatisfied customers tell at least twice as many friends about bad experiences than they tell about good ones.

For many companies, "The Customer Comes First" is a guiding principle (see box "Flying the Customer-Friendly Skies"). It is impossible to overstate the importance of customers to TQ. Customers are at the very center of every TQ activity, and devotion to satisfying them is the first principle of TQ. Customers are recognized as the guarantee of the organization's continued existence. Therefore, a focus on customers, rather than internal issues, is the foundation of the TQ approach to management. Today, organizations are beginning to focus on **customer engagement**, which refers to customers' investment in or commitment to a brand and product offerings.[12]

Customer engagement goes beyond loyalty and is an important outcome of a customer-focused culture and the organization's listening, learning, and performance excellence strategy. Characteristics of customer engagement include customer retention and loyalty, customers' willingness to make an effort to do business with the organization, and customers' willingness to actively advocate for and recommend the brand and product offerings. Customer engagement is influenced by an organization's integrity and the relationships it builds with its customers. As one small business owner stated, "We build customer loyalty by telling our customers the truth, whether it is good or bad news."[13]

The Importance of Suppliers

The quality of goods and services received from suppliers, the upstream portion of the supply chain, has a significant effect on the quality of goods and services that downstream customers receive. Suppliers are those companies that provide the organization with goods and services that help them to satisfy the needs of their

Flying the Customer-Friendly Skies[14]

Southwest Airlines began service on June 18, 1971, with flights to Houston, Dallas, and San Antonio, and has grown to become the fifth-largest U.S. airline in terms of domestic customers carried. The airline operates more than 2,150 flights daily with more than 23,000 employees. Known for its legendary service, the Southwest culture ensures that it serves the needs of its Customers (with a capital C) in a friendly, caring, and enthusiastic manner. Kevin and Jackie Freiberg, authors of *NUTS! Southwest Airlines' Crazy Recipe for Business and Personal Success*, note that legendary service is a key component of Southwest's culture.

Southwest wants its customers to experience service that makes a lasting impression, service that is kind and loving, service that is fun and makes them laugh.... Thus, Southwest will go a long way to defend and support an employee who may violate a company policy to bend toward the customer. The company instills in every employee the idea that happy, satisfied customers who return again and again create job security.

Every one of the approximately 1,000 customers who write to the airline each year get a personal response (not a form letter) within four weeks, and frequent fliers even get birthday cards. The airline even moved a flight up a quarter-hour when five medical students who commuted weekly to an out-of-state medical school complained that the flight got them to class 15 minutes late. Customer focus applies to internal customers also; each operating division identifies an internal customer—mechanics who service planes target the pilots who fly them and marketers treat reservation agents as customers. It is not unusual to find pilots helping ground crews unload baggage. As Executive VP Colleen Barrett stated: "We are not an airline with great customer service. We are a great customer service organization that happens to be in the airline business." Southwest has been one of the most profitable airlines in the United States.

For many years, the airline has been recognized for best baggage handling, fewest customer complaints, and best on-time performance, and has been recognized with numerous honors, including one of America's Most Admired Corporations by *Fortune* magazine.

own customers. A manufacturing company assembling parts made by suppliers illustrates this point: the final product cannot be any better than the parts that comprise it. For example, the U.S. Federal Aviation Administration (FAA), after a widespread and comprehensive review of Boeing's commercial jet unit, concluded that the company failed to maintain adequate control over its supplier base. In one instance, several suppliers provided aluminum parts that were defective and prone to cracking after the parts were installed. Aircraft already in service have had to undergo extensive testing and inspection to eliminate the possibility of catastrophic failure.[15]

If a supplier's performance is of consistently high quality, its customer can decrease or eliminate costly incoming inspections that add no value to the product. For these reasons, many organizations have increasingly demanded tangible progress in quality from all their suppliers. Companies that do not accept this requirement are dropped from supplier lists. The importance of suppliers is at least as great when they provide training, software, or other goods or services that do not physically become part of the final product; they will influence its quality nevertheless by shaping the quality of the processes used to produce it.

However, as Terry A. Carlson, corporate vice president of purchasing for Maytag, stated, "Superior quality, consistent service, and competitive pricing are just the price of entry to get into the game." What sets world-class suppliers apart from the rest are a formal company-wide effort to continually improve their products and services, the ability and willingness to align products, processes, and business strategies with customers for mutual success, and a proven ability to be an industry leader in developing new technologies and products.[16]

In business today, operations are often highly decentralized and dispersed around the world. Consequently, managing a complex network of suppliers becomes a critical interorganizational issue. Suppliers play a vital role throughout the product development process, from design through distribution. Suppliers can provide technology or production processes not internally available, early design advice, and increased capacity, which can result in lower costs, faster time-to-market, and improved quality for their customers. In turn, they are assured of stable and long-term business. At the former Daimler-Chrysler, for example, suppliers were involved early in the design process.[17] As a result, Daimler-Chrysler was able to find out about new materials, parts, and technologies before other automakers.

Increasingly, suppliers are viewed as *partners* with customers, because there usually is a codependent relationship. A powerful example of supplier partnerships is the response that occurred when a fire destroyed the main source of a crucial five-dollar brake valve for Toyota.[18] Without it, Toyota had to shut down its 20 plants in Japan. Within hours of the disaster, other suppliers began taking blueprints, improvising tooling systems, and setting up makeshift production lines. Within days, the 36 suppliers, aided by more than 150 other subcontractors, had almost 50 production lines making small batches of the valve. Even a sewing-machine company that had never made car parts spent 500 person-hours refitting a milling machine to make just 40 valves a day. Toyota promised the suppliers a bonus of about $100 million "as a token of our appreciation."

PRINCIPLES FOR CUSTOMER-SUPPLIER RELATIONSHIPS

Three governing principles describe CSRs under total quality:

- recognition of the strategic importance of customers and suppliers,
- development of win-win relationships between customers and suppliers, and
- establishing relationships based on trust.

First, every organization must recognize that its customers and suppliers are absolutely crucial to its success (see the box "Finding the Special Touch"). Although this may sound obvious, many organizations seem to be driven by the need to observe standard operating procedures and maintain rigid boundaries between jobs, rather than trying to meet customer expectations.

Many employees don't think that it's their "job" to serve customers beyond their job descriptions. For example, a hotel desk clerk's formal job description might be to greet and register guests and process bills. Does this mean that he or

FINDING THAT SPECIAL TOUCH[19]

Many companies in industries not known for great customer service, such as auto dealerships, banks, and hospitals, are learning lessons from luxury hotels that have long prided themselves on exceptional service, such as two-time Baldrige winner The Ritz-Carlton or Four Season's Hotels. A Lexus dealer added valet parking, fresh flowers in the showroom, and a marble floor in the bathroom; customers picking up their cars after they have been serviced find bottled water and Hershey kisses in the cupholders—amenities that are often found at these luxury hotels. After receiving the Baldrige Award, The Ritz-Carlton began offering training courses in its legendary service strategies; today, such companies as Macy's and Starbucks are signing up.

The Ritz-Carlton motto is "We Are Ladies and Gentlemen Serving Ladies and Gentlemen," and all employees are treated as guests would be treated. The company's focus is to develop a "skilled and empowered workforce operating with pride and joy" by ensuring that all employees knows what they are supposed to do, how well they are doing, and have the authority to do whatever is necessary for the customer. For example, employees are empowered to "move heaven and earth to satisfy a customer," to enlist the aid of other employees to resolve a problem swiftly, to spend up to $2,000 to satisfy a guest or resolve a complaint. The role of a restaurant hostess is not simply to seat patrons, but to create a memorable experience for the customer. If a customer asks where the gift shop is, the hostess will take the customer there rather than simply point out the way. Each work shift begins with a 15 minute "huddle" in which managers discuss company values, service processes, and recognize employees' exceptional performance. However, while nearly everyone is impressed with the special touches afforded by The Ritz-Carlton and its competitors, not all industries are able to make them work as seamlessly and effectively; it takes a special culture and discipline to achieve them.

she should not respond to special requests like bringing extra pillows to a room (housekeeping's "job"), or make a restaurant reservation (the "job" of the concierge)? As the first and last contact a guest makes with the hotel, front-desk personnel probably have the largest impact on guest satisfaction. It is frightening to imagine how much damage a poor attitude from a desk clerk might have on his or her organization. Of course, the responsibility for this attitude may ultimately rest with the hotel organization that apparently has created a system in which people are more interested in maintaining boundaries than in serving customers.[20]

Customers must be at the center of the organizational universe (see box "The Boomerang Principle"). Satisfying their needs leads to repeat business and positive referrals, as opposed to one-shot business and negative referrals. Suppliers also must be considered crucial to organizational success, because they make it possible to create customer satisfaction. Neither the quality nor the cost of the organization's product can be brought to competitive levels and continuously improved without the contributions of suppliers.

The second principle of customer-supplier relationships is the need to develop mutually beneficial (often called "win-win") relationships between customers and suppliers. This was discussed previously as working together to increase the size of the pie, rather than competing over how to divide it.

THE BOOMERANG PRINCIPLE[21]

Feargal Quinn is the executive chairman of Superquinn, a 5,600-person, 19-store chain of supermarkets in Ireland. In every deed, Quinn's focus is on persuading the customer to return. Quinn calls it the "boomerang principle." His tireless and inventive exploration of this principle has earned him a reputation as Ireland's "pope of customer service." Superquinn inspires such intense devotion that many customers say that they drive out of their way—and past several of its biggest competitors—to shop there. At Superquinn, you don't have to pay for broccoli stalks and carrot tops you never use; the store provides scissors to cut off what you don't want. The checkout technology provides a running tab on a screen that faces the customer, and then organizes the final receipt by product category, rather than the order in which products were scanned. Every store features a professionally staffed playhouse where mothers can leave young children while they shop. The program costs the company a bundle, but it has earned even more in loyal customers and reputation.

Kindergarten teachers around the country (Ireland doesn't have preschool) recognize "Superquinn kids" as the most socialized and school-ready of each new class. Each month, Superquinn managers are required to spend time in customers' shoes, shopping, asking questions, lodging complaints, waiting in line. Superquinn's fresh produce, butchers, and fishmongers are mixed in with futuristic flat screen displays, digital shelf labels, and kiosks that link customers to their bank, their SuperClub account, as well as to wine recommendations and interactive recipe planners. Quinn notes that, "What seems reasonable or ever valuable from the perspective of the company is often glaringly wrong from the point of view of the customer."

The goal of building partnerships with customers and suppliers can be seen as an extension of the teamwork principle that applies to all TQ activities and as recognition that the needs of both partners must be satisfied if productive long-term relationships are to be created. W. Edwards Deming advocated these principles for decades, as is evident in his 14 Points (Chapter 2). Joseph Juran developed a useful framework to distinguish between adversarial and teamwork relationships with suppliers.[22] Traditionally, customers have used many different suppliers for the same purchased item, and they typically have been awarded short-term (annual) contracts. This practice fosters a competitive situation in which suppliers strive to outbid each other and may sacrifice quality for cost. A teamwork relationship results in the need for fewer suppliers, with many items being single-sourced. With few suppliers, companies do not have to rely on annual bidding, and can award longer-term contracts. This enhances the motivation to work together for mutual benefits. For instance, quality planning, problem-solving activities, and efforts to adjust to market changes are performed jointly, rather than independently. This helps both the customer and supplier focus on "fitness for use" to meet customer needs rather than simply trying to conform to specifications. It also fosters a spirit of continuous improvement, in which larger customers often help smaller suppliers develop their quality management systems and process capabilities. Similar ideas were also advocated by Deming in his 14 Points.

The third principle of effective CSRs is that they must be based on trust rather than suspicion. This point is described by Juran as the "pattern of collaboration." The costs of mistrust are staggering: witness the tremendous number, detail, and rigidity of rules that characterize the U.S. Department of Defense's contracts with its suppliers. The suppliers often incur substantial costs in terms of both money and time because of multiple levels of review and inspection. Although a certain level of rigidity is to be expected in the acquisition of weapons, it is harder to understand when applied to more ordinary items.

Aside from the obvious teamwork implications for relationships based on trust versus suspicion, monitoring supplier or customer behavior does not add any value to the product. If a trusting relationship between customers and suppliers can be developed so that neither must check up on the behavior of the other, the costs of monitoring, such as inspection and auditing, can be avoided. Many Japanese firms do not inspect items purchased from other companies in Japan; they do, however, often inspect those purchased from America. Trust is not a blind leap into the unknown; it is developed over time "through a pattern of success by all parties to fully and faithfully deliver that which was promised."[23] In other words, trust depends upon trustworthy behavior by both parties in a CSR.

PRACTICES FOR DEALING WITH CUSTOMERS

How can these principles be translated into specific practices? The most basic practices for dealing with customers are: (1) to collect information constantly on customer expectations; (2) to disseminate this information widely within the organization; and (3) to use this information to design, produce, and deliver the organization's products and services.

COLLECT CUSTOMER INFORMATION

Acquiring customer information is critical to understanding customer needs and identifying opportunities for improvement. The Japanese auto industry is known for trying to understand customer needs so thoroughly that it can incorporate design features that customers would never have asked for but love once they experience them. Teams of automobile designers visit people at home and observe how they live in order to anticipate their automotive needs. Hideo Sugiura, executive vice president of Honda, comments on his company's efforts to anticipate customer needs: "We should not try to sell things just because the market is there, but rather we should seek to create a new market by accurately understanding the potential needs of customers and society."[24] Lexus, Toyota's luxury car line, has succeeded dramatically in this manner and is consistently at the top of owner satisfaction surveys.

In Chapter 1, we cited the Kano model of customer requirements:

- Dissatisfiers
- Satisfiers
- Exciters/delighters

In trying to understand customer needs, it is important to go beyond what customers say they need and anticipate what will really excite them. It is a well-known principle of innovation that customers will seldom express enthusiasm for a product that is different from anything they have experienced. Thus, the original market survey for computers suggested that only a few would be sold, and it took years for 3M to become convinced that Post-it notes would actually be valuable to people in offices. As Kozo Ohsone of Sony puts it, "When you introduce products that have never been invented before, what good is market research?"[25]

Some of the most popular ways to collect information about customers are surveys, service evaluation cards, focus groups, and listening to what customers say during business transactions, especially when they complain. Some companies, such as Marriott Hotels, have developed elaborate methods for keeping abreast of customer needs. This is not a low-profile activity at Marriott: Chairman Bill Marriott, Jr., himself reads approximately 800 letters from customers and 15,000 guest questionnaires every month![26] The rewards of taking customer information seriously are also apparent at Marriott, where occupancy rates are consistently 10 percent above the industry average.

Getting employees and executives involved in collecting customer information improves worker skills and learning, makes work more meaningful, and enhances motivation (see the discussion of job characteristics theory in Chapter 8). For example, employees at Saturn conducted customer surveys themselves—this makes them more accountable for quality while building relationships with customers.[27] In a similar vein, sending employees into customer facilities, another popular practice, provides not only feedback from customers, but also valuable information to employees about the importance of what they do. A manager in a foundry that follows this practice commented: "We take shop floor people out to the customer's plant. We want them to see the final product in place. It gets our employees out in the world to meet the customers. They get to know the customers better, and by doing that, the employees get to have a better, more caring attitude. Because they know more about what's going on."

Having top managers of a company act as customers of their own organizations—renting a room in their own hotel or buying a suit from a retail outlet—is another way to better understand customer needs. This not only gives them a sense of the quality of service but also makes them more sensitive to how the organizational policies they have created actually affect customers.[28] Credit Suisse executives, for example, practice "experience immersion," by which they watch customers, perform typical customer tasks, such as exchanging foreign currency or navigate the firm's own Web site, and even spend a day in a wheelchair to understand the challenges that disabled customers face. One executive noted that "in some cases, we actually make it hard for customers to do business with us," resulting in initiatives to redesign some of their facilities and services.[29]

A more recent approach to collecting customer information is to monitor the Internet.[30] The Internet offers companies a fertile arena for finding out what consumers think of their products. Internet users frequently seek advice from other users on strengths and weaknesses of products, share experiences on service quality, or pose specific problems they need to resolve. By monitoring the conversations on Usenet discussion groups, managers can obtain valuable insights on customer perceptions and product or service quality problems. In open forums, customer comments can often be translated into creative product improvements. In addition, the Internet can be a good source of information about competitors' products.

The cost of monitoring Internet conversations is minimal compared to the costs of other types of survey approaches, and customers are not biased by any questions that may be asked. However, the conversations may be considerably less structured and unfocused, and thus may contain less usable information. Also, unlike a focus group or telephone interview, inaccurate perceptions or factual errors cannot be corrected.

Beyond getting a thorough understanding of customer needs, companies also need to assess how well their products and services are meeting customer needs. A simple approach is to ask them directly, using a process called the "voice of the customer" (see box "The Good, the Bad, and the Ugly"). Some companies have developed unconventional and innovative ways of understanding customers. British Airways (BA) has installed video kiosks at Heathrow Airport outside London and at Kennedy Airport in New York. When upset, customers can enter the booth and create a video message for BA's management. The videos have proven so informative that, although they were initially viewed only by executives, frontline employees demanded and were given access to them. One important aspect of this method is that it gives people a sense of the emotion associated with customer response to the quality of service ("You lost my *&%$# baggage!"), which cannot easily be conveyed

THE GOOD, THE BAD, AND THE UGLY

One regional chain of restaurants realized that customers know what they want, but have a difficult time expressing their needs in ways that are meaningful to managers. This means that the company must be able to effectively translate customers' language into actionable business terms. Here are some real examples of voice-of-the-customer research that took place in cities in which the chain was considering expanding:

- "So there I was, like herded cattle, standing on the hard concrete floor, cold wind blasting my ankles every time the door opened, waiting and waiting for our name to be called."
- "And then I saw a dirty rag being slopped around a dirty table."
- "This is a great place because you can just come in and plop in a booth, just like at Mom's house."
- "The manager said, 'That's not a gnat—that's black pepper,' so I said, 'I know the difference between black pepper and a gnat—black pepper doesn't have little wings on it!'"
- "I swear! The salad looked like the server ran down to the river bank and picked weeds and grass—I'm never going back!"
- "When they're that age, going to the bathroom is a full-contact sport—they're reaching and grabbing at everything, and you're trying to keep them from touching anything because the bathroom is so dirty. And, by the way, isn't the kitchen just a few steps away?"
- "The server just stood there staring at me, chomping his gum like a cow chewing its cud."

In the first example, what the customer really was saying is, "Make me comfortable!" What do you think the customers were really saying in the other examples?

by checking a number from one through five on a customer satisfaction survey, especially when done weeks later. Texas Instruments created a simulated classroom to understand how mathematics teachers use calculators, and a manager at Levi Strauss used to talk with teens who were lined up to buy rock concert tickets.

A more formal approach to getting into customers' minds is called **imprint analysis.**[31] "Imprint" refers to the collection of associations and emotions unconsciously linked to a word, concept, or experience. The stronger the emotion, the stronger the imprint. Events and experiences imprinted with strong emotions at an early age usually last just below the level of consciousness for a person's entire life. By looking deeply into people's past experiences, imprint analysis can help companies understand what drives today's behavior. Also, imprints of current experiences reveal emerging needs; thus, imprint analysis can actually forecast customer behavior. One ice cream company, faced with responding to a shift to healthier eating, needed to understand whether it should develop a nonfat product or reduce the sugar content. An imprint analysis uncovered a surprising new customer segment whose eating habits defied common sense. During the week, these customers would consume low-fat foods and deprive themselves of desserts. But on weekends, they wanted a super-rich ice cream, acting as a reward for eating healthy during the week! Another paradox the analysis uncovered was that although customers said they wanted many different flavors, they tended to buy those that were fundamentally vanilla. The analysis revealed two senses of taste: one in the body and one in the mind. By creating vanilla variations with exciting names (and premium priced extra-creamy ice cream), the company created loyalty among existing customers while also attracting new customers.

The principles of TQ can help organizations to collect customer information by engaging the participation of everyone who encounters customers in their jobs; focusing on the processes used to collect information, such as segmenting customer groups and prioritizing customer requirements; and continually improving those processes.

Customers generally have different requirements and expectations. For example, Macy's department stores defines four lifestyles of its core customers: "Katherine"—traditional, classic dresser who doesn't take a lot of risks and likes quality; "Julie"—neo-traditional and slightly more edgy but still classic; "Erin"—a contemporary customer who loves newness and shops by brand; and "Alex"—the fashion customer who wants only the latest and greatest (there's a male version too!).[32] Another way of segmenting customers with an eye toward business results is by profitability. The Royal Bank of Canada (RBC), for instance, identified a key customer segment, "snowbirds," Canadians who spend the winter in Florida or Arizona. These individuals want to borrow in the U.S. for condos or houses and want to be served by employees who know Canada as well as the U.S. and even speak French when necessary. So RBC opened a branch in Florida, which achieved exceptional results.[33]

A company usually cannot satisfy all customers with the same products or services. This issue is particularly important for companies that do business globally (just think of the differences in regulations for automobiles in various countries or the differences in electrical power systems in the United States versus Europe). Therefore, companies that segment customers into natural groups and customize the products or services are better able to respond to customers' needs.

Disseminate Customer Information

After people in the organization have gathered information about customer needs, the next step is to broadcast this information within the organization. After all, if the people in the firm are going to work as a team to meet customer expectations, they must all be "singing from the same hymnbook," as the saying goes. Information does little good if it stays with the person or department that brought it into the organization. Wainwright Industries has a unique approach. A room in the headquarters building, named Mission Control (so dubbed by one of the managers who is a Star Trek fan), serves as the company's key information center. Not only are customer report cards displayed on a wall (along with other key quality and business information), but green and red flags are used to designate customers for whom everything is going well or for whom a problem has arisen. Red flags signal the convening of a customer team to address the problem.

AT&T, whose divisions have won several Baldrige Awards, is one organization trying to maintain a constant customer focus. Jerre Stead, president of Global Business Communications Systems, tells people in his unit: "I say if you're in a meeting, any meeting, for 15 minutes and we're not talking about customers or competitors, raise your hand and ask why. If it goes on for half an hour, leave! Leave the meeting!"[34]

Customer information must be translated into the features of the organization's products and services. This is the bottom line of quality customer-supplier relations from the supplier's point of view: giving the customers what they want. Translating customer needs into product features can be done in a structured manner using quality function deployment (QFD), a technique discussed in Chapter 3. QFD allows people to see how aspects of their products and services relate to customer satisfaction, and to make informed decisions about how their products should be improved. The overall process of using information from customers to provide quality products is summarized in Figure 6.2.

Use Customer Information

Customer information is worthless unless it is used. Customer feedback should be integrated into continuous improvement activities. For example, by listening to customers, Bank One opened nearly 60 percent of its 1,377 branches in Ohio and Texas on Saturdays, and 20 percent on Sundays. A 24-hour customer hotline is also available.

Binney & Smith, the company that produces Crayola crayons and markers, makes it a point to improve its products by taking advantage of customer feedback. Many of the letters the company receives from parents laud the role that crayons play in the artistic development of their children. However, some letters complained that the markers created permanent stains in children's clothes. After two years of research, Binney & Smith responded by developing a new line of washable markers. Marker sales doubled, demonstrating the company's ability to learn and provide what customers are looking for.[35] Binney & Smith also sponsored a contest in which customers could name one of 16 new crayon colors the company created for its Big Box. "Part of our reason for introducing new colors

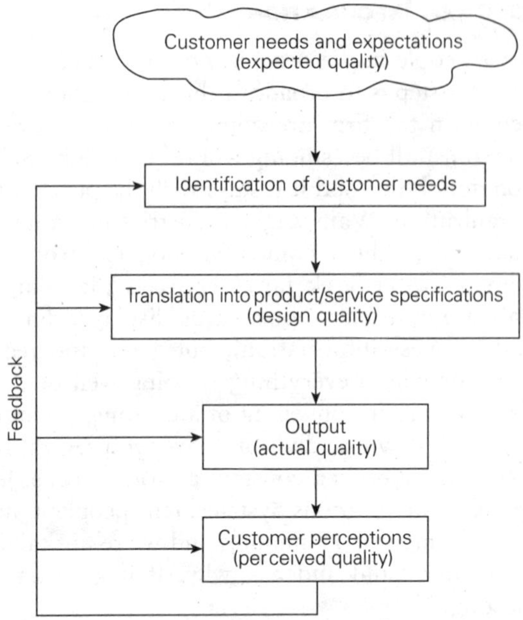

FIGURE 6.2 | THE CUSTOMER-DRIVEN QUALITY CYCLE

came from consumer suggestions. More than 50 percent said they wanted us to expand and add new colors," according to Brad Dexler, a company spokesman. Perhaps the most important use of customer information is in developing business strategies and in designing goods and services (see box "Customer Focus Is Not a Gamble!").

In the Malcolm Baldrige criteria, for example, one of the key questions is how a company collects and analyzes customer and market needs, expectations, and opportunities, and relates them to the development of strategies. Analyzing customer information can uncover a myriad of opportunities for new and improved goods and services. One way to ensure that measurement is appropriate is to collect information on both the importance and the performance of key quality characteristics. For example, a hotel might ask how important check-in speed, check-out speed, and staff attitude are, as well as how the customer rates the hotel on these attributes. Evaluation of such data can be accomplished by plotting mean performance and importance scores for individual attributes on a two-dimensional grid (for example, a scatter diagram as explained in Chapter 4). A firm ideally wants high performance on important characteristics and not to waste resources on characteristics of low importance (that is, to tolerate low performance scores). Results with high performance and low importance indicate that the firm is wasting resources on unimportant customer attributes (overkill), but those with low performance and high importance means that the firm is not performing acceptably on important customer attributes, leaving it vulnerable to competition. Often, competitor data are also plotted, providing a comparison against the competition.

Customer Focus Is Not a Gamble![36]

Dr. Gary Loveman, a Harvard Business School professor who was instrumental in introducing the "Service-Profit Chain" to the business literature, has been chief operating officer and CEO of Harrah's Entertainment, owner of casinos in Las Vegas and other locations. The service-profit chain argues that a direct correlation exists between profitability and a focus on customer loyalty and rewards to front-line employees who have the most contact with customers. Recognizing that gambling is fundamentally entertainment, Loveman focused Harrah's strategy on the casino floor, rather than on peripheral entertainment activities that are characteristic of other casino enterprises. He also directed more attention to the large numbers of loyal customers who could not be classified as "high rollers." For example, he helped devise a three-tiered loyalty card system that encouraged people to spend more to get perks like discounted rooms, no-line check-in, and separate buffet seating. The cards also collect reams of useful customer data. Harrah's also launched a program that gave these customers free or deeply discounted flights on chartered planes, shuttle service to the casino, and even blue margaritas. Of course, customers were expected to return the favor!

Manage Customer Relationships

A company builds customer loyalty by developing trust and effectively managing the interactions and relationships with customers through customer-contact employees. Truly excellent companies foster close and total relationships with customers. These companies also provide easy access to their employees. Customers of Ames Rubber Corporation have immediate access to top division management, manufacturing personnel, quality engineers, sales and service representatives, and technical support staff.

In services, customer satisfaction or dissatisfaction takes place during *moments of truth*—every instance in which a customer comes in contact with an employee of the company. Moments of truth may be direct contacts with customer representatives or service personnel, or when customers read letters, invoices, or other company correspondence. In leading fundamental change at Procter & Gamble (P&G), CEO A. G. Lafley felt that P&G was letting technology rather than consumer needs dictate new products, and that the company was not working closely enough with retailers, where consumers first see the product on the shelf—the "first moment of truth," as he called it—and that the company wasn't concerned enough with the consumer's experience at home—the "second moment of truth." Lafley summed up his strategy for P&G simply: "The consumer is boss."[37]

One study concluded that 70 percent of customers leave a supplier because of poor-quality service, not problems with products per se, and many companies are struggling to bring their service up to the level of their products.[38] One of the main areas on which companies have focused is telephone service, especially how long it takes to get someone on the phone, and to get one's question answered or order taken. Many companies have worked to make sure that phone calls are answered on the third ring, but to AMP, Inc., the world's largest manufacturer of electronic interconnection systems, three rings is an eternity. Customer calls to

AMP are answered within six seconds—that is, on the first ring. Why such an ambitious goal? AMP found that 8 percent of their customers were hanging up before their calls were answered under the three-ring standard. They don't lose many calls now.[39] TQ principles help to view customer service as a process, and focus on improving service delivery and reducing points of failure that can result in dissatisfaction. Well-designed processes for building customer relationships can help to identify early signal of customer dissatisfaction or defection.

Customer-contact employees are particularly important. They are the people whose main responsibilities bring them into regular contact with customers—in person, by telephone, or through other means. Companies must carefully select these employees who are then extensively trained and empowered to meet and exceed customer expectations. Job applicants often go through rigorous screening processes and extensive training. LeBoeuf, Lamb, Greene, & MacRae, LLP, one of the world's leading law firms, created an in-house curriculum with such workshops as "Care and Feeding of the Customer," which reinforces the idea that no matter where people are in the firm, they are customer service employees first, and what they do not only reflects on the firm but also on themselves as individuals. The course presents real work situations, and the discussion relates to "How do you think you are perceived when certain situations happen?" and "Do you realize you might be perceived as…?" with a focus on improvement activities.[40]

Service standards are measurable performance levels or expectations that define the quality of customer contact. Service standards might include technical standards such as response time, (answering the telephone within two rings), or behavioral standards (using a customer's name whenever possible). Companies need to communicate and continually reinforce their service standards. Finally, a company should implement a process for tracking adherence to the standards and providing feedback to the employees to improve their performance. Information technology supplies the data for effectively tracking conformance to customer service standards.

Despite all efforts to satisfy customers, every business experiences unhappy customers. Complaints can adversely affect business if not dealt with effectively. Many customers do not complain because they feel it wouldn't do any good or they are uncomfortable with the process. World-class organizations make it easy for customers to complain. Besides providing easy access to the company using toll-free telephone numbers (which should be adequately staffed and supported), many firms actively solicit complaints. Nissan, for instance, telephones each person who buys a new car or brings one in for significant warranty work. Its objective is to resolve all dissatisfaction within 24 hours.[41] Effective resolution of complaints increases customer loyalty and retention (see box "Don't Brush Off Customer Complaints"). At The Ritz-Carlton Hotel Company, for example, employees can spend up to $2,000 to resolve complaints with no questions asked.

Exploit CRM Technology

Customer relationship management (CRM) software is designed to help companies increase customer loyalty, target their most profitable customers, and streamline

Don't Brush Off Customer Complaints[43]

One Matt Stewart, co-founder of College Works Painting in Irvine, CA, was delighted that his summer house painting company had 95 percent customer satisfaction. After all, the company, which offers college students a way to earn money while learning to run a small business, paints 12,000 houses a year. But then he saw a Web site put up by a dissatisfied customer in North Carolina. Suddenly, the whole world could read bad things about the company. "We have more happy customers than any other painting company in the United States," Stewart said. "That's not good enough. Even one upset customer is too many." So College Works Painting and its affiliated companies have launched a systematic customer service improvement program to push that customer satisfaction toward 100 percent.

College Works Painting had the names of 12 really disgruntled customers, so Stewart and his partner Jeff Gunhus divided them up and started calling. Stewart acknowledged that he was reluctant to make those calls. It would be unpleasant, and he presumed it would cost hundreds of thousands of dollars to make things right. "After the first call, it was easy," he said. "They didn't think we'd call them." Letting customers vent their problems made Stewart realize that virtually all the problems were the company's fault and that they cost relatively little to fix. The biggest problem was the breakdown in communications. Using a consultant, the company broke down every stage of customer interaction. Then managers listed potential problems at each stage, set standards that should happen every time and identified opportunities to go beyond expectation. The person who put up the negative website has since revised it to be less strident and says he might hire College Works Painting in the future because of the way his problems were finally handled.

customer communication processes. More than $11 billion was spent on CRM-related U.S. sales at the turn of the century and is growing significantly.[42] A typical CRM system includes market segmentation and analysis, customer service and relationship building, effective complaint resolution, cross-selling goods and services, order processing, and field service.

CRM helps firms gain and maintain competitive advantage by:

- Segmenting markets based on demographic and behavioral characteristics.
- Tracking sales trends and advertising effectiveness by customer and market segment.
- Identifying and eliminated non-value-adding products that would waste resources as well as those products that better meet customers' needs and provide increased value.
- Identifying which customers should be the focus of targeted marketing initiatives with predicted high customer response rates.
- Forecasting customer retention (and defection) rates and providing feedback as to why customers leave a company.
- Studying which goods and services are purchased together, leading to good ways to bundle them.
- Studying and predicting which Web characteristics are most attractive to customers and how the Web site might be improved.
- Streamlining processes around customers rather than traditional functions, resulting in improved flow of information and cycle times.

Technology is a key enabler of CRM. CRM systems provide a variety of useful operational data to managers, including the average time spent responding to customer questions, comments, and concerns, average order tracking (flow) time, total revenue generated by each customer (and sometimes his or her family or business) from all goods and services bought by the customer—the total picture of economic value of the customer to the firm, cost per marketing campaign, and price discrepancies.

It is important to realize that although CRM can provide many benefits, it is not a solution to customer relationship problems. CRM can help an organization use data wisely to customize its product to better serve its markets, but it first requires an understanding of customer needs. In addition, one can easily capture a lot of useless information simply because it is easy to do. This makes analysis difficult, and can frustrate users.

Don't Ignore Internal Customers

Individual departments and key cross-functional processes within a company have **internal customers** who contribute to the company's mission and depend on the department's or function's products or services to ultimately serve consumers and external customers. For instance, manufacturing is a customer of purchasing, a nursing unit is a customer of the hospital laundry, and reservations is a customer of the information systems department for an airline or hotel. In addition, each employee receives inputs from others and produces some output to internal customers. A customer may be the assembly-line worker at the next station, an executive's secretary, the order-taker who passes along orders to the food preparer at McDonald's, or an X-ray technician who must meet a physician's request. The linkages among internal customers build up the "chain of customers and suppliers" throughout the company that connect every individual and function to the external customers and consumers.

The principle of mutually beneficial relationships also applies to internal customer-supplier relationships (see box "Partnering with Internal Customers").

PRACTICES FOR DEALING WITH SUPPLIERS[44]

In business today, operations are often highly decentralized and dispersed around the world. Consequently, managing a complex network of suppliers becomes a critical interorganizational issue. Suppliers play a vital role throughout the product development process, from design through distribution. Suppliers can provide technology or production processes not internally available, early design advice, and increased capacity, which can result in lower costs, faster time-to-market, and improved quality for their customers. In turn, they are assured of stable and long-term business.

Successful suppliers have a culture where employees and managers share in customers' goals, commitments, and risks to promote such long-term relationships (recall one of Deming's 14 Points about supplier relationships—not purchasing solely on the basis of price). Strong customer/supplier relationships are based on three guiding principles:

PARTNERING WITH INTERNAL CUSTOMERS[45]

GTE Supply negotiates contracts and purchases products and distributes a vast array of goods needed for telephone operations, from office supplies to telecommunications equipment. Its major customers are internal network, business, and telephone operations customer groups at each GTE local telephone company. The company created a systematic, highly effective process of obtaining and using information from internal customers, making partners of previous adversarial groups, reducing costs, and improving customer satisfaction.

This was based on systematically surveying internal customers and using the results as a basis for quality improvement. Respondents are asked to rate GTE Supply on how well it:

- provides complete information,
- understands customers' needs,
- does the job right the first time,
- provides timely responses to questions and requests,
- makes it easy to do business with,
- follows up on services,
- provides clear communication, and
- executes various other attributes.

Other questions seek information about overall satisfaction, quality, and value. Other open-ended questions ask about improvement opportunities. Detailed reports and analyses are provided to managers who use the information to set objectives, develop action plans, and implement them.

The survey and quality improvement process have transformed the organization from one of the worst-regarded to one of the best-regarded organizations in the company. GTE Supply learned that extensive, focused communication with internal customers can produce spectacular increases in satisfaction levels and decrease costs and cycle times.

1. recognizing the strategic importance of suppliers in accomplishing business objectives, particularly minimizing the total cost of ownership,
2. developing win-win relationships through partnerships rather than as adversaries, and
3. establishing trust through openness and honesty, thus leading to mutual advantages.

Although the principles of CSRs are the same in dealing with suppliers as they are with customers, the practices are somewhat different. In many companies, suppliers are treated as if they were actually a part of the organization. For example, functions such as cafeteria service, mailroom operations, and information processing are being performed by suppliers at their customers' facilities. As more and more of this type of outsourcing is done, the lines between the customer and the supplier become increasingly blurred.

To ensure that suppliers can provide high quality and reduce costs associated with incoming inspection or testing, many companies provide many types of assistance to their suppliers in developing quality assurance programs or solving quality problems. Joint conferences, training, incentives, recognition, and long-term agreements help to improve suppliers' abilities to meet key quality requirements. The Delco Moraine Division, a manufacturer of automotive brake controls, uses an awareness program that includes a videotape presentation emphasizing quality shown at supplier plants. After viewing the tape, supplier employees were better able to relate their work to Delco.

Base Purchasing Decisions on Quality and Cost

The first and most obvious practice is that purchasing decisions should be based on the quality of the product and not just its cost.[46] This, however, goes against the grain in most organizations. Generally speaking, the technical people will determine the specifications for a product to be purchased, and then the purchasing department will solicit bids or check prices with several suppliers and negotiate the contract with the one that fills the order. Purchasing personnel traditionally have been rewarded primarily for negotiating low prices, and thus this has been their focus. Supplier firms have often responded to this situation in the obvious way: by doing whatever they need to do (including sacrificing quality) to maintain low prices.

Beyond the compromises this creates for the quality of the final product, there are two other problems with this approach. First, low purchase cost often does not equal low overall cost. If a cheap (in both senses of the word) part causes a large amount of scrap or leads to high warranty costs, it may end up with a higher overall cost, often referred to as life-cycle cost. Second, pressing suppliers for ever-lower prices will minimize their profits. Although this benefits the customer in the short run, in the long run it keeps suppliers operating so close to the bone that they forgo capital investments, maintenance, and other expenses necessary to improve or even maintain their quality.[47]

Reduce the Number of Suppliers

Firms pursuing TQ also reduce the number of suppliers they work with to the point of having only one supplier for some components. Xerox reduced its suppliers by about 90 percent—from more than 4,000 to about 450 in 1990.[48] In the automotive industry, General Motors cut domestic suppliers by 45 percent, from 10,000 down to 5,500, by 1991. Ford Motor Co. likewise reduced its number of suppliers from 1,800 down to 1,000.[49] This also goes against the grain of conventional purchasing practices, as it increases the dependence of the organization on the supplier, thus weakening its bargaining position and exposing it to the possibility of an interruption in supply in the case of a labor stoppage or similar problem with the supplier.

Several advantages offset these disadvantages. For one thing, administrative costs are greatly reduced.[50] (Imagine the time to be saved by eliminating the paperwork associated with 90 percent of suppliers!) Also, cutting the number of suppliers reduces the variability in the incoming products, making it much easier to control the quality of outgoing products. This is because there are fewer "special causes" of variation, to use Deming's term.

The type of intensive CSRs that characterize TQ simply cannot be maintained with a large number of suppliers. The significance of partners (like friends or vice presidents) is lost if you have too many of them. For these reasons, many organizations continue to reduce the number of suppliers with which they do business.

Establish Long-Term Contracts

Related to the idea of fewer suppliers is the practice of establishing long-term contracts with suppliers. Establishing long-term contracts allows suppliers to make greater commitments to improving the quality of products and provides greater opportunity for joint improvement efforts and the development of teamwork across organizational boundaries.

Measure and Certify Supplier Performance

Texas Instruments measures suppliers' quality performance by parts per million defective, percentage of on-time deliveries, and cost of ownership.[51] An electronic requisitioning system allows a paperless procurement process. More than 800 suppliers are linked to Texas Instruments through an information exchange system. Integrated data systems track the incoming quality and timeliness of deliveries as materials are received. Analytical reports and online data are used to identify material defect trends. Performance reports are sent each month to key suppliers. Joint customer-supplier teams are formed to communicate and improve performance. A supplier management task force of top managers directs current and strategic approaches to improving supplier management practices.

Supplier certification is used by many companies as the focal point of their supplier management system. Formal programs typically are established to rate and certify suppliers who provide quality materials in a cost-effective and timely manner. At the Gillette Company, the supplier certification program begins with Gillette identifying those suppliers with a proven ability to meet its specifications.[52] Once a supplier is selected to participate, Gillette expects them to establish a preproduction planning system to assess the capability of their process to meet Gillette's specifications. Feedback is offered in the form of recommended changes that will improve quality, reduce cost, or facilitate ease of manufacture.

Some companies, such as Motorola, have suppliers rate them as customers. Motorola uses a 15-member council of suppliers that rates Motorola's practices and offers suggestions for improving, for example, the accuracy of production schedules or design layouts that Motorola provides.[53] Corning TPD classifies its suppliers in a hierarchy: Level 1 suppliers have a direct impact on customer satisfaction; Level 2 suppliers are important, but do not have direct linkage to customer satisfaction; Level 3 suppliers provide commodity-like products. Level 1 suppliers are supported by cross-functional teams and integrated into development activities. Armstrong conducts site visits and has a five-level scale to help suppliers understand where they stand in meeting the company's expectations. STMicroelectronics developed an annual Supplier Quality & Service Plan, which sets goals for suppliers and specifies how ST will review performance, share data, and carry out other responsibilities in the relationship. Long-term partnerships with quality-minded suppliers enabled Texas Nameplate Company to nearly eliminate inspections of incoming materials. These "ship-direct-to-stock" suppliers are required to be defect-free for at least two years and meet all requirements specified on purchase orders.

Develop Cooperative Relationships and Strategic Alliances

Increasingly, suppliers are viewed as partners with customers, because there usually is a codependent relationship. Thus, the cornerstone of TQ-style customer-supplier relationships is cooperation. In a sense, practices such as long-term contracts and fewer suppliers create an environment in which cooperation can flourish. Similar to the operation of teamwork within an organization (see Chapter 7), quality customer-supplier relations help both parties to achieve their goals.

One common form that cooperation takes is the early involvement of suppliers in the design of new products.[54] Early involvement allows suppliers to make cost-cutting and quality-improving suggestions about the design while changes are relatively easy and inexpensive to make. When the product design is not revealed to suppliers until late in the process, often out of concern that it will be leaked to competitors, such opportunities are lost.

Security concerns can be dealt with through nondisclosure agreements.[55] Another indication of cooperation is the effort of customers to help suppliers improve quality, which can take many forms. Many TQ-oriented corporations present quality-improvement seminars for their suppliers.[56] Juran recommends joint quality planning between customers and suppliers, featuring the exchange of quality-related information.[57] Although customers traditionally have hammered suppliers to lower their prices, in a cooperative relationship the focus is on helping suppliers to lower their costs, which will ultimately benefit both parties.[58]

Today, suppliers are being asked to take on greater responsibilities to help their customers. As companies focus more on their core competencies—the things they do best—they are looking outside their organizations for assistance with noncritical support processes. Customer-supplier partnerships represent an important strategic alliance in achieving excellence and business success. For example, partnerships with suppliers have helped Dell drive down parts inventories from 25 hours to 3 hours. Benefits of such partnerships include access to technology or distribution channels not available internally, shared risks in new investments and product development, improved products through early design recommendations based on supplier capabilities, and reduced operations costs through better communications. For example, FedEx and Jostens formed a strategic partnership that enabled both to benefit from new sales of scholastic jewelry and yearbooks.[59] They took advantage of each other's strengths: Josten provided a high-quality product with superior service, and FedEx provided reliable high-volume, short-interval delivery for these time-critical products.

QUALITY CUSTOMER-SUPPLIER RELATIONSHIPS IN ACTION

Many of the aspects of quality CSRs we have been discussing are illustrated by the relationship between GE Appliance and D.J. Inc., both of Louisville, Kentucky.[60] In nine years, D.J. went from being one of 100 G.E. suppliers of plastic parts to being its sole source. D.J. improved its quality by taking advantage of GE's supplier seminars in statistical process control (SPC). The company must have studied hard, as it has not had a single lot of parts rejected by GE since 1978. Early involvement in product design is commonplace for these two companies. In one typical case, D.J. recommended a minor change in product design that reduced the cost of a part by more than 5 percent and increased its expected life by 16 percent. This example typifies the advantages enjoyed by companies with quality customer-supplier relationships.

Graniterock Company of Watsonville, California, a 1992 Malcolm Baldrige Award winner, has also devoted itself to absorbing and making use of information from customers.[61] Bruce Woolpert, who shares with his brother Steve the CEO title at Graniterock, believes that the role of manager is "to make sure there's a flood of information coming into the company." Where does the flood come from? Graniterock has its customers rate its performance against its competitors in "report cards," longer surveys, quick-response cards, and focus groups. Information on what customers need and what is being done to satisfy them is distributed throughout the company via team meetings, an annual recognition day, and the appropriately titled company newsletter, *Rock Talk*.

Graniterock learned that quarry customers wanted to pick up rock very quickly at any time of the day or night. To satisfy this need, the company invested a great deal of money in Granite Xpress, a system that allows customers to pull up to the quarry, check the computer for their order, and insert a magnetic card to load their own orders. Not only does this system operate 24 hours a day, but it has reduced the time at the quarry for truckers from 30 minutes to 10.

Graniterock personnel also frequently make trips to benchmark other companies, both in their industry (aggregate and concrete producers) and out of their industry (a gold mine). Perhaps the furthest afield they have roamed is to Domino's Pizza, another company that is concerned about on-time delivery. Domino's told Graniterock where to get better maps and suggested that they adopt Domino's practice of writing house numbers on maps.

A third example is EMC Corporation, a manufacturer of data storage systems.[62] On one occasion, a bank in Wisconsin suddenly lost access to its data-storage facility. In quick succession, the screens in the bank's computer center started flashing "Data unavailable"—a message that might as well have read "Closed for business." Within minutes, customer service engineers at EMC headquarters had retrieved, remotely, the logs of EMC's storage systems at the bank and had begun to examine them, but the cause of the problem was not readily evident. Four hours later, the engineers who designed the machine joined the effort. They recreated the bank's setup in a $1 billion facility that EMC created for such simulations, including a double of the EMC machine that was faulty. Only then did they find the problem, and they created a patch that they immediately sent to Wisconsin. But this was just the beginning; the VP of global technical support jumped on a plane to Wisconsin, and walked into the bank's boardroom to help restore faith in the company by answering the questions: "What happened?"; "Why did it happen?"; and "How do we make sure it doesn't happen again?" By the end of the meeting, the VP had sold the bank on a new EMC system that builds a mirror copy of data, which is always available.

CUSTOMER-SUPPLIER RELATIONS IN ORGANIZATION THEORY

Much of the organization literature has argued that firms should consider customers as partners for success.[63] As far back as 1973, Gersuny and Rosengren argued that diverse customer roles require new bonds of interdependence and an increasingly complex social network that crosses traditional organizational boundaries.[64] They identified four distinct roles for customers:

1. resource,
2. worker (or coworker),
3. buyer, and
4. beneficiary (or user).

A fifth role has emerged from work in the human service area: customers can be a key outcome, or product, of value-creating transformation activities, such as education and health delivery. In the first two roles, customers act as inputs to the transformation process, while in the last three, they act as outputs. Each of these roles is instrumental in creating competitive quality within a firm.

In reviewing the organizational literature for these roles, Lengnick-Hall suggests that the following organizational practices are positively related to the competitive quality of production processes and outcomes:

- practices that deliberately select and carefully manage customer resources, foster an effective alliance between the firm and its customer resources, and improve the quality of its customer resources;
- practices that provide clear opportunities for co-production, enhance customer abilities as co-producers, and increase customer motivation toward co-production;
- activities that foster trust, develop interdependence, share information, and initiate friendly, mutually beneficial customer-organization bonds;
- activities that foster unambiguous communication with users, focus on meeting customer needs, offer realistic previews, achieve dimensions of quality that customers truly care about, and ensure that actual use is consistent with intended use; and
- activities that create opportunities for direct communication and interaction between users and production/core service personnel.

Thus, firms should design systems that involve and empower customers throughout the input-transformation-output system, rather than merely rely on customers to define their preferences and evaluate the products and services provided to them. This conclusion is certainly the foundation of modern TQ approaches and is reflected in the Baldrige Award criteria. One example of this in practice is ADAC Laboratories, a manufacturer of high-technology health care equipment and a 1996 Baldrige winner. Not only does ADAC survey customers and potential customers and measure satisfaction, they invite customers to participate in strategic planning meetings, have lunch with customers attending new equipment training sessions, and host formal user group meetings to help prioritize product enhancements, share tips on new uses, and provide other information.

Total quality also can be related to a number of traditional organizational theories. The following sections discuss TQ's relationship with the resource dependence perspective and the theory of integrative bargaining.

The Resource Dependence Perspective

The organizational theory most directly comparable to the TQ view of customer-supplier relations is the Resource Dependence Perspective (RDP) developed by Jeffrey Pfeffer and Gerald Salancik.[65] This perspective—which deals with how organizations manage to get the resources they need from their environment—resembles TQ in some ways, yet differs in others.

The most important similarity between the two perspectives is their mutual emphasis on the idea that the sources of an organization's success lie outside its boundaries. Although the idea that customers ultimately grant the organization its continued existence has become familiar as a fundamental principle of TQ, Pfeffer and Salancik point out that much organization theory focuses on the internal operations of organizations, giving less emphasis to the organization's environment:

> Most current writers give only token consideration to the environmental context of organizations. The environment is there, somewhere outside the organization, and the idea is mentioned that environments constrain or affect organizations.... After this, the task of management is considered. Somehow, the things to be managed are usually within the organization, assumed to be under its control, and often have to do with the direction of low-level hired personnel. When authors get down to the task of describing the running of the organization, the relevance of the environment fades.[66]

According to the RDP, the effectiveness of an organization should be understood in terms of how well it meets the demands of external groups and organizations that are concerned with its actions and products. This is similar to the TQ conception of quality as meeting or exceeding customer expectations. There is an interesting difference, however, between the RDP concept of effectiveness and the TQ concept of quality.

TQ has traditionally focused almost exclusively on the organization's customers—that is, those who purchase the organization's products and provide the wherewithal for the organization's continued survival. The RDP, however, recognizes that organizations must satisfy the demands of not only customers, but also other entities in the environment including various government agencies, interest groups, shareholders, and—to some extent—society as a whole.

A government regulatory agency can make life miserable for an organization it does not believe is following government regulations—for example, a coal mine with inadequate safety procedures or a restaurant with unsanitary practices. In the extreme case, the government can even shut them down. Interest groups can influence customers to boycott a product for reasons unrelated to the quality of the product itself. Certain brands of California wine were boycotted for years because of the alleged mistreatment of the migrant farm workers who picked their grapes.

Shareholders of public corporations in recent years have become a constituency to be reckoned with. They are making increasing demands on how corporations operate, including not only economic but also social and environmental aspects of performance such as minority hiring and use of recyclable materials.

From this perspective it is clear that although customers are important, groups and organizations other than customers can play a major role in determining an organization's success. TQ advocates can take two avenues in dealing with this issue. The first would be to enlarge the concept of customers to include all those who have a stake in the organization. Following this logic, an organization would not be seen as practicing TQ unless it met the expectations of all of its constituencies, not just its customers in the traditional sense. However, different groups are apt to have very different expectations for the behavior of an organization, thus making it quite difficult to satisfy all parties.

The other avenue would be for TQ advocates to recognize that although providing quality to customers is the overriding focus of an organization's activities, satisfying customers alone will not necessarily guarantee continued success, due to the potential influence of other constituencies. Interestingly, this perspective has been incorporated into the Baldrige Award criteria through its core value of Societal Responsibility:

> An organization's leaders should stress its responsibilities to the public and the need to practice good citizenship. These responsibilities refer to basic expectations of our organization related to business ethics and protection of public health, safety, and the environment.... Planning should anticipate adverse impacts from production, distribution, transportation, use, and disposal of your products. Effective planning should prevent problems, provide for a forthright response if problems occur, and make available information and support needed to maintain public awareness, safety, and confidence.... Organizations should not only meet all local, state, and federal laws and regulatory requirements, but they should treat these and related requirements as opportunities for improvement "beyond mere compliance." (2002 Baldrige National Quality Program Criteria for Performance Excellence, p. 3)

Another similarity between TQ and the RDP is in their recognition of interdependence between organizations as a fact of organizational life that must be managed effectively.

> In the current dense environment ... interdependencies are the problem. The dominant problems of the organization have become managing its exchanges and its relationships with the diverse interests affected by its actions.... The increasing density of relationships among diverse interests has led to less willingness to rely on unconstrained market forces. Negotiation, political strategies, the management of the organization's institutional relationships—these have all become more important.[67]

Thus, the RDP shares with TQ the idea that managing interdependencies with other organizations is a key to success. The two perspectives diverge again, however, when it comes to how such interdependencies should be managed. Quality customer-supplier relationships are seen from the TQ perspective as consisting of mutually beneficial partnerships. Such an option, however, is not anticipated in the RDP. From this perspective, interdependence should be managed by some combination of gaining as much control as possible over the other organization, minimizing the other party's control over one's own organization, making it difficult for the other organization to monitor and influence one's behavior, and so on.

When compared to the protection of self-interest inherent in the recommendations of the RDP, the TQ win-win doctrine sounds somewhat naive. Yet most organizations practicing TQ and building partnerships with their customers and suppliers have traditionally managed customer-supplier relationships in the manner suggested by the RDP and have been dissatisfied with the results. The partnership efforts are mostly in their early stages, and there is no guarantee that they will ultimately succeed. As of now, however, they are the preferred method of many firms for managing interdependence.

Integrative Bargaining

The idea of building cooperative relationships that benefit both parties to a negotiation is not something that was created by writers or practitioners of TQ. The idea of mutually beneficial relationships and win-win bargaining comes from a long tradition of research and writing on conflict management and negotiation.[68]

The idea behind this research tradition is that both parties will benefit more in the long run if they work together to help each other, rather than each one striving to win each round of negotiation. This tradition has been appropriated by writers on TQ, perhaps because it is consistent with the idea of customer orientation and teamwork. This is another area where TQ doctrine derives in a straightforward manner from existing organizational theory.

The key ideas of integrative bargaining (or principled negotiation) are

1. separate the people from the problem;
2. focus on interests, not positions;
3. invent options for mutual gain; and
4. insist on using objective criteria.

These principles have significant implications for CSRs in total quality. The first point deals with eliminating emotions from issues, forcing participants to work together to attack the problem and not each other. For example, focus on interests, not positions, means that it is important to search for ways to meet each party's needs, not necessarily the way they have been met in the past. Rather than focusing on the position (I want air-conditioning in the car), one searches for the underlying interest (I spend a lot of time in the car, so it is important to be comfortable), and then finds a way to meet that interest. The second point results from the fact that a negotiating position often obscures what the bargainers really want. Compromising on positions, as is often done in union agreements, may not take care of the true needs that led people to adopt the positions in the first place. For the third point, it is difficult to make decisions in the presence of an adversary. Creatively identifying options without the pressure of adversarial negotiation can reconcile differing interests and "expand the pie." Finally, fair solutions result from deciding on the criteria on which to evaluate the result, not the personalities of the negotiators.

Review and Discussion Questions

1. How does Mercy Health Systems meet the expectations of its customers? How does it exceed expectations?
2. What can be learned about customer-supplier relationships from the story about IBM and its Japanese supplier?
3. What is the difference between customer satisfaction and customer loyalty? Why is it important to distinguish between these two concepts?
4. Draw a diagram of a customer-supplier chain that includes at least four organizations. What attributes of quality are required at each link in the chain? How does quality at the beginning of the chain influence quality at the end?
5. Why are suppliers important to a company's quality efforts?
6. Identify three practices through which companies can better understand their customers' needs.
7. Prepare a list of moments of truth that you encounter during a typical quarter or semester at your college or university.
8. Analyze the remaining voice of the customer statements in the example box "The Good, the Bad, and the Ugly," and try to determine what the customers are saying in actionable terms that are meaningful to the managers of the restaurant.
9. Think of a type of customer that you know reasonably well. Try to identify some unmet needs of this type of customer and to think of some new features of the products and/or services they purchase that would excite them. Why do you think these features are not being offered?
10. Identify a customer-supplier relationship in which you are involved. How does it compare to the principles and practices of TQ relationships? In what specific ways could adopting some of the principles and practices discussed in this chapter improve this relationship?
11. Consider the following customer experiences.[69] What would your reaction be to each of them?
    a. Looking to buy a cell phone, I met a saleswoman who introduced herself, asked my name, went through the features related to my needs, and didn't try to sell me the most expensive phone.
    b. I was shopping in a home-improvement store and encountered a salesman who remarked, "Oh, shopping for your husband?"
    c. At one restaurant, we were stranded in a booth without silverware or a waiter. We finally made contact with a waitress who said, "Your waiter is late, and I can't take your order because this isn't my station."
    d. I was shopping for a TV antenna, and asked the salesman the difference between the models. He replied, "They're all pretty much the same. Some cost more because they look better."
12. How do the terms used for customers in different industries and occupations (e.g., patients, clients, passengers, students) influence how people in these industries think about their customers?
13. Think about a prescription that a doctor may write. Describe the different types of customers involved in the process of filling the prescription.
14. How would TQ and the resource dependence perspective differ in describing the quality and effectiveness of a state university?
15. Can you think of a situation in which customers are not important to the success of an organization?
16. How should an organization go about deciding who its customers are? Identify the customers of a university, a government agency, and a movie producer.

17. Below are listed some key principles of TQ. Describe what steps a company could take upstream in the supply chain to practice these principles.
    a. customer-driven quality
    b. built-in quality at the source
    c. management by fact
    d. a focus on prevention rather than detection
    e. process focus
    f. striving for zero defects
    g. continuous improvement
    h. making quality everyone's responsibility

18. Customer satisfaction is generally discussed from the consumer viewpoint. However, it is equally important from a business-to-business transaction perspective. Discuss what suppliers to other businesses can do to improve satisfaction.

CASES

The Case of the Missing Reservation

Mark, Donna, and their children, along with another family, traditionally attend Easter brunch at a large downtown hotel. This year, as in the past, Donna called and made a reservation about three weeks prior to Easter.

Because half the party consisted of small children, they arrived 20 minutes prior to the 11:30 reservation to assure being seated early. When they arrived, however, the hostess said that they did not have a reservation. The hostess explained that guests sometimes fail to show and that she would probably have a table available for them before long. Mark and Donna were quite upset and insisted that they had made a reservation and expected to be seated promptly. The hostess told them, "I believe that you made a reservation, but I can't seat you until all the people on the reservation list are seated. You are welcome to go to the lounge for complimentary coffee and punch while you wait." When Mark asked to see the manager, the hostess replied, "I am the manager," and turned to other duties. The party was eventually seated at 11:45, but was not at all happy with the experience.

The next day, Mark wrote a letter to the hotel manager explaining the entire incident. Mark was in the MBA program at the local university and was taking a course on total quality management. In the class, they had just studied issues of customer focus and some of the approaches used at The Ritz-Carlton Hotel, a two-time Baldrige Award winner. Mark concluded his letter with the statement, "I doubt that we would have experienced this situation at a hotel that truly believes in quality." About a week later, he received the following letter:

> We enjoy hearing from our valued guests, but wish you had experienced the level of service and accommodations that we strive to achieve here at our hotel. Our restaurant manager received your letter and asked me to respond as Total Quality Lead.
>
> Looking back at our records we did not show a reservation on the books for your family. I have addressed your comments with the appropriate department head so that others will not have to experience the same inconveniences that you did.
>
> Thank you once again for sharing your thoughts with us. We believe in a philosophy of "continuous improvement," and it is through feedback such as yours that we can continue to improve the service to our guests.

Discussion Questions

1. Were the hostess's actions consistent with a customer-focused quality philosophy? What might she have done differently?
2. How would you have reacted to the letter that Mark received? Could the Total Quality Lead have responded differently? What does the fact that the hotel manager did not personally respond to the customer tell you?

Pauli's Restaurant and Microbrewery

You have been appointed general manager of Pauli's Restaurant and Microbrewery, a popular downtown pub in a major city, after working there for several years as a waiter and recently a shift manager. Pauli's has locations in six regional cities and operates a corporate Web site. One of the features of the Web site is a customer feedback section; comments are sent directly to the corporate VP and to the appropriate general manager. After your first weekend on the job, you receive the following comment:

> We had a lousy service experience last Saturday at your restaurant. We eat there several times a year before going to the theater. We make a reservation for 6:15, and we are usually done eating—including dessert—by 7:30 or 7:40 at the latest so we can get to the theater in time. Service was ridiculously slow on

Saturday. We finally ordered dessert around 7:20–7:25. But it took at least 10 min for the waitress to come back and tell us they didn't have the coconut key lime pie that was listed on special; we ordered something else, and waited and waited. Eventually we had to find the waitress and tell her to forget it because we didn't have time. My wife couldn't even flag her down to get her coffee refilled, despite trying for a half-hour. To top it off, we didn't even receive an apology; the only thing the waitress did quickly was to process the check. She was clearly overcommitted to too many tables to provide us with adequate service. It was very disappointing for what we considered one of our favorite places, and bringing friends with us who had never been there before.

Draft a response to this customer. Analyze the responses of your classmates. What makes a good "service recovery" response? Develop some general guidelines.

Landmark Dining

Landmark Dining, Inc. (Landmark), is a family-owned and -operated steak and seafood restaurant small business in south Texas. The first restaurant, Harrisburg Station, and its associated catering business, Harrisburg Station Catering, are located in one of the oldest standing landmarks in Houston—a train station built in 1857 in the small settlement then known as Harrisburg. The second restaurant, Texas Lightkeeper, is located in a restored lighthouse built in 1853 in Galveston. Landmark restaurants offer an exceptional dining experience at a good value to the Houston and Galveston metropolitan areas.

A. The executive team at Landmark Dining has met recently to discuss better ways of listening and learning to its customers. One manager suggested some enhancements to the "voice of the customer" process that she had read about in a quality management book. Her suggestion is summarized in a matrix shown below:

The Voice of Experience refers to knowledge acquired from industry and market sources, and the Voice of the Process refers to data collected from the service delivery process (wait times, for example). To implement this idea, Landmark needs to identify types and sources of data and information that they should collect in each grid of this matrix. Suggest some ideas that would provide the information needed to truly understand the customer experience and provide opportunities for ensuring a high-quality experience as well as potential improvements.

B. During the same meeting, another manager noted that Landmark needs to establish a set of standards for customer contact that convey quality and exceptional service. They identified six categories of staff and employees:

Voice	Before the Dining Experience	During the Dining Experience	After the Dining Experience
Voice of Experience			
Voice of the Customer			
Voice of the Server			
Voice of the Process			

1. All staff that encounter a customer anywhere in the facility
2. Hosts and hostesses
3. Bar service staff
4. Food service staff
5. Chefs
6. Shift managers

Suggest some standards that might be instituted to ensure an outstanding customer experience. As an example, one customer contact requirement might be for staff members to ask customers about any issues that were not resolved in the previous dining service step and verify their continuing satisfaction; for instance, servers might ask customers about their reservations, reception, and bar service.

The Campus Food Court[70]

The manager of the Campus Food Court at a large university conducted a comprehensive student survey to understand how important 20 different customer-focused attributes are, as well as how students perceived the company is doing on these attributes. The attributes used in the survey were

(1) Has a visually attractive dining area.
(2) Has staff members who are clean, neat, and appropriately dressed.
(3) Has a decor in keeping with its image and price range.
(4) Has a menu that is easily readable.
(5) Has dining areas that are thoroughly clean.
(6) Has comfortable seats in the dining area.

(7) Quickly corrects any problems with service that is brought to its attention.
(8) Is dependable and consistent.
(9) During busy times, has employees shift to help each other maintain speed and quality of service.
(10) Provides prompt and quick service.
(11) Makes extra effort to handle special requests.
(12) Has employees who can answer your questions completely.
(13) Has personnel who are willing and able to give you information about menu items, their ingredients, and method of preparation.
(14) Has personnel who seem well trained, competent, and experienced.
(15) Seems to give employees support so they can do their job well.
(16) Has employees who are sensitive to your individual needs and wants, rather than always relying on policies and procedures.
(17) Makes you feel special.
(18) Anticipates your individual needs or wants.
(19) Has employees who are sympathetic and reassuring if something is wrong.
(20) Seems to have customers best interest at heart.

The mean importance and performance ratings, on a scale from 1 (Very poor) to 7 (Very good) for a large sample of students were

Attribute	Importance	Performance
(1)	5.4	5.1
(2)	6.0	4.9
(3)	5.2	4.7
(4)	5.7	5.3
(5)	6.4	5.0
(6)	5.7	4.9
(7)	5.9	4.6
(8)	5.8	4.8
(9)	6.0	4.3
(10)	6.3	4.6
(11)	5.1	4.2
(12)	5.4	4.3
(13)	5.0	4.2
(14)	5.7	4.6
(15)	5.4	4.6
(16)	5.2	4.1
(17)	4.3	3.6
(18)	5.0	4.0
(19)	5.2	4.1
(20)	5.7	4.3

Analyze these data using the Importance-Performance grid below and provide recommendations to the manager.

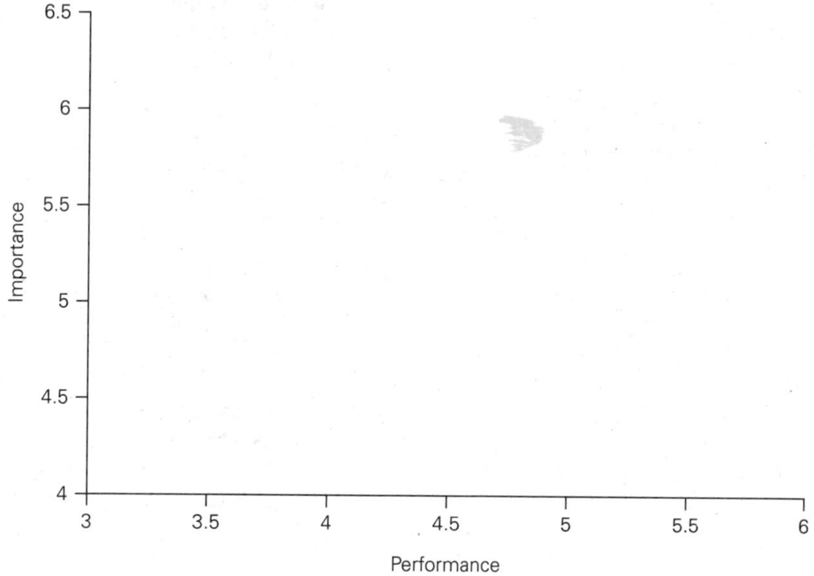

Endnotes

1. 2007 Malcolm Baldrige National Quality Program Award Winner Profile, National Institute of Standards and Technology, U.S. Department of Commerce.
2. Don Peppers and Martha Rogers, "Customers Don't Grow on Trees," *Fast Company*, July 2005, 19–20.
3. Reported in "Total Quality Management and Competitiveness" by G. Pouskouleli, *Engineering Digest*, December 1991, pp. 14–17. The Japanese response is based on a story in the *Toronto Sun* by S. Ford, April 25, 1983, p. 6.
4. This idea has been promoted by Richard J. Schonberger in his book, *Building a Chain of Customers*, New York: Free Press, 1990.
5. Myron Magnet, "The New Golden Rule of Business," *Fortune*, February 21, 1994, 60–64.
6. Patricia C. La Londe, "Surveys As Supplier Relationship Tool" ASQ's 54th Annual Quality Congress proceedings, Indianapolis, IN, 2000, pp. 684–686.
7. Arthur R. Tenner and Irving J. DeToro, *Total Quality Management: Three Steps to Continuous Improvement*, Reading, Mass.: Addison-Wesley, 1992, p. 197.
8. Patricia Sellers, "Companies That Serve You Best," *Fortune*, May 31, 1993, pp. 74–88.
9. Carl Sewell and Paul B. Brown, *Customers for Life*, New York: Doubleday-Currency, 1990.
10. Jane Norman, "Royal Treatment Keeps Customers Loyal," *The Cincinnati Enquirer*, May 31, 1998, E3, E5.
11. The Forum Corporation, Customer Focus Research, Executive Briefing, Boston 1988.
12. Customer engagement was introduced in the 2009-10 Baldrige Criteria for Performance Excellence as a recognition of its increasing importance to organizations that compete in a global marketplace and in competitive local markets.
13. The Forum Corporation, "Customer Focus Research," executive briefing, Boston, 1988.
14. Sources: Southwest Airlines home page, http://iflyswa.com; Richard S. Teitelbaum, "Where Service Flies Right," *Fortune*, August 24, 1992, pp. 117–118; and Kevin Freiberg and Jackie Freiberg, *NUTS! Southwest Airlines' Crazy Recipe for Business and Personal Success*, Austin, Tex.: Bard Press, 1996.
15. Robert J. Trent, "Applying TQM to SCM," *Supply Chain Management Review*, May/June 2001, pp. 70–78.
16. Tim Minahan, "What Makes a Supplier World-Class?" *Purchasing*, Vol. 125, No. 2, August 13, 1998, pp. 50–61.
17. Justin Martin, "Are You as Good as You Think You Are?" *Fortune*, September 30, 1996, pp. 142–152.
18. Valerie Reitman, "Toyota's Fast Rebound after Fire at Supplier Shows Why It's Tough," *Wall Street Journal*, May 8, 1997, p. 1.
19. Based on Jennifer Saranow, "Selling the Special Touch," *Wall Street Journal*, July 18, 2006, B1, B8; 1992 and 1999 The Ritz-Carlton Hotel's Malcolm Baldrige National Quality Award application summaries; Cheri Henderson, "Putting on the Ritz," *The TQM Magazine* 2, No. 5 (November–December 1992), 292–296; and remarks by various Ritz-Carlton managers at the 2000 Quest for Excellence Conference, Washington D.C.
20. David Waldman provided this insight.
21. Adapted from the article on Feargal Quinn by Polly Labarre in "Who's Fast in 2002," *Fast Company*, November 2001, pp. 88–94.
22. Reprinted with the permission of the Free Press, a Division of Macmillan, Inc., from *Juran on Leadership for Quality: An Executive Handbook* by J. M. Juran. Copyright 1989 by Juran Institute Inc.
23. John Carlisle, quoted in Tenner and DeToro, *Total Quality Management*.
24. Richard C. Whiteley, *The Customer-Driven Company, Moving from Talk to Action*, Reading, Mass.: Addison-Wesley, 1991, p. 7.
25. Quoted in "When Customer Research Is a Lousy Idea" by Willard I. Zangwill, *Wall Street Journal*, March 8, 1993.
26. Marriott's approach to gathering information from customers is discussed in detail in Whiteley, *The Customer-Driven Company*.
27. Mark Graham Brown, "And the Survey Says ... Customer Behavior Can't Always Be Predicted," *The Journal for Quality and Participation*, Vol. 23, No. 2, March/April 2000, pp. 30–32.
28. See Benson P. Shapiro, V. Kasturi Rangan, and John J. Sviokla, "Staple Yourself to an Order," *Harvard Business Review*, July-August 1992, pp. 113–122.

29. Ian Wylie, "Talk to Our Customers? Are You Crazy?" *Fast Company*, July/August 2006, 71, 74.
30. Byron J. Finch, "A New Way to Listen to the Customer," *Quality Progress*, Vol. 30, No. 5, May 1997, pp. 73–76.
31. Cristina Afors and Marilyn Zuckerman Michaels, "A Quick, Accurate Way to Determine Customer Needs," *Quality Progress*, July 2001, pp. 82–87.
32. "Here's Mr. Macy," *Fortune*, November 28, 2005, 139–142.
33. Larry Selden and Geoffrey Colvin, "5 Rules for Finding the Next Dell," *Fortune*, July 12, 2004, 103–107.
34. Quoted in "Could AT&T Rule the World?" by David Kirkpatrick, *Fortune*, May 17, 1993.
35. Whiteley, *The Customer-Driven Company*.
36. Julie Schlosser, "Teacher's Bet," *Fortune*, March 8, 2004, pp. 158–164.
37. Robert Berner, "P&G, New and Improved," *Business Week*, July 7, 2003, pp. 52–63.
38. Whiteley, *The Customer-Driven Company*.
39. "Complex Quality: AMP Rings up Service Success," by Dick Schaaf, *The Quality Imperative*, September 1992, pp. 16–26.
40. Ron Zemke, "The Best Customer to Have Is the One You've Already Got," *The Journal for Quality and Participation*, March/April 2000, pp. 33–35.
41. "Focusing on the Customer," *Fortune*, June 5, 1989, p. 226.
42. Painting Company Refuses to Brush Off Customer Complaints, The Orange County Register (CA), January 24, 2008, http://www.asq.org/quality-news/qnt/execute/displaySetup?newsID=2931
43. See "Behind the Numbers," *CIO Magazine*, November 2, 2000, available at http://www2.cio.com/
44. These practices are based on *The Deming Route to Quality and Productivity* by William W. Scherkenbach, Rockville, Md.: Mercury Press, 1988; and on *Juran on Leadership for Quality* by Joseph M. Juran, New York: Free Press, 1989.
45. James H. Drew and Tye R. Fussell, "Becoming Partners with Internal Customers," *Quality Progress*, Vol. 29, No. 10, October 1996, pp. 51–54.
46. This idea has long been championed by Deming. See the discussion of his 14 Points in Chapter 2.
47. For a discussion of these two points, see David N. Burt, "Managing Suppliers Up to Speed," *Harvard Business Review*, July-August 1989, pp. 127–135.
48. Tenner and DeToro, *Total Quality Management*.
49. John R. Emshwiller, "Suppliers Struggle to Improve Quality as Big Firms Slash Their Vendor Rolls," *Wall Street Journal*, August 16, 1991, B2.
50. Patrick J. McMahon, "Supplier Involvement," Chapter 9 in *The Improvement Process* by H. James Harrington, New York: McGraw-Hill, 1987.
51. Texas Instruments Defense Systems & Electronics Group, Malcolm Baldrige Application Summary (1992).
52. Mike Lovitt, "Responsive Suppliers Are Smart Suppliers," *Quality Progress*, June 1989, pp. 50–53.
53. McMahon, op. cit.
54. This point is discussed by Randall S. Schuler and Drew L. Harris in *Managing Quality: The Primer for Middle Managers*, Reading, Mass.: Addison-Wesley, 1992.
55. McMahon, op. cit.
56. McMahon, op. cit.
57. Juran, *Juran on Leadership for Quality*.
58. Schuler and Harris, *Managing Quality*.
59. AT&T Corporate Quality Office, Supplier Quality Management: Foundations, 1994, p. 52.
60. This example is discussed by David N. Burt in "Managing Suppliers up to Speed," *Harvard Business Review*, July-August 1989, pp. 127–135.
61. The section on Granite Rock is based on "The Changemasters," John Case, *Inc.*, March 1992, pp. 58–70.
62. Mike Ruettgers, "When a Customer Believes in You … They'll Stick with You Almost No Matter What," *Fast Company*, June 2001, pp. 138–145.
63. Cynthia A. Lengnick-Hall, "Customer Contributions to Quality: A Different View of the Customer-Oriented Firm," *Academy of Management Review*, Vol. 21, No. 3, 1996, pp. 791–824.
64. C. Gersuny and W. R. Rosengren, *The Service Society*, Cambridge, Mass.: Schenkman Press, 1973.
65. Jeffrey Pfeffer and Gerald R. Salancik, *The External Control of Organizations: A Resource Dependence Perspective*, New York: Harper & Row, 1978.
66. Ibid., pp. 257–258.
67. Pfeffer and Salancik, *The External Control of Organizations*, p. 94.
68. See, for example, David W. Johnson and Frank P. Johnson, *Joining Together: Group Theory and Group Skills*, Englewood Cliffs, N.J.: Prentice

Hall, 1975; Max H. Bazerman and Roy J. Lewicki (eds.), *Negotiating in Organizations*, Beverly Hills, Calif.: Sage Publications, 1983; M. Afzalur Rahim, "A Strategy for Managing Conflict in Complex Organizations," *Human Relations*, Vol. 38, No. 1, 1985, pp. 81–89. From a popular standpoint, the book *Getting to Yes* by Roger Fisher and William Ury, New York: Penguin Books USA, 1981, addresses the principles described in this section in more detail.

69. "Getting to Very Satisfied," *Fast Company*, February 2004, p. 32.
70. Adapted from Henry Aigbedo and Ravi Parameswaran, "Importance-performance analysis for improving quality of campus food service," *International Journal of Quality and Reliability Management*, 21, 8, 2004, pp. 876–896.

Designing Organizations for Performance Excellence

CHAPTER 7

Performance Excellence Profile: Boeing Aerospace Support[1]

Boeing Aerospace Support (AS) is part of the Boeing Company, the largest aerospace company in the world. Boeing AS provides products and services, including aircraft maintenance, modification, and repair, and training for aircrews and maintenance staff, to reduce life-cycle costs and increase the effectiveness of aircraft. Ninety-seven percent of Boeing AS's business comes from military customers. Boeing AS has a workforce of over 13,000 employees based at its headquarters in St. Louis, Missouri, and nine major sites—eight in the United States and one in Australia—as well as more than 129 secondary and smaller sites. In this highly competitive industry, new orders for Boeing AS's products and services have grown each year since 1999 and are significantly higher than its competitors' cumulative growth.

Key factors to the success of Boeing AS are its commitment to customer satisfaction, performance-to-plan, and on-time delivery of quality products and services. Since 1998, the "exceptional" and "very good" responses from government customers regarding Boeing AS's performance have gone up 23 percent. In 2003, the exceptional responses nearly doubled those of 2002. In a survey of customers conducted by an independent third party, positive responses improved from 60 percent in 2001 to more than 75 percent in 2002.

Carefully planned and well-managed processes combined with a culture that encourages knowledge sharing and working together have been essential to Boeing AS's ability to deliver high-quality products and services. Boeing AS has developed a seven-step approach for defining, managing, stabilizing, and improving processes. This process-based management, or PBM, methodology also is used to set goals and performance metrics and requires interaction and agreement among process owners, users, suppliers, and customers.

Teams of employees who "own" and are responsible for the company's complex operations and processes are the core of the company's high-performance work environment. A highly structured process known as the "AS People System" helps to ensure that employees who make up these teams understand priorities and expectations; have the knowledge, training, and tools they need to do the job and to assess performance against goals and objectives; and are rewarded and recognized for their accomplishments. Programs such as the Atlas Award, which recognizes outstanding team achievement, cash awards, and stock options are used to acknowledge employees who develop innovative solutions to problems. Cash awards to individuals and teams for extraordinary performance have tripled over the past three years.

Developing a sound, long-term strategy and then turning that strategic intent into meaningful action is another of Aerospace Support's strengths and competitive advantages. AS uses an Enterprise Planning Process (EPP) composed of four process elements—Key Data Factors, Strategies, Plans, and Execution—and 10 defined steps, including Lessons Learned and Process Improvements, to plan and execute key strategies. Senior leaders and business, strategic planning, and functional councils each have a role in developing and executing the EPP to ensure that all business functions and sites are integrated and aligned with the overall strategic plan.

To improve performance, a five-step system helps Boeing AS select, analyze, and align data and information. The system begins by gathering requirements and expectations from stakeholders and results in a set of action plans and performance goals and metrics. A "Goal Flowdown" process communicates goals and directions not only throughout the organization but also to customers and suppliers. Measurement, analysis, and knowledge management systems provide performance status and other information needed to make decisions. Finally, performance analyses and reviews are conducted regularly, resulting in recommendations or actions needed to improve performance at all levels.

In this large, widespread organization, communication is vital. Employees are encouraged to "shamelessly share" information across businesses, sites, and functions. A continuous flow of information also comes from a wide range of sources, including meetings, roundtable discussions, online newsletters, and functional and business councils.

Boeing Aerospace Support has selected many facets of its organization, such as its carefully designed processes and team-based focus, to support high performance. Many organizations that pursue performance excellence strategies have found it necessary to reconfigure the structures of their organizations. This chapter discusses the changes in organization design necessary to achieve total quality. The chapter will:

- discuss issues related to choosing organizational structures;
- describe the functional structure, the most common structure used in a business;

- show how many aspects of the functional structure stand in the way of quality and what changes are necessary to create organization structures that support quality and high performance;
- provide several examples of how firms are making substantial changes in their organizations in order to implement a better focus on TQ and performance excellence; and
- compare organizational design from a TQ point of view to more conventional perspectives.

ORGANIZATIONAL STRUCTURE

The effectiveness of an organization depends in part on its organizational structure—the clarification of authority, responsibility, reporting lines, and performance standards among individuals at each level of the organization. Traditional organizations tend to develop structures that help them to maintain stability. They tend to be highly structured, both in terms of rules and regulations, as well as the height of the "corporate ladder," sometimes with seven or more layers of managers between the CEO and the first-line worker. In contrast, organizations in the rapidly changing environments characteristic of modern organizations have to build flexibility into their organization structures. Hence, they tend to have fewer written rules and regulations and flatter organizational structures.

Several factors having to do with the context of the organization affect how work is organized. They include the following:[2]

1. *Company operational and organizational guidelines.* Standard practices that have developed over the firm's history often dictate how a company organizes and operates.
2. *Management style.* The management team operates in a manner unique to a given company. For example, management style might be formal or informal, or democratic or autocratic. If the organization operates in a highly structured, formal atmosphere, organizing a quality effort around informal meetings would probably meet with little success.
3. *Customer influences.* Customers, particularly governmental agencies, may require formal specifications or administrative controls. Thus, the organization needs to understand and respond to these requirements.
4. *Company size.* Large companies have the ability to maintain formal systems and records, whereas smaller companies may not.
5. *Diversity and complexity of product line.* An organization suitable for the manufacture of a small number of highly sophisticated products may differ dramatically from an organization that produces a high volume of standard goods.
6. *Stability of the product line.* Stable product lines generate economies of scale that influence supervision, corrective action, and other quality-related issues. Frequent changes in products necessitate more control and commensurate changes to the quality system.
7. *Financial stability.* Quality managers need to recognize that their efforts must fit within the overall budget of the firm.

8. *Availability of personnel.* The lack of certain skills may require other personnel, such as supervisors, to assume duties they ordinarily would not be assigned.

The most common type of organizational structure is the functional structure, which we discuss next.

THE FUNCTIONAL STRUCTURE

In the functional structure shown in Figure 7.1, the organization is divided into functions such as operations and maintenance, each of which is headed by a manager. The title of such managers is often "director" in small organizations and "vice president" in larger ones. In such organizations, communication occurs vertically up or down the chain of command, rather than horizontally across functions.

Functional structures provide organizations with a clear chain of command and allow people to specialize in the aspect of the work for which they are best suited. They also make it easy to evaluate people based on a narrow but clear set of responsibilities. For these reasons, functional structures are common in both manufacturing and service organizations at plant and business unit levels.

PROBLEMS WITH THE FUNCTIONAL STRUCTURE

Despite its popularity, the functional structure is designed primarily for the administrative convenience of the organization, rather than for providing high-quality service to customers. From a TQ point of view, the functional structure has several inadequacies.

The Functional Structure Separates Employees from Customers Few employees in the functional organization have direct contact with customers or even a clear idea of how their work combines with the work of others to satisfy

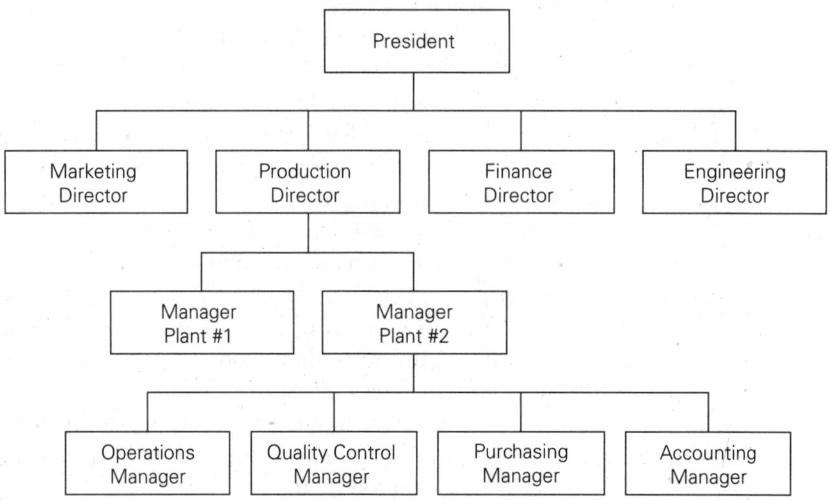

FIGURE 7.1 FUNCTIONAL STRUCTURE FOR A MANUFACTURING COMPANY

customers. The functional structure tends to insulate employees from learning about customer expectations and their degree of satisfaction with the service or product the firm is providing. Being insulated from customers encourages in workers a narrow conception of their responsibilities. This is often expressed in statements such as "It's not my job" or "I just work here." Even when such employees want to help customers, they often have such a limited understanding of how their organizational system works that they are unable to do so. This often results in demotivated workers and poor quality work.

Most of us have experienced this phenomenon when we call a large organization for help and get switched to several different people before (if we're lucky) finding someone willing and able to help us. If our needs as customers relate to the product or service as a whole, but the knowledge and responsibilities of anyone with whom we deal relate only to their function, we are doomed to disappointment.[3] More seriously, the functional structure promotes the idea that one's boss is the customer whom the employee must satisfy. Of course, this manager is trying to satisfy the next-level manager, and so on. If the chain ended at the customer, the structure might work, but this is generally not the case. Managers in functional organizations are usually rewarded for satisfying functional goals, such as meeting design deadlines and limiting manufacturing costs, rather than for providing value to customers.

The focus on vertical reporting relationships to the exclusion of horizontal coordination has led many observers to refer to departments in functional organizations as "chimneys" or "silos." As Myron Tribus describes it, "The enterprise is viewed as a collection of separate, highly specialized individual performers and units.... Lateral connections are made by intermediaries close to the top of the provinces."[4]

Paul Allaire, former Xerox chairman and CEO, presided over a massive restructuring of the corporation. He described the company's problems with the functional organization and its new approach as follows:

> We were an extremely functional organization. If you were in manufacturing, you strived to make manufacturing as good as possible—and only secondarily to make the businesses that manufacturing affected work well. The same was true for sales, R&D, or any other function.... We [now] want people who can hold two things in their heads at the same time, who can think in terms of their individual organizations but also in terms of the company as a whole. Our architecture won't work if people take a narrow view of their jobs and don't work together.[5]

The Functional Structure Inhibits Process Improvement No organizational unit has control over a whole process, although most processes involve a large number of functions. This is because the breakup of the organization into functions is usually unrelated to the processes used to deliver a product to the customer. This structure is likely to create complex, wasteful processes, as people do things in one area that must be redone or undone in another. For example, some organizations maintain a group of engineers whose sole responsibility is to redesign products so that they can be manufactured effectively. The engineers who design the products in the first place worry only about product performance, not manufacturability. Worse yet, if one function tries to improve its part, it may well make things worse (more wasted time and effort, more cost) for another part of the process. In this environment, continuous process improvement doesn't stand a chance.

Richard Palermo, a former vice president for quality and transition at Xerox, explains the problems with functional structures in terms of "Palermo's law," which states: "If a problem has been bothering your company and your customers for years and won't yield, that problem is the result of a cross-functional dispute, where nobody has total control of the whole process." The corollary to Palermo's law? "People who work in different functions hate each other."[6]

Functional Organizations Often Have a Separate Function for Quality, Called Quality Control or Quality Assurance This may send a message to the rest of the organization that there is a group dedicated to quality, so it's not their responsibility. Furthermore, it breaks the feedback loop that informs employees that their work needs to be improved. The QC department is generally responsible for collecting and maintaining quality statistics, which may not seem as valid to the departments actually doing the work.[7] This arrangement obviously stands in the way of continuous process improvement. Organizations pursuing TQ often retain their quality assurance departments, but these units act more as coaches or facilitators to employees, rather than as the group with primary responsibility for quality.

In summary, the functional organization compromises total quality in several ways: It distances people from customers and insulates them from customer expectations. It promotes complex and wasteful processes and inhibits process improvement. It separates the quality function from the rest of the organization, providing people with an excuse for not worrying about quality. The next section discusses some remedies for the quality problems caused by the functional structure.

REDESIGNING ORGANIZATIONS FOR PERFORMANCE EXCELLENCE

Poor organization design can be devastating to a company (see box "Wired for Failure"). One of Deming's 14 Points is to "break down barriers between departments" because "people in various departments must work as a team."[8] This slogan captures in a nutshell what the TQ philosophy entails for organizational design. People cannot contribute to customer satisfaction and continuous improvement if they are confined to functional prisons where they cannot see customers or hear their voices. Some of the more effective ways to break down these barriers are to focus on processes, make quality everybody's job, put external customers first, recognize internal customers, create a team-based organization, reduce hierarchy, and use leadership teams.

FOCUS ON PROCESSES

Process focus is one of the basic principles of TQ, and we introduced many tools and techniques for designing processes in Chapter 3. According to AT&T, a **process** is how work creates value for customers.[9] Common business processes include acquiring customer and market knowledge, fulfilling customer orders,

Wired for Failure

The Internet revolution, or the "New Economy," as many call it, was supposed to revolutionize business. For example, between Thanksgiving and Christmas, 1999, some 22 million shoppers spent more than $5 billion shopping online.[10] Traffic on sites like Yahoo! and KBkids.com grew by 500 percent. Outpost.com, a computer and electronics retailer, sold $2 million of merchandise in one day. However, it wasn't long before Internet message-boards were filled with comments such as, "I doubt I will ever shop again online for Christmas," and other comments unfit to print here. As *Fortune* magazine noted "... it takes much more than a logo and a Website to run an e-tailing operation. Online retailers aren't so different from brick and mortar stores. They run out of stock, sell damaged merchandise, and hire rude sales help.... Hordes of companies flooded the market. Trouble is, many of them spent heavily to market and promote their brands but scrimped on infrastructure—the unglamorous side of the business, which focuses on delivering products to customers. The results were often disastrous." Amazon.com, for example, initially tried to have suppliers maintain inventory but found that it needed to build traditional distribution centers around the country to improve customer service and control over the product.[11]

A. Blanton Godfrey, former CEO of the Juran Institute, notes that many organizations are "wired for failure"—that is, their processes are not designed effectively or aligned with each other.[12] He cites other examples in addition to the problems that confronted e-retailers. One example is over-scheduling at airports. During the 4:15 to 4:30 p.m. time slot, 35 arrivals are scheduled in Atlanta, even though in optimal weather conditions the airport can handle only 25 in 15 minutes; with bad weather, this drops to 17. Another company celebrated its largest sales contract in history only to discover that all qualified suppliers for critical materials were at capacity. A third example is the unwillingness of departments to work together. For example, when products fail in the plant or in service, it isn't because designers choose components they know will fail; they often have insufficient information about the problems that result from their choices.

purchasing, developing new products or services, strategic planning, production or service delivery, distribution, research and development, information management, performance measurement, and training, to name just a few. Individuals or groups, known as **process owners**, are accountable for process performance and have the authority to manage and improve their process. Process owners may range from high-level executives who manage cross-functional processes to workers who run machinery on the shop floor. Assigning process owners ensures that someone is responsible to manage the process and optimize its effectiveness.

Processes that drive the creation of products and services, are critical to customer satisfaction, and have a large impact on the strategic goals of an organization are generally considered **value-creation**, or **core processes** of a business. Value-creation processes are those most important to "running the business" and maintaining or achieving a sustainable competitive advantage. Value-creation processes typically include design, production/delivery, and other critical business processes. Design processes involve all activities that are performed to incorporate customer requirements, new technology, and past learning into the functional specifications of a manufactured good or service, and thus define its fitness for use. Production/delivery processes create or deliver the actual product; examples are manufacturing, assembly, dispensing medications, teaching a class, and so on. These processes must be designed to ensure that the product will conform to specifications (the manufacturing definition of quality) and also be produced economically and efficiently. Because product design greatly influences the efficiency of manufacture as well as the flexibility of service strategies, it must be coordinated with production/delivery processes. The ultimate value of the product and, hence, the perceived quality to the consumer, depend on both these types of processes. **Support processes** are those that are most important to an organization's value creation processes, employees, and daily operations, but generally do not add value directly to the product or service. For many organizations, critical support processes that lead to business success and growth might be research and development, technology acquisition, supply chain management and supplier partnering, mergers and acquisitions, project management, or sales and marketing.

Table 7.1 shows the value creation processes and their requirements defined by Pal's Sudden Service, a regional chain of fast-food restaurants in the southeastern United States. Their support processes include accounting/finance, human resources, maintenance, management information systems, ordering, and stocking.

Value creation and support processes will differ greatly among organizations, depending on the nature of products and services, customer and market requirements, global focus, and other factors. For example, a hospital might define its key value creation processes as pre-admission screening, admission and registration, assessment and diagnosis, treatment, and discharge and follow up; support services might include workforce management, medical records and information technology, financial planning, supply chain management, environmental services, and physical plant operations. A process such as order entry that might be considered a core process for one company (e.g., a direct mail distributor) might be considered as a support process for another (e.g., a custom manufacturer). In general, core

TABLE 7.1 | VALUE CREATION PROCESSES FOR PAL'S SUDDEN SERVICE

Process	Principal Requirements
Order Taking	Accurate, fast, friendly
Cooking	Proper temperature
Product Assembly	Proper sequence, sanitary, correct ingredients and amounts, speed, proper temperature, neat
Cash Collection	Accurate, fast, friendly
Slicing	Cut/size, freshness/color
Chili preparation	Proper temperature, quantity, freshness
Ham/chicken preparation	Proper temperature, quantity, freshness
Supply chain management	Price/cost, order accuracy
Property acquisition	Sales potential, adherence to budget
Construction	On time, within budget
Marketing & advertising	Clear message, brand recognition

Source: Courtesy of Pal's Sudden Service.

Chili, Spaghetti, and Cheese: It's the Process That Counts

You probably would not expect that a regional chain of small chili restaurants takes a formal view of process management, but Gold Star Chili, Inc., based in Cincinnati, Ohio, does just that. The company operates over 100 regional locations (most of which are franchised; the remaining are company restaurants or are co-owned). The Gold Star menu is based on a unique, "Cincinnati-style" chili recipe—the basic "3 way" is a plate of spaghetti, topped with chili that is flavored with a proprietary blend of spices from around the world, followed by finely shredded cheese. (Visit the company's Web site: http://www.goldstarchili.com.)

Figure 7.2 shows a process-based organization of the company. Three major core processes link the operation of the company to its customers and other stakeholders: (1) franchising, (2) restaurant, and (3) manufacturing/distribution. Sustaining these core processes are various support processes, such as research and development, human resources, accounting, purchasing, operations, training, marketing, and customer satisfaction. Even restaurant operations are viewed from a process focus. Key processes such as Cash Register, Steam Table, Drive-Thru, Tables, Bussers, and Management are designed to ensure that customer needs are served in a timely manner. Prior to opening each restaurant, training sessions ensure that these processes are performed correctly and according to company standards.

processes are driven by *external* customer needs while support processes are driven by *internal* customer needs.

A process focus can help define the organization design (see box "Chili, Spaghetti, and Cheese: It's the Process That Counts"). As discussed in Chapter 1, a process focus, as opposed to the functional structure, involves some form of cross-functional cooperation (see Figure 1.1). A process perspective helps managers to recognize that problems arise from processes, not people. By aligning the structure of an organization with the actual work processes that the organization performs, customers may be served more effectively. We will address further details of designing and managing processes in the next chapter.

Make Quality Everyone's Job

As we noted, functional organizations often have separate quality control or quality assurance departments. It is not unusual for TQ-focused organizations to eliminate the quality department and make everyone in the organization a "quality manager." Texas Nameplate Company is one example where this has been done quite successfully.[13]

Founded in 1946, Texas Nameplate Company, Inc. (TNC) manufactures and sells identification and information labels that are affixed to refrigerators, oil-field equipment, computers, and other products. TNC, with only 66 employees, has honed the raw attributes inherent to its small size—from streamlined communications and rapid decision making to shared goals and accessible leaders—into competitive advantages. The result is a closely-knit organization that is finely tuned to the requirements of its customers. TNC aims to create a continuous learning

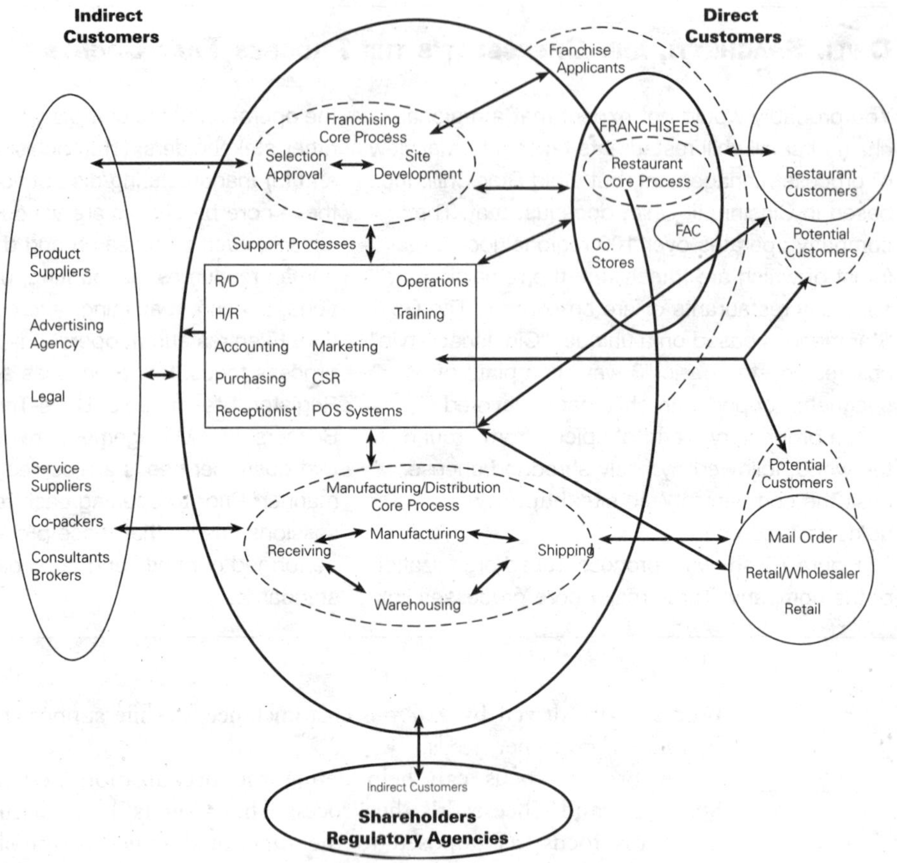

FIGURE 7.2 | GOLD STAR CHILI, INC., ORGANIZATION

environment that enables teams of workers to take charge of processes and deliver products and services with high quality. Long-term partnerships with customers and suppliers are the rule. Sustained relationships with quality-minded suppliers have enabled TNC to nearly eliminate inspections of incoming materials.

Company President and CEO Dale Crownover and his seven top managers make up the Business Excellence Leadership Team, which aligns the focus and direction of all employees with the company's vision to "become the recognized supplier of commercial nameplates in the United States." Primary responsibility for accomplishing company goals rests with work teams—so much that the company disbanded its Quality Control Department in 1998. Because teaming has become so engrained into its culture, TNC no longer needs formal procedures for rotating employee participation. Processes and jobs are designed to allow flexibility so that employees can respond quickly to customer requirements and changing business needs. Production workers are responsible for tailoring processes to optimize contributions to company goals and to meet team-set standards.

PUT EXTERNAL CUSTOMERS FIRST

Many organizations "flip" the organization chart to put customers at the top, as opposed to the traditional functional structure that we illustrated in Figure 7.1. A generic example is shown in Figure 7.3. The City of Coral Springs, Florida, practices this organizational structure.[14] At the top of the organizational chart Florida are Citizens/Customers of Coral Springs (its residents and businesses), followed by 27 Citizen Advisory Committees and Boards, the City Commission, the City Manager, and, finally, operating departments such as Public Works, Police, and Parks and Recreation. This organizational structure supports the City's mission, which is "to be the nation's premier community in which to live, work, and raise a family." Community visioning retreats are held to reach consensus on the direction for the City. The City's organizational culture is expressed in the four core values underlying this vision:

- Customer Focus—Demonstrate a passion for customer service.
- Leadership—Establish an inspiring vision that creates a government that works better and costs less.
- Empowered Employees—Empower the people closest to the customer to continuously improve the organization's quality and services.
- Continuous Improvement—Commit "every day, in every way, to getting better and better."

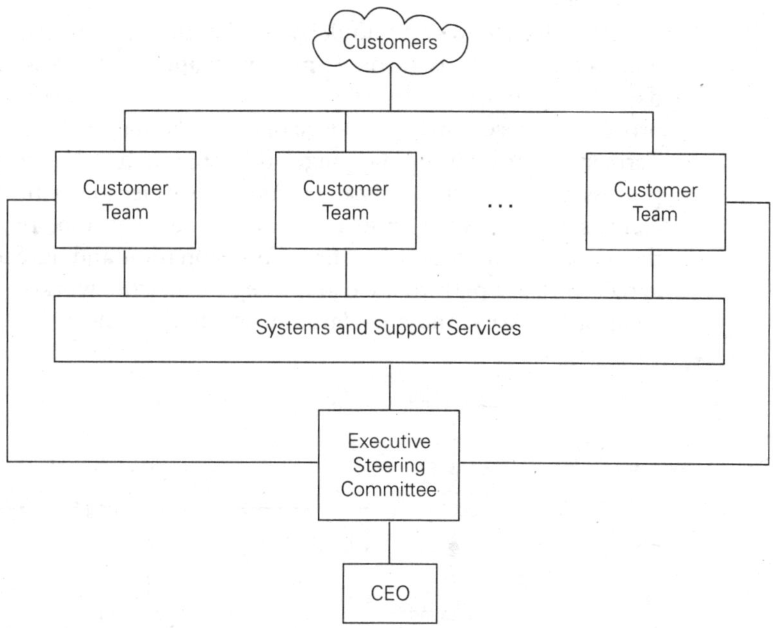

FIGURE 7.3 | TEAM-BASED ORGANIZATIONAL CHART

Recognize Internal Customers

We discussed the concept of internal customers in Chapter 6. An internal customer is another person or group within the organization who depends on one's work to get their own work done. For example, machine operators in a manufacturing plant are customers of maintenance; if maintenance does not do its job well, the machines will not produce quality products (or perhaps not any products at all). In a university, professors and students are customers of the audiovisual staff, who provide and maintain overhead projectors and VCRs.

In a restaurant, the servers are internal customers of the kitchen staff, because the servers' ability to serve appetizing food in a timely manner to customers depends on the kitchen. In Figure 7.4, product design is the internal customer of both research and development and marketing, manufacturing is the customer of product design and purchasing, and sales is the customer of manufacturing. Although not shown in the diagram, all of these departments are customers of staff groups such as human resources and finance.

One way that organizations can promote quality and teamwork is to recognize the existence of internal customers. However, Richard Schonberger, a noted consultant and writer on manufacturing and quality, has taken the internal customer idea one step further by arguing that organizations should be designed as "chains of customers." That is, customer-supplier links should be forged, one at a time, from the organization's suppliers all the way to its external (real) customers.[15] By linking customers and suppliers together at the individual level, the nature of cross-functional processes becomes clearer. Eventually, everyone can better understand their role in satisfying not only their internal customers, but also the external customers.

An effective way to understand internal customer-supplier relationships and improve processes is through **process mapping**. Process maps are generally standard flowcharts that describe a process as a sequence of steps. A rather new approach to process mapping developed by Fernando Flores is gaining popularity.[16] Termed "coordination mapping," this approach is based on the premise that each process activity includes two players, a customer and a provider. Each coordinating conversation between these agents moves through four phases: (1) preparation and the making of a request or offer; (2) negotiation and agreement (or failure to reach agreement); (3) performance and a report that the work is complete; and (4) assessment of the work and a declaration of satisfaction or dissatisfaction.

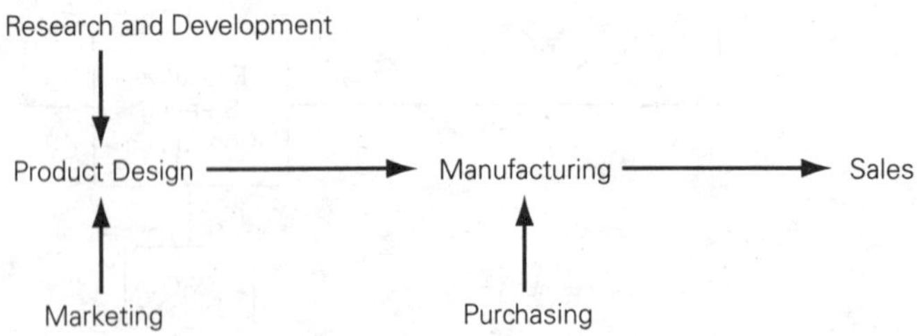

Figure 7.4 | Internal Customers in a Manufacturing Company

This cyclic process is represented graphically by a loop. The mapping process involves identifying each conversation, its customer and provider, the customer's conditions of satisfaction, and how each of the moves is taken, as well as interdependencies among conversations. Working through and analyzing the interactions one by one often reveals hidden or implicit assumptions and discoveries of breakdowns in the process. Figure 7.5 shows an example of a university residence hall

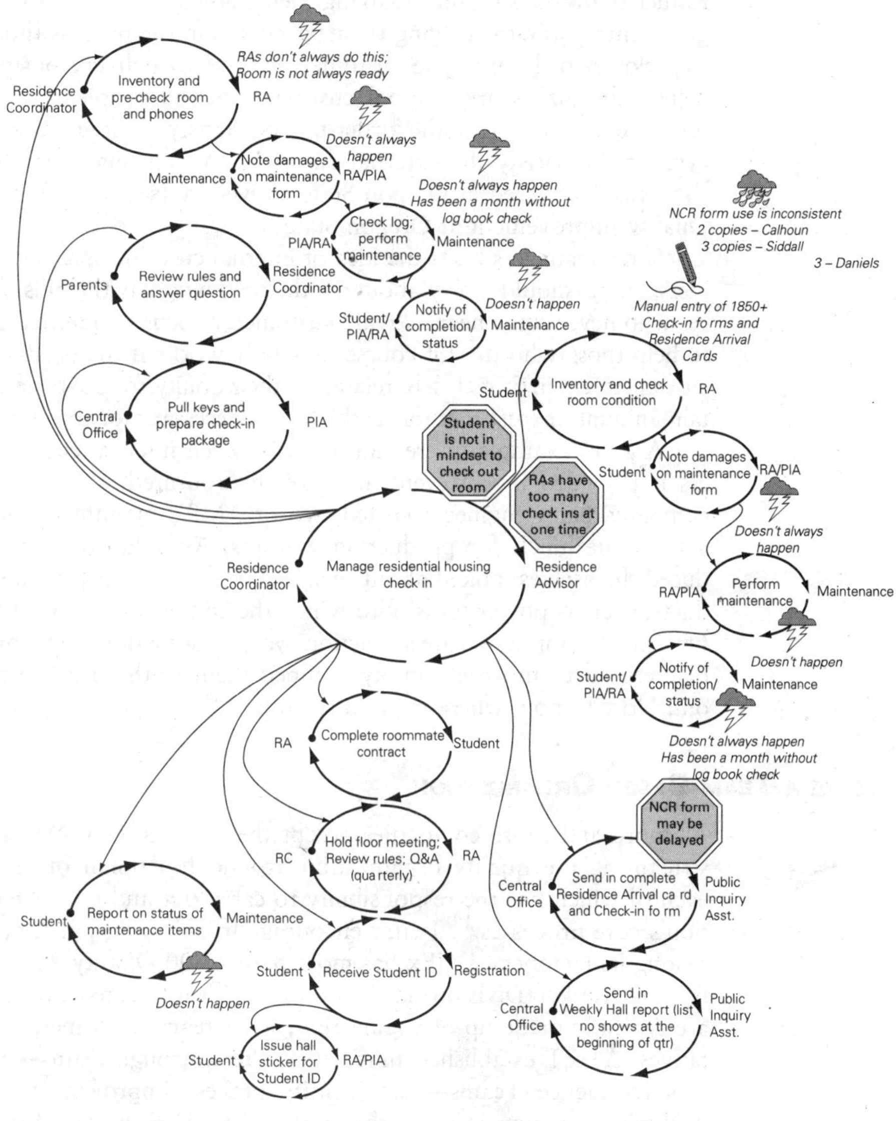

Project: U.C. residence hall as is workflow map. Prepared by: Workflow Dynamics, Inc.

FIGURE 7.5 | COORDINATION MAP FOR RESIDENCE HALL CHECK-IN PROCESS

check-in process developed using this approach by a Cincinnati-based consulting firm, Workflow Dynamics, Inc.[17] What on the surface is a seemingly simple process can indeed be quite complex, resulting in numerous process failures (the "cloudbursts" in the figure). Such maps can provide the basis for reengineering or other types of process improvement efforts.

Promoting the idea of internal customers does not change the organization's structure as much as it changes the way that people think about the structure. Rather than focusing on satisfying their immediate supervisor (vertical), people begin to think about satisfying the next person in the process (horizontal), who is one step closer to the ultimate customer. In a pizza delivery business, the people who deliver the pizzas are internal customers of the people who make them, who in turn are customers of the order-takers. Satisfying internal customers first is the best way to satisfy the external customer. An unusual customer-supplier relationship was uncovered at Oregon State University (see box "Where's the Paperwork? Quality Improvement at Oregon State").

Some managers resist the idea of internal customers, arguing that the only customers people should worry about are the ones who pay the bills. But for those employees who never come near a "real" customer, a focus on internal customers helps them to help those who do. Of course, this only works if the needs expressed by internal customers are in fact closely related to their ability to satisfy actual customers. A certain amount of trust that this is the case is necessary for the system to work.

A good example of creating links between internal customers and their suppliers is provided by an event at AMP Incorporated, a global electronic connector company. Sales engineers visited two of AMP's manufacturing plants and cooked a barbecue lunch for production workers. After lunch, the sales engineers introduced themselves, talked about their customers, and displayed some of the end products, such as power tools, into which the connectors made at the plant are placed. One production associate's reaction was, "I sometimes felt that we made millions of these parts and they simply dumped them in the ocean after we shipped them out. Now I know where most of them go."[18]

Create a Team-Based Organization

As more and more companies accept the process view of organizations, they are structuring the quality organization around functional or cross-functional teams, each of which has the responsibility to carry out and improve one of the organization's core processes.[19] Teams encourage free-flowing participation and interaction among its members. FedEx has more than 4,000 Quality Action teams. Boeing Airlift and Tanker Division has more than 100 integrated product teams (IPTs) that are typically made up of engineering, work-team, customer, and supplier representatives. AT&T established nine expert breakthrough teams—called Achieving Process Excellence Teams—that identify process improvements for developing and deploying products faster in the market. Graniterock, with fewer than 400 employees, has about 100 functioning teams, ranging from 10 corporate quality teams to project teams, purchasing teams, task forces, and function teams composed of people who do the same job at different locations. Special efforts keep the teams relevant and make sure that no teams exist just for the sake of having them.

Texas Nameplate Company builds its leadership system upon a team framework that includes a Business Excellence Leadership Team, a Daily Operations & Innovation Team, teams within each production and support service department for daily work activities, corrective action teams, and various other teams such as the Recognition Committee. Similarly, Stoner Incorporated (a very small chemical specialty manufacturing and sales company with fewer than 50 employees) has a six-member senior leadership team empowered by the owner to manage and lead the company. The leadership team created and refined the Stoner Excellence System to define and communicate to all team members how the business is run. The system is based on Leadership, Strategy, and Process, which are combined with an Assess/Improve/Implement continuous improvement approach. Stakeholder value is at the center of the system to characterize the main focus on the customer. Stoner's leadership approach is built on (1) leadership at all levels, (2) worker leaders, and (3) strong fundamental leadership skills based on Stephen Covey's *Seven Habits of Highly Effective People*.

Mark Kelly provides an example of an organizational structure based on teams in *The Adventures of a Self-Managing Team*.[20] The building blocks of the "Clear Lake Plant" organization are process-based teams. Tasks that transcend processes

Where's the Paperwork? Quality Improvement at Oregon State[21]

Oregon State University was among the first universities to embrace TQ. In 1990, faced with state budget cuts and trying to improve the quality of its operation, Oregon State began the process of quality improvement. Like many schools, it focused first on improving administrative areas.

The physical plant was among the first areas singled out for quality improvement. Specifically, the group that did repair and remodeling at the university tackled the time it took to complete a work order, which its internal customers identified as the number one problem with the service they were receiving. When the group began to address the problem, they found that the average time to complete a job was 195 days, just over six months.

None of the people who actually did the work could believe the entire process took so long, as individually each knew that his or her work lasted only a few days or weeks. In attempting to understand why it took so long, the group set up a flowchart of the process they used in their work.

They discovered that a woman in another group received their work orders first, and it took 10 days for the paperwork to make its way to the repair and remodeling group. Group members approached the woman and asked what she did with the paperwork during the time she kept it. She did her job and she did it well, exactly as she had been instructed, she told them.

What exactly had she been told to do? When the paperwork arrives, put it aside. After 10 days, send it on to the repair and remodeling group! As it turned out, there had been a time when the group had had trouble getting the material they needed for jobs delivered. Having no success in expediting the flow of material, they simply slowed down the flow of paperwork, so that they would have a headstart on the job when the paperwork arrived. Eventually the problems with material delivery were resolved, but no one had remembered to undo the 10-day waiting period. Because the paperwork was held by another functional group, no one in repair and remodeling had a broad enough view of the process to see what was going on. Sometimes process improvement is hard work. But, in this case, the repair and remodeling group could get off to a fast start by immediately knocking 10 days off of their time!

(such as innovation and safety) are handled in task teams made up of members drawn from each of the process teams. This organization is depicted in Figure 7.6. (Compare this to the functional organization in Figure 7.1 to get an idea of the size of the changes we are talking about.)

Another example is that of the former GTE Directories (since acquired by Verizon Information Services), shown in Figure 7.7. In this organizational structure, the management board leads the quality effort, meeting twice each month to discuss and review management and quality issues. Quality is implemented through various teams: core process business team, cross-functional coordinating committee, regional management councils, major business process management teams (PMTs), Malcolm Baldrige National Quality Award (MBNQA) teams, and quality improvement teams. The regional management councils identify and address key regional issues; the cross-functional coordinating committee reviews major proposals for consistency with the strategic plan and business priorities. Such team-based organization structures spread the ownership, and the accountability, for quality throughout the organization. The "quality department" serves as an internal consulting group, providing advice, training, and organizational development to the teams. Clearly, each organization needs to create a structure that meets its own unique needs.

Depending on the size of the organization and the nature of the processes, teams may include everyone who contributes to a given process or only a representative subset. Similarly, the teams may meet continuously on a crash basis until their new process design is complete, after which they may meet periodically or on an ad hoc basis whenever necessary. For example, Solectron Corporation, a two-time Baldrige recipient, has a customer focus team for each customer that includes personnel from quality, manufacturing management, project engineering, sales, production control, test engineering, and a project buyer and program manager.

FIGURE 7.6 ORGANIZATIONAL STRUCTURE OF THE CLEAR LAKE PLANT

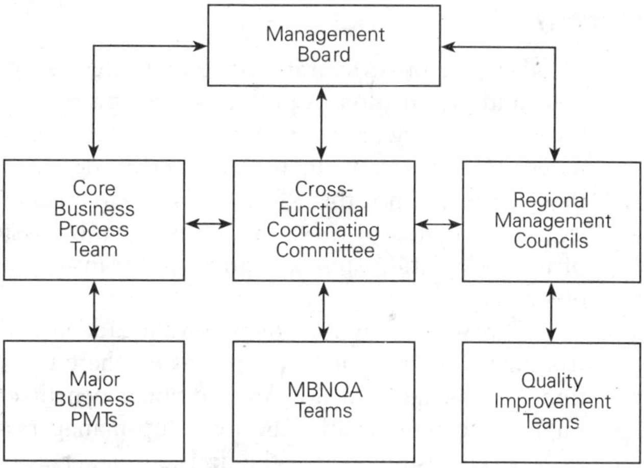

Courtesy of Verizon Information Services.

FIGURE 7.7 FORMER GTE DIRECTORIES MANAGEMENT STRUCTURE

This approach eliminates many of the problems with the functional structure. By bringing together everyone associated with a process, practices that are wasteful or compromise quality become much easier to identify and eliminate. If a team has responsibility for an entire process, they don't have to worry that their improvement efforts will be undermined—intentionally or unintentionally—by the actions of another group.

Using processes as a grouping method can create substantial improvement in organizations by allowing people to see and change procedures they couldn't see or change in the functional structure. As Robert Brookhouse, member of a process organization at Xerox, puts it, "When you create a flow [Xerox's term for process organization], you find where you're wasting time, doing things twice. And because we own the entire process, we can change it."[22]

This is not to suggest that changing to a process-based organization is simple or easy. On the contrary, it takes a lot of thought, because it means essentially taking the organization apart and putting it back together again. As Robert Knorr and Edward Thiede describe it: "The restructuring should begin by defining each process in terms of its operations, information, and skill needs.... Process definition also answers key questions about the lines of integration needed among processes and functions, such as who must interact and when? What changes are needed in upstream processes to accommodate the needs of those downstream, and vice versa?"[23]

Project teams are fundamental to Six Sigma. Six Sigma projects require a diversity of skills that range from technical analysis, creative solution development, and implementation. Thus, Six Sigma teams not only address immediate problems but also provide an environment for individual learning, management development, and career advancement. Six Sigma teams will be discussed further in Chapter 8.

Reduce Hierarchy

Another type of structural change that often results from a focus on internal customers and the creation of process teams is a reduction in the number of hierarchical layers in the organization. Several levels of middle management are often eliminated. (Of course, if an organization is designed for quality from its inception, those levels are not there in the first place.) This reduction in middle management is also facilitated by advances in information systems that have taken over many of the information summarization and transmission roles formerly played by middle managers.

With the elimination of non–value-added activities and the empowerment of frontline workers to improve processes, there is also less supervision and coordination for managers to do. An additional benefit of such "flatter" organizations is improved communication between top managers and frontline employees, as well as between customers and the decision makers.

This is not to say that the flattening of organizational structures is without its drawbacks. People—sometimes many people—lose their jobs. This is not only a significant disruption in the lives of the individuals affected but also a loss to the organization of their experience. Furthermore, the morale of the people who remain in the organization may suffer. For all of these reasons, organizations should approach flattening with an attitude of caution and concern.

Use Leadership Teams

One type of structural change associated with TQ is the creation of a high-level planning group, as opposed to a single individual, invested with the responsibility for guiding the organization's performance excellence efforts. Such groups—traditionally called *steering committees* or *quality councils*, but which are more commonly known today as simply *leadership teams*—are a key part of many organizations' leadership structures. At Custom Research Inc., for example, a four-person steering committee is the center of the leadership system (see Figure 7.8). The steering committee sets the company directions, integrates performance excellence goals, and promotes the development of all employees. Leadership team members have frequent interaction with associates, and review overall company performance daily. They meet formally each month to evaluate performance and identify areas for improvement. Park Place Lexus, a Baldrige recipient located in Texas, has a corporate leadership team that consists of the chairman, presidents of dealership groups, VP of human resources, and the CFO, and management teams at individual dealerships that consist of the president, general managers, and various other managers.

Leadership teams are often characterized by four elements:[24]

- *Leadership*: promoting and articulating the quality vision, communicating responsibilities and expectations for management action, aligning the business management process with the quality approach, maintaining high visibility for commitment and involvement, and ensuring that business-wide support is available in the form of education, consulting, methods, and tools.

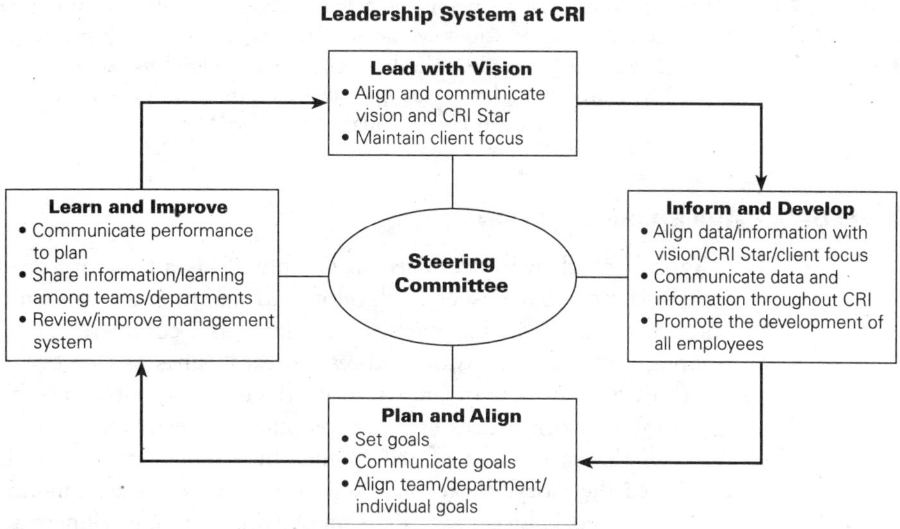

FIGURE 7.8 | CUSTOM RESEARCH INC. LEADERSHIP SYSTEM

- *Planning*: planning strategic quality goals, understanding basic customer needs and business capabilities, developing long-term goals and near-term priorities, formulating human resource goals and policies, understanding employees' perceptions about quality and work, ensuring that all employees have the opportunity and skills to participate, and aligning reward and recognition systems to support the quality approach.
- *Implementation*: forming key business process teams, chartering teams to manage and improve these processes, reviewing improvement plans, providing resources for improvement, enlisting all managers in the process, reviewing quality plans of major organizational units, and working with suppliers and business partners in joint quality planning.
- *Review*: tracking progress through customer satisfaction and internal measures of quality, monitoring progress in attaining improvement objectives, celebrating successes, improving the quality system through auditing and identifying improvement opportunities, planning improvements, and validating the impact of improvements.

Although many firms use only top managers in such groups, Portman Equipment Company—an industrial equipment sales, service, and rental company—uses people from all types of jobs. Richard Buck, Portman's vice president for quality, argues that the presence of frontline associates in the committee has made a big difference in the decisions the group has made:

> We have general managers, we have some supervisory people, and we have some hourly people. It was our decision in forming a steering committee to break precedence from every company we've studied that used only executives on the steering committee. We opted to break that pattern and listen to the voices of all of our people as we formulate our plans. I think it's one of the better decisions we've made. And looking back

on decisions we have made in the steering committee, I think there's good evidence that some of our decisions would not have been the same if we did not have representation from hourly people. I think as managers we tend to learn to think the way managers think ... having hourly people gives us a different perspective. We see a broader picture and it's been good for our quality initiative.[25]

Develop an Agile Organization

Agility, which we introduced in Chapter 5, is an important characteristic for any organization that wishes to develop and maintain a focus on the customer and react to competitive challenges, particularly as e-commerce grows and requires more rapid, flexible, and customized responses. Businesses face ever shorter cycles for the introduction of new or improved products and services. These often require simplification of work processes and rapid changeover from one process to another.

In the early days of the quality movement, it was the large companies that received the glory. Motorola, Xerox, and AT&T were among the large companies that received Baldrige awards, some having multiple winners across divisions. Large companies were early adopters of quality tools and processes, and had the resources to implement them. Although some large organizations such as Boeing continue to excel in performance excellence, many smaller companies, for example, Stoner, Inc. and Texas Nameplate, both with under 50 employees, and Custom Research Incorporated with about 100 employees, for example, have received Baldrige awards and have outstanding quality systems and business results. Small organizations are often more agile, meaning that they can adapt quickly and flexibly to changing customer requirements and demand, a key characteristic in today's globally competitive markets. Small organizations also often have simple leadership systems, highly motivated employees, and are closer to customers. In addition, small organizations avoid bureaucratic barriers that stifle innovation and lead to complex processes, and thus they can implement changes more effectively and smoothly.

In recent years, evidence suggests that many large companies, including Johnson & Johnson, AT&T, IBM, and Microsoft, are undergoing massive reorganizations by forming groups of small companies or divisions. The reorganization is aimed at embracing a large company/small company hybrid that combines a large company's resources, market share, and capital with a small company's mindset of simplicity, flexibility, and ability to get closer to the customer.

Research has suggested that organization size can have a significant effect on employee job satisfaction and customer satisfaction; thus, organizations that are attempting to make a transformation to a large company/small company hybrid should pay close attention to employee satisfaction.[26]

Redesign Work Systems

It's difficult to make any fundamental changes in organizational structure or strategic direction without considering their impacts on work systems. TQ organizations design work systems to achieve high performance. **Performance** simply means the extent to which an individual contributes to achieving the goals and objectives of an organization. **High-performance work** is characterized by flexibility, innovation, knowledge and skill sharing, alignment with organizational directions, customer focus, and rapid response to changing business needs and marketplace requirements. Teams, as we have already suggested, often provide the infrastructure for high performance work systems.

Organizations may be viewed at three levels: the individual job level, the process level, and the organizational level (think of front-line or shop floor workers, middle managers, and senior executives). The design of high-performance work systems can be addressed using this framework. At the individual level, work systems should enable effective accomplishment of work activities and promote flexibility and individual initiative in managing and improving work processes. Empowering employees and using work teams are ways to achieve these objectives. At the process level, work systems must promote cooperation, cross-functional teamwork, and communication. This often is done through project teams and other forms of cross-functional communication (such as product design teams). At the organizational level, senior managers must design a supportive work environment through compensation and recognition policies, and health, safety, and support services.

Several common approaches to work design—job enlargement, job rotation, and job enrichment—support TQ-based work systems. IBM was apparently the first user of **job enlargement**, in which workers' jobs were expanded to include several tasks rather than one single, low-level task. This approach reduced fragmentation of jobs and generally resulted in lower production costs, greater worker satisfaction, and higher quality, but it required higher wage rates and the purchase of more inspection equipment. **Job rotation** is a technique by which individual workers learn several tasks by rotating from one to another. The purpose of job rotation is to renew interest or motivation of the individual and to increase his or her complement of skills. However, several studies showed that the main benefit was to increase workers' skills but that little, if any, motivational benefit could be expected.[27] Finally, **job enrichment** entails "vertical job loading" in which workers are given more authority, responsibility, and autonomy rather than simply more or different work to do. Job enrichment has been used successfully in a number of firms, notably AT&T, which experienced better employee attitudes and performance, as well as Texas Instruments, IBM, and General Foods. See box "No Egg on Their Faces" for a good example of the value of these approaches.

In today's technology-dominated world, the nature of work is constantly changing. Today's entry-level workers are accustomed to new ways of interacting, such as blogs and wikis (editable Web sites). For instance, about 1,500 employees of the financial firm Dresdner Kleinwort Wasserstein use wikis and blogs as virtual workspaces to create, edit, comment, and revise projects in real time. Another example is Basecamp®, a collaborative project-management service that lets groups of people post messages and files, create to-do lists, and set milestones for a project, all on simple private Web pages. One firm cut the time to complete a massive redesign project from at least two years to about eight months by using Basecamp®. New capabilities to use Basecamp® for interactive collaboration anywhere and anytime are available now via an iPhone application.[28] Thus, with new technologies constantly becoming available, managers face new challenges to design work and jobs that are effective in meeting organizational goals and objectives as well as being motivating and satisfying to the people in their organizations.

No Egg on Their Faces[29]

Sunny Fresh Foods (SFF) manufactures and distributes more than 160 different types of egg-based food products to more than 2,000 customers, such as quick-service restaurants, schools, hospitals, convenience stores, and food processors. A subsidiary of Cargill, Inc., SFF operates five manufacturing facilities with a total of about 620 employees. At SFF, a satisfied, motivated workforce is a vital ingredient of the company's successful operational and business performance.

SFF refers to its workers as "stakeholders," and ensures that they share in the benefits of continuous improvement. For example, although the base pay is set slightly below the industry midpoint for salaried workers, incentives can increase earnings above the 75th percentile. In addition, extensive reward and recognition systems, including monetary rewards for exemplary safety performance to extra vacation days for quality achievements, also help to motivate employees to contribute to the company's progress toward its improvement goals.

Sunny Fresh Foods designs its work systems to emphasize safety, quality, compensation and recognition, and employee development in support of individual development and SFF's long-term goals. Many of its work systems are unique to the industry. Examples are a "ramp-in" schedule in which new employees are allowed to work for only a specified number of hours to learn their jobs and minimize the potential for repetitive-stress injuries; and a rotation system by which employees rotate to another workstation every 20 minutes. This format ensures that workers can understand and respond to product quality issues at any stage of the process and understand their internal customers; it also fights boredom, reduces repetitive-stress injuries, and promotes learning. In addition, SFF uses a "buddy" system in which new employees are matched with high-performing experienced employees who serve as role models for operational excellence and behavioral competencies. SFF has recently changed its name to Cargill Kitchen Solutions.

ORGANIZATIONAL DESIGN FOR QUALITY IN ACTION

Promoting the concept of internal customers, forming process teams, reducing hierarchy, and creating leadership teams all facilitate quality. This section presents examples of organizations that use these ideas to ensure or improve quality in their operations.

Boeing Airlift and Tanker Programs[30]

Boeing Airlift and Tanker (A&T) Programs designs, develops, and produces the C-17 airlifter used by the U.S. Air Force to transport large, heavy cargo to sites around the world. In 1996, A&T signed a $14.2 billion agreement to deliver 80 C-17s to the Air Force. A few years earlier, the U.S. Defense Department had threatened to cancel the C-17 program because of technical problems, cost overruns, and late deliveries. The organization, then a unit of McDonnell Douglas Corp., responded with a complete overhaul of its business, aiming to become "process-focused and customer-driven." It initiated partnerships with customers, unions, and suppliers and replaced manager-controlled teams with empowered teams that now function like small businesses motivated by common, systematically developed goals. A&T directly involved its 7,000 Air Force customers and suppliers in planning and decision making at all organizational levels.

Interdependence and integration characterize A&T's organizational structure and its approaches to performance improvement. A high-level "enterprise process model" defines the entire business as eight interconnected process "families." These major groupings range from enterprise leadership and new business development to production and post-delivery product support.

Each family encompasses up to 10 major processes, which, in turn, are made up of several tiers of supporting subprocesses. The result is a coherent framework for process management. The model provides a direct line-of-sight from A&T-wide initiatives to the work plans and goals of teams and workers. It also helps to identify apparent operational dependencies that link subsets of process families. A&T manages these cross-cutting relationships as "megaprocesses" that typically extend to suppliers and customers.

VA HOSPITALS[31]

The Veterans' Affairs health system was once considered one of the worst health care systems in America, and even ridiculed in popular movies such as *Born on the Fourth of July* with Tom Cruise. Today the VA health system—which provides lifetime medical care to veterans with service-related disabilities, as well as to low-income and other qualifying vets and their families—has turned that reputation around. The nation's largest health network, with 1,300 hospitals, community clinics, and other facilities, the VA beats most other medical providers on dozens of quality indicators, such as administering regular cancer screenings or prescribing beta-blockers to heart-attack survivors.

This transformation was accomplished by improving the organizational design using many of the ideas described in this chapter. In the mid-1990s, Dr. Kenneth W. Kizer, the VA Under Secretary for Health, installed the most extensive electronic medical-records system in the U.S. Kizer also decentralized decision-making, closed underused hospitals, reallocated resources, and, most critically, instituted a culture of accountability and quality measurements. "Our whole motivation was to make the system work for the patient," says Kizer, now director of the National Quality Forum, a nonprofit dedicated to improving health care. "We did a top-to-bottom makeover with that goal always in mind."

Soon after taking over, Kizer summoned a dozen top managers for a week-long brainstorming session. They decided to change the organizational structure, ending Washington's centralized decision-making and creating a dozen territories, each with its own budget, managers, and performance goals. And over the next several years the agency shifted away from an expensive, hospital-based model to one that emphasized outpatient community clinics and primary care.

Kizer also encouraged creative thinking. During a monthly meeting with his top managers in 1998, a VA staffer mentioned a project at the medical center in Topeka that had reduced medication errors 70 percent by using barcode scanners to match patients, drugs, and doctors' orders. Sue Kinnick, a longtime nurse at the hospital, had conceived the idea after watching a car-rental agent wield a wireless barcode scanner to check in her car. Intrigued, Kizer hopped on a flight to Topeka, liked what he saw, and decided to install the technology. By September 2000 the system was operating in every VA hospital.

Technology is at the heart of the transformation. A networked software program—dubbed Vista—runs a powerful electronic medical recordkeeping system that acts as the VA's brain. Through Vista, doctors submit prescriptions electronically, minimizing errors that stem from illegible handwriting. They are notified when their patient needs a flu shot, a chest X-ray, or other follow-up care. (In a pilot program, many vets also get reminders over home computers.) By using technology to practice preventive medicine and reduce unnecessary doctor visits, the VA has proved that quality can actually save money. "The VA turns the paradigm on its head," says Margaret O'Kane, president of the National Committee for Quality Assurance, a private nonprofit that accredits health organizations based on various performance measures. "It shows that better quality pays."

Solar Turbines, Inc.[32]

Solar Turbines, Inc. is a wholly owned subsidiary of Caterpillar and one of the world's largest suppliers of midrange industrial gas turbine systems. Solar Turbines combines both a traditional functional organizational structure with team-based approaches. First, through a functional organizational structure led by the president's staff, Solar maintains a focus on functional excellence through recruitment, hiring, development of critical skills, and the application of tools and common processes to continuously improve functional effectiveness. Second, three cross-functional leadership structures, made up of managers and technical experts selected from multiple levels of the organization, facilitate company-wide teamwork and decision making.

This Expanded Leadership Team, consisting of the Operations Council (74 leaders from across the business) and the Expanded Leadership Group (more than 400 managers and supervisors), enable Solar to develop the next generation of business leaders. It also promotes rapid, effective communication among employees with cross-functional teams at all levels of the organization.

The third organizational structure is the set of 10 interlocking committees that coordinate and integrate all business areas. These committees, which include sales and operations planning, products committee, ERP/IT committee, and ethics and compliance committee, provide a mechanism to strengthen organizational learning through cross-functional sharing, company-wide communication, and strategic direction setting. Members of the president's staff chair key committees and, along with other senior business leaders, actively participate to provide guidance, learn, share, and support each other's decisions.

Oticon[33]

It sounds like the corporate paradise of the future. Workers organize themselves, coalescing around natural leaders and gravitating to the most exciting projects. There are no middle managers, no hierarchies, no fixed assignments. At Oticon, a midsize Danish maker of hearing aids, the future started back in 1991. That's when its chief executive, Lars Kolind, turned traditional notions of the workplace upside down. Kolind, a corporate renegade trained as a mathematician, swept away old structures. Workers were suddenly free to concentrate on any project and join any team.

Kolind's radical idea was to transform the company's once-stodgy culture into a free marketplace of ideas. He moved headquarters to a new location where none of the 150 employees had a permanent desk or office, only filing cabinets on wheels that they pushed from project to project. Meeting areas had no tables or chairs. He called it the "spaghetti organization," because the place had no fixed structure yet somehow held together. Ideas bubbled up and turned into hits such as a new hearing aid that required less adjustment. Sales and profits soared. The company became a model for management creativity. Even CNN showed up to tape a segment. Yet as the company grew and went public, many of the old structures crept back.

Kolind eventually left, and these days there's not much talk about his spaghetti revolution. Everyone has a boss to whom they report and they no longer have total freedom to choose projects. Still, its spirit survives. None of the 500 head-office employees at Oticon has even a cubicle. The latest headquarters features few interior walls. Workers sit around the perimeter of the building at simple desks. They attend meetings on sofas in the middle of each floor. The relaxed atmosphere helps retain top engineers, keeping Oticon at the forefront of innovation. Its unobtrusive Delta hearing aid has been a success. Sales of parent William Demant Holding Group, of which Oticon is the largest business, have grown 36 percent since 2002, to $927 million, while operating profit has risen 57 percent, to $232 million.

The San Diego Zoo[34]

With $75 million in revenues, 1,200 employees, and 5 million visitors annually, the Zoological Society of San Diego (a.k.a. the San Diego Zoo) is a force to be reckoned with in the animal world. Even during the recession of the early 1990s, the zoo (and its Wild Animal Park) managed to increase attendance. Its overall objectives include recreation, education, and conservation.

One of the reasons for the zoo's success may be its reorganization. In the old system, the animals were organized by species (e.g., *phascolarctos cinereus*) and the humans by functions (e.g., *homo sapiens beancounterus*). In fact, the humans were divided into 50 different departments, each of which played a role in the care and feeding of either animals, customers, or both.

This led to a somewhat sterile and unrealistic environment for everyone involved. For example, a groundskeeper confessed to occasionally sweeping a cigarette butt from the path under a bush, so it would become the gardener's responsibility instead of his own.

In the new organization, the animals are grouped into bioclimatic zones that mirror their natural habitats. Gorilla Tropics groups the animals normally found in an African rain forest, while Tiger River recreates the environment of a jungle in Asia. The humans haven't been forgotten in the new zoo design. They are now organized into teams, each of which has responsibility for one of the bioclimatic zones. The team that runs Tiger River includes specialists in mammals and birds, as well as maintenance and construction personnel. Although turf was jealously guarded in the old organization, team members are now learning one another's skills and cooperate in making improvements that transcend the old functional boundaries. As the teams have taken over responsibility for activities that were previously the prerogatives of management, managers have been freed up to find ways to bring more people to the zoo. (As in any organization with a high level of fixed costs, maintaining a consistently high level of revenues is crucial to its survival.)

COMPARISON TO ORGANIZATIONAL DESIGN THEORY

This section compares the total quality view of organizational design to the viewpoint from organization theory. Topics discussed are structural contingency theory and the institutional theory of organization structure, and the impact of contextual factors on TQ practices and performance.

STRUCTURAL CONTINGENCY THEORY

The structural contingency model, which originated in the 1960s, is the dominant view of organizational design in the management literature. According to this view, the two principal types of organization structures are mechanistic (centralized, many rules, strict division of labor, formal coordination across departments) and organic (decentralized, few rules, loose division of labor, informal coordination across departments).[35] These structures are described in detail in most management and organizational theory textbooks. The structural contingency model holds that there is no "one best way" to organize and that the choice between mechanistic and organic structures should be a function of certain contingencies, most often characteristics of the organization's environment and technology.

The choice between mechanistic and organic structures is usually seen as a function of uncertainty. Organizations face a great deal of uncertainty if their environments are complex and changing and if the technology they use in creating their products is not well understood. The microcomputer industry is a good example of this type of industry. The contingency model says that organizations facing uncertainty should adopt an organic structure. By contrast, organizations that experience little uncertainty—their environments are simple and stable, and their technology is well understood—are seen as needing a mechanistic structure.

The rationale for these recommendations is that organic organizations are better able to process the information necessary to deal with a complex environment and uncertain technology. They also are more flexible and can adapt to the changing circumstances associated with an unstable environment.

However, this information processing and adaptive capacity comes at the expense of efficiency and control. Although mechanistic organizations may not be able to accomplish uncertain tasks or to change rapidly, they are better suited for accomplishing straightforward tasks in a predictable environment. The mechanistic organization will accomplish such tasks quite reliably, with little danger of employees engaging in costly experiments to see whether there is a better way to do the job. The organic organization sacrifices reliability for flexibility.

Clearly a quality-oriented organization practicing continuous improvement cannot afford to freeze its processes by using a mechanistic structure, although some do. Some organizations view quality as a set of rigid procedures and formal coordination activities among groups. These organizations often plateau or eventually disband their quality efforts. Most organizations practicing total quality move in the direction of organic structures. The number of levels in their hierarchy decreases, teams are created, and employees are given the authority (and even the responsibility) to develop new and better ways of accomplishing their tasks. Coordination also tends toward the informal, as people who are interdependent are able to coordinate their work on a personal basis without the interference of a bureaucratic hierarchy. The relatively broader jobs in a TQ company give employees a better sense of how their work contributes to customer satisfaction, whether their customers are internal or external.

John Akers, the former CEO of IBM who presided over a substantial reorganization of his company, stated that, "Every reorganization solves some problems and creates some problems."[36] Are problems created by the adoption of organic-type TQ organizational designs? It is too early to tell. Few organizations are more than a few years into TQ, so there is not enough of a track record on which to judge. Even fewer, however, have reverted from a TQ-type design to a more mechanistic design, and more organizations all the time are adopting a design that features internal customers, process teams, broad employee responsibilities, and quality steering committees. This indicates that such structures are seen as viable and necessary by an increasing number of managers and organizations.

How can the "one best way" approach of the quality movement be justified in light of organization theory's historical endorsement of a contingency approach to design? It may be that few industries and technologies are simple and stable enough for a mechanistic design to operate effectively.

A second possibility is that TQ designs have capacities for producing efficiencies unanticipated in the old mechanistic-organic distinction. Once the improvement of a particular process has reached the point where it is impractical to search for further gains, teams may establish the process as their standard and attempt to recreate it perfectly each time without the involvement of their managers. In other words, efficiencies would be created through different methods than those used in mechanistic firms.

A third possibility is that TQ-oriented firms pay a price in efficiency for their organizational structures, but that the superior quality of their products more than makes up for the higher prices that a lack of efficiency entails. Such firms would be unlikely to compete effectively in markets, such as textiles, where price is the overriding competitive factor.

A final possibility is that firms structured to achieve quality are paying a price for inefficiency that is not offset by their advantages. In this case such structures are not viable in the long run. This possibility does not seem to be the case, based on the limited information currently available.

Institutional Theory

Structural contingency theory, like most organizational design theories, is based on the assumption that organizations choose structures to help them perform better—provide high quality, low costs, and so forth. Institutional theory, by contrast, holds that organizations try to succeed by creating structures that will be seen as appropriate by important external constituencies—customers, other organizations in the industry, government agencies, and so on.[37]

According to institutional theory, an aspect of organizational structure need not contribute to organizational performance to be worthwhile. If the adoption of a certain structure helps the organization to be seen as legitimate in the eyes of those who have power to determine the organization's fate, then it is worthwhile. For example, many businesses have departments devoted to achieving environmental goals. Whether these departments help achieve these goals is debatable, but the existence of such departments helps to promote the legitimacy of these organizations as being concerned about the environment.

From an institutional theory standpoint, it is important to ask whether quality-oriented organization designs that include steering committees and extensive use of teams are actually intended to promote quality or are merely a means of legitimizing the organization as a progressive, quality-conscious organization. Little evidence has been generated to suggest that such structures demonstrably improve performance, yet they continue to be adopted in huge numbers by organizations in all sectors of the economy. Some writers describe these structures as "fads" or "fashions."[38] A fad is something that is normally a new idea, developed in a vague and previously undefined area, and about which users are initially enthusiastic, but can quickly lose interest. A fashion has been defined as the pursuit of novelty for its own sake. Both are temporary phases in an organization, and unless they become entrenched in the organization, they will never achieve their purpose or endure for the long haul.

In some settings, the adoption of quality-oriented structures is motivated primarily by institution concerns. For example, any company that wishes to compete in Europe must be certified as complying with the ISO 9000 quality standards. Suppliers to American automobile producers must also have elaborate quality programs in place. Many organizations have adopted a Six Sigma approach, primarily because of the publicity surrounding the use of Six Sigma by Jack Welch at General Electric. Thus, institutional theory provides another way of thinking about the rapid proliferation of quality-oriented structures in organizations. Although some organizations may be primarily seeking higher performance through the adoption of teams and steering committees, others may be primarily seeking the approval of important constituencies.

Contextual Factors and TQ Performance

Although much has been written about quality, little attention has been paid to the potential effects of contextual factors on quality and performance.[39] The use of organizational theory to formulate propositions regarding the effects of such factors is especially scarce in the literature. However, one research study used institutional theory and contingency theory to derive and test a number of interesting propositions. Using data obtained from a survey, the effects of five contextual factors—three institutional factors and two contingency factors—on the implementation of TQ practices and on the impact of TQ on key organizational performance measures were analyzed. The three institutional factors included TQ implementation,

ISO 9000 registration, and country of origin; and the two contingency factors included company size and scope of operations. The four performance measures were organizational effectiveness, human resource results, financial and market results, and customer results.

The results showed that the implementation of TQ practices is similar across subgroups of companies within each contextual factor. In addition, the effects of TQ on four performance measures, as well as the relationships among these measures, are generally similar across subgroup companies. Thus, for the five contextual factors analyzed, the overall findings suggest that TQ and TQ-performance relationships are not dependent on context, and that the holistic implementation of TQ practices contributes to improved performance consistently across subgroups of companies within each institutional and contingency factor. By implementing these practices effectively, managers can expect to realize improvements in all of the four performance areas. However, improvements in human resource results, customer results, and organizational effectiveness would be more immediate than those in financial and market results. This finding supports the argument that a long-term view should be taken in implementing TQ and that TQ initiatives should not be terminated if there are no significant improvements in the bottom line in the short-term.

The research findings between TQ companies and non-TQ companies show that for a company to be a TQ company, it does not have to formally implement TQ. There was also no difference between ISO-registered companies and non–ISO-registered companies. These results could be explained by the fact that a large number of companies responding to the survey had a number of other quality initiatives such as kaizen, lean manufacturing, constraint management, and Juran training, as well as other quality initiatives with no formal name. Therefore, the important question is how effectively these companies are implementing the various components of TQ in the absence of a formal quality program. This suggests that companies need to decide whether significant resources and effort should be allocated to the implementation of a TQ program to achieve desired performance outcomes. Companies that already have other quality initiatives in place have to determine whether they will reap extra benefits by implementing a separate TQ program. The results suggest that similar performance outcomes can be achieved by either undertaking other quality initiatives or simply establishing organizational systems that incorporate common TQ practices.

This study also indicates that the TQ practices of U.S. and non-U.S. companies operating in the U.S. are similar. This finding should be useful to the managers of these companies in planning and implementing the appropriate TQ practices. However, they should expect to see different results in some of the performance areas. Although TQ practices were first implemented in large companies, this study shows that small- and medium-size companies have come a long way in employing the same practices and that they can benefit similarly from the same concepts. These findings support prior research, which found that small companies could implement TQ practices as effectively as large companies and obtain high product quality. Similarly, the fit of TQ practices is similar across domestic and international operating companies. This suggests that domestic operating companies have developed comparable TQ practices. Even though learning and adoption of new management techniques in international companies may be faster, the fact that the TQ philosophy has been in practice for a long time may have narrowed the TQ knowledge gap between the two subgroups.

Review and Discussion Questions

1. Many managers think that process thinking is only relevant in operations (e.g., manufacturing and service delivery). How is a process focus reflected in nearly everything that Boeing AS does in the Performance Excellence Profile at the beginning of this chapter and what does this suggest to the managers in the first question?
2. What are the advantages and disadvantages of the functional structure? How does a process focus overcome some of the disadvantages?
3. What are the major types of structural change exhibited by organizations pursuing total quality?
4. Think back to an experience you have had with poor customer service from an organization. Whom did you blame for it? Do you know anything about the design of the organization involved? Do you think it was the fault of the individual(s) involved or could the problem have resulted from a poorly designed system? Would what you have learned in this chapter change your reaction to receiving poor quality service? How?
5. What are the core processes in a video rental store? A department store? A grocery store? How could these organizations be redesigned around these processes? What barriers would need to be overcome to accomplish this?
6. Find an organizational chart for your college or university. Is it primarily functional or process-focused? What advantages or problems do you see with this organizational structure? How might the structure be redesigned to better meet the needs of students and other stakeholders?
7. How does the organizational structure of Gold Star Chili reflect Deming's view of a production system? (See the introduction to Chapter 6.)
8. Explain how a focus on internal customers and a team-based organization supports the process view of organizations.
9. How do teams support organizational design for TQ?
10. What is high-performance work? What types of HR practices contribute to a high performance work environment?
11. Explain the differences between job enlargement, job enrichment, and job rotation. Provide some examples from your experience.
12. Discuss how each of the organizations described in the section "Organizational Design for Quality in Action" apply the principles presented in the section on "Redesigning Organizations for Quality."
13. Richard Palermo of Xerox was quoted in *Fortune* as saying that "people in different functions hate each other." Allowing for some exaggeration because of dramatic license, do you find this to be true? Talk to several people in a functional organization, and ask them about their feelings for people in other functions. How would you explain the variation in attitudes? If you were assigned to try to solve the problem of bad feelings between departments, how would you begin?
14. Could total quality be effective in a company with a mechanistic structure? How would it work?
15. Do you feel that the institutional theory of structure is a good description of why organizations choose quality-oriented organization designs? Why or why not?

CASES

The State University Experience

Wow! That State University video was really cool. It has lots of majors; it's close to home so I can keep my job; and Mom and Dad loved it when they visited. I wish I could know what it's really like to be a student at State. Hmmm, I think I'll ask Mom and Dad to take a campus tour with me....

I'm sure that we took our tour on the hottest day of the summer. The campus is huge—it took us about two hours to complete the tour and we didn't even see everything! I wasn't sure that the tour guide knew what he was doing. We went into a gigantic lecture hall and the lights weren't even on. Our tour guide couldn't find them so we had to hold the doors open so the sunlight could come in. About three-fourths of the way through the tour, our guide said, "State University isn't really a bad place to go to school; you just have to learn the system." I wonder what he meant by that?...

This application is really confusing. How do I let the admissions office know that I am interested in physics, mechanical engineering, and industrial design? Even my parents can't figure it out. I guess I'll call the admissions office for some help....

I'm so excited! Mom just handed me a letter from State! Maybe they've already accepted me. What? What's this? They say I need to send my transcript. I did that when I mailed in my application two weeks ago. What's going on? I hope it won't affect my application. I'd better check with Admissions....

You can't find my file? I thought you were missing only my transcript. I asked my counselor if she had sent it in yet. She told me that she sent it last week. Oh, you'll call me back when you locate my file? OK.

Finally, I've been accepted! Wait a minute. I didn't apply to University College; that's a two-year program. I wanted physics, M.E., or industrial design. Well, since my only choice is U. College and I really want to go to State, I guess I'll send in the confirmation form. It really looks a lot like the application. In fact, I know I gave them a lot of the same information. I wonder why they need it again? Seems like a waste of time....

Orientation was a lot of fun. I'm glad they straightened out my acceptance at U. College. I think I will enjoy State after all. I met lots of other students. I saw my advisor and I signed up for classes. All I have left to do is pay my tuition bill. Whoops. None of my financial aid is on this bill. I know I filled out all of the forms because I got an award letter from State. There is no way my parents and I can pay for this without financial aid. It says at the bottom, I'll lose all of my classes if I don't pay the bill on time....

I'm not confirmed on the computer? I sent in my form and the fee a long time ago. What am I going to do? I don't want to lose all of my classes. I have to go to the admissions office or my college office and get a letter that says I am a confirmed student. OK. If I do that tomorrow, will I still have all of my classes? ...I can't sleep; I'm so nervous about my first day....

Discussion Questions

1. What breakdowns in service processes has this student experienced? How might these be a function of organizational design?
2. What types of process management activities should State University administrators undertake?

You Want Us to Work with Marketing???[40]

On her second day as division level financial manager, one of Kay's employees (someone she had known for several years) told her about a transactional problem with sales data. Kay suggested that the employee resolve the issue with someone in marketing. The response was the last thing she expected: "Our department hasn't talked to marketing about these kinds of problems for seven years."

Shocked, Kay decided to do some investigating. She called one of the marketing managers she had known for many years and asked what he knew about this problem. He confirmed there was an issue between the two departments but said he didn't understand the details. What made this situation even more puzzling was that this barrier had survived a move of the entire division (85 people) from Denver to Phoenix six years earlier. Significant synergy could be gained by having the two groups work closely. How could managers in either department have permitted these silos? Did they lack the courage to address the problem, or were they so disengaged from the day-to-day activities that they didn't even see it?

To address this issue, Kay wanted to have both groups share their process flows with each other in a series of joint departmental meetings. Each session would develop process thinking and help the groups understand how to support each other by seeing themselves as customers and suppliers of each other. She called the marketing manager again and shared her plan. Without hesitation, he agreed to help. The marketing department already had process maps it shared with customers. They agreed not to tell their groups what situation had initiated these sessions.

Within a week, the first session was scheduled. It was interesting to watch everyone find a seat. One group gathered on the right side of the room and the other on the left. The meeting went well. At first, there were no questions or discussion, but toward the end, employees from both groups began exchanging ideas about how they could better support each other at their process touchpoints—the points at which the two departments' processes overlapped. The morning after the first session, one of the marketing employees came to our department to ask for help with a process problem. Within three weeks, a customer service manager asked my group to participate in a conference call to the computer support department. The purpose of the call was to raise the priority for fixing a marketing system problem that resulted in data errors for both marketing and my department.

Because marketing now understood more about the data flow connection between our departments, they also understood the impact of the system error reached beyond the marketing group and recognized the potential to help both groups by correcting the problem. This joint effort was the first of many synergistic efforts between the departments. Remaining process review sessions were scheduled regularly, and cooperation between both groups continued to grow.

Discussion Questions

1. What are some symptoms of typical cultural barriers that create obstacles to improvement?
2. How can a process focus help to break down silos in an organization?
3. What types of tools and techniques can be used to help to support a process focus and improve the process of change?

Walker Auto Sales and Service

The organization chart for Walker Auto Sales and Service is shown in Figure 7.9. Use this to address the discussion questions below.

Discussion Questions

1. Specifically in the context of an automobile dealership, discuss the problems that this functional structure might have.
2. Using the principles discussed in this chapter, suggest some organizational redesign proposals that might better help this company pursue a performance excellence strategy.

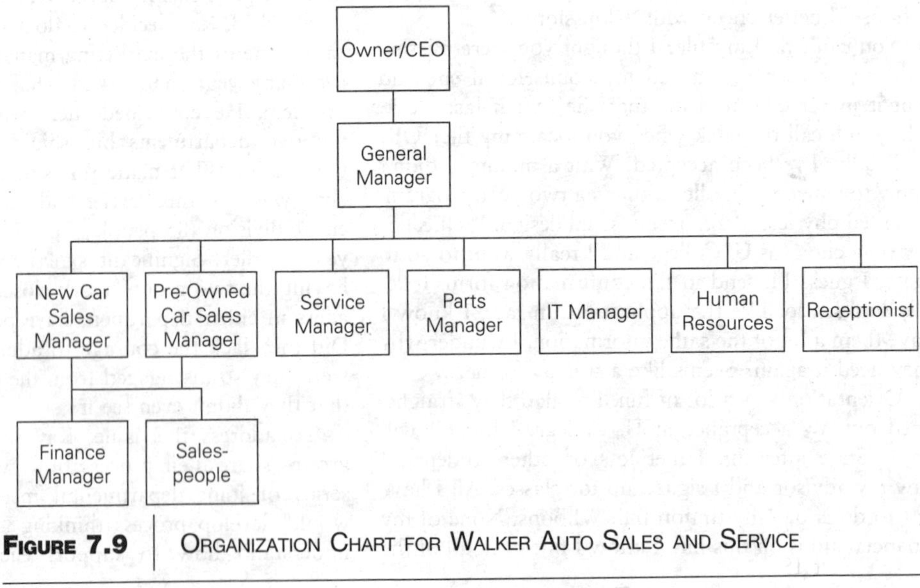

FIGURE 7.9 | ORGANIZATION CHART FOR WALKER AUTO SALES AND SERVICE

Child Focus, Inc.[41]

Child Focus, Inc. (CFI), whose mission is to join with communities in strengthening families and improving the quality of life for children, offers a wide variety of programs in Clermont, Hamilton, and Brown counties in Ohio. With an agency budget in excess of $11 million dollars, the spectrum of services includes Head Start programs for children ages 0–5, parenting education, family literacy, GED test preparation, substance abuse prevention, partial hospitalization, mental health prevention and counseling services in schools, foster care, independent living, case management, outpatient individual, family, and group therapy, diagnostic testing, psychiatric services, and professional training. CFI's 240 employees have a broad range of professional education, including high school, associate's, bachelor's, master's, Ph.D., R.N., and M.D. degrees. All staff share the authority, dedication, and commitment to promote the mission of serving children and families.

Facilities include intranet, Internet, a Web site (http://www.child-focus.org), specifically designed management information systems with necessary office equipment, 22 vehicles to provide client transportation, and two commercial kitchens that serve more than 800 meals a day. Facilities and programs are supervised by a volunteer Board of Trustees and by the accreditation standards of the National Association for the Education of the Young Child, Day Care Licensing Regulations, Head Start Performance Standards, and Ohio Departments of Education, Mental Health, Alcohol and Drug Addiction Services, and Job and Family Services.

As CFI continues to expand its programs through new and larger contracts, the biggest challenge is to provide quality services. Personnel and human resources issues are another challenge. They continually strive to find qualified staff who are willing to work with some of the most challenging children and dysfunctional families. Although their turnover rate is approximately 15 percent, most of it is in less-skilled positions. Consequently, this loss of staff increases training costs. Training existing staff to meet higher educational standards and continuing to find office and service space to meet growing needs is also a challenge.

CFI's diversity of programming, reporting, and funding to multiple agencies and organizations requires continuous management at all levels within the agency. The governing Board of Trustees for Child Focus is a diverse group of volunteers that have experience as attorneys, teachers, homemakers, and CFI consumers. Federal, state, and county legislative and regulatory changes can affect programming or present financial challenges. These entities, in turn, may have competing philosophies, which complicate administration or delay program implementation.

CFI management has several procedures in place to identify and manage these organizational challenges. Customer, staff, and collaborators' recommendations and complaints are identified through evaluation and administrative programs in both the Early Childhood and Behavioral Health divisions and are continuously monitored by staff, management, and the Board of Trustees. Through a continuous strategic planning process, CFI identifies ways in which to improve and expand its services through program modification or development.

The CEO is committed to building a total quality organization. If you were asked to help in this quality journey, what questions would you want answered? What advice concerning organizational design would you provide?

Endnotes

1. 2003 Malcolm Baldrige National Quality Award Recipient Profile, U.S. Department of Commerce.
2. Kermit F. Wasmuth, "Organization and Planning," in Loren Walsh, Ralph Wurster, and Raymond J. Kimber (eds.), *Quality Management Handbook*, Wheaton, IL: Hitchcock Publishing Company, 1986, pp. 9–34.
3. An interesting perspective on this problem is provided by Benson P. Shapiro, V. Kasturi Rangan, and John J. Sviokla, in "Staple Yourself to an Order," *Harvard Business Review*, July-August 1992, pp. 113–122.
4. Myron Tribus, "Total Quality in Education," unpublished manuscript. Hayward, Calif.: Exergy, Inc.
5. Quoted from "The CEO as Organizational Architect: An Interview with Xerox's Paul Allaire" by Robert Howard, in *Harvard Business Review*, September–October 1992, pp. 106–121.
6. Thomas A. Stewart, "The Search for the Organization of Tomorrow," *Fortune*, May 18, 1992.
7. J. M. Juran, *Juran on Leadership for Quality: An Executive Handbook*, New York: Free Press, 1989.

8. W. E. Deming, *Out of the Crisis*. Cambridge, Mass.: MIT Center for Advanced Engineering Study, 1986.
9. *AT&T's Total Quality Approach*, AT&T Corporate Quality Office, 1992, p. 6.
10. Adapted from Katrina Brooker, "The Nightmare before Christmas," *Fortune*, January 24, 2000, pp. 24–25.
11. Robert Hof, Debra Sparks, Ellen Neuborne, and Wendy Zellner. "Can Amazon Make It?" *Business Week*, July 10, 2000, pp. 38–43.
12. A. Blanton Godfrey, "Planned Failures," *Quality Digest*, March 2000, p. 16.
13. Adapted from Texas Nameplate Company, Inc. 1998 Award Winner Profile, Baldrige National Quality Program, U.S. Department of Commerce.
14. City of Coral Springs Florida 2007 Baldrige Award Application
15. R.J. Schonberger, *Building a Chain of Customers*, New York: Free Press, 1990.
16. See Jack Reilly, "Using the Methods of Fernando Flores," *Center for Quality of Management Journal*, Vol. 6, No. 1, Spring 1997; and Grant Harris and Steve Taylor, "Escaping from the Box: Using a New Process Model to Support Participation and Improve Coordination," *Center for Quality of Management Journal*, Vol. 6, No. 3, Winter 1997.
17. The author is indebted to Jackie Messerschmidt of Workflow Dynamics for graciously providing this example.
18. Jerry G. Bowles, "Leading the World-Class Company," *Fortune*, September 21, 1992.
19. Jeannie Coyle, "Aligning Human Resource Processes with Total Quality," *Employment Relations Today*, Vol. 18, No. 3, Fall 1991.
20. Mark Kelly, *The Adventures of a Self-Managing Team*, Raleigh, N.C.: Mark Kelly Books, 1990.
21. Based on "TQM-Quality with Reduced Resources," a talk given by Dr. Edwin Coate, vice president for finance and administration, Oregon State University, presented via teleconference by Cuyahoga Community College, September 9, 1992.
22. Stewart, "The Search for the Organization of Tomorrow."
23. Robert O. Knorr and Edward F. Thiede, Jr., "Making New Technologies Work," *The Journal of Business Strategy*, Vol. 12, No. 1, pp. 46–49.
24. AT&T Quality Steering Committee, *Leading the Quality Initiative*, AT&T Bell Laboratories, 1990, pp. 13–14.
25. Interview by former co-author James W. Dean, Jr. with Richard Buck.
26. Nadav Goldschmidt and Beth G. Chung, "Size Does Matter: The Effect of Organizational Size on Customer Satisfaction," *Journal of Quality Management*, Vol. 6, 2001, pp. 47–60.
27. J. R. Hackman and G. R. Oldham, *Work Redesign*, Reading, Mass.: Addison-Wesley, 1980.
28. Robert D. Hof, "Teamwork, Supercharged," Business Week, November 21, 2005, 90–94.
29. Malcolm Baldrige National Quality Award, Profiles of Winners, National Institute of Standards and Technology, U.S. Department of Commerce.
30. Adapted from Boeing Airlift and Tanker Programs 1998 Award Winner Profile, Baldrige National Quality Program, U.S. Department of Commerce.
31. Sources: David Stires, "How the VA Healed Itself," *Fortune*, May 15, 2006, 128–136; Catherine Arnst, "The Best Medical Care in the U.S.," *Business Week*, July 17, 2006, 50–56.
32. Solar Turbines, Inc. Malcolm Baldrige National Quality Award Application Summary, 1999, p. 4.
33. Jack Ewing, "No Cubicle Culture" *Business Week*, August 20, 2007. http://www.businessweek.com/magazine/content/07_34/b4047412.htm
34. Based on Stewart, "The Search for the Organization of Tomorrow."
35. This version of the contingency model comes from T. Burns and G. M. Stalker, *The Management of Innovation*. London: Tavistock, 1961.
36. Quoted in D. Hellriegel, J. W. Slocum and R. W. Woodman, *Organizational Behavior, 5th ed.*, St. Paul, Minn.: West Publishing Company, 1989.
37. See J. W. Meyer and B. Rowan, "Institutionalized Organizations: Formal Structure as Myth and Ceremony," *American Journal of Sociology*, Vol. 83, 1977, pp. 340–363, and W. R. Scott, "The Adolescence of Institutional Theory," *Administrative Science Quarterly*, Vol. 32, 1987, pp. 493–511.
38. R. E. Cole, *Managing Quality Fads*, Oxford University Press, New York, 1999; B. G. Dale, M. B. F. Elkjaer, A. van der Wiele, and A. R. T. Williams, "Fad, Fashion, and Fit: An Examination of Quality Circles, Business Process Re-engineering and Statistical Process Control," *International Journal of Production Economics*, Vol. 73, 2001, pp. 137–152; Gerald Zeitz, Vikas Mittal, and Brian McAulay, "Distinguishing Adoption and Entrenchment of Management

Practices: A Framework for Analysis," *Organization Studies*, Vol. 20, No. 5, 1999, pp. 741–776.

39. Ismail Sila, "Examining the effects of contextual factors on TQM and performance through the lens of organizational theories: An empirical study," *Journal of Operations Management*, 25, 2007, pp. 83–109.
40. Based on Kay Sever, "The Power of Process Orientation," *Quality Progress*, January 2007, 46–52.
41. Child Focus, Inc., 2003 Greater Cincinnati Chamber of Commerce Small Business Awards Application. Our thanks go to Tara Dawson for providing this information.

PART 3

PERFORMANCE EXCELLENCE AND ORGANIZATIONAL BEHAVIOR

CHAPTER 8 Quality Teamwork 303

CHAPTER 9 Engagement, Empowerment, and Motivation 334

QUALITY TEAMWORK

CHAPTER 8

Performance Excellence Profile: KARLEE Company, Inc.[1]

Located in Garland, Texas, KARLEE is a contract manufacturer of precision sheet metal and machined components for customers in the telecommunications, semiconductor, and medical-equipment industries. Since beginning in 1974 as a one-man, garage-based machine shop, the company has developed into a one-stop supplier of manufacturing services. Its work ranges from initial design and prototyping to painting and assembly to integration of cabling and power elements. KARLEE won the Texas Quality Award in 1999, and was named Texas Business of the Year in 2000, the same year in which it received the Baldrige Award.

KARLEE is organized as a team of teams that are unified by a shared mission. Whether executive, managerial, operational, administrative, or support, each team aims "to exceed stakeholders' expectations." Although this organizational ambition is not unique to KARLEE, the manufacturer does distinguish itself in the way it uses team approaches to promote an intense focus on the customer throughout the company. The company encourages open communications among teams, team participation in setting goals, and team responsibility for managing and improving processes. To foster a common sense of business direction, for example, KARLEE shuts down its manufacturing cells so that everyone can be included in company-wide meetings. The company's chief asset in motivating a shared commitment, however, may be the culture of mutual trust, honesty, and respect that KARLEE leadership actively encourages.

An integrated leadership system links KARLEE's present operational course to its future direction. The Senior Executive Leader (SEL) team concentrates on identifying and clarifying long-term strategic issues and opportunities, including future customer requirements. The KARLEE Steering Committee, consisting of the seven senior executives and the leaders of departmental teams, distills the SEL's five-year plan and its forward-looking performance targets into annual business and operational objectives. Decisions are guided by customer assessments—based on annual survey results and almost daily customer feedback—and by equally detailed reviews of KARLEE's performance, workforce, and operational capabilities.

Annual goals are aligned with the company's five key business drivers—customer satisfaction; operational performance; financial performance; community service; and team member safety, satisfaction, and development. Members of the Steering Committee work with functional and cross-functional teams to translate the goals into improvement projects with measurable objectives.

Manufacturing teams use statistical process control methods to monitor process performance. In addition, teams in all areas conduct monthly self-audits, and the Quality Assurance Department performs a monthly assessment of team performance, yielding a weighted quality rating for each team and each department. Results of these evaluations are posted on team, department, and corporate bulletin boards. This permits all team members to check progress toward accomplishing company objectives.

KARLEE promotes cooperation, collaboration, and initiative through its team structure. Teams are expected to perform at high levels and to take full responsibility for meeting the requirements of internal and external customers. Cross-training and job rotation are encouraged because they foster organizational flexibility and broaden the base of skills and knowledge needed to respond quickly to changing customer demands.

Manufacturing cell teams are empowered to schedule work, manage inventory, and design the layout of their work areas. Every team has a budget for recognition and celebration, which complements the company's broader program of rewards and recognition. These range from free movie passes to monthly and quarterly awards for outstanding performance by team members and leaders.

New approaches to cultivate the company's family atmosphere and to reinforce team member commitment to KARLEE's mission are recommended by the Cultural Advisory Committee. Members of this committee are chosen specifically to reflect the ethnic diversity of the company's workforce. Other vehicles for creating a climate of teamwork and mutual support include the KARLEE Cares Team, which members formed to help fellow workers during times of personal crisis.

Deming urged leaders to abandon competition and to seek cooperation. Teams provide a way of doing this, as well as enhancing Deming's concept of "pride and joy in work." A **team** is a small number of people with complementary skills who are committed to a common purpose, a set of performance goals, and an approach for which they hold themselves mutually accountable.[2] Teams are everywhere in our world—on the football or baseball field, reality shows such as the *Amazing Race*, the Navy SEALS, the Tokyo String Quartet, and Jeff Gordon's pit crew, to name just a few. Teams also are a central facet of performance excellence initiatives, as the KARLEE Company illustrates in this chapter's opening profile.

Although many types of teams exist in organizations pursuing quality and performance excellence, the concept of teamwork is widespread and is a key contributor to success in just about any setting. This chapter will:

- explain the importance of teams in a quality environment,
- identify the different types of teams used in organizations,
- explain some of the factors associated with the successful use of teams,
- give examples of effective teams in action, and
- relate the use of quality-focused teams to organizational behavior theories.

THE IMPORTANCE OF TEAMS

Teams are everywhere in high-performing organizations: at the top and bottom and in every function and department in between. For instance, Corning Telecommunications Product's Division, a former Baldrige recipient, has employee-designed work teams, customer account teams, market teams, new product development teams, and manufacturing operation teams. FedEx has more than 4,000 Quality Action teams; Boeing Airlift and Tanker Division has more than 100 integrated product teams (IPTs) that are typically made up of engineering, work-team, customer, and supplier representatives. Graniterock, with fewer than 400 employees, has about 100 functioning teams, ranging from 10 corporate quality teams to project teams, purchasing teams, task forces, and function teams composed of people who do the same job at different locations.

Why are there so many teams? The principles of total quality recognize the interdependence of various parts of the organization and uses teams as a way to coordinate work. Teamwork enables various parts of the organization to work together in meeting customer needs that can seldom be fulfilled by employees limited to one specialty. Teams promote equality among individuals, encouraging a positive attitude and trust. The diversity inherent in teams often provides unique perspectives on work, spontaneous thought, and creativity. In addition, teams develop a greater sense of responsibility for achieving goals and performing tasks. In short, teams provide a variety of benefits that are not derived from individuals working alone.

High-performing organizations recognize that the potential contributions of employees are much greater than in the traditional organization, and teams are an attempt to take advantage of this potential. Furthermore, the competitive environment of modern business requires flexible, fast reaction to changes in customer demands or technological capacity. Teams can provide the capacity for rapid response. Many companies have gone public with stories of their successful teams as well as sharing their recognition efforts (see box "Teams are Motivating"). Managers are always looking for ideas that produce results, and teams certainly fall squarely within this category.

Teams Are Motivating[3]

Several teams from Boeing received awards in the 2007 International Team Excellence Competition sponsored by the American Society for Quality's Team and Workplace Excellence Forum. Using a variety of quality tools, the first-place team developed a solution that eliminated unsafe conditions that occurred during installation of details in C-17 aircraft tailcones. The team also initiated process improvements with positive results in areas of quality, cost, and schedule with direct impact on organizational goals. Perhaps the most encouraging aspect of the team experience was the reaction from one of the team members:

> Watching the [other] Boeing teams receive their awards brought a great feeling of pride for the company we work for, but it also brought a momentary feeling of going home empty-handed... "The 2007 ASQ International Team Excellence Gold winning team is ... the C-17..." That was all we needed to hear to know we had just won the biggest prize in the quality team competition. By the time they had finished announcing us, we were on our feet and headed to the stage. Far from the accolades and congratulations, I take from this experience a renewed desire to achieve even higher levels of quality in the projects I am a part of at Boeing. I understand more about the essence of using quality tools, how they help to define direction and substance in managing a project, and how to better prepare a team for future competitions.
>
> —Daniel Munoz

TYPES OF TEAMS

Organizations use so many different types of teams that sometimes it is difficult to tell one from another. Some common types of teams include:

- *Leadership teams* (often termed *steering committees or quality councils*)—teams that lead quality initiatives in an organization and provide direction and focus.
- *Problem-solving teams*—teams of workers and supervisors that meet to address workplace problems involving quality and productivity, or ad-hoc teams with a specific mission such as organizational design teams that act as architects of change as discussed in the previous chapter.
- *Natural work teams*—people who work together every day to perform a complete unit of work.
- *Self-managed teams*—Work teams that are empowered to make and control their own decisions.
- *Virtual teams*—teams whose members communicate electronically, take turns as leaders, and jump in and out as necessary. These types of teams use a combination of Internet, e-mail, phone, fax, video conferencing, PC-to-PC connections, and shared computer screen technologies to get their jobs done.
- *Project teams*—teams with a specific mission to develop something new or to accomplish a complex task. Project teams have recently gained a new measure of importance and respect in the context of Six Sigma.

Leadership teams, natural work teams, self-managed teams, and virtual teams typically work on routine business activities—managing an organization, building a product, or designing an electronic system—and are an integral part of how work is organized and designed. Problem-solving teams and project teams, by contrast, work more on an ad hoc basis to address specific tasks or issues, often relating to quality improvement.

Leadership Teams

Quality leadership teams, which we introduced in Chapter 7, have long been promoted by quality gurus such as Juran and Crosby. Juran advocated the use of steering committees, called **quality councils,**[4] while Crosby suggested the use of **quality improvement teams.**[5] Steering committees are responsible for establishing overall quality policy and for guiding the implementation and evolution of quality throughout the organization. Quality improvement teams provide the leadership for quality at mid- and lower levels of the organization.

The top manager of the organization is usually on the quality council, as is the manager with overall responsibility for quality—for example, the Vice President/Director of Performance Excellence. The steering committee may meet fairly often when a quality initiative is getting started, but usually meets only monthly or quarterly once things are under way. This group makes key decisions about the quality process—how quality should be measured and what structures and approaches should be used to improve quality. The steering committee also periodically reviews the status of the effort and makes the adjustments necessary to ensure customer satisfaction and continuous improvement. In general, the steering committee has overall responsibility for the progress and success of the entire performance excellence effort. Often, this revolves around using the Baldrige Criteria and conducting routine self- or external-assessments to measure progress and identify improvement opportunities (see Chapter 11 for further discussion of this topic).

As performance excellence became a routine part of overall business management, the roles of independent quality councils have been assimilated into executive leadership teams in many organizations, signifying that quality planning is not a separate activity, but rather an integrated part of overall business planning. Thus, the executive leadership team acts both as a quality council and a business leadership team. At Custom Research, Inc., for example, a four-person steering committee sets company directions, integrates performance excellence goals, and promotes the development of all employees. Committee members have frequent interaction with associates, review overall company performance daily, and meet formally each month to identify areas for improvement.

Problem-Solving Teams

The second, and probably most common, type of team used in quality is the problem-solving team. As the name implies, problem-solving teams work to improve quality by identifying and solving specific quality-related problems facing the organization. Such teams are sometimes referred to as *corrective action teams*, or *quality circles* (see box "Quality Circles in Japan: Still Unbroken"), although many organizations have created their own names for them. Two basic types of problem-solving teams are departmental and cross-functional.

These teams are limited in membership to employees of a specific department and are limited in scope to problems within that department. Such groups typically meet once a week for one to two hours and progress through a standardized problem-solving methodology. First they identify a set of problems and select one to work on. Then they collect data about the causes of the problem and determine the best approach to solving it. (Often this will entail using many of the techniques described in Chapter 7.)

If the solution does not require any major changes in procedures or substantial resources, the group frequently can implement its own solution. If this is not the case, group members will make a presentation to some level of management, requesting approval for their solution and the resources to implement it. These teams typically remain relatively intact as they address a number of problems in succession.

The problems that such teams work on can be quite diverse. A team of hourly workers at U.S. Steel's Gary Works has solved a number of crippling quality problems, helping to reduce the amount of steel rejected by automotive customers by

Quality Circles in Japan: Still Unbroken

Quality circles were among the first Japanese management practices used in the United States. When visiting Japan in the 1970s, American managers noticed groups of workers meeting to address quality problems. The managers recognized this is a practice that could easily be copied and returned home to institute it in their own companies. Quality circles (QCs) took off in the United States as the Japanese management mania peaked, and firms like Lockheed and Westinghouse reported early successes with QCs. The movement boomed in the early 1980s as most large American companies introduced the practice.

The bloom was soon off the rose, however, as firms found themselves devoting a lot of time and attention to QCs and receiving relatively little in return. There were a number of reasons for the lack of results. Employees were only encouraged to work on quality problems during their meetings (usually about an hour a week) and spent the rest of their week just "doing their job." Supervisors were often not involved in the program and were indifferent, if not downright hostile, to it. Perhaps the biggest problem was that QCs were "just a program," cut off from and often opposed to the way the organization usually worked. Managers preached about the importance of quality work during their QC events, but when crunch time came, their attitude was, in the words of one QC member, "If it doesn't smoke, ship it!" Not surprisingly, companies started to disband their QC programs, which were soon dismissed as just another passing fad. In the context of the current interest in total quality, many managers look back on QCs as essentially a false start on the road to quality. It is interesting in this light to note that many Japanese companies still operate QCs and that they are seen as a critical part of the total quality control (TQC) effort in these companies.[6]

According to the Union of Japanese Scientists and Engineers, 5.5 million workers take part in 750,000 circles. Managers as well as frontline employees are involved, and the circles are considered a normal part of working life, rather than a "program." In fact, QCs often work to achieve the objectives set in the kaizen process (see Chapter 4), which puts them in the mainstream of TQC activity. Some organizations provide monetary incentives for suggestions provided by circles, and employees in some firms make dozens of suggestions per year. It appears that the mistake made in the U.S. introduction of quality circles was not in introducing them, but in not taking them seriously.

80 percent.[7] A team of service technicians at an equipment rental company simplified the form used to perform preventive maintenance, saving the company considerable time in the process. A team of people from the "re-sort" department at Federal Express improved the process of package sorting, which created savings in labor costs and helped to avoid the cost and embarrassment of having to send overnight packages via commercial airlines.[8] An information systems team for a manufacturing company addressed a serious problem with internal customer satisfaction about its response to requests for application changes and help with using new software.[9]

Natural Work Teams

Natural work teams are organized to perform a complete unit of work, such as assembling a motorcycle, creating circuit plans for a television set, or performing a market research study from beginning to end. The "unit of work" need not be the final product, but some intermediate component. Natural work teams replace rather than complement the traditional organization of work. What is different in this work design structure is that work tasks are not narrowly defined as they would be on an assembly line, for instance.

Team members share responsibility for completing the job and are usually cross-trained to perform all work tasks and often rotate among them. A team in an automotive manufacturing plant placed an advertisement in the classified section of their local newspaper that read in part:

> Our team is down one good player. Join our group of multiskilled Maintenance Associates who work together to support our assembly teams.... We are looking for a versatile person with ... ability to set up and operate various welding machinery... willingness to work on detailed projects for extended time periods, and general overall knowledge of the automobile manufacturing process.... You must be a real team player, have excellent interpersonal skills, and be motivated to work in a highly participative environment.[10]

This ad illustrates many of the differences between natural work teams and the traditional organization of work for non-managerial employees. For example, members of such teams are expected to actually work as a team, rather than just perform their own jobs capably. Their knowledge must be broad rather than narrow, their skills interpersonal as well as technical. Natural work teams lead to self-managed teams, which are discussed next.

Self-Managed Teams

Self-managed teams (SMTs), also known as self-directed teams or autonomous work groups, are natural work teams with broad responsibilities, including the responsibility to manage themselves. SMTs are empowered to take corrective action and resolve day-to-day problems; they also have direct access to information that allows them to plan, control, and improve their operations. Self-managed teams have been used for decades, (the SMT concept was developed in Britain and Sweden in the 1950s, and one of the early companies to adopt it was Volvo, the Swedish auto manufacturer), and are common in TQ organizations.

In the absence of a supervisor, SMTs often handle budgeting, scheduling, setting goals, and ordering supplies. Some teams even evaluate one another's performance and hire replacements for departing team members. For example, the GE aircraft-engine plant in Durham, North Carolina, is a totally self-managing facility. Workers manage everything from process-improvement and work schedules to overtime budgets. Each engine is built by a single group of people, and that group "owns" the engine—from initial assembly to the moment it's put on the truck. GE/Durham team members take such pride in the engines they make that they routinely take brooms in hand to sweep out the beds of the 18-wheelers that transport those engines—just to make sure that no damage occurs in transit. Equipment maintenance and the cleaning of areas like bathrooms are contracted out, but team members keep their own areas clean.[11] In short, members of such teams are more like managers than employees in the traditional sense, hence the term self-managed teams (see box "A Little Spice and a Heaping Scoop of Teamwork").

SMTs have resulted in improved quality and customer service, greater flexibility, reduced costs, faster response, simpler job classifications, increased employee commitment to the organization, and the ability to attract and retain the best people.[12] Experts estimate that SMTs are 30 to 50 percent more productive than conventional teams. FedEx, for instance, reduced service errors by 13 percent; one 3M facility increased production by 300 percent; in a Mercedes-Benz plant, defects were reduced by 50 percent. A study of 22 manufacturing plants using SMTs

A Little Spice and a Heaping Scoop of Teamwork[13]

A great restaurant has superb cuisine, a special ambience, and a chef with presence. Radius, a hot restaurant in Boston's Financial District, has another ingredient: a real commitment to teamwork. Great teamwork starts in the kitchen. The Radius kitchen is made up of stations: the meat station, the fish station, the garde-manger station, the pastry station. Two people work at each station, and they have full responsibility for their part of the meal. In other words, the team at the meat station not only cooks the meat but also butchers it and seasons it—a sharp departure from the standard procedure at most restaurants.

Radius has also developed a series of meetings in which both the spirit and the practice of teamwork get reinforced. One weekly meeting focuses on frontline service. The sous-chefs and the pastry chefs meet with the back waiters and the food runners (the waiters' support staff) to review dishes and procedures. Because servers at Radius announce each course, they need to know what is on each plate, how to put it down in front of a guest, and how to pronounce it.

A daily meeting (the kitchen-staff session) focuses on behind-the-scenes operations. About 30 staffers gather around Chef Michael Schlow to discuss plans for the evening. He reminds them about his obsession with using as much of every ingredient as possible. "Can we make a sauce with that extra crème fraîche?" he asks. Then there's the daily service meeting. This meeting includes all of the waitstaff, the floor managers, and the hosts and hostesses. The general manager begins by going over that night's reservations: who the customers are—their names, what they do, if they've been to Radius before. Then all eyes shift to a plate of food. The general manager calls on a server to describe the dish. She follows with a series of highly detailed questions. "What are the red beads around the plate?" she asks. "Spicy tomato oil," the server answers.

found that more than half of them made improvements in quality and productivity, removed at least one layer of management or supervision, and decreased their levels of grievances, absenteeism, and turnover.[14]

Virtual Teams

Virtual teams are groups of people who work closely together despite being geographically separated. Virtual teams rarely meet face-to-face; their primary interaction is through technologies such as telephone, fax, shared databases and collaborative software systems, the Internet, e-mail, and video conferencing. In 1998, over eight million workers were members of such teams, and this number has undoubtedly grown as new technology has proliferated.

Virtual teams are becoming important because of increasing globalization, flatter organizational structures, an increasing shift to knowledge work, and the need to bring diverse talents and expertise to complex projects and customize solutions to meet market demands. For example, a product design team in the United States can hand off its work to another team in Asia or Australia, resulting in an almost continuous work effort that speeds up development time considerably.

Because of their physical separation, some have difficulty applying the team concept to virtual teams. Virtual teams can face some unique challenges including

Virtual Teaming at MySQL[15]

It seemed like a typical company holiday party. The brandy and eggnog flowed freely, although it didn't seem to loosen up any of the attendees. "Smile and make pleasant talk while you serve, please," instructed the fellow who had cast himself as Santa. There were plenty of gag gifts: a luxury flat overlooking the Kremlin for Victoria, who was moving to Moscow; growth-enhancing supplements for Domas, who hovers at 6-foot-4. And, of course, the requisite tasteless humor. All standard fare for an office party—except that there was no office.

Thomas Basil, director of support at MySQL (pronounced "my S-Q-L"), a $40 million software maker, staged the event online, playing Santa while dispensing virtual drinks and gifts to staffers scattered in such outposts as Russia, England, and Germany. Few businesses are as spread out as MySQL, which employs 320 workers in 25 countries, 70 percent of whom work from home. (MySQL's database software is open source. That is, it offers free access to its software's source code and hopes in return to get its customers' help in identifying and fixing bugs and creating new features.)

In the MySQL mode, effective team-building may come from knowing when not to send an emotional e-mail or why the phone is necessary for certain interactions. Basil has developed strict guidelines that govern his online conduct. In the morning, when he first signs on to the company's Internet Relay Chat (IRC)—a postmodern version of the CB radio that acts as a companywide chatroom and offsets the isolating aspects of e-mail—Basil makes sure to greet every support-team member by name.

People at MySQL match the technology to the task. In addition to IRC, the company relies on Skype to allow people to make free voice calls over the Internet—and, just as important, to keep themselves from perishing in what can quickly intensify into Category 5 e-mail storms. MySQLers are also known to fire up a chat session on the side while on a conference call with a customer—the digital equivalent of kicking each other under the conference table.

language, culture, style differences, and the lack of social relationships that can lessen team commitment.[16] These require special efforts to ensure that a team environment is truly realized, particularly paying attention to communication, strong interpersonal relationships, and formal structures that support their work. For example, team member roles and objectives often must be made more explicit. All the issues that we describe in subsequent sections affect virtual teams in the same fashion as co-located teams, and should be incorporated into their design. See box "Virtual Teaming at MySQL" for an interesting example of some of these issues.

Project Teams

Project teams are chartered to perform one-time tasks such as technology implementation. They are fundamental to Six Sigma. Six Sigma projects require a diversity of skills that range from technical analysis, creative solution development, and implementation. Thus, Six Sigma teams not only address immediate problems, but also provide an environment for individual learning, management development, and career advancement. Six Sigma teams are comprised of several types of individuals:

- *Champions*: Senior-level managers who promote and lead the deployment of Six Sigma in a significant area of the business. Champions understand the philosophy and tools of Six Sigma, select projects, set objectives, allocate resources, and mentor teams. Champions own Six Sigma projects and are responsible for their completion and results; typically they also own the process that the project is focused on improving. They select teams, set strategic direction, create measurable objectives, provide resources, monitor performance, make key implementation decisions, and report results to top management. More importantly, champions work toward removing barriers—organizational, financial, personal—that might inhibit the successful implementation of a Six Sigma project.
- *Master Black Belts*: Full-time Six Sigma experts who are responsible for Six Sigma strategy, training, mentoring, deployment, and results. Master Black Belts are highly trained in how to use Six Sigma tools and methods and provide advanced technical expertise. They work across the organization to develop and coach teams, conduct training, and lead change, but are typically not members of Six Sigma project teams.
- *Black Belts*: Fully-trained Six Sigma experts with up to 160 hours of training who perform much of the technical analyses required of Six Sigma projects, usually on a full-time basis. They have advanced knowledge of tools and DMAIC methods, and can apply them either individually or as team leaders. They also mentor and develop Green Belts. Black Belts need good leadership and communication skills in addition to technical skills and process knowledge. They should be highly motivated, eager to gain new knowledge, and well-respected among their peers. As such, Black Belts are often targeted by the organization as future business leaders.
- *Green Belts*: Functional employees who are trained in introductory Six Sigma tools and methodology and work on projects on a part-time basis, assisting Black Belts while developing their own knowledge and expertise. Typically, one of the requirements for receiving a Green Belt designation is to successfully

complete a Six Sigma project. Successful Green Belts are often promoted to Black Belts.

- *Team Members*: Individuals from various functional areas who support specific projects. The roles of the Six Sigma champion and the Master Black Belt leader are similar to those of the champion and sponsor. The role of a Black Belt is similar to a staff quality expert, while Green Belts are typically given the team leadership role.

CROSS-FUNCTIONAL TEAMWORK

Natural work teams, self-managed teams, and problem-solving teams typically are intraorganizational; that is, members usually come from the same department or function. Leadership teams, virtual teams, and project teams, are usually cross-functional; they work on specific tasks or processes that cut across boundaries of several different departments regardless of their organizational home. Cross-functional teams are not unique to quality—they are commonly used in new product development, for example—but are increasingly becoming a mainstay of quality initiatives. These teams are similar in many ways to the departmental teams just discussed: they receive training in problem solving, identify and solve problems, and either implement or recommend solutions.

The differences are that members of cross-functional teams come from several departments or functions, deal with problems that involve a variety of functions, and typically dissolve after the problem is solved. For example, a cross-functional team in a brokerage might deal with problems in handling questions from clients. The issues raised would not be limited to stocks, bonds, or mutual funds, so people from all of these areas would be involved.

Cross-functional teams make a great deal of sense in an organization devoted to process improvement, because most processes do not respect functional boundaries. If a process is to be comprehensively addressed, the team addressing it cannot be limited, by either membership or charter, to only one function. To be effective, cross-functional teams should include people from several departments: those who are feeling the effects of the problem, those who may be causing it, those who can provide remedies, and those who can furnish data.[17]

Cross-functional teams are often used for solving specific problems. For example, one cross-functional team made up of nurses, dieticians, and other nursing unit and food services staff addressed the problem of patients receiving their dinners late. This problem was quite aggravating to patients, but if it had been addressed by only the nursing unit, ignorance or apathy in the food services department would most likely have been blamed. Had the problem been addressed by food services, nursing would likely have been blamed. In either case, little would have been accomplished. A cross-functional team was required to unravel the complex scheduling and delivery issues associated with the problem. Similarly, a cross-functional team at New York Life Insurance Company addressed the problem of returned mail. This was crucial for the company, because if policyholders do not receive their premium notices, New York Life does not get paid (see box "Gravedigging in New York").

Cross-functional teams are natural vehicles for implementing large-scale organizational changes. A large North American wholesale and retail grocery company

GRAVEDIGGING IN NEW YORK[18]

Have you ever sent a letter only to have it returned as "undeliverable" by the post office? How about 7,000 undeliverable pieces of mail every week? This was the problem faced by New York Life Insurance Company. Most of the mail being returned was notices to people that their premiums were due, so a great deal of revenue was being lost. In fact, the company estimated the problem to be costing them as much as $80 million.

The team formed to attack this problem became known as the Gravediggers, because of their relentlessness in "digging up" addresses so that premium notices could be delivered. The 18-member team, whose members were drawn from around the nation, met via teleconference once or twice a week. Following total quality principles, the team began by looking for the root causes of undeliverable mail. Some of the most common were: (1) policyholders who forgot to notify New York Life when they moved, and (2) long addresses that did not fit into the window on the mailing envelope.

The Gravediggers instituted a number of corrective measures to deal with the problem. They created units in each of the company's service offices to find addresses and keep company records up to date, they worked out a deal with the post office to forward mail and provide the company with corrected addresses, and they used a more elaborate mail-sorting system with bar codes. Early results found that the volume of returned mail was reduced by more than 20 percent, and the postal service provided the company with 61,000 correct addresses in a nine-month period. In fact, the Gravediggers are already among the most successful teams in the history of New York Life's total quality effort.

had embarked on a major organizational transformation because of competitive threats. Several cross-functional teams were established to support the transformation effort. Some were leadership teams that focused on organizational change and improvement; others were more specific design and development teams.[19]

An example of the cross-functional nature of teams is the platform team approach to automotive vehicle development introduced by Chrysler.[20] This cross-functional team approach brings together professionals from engineering, design, quality, manufacturing, business planning, program management, purchasing, sales, marketing, and finance to work together to get a new vehicle to market. This idea, brought to Chrysler by its merger with smaller, more innovative AMC/Jeep was not accepted at Chrysler without significant upheaval and struggles. "You talk about internal strife," recalls one Chrysler loyalist, "This was war!"[21] Nevertheless, the concept was just what was needed to pull the company from bankruptcy and near collapse. The Dodge Viper, introduced in 1992, and the 1993 Jeep Grand Cherokee tested this approach, which led to the development of the Chrysler Concorde, Dodge Intrepid, and Eagle Vision in just 39 months, not only on time and under budget, but exceeding 230 product excellence targets. Today, all automobile manufacturers develop products using similar cross-functional team approaches.

EFFECTIVE TEAMWORK

Teams are the main structure of many high-performing organizations.[22] Thus, effective teamwork is critical to a successful quality effort. If teams are not effective, key business processes will suffer. Steering committees will choose poor directions and policies for the organization; departmental and cross-functional problem-solving teams will choose inappropriate problems or won't be able to solve the problems they identify; and self-managed teams will not be able to fulfill the promise of an empowered, creative workforce.

This section explores what it takes for teams to be effective in a high-performance environment. Although the relative importance of these factors will vary from one type of team to another, they generally apply to any type of team. As you read this section, consider the ideas in light of your own experiences, rewarding or otherwise, on teams. If you are currently on a team, you may identify some ideas for improvement.

Criteria for Team Effectiveness

There are several criteria for team effectiveness. First, the team must achieve its goals of quality improvement. For example, a steering committee must move the performance excellence effort ahead, a problem-solving team must identify and solve important problems, a self-managed team must operate and improve a set of production or service processes.

Second, teams that improve quality performance quickly are more effective than those that take a long period of time to do so. One of the strengths of teams is their potential for rapid adaptation to changing conditions. A team that takes a long time to accomplish anything is losing the potential benefits of having problems solved sooner and is consuming a greater-than-necessary amount of resources, including the time devoted to team meetings. In short, it is inefficient.

Third, the team must maintain or increase its strength as a unit. Think of the team as representing an asset—a quantity of human capital—beyond that represented by its individual members. This additional human capital is based on the ability to understand and adjust to one another's work styles, the development of an effective set of routines, the growth of trust among team members, and so on. A team that remains intact over a period of time preserves and enhances this human capital. A team that solves an important problem, but has such miserable relations that it dissolves, does not. It may make a contribution to the quality effort, but it squanders a considerable amount of human capital in the process.

Fourth, the team must preserve or strengthen its relationship with the rest of the organization. With apologies to John Donne, "no team is an island," especially in a high-quality environment. A team that accomplishes its goals at the cost of alienating others in the organization violates the TQ principle of teamwork and compromises its ability to perform successfully in the future, when the collaboration of others may well be needed.

Peter Scholtes, a leading authority on teams for quality improvement, has suggested 10 ingredients for a successful team:

1. *Clarity in team goals.* As a sound basis, a team agrees on a mission, purpose, and goals.
2. *An improvement plan.* A plan guides the team in determining schedules and mileposts by helping the team decide what advice, assistance, training, materials, and other resources it may need.
3. *Clearly defined roles.* All members must understand their duties and know who is responsible for what issues and tasks.

4. *Clear communication.* Team members should speak with clarity, listen actively, and share information.
5. *Beneficial team behaviors.* Teams should encourage members to use effective skills and practices to facilitate discussions and meetings.
6. *Well-defined decision procedures.* Teams should use data as the basis for decisions and learn to reach consensus on important issues.
7. *Balanced participation.* Everyone should participate, contribute their talents, and share commitment to the team's success.
8. *Established ground rules.* The group outlines acceptable and unacceptable behaviors.
9. *Awareness of group process.* Team members exhibit sensitivity to nonverbal communication, understand group dynamics, and work on group process issues.
10. *Use of the scientific approach.* With structured problem-solving processes, teams can more easily find root causes of problems.[23]

TEAM MEMBERSHIP AND ROLES

Like any system, teams cannot function effectively without high-quality input. On the surface, this might suggest the "dream team" approach—assemble a group of stars like the 1992 U.S. basketball team that won the gold medal in the Barcelona Olympics. That approach has failed more often than not (the 2004 U.S. Olympic team also consisted entirely of NBA stars, lost to Lithuania, and finished third). In contrast, the 1980 U.S. hockey team that shocked the world in the Lake Placid Olympics left out the best players; it was built on team chemistry.

One company that has been successful in choosing team members is Worthington Industries, an Ohio-based steel processor. When an employee is hired to join a plant-floor team, he works for a 90-day probationary period, after which the team votes to determine whether he can stay. The system works because much of the team's pay is based on performance, so members are clear-eyed and unsparing in evaluating a new candidate's contribution. Worthington's CEO, John McConnell, could be talking about teams at any level when he says, "Give us people who are dedicated to making the team work, as opposed to a bunch of talented people with big egos, and we'll win every time."[24]

The most important elements of team processes are the team members themselves. Managers need to understand why people do and do not join teams. People participate on teams for many reasons:[25]

- They want to be progressive in making decisions that affect their work.
- They believe that being involved in teams will enhance their potential for promotion or other job opportunities.
- They believe that teams will be privy to information that typically is not available to individuals.
- They enjoy the feeling of accomplishment and believe that teams provide greater possibilities.
- They want to use team meetings to address personal agendas.
- They are genuinely concerned about the future of the organization and feel a sense of obligation to help improve it.

- They enjoy the recognition and rewards associated with team activity.
- They find teams to be a comfortable social environment.

Likewise, many people refuse to join teams for reasons such as outside commitments, fear or embarrassment, an overwhelming workload, mistrust of management, fear of failure or losing one's job, or simply an "I don't care" attitude. True leaders need to develop strategies for dealing with these issues.

To be effective, team members must be representative of the departments or functions related to the problem being addressed. For example, a steering committee made up of members from one part of the organization would be insufficiently representative of the organization to be effective. Representation is particularly important for cross-functional teams.

Team members assume a variety of roles in performing their duties. Some are task-oriented, for example, initiating projects, collecting information, analyzing data, using quality tools (flowcharts, cause-and-effect diagrams, etc.), creating action plans, writing reports, and so on. Others are relationship-oriented, such as encouraging other team members, listening carefully, and respecting others' opinions. Both types of roles are necessary for teams to function effectively, and proper selection and training of team members is important to ensure that they possess both technical and interpersonal skills to perform these roles. In fact, one study of cross-functional organizational design teams suggests that team skills, as well as a clear purpose and expectations, are significant predictors of team performance.[26]

Team members must possess the necessary technical knowledge to solve the problem at hand. This may mean understanding metallurgy for a team in a steel mill or understanding credit approval for a team in a bank. All members need not share the same knowledge, and in fact team members are often selected on the basis of specialized knowledge, but all of the appropriate technical bases must be covered for the team to be effective.

The critical importance of interpersonal skills is demonstrated by the following passage from a book on self-managed teams: "We often hear experienced team leaders and members make remarks like this one: 'I'll take someone with a good attitude over someone with just technical skills any day. I can train technical skills.' With further prodding, we usually discover that they are really talking about interpersonal skills.... Because these qualities can be difficult to detect in a casual selection process, they are often overlooked in the pursuit of apparent, more objectively measured technical skills."[27]

What is meant by interpersonal skills? Think of people who are easy to work with in a group. They are good listeners and do not ignore or downgrade someone else's ideas in order to promote their own. They try to understand other people's positions, even when they do not agree with them. They offer help to other group members, rather than waiting to be asked. They are willing and able to communicate their opinions, ideas, and any information that needs to be shared. They can deal with conflict without turning it into a personal issue. Finally, they are willing to share credit for accomplishments with other members of the group, rather than trying to keep the limelight for themselves.[28] If you have worked on a team with people who possess even most of these skills, you are lucky indeed!

Another important attribute of team membership is diversity. Many organizations have found that the best decisions stem from cross-fertilization of ideas from individuals with varied backgrounds, experiences, and interests; it has become a cliché that decisions emanating from groups of aging white males won't do.[29] Kraft Foods, for example, has developed a course for every new employee called The Power of Differences. The course focuses on the company's conviction that it is a team-based organization, that innovation and ideas are critical to its business, and that the diversity of thought gives the best solution. The course teaches that these solutions arise from the interactions of style and approach and personality types. It gets people thinking in terms of What's our skill set?, What's our match?, and How do we know when we've actually got a blind spot?

Team Processes

Many processes are undertaken within TQ teams, including quality planning, problem selection and diagnosis, communication, data collection, and implementation of solutions. Team processes are not fundamentally different from other processes, such as assembling an electronic device, taking a patient's vital signs, or preparing coq au vin. The customers of all these processes can be identified, their elements can be placed in a flowchart, steps that do not add value can be removed, and their quality can be improved continuously.

Most people, however, are not accustomed to thinking of group processes in this manner. This may be why group meetings are often long and boring and why so many people try to escape committee assignments and avoid committee meetings like the plague. A willingness to tolerate poor quality group processes has no place in organizations practicing total quality. This section identifies a few of the processes used in teams and provides some ideas about how teams can use them to operate effectively.

Problem Selection One of the processes undertaken at least occasionally by most teams and frequently by problem-solving teams is the choice of problems or issues on which to work. This process can be particularly difficult for newly empowered employees, who are more accustomed to being told what to do than they are to establishing their own agenda. New teams are often tempted to select the biggest, most glaring problem in sight that has been haunting them for years. Selecting such problems—often called "world hunger" problems—is usually a mistake.

New teams generally are not skilled enough to solve massive problems, and a failure to address such a visible problem successfully may be difficult for the team to overcome. It makes more sense for a team initially to select a problem of moderate importance and difficulty and to move on to more complex and difficult problems when the team is better established. This approach is more likely to lead to successful solutions, which will build momentum for each team and for the quality effort as a whole.

Another common problem among new teams is that they select problems that are not associated—at least in management's eyes—with important business or quality issues. When given a voice for the first time, many teams ask for things they have been denied in the past, such as a better lunch area or break room. Although managers often consider such behavior an indictment of quality teams, it is in fact an indictment of management itself. It is unrealistic to expect employees to focus on business issues when managers have not taken seriously employee requests for adequate facilities. In fact, it is better for issues such as these to be worked out prior to initiating a team-based quality effort, rather than allowing them to undermine such efforts.

The selection of "trivial" problems by teams may also indicate that management has not done an effective job of sharing information about the business with team members. If they truly understand the nature of the important problems faced by the organization, teams are much more likely to choose worthwhile issues on which to work.

Problem Diagnosis After problems to be addressed are identified, their causes must be ascertained. Thus a second critical process in TQ groups is problem diagnosis, the process by which the team investigates potential causes of problems to identify potential solutions. Juran refers to this step as the "diagnostic journey" and explains that it consists of three parts:

1. understanding the symptoms (for example, a process out of control),
2. theorizing as to causes (for example, preventive maintenance neglected), and
3. testing the theories (for example, reviewing preventive maintenance records to see whether they relate to the problems experienced).

Many teams want to bypass problem diagnosis and begin problem solving as soon as possible, usually because they mistakenly believe that the problem's causes are obvious. Teams that spend more time diagnosing problems have been shown to be much more effective than those that proceed immediately to solutions. Spending time pinning down the sources of problems is consistent with the TQ principle of decision making based on facts and reduces the potential for what are sometimes called "type 3 errors"—solving the wrong problem. Training in methods of diagnosis and analysis is important for team effectiveness.

Work Allocation Another important process is the allocation of work within the team. Many teams approach this process haphazardly, assigning tasks to the next in line or the first person who volunteers. Assigning tasks is one of the keys to team effectiveness and should not be taken so lightly.[30] Each team member has certain skills and will perform well on tasks that use those skills and not so well on tasks that use other skills. The team needs to assign people tasks that will utilize their skills to the greatest extent possible.

Imagine a women's college basketball team that consists of some tall women who are excellent rebounders and inside shooters and some shorter (vertically challenged?) women who are skilled ball handlers and outside shooters. This team will be much more successful if the coach takes the time to assess the skills of each player and assigns them to the position where they can best help the team.

When explained in this context, the point is obvious, but you would be amazed at how many teams have the tall members bring the ball down the floor and pass to the short members underneath the basket! Differences in status within the group can be a problem if team members in higher positions are assigned the more glamorous roles, even when others are more qualified to fulfill them.[31] The status problem is particularly acute in organizations that have very high- and very low-status members, especially when (as in medicine) these differences are institutionalized in society. The vice president of quality at one hospital described a team with this problem: "We had an emergency room physician who was a disaster. He was very much the old-school expert and he was not about to be egalitarian in his approach. This created a lot of problems for that team. In spite of that, we were able to achieve some success with that team but it was, I'm sure, limited. If there was one factor [that hurt us], it was probably his impact on the team."

Communication Communication is a key process for any team attempting to improve quality. Steering committees communicate priorities to employees. Members of problem-solving teams communicate among themselves and to their internal and external customers. For example, problem-solving teams often have to present their recommendations to management. Self-managed teams have similar communication needs and often must communicate effectively across shifts.

Three times every day in thousands of hospitals, mines, and manufacturing plants, teams of nurses, miners, and machine operators explain to the next shift what has happened in the last eight hours and what needs to be done in the next. The quality of this communication can dramatically affect the performance of the team on the next shift. The communication process can be improved by carefully assigning people to key communication tasks and by training people in communication.

We spend so much time communicating in our daily lives that we sometimes forget that skills such as listening and asking questions are vital to effective communication. Communication within and across teams also can be enhanced by using a variety of media. Many teams use e-mail and fax machines, but also benefit from such low-tech media as posters and graphs posted on the walls. As with many team processes, any specific recommendations are less important than the general idea of recognizing communication as a process that consists of a series of steps that can be improved.

Coordination Another key process is coordinating the team's work with other teams and departments in the organization. Teams cannot work in isolation, and maintaining good relationships outside the team is one criterion of team effectiveness.

New product teams, for example, depend on other parts of the organization for resources, information, and support while also acting as primary internal suppliers. One of the reasons for the success of Lockheed's Skunk Works operations, which pushed the envelop of aeronautics research and development that resulted in the F-104 Starfighter and the U-2 and SR-71 spy planes, was the fact that its leader put designers right next to metalworkers so they didn't draft anything unbuildable.[32] Coordination often involves resolving issues of interdependent schedules, but may also include some negotiation. Thus, teams often play a "boundary spanner" role.[33] The boundary-spanning literature shows positive relationships between communication and performance. However, researchers have often found a tendency among teams to turn inward, believing that their own needs, ideas, and plans are more valid than those of "outsiders." Ironically, the more cohesive the team becomes, the greater the likelihood of this occurring.[34]

Such a tendency is antithetical to TQ, but it is a danger faced by virtually all groups. Teams can try to overcome this problem by keeping their customers in mind and using customer satisfaction as the yardstick against which ideas and plans are measured. Remaining aware of the need to improve team processes should also guard against the tendency to downplay the potential contributions of non–team members, as outsiders are often the source of ideas for improvement that team members have overlooked.

Finally, good communication should also help to coordinate work with other teams and departments. The likelihood of following a path that works against the needs or plans of other groups will be diminished if teams communicate with other groups early and often. Tools such as quality function deployment and affinity diagrams, discussed in Chapter 3, can be used to enhance such communication.

In a sense, quality-oriented process improvement and problem solving are a minefield for the unsuspecting team. Whenever changes are made in an organization, vested interests are challenged. By carefully managing the coordination process, teams will reduce the potential for unnecessary conflict with groups outside the team and will greatly enhance their potential for long-term effectiveness.

In summary, team processes can be improved just like any other process. Several key processes that are candidates for improvement are problem identification and diagnosis, work allocation, communication, and coordination of work with other teams and departments.

Organizational Support However skillful the team, they will find it hard to be successful unless their efforts are supported by the organization in general and by management in particular. Organizational support is the foundation for effective teamwork.

Management must provide the following if a team is to be successful. First, management must issue a clear charge to the group; that is, a description of what the group is and is not expected to do. Many teams have wasted a great deal of time and energy on issues that they later found they were not authorized to pursue. Management's guidance as to the quality priorities of the organization is crucial, especially in the early stages of a team's work. Second, human resource management (HRM) systems often must be adjusted. Conventional HRM systems may be barriers to effective teamwork that will undermine TQ if not changed.[35] The need for enhanced training is particularly acute, as team members must be brought up to speed on the various types of skills necessary for effective teamwork.

Performance appraisal and reward systems are also a concern. Many of these systems are designed to reward individual effort or the attainment of functional goals, rather than teamwork. Numerous research studies over the past several decades have pointed out the problems and pitfalls of performance appraisals.[36] Many legitimate objections can be made:[37]

- They tend to foster mediocrity and discourage risk taking.
- They focus on short-term and measurable results, thereby discouraging long-term planning or thinking and ignoring important behaviors that are more difficult to measure.
- They focus on the individual and therefore tend to discourage or destroy teamwork within and between departments.
- The process is detection-oriented rather than prevention-oriented.

- They are often unfair, since managers frequently do not possess observational accuracy.
- They fail to distinguish between factors that are within the employees' control and system-determined factors that are beyond their control.

This can greatly undermine teamwork and can be fatal to the team if not addressed.

Performance appraisals are most effective when they are based on the objectives of the work teams that support the organization.[38] In this respect, they act as a diagnostic tool and review process for individual, team, and organizational development and achievement. The performance appraisal can also be a motivator when it is developed and used by the work team itself. Team efforts are harnessed when team members are empowered to monitor their own workplace activities. In a performance excellence culture, quality improvement is one of the major dimensions on which employees are evaluated.

Xerox, for instance, changed its performance review criteria by replacing traditional measures such as "follows procedures" and "meets standards" to evaluating employees on the basis of quality improvement, problem solving, and team contributions. Many companies use peer review, customer evaluations, and self-assessments as a part of the appraisal process.

Selection processes may also be changed in a performance excellence environment. Companies like Procter & Gamble seek entry-level college graduates who understand total quality principles. They specifically want their new employees to think in terms of creating quality and value for consumers, to understand their customers and needs, and to work toward results despite obstacles. The members of self-managed teams often take much of the responsibility for hiring people for their team. Human resource professionals should play a consultative role in such efforts, however, to make sure that selection is done in a fair and legal manner.

Third, management must provide the team with the resources necessary to be successful. These include a place and time to meet and the tools to get the job done. Human resources are also important: management should avoid moving people on and off teams frequently, as this can disrupt teamwork and send a message that quality and teamwork are really not a high priority for the organization.

Fourth, when teams make a proposal, management must respond swiftly and constructively. It is not realistic to expect that every quality improvement proposal made by a team will be implemented. For those proposals that cannot be implemented, management owes the team a reasonable explanation as to why it is not feasible and some guidance as to how the proposal might be modified so that it would be acceptable. Few experiences are as demoralizing to quality teams as making an elaborate, reasoned presentation, only to be met with deafening silence from management. This was one of the problems that undermined quality circle programs. It is less of a problem for self-managed teams that generally have broad authority to implement their own solutions.

For those proposals that are accepted, some form of recognition for the team is in order. At The Ritz-Carlton Hotel Company, L.L.C., team awards include bonus pools and sharing in the gratuity system. Many companies have formal corporate recognition programs, such as IBM's Market Driven Quality Award for outstanding individual and team achievements in quality improvement, or the Xerox President's

Award and Team Excellence Award. Often the most effective forms of recognition are symbolic, such as a citation or picture in the company newspaper.

Many organizations view team development as an important business process and manage it accordingly. See box "Team Effectiveness and Organizational Design" for some research-based perspectives on managing for effective team performance.

Team Charters Team responsibilities and processes are often summarized in a team charter. A **team charter** is an explicit, written document that offers guidelines, rules, and policies for team members. It often includes a mission statement; values that guide behavior; structural issues such as logistics, meeting agendas, task responsibilities, and target dates; methods for group decision making; processes for dealing with conflicts; and methods for resolving problems with team members. Several organizational researchers have found that team performance improved for teams with charters and clear expectations.[39] Benefits include reduced intragroup conflict, improved speed of making decisions, better decision quality, stronger shared values, higher group member satisfaction, and reduced exposure to litigation.

TEAM EFFECTIVENESS AND ORGANIZATIONAL DESIGN[40]

Using in-depth case study analysis, researchers from the University of Valencia, Spain, examined the relationship between organizational design variables and team effectiveness. Their main conclusions were

- The more intense the level of decentralization, the more powerful the degree of coordination within and among teams and the degree of team autonomy and, consequently, the more effective the team becomes.
- The more intense the level of formalization in the firm, the more powerful the degree of coordination and the link between functions (in cross-functional teams) and, as a result, the more effective the team turns out to be.
- The more participative the leadership style and the more intense the level of decentralization, the more intense the degree of team autonomy and the level of resources required to exercise that power, so the more effective the team becomes.
- Motivational human resource policies and a high level of socialization and values in the organization will strengthen the team's interiorization of the firm's mission and, as a result, its effectiveness.
- The higher the hierarchical level at which the team is inserted, the more developed the reward system designed for the team becomes.
- The existence of TQM practices reinforces the use of the different design variables (decentralization, leadership style, motivational policies) and increases, as a result, the relevance of socialization and values in the firm, contributing to the effectiveness of the teams created within this framework.

From these results, managers can better understand the functioning of teams by recognizing the impact of these key design variables (specialization, decentralization, human resource policies, leadership styles, and rewards), and they can modify a team's organizational context by changing these variables to improve team effectiveness.

TEAMWORK IN ACTION

This section provides several examples of quality teamwork, including a problem-solving team in a general hospital and a high-tech team at Analog Devices. As you read these examples, reflect on whether the teams are effectively practicing the team processes we have discussed. For other examples of teamwork in action, see box "The ASQ Team Excellence Awards."

A Team with a Transparent Problem[41]

Have you ever had tests done in a hospital and wondered why it takes so long to get the results back? So did the employees and managers in the radiology department at Sentara Norfolk General Hospital in Norfolk, Virginia.

Although everyone associated with the process felt that they were working as fast as they could, performing and reporting the results of an X-ray or CAT scan was taking three days on average (72.5 hours, to be precise). A nine-person team was formed to address the problem, and they vowed to cut the time down to 24 hours.

The ASQ Team Excellence Awards[42]

The International Team Excellence Award competition was launched in 1985. Sponsored by the American Society for Quality, it has drawn participants from the U.S., Costa Rica, and Mexico, and as far away as China. Teams submit a 25-minute video explaining their project and process, and are judged on how well they meet 36 criteria that ranges from project selection and action planning to results and the project's impact on organizational goals. Some examples of finalists are:

Fidelity Wide Processing Bulk Shipping Process Management Team (Gold Award Winner)
The purpose of the team was to reduce controllable shipping costs and operating unit costs, and improve productivity in the bulk shipping operations area. Through implementation of a cross-functional process management team and utilization of quality tools, shipping costs were reduced by 20%, productivity improved by 30%, and unit costs were lowered by 36%.

DynMcDermott Petroleum Operations Company, Vehicle Accident Performance Improvement Team
The Vehicle Accident Prevention Team was chartered to develop strategies to reduce the number of vehicle accidents involving government vehicles. As a result of the team's activities, the rate was reduced from 5.6 vehicle accidents per million miles traveled to 1.8.

Baxter, Cartago, Costa Rica, Anesthesia Circuits Problem Solving Team
This team faced the problem of easy separation of components on Anesthesia Circuits. The root cause was identified as Adult Isoflex tubing cuff design. Solutions included new cuff design, new resin, and improvement of assembly operation. This resulted in a 100% reduction of complaints, a savings of $240,000, and a better ergonomic assembly process.

JPMorgan Chase, Right the First Time
The team used Six Sigma methodology to analyze data and internal processes and reduce adjustments in northeast item processing by 50 percent. This cross-functional team of 72 employees worked together to improve the customer experience, streamline internal processes, and reduce operating costs by $1.4 million annually.

The first step was to focus the team on the process, rather than on individual performance, and to create a sense of teamwork that would override the differences in status that sometimes hamper the work of medical professionals. Pat Curtis, head of cardiac nursing, was chosen as the team's facilitator, partially for her recognized skills but also because she was from outside radiology and had no formal authority over team members.

Although the team met infrequently, the members had plenty of work to do between meetings, mostly on collecting information. Using techniques associated with Norfolk General's CQI effort (Continuous Quality Improvement, as TQ is often known in health care), the team identified 40 steps in the X-ray process and 50 possible causes of delay, only a few of which were causing most of the problems. Rather than waiting for a grand changeover at the culmination of their work, the team made improvements to the process as they discovered them. This was greatly facilitated by the cross-functional representation and the presence of managers on the team. As one member put it, "Folks who could effect change were part of the decision making." None of the changes the team made were particularly dramatic. Curtis helped the nursing department to reduce errors such as forgetting to note whether patients would need stretchers or oxygen. X-ray technologists began to deliver developed films to the next person in the process, rather than waiting for the internal mail service to move them. Fourteen of the 40 steps were redesigned out of the process.

The results were clearly dramatic. The average time to process an X-ray dropped to 13.8 hours, an 81 percent improvement! This achievement was impressive enough to win the team a Rochester Institute of Technology/USA Today Quality Cup for team accomplishment in the not-for-profit category.

Physicians in the hospital report that the faster availability of diagnostic information is helping them to improve their own processes, and other companies and government agencies in the Norfolk area are looking to the hospital for help with their own quality improvement challenges.

The team has responded to its success with a renewed commitment to continuous improvement. The introduction of a CD-based digital system to replace tapes for dictating physician comments is expected to cut the time down to 11 hours. The team's new goal? Eight hours.

Self-Managed Teams at Analog Devices[43]

In 1996 one unit of Analog Devices was under intense time pressure to get a new wafer fabrication plant up and running in an empty building in Cambridge, Massachusetts. The new "wafer fab" (as such plants are typically called in the semiconductor industry) was for a new division and would be relatively small, as wafer fabs go. At an early step of the process, it became clear they needed people who were very experienced, unusually flexible, and highly cross-trained, and who had unusually effective and efficient communication mechanisms available. The director of manufacturing saw this small-scale, clean-slate situation as an appropriate opportunity for him to deploy self-directed work teams (SDWT).

The Analog Devices Cambridge wafer fab runs 24 hours a day, seven days a week. Four separate teams handle a continuous operations schedule of shifts. During any one shift, the one team on duty for that shift runs the plant. Each team must cover the areas of chemical vapor deposition, trim, diffusion, etch, implant, photolithography, and thin film. Each area includes several relevant functions, and it is desirable for team members to become certified for all functions within multiple areas. These teams do not have supervisors on their shifts. In fact, all of the operators (called manufacturing technicians or MTs in the Cambridge operation) on all four teams report to the production manager. These supervisorless teams completely run the plant day by day, planning and deciding everything that must be done.

Because various aspects of operation require specific attention, each team rotates members through roles: production representative, yield representative, safety representative, continuous improvement representative, and training representative, to push cross-training. The people in some of these roles need to coordinate with engineering and with the senior managers of the plant, and appropriate meetings are held. The relevant representatives are expected to attend these meetings, which may be at times when the people are not on shift. Someone on each team is also designated "site manager": the person who is to speak for the plant in case of some sort of emergency.

In addition to getting the new plant up and running well with a small staff over a short time, the company found that in the long run, productivity has been higher than expected because the self-directed work teams run the plant very effectively and efficiently.

Some comments from team members show their perspectives on SDWTs:

> The biggest pro is that SDWT enables a group of people to manage themselves using a set of predetermined guidelines through constant communication and redefinition of these guidelines for the common goals of an organization. In addition, it provides a sense of worth that one usually doesn't feel in a normal work environment.
>
> Cons? It takes a strong amount of respect, both for yourself and for your teammates, to communicate on an even plane. Most people do not have it in them; and because of this a lot of issues arise and, many times, never go away.
>
> Trust is an important factor for the SDWT to succeed. When one member of the team loses trust, the team breaks down, causing animosity. Regaining the trust is essential. Maintaining a positive attitude and an open mind gives you flexibility and encourages participation from all members. Opinions shouldn't be taken personally but understood professionally and utilized in formulating decisions.

A Team of Thousands

Wikipedia is an online encyclopedia that has over one million entries and is operated by the nonprofit Wikipedia Foundation. It has a paid staff of only four people, but thousands of active volunteers. Since its launch in 2001, founder Jimmy Wales has made it easy for contributors to monitor one another's activities. Wikipedians (those who contribute to Wikipedia) are alerted when any changes are made on pages they've worked on. Every edit can be traced to its originator, and most versions of each entry, along with online conversations about it, can be retrieved. Though vandals strike occasionally, virtual vigilantes are always on patrol. Volunteers who misbehave risk banishment. Official policy requires that entries stay neutral and that members treat each other civilly.[44]

COMPARISON TO ORGANIZATIONAL BEHAVIOR THEORIES

Little conflict exists between the use of teams in TQ and theories of organizational behavior, but there are differences in emphasis. Along with social psychology and sociology, organizational behavior (OB) is the source of much of what is known about groups or teams. Since there is no separate tradition of research or thinking about groups within TQ, virtually all of the practices and recommendations ultimately derive from conventional (or unconventional) management theory.

The sociotechnical systems (STS) approach is devoted to the effective blending of both the technical (job requirements) and social aspects of the work environment. These two factors must be considered jointly, because work designs that optimize one factor may not be optimal for the other. The STS approach has been prevalent since the 1950s, and its principles were first developed in manufacturing by Eric Trist, its leading founder, who was guided by earlier systems thinking, research on participation, and the action research work of Kurt Lewin. More recently, this approach has been adapted and refined to non-manufacturing organizations. The approach has more relevance today than ever before, as organizational personnel seek more fruitful means of empowerment and as their organizations strive for greater productivity and viability in increasingly turbulent environments.[45] Teams—particularly self-directed teams—support many of the benefits of STS approaches.

Research knowledge about groups is most heavily emphasized in organizational development (OD), the branch of the organizational sciences that deals with changing and improving organizations. Most team-based practices in TQ come from OD. Some of these practices, such as the nominal group technique, are based on research in organizational behavior or social psychology; others are not.

Teams are actually a subset of the organizational behavior/social psychology concept of groups. All teams are groups, but not all groups are teams. Compare our definition of a team as "people working together to achieve a goal" to the following definition of a group: "A number of persons who communicate with one another often over a span of time, and who are few enough in number that each person may communicate with all the others."[46]

Clearly we ask more of our teams than we do of our groups! Organizational behavior has traditionally focused on workgroups, people who work together in the same function. Theory has addressed why some groups are more cohesive or productive than others and whether groups are likely to support or undermine organizational goals.

The specific types of teams used in TQ efforts are also derived from OB research. Self-managed teams are a modern version of semiautonomous work groups, which were championed for use in underground coal mines by researchers from Britain's Tavistock Institute more than 40 years ago.[42] Similarly, cross-functional teams have been discussed within OB for many years as a way to integrate work across interdependent functions.[47]

Much of the knowledge from OB research on groups has not yet been absorbed into TQ thinking in a widespread manner, but it probably should be. This includes the research on the relative advantages of homogeneous and heterogeneous groups, which appears to be relevant to effective team building. Research has shown that homogenous groups (those in which members are similar in age, race, gender, experience, and so on) are better suited to well-defined, familiar tasks, where the emphasis is on efficient production.

Heterogeneous groups, on the other hand, are better at tasks that require creative thinking. This implies that teams used in TQ efforts generally should be quite diverse, due to the heavy emphasis on creativity and fresh thinking in the tasks they face. Based on this research, managers selecting people for teams should make heterogeneity their goal.

Research also suggests that cultural values play a role in an employee's support of, or resistance to, self-managed teams (SMTs).[48] This is particularly important as companies expand globally. (Motorola and Eastman Kodak, for example, each have operations in more than 50 countries.) People from collectivistic cultures—those who value the welfare of the group more than the individual, such as South Korea, China, and Sweden—appear to have more of the skills and attitudes that lead to the acceptance of SMTs. In contrast, people in individualistic cultures like the United States have more of a tendency to resist SMTs. The success of SMTs is therefore related to the extent to which organizations manage culture-based resistance. Practitioners should consider using selection systems in each country to obtain employees having those values most compatible with SMT requirements and adopt SMTs that mesh with the cultural values of the country.

Recently, more research on the impacts of diversity is being conducted.[49] Although the anecdotal thinking promotes diversity as beneficial, research results suggest some contingencies. For instance, a multimethod field study of 92 workgroups explored the influence of three types of workgroup diversity (social category diversity, value diversity, and informational diversity) and two moderators (task type and task interdependence) on workgroup outcomes. Informational diversity positively influenced group performance, while social category diversity positively influenced group member morale.

However, value diversity decreased satisfaction, intent to remain, and commitment to the group. Another study found that social category diversity resulted in increased relationship conflict, even though group members reported increased morale, which runs counter to both conventional wisdom and past research. This study also shed light on patterns that practitioners can expect in diverse work groups. In particular, task conflict is likely in these teams and such conflict may enhance performance, something that managers and members of cross-functional teams can take comfort in. At the same time, race and tenure diversity may increase emotional conflict, especially in new groups with non-routine tasks. Anticipating such a possibility may be critical if organizations hope to manage employees' background differences successfully.

Review and Discussion Questions

1. Describe the use of teams at KARLEE in the Performance Excellence Profile. How does the team-based structure support performance excellence?
2. Donald Peterson, former CEO of Ford, said "No matter what you are trying to do, teams are the most effective way to get the job done." Do you agree? Why or why not?
3. Petronius, a Roman satirist, noted back in 66 A.D.: "We trained hard—but it seemed that every time we were beginning to form up into teams, we would be reorganized. I was to learn later in life we tend to meet any new situation by reorganizing, and a wonderful method it can be for creating the illusion of progress while producing confusion,

inefficiency, and demoralization." What implications does this quote have for modern managers?

4. How might a jazz quartet be viewed as a metaphor for a team in a business situation? If possible, watch the individuals in a jazz quartet in action in addition to simply listening to the music (the author's favorite is Diana Krall's *Live in Paris* DVD!).
5. What are the similarities and differences among the types of teams used in TQ?
6. Think of a team that you are on, or have been on recently. How does it stack up against the criteria for quality teamwork? What specific steps could be used to improve the performance of your team? How could TQ techniques be used to improve team processes?
7. How are Six Sigma project teams different from the other types of teams discussed in this chapter?
8. How did the team at Norfolk General Hospital illustrate the effective teamwork practices discussed in the text?
9. If self-managed teams can succeed without active intervention from managers, what—if anything—does this imply about the traditional roles of management (to plan, organize, and control) in organizations? Should a new set of roles be identified for such situations?
10. Do you think that the current popularity of teams in organizations is a fad or a fundamental change in the way we manage organizations? Why?
11. Are teams absolutely necessary for total quality to be successful? Sketch out a plan for a total quality effort that does not involve teams.
12. Discuss the conditions under which team incentives may work. When is it a poor idea to install such systems?
13. How might a team leader deal with "social loafing," when members of the team are freeloaders, willing to receive the benefits of teamwork without doing the work themselves? How would you deal with it if it occurred in a class project?
14. How does the Wikipedia virtual team environment reflect the principles discussed in this chapter? For instance, which of Peter Scholtes' ingredients for a successful team are evident? Can you suggest any improvements to the Wikipedia approach based on these principles?
15. You have undoubtedly been assigned to teams for student projects. Suppose that you are assigned to work with a group of your fellow students on a term project. Draft a team charter that will guide your work. Compare your charter with those of other classmates and discuss similarities and differences.

CASES

Golden Plaza Hotel

Sandra Wilford was recently promoted to general manager of the Golden Plaza Hotel, San Francisco. She had previously been an assistant manager at the corporation's hotel in Denver. The Denver hotel was truly a team-based organization. Sandra had seen the benefits from teamwork that propelled the hotel to the top of the corporation in customer satisfaction ratings. In fact, it was one of the reasons she was asked to take over the San Francisco property. The previous general manager's policies had created large turnover among the staff and continuing loss of market share that led to his firing.

Sandra was reviewing her notes from a meeting with all the hotel's supervisors and assistant managers. The meeting had tried to identify why many employees were reluctant to be "team players" or even to participate on teams that she was trying to initiate based on her experiences in Denver. Among the reasons that surfaced were the following

- Child care obligations, classes, and other outside commitments made it difficult for some associates to meet before or after shifts.
- Many of the custodial workers who were functionally illiterate seemed to be uncomfortable in interactions with other associates.

- Several associates feel that their current jobs are simply too demanding to take on the additional meetings that would be necessary.
- One assistant manager felt that some of her people preferred to work alone and usually disrupted meetings in which they were involved.
- Because of the previous general manager, there was a lot of cynicism among the associates and many didn't trust management. They felt that teams were simply a political ploy to get support for unpopular decisions. The previous GM had established some teams that had failed miserably and many associates were bitter and had conflicts with other departments. There seemed to be a widespread attitude of "What's in it for me?"
- Some associates thought that the expectations of team processes would be overwhelming and were afraid that if the team failed, they would be held personally responsible and their careers would be in jeopardy. Others thought that their jobs might be eliminated.

Sandra stared at this list and wondered what she had gotten herself into. What recommendations would you make to her to address these issues?

The Power of Leadership Teams[50]

When the top management group at Georgia Power Company's Plant Hammond decided to become a team, everyone was quite sure that they were already a team and worked pretty well together. The top leadership group in early 1995 was 10 people from three management levels and two individual contributors. The management style was much the same as they had been using for many years in the utility industry and was characterized by an emphasis on the chain of command for most decisions—with the important ones made by one or two people. Information and business results were communicated on a "need to know" basis. For the most part, each department operated and made decisions independently.

This management style served the utility business well, given its business requirements. The business was relatively predictable and structured with a regulated rate of return, regional market protection, and 100 percent control of access to its own distribution facilities. A watershed development, however, occurred in the early 1990s—a move toward deregulation. This demanded fundamental changes in the way Plant Hammond operated and managed its resources.

In the early 1990s, the plant had reduced the number of employees by about one third, resulting in fewer management levels and fewer managers in those levels. In early 1995, the parent organization, Southern Company, implemented a transformation process to improve the plant's ability to compete.

This transformation process required an emphasis on business results at all levels and creation of an organization culture that could deal with uncertainty and competition.

As the plant manager considered the requirements for the future, he determined that the structure, processes, and culture of the plant would need to change. Therefore, top management must change how it operated, broadening capabilities at all levels. Processes were needed to manage decision-making risk and gain consensus on direction. A new organizational structure was one of the early steps in their transformation. The structure provided an "outside in" focus—identifying the operations function as the primary internal customer, and grouped plant activities into several functional areas.

However, plant management knew that simply changing the boxes on an organization chart was not sufficient for real change. In the summer of 1995, the plant manager and nine other employees took their first step toward becoming a team when they came together at a facilitated off-site meeting. They clarified individual roles and responsibilities on this new team and began developing team relationships. They agreed that the role of each leadership-team member should be one of "shared responsibilities with a functional focus." Top managers at the plant could no longer make decisions from only their own departments' view. In fact, managers were required to consider the impact of their decisions—not only on the total plant but also on the total operating system of the Southern Company.

Each member took on the responsibility to champion specific transformation activities for the leadership team. The team began to have regular one-day session meetings where they discussed and made decisions on strategic and operational issues. This management team took a key developmental step in 1996 by setting expectations for their behavior and presenting them to their organizations during reviews of the 1996 plant strategic plan. Putting these expectations "on the record" built incentives to act accordingly.

The team found several tools to be helpful in its operation and development. One was a *common work plan* that served multiple purposes: (1) to ensure integration of their efforts and to track team results; (2) to establish member accountability; (3) to facilitate the delegation of traditional plant manager tasks; and (4) as a catalyst to surface strategic issues. Each team member took responsibility for the accomplishment of particular parts of the work plan.

The team also used various *assessment instruments* to understand and deal with the different individual styles of team members. Each team member discussed his or her assessment in an open forum. As a result, members made commitments for change and support. Each team member also formulated his or her own development plan based on these and other assessments.

Because one of the plant's strategies was to improve the capabilities of the management team, the team worked with an outside consultant to identify strengths and weaknesses. The consultant observed each of the team members in work situations and provided specific personal feedback and suggestions over an extended period of time. Each team member reviewed his or her assessment with the group and asked for reactions and recommendations.

The consultant also provided feedback on group processes and worked in concert with an internal consultant to improve teamwork processes.

Discussion Questions

1. What lessons do you think the company learned about transforming its leadership system to a team-based organization?
2. What conditions do you think are necessary for management teams to become "real teams" and not just a grouping of independent functional managers who cooperate with each other?
3. What challenges do leadership teams like these face?

Landmark Dining: Team Processes

Landmark Dining, Inc. (Landmark) is a family-owned and operated steak and seafood restaurant small business in south Texas. The first restaurant, Harrisburg Station, and its associated catering business, Harrisburg Station Catering, are located in one of the oldest standing landmarks in Houston—a train station built in 1857 in the small settlement then known as Harrisburg. The second restaurant, Texas Lightkeeper, is located in a restored lighthouse built in 1853 in Galveston. Landmark restaurants offer an exceptional dining experience at a good value to the Houston and Galveston metropolitan areas.

As a key strategic challenge, the availability of skilled, motivated employees is essential to Landmark's competitive success factor of superior service and to its Value of Employee Development. To address that challenge, a focus on teamwork and the development of employees improves service and reduces turnover. Until the early 1990s, work and jobs were organized according to accepted industry practices. Employees were hired for specific jobs, worked specific hours, and had very little input into how tasks were performed. With the initiation of a formal Strategic Planning Process and the articulation of its Vision, Mission, and Values, Landmark began to develop innovative processes to manage work and jobs in support of high performance.

In order to facilitate cooperation and empowerment, employees in all business divisions, including Catering, Dinner Delivery Service, and Administration, are organized in empowered process teams that align with its key processes (see Figure 8.1). Each team is responsible for its own scheduling and process improvement, and each has a

	Process	Requirements
Restaurants	Reservations and Greeting	Accurate reservations
		Prompt seating
		Timely/courteous greeting
	Order Taking	Short wait time
		Accurate order
		Responsive/informed server
	Food Preparation	Healthy meals
		Attractive presentation
		Good taste
		As described in menu
	Table Service	Appropriate tempo/pace
	Table Bussing	Dishes removed as finished
Catering	Event Planning	Timely event scheduling Positive client relations
	Food Prep.	(Same as for restaurants)
	Delivery and Event Cleanup	Delivered/served as planned
HMR	HMR Delivery Order Taking	Accurate orders
	HMR Delivery Service	Accurate, on-time delivery
All Business Lines	New Product Introduction	New products and services valued by customers
	Menu Design and Re-engineering	Favorable menu performance semi-annual menu review Menu changes quarterly
	Purchasing Consortium	Accurate delivery of products
	Facility Cleaning	Restaurants, restrooms, and kitchens clean and free of pests

FIGURE 8.1 LANDMARK DINING VALUE CREATION PROCESSES

member in the role of team leader. The team leader is not considered a part of management, but is compensated for assuming required extra duties, including (1) ensuring the team schedule is developed, (2) training new employees and providing refresher training for all team members, (3) monitoring and coordinating improvement of the team's processes (including reporting metrics), and (4) providing input for team members' performance appraisals.

Assignment: Examine Landmark's processes in Figure 8.1 and develop a "white paper" proposing how teams can best accomplish their work in ensuring that process requirements are accomplished. Address such issues as team membership and roles and team processes in your response.

Endnotes

1. 2000 Malcolm Baldrige National Quality Award Recipient Profile, U.S Department of Commerce.
2. Jon R. Katzenback and Douglas K. Smith, "The Discipline of Teams," *Harvard Business Review*, March/April 1993, pp. 111–120.
3. Nicole Adrian, "A Gold Medal Solution," *Quality Progress*, March 2008, pp. 44–49.
4. J.M. Juran, *Juran on Leadership for Quality: An Executive Handbook*. New York: Free Press, 1989.
5. P.B. Crosby, *Quality Is Free: The Art of Making Quality Certain*, New York: McGraw-Hill, 1979.
6. The information on quality circles in Japan is from B.G. Dale and J. Tidd, "Japanese Total Quality Control: A Study of Best Practice," *Proceedings of the Institution of Mechanical Engineers*, Vol. 205, No. 4, pp. 221–232.
7. James R. Healey, "U.S. Steel Learns from Experience," *USA Today*, April 10, 1992.
8. Martha T. Moore, "Hourly Workers Apply Training in Problem Solving," *USA Today*, April 10, 1992.
9. Helene F. Uhlfelder, "It's All About Improving Performance," *Quality Progress*, February 2000, pp. 47–52.
10. Richard S. Wellins, William C. Byham, and Jeanne M. Wilson, *Empowered Teams: Creating Self-Directed Work Groups That Improve Quality, Productivity, and Participation*, San Francisco: Jossey-Bass, 1991, p. 21.
11. Charles Fishman, "How Teamwork Took Flight," *Fast Company*, October 1999, p. 188.
12. Ron Williams, "Self-Directed Work Teams: A Competitive Advantage," *Quality Digest*, November 1995, pp. 50–52.
13. Gina Imperato, "Their Specialty? Teamwork," *Fast Company*, January 2000, p. 54.
14. Peter Lazes and Marty Falkenberg, "Work Groups in America Today," *The Journal for Quality and Participation*, Vol. 14, No. 3, June 1991, pp. 58–69.
15. Josh Hyatt, "The Soul of a New Team," *Fortune*, June 12, 2006, pp. 134–143.
16. Jane E. Henry, and Meg Hartzler, "Virtual Teams: Today's Reality, Today's Challenge," *Quality Progress*, May 1997, pp. 108–109.
17. Juran, *Juran on Leadership for Quality*.
18. Based on Jerry G. Bowles, "Leading the World-Class Company," *Fortune*, September 21, 1992.
19. Eileen M. van Aken and Brian M. Kleiner, "Determinants of Effectiveness for Cross-Functional Organizational Design Teams," *Quality Management Journal*, Vol. 4, No. 2, 1997, pp. 51–79.
20. "Platform Approach at Chrysler," *Quality '93: Empowering People with Technology, Fortune*, September 20, 1993, advertisement.
21. Brock Yates, *The Critical Path*, Boston: Little, Brown and Co., 1996, p. 76.
22. P. Alexander, M. Biro, E. G. Garry, D. Seamon, T. Slaughter, and D. Valerio, "New Organizational Structures and New Quality Systems," in J.P. Kern, J.J. Riley, and L.N. Jones (eds.), ASQC Quality Press *Human Resources Management, Milwaukee*, 1987, pp. 203–268.
23. Peter R. Scholtes, et al., *The Team Handbook: How to Use Teams to Improve Quality*, Madison, Wisc.: Joiner Associates, Inc., 1988, pp. 6-10–6-22.
24. Geoffrey Colvin, "Why Dream Teams Fail," *Fortune*, June 12, 2006, pp. 87–92.
25. Michael Jaycox, "How to Get Nonbelievers to Participate in Teams," *Quality Progress*, March 1996, pp. 45–49.
26. Van Aken and Kleiner, op. cit.

27. Wellins et al., *Empowered Teams*, p. 147.
28. Partially based on Wellins et al., *Empowered Teams*, and H. J. Harrington, *The Improvement Process: How America's Leading Companies Improve Quality*, New York: McGraw-Hill, 1987.
29. Willard C. Rappleye, Jr., "Diversity in the Workforce," *Across the Board*, Vol. XXXVII, No. 10, Nov/Dec 2000, special advertising section.
30. This point is based on a model developed by I. Steiner in his book *Group Process and Productivity*, New York: Academic Press, 1972.
31. The problems of differential status in groups are discussed by Alvin Zander in *Making Groups Effective*, San Francisco: Jossey-Bass, 1982.
32. Stuart F. Brown, "The Right Stuff," *Fortune*, June 12, 2006, special insert: "The Secrets of Greatness."
33. Deborah G. Ancona and David F. Caldwell, "Bridging the Boundary: External Activity and Performance," *Administrative Science Quarterly*, Vol. 37, No. 4, December 1992, p. 634.
34. The classic statement of this problem is by Irving Janis in his book *Groupthink*, 2nd ed. Boston: Houghton-Mifflin, 1982.
35. Wellins et al., *Empowered Teams*. See also S.A. Snell and J.W. Dean, Jr., "Integrated Manufacturing and Human Resource Management: A Human Capital Perspective," *Academy of Management Journal*, August 1992, pp. 467–504.
36. Douglas McGregor, "An Uneasy Look at Performance Appraisal," *Harvard Business Review*, September/October 1972; Herbert H. Meyer, Emanuel Kay, and John R. P. French, Jr., "Split Roles in Performance Appraisal," *Harvard Business Review*, January/February 1965; Harry Levinson, "Appraisal of What Performance?" *Harvard Business Review*, January/February 1965; A. M. Mohrman, *Deming versus Performance Appraisal: Is There a Resolution?* Los Angeles: Center for Effective Organizations, University of Southern California, 1989.
37. John F. Milliman and Fred R. McFadden, "Toward Changing Performance Appraisal to Address TQM Concerns: The 360-Degree Feedback Process," *Quality Management Journal*, Vol. 4, No. 3, 1997, pp. 44–64.
38. Stanley M. Moss, "Appraise Your Performance Appraisal Process," *Quality Progress*, November 1989, p. 60.
39. William I. Norton Jr. and Lyle Sussman, "Team Charters: Theoretical Foundations and Practical Implications or Quality and Performance," *Quality Management Journal*, 16, 1, pp. 7–17. Also see Van Aken and Kleiner, op. cit.
40. M. Ángeles Escribá-Moreno, Maria Teresa Canet-Giner, and María Moreno-Luzón, "TQM and Teamwork Effectiveness: The Intermediate Role of Organizational Design," *Quality Management Journal*, 15, 3, pp. 41–59.
41. Based on Kevin Anderson, "X-Ray Processing Time Cut 81%," *USA Today*, April 10, 1992.
42. n.a. "The International Team Excellence Award," *The Journal for Quality & Participation*, Summer 2004, pp. 34–41.
43. Adapted from Ira Moskowitz and Ken Bethea, "Self-Directed Work Teams at Analog Devices," *Center for Quality of Management Journal*, Vol. 9, No. 1, Summer 2000, pp. 17–24.
44. "The Wonder of Wikipedia," *Fortune*, June 12, 2006, p. 140.
45. William M. Fox, "Sociotechnical System Principles and Guidelines: Past and Present," *The Journal of Applied Behavioral Science*, Vol. 3, No. 1, March 1995.
46. G. C. Homans, *The Human Group*, New York: Harcourt, Brace, and World, 1959, p. 2.
47. E. Trist and K.W. Bamforth, "Some Social and Psychological Consequences of the Long Wall Method of Coal-Getting," *Human Relations*, Vol. 4, No. 1, 1952, pp. 3–38.
48. Bradley L. Kirkman and Debra L. Shapiro, "The Impact of Cultural Values on Employee Resistance to Teams: Toward a Model of Globalized Self-Managing Work Team Effectiveness," *Academy of Management Review*, Vol. 22, No. 3, 1997, pp. 730–757.
49. This discussion stems from Karen A. Jehn, Gregory B. Northcraf, and Margaret A. Nealeand, "Why Differences Make a Difference: A Field Study of Diversity, Conflict, and Performance in Workgroups," *Administrative Science Quarterly*, Vol. 44, No. 4, December 1999, pp. 741–763; and Lisa Hope Pelled, Kathleen M. Eisenhardt, and Katherine R. Xin, "Exploring the Black Box: An Analysis of Work Group Diversity, Conflict, and Performance," *Administrative Science Quarterly*, Vol. 44, No. 1, March 1999, pp. 1–28.
50. Adapted from Billie R. Day and Michael Moore, "Plugging Into the Power of Leadership Teams," *The Journal for Quality and Participation*, May/June 1998, pp. 21–24.

CHAPTER 9

Engagement, Empowerment, and Motivation

Performance Excellence Profile: PRO-TEC Coating Company[1]

Established in 1990 as a joint venture between United States Steel Corporation and Kobe Steel Ltd. of Japan, PRO-TEC Coating Company provides coated sheet steel primarily to the U.S. automotive industry for use in manufacturing cars, trucks, and sport utility vehicles. PRO-TEC's 236 employees, called Associates, work in a state-of-the-art 730,000-square-foot facility in the small rural town of Leipsic, Ohio. With its heritage from U.S. Steel and Kobe Steel, PRO-TEC has developed its own unique culture centered around three fundamental concepts—ownership, responsibility, and accountability. Since its inception, PRO-TEC's success has been driven by its vision:

- BE totally committed to personal safety and wellness, consistently profitable, and recognized as the industry technology leader in both product and process;
- DO maintain high standards for community, citizenship, and service; provide on-time delivery with world-class quality; and develop/maintain world-class facility/business systems;
- HAVE a highly skilled, engaged workforce committed to ongoing performance excellence; optimal utilization of production capacity/capability; and valuable vendor/supplier relationships.

From the beginning, the company incorporated numerous best-management practices, including lean manufacturing and continuous improvement, and relied on a well-trained, self-directed, empowered workforce to help the company become an industry leader. Its mission statement, "To foster human potential, a spirit of cooperation, and technical innovation for the betterment of our industry, Associates and our community," further defines its culture. The statement appears on company business cards and is displayed prominently throughout the PRO-TEC facility. From the beginning, the company incorporated numerous best-management practices, including lean manufacturing and continuous improvement, and relied on a well-trained, self-directed, empowered workforce to help the company become an industry leader. PRO-TEC routinely scores better than its competition in product quality, on-time delivery, service, product development, and overall quality.

PRO-TEC's Associates work in self-directed teams and are empowered, innovative leaders who fix problems as they are identified and use a continuous improvement process called "I-to-I" to Initiate and Implement process and product improvements. New Associates go through three weeks of orientation and training, followed by six months of mentoring. The company's commitment to Associate quality of life through safety, education and training, and an above-average compensation and "cafeteria-style" benefits package reflects the value PRO-TEC places on attracting and retaining its workforce. All Associates are salaried and participate in a profit sharing plan that has provided an average payout of approximately 15 percent of annual base pay. In a survey, Associates agreed or strongly agreed with the following statements: "The people I work with cooperate and work as a team," "I know what is expected of me at work, "I am supported when responding to customers' questions or problems," and "I am satisfied with my job." PRO-TEC has a turnover rate of less than 2 percent and has never had a layoff.

In a manufacturing environment that poses potential hazards, PRO-TEC's facility was designed with safety, health, and security in mind, along with minimizing environmental impacts. During an emergency, PRO-TEC's hierarchy of priorities are to first, preserve human life and the safety of Associates, responders, and the public; second, minimize impact to the environment; and, third, minimize property damage and disruption of operations. PRO-TEC has developed comprehensive procedures to prepare for and respond to emergencies such as fires, explosions, natural disasters, and the release of hazardous materials. Associates participate in ongoing safety initiatives, which establish safety rules and procedures, requirements for personal protection and emergency response equipment, and safety training. Senior leaders and others have been trained on incident command, and PRO-TEC has a staff of 31 emergency medical technicians on-site to respond to emergencies. Since 2004, PRO-TEC has shown a 1.65 recordable injury frequency or below per 200,000 man-hours.

In 1988, Takeo Miura of Hitachi Corporation made the following statement to a group of senior U.S. business executives:

> We are going to win and the industrial West is going to lose out; there's nothing much you can do about it, because the reasons for your failure are within yourselves.... With your bosses doing the thinking while the workers wield the screwdrivers, you're convinced deep down that this is the right way to run a business. For you, the essence of management is getting the ideas out of the heads of the bosses and into the hands of labor. We are beyond the Taylor model: business, we know, is so complex and difficult that survival for firms ... depends on the day-to-day mobilization of every ounce of intelligence.[2]

Miura threw down the gauntlet to American business: bring the brainpower of your entire organization to the competition, or prepare to lose permanently.

High-performing organizations like PRO-TEC Coating Company have recognized that engaged employees (associates, team members, stakeholders, or whatever term may be used to describe employees) deliver better performance and generate satisfied customers. However, the Gallup organization estimates that over half of the nation's employees are not engaged and a significant percentage are actually *actively disengaged* in their work.

This chapter will:

- explain the scope of employee engagement,
- explain the importance of empowerment and principles of successful empowerment,
- provide examples of firms practicing employee engagement, and
- link engagement and empowerment to theories of motivation.

EMPLOYEE ENGAGEMENT

Businesses have learned that to satisfy customers, they must first satisfy employees. FedEx, for instance, has found direct statistical correlation between customer and employee satisfaction; a drop in employee satisfaction scores precedes a drop in customer satisfaction by about two months. Academic research has found similar relationships.[3] For example, in a study of service operations in industries ranging from communications to banking to fast food, researchers found that as employee satisfaction increased, so did customer satisfaction and loyalty to the organization. If employees were satisfied with their working conditions and jobs, they stayed with the company, became familiar with customers and their needs, had the opportunity to correct errors because the customers knew and trusted them, and had outcomes of higher productivity and high service quality. Customers of these firms became more loyal, thus providing more repeat business, were willing to complain about service problems so that employees could fix them, and benefited from the relationship by seeing lower costs and better service, thus leading to a new cycle of increased customer satisfaction.

So how can organizations create more satisfied employees? One way is to engage them in their work and make them a part of the "fabric" of the organization. **Employee engagement** simply means that workers have a strong emotional bond to their organization, are actively involved in and committed to their work, feel that their jobs are important, know that their opinions and ideas have value, and often go beyond their immediate job responsibilities for the good of the organization. Engagement leads to greater levels of satisfaction among the workforce.[4] Furthermore, engagement improves organizational performance.[5] A survey of 55,000 workers by the Gallup Organization found that four key employee attitudes, taken together, correlate strongly with higher profits:

- Workers feel they are given the opportunity to do what they do best every day.
- They believe their opinions count.
- They sense their fellow workers are committed to quality.
- They've made a direct connection between their work and the company's mission.

Related research supported the conclusions that employee satisfaction and engagement is strongly correlated with business-unit outcomes of customer satisfaction, productivity, profit, employee retention, and employee safety, and that these results generalize across organizations. For example, a study of Spanish firms suggested that organizational success depends to a greater extent on the leadership, human resource management, and learning factors and quality planning, and to a lower extent upon other practices. Firms showing a higher concern for empowerment, personnel policies, and work knowledge were those with a wider implementation of TQ practices and better performance. Another study comparing U.S. and Japanese firms found that innovative human resource practices lead to higher productivity.[6]

The benefits of employee engagement have become obvious to many managers, such as Art Wegner, president of Pratt & Whitney, a producer of jet engines: "If I try to make a lot of decisions with the goal of reducing costs by 30 percent, I'm not likely to understand all the issues very well. But if you get everybody—all those people in the organization—asking themselves, 'How am I going to get 30 percent of the costs out of there?' the power of that is unbelievable."[7]

Engagement is manifest in Deming's concept of "pride and joy" in work. A compelling example occurred in 2002 when former Southwest Airlines CEO Herb Kelleher sent a letter concerning the current fuel cost crisis to the home of every employee. "Jet fuel costs three times what it did one year ago. Southwest uses 19 million gallons a week. Our profitability is in jeopardy," he wrote. He asked each worker to help by identifying a way to save $5 a day. That would, he explained in the letter, save Southwest $51 million annually. The response was immediate. A group of mechanics figured out how to reduce the costs of heating the aircraft. Another department offered to do its own janitorial work. Within six weeks of the letter being sent to the employees, this large organization found ways to save more than $2M.[8]

Although engagement is relevant for all aspects of organizational performance, it plays a special role in quality improvement. Total quality requires people to make real changes in the way work is done and relies on in-depth understanding of the current system. Only employees involved in the system day to day possess such an understanding, which is why so many managers see involved employees as an integral part of total quality. As one survey concluded, "Employee involvement ... may be viewed as creating the organizational context needed to support quality improvement processes."[9] The relationship between engagement and quality is summarized in Figure 9.1.

Organizations that provide an environment in which workers can do their best every single day foster engagement. This includes providing job autonomy, the right tools and equipment to do a quality job, challenging work and continuous learning opportunities, flexible work options, involvement in decision-making, recognition for a job well done, mangers and supervisors showing sincere care and encouragement along with effective communication, and a healthful and safe work environment with satisfying social relationships. One need only look at *Fortune* magazine's annual list of the "100 Best Companies to Work For" to support these findings (see box "How Can You Not Love This Job?!"). As Hal Rosenbluth, president of Rosenbluth Travel, puts it, "By maintaining an enjoyable, bureaucracy-free

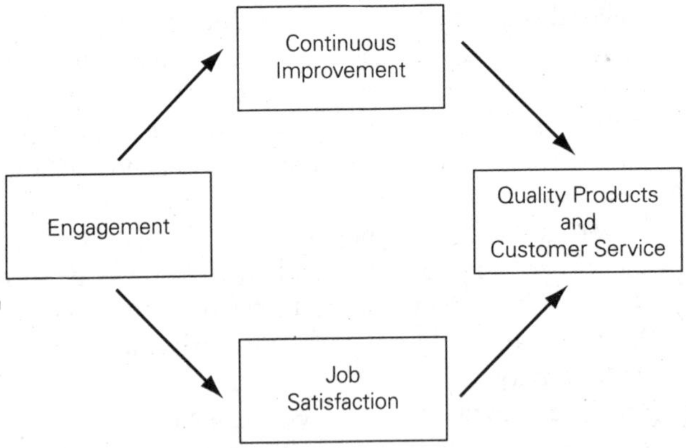

FIGURE 9.1 | HOW ENGAGEMENT LEADS TO QUALITY

work environment, one that encourages innovative thinking … and honest communication, people are freed to concentrate solely on the needs of the clients."[10]

Employee engagement is rooted in the psychology of human needs and supported by the motivation models of Maslow, Herzberg, and McGregor. Employees are motivated through exciting work, responsibility, and recognition. Engagement provides a powerful means of achieving the highest order individual needs of self-realization and fulfillment. Employee engagement offers many advantages over traditional management practices as it:

- Replaces the adversarial mentality with trust and cooperation
- Develops the skills and leadership capability of individuals, creating a sense of mission and fostering trust
- Increases employee morale and commitment to the organization
- Fosters creativity and innovation, the source of competitive advantage
- Helps people understand quality principles and instills these principles into the corporate culture

HOW CAN YOU NOT LOVE THIS JOB?![11]

At Google, you can do your laundry; drop off your dry cleaning; get an oil change, then have your car washed; work out in the gym; attend subsidized exercise classes; get a massage; study Mandarin, Japanese, Spanish, and French; and ask a personal concierge to arrange dinner reservations. Naturally, you can get haircuts onsite. Want to buy a hybrid car? The company will give you $5,000 toward that environmentally friendly end. Care to refer a friend to work at Google? Google would like that too, and it'll give you a $2,000 reward. Just had a new baby? Congratulations! Your employer will reimburse you for up to $500 in takeout food to ease your first four weeks at home. Looking to make new friends? Attend a weekly TGIF party, where there's usually a band playing. Five onsite doctors are available to give you a checkup, free of charge.

- Allows employees to solve problems at the source immediately
- Improves quality and productivity[12]

Engagement begins with involvement. **Employee involvement (EI)** refers to any activity by which employees participate in work-related decisions and improvement activities, with the objectives of tapping the creative energies of all employees and improving their motivation. Tom Peters suggested involving everyone in everything, in such activities as quality and productivity improvement, measuring and monitoring results, budget development, new technology assessment, recruiting and hiring, making customer calls, and participating in customer visits.[13] Pete Coors, CEO of Coors Brewing, explained it simply, "We're moving from an environment where the supervisor says, 'This is the way it is going to be done and if you don't like it, go someplace else,' to an environment where the supervisor can grow with the changes, get his troops together and say, 'Look, you guys are operating the equipment, what do you think we ought to do?'"[14] EI approaches can range from simple sharing of information or providing input on work-related issues and making suggestions to self-directed responsibilities such as setting goals, making business decisions, and solving problems, often in cross-functional teams.

EI initiatives are by no means new. Many programs and experiments have been implemented over more than 100 years by industrial engineers, statisticians, and behavioral scientists. Early attempts influenced modern practices considerably. Unfortunately, these approaches lacked the complementary elements of TQ, such as a customer orientation, top management leadership and support, and a common set of tools for problem solving and continuous improvement.

One of the easiest ways to involve employees on an individual basis is the suggestion system. An employee suggestion system is a management tool for the submission, evaluation, and implementation of an employee's idea to save cost, increase quality, or improve other elements of work such as safety. Companies typically reward employees for implemented suggestions. At Toyota, for instance, employees generate nearly 3 million ideas each year—an average of 60 per employee—of which 85 percent are implemented by management. Suggestion systems are often tied to incentives.

Wainwright Industries developed a unique and effective approach that has been benchmarked extensively.[15] Suggestion programs were viewed as neither systematic nor continuous, and not woven into the fabric of daily operations. Their approach was designed to overcome these shortcomings in the following ways:

- Focusing employees on small, incremental improvements within their own areas of responsibility and control
- Recognizing all employees for their level of participation regardless of the value of the improvement
- Scaling team-based improvement efforts in a way that minimizes downtime and provides people with the tools and techniques to produce successful outcomes
- Positioning supervisors as the catalyst for cultural change through a coaching and support role in the employee involvement and improvement process

The process contains two main components: individual implemented improvements and team-based system improvements. Rather than submitting suggestions for someone else to approve and implement, employees are provided with training and given the responsibility to take the initiative to make improvements on their own without prior approval within the scope of their main job responsibilities. Upon making improvements, they complete a form to document what they have done and present it to the supervisors, whose role is not to approve or disapprove, but to acknowledge the improvement and to point out any issues that the employee needs to understand. All forms submitted during the week are placed into a random drawing for some type of award determined by the individual unit. At the end of each quarter, every individual who met his or her goal of implemented improvements receives some type of valued recognition. The team-based approach breaks large initiatives into smaller manageable projects. Breaking down large tasks allows employees to understand how their individual jobs fit into the big picture and maximizes participation reduces time requirements for any particular employee. Wainwright was able to cite more than 50 implemented improvements per employee per year, far exceeding those of most American and Japanese companies.

Fostering employee creativity has many benefits. Thinking about solutions to problems at work makes even routine work enjoyable; writing down the suggestions improves workers' reasoning ability and writing skills. Satisfaction is the by-product of an implemented idea and a job made easier, safer, or better. Recognition for suggestions leads to higher levels of motivation, peer recognition, and possible monetary rewards. Workers gain an increased understanding of their work, which may lead to promotions and better interpersonal relationships in the workplace.

EMPOWERMENT

Empowerment represents the highest level of engagement. **Empowerment** means giving someone power—granting the authority to do whatever is necessary to satisfy customers, and trusting employees to make the right choices without waiting for management approval. The objective of empowerment is "to tap the creative and intellectual energy of everybody in the company, not just those in the executive suite ... to provide everyone with the responsibility and the resources to display real leadership within their own individual spheres of competence."[16] By empowering employees, organizations drive decision making down to its lowest possible level. Empowerment allows organizations to flatten their organizational structure because fewer managers are needed to "direct and control" employees. Giving employees responsibility for their own work has led not only to improvements in motivation, customer service, and morale, but also to improvements in quality, productivity, and the speed of decision making.[17]

Empowerment is a natural extension of employee involvement concepts. In some companies empowerment is used as the umbrella term for increasing employee involvement in decision making. Empowerment is more than another term for involvement, however. It represents a high degree of involvement in which employees make decisions themselves and are responsible for their outcomes. This is a more radical change than having employees merely participate in managers' decisions, even when they are given some influence (see Figure 9.2).

Examples of empowerment abound. Self-managed teams discussed in the previous chapter are perfect examples. Workers in the Coors Brewery container operation

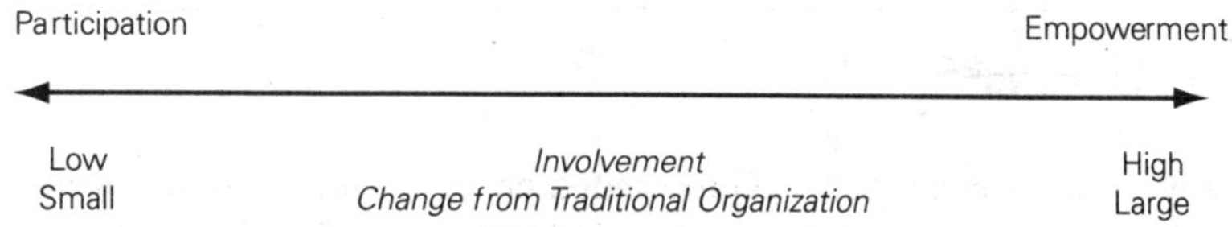

FIGURE 9.2 | CONTINUUM OF EMPLOYEE INVOLVEMENT PRACTICES

give each other performance evaluations, and even screen, interview, and hire new people for the line. At Motorola, sales representatives have the authority to replace defective products up to six years after purchase, a decision that used to require top management approval. Hourly employees at GM's antilock brake system plant in Dayton, Ohio, can call in suppliers to help solve problems, and manage scrap, machine downtime, absences, and rework. See box "Stuff Happens" for a good example.

One survey found that more than 40 percent of the largest U.S. corporations are moderate to high users of employee involvement practices such as empowerment.[18] Manufacturing, especially in the chemical and electronics industries, has tended to empower employees more than service organizations, although the financial services industry has taken a leading role.

Empowerment has even played a role in such business successes as the Ford Taurus program.[19] Employee ideas were responsible for reducing the number of different welding guns on the assembly line from three to one and for developing a standard screw size for use in the car's interior plastic moldings. Although these changes may not sound very dramatic, a Ford executive estimated that such ideas often are worth more than $300,000 each.

The need to empower the entire workforce in order for quality to succeed has long been recognized, even if it is only recently coming into practice. Five of Deming's 14 Points relate directly to the notion of empowerment.

Point 6: Institute training.

Point 7: Teach and institute leadership.

Point 8: Drive out fear. Create trust. Create a climate for innovation.

Point 10: Eliminate exhortations for the workforce.

Point 13: Encourage education and self-improvement for everyone.[20]

Juran wrote that "ideally, quality control should be delegated to the workforce to the maximum extent possible."[21] Empowerment resembles Juran's concept of "self-control." For employees to practice self-control, they must know their unit's goals and their actual performance and have a means for changing performance if the goals are not being met.[22] Although it is a difficult struggle, organizations are increasingly meeting these conditions.

For empowerment to occur, managers must undertake two major initiatives:[23]

1. identify and change organizational conditions that make people powerless, and
2. increase people's confidence that their efforts to accomplish something important will be successful.

Stuff Happens[24]

Jim Kelly, UPS chairman and CEO recounted an example of empowerment in a speech to Rutgers University:

> At UPS, we've got thousands of heroes every day. Not the kind that make headlines, but the kind that do make a difference.
>
> For instance, there's the story of an account executive who took responsibility for a damaged parcel that was packed incorrectly. This particular parcel was a rare numbered art print sent by an elderly homebound couple in Florida to their son in Wisconsin.
>
> The print was valued at $350, but it had much greater emotional value. It was a beautiful limited edition of an elk in a forest, and the couple sent it as a best wishes offering to their son who raised elk on his farm. It arrived in Wisconsin badly damaged. The elderly couple was devastated.
>
> However, our account executive in Wisconsin wanted to help. A wildlife art collector himself, he knew that most artists keep a couple of extra unnumbered prints around for such misfortunes. He contacted the artist in Florida, had a new print renumbered and shipped back to Wisconsin. He then personally delivered it to the delighted son. The son was impressed. His parents were overjoyed. The point is, one of our people took a lot of initiative and responsibility for a problem he didn't even directly cause. He took a bad situation and turned it into a customer-for-life situation.

The need to do both of these implies that organizational systems often create powerless employees and that these systems must be changed first. Examples of systems in need of change are those that specify who can (and cannot) make certain types of decisions and systems of standard operating procedures (and who can override them). Even when systems are changed to permit empowerment, individuals who have lived under those systems are not readily able to operate in an empowered manner. The other need in empowering people is to deal with the psychological aftereffects of powerlessness by convincing people that they are in fact able to "make a difference." Empowerment is an application of the teamwork principle of total quality, embodying "vertical" teamwork between managerial and nonmanagerial personnel. If employees are given important responsibilities—and the authority that goes along with them—it is more realistic to describe their relationship with management as teamwork than it would be in a hierarchical system. After all, people can hardly be seen as team members if they only execute decisions made by others.

The traditional treatment of employees by American managers led W. Edwards Deming to plead with managers to drive out fear—defined as "feeling threatened by possible repercussions as a result of speaking up about work-related concerns."[25] Today, managers in quality-oriented companies, hampered by decades of policies encouraging employees to keep their ideas to themselves, struggle to find ways to encourage employees to take responsibility for their work.

Principles of Empowerment

Although many organizations have undertaken the journey toward empowerment, many have become lost along the way. Empowerment may sound easy, but there is a lot more to it than telling employees they are (poof!) empowered, like the Fairy

Godmother's transformation of Cinderella before the ball. A number of principles are involved in successfully giving power to employees.

Empower Sincerely and Completely It should go without saying that empowerment must be done sincerely. It cannot be done superficially. One executive observed that in many large companies, empowerment is 90 percent psychological and only fractionally real.[26] To gain its benefits, managers must empower for its improvement value, not for its public relations value. As Dan Ciampa, a consultant with expertise in empowerment, puts it: "Simply bringing employees together once a month and exhorting them to work harder to achieve the business's objectives is not enough."[27]

A process is needed that enables them to make significant improvements in their own work area that help meet the business imperatives in a way that will satisfy the needs of the individual employee.[28] Furthermore, nothing could be worse for employees than to be told they are responsible for something, only to be jerked back at the first sign of trouble or uncertainty. Managers must think long and hard before making the commitment to empowerment—once done, it can't be done halfway. Semi-empowerment just doesn't work. Senior managers need to ask three critical questions:

1. How can I make fewer decisions, thereby letting others become more involved in managing the business?
2. How can I teach others how to make solid decisions once they're given the chance?
3. How can I recruit others to be more aware of changes that need to be made in order to keep our company competitive—and then help them feel they can make these changes without begging for permission each and every time?[29]

This does not mean that there should be no limits. On the contrary, managers must be clear on exactly what responsibility and authority rests with employees. Questions such as "What procedures can we change?" and "How much money can we commit?" must be answered ahead of time. Finally, managers must be willing to wait for results, as miracles do not happen overnight.[30]

Establish Mutual Trust

As Juran has put it, "The managers must trust the workforce enough to be willing to make the delegation, and the workforce must have enough confidence in the managers to be willing to accept the responsibility."[31] Trust is not created just by saying you trust someone; it must be backed up by actions (see box "All You Need Is Trust").

In one plant utilizing self-managed teams, trust was symbolized by giving each new employee a key to the plant, a highly unusual practice.[32] The ultimate issue for many employees, however, is job security. They must trust that management will not take advantage of productivity increases to cut the workforce, in effect working themselves out of a job. Firms embarking on employee involvement activities often make explicit commitments to this effect to employees.[33] Southwest Airlines, for example, has never downsized a single employee, even through jet fuel spikes, recessions, and the Gulf War.

ALL YOU NEED IS TRUST[34]

Texas Nameplate Company (TNC), a small (only about 50 people), privately-held firm founded in 1946, makes nameplates, the small metal tags with etched lettering that get riveted to refrigerators, computers, high-pressure valves, and military equipment. When serious work started on reducing nonconformances through statistical process control in 1992, total nonconformances amounted to about 15–18 percent of billing—a significant amount of lost profit. Improvement activities were able to drive that rate down to 3.7 percent by 1997, in an industry that averages around 10 percent. But Dale Crownover, the company president, wasn't happy.

TNC started a gainsharing plan that distributed bonuses equally to all employees, beginning with nonconformance rates of less than 5 percent. Results were posted daily. By the end of 1997, TNC employees whittled nonconformances down to 1 percent. In January 1998, in an attempt to further carve away at the problem, TNC did away with its quality control department. In the first month following that move, which Crownover said was part of the company's strategic plan, nonconformances were cut in half.

Quality improvement now comes through DOIT—Daily Operation Innovation Team—consisting of supervisors who meet every other week to discuss accomplishments and opportunities for further improvements. They are charged with sharing information discussed at meetings with their employees.

"People on the floor can figure out what's happening and make adjustments the fastest," says Troy Knowlton, company operations manager. He added that they are quick to help out when one person is having a problem; they know what's at stake. "People listen to peers more than supervisors. We tried that for 45 years, and it didn't work. We have found the value of letting people do the work, with management providing the guidance." Not surprisingly, in 1998 TNC became the smallest company ever to win a Baldrige Award and repeated this accomplishment a second time (see the opening Performance Excellence Profile in Chapter 7).

Even in the aftermath of the September 11, 2001, terrorist attacks, when competitors announced job cuts of 20 percent, Southwest managers schemed how to cut costs by delaying deliveries of new planes and scrapping plans to renovate headquarters. CEO James F. Parker noted, "We are willing to suffer some damage, even to our stock price, to protect the jobs of our people." Think employees are fiercely loyal? You bet. And empowerment is a major principle of the airline's philosophy, as the example in Chapter 6 illustrated.

PROVIDE EMPLOYEES WITH BUSINESS INFORMATION

For empowerment to succeed, it must focus on making the organization more competitive.[35] Empowerment can contribute to organizational performance only if employees have access to the necessary information about the business and its performance, such as their personnel files and resources such as the quality improvement budget.[36] Information about the employees' department or other subunit is particularly necessary, as this is the level of performance that they can affect. Sharing business information with employees relates directly to quality, customer service, and competitiveness.[37] At DuPont's Delaware River plant, for example, management shares cost figures with all workers.[38] By sharing this information, management believes that workers will think more for themselves and identify with company goals. To help employees make decisions on issues affecting production, a department manager at Texas Eastman Chemicals Plant supplied operators with a daily financial report that showed how their decisions affected the bottom line. As a result, department profits doubled in four months and quality improved by 50 percent as employees began suggesting cost-saving improvements.[39]

In the absence of appropriate information, empowered employees may squander their power on problems that are not very important. As Peter Senge has put it, "Empowering the individual where there is a relatively low level of alignment [between organizational and employee goals] worsens the chaos and makes managing ... even more difficult."[40]

The criticism of misplaced goals was often leveled at earlier employee involvement efforts, such as quality circles. Although managers formerly blamed employees for having the wrong priorities, sophisticated managers today recognize that they are responsible for providing employees with the information necessary to develop educated priorities.

Ensure That Employees Are Capable

"You can't empower incompetence," says one manager. If employees are going to take on important organizational responsibilities, they must be prepared to do so. To operate in an empowered, TQ environment, employees must possess not only technical skills (including statistics) but also interpersonal and problem-solving skills (see box "Spilling the Beans: Secrets of Starbucks' Success"). Unfortunately, many people entering the workforce today lack even the most basic skills in reading and math, let alone these relatively advanced skills.[41]

Employee capability can be ensured through selection and training processes. Unless the human resource processes are adapted to provide capable employees, empowerment cannot succeed, and management's worst nightmares will be realized. Unfortunately, many employees are not trained in these areas, which helps explain the mixed results many organizations have had with empowerment.[42]

A Corning Glass plant in Erwin, New York, exemplifies this principle.[43] The union agreed to replace 21 different jobs with one "specialist" job. Employees were placed in teams and given broad authority over production scheduling and the division of labor. Did a bright new day dawn at Erwin? Not exactly. Conflict and confusion went up, and productivity went down. Plant manager Gary Vogt concluded: "We took steps to empower people, but the desired outcomes were not reached because we had not prepared them." An elaborate training program was created, and workers now become certified for the various tasks in the operation through testing. The promise of empowerment is now being fulfilled, and quality and productivity have increased.

Empowerment also requires that employees understand their appropriate limits of discretion. At The Ritz-Carlton Hotel Company, L.L.C., each employee can "Move heaven and earth" and spend up to $2,000 to satisfy a customer. However, whenever they apply this privilege, they must complete a report that explains the problem and actions taken, which is evaluated to determine why the problem occurred, take preventive measures, and ensure that the empowered action taken was appropriate.

Spilling the Beans: Secrets of Starbucks' Success[44]

Starbucks Coffee, which grew from a small Seattle retailer to a national phenomenon, can be found in cities and airports across America, as well as up in the friendly skies. Its consistency and precision stem from its employee training program. All "partners," as employees are called, complete five classes during their first six weeks with the company, including "Brewing the Perfect Cup," "Coffee Knowledge," and "Customer Service." All partners have to memorize and practice the rules. Milk must be steamed to at least 150° F but never more than 170° F. Every espresso shot must be pulled within 23 seconds—or tossed. Trainers demonstrate how to wipe oil from the coffee bin, open a giant bag of beans ("In a sanitary manner! You never put your hand in there!"), and clean the milk wand on the espresso machine ("It's like blowing a little boy's nose"). They demonstrate how to fill sacks with coffee and affix a sticker exactly one-half inch over the Starbucks logo. Practicing on lattes, the trainer cries out, "Fabulous foam! It's okay to practice in your stores. Pull ten shots and dump 'em. And what does it taste like when the milk in your latte is 190° F? Be a mad scientist behind the bar ... you'll understand why customers complain."

Three guidelines (Star Skills) govern interpersonal relations: maintain and enhance self-esteem, listen and acknowledge, and ask for help. Throughout the training, partners are encouraged to share their feelings about selling, about coffee, about working for the company. They also learn relaxation techniques so they can focus on the cappuccinos, to take personal responsibility for the cleanliness of the coffee bins—even when it's someone else's job—and to treat partners respectfully and do the right thing when one of them spills a gallon of milk.

Don't Ignore Middle Management

A well-known principle of organization theory popularized by Deming is that organizations are systems. When changing one part of an organization, it is necessary to consider the effects of the change on other parts of the system. Thus, managers must consider how empowering lower-level employees will affect middle managers. If the needs and expectations of middle managers are ignored, empowerment will be confusing at best and disastrous at worst. One manager described the situation with middle managers in his company like this:

> We pretty much promoted people because of their technical knowledge, not their management skills. Therefore we have a group of people in supervisory positions who aren't people-oriented; they don't know how to get the ideas and the solutions and better ways of doing things out of their people. And they are not receptive to employee-involvement programs, they are not receptive to too much change in their lives, they feel comfortable in this doing role rather than a coaching or facilitator's role. So therefore we have to train these people to think differently and manage their departments from a management point of view rather than a doer's point of view.... It's the middle management transition from the old style of management to today's new style of management that's the problem, that stops companies from getting where they need to be as fast as they need to get there.

Among the roles for middle managers in organizations with empowered workforces are:[45]

- maintaining focus on the organization's values,

- managing solutions to system-level problems (those that involve many functions and departments), and
- acting as teachers and coaches.

It's tempting to think of middle managers faced with empowerment efforts as dinosaurs, rapidly becoming extinct because the world has changed too quickly for them. However, remember that most middle managers are a product of their organizations and have attained their level of success in an environment that rewarded different things than are needed from managers now. Given a new set of instructions from top management, backed up by new performance appraisal criteria, many (but far from all) managers will be able to make the necessary transition.

Change the Reward System

Rarely can substantial organizational change be created without changing the reward system. When organizations ask employees to assume new challenges and responsibilities, the question "What's in it for me?" ultimately gets asked. The reward system includes all of the rewards that employees receive, as well as the criteria for distributing these rewards. An organization is to its reward system like a boat is to its anchor: unless the reward system is changed, the organization may drift a little bit in one direction or another, but it won't get very far.

It is hard to specify exactly what kind of reward systems will be needed to complement empowerment. Some of the practices common to organizations utilizing employee involvement include pay-for-skills, in which employees' pay increases as they learn new job-relevant skills, and profitsharing, in which employees receive bonuses related to the profits of their organization.[46] (The box "All You Need Is Trust" describes Texas Nameplate's gainsharing plan.) Nor should intrinsic rewards be overlooked: simple but sincere expressions of appreciation by supervisors, a picture in the company newsletter, or an evening of celebration upon a major accomplishment may be of tremendous value to employees who have seldom received any recognition at all in the past (see box "Caught Doing Things Right"). In fact, a Conference Board survey found that noncash recognition for hourly/production workers was found to be effective to "great/ some extent" by 84 percent of business units in contrast to only 63 percent for cash recognition.[47]

As one example, in October 1994, Continental Airlines' new CEO Gordon Bethune calculated that late and canceled flights were costing the company $6 million per month to put passengers on rival airlines or send them to hotels. He declared that if Continental ranked among the top three airlines for on-time performance in any month, he would split half the savings (about $65 per person) with all non-executive employees. Within two months, Continental was first. To ensure that the bonuses made a vivid impression, Bethune issued the checks separately and traveled around the country to distribute thousands of them personally. The behavioral changes are best illustrated by a story executives like to retell. A catering truck pulls up to a plane but is 10 meals short. In the old days, the flight attendant would have told the driver to get the extra meals while the plane sat at the gate for 40 minutes. The newly gung ho flight attendant, however, crisply tells the catering guy not to screw up again and shuts the cabin door. The plane pushes back on schedule, and she finds a bunch of investment bankers and offers them free liquor in place of the meal.[48]

Caught Doing Things Right[49]

When the chicken strips at a KFC sold out that day, a customer had to wait while employees cooked up a fresh batch. Gardner, working the lunch shift, apologized for the delay and offered the man a free side item so he wouldn't go hungry. She and her team members "were just so attentive to me," the customer recalls. It was no ordinary customer experience—and the man, it turned out, was no ordinary customer. As senior VP of public affairs at Yum Brands Inc. (formerly Tricon Global Restaurants), KFC's parent company, Jonathan Blum was in a position to recognize employees going the extra mile. Blum hurried back to nearby Yum headquarters, grabbed one of his signature awards—a seat belt on a plaque, symbolizing the "roller coaster" nature of the restaurant business—and returned to the KFC to fete Gardner. "In front of all her peers, I said, 'You didn't know that I work at Yum. I want you to know how proud I am of you.'" Today, a photo of a beaming Gardner hangs in Blum's office.

In Yum parlance, they call it "catching people doing things right"—taking time to notice and publicly reward employees who exceed expectations. "People innately want to be recognized for their hard work," says Yum chairman and CEO David Novak.

When Empowerment Doesn't Work

Beverly Reynolds thought she wanted to be an empowered worker.[50] After nine months at an Eaton Corporation plant, however, she left for another job. Although she liked the idea of being her own boss, she hated the headaches that came with it—fixing broken machines and having to learn a wide variety of jobs.

Many workers prefer the old-style approach with narrowly defined tasks and find that an empowered organizational culture is simply not for them. Saturn Corporation, for instance, found that many job candidates from old-style General Motors plants just couldn't adjust to a new style of work. This provides a big challenge to organizations to recruit the right people at the outset.

Other efforts at empowerment have failed because of the inability of management to understand and implement it properly. Among the reasons for failure are:[51]

- Management support and commitment is nonexistent or not sustained.
- Empowerment is used as a manipulative tool to ensure employees complete tasks and assignments without giving them any real responsibility or authority.
- Managers use empowerment to abdicate responsibility or task accountability, accepting accolades for successes and assigning fault to others for failure.
- Empowerment is deployed selectively, segmenting the workforce into those who are empowered and those who are not.
- Empowerment is used as an excuse to not invest in training or employee development.
- Managers fail to provide feedback and do not recognize achievements.

These problems can be avoided by applying the principles discussed earlier in this chapter.

EMPLOYEE ENGAGEMENT IN ACTION

We present three examples of how empowerment is practiced followed by some observations as to its lack of universal appeal.

DynMcDermott[52]

DynMcDermott (DM) Petroleum Operations Company is the sole contractor responsible for managing the U.S. Strategic Petroleum Reserve for the Department of Energy. DM addresses many of the factors discussed in this chapter with respect to employee engagement and empowerment. Cooperation, initiative, innovation, and empowerment are the basis of their high performance values-based culture. All employees are empowered to innovate and improve processes and complete their work in self-directed informal and formal functionally diverse work groups and/or teams. Formal teams are chartered, managed, and members trained just in time during the Performance Improvement (PI) process, which uses Six Sigma and lean tools to systematically analyze processes and reduce variation and waste.

DM adapts to changing business needs through individual empowerment and authority and when additional resources are required, uses teams with members from different functions, disciplines, and locations, including supplier/contractor personnel, to capitalize on diverse skills and facilitate interdepartmental cooperation. They use teams for major initiatives, continuing responsibilities, and improvements. One major DM initiative, Vapor Pressure, was a new requirement developed as a result of using leading indicator measures. To maximize cooperation, coordination, and ensure that appropriate skills were in place to support this initiative, this project was managed by a cross-functional project team. This included development of work task assignments, job descriptions, recruitment, and training resulting in a successful start-up of the Vapor Pressure plant in April 2004.

The DM employee performance management system uses performance evaluations to manage an employee's career, set work goals, reinforce and reward good performance, provide timely feedback to each employee on their performance, and to establish Individual Development Plans (IDP) that ensure the employee has support for career development. DM strongly supports training and allots resources for individual development. Employee performance evaluation procedures require that employees' goals directly support organizational goals, action plans, and reinforce an understanding of how their performance contributes to DM's success. Periodically, HR also conducts a complete review of each job to ensure that job descriptions remain relevant to the DM mission and that employee skill requirements remain aligned with business needs and customer requirements. This systematic process provides each employee with the opportunity to participate in the overall evaluation process; supports employee job ownership in support of DM's action plans to achieve the Mission; and facilitates the timely identification of employee training and development needs, as required, to maximize agility and responsiveness to changing mission requirements. One of the most important rewards is employee profit sharing based on DM's performance fee received from DOE, which is based on overall company performance.

As part of DM's annual merit increase funding process, HR conducts a comprehensive evaluation of the compensation program, which includes a thorough review of industry practices and measurement of key program components, such as salary range structures to ensure that this program is capable of attracting and retaining high-performing employees with the appropriate skills. DM participates in a number of national salary benchmarking studies to support this effort and, by using this comparative benchmarking data, DM is able to gauge the competitive market and determine adjustments needed to sustain its competitive position as defined in its Compensation Plan.

DM recognizes the need to maintain a highly talented workforce, especially due to the special needs of the SPR and recent budget reductions. To accomplish this, each manager works with his employees during the performance evaluation process to review organizational goals and personal goals in relation to the employees' position. They review the previously agreed-upon training plan and update it to enable the employee to achieve his/her stated goals. DM offers a continuing education reimbursement program for employees. Employees are able to pursue undergraduate, graduate, and single course study programs. In addition, employees can choose conferences and seminars to develop their potential. Job and career development are part of the annual performance evaluation process. Employees work with their managers to select development objectives for the coming year and together review accomplishment of the previous year's goals.

HEWITT ASSOCIATES[53]

Hewitt Associates, based in Lincolnshire, IL, is a human resources (HR) outsourcing and consulting company. The customer service (CS) role at Hewitt—and many other companies that rely heavily on CS to deliver outsourced processes—requires significant training in the proprietary systems used to handle data from client organizations. Maintaining CS talent, which typically has a high turnover rate, is a top priority. One way to do this is to increase employee engagement. Based on the work Hewitt does with its HR consulting clients, the company knows that there is a strong positive relationship between engagement and organizational performance. Specifically, companies with higher levels of engagement are likely to have greater sales growth and higher total shareholder return.

Hewitt conducts an annual associate engagement survey that measures not only all the standard employee opinion survey components, such as satisfaction with opportunities, but also intent to display certain behaviors known to have an impact on business results. One of those survey items asked: "How likely is it that you will be working at Hewitt one year from now?" Predictive analysis has shown that of the representatives who respond that it is unlikely they will be working at Hewitt, about half actually leave within one year, making this item an important leading indicator of retention. Hewitt also uses regression analysis to determine the most important drivers of retention for the CS representatives. Elements of the work environment in which satisfaction is low but the relationship to retention is high were identified as opportunities for growth and training and rewards (pay and recognition). Elements of the work environment in which satisfaction is high but the threat to retention is high if the area is neglected were work activities and managers and leadership. Understanding these factors has helped the company to make better decisions on recruiting, compensation, and other workforce practices.

Los Alamos National Bank

Los Alamos National Bank (LANB) is the largest independent bank in New Mexico.[54] In the mid-1990s, employee survey results revealed that workers did not understand their role in the bank's strategic direction. Under the leadership of LANB's Quality Council, which has members from every area and level of the company, the performance appraisal system was redesigned to magnify the direct link between job performance and corporate performance.

The form used for this system lists corporate goals, departmental objectives, and the annual and long-term goals of the employee, which he or she writes in consultation with a supervisor. Employees also complete a personal self-assessment of their strengths and of opportunities to improve their customer-service skills and technical competence. Once they complete the annual appraisal process, employees have a complete snapshot of what they must do to perform at a high level and to earn the attendant incentives and rewards, which include profit sharing and employee stock ownership. Such incentive payouts average over 21 percent of an employee's annual salary.

Employee empowerment is vital to accomplishing LANB's goals for performance improvement and double-digit growth in annual income. Management consciously acts to distribute leadership responsibilities throughout the organization. In fact, over 90 percent of LANB's employees received leadership training in 1999 as compared to 8 percent of bank employees nationally.

Employees are expected to create value for customers, and they are given the authority and resources to act proactively and decisively. For example, all workers have the authority to resolve complaints on the spot. Also, high lending limits and flexible underwriting standards enable loan officers to respond innovatively to loan applicants with special circumstances. Yet, LANB's charge-offs for loan losses (as a percentage of average assets) have been declining since 1997 to about one-third the average percentage for local competitors. The bank's empowerment strategies were clearly evident during the 2000 Cerro Grande fire that ravaged over 48,000 acres and destroyed 280 homes, when employees set up shop without direct supervision in schools and other locations to keep the bank running and provide extraordinary measures to help the community overcome the crisis.

MOTIVATION

Without willing, sustained, individual effort and coordinated teamwork focused on meeting organizational goals, TQ is an impossible dream. However, when organizations ask employees to assume new challenges and responsibilities, the question "What's in it for me?" ultimately gets asked. Understanding human behavior and motivation are major elements of Deming's Profound Knowledge discussed in Chapter 1. Deming spoke of motivation as being primarily intrinsic (internal), and was suspicious of extrinsic (external) forms of motivation, such as incentives and bonuses, even though they are popular with business organizations and appear to positively reinforce employees.

Both extrinsic and intrinsic rewards are vital to sustained individual efforts. As managers in a TQ environment increasingly take on the roles of coaches and facilitators, their skills in motivating employees become even more crucial. There is no such thing as an unmotivated employee, but the system within which people work can either seriously impede motivation or enhance it. Compensation, recognition/reward systems, and the work environment must be carefully designed to motivate employees to achieve organizational as well as personal objectives.

COMPENSATION

Compensation is always a sticky issue, closely tied to the subject of motivation and employee satisfaction. Although money can be a motivator, it often causes employees to believe they are being treated unfairly, and forces managers to deliver negative messages. Eventually, it diminishes intrinsic motivation and creates win-lose situations. The objectives of a good compensation system should be to attract, retain, and not demotivate employees. Other objectives include reducing unexplainable variation in pay (think about Deming's principles) and encouraging internal cooperation rather than competition. Most companies still use traditional financial measures, such as revenue growth, profitability, and cost management, as a basis for compensation; more progressive organizations use quality measures such as customer satisfaction, defect prevention, and cycle time reduction to make compensation decisions.

Many companies link compensation to company track records, unit performance, team success, or individual achievement (see box "Compensation for Motivation").[55] For instance, Medrad bases its pay range on market pricing rather than on an internally focused job evaluation process. In 2001, a cross-functional project team developed a market-based compensation system that reinforced the goals and objectives of the company and pays base pay in the top quartile of similar positions in the market. The team redesigned the pay structure to:

- Retain and attract high performance individuals at all levels of the company;
- Align individuals and teams with corporate goals;
- Support Medrad's culture and employee growth and development; and,
- Maintain the view of base pay as one component of total compensation that also includes variable incentive pay, gainsharing, benefits, and other rewards and programs.

Medrad uses role profiles to match all jobs to market salary data. The new pay equation combines market value for a given job with the unique qualities of the individual. Every job now has a market range with a target zone. Medrad's goal is to move employees to their target zone over time, based on their performance and experience.

Team-based pay and gainsharing, an approach in which all employees share savings equally, are gaining in popularity and importance. Compensation for individuals is sometimes tied to the acquisition of new skills, often within the context of a continuous improvement program in which all employees are given opportunities to broaden their work-related competencies.

Compensation for Motivation

Nucor Corporation, one of the nation's largest steel producers, is well-known for having succeeded in attacking quality, productivity, participation, and compensation issues.[56] Nucor has more than 6,000 employees in plants in the United States. All employees, from the president on down, have the same benefits; the only differences in individual pay are related to responsibilities. Workers at Nucor's five nonunion steel mills earn base hourly rates that are less than half of the going rate for unionized steelworkers. Nucor uses pay incentives designed around groups of 40 to 50 workers, including secretaries and senior managers. They offer four basic compensation plans:

1. Production Incentive Plan. Employees involved directly in manufacturing are paid weekly bonuses on the basis of production of their work groups, which range from 20 to 40 workers each, and can average 80–150 percent of the base wage. The bonuses are paid every week to reinforce motivation. The average worker at Nucor earns several thousand dollars per year more than the average worker in the industry, whereas the company is able to sell its steel at competitive worldwide market prices.
2. Department Manager Incentive Plan. Department managers earn incentive bonuses paid annually based primarily on the return on assets of their facility.
3. Nonproduction and Nondepartment Manager Incentive Plan. Participants include accountants, engineers, secretaries, and other employees. The bonus is based on the facility's return on assets. Each month every operation receives a report showing progress, which is posted in the employee cafeteria or break area to keep employees appraised of their expected bonus levels throughout the year.
4. Senior Officers Incentive Plan. Senior officers do not receive profit sharing, pension, discretionary bonuses, or retirement plans. A significant part of their compensation is based on Nucor's return on stockholder's equity above a certain minimum earnings. If Nucor does well, compensation is well above average, as much as several times base salary. If the company does poorly, compensation is limited to base salary, which is below the average pay at comparable companies.

During downturns, managers at Nucor frequently find that their bonuses are cut, even while hourly workers continue to receive theirs, based on production rates. However, even in tough times, Nucor maintained its policy of no layoffs as it had throughout the history of the current company. More about the Nucor story can be found on its Web site at http://www.nucor.com.

Recognition and Rewards

Special recognition and rewards can be monetary or nonmonetary, formal or informal, individual or group. These rewards might include trips, promotional gifts, clothing, time off, or special company-sponsored awards and events. Most important, rewards should lead to behaviors that increase customer satisfaction. Whatever the recognition, it should have symbolic value that employees can inspire employees in the future. A Conference Board study found that a combination of cash and noncash recognition works better for clerical and hourly workers than for managers and professional/technical employees; for these groups, compensation-based incentives such as stock options are more successful.

Recognition provides a visible means of promoting quality efforts and telling employees that the organization values their efforts, which stimulates their motivation to improve. Employees should contribute to the company's performance and recognition approaches. L.L. Bean, for example, gives dinners or certificates exchangeable for merchandise. Winners of "Bean's Best Awards" are selected by cross-functional teams based on innovative ideas, exceptional customer service, role modeling, expertise at their jobs, and exceptional management ability.[57]

Certain key practices lead to effective employee recognition and rewards:

- Giving both individual and team awards. At The Ritz-Carlton, individual awards include verbal and written praise and the most desirable job assignments. Team awards include bonus pools and sharing in the gratuity system. Many companies have formal corporate recognition programs, such as IBM's Market Driven Quality Award for outstanding individual and team achievements in quality improvement, or the Xerox President's Award and Team Excellence Award.
- Involving everyone. Recognition programs should be available to everyone in the organization, including both front-line employees and senior management. A Monsanto Company chemical plant ties worker bonuses to results at individual units and rewards workers for helping to prevent accidents.[58] What is particularly interesting is that different programs exist in different Monsanto plants—all developed with the participation of workers. Bonus plans that failed had been ones decreed by corporate headquarters, rather than those formulated in cooperation with employees.
- Tying rewards to quality based on measurable objectives. Rewards should lead to behaviors that increase customer satisfaction and quality. When Custom Research, Inc. attains a specific corporate goal, the entire company is taken on a trip to destinations such as San Francisco and Disney World!
- Allowing peers and customers to nominate and recognize superior performance. Employees at FedEx who receive favorable comments from a customer are automatically nominated for the Golden Falcon Award. Recipients chosen by a review committee receive a gold pin, a congratulatory call from the CEO, recognition in the company newsletter, and 10 shares of company stock.
- Publicizing extensively. Many companies recognize employees through newsletters, certificates and pins, special breakfasts or luncheons, and annual events such as competitions. Making recognition public reinforces its significance, and having top managers preside in giving recognition sends an important message that they really understand and appreciate employees' efforts.
- Making recognition fun. Domino's Pizza stages a national Olympics, in which teams from the company's three regions compete in 15 events based on 15 job categories, such as doughmaking, driving, answering the telephone, and delivery. Winners, standing on platforms while the Olympic theme is played, receive medals, checks, and other forms of recognition. The finals are broadcast live to commissaries around the country.[59]

WORK ENVIRONMENT

Working in an organization that cares for its employees is perhaps the best form of motivation (see the box "How Can You Not Love This Job?!" about Google earlier in this chapter). Most companies provide many opportunities to enhance the quality of working life. They can provide personal and career counseling, career development and employability services, recreational or cultural activities, daycare, special leave for family responsibilities or for community services, flexible work hours, outplacement services, and extended health care for retirees. Johnson & Johnson's Ethicon Endo-surgery Division, in Blue Ash, Ohio, has a Wellness Center with exercise rooms and equipment to support employees in their manufacturing and R&D facility. Employees can use the center before or after working hours or during their breaks. In addition, those workers who are assembling products get regular, programmed "ergonomic" breaks every few hours, where they are required to do exercises designed to prevent repetitive motion injuries. All of these opportunities contribute to creating a more productive, safer, and more enjoyable work environment.

EMPLOYEE ENGAGEMENT AND THEORIES OF MOTIVATION

The TQ perspective of employee engagement, and empowerment in particular, are quite consistent with organizational behavior (OB) theory. In fact, most TQ-based thinking about empowerment and motivation is derived, directly or indirectly, from OB theory. Managers' willingness to accept these ideas and put them into practice, however, has been greatly increased by the incorporation of these ideas into the total quality package.

A few examples should serve to make our point. The idea that quality problems are usually attributable to management-created systems rather than employee motivation was proposed by organizational psychologist Chris Argyris.[60] Rensis Likert described an organizational system he called "System IV," which featured empowered workgroups and cross-functional teams. Douglas McGregor developed the well-known "Theory Y" approach to managing employees, which is based on the assumption that people wish to do a good job and emphasizes that people in organizations should make decisions for themselves. These are the fundamental principles of the human side of performance excellence, but they were developed decades ago by theorists concerned with reconciling the psychological needs of people and the economic needs of businesses.

The performance excellence philosophy is also consistent with several more recent theories of work motivation. This means that implementing the principles of TQ should result in increased employee motivation, because the kinds of changes that TQ represents are among those that theories say will result in increased effort on the job. Specifically, the following sections discuss performance excellence in terms of job characteristics theory, acquired need theory, and goal setting theory. The theories themselves are not described in detail, as they are covered in OB and management textbooks. Here they are compared to total quality practices.

Job Characteristics Theory

The job characteristics theory (JCT) states that people will be more motivated to work and more satisfied with their jobs to the extent that their jobs possess certain core characteristics: skill variety, task identity (doing a meaningful unit of work), task significance, autonomy, and feedback. If jobs do not have such characteristics—that is, involve few skills and give workers little control over what they do—most employees are likely to be unmotivated and dissatisfied.[61]

In general, we would expect a performance excellence focus to increase the motivating potential of jobs through increases in the foregoing task characteristics. In fact, performance excellence practices resemble some of the steps recommended by job design experts for making jobs more motivating. For example, getting people involved in problem solving and other quality improvement activities should increase both the variety of skills they use in their jobs and their perception of doing a meaningful unit of work. Empowerment should increase the degree of autonomy people feel they have in doing their work. Focusing their efforts on increasing customer satisfaction should increase people's perception of the significance of their roles in the organization.

Three factors have been identified that will influence the way people react to jobs that have high levels of the task characteristics: knowledge and skill, growth-need strength, and satisfaction with contextual factors.[62] Knowledge of how to do one's job should be enhanced by the training that often accompanies performance excellence initiatives and empowerment. Growth-need strength, by contrast, is rooted in people's personalities and is unlikely to be affected by TQ. Satisfaction with contextual factors (company policies, working conditions) may increase with implementation of performance excellence, as various groups in the organization make improvements to satisfy internal customers. This means it is likely not only to increase the levels of task characteristics that people find motivating, but also to change two of the three factors that influence how people react to these characteristics, in such a way that they are more likely to find such jobs motivating. Such work design practices prevalent in high-performing organizations as job enlargement, job rotation, and job enrichment are supported by this theory.

Acquired Needs Theory

Another perspective on employee motivation states that people are motivated by work that fulfills their needs. Specifically, the need for achievement, the need for affiliation, and the need for power have been the subjects of extensive research.[63] People who have a strong need for achievement will work hard to reach a high standard of excellence. The need for affiliation refers to the desire to have close relationships with other people, for example as part of a team. The need for power is the desire to have influence over one's environment and the people in it.

How will the implementation of performance excellence, including empowerment practices, influence people who are motivated by these needs? As research has not addressed this question, we can only speculate. The need most likely to be fulfilled by participation in quality-based initiatives is the need for affiliation. The most obvious way this would occur is through the formation of self-managed or cross-functional teams. A TQ focus promotes close relationships between people in the same or different subunits, and even in different organizations in the customer-supplier chain.

The connection between quality and the need for achievement is a bit murkier. Effective utilization of quality principles should allow organizations to achieve higher levels of performance in such areas as quality and customer satisfaction, but these achievements are likely to come through team, rather than individual, efforts. Thus, the opportunity to participate in such efforts is likely to motivate people with high achievement motivation only if they can see the relationship between their own work and team performance and feel a sense of achievement on that basis. Performance excellence and empowerment are likely to be motivating for employees with a high need for power. In fact, employees with a high need for power are likely to be quite frustrated with traditional organizations that give them little influence. Empowerment, if it follows the principles described in this chapter, should go a long way toward reducing this frustration and provide newfound motivation for individuals with a high need for power.

However, empowerment can be a double-edged sword. Middle managers whose subordinates are being empowered may feel that their own needs for power are less fulfilled in a performance excellence environment. This need not occur, as empowerment of lower-level employees should be accompanied by finding new and fulfilling roles for middle managers. Many organizations will not be able to accomplish this, however, and even if they do, a certain number of middle managers with a high need for power will miss the old "command and control" type of organization.

Goal-Setting Theory

The central insight of goal-setting theory is that people whose goals are clear will work more quickly, perform better, and generally be more motivated than people who lack clear goals (you might look back on the Los Alamos National Bank case as a practical example of this concept). A great deal of research has been performed on goal-setting theory and generally supports the theory's predictions. According to the theory, goals will be motivating to people when they are specific and difficult, and people accept them as their own.[64] However, goals should also be attainable; specific, challenging goals that seem impossible are demotivating.

How does goal-setting theory relate to total quality in general and empowerment in particular? This connection has not been the subject of research, but we can offer some conjecture about it. One likely link between empowerment and goal setting is the goal-acceptance aspect of the theory. Although there has been some debate about this among scholars, it seems that people who set their own goals (as in empowerment) are likely to be more motivated by them than are people whose goals are set by others (as in the traditional organization). People who set their own goals may also find that their goals are clearer (to them, at least).

The principle that goals should be specific and difficult can be related to total quality and empowerment. In general, the principle of breakthrough improvement leads to fairly difficult goals. In traditional management, when an acceptable level of performance is reached, people simply try to maintain it. In a quality-focused environment, an acceptable performance level would be a stepping-stone to further improvements. Therefore, the difficulty of goals would be enhanced by performance excellence approaches. Goals need not be impossible; even incremental (and thus seemingly achievable) improvement goals supported by the kaizen philosophy fall into this realm. One wonders whether this compromises the long-run specificity of goals.

Continuous improvement is a noble ideal, likely to spur heroic efforts in many cases. When, if ever, is the goal reached? Can workers be motivated by a goal of eternal improvement or must milestones be placed along the way to maintain motivation and enthusiasm? Perhaps as organizations gain more experience with performance excellence, such questions will be answered. Given the increasing importance of continuous improvement for competitiveness, organizations will need to find ways to motivate employees for sustained improvement in order to be economically viable in today's complex business environment.

Review and Discussion Questions

1. Describe how the practices at PRO-TEC in the Performance Excellence Profile illustrate principles of employee engagement, empowerment, and motivation. What does the company do to foster employee engagement? How might employee engagement activities be linked to its performance improvement, customer-focused, and strategic planning processes?
2. Explain the concept of employee engagement. How does it differ from employee involvement?
3. What might you see in an organization that provides evidence that employees are truly engaged?
4. Provide several examples of employee involvement. How might these fall in the continuum shown in Figure 9.1?
5. What is employee empowerment? What do you see as the most important barriers to employee empowerment?
6. How might the concept of empowerment be employed in a classroom?
7. Have you ever experienced fear in the workplace? What impact did it have on your performance? Is a little bit of fear a good thing for motivating performance?
8. Are there circumstances in which employee empowerment would hurt rather than improve quality? Why would this occur?
9. What risks does an organization face in empowering its employees?
10. How will employees know when they are empowered?
11. What sort of performance appraisal process would be appropriate for empowered workers in a total quality company?
12. Which of the principles of empowerment do you think is most important? Why?
13. Have you ever received exceptional service from an empowered employee? What happened? How did you react to it?
14. In what ways do DynMcDermott, Hewitt, and LANB exemplify the principles of employee engagement?
15. What can managers do to mitigate the risks of failure associated with employee engagement?
16. Which theory of motivation do you see as most consistent with empowerment? Why?
17. Philip Atkinson tells the story of a government agency that fired up its employees to do great things with a wilderness training experience.[65] One young man, on his return to work, noticed some parking spaces owned by the organization in a busy part of the city. The spaces were always free and could be rented for a substantial sum. The young man made a proposal to do so, but it was rejected out of hand. Undeterred, he rented the

spaces himself, only to find that there was no mechanism to deposit the checks into corporate accounts. Eventually, the young man left the company to work for one in which people's ideas were taken more seriously, and initiative was valued. How does this story illustrate the principles of empowerment discussed in this chapter?

18. Think of a job you have had. Apply the Hackman and Oldham model to evaluate how the job design impacted your motivation and satisfaction, as well as organizational effectiveness.
19. How does empowerment differ from such approaches as job enrichment and other forms of employee involvement?

CASES

The Frustrated Manager

A professional colleague who teaches total quality concepts received the following e-mail from a former student:[66]

> I was wondering if you could offer me some thoughts on a particular situation that plagues the company I work for. Our workforce is unionized and has a long history of anti-company sentiment. Upper management has set up the assembly area as an example of employee involvement and the blossoming empowered workforce to show off to customers. They often bring in customers to help gain future contracts. One customer in particular is very sensitive to cost, quality, and schedule, and has had some bad experiences with us in the past. The customer has clearly told us that it wants to see an empowered workforce making key decisions. If this does not happen, it will not award the contract. This information has been relayed to the work teams in the area, but several work teams, in their team meetings, tell us they don't want to be empowered. The attitude (as I see it) appears to be as follows: "We know how to build our products, the customers do not. So, get the customers out of our business and tell them to take the product when we're done with it, regardless of how we choose to build it." As many times as I inform them that customers will not buy our products in that manner, I am given the same answer. How would you suggest I get these teams to take the gun away from their own heads? They have a management who is willing to hand over the power. They have the tools necessary to make informed decisions on the shop floor. They just don't have the inspiration to take the power and to run with it. My question is simple: Is it possible to create an empowered workforce in an old union environment?

How would you advise him?

Landmark Dining: Employee Engagement and Motivation

Landmark Dining closely monitors employee turnover, the rate of completion of individual development plans, absenteeism, sales per server, results from exit interviews, and the work environment. When declining results occur in any of these areas, they are investigated and improved through the use of cross-functional improvement teams. For example, last year, a team investigated a decrease in the completion of exit interviews. The team found that the lower numbers reflected a large decline in interviews with servers and then linked this to a lack of time for the Business Excellence Director to manage the interview process. The methodology was streamlined and the process was delegated to Staffing Solutions, Inc. The current completion rate has improved to higher levels than in previous years.

However, the company doesn't feel that this information, being somewhat passive and after-the-fact, provides a complete picture of employee satisfaction. Thus, it believes that it should develop a formal employee satisfaction survey as the key tool for determining employee satisfaction. What specific factors should it address in such a survey? (See the Landmark Dining case in Chapter 8 also for a description of team processes that may be relevant here.) How should it use the results in conjunction with the Voices system (see the Landmark Dining case in Chapter 6)?

The MBA Candidate

Gretchen Faulkner was interviewing for an MBA program. She was a liberal arts major in college, and for the last several years had worked at the art museum in the city where she attended college. During the conversation, the MBA program director asked her why she decided to quit and pursue an MBA. "Actually, I had been quite happy with the job," she said. "After I'd been there for three years, I was able to work more autonomously, troubleshooting problems, taking steps to resolve those problems, and taking the initiative to improve my job. Guided by the mission statements of the museum and my department, I felt empowered to make changes or take steps to achieve the museum's strategic goals. After a while, I learned that my job wasn't entirely about following strict procedures. It was a real epiphany for me to figure out that I could make decisions and think on my feet to benefit a visitor, a volunteer, a co-worker, etc. For example, every year in May, the museum experiences a rush of school tours. It's the busiest time of year with school groups touring every day, Tuesday through Friday, on the hour or half-hour. The more years I worked through this crunch, the better equipped I was to promote positive changes for the 'spring rush.' Two years ago, the museum had a spring exhibit of Egyptian artifacts that was expected to attract many school tours. Working with many other departments like Security and Marketing, I was able to help implement school tours on Mondays when we were normally closed to the public and relieve some of the problems associated with the high demand. That said, though, I ended up leaving the museum because there was no place for me to go in my position."

How does Gretchen's job relate to the Hackman and Oldham job characteristics theory? What aspects motivated her? What positive outcomes in the model were evident? What aspects of the theory explain her decision to leave?

Endnotes

1. 2003 Malcolm Baldrige National Quality Award Recipient Profile, U.S Department of Commerce.
2. Quoted in David Ulrich and Dale Lake, "Organizational Capability: Creating Competitive Advantage," *Academy of Management Executive*, Vol. 5, No. 1, 1991, pp. 77–92.
3. James L. Heskett, W. Earl Sasser, Jr., and Leonard A. Schlesinger, *The Service Profit Chain*, New York: Free Press, 1997, p. 101.
4. Lawler, Mohrman, and Ledford, *Employee Involvement*, p. 60.
5. Linda Grant, "Happy Workers, High Returns," *Fortune*, January 12, 1998, p. 81. A formal research study of the relationship between employee engagement and business outcomes is reported in James K. Harter, Frank L. Schmidt, and Theodore L. Hayes, "Business-Unit-Level Relationship Between Employee Satisfaction, Employee Engagement, and Business Outcomes: A Meta-Analysis," *Journal of Applied Psychology*, 87, 2, 2002, pp. 268–279.
6. See Casey Ichniowski and Kathryn Shaw, "The effects of human resource management systems on economic performance: An International Comparison of U.S. and Japanese Plants," *Management Science*, May 1999, Vol. 45, No. 5 pp. 704–721; Juan J. Tarı´ and Vicente Sabater, "Human aspects in a quality management context and their effects on performance." Int. J. of Human Resource Management, Vol. 17, No. 3, March 2006, pp. 484–503.
7. Quoted in Whiteley, *The Customer-Driven Company*, p. 180.
8. The Employee Involvement Association's e-newsletter *Ideas & Inspirations*, which gave credit to *The CEO Refresher* by Freda Turner, PhD. http://www.bcpublicservice.ca/awards/ai/ai_index/emp_engage/emp_engage.htm.
9. Lawler, Mohrman, and Ledford, *Employee Involvement*, p. 105.
10. Hal F. Rosenbluth, "Have Quality, Will Travel," *The TQM Magazine*, November/December 1992, pp. 267–270.
11. Adam Lashinski, "Google is No. 1: Search and enjoy," *Fortune*, January 8, 2007. http://money.cnn.com/magazines/fortune/fortune_archive/2007/01/22/8397996/index.htm vaccessed on 4/9/09.
12. Joseph J. Gufreda, Larry A. Maynard, and Lucy N. Lytle, "Employee Involvement in the Quality Process," in Ernst & Young Quality Improvement Consulting Group, *Total Quality!: An Executive's Guide for the 1990s* (Homewood, IL: Richard D. Irwin, 1990).
13. Tom J. Peters, *Thriving on Chaos: Handbook for a Management Revolution* (New York: Alfred A. Knopf, 1988).
14. Alan Wolf, "Golden Opportunities," *Beverage World*, February 1991.
15. From materials provided by Mike Simms, former plant manager.
16. M.J. Kiernan, "The New Strategic Architecture: Learning to Compete in the Twenty-First

Century," *Academy of Management Executive*, Vol. 7, No. 1, 1993, p. 14.

17. Lawler, Mohrman, and Ledford, *Employee Involvement;* Dan Ciampa, *Total Quality: A User's Guide for Implementation*, Reading, Mass.: Addison-Wesley, 1992.
18. E.E. Lawler, S.A. Mohrman, and G.E. Ledford, *Employee Involvement and Total Quality Management*, San Francisco: Jossey-Bass, 1992.
19. Richard C. Whiteley, *The Customer-Driven Company: Moving from Talk to Action*, Reading, Mass.: Addison-Wesley, 1991.
20. Phillip A. Smith, William D. Anderson, and Stanley A. Brooking, "Employee Empowerment: A Case Study," *Production and Inventory Management*, Vol. 34, No. 3, 1993, pp. 45–50.
21. J.M. Juran, *Juran on Leadership for Quality: An Executive Handbook*, New York: Free Press, 1989, p. 264.
22. Juran, *Juran on Leadership for Quality*, pp. 147–148.
23. J.A. Conger and R.N. Kanungo, "The Empowerment Process: Integrating Theory and Practice," *Academy of Management Review*, Vol. 13, No. 3, 1988, pp. 471–482.
24. Brad Stratton, "UPS: Its Long-Term Design Delivers Quality Millions of Times Each Day," *Quality Progress*, October 1998, pp. 37–38.
25. Kathleen D. Ryan and Daniel K. Oestreich, *Driving Fear Out of the Workplace*, San Francisco: Jossey-Bass, 1991.
26. Tom Brown, "The Empowerment Myth," *Across the Board*, March/April 2001, pp. 71–72.
27. Dan Ciampa, *Total Quality: A User's Guide for Implementation*, Reading, Mass: Addison-Wesley, 1991.
28. Ciampa, ibid.
29. Brown, ibid.
30. Lawler, Mohrman, and Ledford, *Employee Involvement*, p. 51.
31. Juran, *Juran on Leadership for Quality*, p. 277.
32. Mark Kelly, *The Adventures of a Self-Managing Team*, Raleigh, N.C.: Mark Kelly Books, 1990.
33. Lawler, Mohrman, and Ledford, *Employee Involvement*, p. 47.
34. Adapted from Brad Stratton, "Texas Nameplate Company: All You Need Is Trust," *Quality Progress*, October 1998, pp. 29–32.
35. Ciampa, *Total Quality*.
36. A.R. Tenner and I.J. DeToro, *Total Quality Management: Three Steps to Continuous Improvement*, Reading, Mass.: Addison-Wesley, 1992.
37. Lawler, Mohrman, and Ledford, *Employee Involvement*, p. 60.
38. "Changing a Culture: DuPont Tries to Make Sure That Its Research Wizardry Serves the Bottom Line," *Wall Street Journal*, March 27, 1992, p. A5.
39. Robert S. Kaplan, "Texas Eastman Company," Harvard Business School Case, No. 9-190-039.
40. Peter M. Senge, *The Fifth Discipline: The Art and Practice of the Learning Organization*, New York: Doubleday Currency, 1990.
41. See *America's Choice: High Skills or Low Wages!*, National Center on Education and the Economy's Commission on the Skills of the American Workforce, National Center on Education and the Economy, 1990.
42. Lawler, Mohrman, and Ledford, *Employee Involvement*, p. 16.
43. Based on Ronald Henkoff, "Companies That Train Best," *Fortune*, March 22, 1993, pp. 62–75.
44. Jennifer Reese, "Starbucks: Inside the Coffee Cult," *Fortune*, December 9, 1996, pp. 190–200.
45. Based on Jack Johnson and Jack T. Mollen, "Ten Tasks for Managers in the Empowered Workplace," *Journal for Quality and Participation*, December 1992, pp. 18–20.
46. Lawler, Mohrman, and Ledford, *Employee Involvement*, p. 20.
47. The Conference Board, "Innovative Reward and Recognition Strategies in TQM," Report Number 1051, 1993, p. 15.
48. Brian O'Reilly, "The Mechanic Who Fixed Continental," *Fortune*, December 20, 1999, pp. 176–186.
49. Curtis Sittenfeld, "Great Job! Here's a Seat Belt!" *Fast Company*, January 2004, p. 29.
50. Timothy Aeppel, "Not All Workers Find Idea of Empowerment as Neat as It Sounds," *Wall Street Journal*, September 8, 1998, pp. A1, A13.
51. Sharafat Khan, "The Key to Being a Leader Company: Empowerment," *Journal for Quality and Participation*, January/February 1997, pp. 44–50.
52. 2005 Malcolm Baldrige National Quality Award Program Application Summary.
53. Adapted from Jon Leatherbury, "Talent Show," *Quality Progress*, Vol. 41, No. 11, November 2008, 48–55. Copyright © 2008, American Society for Quality.

54. Los Alamos National Bank 2000 Award Winner Profile, Baldrige National Quality Program, U.S. Department of Commerce, and Los Alamos National Bank Baldrige National Quality Award Application Summary.
55. "Bonus Pay: Buzzword or Bonanza?" *Business Week*, November 14, 1994, pp. 62–64.
56. Nancy J. Perry, "Here Come Richer, Riskier Pay Plans," *Fortune*, December 19, 1988, pp. 50–58; "The Nucor Story," available at http://www.nucor.com.
57. Dawn Anfuso, "L.L. Bean's TQM Efforts Put People Before Processes," *Personnel Journal*, July 1994, pp. 73–83.
58. "Bonus Pay: Buzzword or Bonanza?" *Business Week*, November 14, 1994, pp. 62–64.
59. "Domino's Pizza, Inc.," *Profiles in Quality* (Boston: Allyn and Bacon, 1991), pp. 90–93.
60. This discussion of organizational behavior theory's contribution to TQ thinking is based on J.J. Riley, "Human Resource Development: An Overview," in J.P. Kern, J.J. Riley, and L.N. Jones (eds.), *Human Resources Management*, Milwaukee: ASQC Quality Press, 1987.
61. Job characteristics theory is described in J.R. Hackman and G.R. Oldham, *Work Redesign*, Reading, Mass.: Addison-Wesley Publishing Company, 1980.
62. Hackman and Oldham, *Work Redesign*.
63. D.C. McClelland, *Assessing Human Motivation*, Morristown, N.J.: General Learning Press, 1971. See also D.C. McClelland and R. E. Boyatzis, "Leadership Motive Pattern and Long-Term Success in Management," *Journal of Applied Psychology*, 1982, pp. 67, 737–743.
64. Edwin Locke, "Toward a Theory of Task Performance and Incentives," *Organizational Behavior and Human Performance*, Fall 1968, pp. 167–189. For a more recent treatment of goal-setting, see Mark E. Tubbs and Steven E. Ekeberg, "The Role of Intentions in Work Motivation: Implications for Goal-Setting Theory and Research," *Academy of Management Review*, January 1991, pp. 180–199.
65. Philip Atkinson, "Leadership, Total Quality, and Cultural Change," *Management Services*, Vol. 35, No. 6, 1991, pp. 16–19.
66. My thanks go to Professor James Thom of Purdue University for sharing this anecdote. The actual letter was edited to preserve the confidentially of the company.

Leadership and Organizational Change

PART 4

CHAPTER 10 Leadership for Performance Excellence 365

CHAPTER 11 Performance Excellence and Organizational Change 393

LEADERSHIP FOR PERFORMANCE EXCELLENCE

CHAPTER 10

Performance Excellence Profile: Stoner, Inc.[1]

Stoner, Inc. is a small, family-owned business located in Lancaster County, the heart of Pennsylvania Amish country. The company was founded more than 60 years ago by Paul Stoner, an orphan, chemist, and entrepreneur who started the business by making printing inks. In 1986, the company was purchased by Paul Stoner's grandson, Rob Ecklin, who repositioned the company for growth and evolved the product line to more than 300 specialized cleaners, lubricants, coatings, and car care products. Today, Stoner is the largest supplier in the United States of aerosol and bulk release agents for plastics and other molded materials. In other markets, which include automotive car care and electronics cleaning, Stoner is a niche player but is still highly competitive with much larger companies.

Stoner, Inc. President Rob Ecklin personally managed the company throughout the 1980s. Although Ecklin is still the sole owner, in 1990 he empowered a six-member senior leadership team to manage the business. These hands-on leaders facilitate strategic planning, develop team processes, and mentor team members to implement the company's strategy. The company's core values—exceed customer expectations, foster and develop a motivated team, be safety/health/environment responsible, innovate new and better solutions, and continuously improve—guide all aspects of Stoner's business culture.

At the heart of Stoner's success is the Stoner Excellence System, visualized as a pyramid with leadership at the top, supported by strategy and process. Stakeholder Value has a prominent place in the center of the system and is surrounded by Assess, Improve, Implement—the company's simple, but effective, three-step process for continuous improvement. All Stoner employees, known as team members, understand that continuous improvement is the key to sustaining competitive success and are focused on finding and implementing ways to add value for customers. Stoner's Advisory Board, which includes people outside of the company, is another resource to help provide direction and focus to the strategic planning process and advice on priority improvements.

The board helps evaluate risk, assess leadership effectiveness, and oversee financial and ethical governance.

The leadership team uses a scorecard called "Stoner 60" to set goals and measure business initiatives. The scorecard identifies 60 key operational measurements, linked goals, and strategic milestones for each of the next five years. Senior leaders regularly monitor and discuss business results; compare them to the Stoner 60 goals; and develop improvement action items at weekly, monthly, and quarterly meetings. Stoner also uses an integrated key indicator database, known as "Key 1," to collect, analyze, and deploy data to help in daily decision-making. The database helps to spot emerging trends that require corrective action or reallocation of resources. To manage data and increase customer satisfaction, Stoner has implemented an enterprise resource planning system that helps ensure that 100 percent of orders are shipped on the same day they are received and has reduced shipping errors to less than 0.05 percent of all orders shipped.

Creating stakeholder value at Stoner begins with the customer. Product managers meet with more than 100 customers per year and sales team members speak by phone with more than 1,000 customers each week to help define the company's direction based on what their customers want or need. Since 2000, Stoner has won three times as many customers as it has lost and over the past five years has retained more than 98 percent of its top customers—those accounting for over 60 percent of the business. Results from a national industry survey show that Stoner's attention to its customers pays off. The company ranks first in satisfaction on four of the five factors most important to its customers: quality, delivery, service, and value. It is in the top quartile for the fifth factor, price. Other stakeholders include Stoner's owner, Rob Ecklin; team members; suppliers; and the community.

Through clearly articulated goals, the company's vision and mission, its strategic objectives, its values and beliefs, and the established Stoner Excellence System process, Team Stoner has achieved remarkable results. Stoner, Inc. has sustained consistent profitability that has grown along with its sales, fueling the company's improvement initiatives and growth. Manufacturing productivity has increased 150 percent since 1991, and weekly average output of aerosol can products has increased 33 percent from 1998 to 2003. Stoner's 39 percent return on assets exceeds the industry average by 29 percent and its best competitor by 14 percent.

Leadership is fundamental to management and organizational behavior and is on just about everyone's short list of prerequisites for organizational success. Thus, it is not surprising that leadership plays a crucial role in high-performing organizations like Stoner, Inc. Virtually every article and book written about quality emphasizes leadership. Deming set the stage for leadership for quality. Several of his 14 Points refer to leadership either directly or indirectly:

- Point 1. Create and publish to all employees a statement of the aims and purposes of the company or other organization. The management must demonstrate constantly their commitment to this statement.

- Point 7. Teach and institute leadership.
- Point 8. Drive out fear. Create trust. Create a climate for innovation.
- Point 12. Remove barriers that rob people of pride in workmanship.
- Point 14. Take action to accomplish the transformation.

One can safely say that the other points also require the necessity of strong leadership to accomplish them.

Leadership is the first category in the Malcolm Baldrige National Quality Award and is recognized as the "driver" of performance excellence. Indeed, leadership is seen by many experts as the *sine qua non* (if you don't have it, you have nothing) of quality and performance excellence. A compelling example is Motorola's former CEO, Bob Galvin, who made a habit of making quality the first item on the agenda of executive staff meetings—and leaving the meeting before discussion of financials. His actions spoke louder than words: if quality was taken care of, financial performance would follow. His leadership guided Motorola to become one of the first winners of the Malcolm Baldrige National Quality Award. A co-director of the Juran Center for Leadership in Quality at the University of Minnesota observed:

- Despite substantial efforts, only a few U.S. organizations have reached world-class excellence.
- Even fewer companies have sustained such excellence during changes in leadership.
- Most corporate quality failures rest with leadership.[2]

This chapter will:

- discuss the importance of leadership for quality,
- describe the role of leaders in performance excellence,
- provide some examples of leaders who have inspired their organizations to achieve quality and performance excellence in businesses,
- provide examples of leadership practices in high-performing organizations, and
- compare the TQ view of leadership to several prominent leadership theories.

PERSPECTIVES ON LEADERSHIP

In practice, the notion of leadership can be as elusive as the notion of quality itself. Most definitions of leadership reflect an assortment of behaviors, for example:

- vision that stimulates hope and mission that transforms hope into reality;
- radical servanthood that saturates the organization;
- stewardship that shepherds its resources;
- integration that drives its economy;
- the courage to sacrifice personal or team goals for the greater community good;
- communication that coordinates its efforts;
- consensus that drives unity of purpose;
- empowerment that grants permission to make mistakes, encourages the honesty to admit them, and gives the opportunity to learn from them; and

- conviction that provides the stamina to continually strive toward business excellence.[3]

A more formal perspective of leadership described by the Human Development and Leadership Division of the American Society for Quality summarizes six competencies for leadership based on more than 50 authors' thoughts on leadership:[4]

- *Navigator* – creates shared meaning and provides direction toward a vision, mission, goal, or end result. This competency may entail risk taking and requires constant evaluation of the operating environment to ensure that progress in the appropriate direction is achieved.
- *Communicator* – effectively listens and articulates messages to provide shared meaning. This competency involves the creation of an environment that reduces barriers and fosters open, honest, and honorable communication.
- *Mentor* – provides others with a role to guide their actions. This competency requires the development of personal relationships that help others develop trust, integrity, and ethical decision making.
- *Learner* – continuously develops personal knowledge, skills, and abilities through formal study, experience, reflection, and recreation.
- *Builder* – shapes processes and structures to allow for the achievement of goals and outcomes. This competency also entails assuming responsibility for ensuring that necessary resources are available and the evaluation of processes to ensure effective resource use.
- *Motivator* – influences others to take action in a desirable manner. This competency also includes the evaluation of people's actions to ensure that they are performing consistently with the mission, goal, or end result.

A collection of personal leadership characteristics underlies these six competencies:

1. *Accountability* – taking responsibility for the organization or community that the leader serves, along with accountability for his or her own actions. This provides the means for measuring performance and dealing with performance that is unsatisfactory.
2. *Courage* – the mental or moral strength to venture forward, persevere, and withstand danger, fear, or difficulty with a firmness of mind and will, allowing leaders to navigate into the unknown.
3. *Humility* – the quality that gives excellent leaders their ability to mentor, communicate, and learn, and to understand that they are servants of those that follow.
4. *Integrity* – the ability to discern what is right from wrong and commit to the right path.
5. *Creativity* – the ability to see possibilities, horizons, and futures that don't yet exist, enabling the leader to help create a shared vision for the organization.
6. *Perseverance* – sticking to a task or purpose, no matter how hard or troublesome. This is vital to overcoming obstacles and motivating subordinates.

7. *Well-being* – the ability to stay healthy in both work and play, demonstrating the importance of being ready to implement leadership competencies when needed.

These characteristics provide the foundation for exercising the competencies. Many notable leaders, from presidents to CEOs, have exhibited these characteristics, and they are reflected in the Baldrige Leadership category criteria.

Although true leadership applies to everyone in an organization, we generally think of *executive leadership*, which focuses on the roles of senior managers in guiding an organization to fulfill its mission and meet its goals, when we use the term. The many activities that senior executives perform include the following:

- defining and communicating business directions
- ensuring that goals and expectations are met
- reviewing business performance and taking appropriate action
- creating an enjoyable work environment that promotes creativity, innovation, and continual improvement
- soliciting input and feedback from customers
- ensuring that employees are effective contributors to the business
- motivating, inspiring, and energizing employees
- recognizing employee contributions
- providing honest feedback

Effective leaders empower employees to assume ownership of problems or opportunities, and to be proactive in implementing improvements and making decisions in the best interests of the organization. The philosophy of the CEO at the former GTE Directories Corporation (now part of Verizon) summarizes this facet of leadership nicely: *Put a stake in the ground, get out of the way, and stay the course.*

Why is leadership so important to quality and performance excellence? Leaders establish plans and goals for the organization. If the plans and goals do not include quality or, worse yet, are antithetical to quality, the quality effort will die. Leaders help to shape the culture of the organization through key decisions and symbolic actions. If they help to shape a culture that puts convenience or short-term benefits ahead of quality, it will die. Leaders distribute resources. If resources are showered on programs that cut short-term costs while quality is starved for resources, quality will die. This list could go on. Virtually everything that an organization needs to succeed in meeting its customers' expectations—goals, plans, culture, resources—can either be helped or hurt by leaders (see box "The Man Who Hated Quality"). With this in mind, let us examine in more detail the roles that leaders play in a total quality company.

Many writers and managers have tried to define what a manager must do as an effective quality leader. Edwin L. Artzt was Chairman of Procter & Gamble, one of the nation's oldest and most successful companies and one of the earliest to emphasize quality. He stated: "To lead quality—and I'm talking about leaders at every level in an organization—means providing the clear strategic choices, the guiding principles, and the disciplined application to continually improve and reinvent ourselves ... and to do that with a focus on the good of the whole."[5]

The criteria for the Malcolm Baldrige National Quality Award also dwell heavily on leadership. Here is the philosophy of leadership within the Baldrige criteria: "An organization's senior leaders should set directions and create a customer focus, clear and visible values, and high expectations.... The directions, values, and expectations should balance the needs of all your stakeholders. Your leaders should ensure the creation of strategies, systems, and methods for achieving excellence, stimulating innovation, and building knowledge and capabilities. The values and strategies should help guide all activities and decisions of your organization."[6]

Senior leaders should inspire and motivate the entire workforce and should encourage all employees to contribute, to develop and learn, to be innovative, and to be creative. Senior leaders should serve as role models through their ethical behavior and their personal involvement in planning, communications, coaching, development of future leaders, review of organizational performance, and employee recognition. As role models, they can reinforce values and expectations when building leadership, commitment, and initiative throughout the organization.[7]

A final overview of the concept of quality leadership comes from Dan Ciampa, president and chief executive officer of Rath & Strong, a consulting group specializing in total quality: The mandate is to inspire, to invoke commitment, to enable employees to form a different concept of the organization in which they believe deeply, and to change without being threatened.[8]

The Man Who Hated Quality[9]

Jack Welch, CEO of General Electric, is probably regarded as the most admired CEO of his generation. The following dialog about General Electric's Six Sigma quality initiative (see Chapter 3) took place between a *Fortune* magazine reporter and Welch in 1999, prior to his retirement from GE:

> *Fortune*: Jack, you're doing a total-quality thing 10 or 15 years after the rest of corporate America did it. Why are you doing it, and why now?
>
> Welch: There was only one guy in the whole country who hated quality more than me. I always believed quality would come from just operating well and fast, and all these slogans were nonsense. The guy who hated quality more was Larry Bossidy. He hated quality totally. Then he left GE and went to Allied Signal. In order to resurrect Allied Signal, Larry went out, saw Motorola, and did some stuff on Six Sigma. And he called me one day and he said, "Jack, this ain't b.s.—this is real stuff, this is really great stuff." We poll 10,000 employees every year. In '95 they came back and said, "We desperately need a quality issue." So Six Sigma was something we adopted then. The results are fantastic. We're going to get $1.2 billion of gain this year. For years our operating margin was never over 10. It's been improving, and it's going to be 16.7 this year. Our working-capital turns were four for 35 years. It will be nine this year.

Jack Welch showed that not only was he a strong leader but also that he didn't have all the answers. Welch needed to continually learn—which is one of the hallmarks of leadership for quality.

THE ROLES OF A QUALITY LEADER

Underlying the concept of quality leadership are three clear imperatives for managers who aspire to quality leadership. First, they must establish a vision. Second, they must live the values. Third, they must lead the improvement efforts. Let's examine each of these in turn.

ESTABLISH A VISION

Leaders are visionaries; they manage for the future, not the past (think back to the first of Deming's 14 Points). Vision is crucial at every level during times of change. Leaders recognize the radical organizational changes taking place today as opportunities to move closer to total quality. Jack Welch, for example, pushed GE to become a leader among traditional Old Economy companies in embracing the Internet after noticing his wife Christmas shopping on the Web. "I realized that if I didn't watch it, I would retire as a Neanderthal," he was reported as saying, "So I just started reading everything I could about it." He began by pairing 1,000 Web-savvy mentors with senior people to get his top teams up to Internet speed quickly.[10] Visionary leaders create mental and verbal pictures of desirable future states and share these visions with their organizational partners, including customers, suppliers, and employees.

A **vision** is a vivid concept of what an organization could be (we introduced this in Chapter 5 in the context of strategic planning). For Texas Nameplate Company, the vision is simple: *We want to be the best.* A vision is a striking depiction of possibilities, of potential. It is a dream, both in the sense of being desirable and in the sense of being a long way from the current reality, but it is not an "impossible dream." "Establishing" a vision implies both the intellectual and emotional work of conceiving the vision and the interpersonal and managerial work of communicating the vision to the organization and leading employees to embrace it, and this process is the responsibility of leadership.

Quality-oriented visions have inspired some of the most dramatic corporate success stories in business history. IBM was founded on the idea of exceptional customer service and fair treatment of employees. Federal Express sought what at the time was seen as almost inconceivable speed and reliability in the package delivery market. Apple Computers wanted to make computing accessible to the masses.[11] These visions were creative, captivating, and most of all achievable.

Jane Carroll, president of The Forum Corporation, Europe/Asia, emphasizes the visionary role of leadership for quality, which she calls focus. She believes that most managers do not understand the need for a quality vision and their personal involvement in establishing it: "In our experience, very few CEOs have a real sense of what their role is in the quality improvement process. It goes far beyond simply being a cheerleader and handing out an occasional award. Top management has to provide the proper focus for the organization. This is not something that can be delegated."[12]

Putting together a vision is hard work, but quality leaders do not have to do it alone. They can draw on the talents and imagination of all the members of their organizations in developing their vision. In fact, in many organizations, people are walking around with "minivisions" of their own that sound like "if only we could [do something they have been told can't be done], things would be so much better around here." The raw material for a vision may be all around leaders in the organization. The first step may be simply listening for it. Leaders who are open to the ideas of people throughout the organization will be much better prepared to develop a vision that people will accept.

In the current competitive environment, if a given organization is not pursuing a customer-oriented vision, competing organizations probably are and are planning to use their vision to win over the competition's customers (or are already doing so). This is why a quality vision is such a crucial first step in quality leadership. An organization with no vision about how to create long-term customer loyalty has little chance of survival (unless, of course, it's a monopoly).

The second part of establishing a vision is instilling it in all the members of the organization. This will be a lot easier if many people were involved in the first part of the process, and the leader doesn't act like Moses coming down the mountain with the stone tablets. When Corning Glass instituted a quality vision, Chairman Jamie Houghton introduced it to employees at all levels in countries all over the world. Communication is vitally important. A leader who is able to present the vision in an intriguing way has an advantage in trying to capture the imagination of the people in the organization, according to Francis Adamson, manager of quality engineering/TQM at Heinz U.S.A.: "The ability to fascinate is one of the most powerful tools of the charismatic leader. Leaders can use it to weave a fabric of commitment throughout the organization. This is the empowering function of the leader: allowing everyone to buy into the vision."[13]

Live the Values

Pursuing the quality vision commits the organization to living by a set of values such as devotion to customers, continuous improvement, and teamwork. A manager who hopes the organization will embrace and live by these values must live them to the utmost. As former Procter & Gamble Chairman and CEO Edwin Artzt puts it, "Leaders of the best companies profoundly believe in, and promote, the core values of customer-focused quality."[14] By "walking the talk," leaders serve as role models for the whole organization.

Many CEOs lead quality training sessions, serve on quality improvement teams, work on projects that do not usually require top-level input, and personally visit customers. For example, senior managers at Texas Instruments Defense Systems and Electronics Group (now part of Raytheon) led 150 of 1,900 cross-functional teams. At Custom Research, Inc., the top four senior leaders ensure that employees have the responsibility, training, and information they need to do their jobs through empowering everyone to do what it takes to serve clients, work with nine other senior people to set strategy, and make middle managers the real leaders.

When dramatic organizational changes are taking place, people in organizations are very sensitive to any sign of hypocrisy. A leader can undermine 100 hours of speeches with one decision that reveals his or her commitment to quality values to be superficial. This is not just a symbolic issue: Harvard's David Garvin found in a study of the air conditioner industry that the quality of a firm's products was strongly related to the quality values expressed by management.[15]

Managers' actions can symbolize their commitment to quality-oriented values in many concrete ways. For example, they can attend training programs on various aspects of quality, instead of just sending others. They can practice continuous improvement in processes that they control, such as strategic planning and capital budgeting. Perhaps most importantly, they can provide adequate funding for quality efforts, so that TQ will not be the "poor cousin" to other business issues.[16]

Virtually every management team that has staged a major quality turnaround has recognized this need to "walk," not just "talk," quality. In looking back on the return to financial success from near-bankruptcy of his company, Harley-Davidson's Ron Hutchinson stated: "We realized that, if we really wanted to communicate to our people a change in the company's direction and approach, what we needed to do as senior managers was demonstrate that we were going to live by a new set of rules."

Lead Continuous Improvement

Beyond establishing a vision for the organization and expressing quality values through their decisions and actions, quality-oriented leaders must lead the continuous process improvement efforts that are the meat and potatoes of total quality management. All of the vision and values in the world are worthless if the organization is not continuously making strides to improve its performance in the eyes of customers. Visions of world-class quality and competitiveness can only be achieved if an organization keeps finding ways to do things a little better and a little faster. Leaders must be at the center of these efforts.

Managers are sometimes reluctant to take an active role in the organization's improvement efforts for fear of dominating or undercutting their newly empowered workers. Like many aspects of management, this is a question of balance, but it is a mistake for managers to remain uninvolved in process improvement efforts. Harry Levinson and Chuck DeHont, quality leaders at Sierra Semiconductor, have thought about this dilemma and concluded: "It is often perceived, incorrectly, that management should never specify how problems should be solved, that to do so would be considered improper delegation. What is actually true is that managers who set no rules for how problems should be solved have abdicated their leadership roles."[17]

There are a number of ways for managers to lead continuous improvement, and which ones make the most sense will depend on the specific organization. One option already mentioned is for leaders to lead by example, by working continuously to improve the processes that they control. For some of these processes, organizational members are among the customers, which gives management the opportunity to model for them the behaviors associated with obtaining and acting on customer input.[18] If management were to streamline the capital budgeting procedure by speeding up the process and eliminating non–value-added activities, it would provide a powerful example for people to emulate.

A second way that managers can lead process improvement is to help organization members prioritize processes to work on. Here managers can take advantage of their knowledge of the "big picture" and suggest avenues of improvement that are likely to have big payoffs in terms of quality improvement and customer satisfaction. This point was underscored by a recent statement by Gerhard Schulmeyer, president and CEO of Asea Brown Boveri, a multinational company headquartered in Germany: It doesn't help simply to encourage everybody to work harder. The issue is to take a fresh look at the problems and concentrate our efforts on core processes that have the largest leverage in improving our position in the market.[19]

A third way is to inspire people to do things they do not believe they can do. Motorola set aggressive goals of reducing defects per unit of output in every operation by 100-fold in four years and reducing cycle time by 50 percent each year. One of Hewlett-Packard's goals is to reduce the interval between product concept and investment payback by one half in five years. The 3M Company seeks to generate 25 percent of sales from products less than two years old. To promote such "stretch goals," leaders provide the resources and support necessary to meet them, especially training.

Of course, managers leading process improvement bear some responsibility for educating all their associates as to how the various processes within the company fit together. If this is done effectively, organization members will be able eventually to set their own priorities for process improvement.

Managers also can lead this effort by removing barriers to success in process improvement.[20] Barriers may consist of a nettlesome standard operating procedure or a recalcitrant manager in a key position. Without leadership from management, such barriers may undermine efforts at process improvement. Of course, in dealing with such barriers managers must continue to operate in a manner consistent with quality values. For example, managers who balk at changes must be treated with respect and their reservations considered seriously, even if they are eventually overruled.

One final way for managers to lead process improvement is to keep track of improvement efforts, to encourage them, and to provide recognition when key milestones are reached. Companies often recognize and reward groups of employees for exceptional performance. Besides monetary awards, they might buy lunch for an entire division or bring in ice cream for the whole corporation. One top manager of our acquaintance makes it a practice always to be present for such recognition ceremonies. If he cannot attend, the ceremony is rescheduled. By doing this, the manager is accomplishing several things at once: he is showing his sincere interest in the process, he is providing reinforcement for those people working to make key changes, and he is letting his subordinates know that it is not acceptable to make excuses for missing quality-related functions. (For an additional and unusual example of leadership for continuous improvement, see box "*Tampopo:* The Quest for the Perfect Noodle Soup.")

LEADERSHIP FOR PERFORMANCE EXCELLENCE IN ACTION

Some of the best examples of leadership come from Baldrige Award recipients. In this section we describe some of the leadership activities of two of them, Branch-Smith Printing Division, and SSM Health Care, focusing on the three key roles of

Tampopo: The Quest for the Perfect Noodle Soup[21]

Like many aspects of organizations, the nature of leadership is changed dramatically by TQ. Moving beyond a command-and-control mentality, leaders in a TQ organization help their associates to provide better products and services to customers. This style of leadership is personified by Goro, a truck driver and noodle expert who, in the film *Tampopo*, helps Tampopo in her quest to create the perfect noodle soup. An unlikely blend of western and samurai movie clichés, *Tampopo* is at the same time a parody and a virtual roadmap for continuous quality improvement.

Goro and his friend Guntu meet Tampopo when they stop in at the Lai Lai noodle stand for a quick bite. When Goro tells a drunken customer that Tampopo's noodles are mediocre, he gets taken outside and beaten up, a fate that (metaphorically at least) awaits many leaders who publicly state that the status quo is not good enough. But Tampopo is wise enough to accept Goro's judgment on the poor quality of her noodles and asks for his help.

One of Goro's first suggestions is to study her customers as they enter the shop, so that she can adjust her service to their needs. Tampopo soon begins to recognize that quality noodle soup involves a lot more than just cooking. She closes her shop until further notice and devotes herself to elevating the quality of her noodle business. In a scene reminiscent of Rocky, Tampopo (now in a sweat suit) runs through the park, with Goro following on a bicycle. She then practices lifting pots of boiling water, working to reduce her soup production time below three minutes.

The next step is to learn from the competition. The nearby shop that Goro and Tampopo visit first is full, demonstrating that customers are there, if Tampopo is good enough. In the second shop, the cooks talk to each other too much and forget people's orders. In the third, the cook's motions are elegant, with no wasted motion. In the fourth, a busy place by a rail station, the cook must keep track of many orders at once. Tampopo shows her progress by rattling off all the orders that have been given. At the fifth shop, the broth is so good that Goro and Tampopo stoop to spying to try to duplicate the recipe. At the sixth, the owners see what is going on and kick them out, but Tampopo tells them they have nothing worth stealing: their dough sat out too long, their pork is overcooked, and their soup tasteless.

Although this noodle benchmarking tour has greatly improved the quality of Tampopo's soup, she recognizes that it is not yet good enough. Help then comes from an unlikely source, an old friend of Goro's living in a hobo camp where everyone is a gastronome. He takes them to yet more restaurants, including one where they rescue a man from choking. The man lends them his chauffeur, who against all odds is also a noodle expert, and takes them to even more restaurants. (The quest for quality can be exhausting, and in this case pretty rough on the waistline.)

In the shop with the best-tasting noodles, Tampopo has to trick the proprietor into divulging his process: "These noodles are not as good as usual, perhaps you did not let them sit long enough." "I left them overnight, as usual," he growls, and so on until Tampopo has the entire recipe.

At this point, Goro and Tampopo's other advisors urge her to reopen her shop, now renamed after her. The drunken customer from her old shop turns out to be a contractor and decorator, who remodels the shop for efficiency and attractiveness. Tampopo herself also gets remodeled, as she drops her dumpy old outfit for a new chef's uniform. The transformation is remarkable.

Still the quest for improvement continues. The experts tell Tampopo that her soup "lacks profundity" and suggest adding spring onions. Although the other elements are nearly perfect, there is nothing to distinguish it, no unexpected element to delight customers and exceed their expectations. With the spring onions added, she tries again. The experts drink her soup to the bottom of the bowl.

Success! Soon customers are swarming to her new shop, and Goro and the others drift away, as Tampopo no longer needs them. A cycle of quality leadership is complete, and Goro rides off into the sunset.

quality leadership that we have discussed. These organizations provide an interesting contrast because of the differences in their size and scope.

Branch-Smith Printing Division[22]

Branch-Smith, Inc. is a fourth-generation, family business. Branch-Smith Printing Division is one of two divisions within Branch-Smith, Inc. The Branch-Smith Printing Division is a small company with under 100 employees that specializes in creating multi-page, bound materials with services ranging from design to mailing for specialty customers. They offer a complete array of turnkey services to customers, including design, image scanning, electronic and conventional prepress work, printing, binding, and mailing/delivery.

Leadership Role: Establish a Vision Organizational values and stakeholder expectations are set at multiple levels of the organization. At the top level, the Board of Directors and Corporate Leadership Team (CLT) created the Corporate Values Statement to focus all divisions on the needs of customers, employees, owners, and society. These values are

- To honor God in all that we do,
- To pursue excellence with integrity and commitment,
- To help people develop as individuals and as a team,
- To grow profitably by committing ourselves to our customers' success.

This mission is embraced and affirmed by the Print Leadership Team (PLT) and used as a foundation for the Division Mission Statement, which is "to provide expert solutions for publishers." From the Corporate Values and Division Mission Statements comes a focus on the importance of quality and a Division-wide focus on meeting customer and stakeholder needs. This is described in the Quality Policy—"Branch-Smith Printing will seek to continuously improve results for all stakeholders through the application of its Innovating Excellence Process," and is embodied in the Division Objectives, which are the firm's highest-level directions and performance expectations. These Division Objectives are

- Continuously Improve Business Results,
- Become the Partner of Choice for Our Customers, and
- Become the Employer of Choice.

The company's senior leadership reviews organizational values, expectations, and directions for alignment each year during the strategic planning process. From those, they develop more detailed short- and longer-term directions and expectations of their organization and their employees based upon input collected from all stakeholders. During the year, through the Management Review Process and PLT decisions, they continue to update directions through Action Plans (AP) and Quality Improvement Process (QIP) activities.

Leadership Role: Live the Values Ensuring that the values, directions, and expectations are communicated to all employees begins with a meeting following strategic planning. Senior leaders introduce the directions for the year and their roles in achieving these directions. This meeting is followed by communication meetings in each department facilitated by the leaders of those groups. Each team/department works through an understanding of their role in the organization's success and creates a mission statement that describes its role in fulfilling the Division mission. Based on their particular mission, each team develops strategies that support the Division Objectives and Strategies. All employees develop work objectives to support Division and department directions. This drives the focus on all stakeholder needs down throughout the organization. These work objectives are created with the assistance of managers who help employees set and achieve these results. Values and expectations of employee responsibility and productive work are communicated and reinforced to employees through an employee handbook, job descriptions, and ISO work instructions.

Senior leaders encourage and motivate employees to engage in innovation and continuous improvement through an expectation that they actively participate in performance improvement activities after receiving training in quality and problem solving. All employees receive training in the meaning of quality, elements of teamwork, and problem-solving skills when they begin with the company. The Quality Manager along with departmental QIP teams deliver ongoing training. The Quality Manager also oversees the use of SPC and continuous improvement tools.

Leadership Role: Lead Continuous Improvement Senior leaders review performance using a structured, comprehensive approach. Reviews are ordered consecutively with individuals and teams first reviewing their work and results, and then rolling results up through the organization in consecutive meetings. This bottom-up approach ensures accurate information, involvement, broad communications, and accountability at all levels. The Management Review is the core meeting of senior leaders. The meeting is designed to ensure they have full current situation and future outlook knowledge as it affects the company's strategic position and direction. The senior leaders have comprehensive knowledge of business and industry activities because of their external involvement and the most up-to-date knowledge of their current position because of their roll-up meetings with departments and functions.

The primary driver of the meeting is the Quality Improvement Database (QID), which outlines measures and actions reviewed. All customer complaints, supplier non-conformances, internal non-conformances, productivity, progress toward department and Division goals, and other quality data are entered into this system by area leaders based on the outcomes of their reviews. Progress against goals for each team is reported through "Resource performance charts" and reviewed at that level in monthly meetings and posted as bar charts on their bulletin board. Progress made by QIP teams is also reported into the QID and reviewed by the MRT at this meeting. The QID automatically performs a Division-level roll-up of the data for review at the Management Review (MR). This database ensures that all vital performance information is available to assist senior managers' analysis for prioritization and action. In addition, senior leaders conduct a series of reviews for their annual strategic planning meetings. These result in the culmination of the prior year performance results and dictate actions for the coming year and beyond.

Through the MR process, every customer complaint, supplier non-conformance, employee suggestion, and open QIP, internal nonconformance, and on-time delivery issue are reviewed for status, prioritized for action, or reviewed for closure or referral to a team or individual. These involve the establishment of QIPs—the central problem-solving, implementation, and evaluation mechanisms in their management system. QIPs link to a specific Objective and Strategy. Open QIPs related to the current plan are posted on the PLT bulletin board. Before closure, QIP owner(s) rate QIP effectiveness against its selected indicator, and an effort may be initiated to improve the solution's effectiveness.

SSM Health Care[23]

Sponsored by the Franciscan Sisters of Mary, SSM Health Care (SSMHC) is based in St. Louis, Missouri, and operates as a private, not-for-profit health care system. SSMHC delivers its health care services in inpatient, outpatient, emergency department, and ambulatory surgery settings associated with 17 acute care hospitals in Missouri, Illinois, Wisconsin, and Oklahoma.

Leadership Role: Establish a Vision SSM Health Care is committed to providing exceptional health care services to every person who seeks need of care. SSMHC's Board of Directors sets the organization's Vision Statement and affirms the Mission and Core Values statements developed by employees throughout the system. The Board consists of nine members, both religious and lay persons, and meets four times a year. Four regional boards and three local boards, operating under guidelines established by the SSMHC Board, are responsible for medical staff credentialing and performance assessment and improvement for SSMHC entities within their service areas.

Approximately 190 regional and system executives, entity presidents and administrative council (AC) members, physicians, and corporate vice presidents make up SSMHC's leadership system. Physician executive leaders, who are typically vice presidents of medical affairs, medical directors, or chief medical officers at the entities or networks, are fully participating members of the leadership system. The leadership system contains the following primary mandated groups:

- System Management, 11 senior leaders, who meet monthly.
- Operations Council, 9 senior leaders, subset of System Management, who meet monthly.
- Innsbrook Group, 31 system, network, and entity senior leaders, who meet three times a year. The Innsbrook Group consists of all members of System Management and all hospital presidents, plus representative physician organization, network, home care, and information systems executives.

- Network leadership, network president/CEO and his or her direct reports, 8 to 10 people, who meet weekly or biweekly.
- Entity leadership, presidents and members of their leadership teams, called administrative councils, and medical staff leaders, 8 to 10 people, who meet weekly or biweekly.

Nearly 3,000 SSM Health Care employees and physicians participated in focus groups across the system to define the organization's mission and values during 1999. Out of this discussion came recommended wording for a single, more concise, and memorable mission statement and core values. During 2000, educational sessions were conducted at each of the entities to communicate the new mission and core values to all physicians and employees. The education, designed to give definition to the mission and values, included group discussions of the personal meaning of the mission and values to individuals. A "Meeting in a Box" tool kit, including a video, brochures and pocket cards was used to facilitate consistent deployment. Educational programs conducted in 2001 for the deployment of the 2002-4 Strategic, Financial & HR Plan (SFP) served to reinforce the mission and values.

Leadership Role: Live the Values SSMHC is a mission-and-values-driven organization. Every executive leader throughout the system is responsible for ensuring that SSMHC's mission and values are communicated and deployed. The corporate vice president-mission awareness develops SSMHC's mission initiatives with input from the Mission Think Tank of about a dozen employees and entity/network mission awareness representatives. System Management requires each entity to have a mission awareness team (MAT), made up of a cross section of employees. These teams sponsor an annual retreat day for their co-workers and a variety of works of mercy (for example, fundraising for local charities), that emulate the mission and values. Mission and values statements and Quality Principles are reinforced in system, network and entity publications, such as SSM Network, SSMHC's bimonthly newspaper, and posted in conference rooms throughout the system.

The Innsbrook Group sets the organization's short- and long-term strategic directions and performance expectations through the Strategic, Financial & HR Planning Process (SFPP). They develop goals that support the Vision and Mission statements. Interactive processes occur within each entity and network to finalize the entity/network Strategic, Financial & HR Plans (SFPs). Use of the SFPP also enables the Innsbrook Group to create and balance value for all of its stakeholders (patients and their families; employees; all active and associate physicians; major suppliers; and payors) by ensuring the goals reflect each stakeholder's requirements.

System Management translates short- and long-term directions and communicates organizational values and performance expectations to all employees through a system-wide tool called "Passport." SSMHC employees receive a "Passport"—a card that contains the SSMHC mission and values; the characteristics of exceptional health care services identified in the 2002-4 SFP; spaces for entity, departmental, and personal goals and measures; and a place for the employee and manager signatures and date. The Passport creates "line of sight" from personal goals to the organization's goals. SSMHC's senior leaders use communication plans (which identify key messages, audiences, leader spokespersons, methods, and timelines) and tools like "Meeting in a Box" to ensure consistent communication of values, directions, and expectations throughout the leadership system and to all employees and employed physicians.

Leadership Role: Lead Continuous Improvement SSMHC committed to continuous quality improvement (CQI) system-wide in 1990, and was among the first health care systems in the nation to do so. Sr. Mary Jean Ryan, FSM, president/CEO, and the system's senior leadership team made this commitment after research showed strong parallels between SSMHC's values and quality principles. SSMHC has become a national role model for health care organizations across the country, even internationally, that are striving to create a culture of continuous improvement.

SSMHC executive leaders use a system-wide Performance Management Process to review and assess organizational performance as it relates to achieving the SFPP short- and long-term goals; and in meeting changing health care service needs. The process facilitates identification of the root causes of performance variations and establishes clear accountabilities for implementing corrective action. This Performance Management Process was developed during 2000 by the system-wide Accountability Team. The process improves accountability and monitoring of performance at all levels of the organization. The Performance Management Process defines the roles and responsibilities of leadership groups in managing the performance of SSMHC and its entities; defines a consistent set of performance reporting tools used throughout SSMHC; and establishes standardized definitions and indicators to ensure consistency in the measurement and evaluation of performance. The operational process covers three general areas of reporting: financial, customer satisfaction, and clinical quality performance.

System Management assesses the overall health of SSMHC monthly by examining the Combined Financial Statements and 16 System Level Indicators on a consolidated basis for the services of hospital operations, home health, long-term (nursing home) care, and physician practices. The Operations Council analyzes the operational performance of SSMHC monthly using the SSMHC Operations Performance Indicator Report (IPR), also known as the Stoplight Report, which contains the same 16 indicators reviewed by System Management plus other key measures. This report covers performance by network and freestanding campuses. If an unfavorable variance occurs for one of these system level indicators, the Operations Council looks at the Hospital Operations Performance Report to determine causal factors.

System, network, and entity leadership groups and the regional boards assess quality improvement and patient safety at SSMHC hospitals through the Quality Report. This quarterly electronic report contains 14 indicators in four categories: customer satisfaction, employee safety, clinical quality, and patient safety. It also contains information related to risk management, infection control and environment of care issues. Corrective action plans are required to remedy unfavorable variances. If an unfavorable variance occurs beyond an established performance threshold in any of the 16 System Level Indicators, a network or freestanding (non-network) entity is required to develop and implement a corrective action plan using a standardized format. Corrective action plans include a root cause analysis, detailed implementation plans, description of the support needed, timelines, and responsibilities. These plans are reviewed by the SSMHC's executive vice president and the Operations Council. The network/entity has implementation responsibility with oversight provided by the executive vice president/COO and Operations Council.

SSMHC's senior leaders deploy the organization's performance results to employees at the appropriate system, network and entity levels. They communicate system performance review findings, priorities for improvement, and opportunities for innovation in their areas at System Management, Operations Council and Innsbrook Group meetings. The network/entity presidents communicate findings, priorities and opportunities for their network/entity at administrative council and entity department meetings. Network/entity presidents appoint teams or other accountable groups to deploy the corrective action plans. Entity presidents and other leaders deploy performance results to physicians at medical executive committee meetings (monthly), medical staff meetings (at least annually), and employed physician board meetings (monthly).

LEADERSHIP SYSTEMS

In complex organizations, the ability to successfully lead requires an effective leadership system. The **leadership system** refers to how leadership is exercised, formally and informally, throughout an organization. These elements include how key decisions are made, communicated, and carried out at all levels. The leadership system includes structures and mechanisms for decision making; selection and development of leaders and managers; and reinforcement of values, directions, and performance expectations. It builds loyalties and teamwork based upon shared values, encourages initiative and risk taking, and subordinates organization to purpose and function. It respects the capabilities and requirements of employees and other stakeholders and sets high expectations for performance and performance improvements. An effective leadership system also includes mechanisms for leaders' self-examination and self-improvement.

To illustrate these themes, the leadership system at Solar Turbines, Inc., a division of Caterpillar, operates in three distinct yet highly integrated modes. First, through a functional organizational structure led by the president's staff, Solar maintains a focus on functional excellence through the recruitment, hiring, development of critical skills, and the application of tools and common processes to continuously improve functional effectiveness. Second, three cross-functional leadership structures, made up of managers and technical experts selected from multiple levels of the organization, facilitate companywide teamwork and decision making. This Expanded Leadership Team, consisting of the Operations Council (74 leaders from across the business) and the Expanded Leadership Group (more than 400 managers and supervisors), enables Solar to develop the next generation of business leaders. It also promotes rapid, effective communication among employees with cross-functional teaming occurring at all levels of the organization. The third leadership structure is the set of 10 interlocking committees that coordinate and integrate all business areas. These committees provide a mechanism to strengthen organizational learning through cross-functional sharing, companywide communication, and strategic direction setting. Members of the president's staff chair key committees and, along with other senior business leaders, actively participate to provide guidance, learn, share, and support each other's decisions as a leadership team.[24]

In contrast to the large manufacturing environment at Solar, Stoner Incorporated (profiled at the beginning of this chapter) has a six-member senior leadership team empowered by the owner to manage and lead the company. The leadership team created and refined the Stoner Excellence System to define and communicate to all team members how the business is run. The system is based on Leadership, Strategy, and Process, which are combined with an Assess/Improve/Implement continuous improvement approach. Stakeholder value is at the center of the system to characterize the main focus on the customer. Stoner's leadership approach is built on (1) leadership at all levels, (2) worker leaders, and (3) strong fundamental leadership skills based on Stephen Covey's *Seven Habits of Highly Effective People*.

These examples show that the leadership system in every organization is unique and reflects the vision and culture of the organization.

PERFORMANCE EXCELLENCE AND LEADERSHIP THEORY

There are a great number of theories of leadership; we can discuss the relationship of TQ principles and performance excellence to only a few of them. This section outlines some of theories that seem to relate most closely to quality management philosophies.

The Roles of Managers

One well-known model, advanced by Henry Mintzberg, categorizes the work of managers into 10 roles. Although this is a model of managerial roles, rather than leadership per se, it is useful to explore how roles may change as managers attempt to practice leadership for performance excellence.

There are *interpersonal roles* (figurehead, leader, and liaison), *informational roles* (monitor, disseminator, and spokesperson), and *decisional roles* (entrepreneur, disturbance handler, resource allocator, and negotiator).[25] Each of these roles is likely to be played by managers practicing total quality, although the relative importance of the roles, and the ways in which they are played, may differ from more traditional organizations.

Interpersonal Roles The figurehead role, which involves the ceremonial or symbolic tasks of managers, is certainly played in TQ organizations. A manager presiding at a recognition ceremony for a team's quality accomplishments would be fulfilling this role. The leadership role would obviously be important for TQ-oriented managers, but the directing and controlling aspects of this role would be downplayed.

The liaison role—dealing with customers, suppliers, and others—would still be played, but also it would be fulfilled to an increasing extent by employees, as an outgrowth of their empowerment.

Informational Roles The informational roles of management would continue to be played, but nonmanagerial personnel would be more involved in these activities, rather than looking to managers as the source of all information. Employees involved in benchmarking, for example, would play an important part in monitoring and disseminating information. Whereas top managers would retain an important role as spokespersons, this role also would be increasingly shared with people throughout the organization. By now, probably hundreds, if not thousands, of nonmanagerial personnel have stepped up to the microphone to share their teams' accomplishments with the world.

Decisional Roles Many of the behaviors leaders use to initiate and support a focus on performance excellence are characterized by the entrepreneurial role, one of the decisional roles. In this role, managers try to improve their organization by identifying problems and instituting processes to solve them. The disturbance-handler role—in which leaders resolve conflicts among subunits—should be diminished, at least in the long run, as people take on a more holistic view of the organizational mission. The resource-allocator role continues to be key, as performance excellence will not be achieved unless leaders are unswerving in their commitment of resources to continuous improvement and customer satisfaction. Finally, the negotiator role will still be played, but it will be different, as companies try to create long-term, win-win arrangements with suppliers, unions, and customers.

The Mintzberg model attempts to describe the behavior of managers, not to prescribe what they should do. It also attempts to capture the broad scope of managerial activities across many types of organizations. For this reason it is difficult to compare it directly to the more limited, but explicitly prescriptive, content of leadership for performance excellence. Nevertheless, the comparison is instructive in linking this discussion to the mainstream management literature on leadership: Managers in TQ settings will play some roles (entrepreneurial) more than other managers, other roles (disturbance handler) less often, and others (leader) differently.

Consideration and Initiating Structure

In a series of studies done several decades ago at Ohio State University, researchers tried to identify the behaviors associated with effective leadership. These studies concluded that many of these behaviors could be captured by two dimensions: consideration and initiating structure.

Consideration (also known as socioemotional orientation) means taking care of subordinates, explaining things to them, being approachable, and generally being concerned about their welfare. **Initiating structure** (also known as task orientation) means getting people organized, including setting goals and instituting and enforcing deadlines and standard operating procedures. Research has indicated that, although different situations will require different leadership behaviors, most organizational units over a period of time will require both types of leadership in order to be successful.[26]

One apparent difference between this classic view of leadership and the TQ view is that the former emphasizes leadership at the workgroup level, whereas the latter deals with the more global level of organizations or major subunits. Writers on performance excellence leadership have focused less on lower-level leaders, due perhaps to the emphasis on self-management at those levels.

Despite these differences, consideration and initiating structure are not irrelevant for organizations pursuing performance excellence. Such organizations recognize the importance of employees for the success of their quality efforts and for their performance in general. Thus leaders will certainly need to be considerate of employee needs. The section on Rosenbluth in Chapter 8 illustrated how consideration of employees minimizes their frustration and allows them to focus on customer service and continuous improvement. In a TQ environment, consideration would not be done in a paternalistic manner, emphasizing the power of leaders over subordinates. On the contrary, people would be treated as respected associates.

Initiating structure also will be appropriate in the TQ environment but perhaps will be accomplished differently than in the traditional organizational setting. Traditionally, leaders were responsible for the whole gamut of activities associated with initiating structure-setting goals, establishing deadlines, enforcing rules, and so on. In organizations striving for empowerment, many of these activities will be taken over by employees.

The discussion of leadership for performance excellence suggests that quality leadership consists more of setting a direction for people through establishing a vision and identifying values. By leading continuous improvement efforts, leaders will establish priorities for activities throughout the organization. Such activities will provide the necessary context for employees to initiate structure for themselves.

Transformational and Transactional Leadership Theory

Another model that has important implications for performance excellence is Transformational Leadership Theory.[27] According to this model, leadership has four principal dimensions:

1. Inspirational motivation—providing followers with a sense of meaning and challenge in their work;
2. Intellectual stimulation—encouraging followers to question assumptions, explore new ideas and methods, and adopt new perspectives;
3. Idealized influence—behaviors that followers strive to emulate or mirror;
4. Individualized consideration—special attention to each follower's needs for achievement and growth.

Leaders who wish to have a major impact on their organizations must take a long-term perspective, work to stimulate their organizations intellectually, invest in training to develop individuals and groups, take some risks, promote a shared vision and values, and focus on customers and employees as individuals.

Transactional Leadership Theory assumes that certain leaders may develop the ability to inspire their subordinates to exert extraordinary efforts to achieve organizational goals, through behaviors that may include contingent rewards, and active and passive management by exception. Contingent reward behavior includes clarification of the work required to obtain rewards to influence motivation. Passive management by exception includes use of contingent punishments and other corrective actions in response to deviations from acceptable performance standards. Active management by exception is defined in terms of looking for mistakes and enforcing rules to avoid mistakes. Bernard Bass differentiated transformational from transactional leadership behavior, stating: "Transformational leaders have greater interest in continuous organizational change and improvement transcending or aligning self-interests for the longer-range greater good of the organization and its members. This is in contrast to transactional leaders, who are more focused on the satisfaction of self-interests and the maintenance of the organization's status quo."[28]

Transformational leadership is more aligned with organizational change required by total quality and Baldrige-like performance excellence models. The CEOs and executive team members of nearly every Malcolm Baldrige Award recipient have generally modeled this leadership behavior, and some empirical evidence found in research suggests that transformational leadership behavior is strongly correlated with lower turnover, higher productivity and quality, and higher employee satisfaction than other approaches. Many of its aspects (emphasis on vision and focus on customers and employees as individuals) are right out of the Baldrige playbook, while others are generally consistent with performance excellence principles. For instance, Deming emphasized the necessity for managers to have "constancy of purpose"—to pursue diligently the long-term goal of remaining competitive through continuous improvement processes. They should also communicate an appealing vision emphasizing continuous improvement, teamwork, and customer service in order to inspire followers. Moreover, managers can act as role models by taking a personal interest in activities geared toward improving processes and customer relationships.[29]

It would be tempting to say that all managers in TQ organizations should be transformational leaders, but this is unrealistic and probably unwise. It is not realistic because few, if any, organizations have such a concentration of transformational leaders. It is not wise because such a concentration would likely breed more chaos than quality. An organization pursuing performance excellence needs both those who establish visions and those who are effective at the day-to-day tasks needed to achieve them.[30] These "transactional leaders" play an important role in promoting total quality. See box "Transformational or Transactional? A Research Perspective" for some empirical evidence on these theories.

Situational Leadership

Ken Blanchard and Paul Hersey concluded that no single theory of leadership works in every situation, and they developed a simple model known as *situational leadership* in the late 1960s. This model suggests that the style of leadership that one should use depends on the maturity of those being led. The premise behind

TRANSFORMATIONAL OR TRANSACTIONAL? A RESEARCH PERSPECTIVE[31]

A study was conducted to investigate the importance of transformational and transactional leadership to effective quality improvement. The study measured six dimensions of transformational leadership and two dimensions of transactional leadership using items from prior literature. The items were measured on a seven-point Likert scale. A questionnaire was administered to a sample of quality managers representing 163 companies. Based on the data collected, the companies were classified as successful or unsuccessful in terms of quality improvement. The authors found that transfomational leadership significantly affects both infrastructure and core quality management practices, while transactional leadership does not significantly affect either set of practices. There were, however, significantly higher levels of both types of leadership behavior exhibited in the successful firms compared to the unsuccessful firms. The finding that transformational leadership is associated with successful quality improvement supports theoretical arguments that it provides the visionary leadership needed for successful quality management. Some prior theories had argued that transactional leadership would decrease quality improvement because using contingent reward and contingent punishment would encourage employees to pursue their own goals at the expense of the company's quality improvement goals. These findings support the arguments that transactional leadership is not in opposition to transformational leadership, but actually is a necessary type of leadership.Thus, leaders must not only provide visionary leadership but they also should use their reward and punishment power to direct employee behaviors.

the situation leadership model is that leadership styles might vary from one person to another, depending on their "readiness," which is characterized by their skills and abilities to perform the work, and their confidence, commitment, and motivation to do it. The Situational Leadership model defines four levels of readiness:

1. Unable and unwilling
2. Unable but willing
3. Able but unwilling
4. Able and willing

Blanchard and Hersey defined four leadership styles that best address these four levels of readiness:

1. *Directing*. In this style of leadership, managers define tasks and roles, and closely supervise work. Communication is generally one way—top down. This style applies best to people who lack the skills and knowledge to perform a job and lack the confidence or commitment to their work (unable and unwilling).
2. *Coaching*. In this style, leaders set the overall approach and direction but work with subordinates and allow them to manage the details. Leaders might need to provide some experience or support to individuals having the drive and motivation to do a good job, but who might lack some experience or skills (unable but willing).

3. *Supporting.* Here, leaders allocate tasks and set direction, but the subordinate has full control over the performance of the work. These individuals do not need much supervision or direction, but may require motivation and confidence (able but unwilling), particularly if the task is new.
4. *Delegating.* In this style, subordinates can do their work with little supervision or support. Once the work is delegated, leaders take a hands-off approach, except when asked to provide assistance by the subordinate. They are both able and willing to work on a project by themselves with little supervision or support.

A leader also might apply different styles to the same person at different times. This can be difficult, as most people seem to be more comfortable in one style. However, the choice should not be driven by personal preference but, rather, the needs of the subordinates. In fully empowered organizations and those with strong self-directed teams, you would probably find the delegating style to be most prevalent. However, when introducing new skills, such as Six Sigma, into an organization, it may be necessary to provide more direct control, coaching, or support when individuals are learning and practicing new skills or are transitioning into new job responsibilities. As managers work with different individuals in different stages of careers and maturity, it is his or her responsibility to adapt the leadership style to the individual and the situation.

The situational leadership model is directly reflected in the process model for creating self-directed teams. Thus, it provides a structure for transitioning to an empowered organization. In fact, some research has suggested that the model provides a natural basis for leading organizational change processes as organizations pursue performance excellence.[32]

Management and Leadership

A recent treatment of leadership by John Kotter compares the concept of leadership to the concept of management.[33] According to this view, management is needed to create order amid complexity, and leadership is needed to stimulate the organizational change necessary to keep up with a changing environment. This view avoids the simplistic ideas that management is somehow trivial, generally unnecessary, and should be replaced by leadership, and that the same person cannot practice both management and leadership.

Kotter differentiates leadership from management by contrasting the activities central to each. Although management begins with planning and budgeting, leadership begins with setting a direction. Direction-setting involves creating a vision of the future, as well as a set of approaches for achieving the vision. To promote goal achievement, management practices organizing and staffing, whereas leadership works on aligning people—communicating the vision and developing commitment to it. Management achieves plans through controlling and problem solving, whereas leadership achieves its vision through motivating and inspiring.

Kotter's view of leadership—similar to transformational theory—dovetails with our depiction of quality leadership. Both focus on developing and communicating a vision. Kotter's view of inspiring resembles our discussion of giving people values to embrace and then making sure that the leader is practicing them. The idea of aligning people is consistent with the idea of empowerment, because it gives people a goal, then leaves them to move in that direction. Our description of the role of leaders in continuous improvement is more hands-on than Kotter's description, perhaps suggesting that some management behaviors will continue to be important to leaders in total quality organizations.

Review and Discussion Questions

1. How is leadership exercised at Stoner, Inc. in the Performance Excellence Profile? How might leadership differ at a very small company like Stoner compared to much larger companies (for example, Boeing, Xerox, and so on)?
2. What three processes must leaders undertake to promote total quality in their organizations?
3. Joseph Conklin proposes 10 questions for self-examination to help you understand your capacity for leadership.[34] Answer the following questions, and discuss why they are important for leadership.
   a. How much do I like my job?
   b. How often do I have to repeat myself?
   c. How do I respond to failure?
   d. How well do I put up with second-guessing?
   e. How early do I ask questions when making a decision?
   f. How often do I say "thank you"?
   g. Do I tend to favor a loose or strict interpretation of the rules?
   h. Can I tell an obstacle from an excuse?
   i. Is respect enough?
   j. Have I dispensed with feeling indispensable?
4. State some examples in which leaders you have worked for have exhibited leadership practices discussed in this chapter. Can you provide examples for which they have not? How did their behavior affect you and your co-workers?
5. Review Deming's 14 Points in Chapter 2. What aspects of leadership theories are evident in them, either individually or as a holistic philosophy?
6. Most of the talk on leadership for quality focuses on top managers. What can middle- and first-level managers do to promote quality in their organizations? How does this differ from the role of top management?
7. John Young, former president and CEO of Hewlett-Packard, has summarized the role of the CEO in quality improvement in the following recommendations.[35]
   a. Dramatize the importance of quality to the organization.
   b. Establish agreed-on measures of quality.
   c. Set challenging and motivating goals.
   d. Give people the resources and information needed to do the job.
   e. Reward results.
   f. Keep an attitude that high quality is not only desirable, but possible. How do these recommendations differ from those given in this chapter? Are they really different or do they capture the same ideas in different words?
8. The Baldrige criteria defined the *leadership system* as "how leadership is exercised, formally and informally, throughout the company—the basis for and the way that key decisions are made, communicated, and carried out. It includes structures and mechanisms for decision making, selection and development of leaders and managers, and reinforcing values, practices, and behaviors." What are some attributes of an effective leadership system? How would you design one for an organization?

9. William Scherkenbach, a quality expert and Deming disciple, states: "If management is to improve their organization, they must change the process. This means that they cannot accept conference room promises, but must work directly with their people on the process, the how and the why. During this period of transition, everyone must be willing to learn.... No one is too senior to be involved in the how."[36] Do you agree or disagree? Why?
10. What aspects of an organization's culture or structure could keep managers from leading effectively?
11. Sir John Harvey-Jones, head of Britain's Imperial Chemical Industries from 1982 to 1987, once commented, "The task of leadership is really to make the status quo more dangerous than launching into the unknown."[37] Do you think this statement represents a good approach to total quality leadership? Why or why not?
12. Compare the leadership practices of Branch-Smith Printing and SSM Health Care. How do these practices relate to the concepts developed in this chapter? What differences and similarities can you point to?
13. Can leadership be viewed as a business process? If so, how? How might an organization quantify the performance of its leadership system?
14. Which situational leadership style would be most appropriate for managing a team under the following circumstances? Explain your reasoning.
    a. Team members have the skills to do the job, but don't have the experience or confidence to work as a self-managed team.
    b. Team members have minimal knowledge and experience in performing a task and lack motivation.
    c. Team members have a desire to excel, are highly motivated, and have the skills and knowledge to perform a task.
    d. Team members have a relatively low skill level to perform a task and little prior experience.

CASES

David Kearns and the Transformation of Xerox[38]

David Kearns, former chairman and CEO of Xerox, provides an excellent example of leadership for quality. Xerox's problems in the early 1980s were legion and typical of American manufacturers facing serious foreign competition for the first time. Xerox discovered to its horror that Japanese companies were able to sell copiers in the United States for roughly what it cost Xerox to build them. Its former lion's share of the copier market had dwindled to a paltry 8 percent. Even at the time, Xerox was hardly complacent: productivity was increasing by as much as 7 or 8 percent every year. Kearns calculated that gains closer to 18 percent a year were needed to catch Xerox's competitors.

About this time, Kearns read Philip Crosby's book, *Quality Is Free*, and invited Crosby to address Xerox's management. Kearns's pleas for change initially were resisted by a management team who said they were already doing everything they could. This led Kearns to tell his managers that trying to change Xerox was like "pushing a wet noodle." It was time for more drastic action.

In 1983, the top management team at Xerox designed a new approach to quality that was dubbed "Leadership through Quality." The central principle of the new approach was that quality would be defined as customer satisfaction, not internal standards. If customers were not satisfied, quality had not been attained. A second principle was to focus on processes, not just outcomes.

In the past, poor outcomes were an occasion to blame someone and to hammer into them the importance of doing better. This was replaced with an approach that focused on examining the process that had created the outcome and improving it.

In order to operate according to these principles, a number of specific practices were undertaken. Xerox is perhaps best known for its extensive use of benchmarking—a process by which a company compares its operations to the best practices of other companies. The company's approach is to benchmark against the best, in whatever industry it is found. Xerox has benchmarked its billing processes against American Express and its distribution processes against L.L. Bean.

To demonstrate their commitment to these principles, Kearns and his management team were the first to undergo the newly devised quality training. They then became the teachers for the next level of management, and training flowed throughout the organization in this manner. In a move that represented a major departure from tradition, each senior manager was made responsible for taking calls from customers one day a month. Xerox managers still interrupt their meetings to take such calls.

Although Kearns's efforts were crucial to this process, he believed that leadership must (and in this case did) come from other sources as well, including the Amalgamated Clothing & Textile Workers, the union representing Xerox's production employees. Xerox also learned that it was important to have union leaders as deeply committed to the quality process as management. A strong and enlightened union leadership shared management's vision and understood that changes had to be made if there was to be a future for all Xerox employees. The union leadership and management shared each other's trust.[39]

Xerox's competitive resurgence was dramatic. Market share, revenues, and profits recovered substantially. In 1989, Xerox became one of the first winners of both the American and Canadian National Quality Awards.

Kearns believed that "Xerox was probably the first American company in an industry targeted by the Japanese to regain market share without the aid of tariffs or government help."[40] Despite the recovery and the awards, however, Kearns did not abandon the principle of continuous improvement. At the time, he stated: "We take great satisfaction in winning these awards, but the fact is that we're far from finished with our drive to improve. We have learned that the pursuit of quality is a race with no finish line. We see an upward and never-ending spiral of increased competition and heightened customer expectations."[41]

David Kearns was succeeded as Xerox's chairman in 1991 by Paul Allaire. Kearns is now working within the U.S. Department of Education to bring the quality perspective to America's schools.

Discussion Questions

1. How did David Kearns fulfill the roles of a quality leader at Xerox?
2. Is Kearns's approach broadly applicable, or would different approaches be needed in other settings?
3. Kearns began a practice of having senior managers personally take phone calls from customers with problems. Call the president of an organization of which you are a customer and report a quality or service problem you are experiencing. Will the president take the call? Will the president or someone else return your call? (If you get to talk to someone, congratulate them on their responsiveness, and be as constructive as possible in describing your problem.)

Situational Leadership in Action[42]

A large pharmaceutical manufacturer was highly motivated to meet quality challenges. It implemented an ISO 9000–compatible quality system to ensure not only FDA compliance requirements, but also customer satisfaction. As the manufacturing plants of the organization were audited by the internal audit division, it became apparent that some plants were meeting the challenge, while others continued to struggle in both the quality and the regulatory aspects of production. This fact was evident in the reports of internal findings and in FDA inspection reports.

For the most part, the manufacturing plants share consistent resources and face similar environments. All were issued the responsibility of meeting the expectations of the quality system through the same mechanism. All understood the consequence of not conforming, that is, of jeopardizing their manufacturing license as bound by the consent decree. The issue then became why some plants could successfully design and implement the requirements of the quality system, whereas others could not and still cannot.

Although the plants are similar in many ways, they differ in terms of leadership, as each plant has its own CEO. The CEO, as the leader of his or her plant, has the responsibility of ensuring the successful implementation of a quality system. The plants also differ in their organizational members, those who are to be led by the CEO. The relationship between the leader and the organizational members is critical to a plant's ability to implement an effective quality system, with effectiveness being a measure of how successfully a plant can comply with FDA regulations and internal quality standards.

Both plants have a similar culture that can be best described as conserving, reflecting a level of rigidity in response to the external environment, but demonstrating organizational commitment. The strategy used by the leader in Plant A was a combination of moderate to high amounts of structuring actions, with high to moderate amounts of inspiring actions, whereas the strategy used by Plant B's CEO was a combination of moderate to low amounts of structuring actions, with moderate to high amounts of inspiring actions.

Discussion Questions

1. What type of situational leadership style did the CEO of each plant demonstrate?
2. Which of these styles was more appropriate in view of the Situational Leadership model? Why?
3. Would it be surprising to find out that Plant A was more successful in achieving the goals of the quality system?

Building a Leadership System for Landmark Dining

The Malcolm Baldrige Criteria for Performance Excellence asks organizations to describe how senior leaders guide and sustain their organizations. A subset of the questions asked in the criteria are

> How do senior leaders set organizational vision and values? How do senior leaders deploy your organization's vision and values through your leadership system, to the workforce, to key suppliers and partners, and to customers and other stakeholders, as appropriate? How do senior leaders' personal actions reflect a commitment to the organization's values?
>
> How do senior leaders create a sustainable organization? How do they create an environment for organizational performance improvement, the accomplishment of your mission and strategic objectives, innovation, competitive or role-model performance leadership, and organizational agility? How do they create an environment for organizational and workforce learning? How do they develop and enhance their personal leadership skills? How do they participate in organizational learning, in succession planning, and in the development of future organizational leaders?

Read the background of the Landmark Dining case in Chapter 8. Thinking of an "ideal" leadership system for the company, how would you address these questions? Specifically, develop a leadership system for this organization and describe performance excellence practices that the company might pursue to address these questions.

Endnotes

1. 2003 Malcolm Baldrige National Quality Award Recipient Profile, U.S. Department of Commerce.
2. Debbie Phillips-Donaldson, "On Leadership," *Quality Progress*, August 2002.
3. Rick Edgeman, Su Mi Park Dahlgaard, Jens J. Dalhgaard, and Franz Scherer, "On Leaders and Leadership," *Quality Progress*, October 1999, pp. 49–54.
4. Rudolph C. Hirzel, "Leadership Characteristics for Quality Performance," The Quality Management Forum, Winter 2004, Vol. 30, No. 1, 3–4
5. Quoted in Jerry G. Bowles, "Leading the World-Class Company," *Fortune*, September 21, 1992.
6. 2006 Malcolm Baldrige National Quality Award Criteria for Performance Excellence, U.S. Department of Commerce.
7. 2004 Criteria for Performance Excellence, Baldrige National Quality Program.
8. Dan Ciampa, *Total Quality: A User's Guide for Implementation*, Reading, Mass.: Addison-Wesley, 1992, p. 115.
9. Jack Welch, Herb Kelleher, Geoffrey Colvin, and John Huey, "How to Create Great Companies and Keep Them That Way," *Fortune*, Vol. 139, No. 1, January 11, 1999, p. 163.
10. Award, the Newsletter of Baldrigeplus, May 7, 2000. Available at http://www.baldrigeplus.com.
11. These examples are from A.R. Tenner and I.J. DeToro, *Total Quality Management*, Reading, Mass.: Addison-Wesley, 1992.
12. Quoted in Bowles, "Leading the World-Class Company."
13. F.B. Adamson, "Cultivating a Charismatic Quality Leader," *Quality Progress*, July 1989, pp. 56–57.
14. Quoted in Bowles, "Leading the World-Class Company."

15. D. Garvin, "Quality Problems, Policies, and Attitudes in the United States and Japan: An Exploratory Study," *Academy of Management Journal*, 1986, Vol. 29, No. 4, pp. 653–673.
16. These and other means of demonstrating commitment to TQ values were suggested by Tenner and DeToro, *Total Quality Management*.
17. Levinson and DeHont, "Leading to Quality," p. 56.
18. See P. Richards, "Right-Side-Up Organization," *Quality Progress*, October 1991, pp. 95–96.
19. Quoted in Bowles, "Leading the World-Class Company."
20. This idea is discussed in Howard S. Gitlow and Shelly J. Gitlow, *The Deming Guide to Quality and Competitive Position*, Englewood Cliffs, N.J.: Prentice Hall, 1987.
21. Based on James C. Spee, "What the Film *Tampopo* Teaches about Total Quality Management." *Tampopo* is directed by Juzo Itami and stars Nobuko Miyamoto and Tsutomu Yamazaki (1987 Itami Productions). Available on Republic Pictures Home Video in Japanese with English subtitles.
22. Adapted from Branch-Smith Printing Division Malcolm Baldrige National Quality Award Application Summary, 2002.
23. Adapted from SSM Health Care Malcolm Baldrige National Quality Award Application Summary.
24. Solar Turbines, Inc., Malcolm Baldrige National Quality Award Application Summary, 1999
25. Henry Mintzberg, *The Nature of Managerial Work*, New York: Harper & Row, 1973.
26. R. House and M. Baetz, "Leadership: Some Generalizations and New Research Directions," in B.M. Staw (ed.), *Research in Organizational Behavior*, Greenwich, Conn.: JAI Press, 1979, p. 359.
27. B.M. Bass, *Leadership and Performance Beyond Expectations*, New York: Free Press, 1985. This discussion is based on David A. Waldman, "A Theoretical Consideration of Leadership and Total Quality Management," *Leadership Quarterly*, 1993, Vol. 4, pp. 65–79. See also J. Conger and R. Kanungo, "Toward a Behavioral Theory of Charismatic Leadership in Organizational Settings," *Academy of Management Review*, October 1987, pp. 637–647.
28. Bruce J. Avolio and Bernard M. Bass, eds., *Developing Potential Across a Full Range of Leadership: Cases on Transactional and Transformational Leadership*, Mahwah, N.J.: Lawrence Erlbaum Associates, 2002, pp. 117–118.
29. David A. Waldman, "The Contributions of Total Quality Management to a Theory of Work Performance," *Academy of Management Review*, Vol. 19, No. 3, pp. 510–536.
30. Philip Atkinson, "Leadership, Total Quality and Cultural Change," *Management Services*, June 1991, pp. 16–19.
31. Tipparat Laohavichien, Lawrence D. Fredendall, and R. Steven Cantrell, "The Effects of Transformational and Transactional Leadership on Quality Improvement," *Quality Management Journal*, 16, 2, 2009, pp. 7–24
32. Richard A. Grover and H. Fred Walker, "Changing from Production to Quality: Application of the Situational Leadership and Transtheoretical Change Models," *Quality Management Journal*, 10, 3, 2003, pp. 8–24.
33. J.P. Kotter, "What Leaders Really Do," in J. J. Gabarro (ed.), *Managing People and Organizations*, Boston: Harvard Business School Press, 1992, pp. 102–114.
34. Joe Conklin, "What It Takes to Be a Leader," *Quality Progress*, November 2001, p. 83.
35. John A. Young, "The Quality Focus at Hewlett-Packard," *The Journal of Business Strategy*, Vol. 5, No. 3, 1985, pp. 6–9.
36. William W. Scherkenbach, *The Deming Route to Quality and Productivity*, Washington, D.C.: SPC Press Books, George Washington University, 1986, p. 139.
37. Quoted in Sir John Harvey-Jones, Harvard Business School Case 9-490013, p. 8.
38. This case is based on David Kearns, "Leadership through Quality," *Academy of Management Executive*, 1990, Vol. 4, No. 2, pp. 86–89; "A CEO's Odyssey Toward World-Class Manufacturing," *Chief Executive*, September 1990; and Alan C. Fenwick, "Five Easy Lessons," *Quality Progress*, December 1991.
39. Kearns, "Leadership through Quality," p. 88.
40. Ibid.
41. Ibid.
42. Adapted from Lisa Walters, "Leading for Quality: The Implications of Situational Leadership," *Quality Management Journal*, 8, 4, October 2001, pp. 48–63.

Performance Excellence and Organizational Change

CHAPTER 11

Performance Excellence Profile: Park Place Lexus[1]

At its two locations in Plano and Grapevine, Texas, Park Place Lexus (PPL) sells and services new and pre-owned Lexus vehicles, and sells Lexus parts to the wholesale and retail markets. PPL is part of the family of Park Place Dealerships (PPD), which includes eight dealerships with 12 franchises.

In 1994, PPL began benchmarking business practices outside of the automobile industry, with the intent of emulating the best business practices it could find and bringing innovation to the industry. Four years later, the company conducted its first internal assessment using the Baldrige criteria for performance excellence to identify areas for improvement, and adopted the brand "Experts in Excellence" as a sign of its dedication to quality. Today, PPL ranks among the country's top Lexus dealers.

With its mission, "To provide an extraordinary automotive purchase and ownership experience" as a foundation, the dealership's "House of Quality" graphically depicts the organization's direction and represents its culture. The four Core Convictions—integrity, outstanding client experience, commitment, and winning—provide the structure of the house. Known as "The Big Hairy Audacious Goal," the organization's vision, "Be the unparalleled retail automotive group in the United States," forms the roof of the house.

The dealership uses many means to identify ways to improve, including an annual strategic planning process and self-assessment using the Baldrige criteria for performance excellence. A quarterly meeting, called "Driving Excellence," is used by dealership leaders to assess progress to goals and performance levels. Improvement activities are planned, executed, tracked, and standardized using action plans that result from the strategic planning process or through PPL's problem-solving process known as DRIVE—Define the problem, Recognize the cause, Identify the solution, Verify the actions, and Evaluate the results.

PPL's Listening and Learning process provides a systematic way to identify client needs and then deliver the best service possible. PPL acquires information about its clients from a variety of sources, including client comments and concerns, follow-up interactions after sales, customer surveys, and focus groups. This information is used to develop detailed profiles of clients, identify key customer needs and preferences, refine its service offerings, establish corporate and Member performance goals, and target marketing and improvement opportunities. A database that includes all interactions with clients is available through an extensive IT network to all Members who deal directly with customers, from sales consultants and finance managers to service and parts department Members.

Leaving nothing to chance, PPL has established performance standards for almost every activity that requires contact with clients, including requiring phones to be answered within three rings and e-mail to be responded to within 24 hours. It has determined the key requirements of clients for both its sales and service departments. For example, clients require that sales consultants be courteous, knowledgeable, respect the clients' time, and honor commitments. For service, requirements include fixing the car right the first time and providing an accurate time estimate for repairs or service.

In a highly competitive job market, PPL has a stringent hiring process that includes aptitude and personality tests to ensure that the organization has the right people for the right job. Once hired, Members follow their training plan that includes classroom training, on-the-job training, and coaching and mentoring aimed at helping them be successful. In addition, Members who deal with clients receive Client Delight training. The company also conducts specialized training related to health, safety, and wellness; quality improvement and measurement; computer skills; documentation and reporting; and tuition reimbursement for technical school training and for other higher education pursuits that contribute to job performance. To encourage empowerment and innovation, employees hold a monthly "50/50" meeting. Half of the meeting focuses on ideas and concerns and half on solutions, such as authorizing Members to spend up to $250 on the spot to resolve a client concern.

All of this attention to detail and PPL's insistence on quality and continual improvement has led to outstanding customer and performance results. PPL's Customer Satisfaction Index (CSI) for clients of new cars approaches 100 percent at both locations, placing them among the top 10 percent of Lexus dealers nationwide. Satisfaction among its pre-owned vehicle clients at both locations increased from 96 percent in 2000 to 98 percent in 2004.

Psychologists suggest that individuals go through four stages of learning:

1. Unconscious incompetence: You don't know that you don't know.
2. Conscious incompetence: You realize that you don't know.
3. Conscious competence: You learn to do, but with conscious effort.
4. Unconscious competence: Performance comes effortlessly.

Organizations seem to follow the same paradigm. Many companies in the United States languished in stage 1 until receiving a wake-up call in the 1980s with regard to quality. Many today are finding themselves in the same situation. Unfortunately, as many organizations move into stage 2, they tend to shoot the messenger and refuse to accept their state of "incompetence." To move from stage 2 to stages 3 and 4, organizations must change. Drawing from best practices outside of its industry, Park Place Lexus provides a good illustration of an organization that has embraced change, something certainly unusual in the automobile sales and service industry.

Lewis Lehr, former CEO of 3M Corporation, once observed, "Our successes of the past are no guarantee of the future. Perhaps our biggest need at 3M is for people who are uncomfortable without change."[2] Organizational change is fundamental to performance excellence. Anyone concerned with managing an organization dedicated to performance excellence must understand what types of change are necessary in such an organization, how to make them happen, and how to manage them. This chapter explores these issues. Specifically, we will:

- explain the importance and scope of organizational change to achieving performance excellence;
- explore how organizations build a strong quality culture, sustain performance, and continually improve organizational effectiveness;
- provide some examples of firms undertaking these changes and the approaches they use; and
- explain how TQ perspectives on organizational change relate to organization theory.

THE IMPORTANCE OF CHANGE

For organizations committed to pursuing performance excellence, change is a way of life. Organizational change is needed to initiate performance excellence initiatives and constantly thereafter. In the initial stage, an effort must be mounted to begin to change the culture of the organization. Once a quality mindset is rooted in an organization, continuous improvement efforts will relentlessly create changes in product designs, standard operating procedures, and virtually every other aspect of organizations. Unless a culture based on customers, continuous improvement, and teamwork is established, quality will be little more than "just another one of management's programs." Indeed, this is often the cause of failure of TQ initiatives.

Why do organizations find themselves in need of change? The major reason is that customer expectations and the external environment continuously evolve. Features or services that delight customers one year may be taken for granted the next, and products that customers find acceptable one year may be perceived as substandard the next. Competition continues to raise the standard for quality, and organizations must keep up (see box "Quality Never Goes Out of Style"). When first published, *USA Today*'s use of color and graphics was exceptional. In short order, however, newspapers copied these features so widely that exclusive use of black and white on the front page began to look old-fashioned. With the ubiquitous presence of the Internet today, traditional newspapers are finding themselves turning more attention to online content and services.

Quality Never Goes Out of Style[3]

In 1853 a young German immigrant named Strauss took a 17,000-mile trip on a clipper ship from New York around South America to San Francisco. He intended to set up shop selling dry goods to people lured to California by the Gold Rush. By the time he reached San Francisco, however, he had sold all the goods he brought except for some canvas for tents.

The miners told him he should have brought pants instead of canvas to sell, because most pants fell apart too quickly while they dug for gold. The enterprising young Strauss immediately took the heavy brown canvas to a tailor and created the world's first pair of jeans. Those "pants of Levi's" (Strauss's first name) were so popular that he quickly sold all of his canvas and switched to a heavy serge fabric made in Nimes, France ("serge de Nimes," eventually shortened to "denim"). When the new fabric was treated with indigo dye, it attained its familiar deep blue cover.

Levi never liked the term "jeans" so he called his pants "waist-high overalls." In fact, his company did not use the term—derived from the French word "genes" for a type of cotton trousers—until long after his death.

Levi noticed that miners often complained that the weight of gold nuggets was causing their pockets to tear. Always looking for ways to improve the quality of his pants, Levi and tailor Jacob Davis patented in 1873 the innovation of riveting pocket corners to add strength. By the 1930s, Levi's were worn by everyone from cowboys to school children. The rivets, much appreciated by miners, caused the company problems with other customers, which they quickly addressed. In 1937, the company covered the rivets on the rear pockets in response to complaints that they scratched both saddles and school desks.

The rivet at the base of the fly was removed by executive order after company president Walter Haas crouched a little too close to a roaring campfire for a little too long and discovered what the cowboys had been complaining about.

The popularity of Levi's jeans surged again in the 1950s when actor James Dean wore them in the movie *Rebel Without a Cause*. Today, Levi's jeans are sold in more than 70 nations. The company says that they are made with "the choicest fabric, the strongest thread, first-class buttons, rivets, and snaps, precise sewing, and careful inspection." The jeans carry a "Levi's promise" card guaranteeing customer satisfaction. With this history of continuous improvement in response to customer needs, it's no wonder that, as the company's slogan puts it, "quality never goes out of style."

Any organization that focuses on meeting a fixed set of quality goals quickly will find itself trampled into the dust by competitors racing to keep up with customers. As one Xerox executive stated, "Quality is a race without a finish line." Change is also required because processes tend to become unnecessarily complicated over a period of time, even when they are initially designed in a sensible manner. Each new person working on a process adds a wrinkle or two until, eventually, a monster has been created.

Strategic Change versus Process Change[4]

It is important to differentiate between organizational changes resulting from strategy development and implementation (i.e., "strategic change"), and organizational changes resulting from operational assessment activities (i.e., "process change").

TABLE 11.1 STRATEGIC VERSUS PROCESS CHANGE

	Strategic Change	Process Change
Theme of change	Shift in organizational direction	Adjustment of organizational processes
Driving force	Usually environmental forces—market, rival, technological change	Usually internal—"How can we better align our processes?"
Typical antecedent	Strategic planning process	Self-assessment of management system
How much of the organization changes?	Typically widespread	Often narrow—divisional or functional
Examples	Entering new markets Seeking low-cost position Mergers and acquisitions	Improving information systems Establishing hiring guidelines Developing improved customer satisfaction measures

Strategic change stems from strategic objectives, which are generally externally focused and relate to significant customer, market, product/service, or technological opportunities and challenges. This is what an organization must change to remain or become competitive. Strategic change is broad in scope, is driven by environmental forces, and is tied closely to the organization's ability to achieve its goals. Some examples are General Electric's implementation of Six Sigma throughout the corporation, and Hewlett-Packard's decision to merge with Compaq. In contrast, process change deals with the operations of an organization. Some examples of process change are a health care organization that discovered weaknesses in the organization's ability to collect and analyze information, followed by a $50 million information system upgrade; or an AT&T division that found that many employees did not recall the division's strategic vision, which prompted managers to increase meetings and interactions with employees to improve communication.

Although change to a business process tends to have lasting effects, the change tends to be narrow in scope. Unlike strategic change, which motivates organization-wide changes in behavior, process change is often confined to a particular unit, division, or function of the organization. For example, changing an organization's process for measuring customer satisfaction usually requires substantive adjustment to a limited number of functional areas, such as marketing or information systems. In Table 11.1, we describe the characteristics of strategic change in contrast with process change. Strategic changes are the ones that impact culture the most.

CULTURAL CHANGE

A major strategic change that organizations must make in pursuing performance excellence is a change in culture. Culture is the set of beliefs and values shared by the people in an organization. It is what binds them together and helps them make sense of what happens in their company. Cultures can vary dramatically between one company and another. In some firms, raw ambition is taken for granted, while in others, subordination of one's own agenda to the good of the organization is expected. Some companies create a status hierarchy reminiscent of the court of Louis XIV, whereas others downplay status differences.

Culture is a powerful influence on people's behavior; historically, most employees at IBM would never wear anything other than a white shirt, whereas most people at Apple wouldn't be caught dead in one. Culture has such power because it is shared widely within an organization, and because it operates without being talked about, indeed, often without even being thought of.

Organizations are in some ways like a circle of high school friends who share strong beliefs about which activities, people, and music are okay, and which are not. A new employee who did something that violated the culture might be told, "That's just not how we do things around here." The employee could be forgiven both for the error and for being perplexed at what was wrong, because the rules of culture are often not written down and must be deciphered.

Despite its intangibility, one can learn about an organization's culture in a number of ways. How people dress and how they address one another provide clues. The layout of offices, plant floors, and lounges may also reveal what is important in the organization. For example, do managers but not employees have reserved parking spots? Do offices have doors? Are there any private offices? Culture is expressed in the stories and jokes people tell, in how they spend their time at work, in what they display in their offices, and in a thousand other large and small ways. Culture is also reflected by the management policies and actions that a company practices. Therefore, organizations that believe in the principles of total quality are more likely to successfully implement the practices. Conversely, actions set culture in motion: Behavior leads people to think in certain ways. Thus, as total quality practices are used routinely within an organization, its people learn to believe in the principles, and cultural changes can occur.

From this description, it should be clear why firms deciding to pursue total quality need cultural change. If a quality initiative is inconsistent with the organizational culture, it will be undermined. For example, employees in a company in which status is jealously guarded will feel uncomfortable participating on an equal basis in team meetings with individuals from three different levels of management. People who share the belief that stability is the source of business success will be skeptical about continuous improvement. In situations like these, TQ is like an organ transplanted to a poorly matched donor and will be rejected.

A concept related to culture is *organizational climate*. Although some writers interchange the two concepts, many feel that organizational climate is separate from culture. Climate has been likened to an organization's personality—its hopes, attitudes, and biases—in essence, its mood. Some researchers suggest that organizations have one overall culture, but many underlying climates, which are specific to different areas. For example, there may be a climate for quality, a climate for safety, a climate for ethics, each of which is driven by different management practices and policies.[5] Thus, although an organization may have a culture that supports teamwork and participation, it may not necessarily have a climate that facilitates the full adoption of TQ principles.

Elements of a Performance Excellence Culture

The organizational culture needed to support performance excellence is one that values customers, improvement, and teamwork. In an organization with a quality-friendly culture, everyone believes that customers are the key to the organization's future and that their needs must come first. If two employees are having a conversation and a customer enters the shop, the conversation ends until the customer is served.

In a culture supportive of performance excellence, people expect their jobs to change due to improvements dictated by customer needs. They are always looking for better (faster, simpler, less expensive) ways to do things. "Because that's the way we've always done it" is not a valid reason for doing anything. The culture of improvement is exemplified by the Levi Strauss and Eastman Chemical stories (see also the box "Defining a Performance-Based Culture").

Employees in a quality-oriented culture instinctively act as a team. If someone is away from her desk and her phone rings, another employee will answer it rather than leave a customer hanging. Organizations where a focus on customers, continuous improvement, and teamwork are taken for granted have a good chance of succeeding at total quality. Most organizations do not have such a culture prior to exposure to TQ principles; some degree of cultural change is necessary.

These elements, along with several others, are reflected clearly in the Baldrige National Quality Program Criteria for Performance Excellence. The criteria are built upon a set of "core values and concepts":

- visionary leadership,
- customer-driven excellence,

Defining a Performance-Based Culture[6]

Julia Graham summarized the characteristics of a performance-based culture from a variety of articles and books:

- In a performance-based culture, a premium is placed on excellence in performance—obtaining desired behaviors and results. Seniority-based cultures emphasize "sticking around longer than other people." In best-effort cultures, trying hard is the focus—even if the expected results haven't been achieved.
- Organizations with performance-based cultures acknowledge that their success is contingent upon the successful performance of their employees. They recognize that the ability of the organization to carry out its mission and achieve results is dependent on the competence, innovation, and productivity of its work force.
- Strategic outcomes drive the work of organizations with performance-based cultures. Their people work to achieve the goals, not to the rules. The mindset of both managers and employees is to work together, cooperatively and effectively, toward a common goal, ensuring the success of the organization by delivering timely, high quality products/services to customers. Management in these organizations is strongly committed to creating conditions and consequences that support and sustain strong performance. Desired performance is fostered and rewarded; poor performance is not tolerated. All possible policies and practices are put in place to support sustained, high performance.

- organizational and personal learning,
- valuing workforce members and partners,
- agility,
- focus on the future,
- managing for innovation,
- management by fact,
- societal responsibility,
- focus on results and creating value, and
- systems perspective.

These values provide a solid list of the cultural elements necessary to sustain a total quality environment and are embedded in the beliefs and behaviors of high-performing organizations.

The existence of a set of cultural values necessary for achieving performance excellence does not mean that all organizations that wish to practice total quality must have the same culture. Many aspects of culture differ greatly from one quality-oriented company to another. Company personnel may prefer to communicate in person or in writing; they may serve smoked salmon and champagne or a bushel of crabs and a keg of beer at the company picnic; they may wear uniforms, gray flannel suits, or jeans. As long as they hold the core values of TQ, quality can find a home in their organization.

Changing Organizational Culture for Performance Excellence

Perhaps the first question to address is why organizations decide to pursue a performance excellence-based organizational culture. A reluctance to pursue performance excellence often results from some common misconceptions, such as that it means doing lots of "things" like collecting data and organizing teams, or that it only applies to large companies. A focus on quality does, however, require significant changes in organization design, processes, and culture. Such broad change has been a stumbling block for many companies.

Companies make the decision to adopt a performance excellence philosophy for two basic reasons:

1. A firm reacts to competition that poses a threat to its profitable survival by turning to quality.
2. Performance excellence represents an opportunity to improve.

Most firms—even Baldrige Award recipients—have made the decision because of the first reason. Xerox, for example, watched its market share fall from 90 percent to 13 percent in a little over a decade; Milliken faced increased competition from Asian textile manufacturers; Boeing Airlift and Tankers Programs was on the brink of losing its only customer, the Department of Defense. Although they were not facing dire crises, perceived future threats were the impetus for FedEx and Wainwright Industries. When faced with a threat to survival, a company effects cultural change more easily; under these circumstances, organizations generally implement TQ effectively. A company will generally have more difficulty gaining support for change when not facing a crisis. This reluctance is a reflection of the attitude "If it ain't broke, don't fix it." In such cases, a company might attempt to manufacture a crisis mentality to effect change. Nevertheless, many organizations, like Texas

Nameplate, SSM Healthcare, and Cargill Corn Milling, have pursued performance excellence simply because they recognized that it will make them stronger and more competitive.

The biggest dangers lie in the lack of complete understanding and the tendency to imitate others—the easy way out. Many of the experts and consultants have rewritten total quality management around their own discipline, such as accounting, engineering, human resources, or statistics. The "one best model" of performance excellence may not mesh with an organization's culture; most successful companies have developed their own unique approaches to fit their own requirements. Research has shown that imitation of efforts made by one successful organization may not lead to good results in another (see box "Why Silver Bullets Can Kill"). Building and sustaining performance excellence requires a readiness for change, the adoption of sound practices and implementation strategies, and an effective organization.

How can a company change its culture to be more consistent with quality? As with most aspects of performance excellence, it begins with leadership (see box "A Sincere Belief and Trust in People").[7] Leaders must articulate to employees the direction in which they want the company to go. They must set an example by expressing TQ values in their own behavior and by recognizing and rewarding others who do the same. The efforts of the new leadership team in a foundry to establish the values of continuous improvement and teamwork are described in this statement by the quality director, whose efforts had been frustrated under the old regime:[8]

> They brought in a people-oriented environment. They made the environment conducive to change and tried to get to the point where employees felt safe to make change.

Why Silver Bullets Can Kill[9]

Mike Carnell provides some insights into why "silver bullets" don't often work for organizations. Many have tried to imitate the now legendary Toyota Production System but were unable to achieve the outstanding results that Toyota did. Why? The company had a vision and strategy for a system that would create value for their organization:

- They stayed the course, developing, implementing, and tweaking that system until it fit the organization like a glove.
- They did not spend their time looking for a prefabricated answer to all their problems that might or might not work in their organization.
- They took the time to understand their organization and their business and created a system that delivered the things they knew would make them a force in their industry.

A similar situation occurred when General Electric's (GE) Six Sigma program became visible to the public. People rushed to benchmark GE. Unfortunately, people who spend their lives rushing from one benchmark to the next because they have an innate lack of creativity typically lack the same creativity when they benchmark. They benchmark the convenient, the obvious, and, oftentimes, the irrelevant. They ask: "Did the GE program succeed because Black Belts did X number of projects per year in X amount of time per project? Was the average value per project one of the real factors that drove the GE success?" The reality is that GE was already a fast moving train when they began Six Sigma. Several initiatives, such as Work Out and their change acceleration process, were already in place, as was the experience of the Jack Welch leadership team.

A Sincere Belief and Trust in People[10]

One powerful example of the importance of cultural change is the case of Wainwright Industries, a former Baldrige recipient. During the 1970s and 1980s, Wainwright lost millions in sales; operations slowed to three days a week; and tensions grew between employees and management. Recognizing the problem lay with management, the CEO made some radical changes. Workers were called "associates," and everyone was put on salary. Associates are paid even if they miss work and they still receive time-and-a-half for overtime. The company has maintained over 99 percent attendance since this change.

Managers shed their white shirts and ties, and everyone from the CEO down wears a common uniform, embroidered with the label Team Wainwright. A team of associates developed a profit-sharing plan, whereby everyone receives the same bonus every six months. Everyone has access to the privately held company's financial records. In addition, all reserved parking spaces were removed; walls—including those for the CEO's office—were replaced with glass. Customers, both external and internal, are treated as partners with extensive communication. The most striking example occurred when one worker admitted accidentally damaging some equipment, even though most workers were afraid to report such incidents. The CEO called a plantwide meeting and explained what had happened. Then he called the man up, shook his hand, and thanked him for reporting the accident. Accident reporting increased from zero to 90 percent, along with suggestions on how to prevent them. Wainwright's culture can be summed up as a sincere belief and trust in people. One measure of Wainwright's success is that the number of implemented suggestions per person per year exceeds 50, while the previous benchmark that Wainwright identified was 15!

> Before, you did what the boss told you to do and if you didn't you're probably going to get fired. Now we have some coaches in place and facilitators, and they want the ideas from the employees and it's a hell of a lot easier with their input.

A great deal of the effort leaders expend in cultural change is devoted to communication. Employees company-wide must be informed of the new values and practices desired. Any early successes of the new approach must also be publicized. This is not always easy, especially when the company's employees are geographically dispersed. In attempting to change the culture at Southern Pacific Lines, railroad executives held 125 "town meetings" at sites where employees worked, sometimes in groups as small as 5 to 10.[11]

In promoting a new culture, leaders also must personally practice behaviors associated with the new culture. This both provides a role model for employees and symbolizes management's sincerity about the new approach. When the Indian soap company, Godrej Soaps, tried to initiate continuous improvement, workers were reluctant to unwrap defective soaps to see how mistakes could be avoided in the future. When informed of this, the managing director said he would go into the plant to unwrap the soaps. As it turned out, he didn't need to do it. When workers heard that the top manager was willing to do this kind of work, they agreed to do it themselves.[12]

None of this should be interpreted to mean that cultural change is easy. On the contrary, it is very difficult, takes several years to complete, and often fails.[13]

One reason for the difficulty is resistance by middle management. Managers resist change because it creates more work for them when they often feel overburdened and disrupts the steady flow of work in the organization.[14] Getting on board for a change in culture requires managers to acknowledge that the current approach is somehow lacking, despite any of their previous statements to the contrary. They also may be afraid that they will not be able to perform effectively in the new culture.

Often, reward systems get in the way of cultural change and must be adjusted for the new culture to take hold. In many companies, telephone operators are rewarded for the speed with which they process calls, rather than for how completely they satisfy the customers who call. Unless this type of reward system is changed, management's pleas to increase customer satisfaction will fall on deaf ears. Willingness to make such changes indicates management's commitment to the new culture.

Managing change often requires a well-defined process, just like any other business process. In fact, an organization that doesn't realize that change is a process probably won't do a good job in TQ. This is critical because about 70 percent of all change efforts fail.[15] Thinking of change management as a process helps to define the steps necessary to achieve the desired outcomes.

It also forces the organization to think of its employees as customers who will be affected by the change. American Express, for example, views its change process as consisting of five steps:[16]

1. Scope the change—why are we doing this?
2. Create a vision—what will the change look like?
3. Drive commitment—what needs to happen to make the change work?
4. Accelerate the transition—how are we going to manage the effort on an ongoing basis?
5. Sustain momentum—what have we learned and how can we leverage it?

People Roles in Organizational Change

Senior management, middle management, and the workforce each have a critical role to play in changing culture. Senior managers must ensure that their vision of performance excellence is successfully executed within the organization. Middle managers provide the leadership to design the systems and processes. In the end, it is the workforce that delivers quality.

Senior Management Senior managers must understand how quality can further the mission, vision, and values of the company and its impact on customers and stakeholders. Senior managers must identify the critical processes that need attention and improvement and the resources and tradeoffs that must be made to fund the initiative. They must review progress and remove barriers to implementation. Finally, they must improve the processes in which they are involved (strategic planning, for example), both to improve the performance of the process and to demonstrate their ability to use quality tools for problem solving.[17]

Middle Management Middle management has been viewed by many as a direct obstacle to creating a supportive environment for performance excellence.[18] Middle managers are often seen as feeding territorial competition, stifling information flow, not developing and/or preparing employees for change, and feeling threatened by continuous improvement efforts. However, middle management's role in creating and sustaining a quality-focused culture is critical. Middle managers improve the operational processes that are the foundation of customer satisfaction; they can make or break cooperation and teamwork; and they are the principal means by which the workforce prepares for change.

Mark Samuel suggests that transforming middle managers into change agents requires a systematic process that dissolves traditional management boundaries and replaces them with an empowered and team-oriented state of accountability for organizational performance.[19] This process involves the following:

1. Empowerment. Middle managers must be accountable for the performance of the organization in meeting objectives.
2. Creating a common vision of excellence. This vision is then transformed into critical success factors that describe key areas of performance that relate to internal and external customer satisfaction.
3. New rules for playing the organizational game. Territorial walls must be broken, yielding a spirit of teamwork. One new approach is interlocking accountability, in which all managers are accountable to one another for their performance. The second is team representation, in which each manager is responsible for accurately representing the ideas and decisions of the team to others outside the team.
4. Implementing a continuous improvement process. These projects should improve operational systems and processes.
5. Developing and retaining peak performers. Middle managers must identify and develop future leaders of the organization.

The Workforce The workforce must develop ownership of the quality process. Ownership and empowerment gives employees the right to have a voice in deciding what needs to be done and how to do it.[20] It is based on a belief that what is good for the organization is also good for the individual and vice versa.

At Westinghouse, ownership is defined as "... taking personal responsibility for our jobs ... for assuring that we meet or exceed our customers' standards and our own. We believe that ownership is a state of mind and heart that is characterized by a personal and emotional commitment to approach every decision and task with the confidence and leadership of an owner." Self-managed teams, discussed in Chapter 7, are one form of ownership.

Training, recognition, and better communication are key success factors for transferring ownership to the workforce. With increased ownership, however, comes a flatter organization—and the elimination of some middle managers. Increased ownership also requires increased sharing of information with the workforce and a commitment to the workforce in good times and in bad. This might mean reducing stock dividends and executive bonuses before laying off the workforce during economic downturns. This is what Japanese companies do when the business climate turns south.

Common Implementation Mistakes

Performance excellence initiatives are often attempted without a full grasp of its nature, and certain mistakes are made repeatedly. The most frequent errors are as follows:[21]

1. The effort is regarded as a short-term program, despite rhetoric to the contrary.
2. Compelling results are not obtained quickly. There may be no attempt to get short-term results, or management may believe that measurable benefits lie only in the distant future.
3. The process is not driven by a focus on the customer, strategic business issues, and senior management.
4. Structural elements in the organization (such as compensation systems, promotion systems, accounting systems, rigid policies and procedures, specialization and functionalization, and status symbols such as offices and perks) block change.
5. Goals are set too low. Management does not shoot for stretch goals or use outside benchmarks as targets.
6. The organizational culture remains one of "command and control," and is driven by fear or game playing, budgets, schedules, or bureaucracy.
7. Training is not properly addressed. There is too little training of the workforce. Training may be of the wrong kind; for example, providing only classroom training without on-the-job reinforcement, or focusing on the mechanics of tools and not on identifying problems.
8. The focus is mainly on products, not processes.
9. Little real empowerment is given and what is given is not supported in actions.
10. The organization is too successful and complacent. It is not receptive to change and learning and clings to the "not invented here" syndrome.
11. The organization fails to address three fundamental questions: Is this another program? What's in it for me? How can I do this on top of everything else?
12. Senior management is not personally and visibly committed and actively participating.
13. The use of teams to solve cross-functional problems is overemphasized to the neglect of individual efforts at local improvements.
14. The belief prevails that more data are always desirable, regardless of relevance—"paralysis by analysis."
15. Management fails to recognize that quality improvement is a personal responsibility at all levels of the organization.
16. The organization does not see itself as a collection of interrelated processes making up an overall system. Both the individual processes and the overall system need to be identified and understood.

Although this list is extensive, it is by no means exhaustive. It reflects the continued difficulty of change in organizations. Performance excellence requires a new set of skills and learning, including interpersonal awareness and competence, team building, encouraging openness and trust, listening, giving and getting feedback, group participation, problem solving, clarifying goals, resolving conflicts, delegating and coaching, empowerment, and continuous improvement as a way of life.[22] The process must begin by creating a set of feelings and attitudes that lead to lasting values.

SUSTAINING QUALITY AND PERFORMANCE EXCELLENCE

Successful organizations realize that the process of quality and performance excellence is a never-ending journey. As an old Chinese proverb says, a journey begins with a single step. Getting started often seems easy by comparison with sustaining a performance excellence focus. Numerous organizational barriers and challenges get in the way. New efforts usually begin with much enthusiasm, in part because of the sheer novelty of the effort. After a while, reality sets in and doubts surface. Real problems develop as early supporters begin to question the process. At this point, the organization can resign itself to inevitable failure or persist and seek to overcome the obstacles.

THE LIFE CYCLE OF QUALITY INITIATIVES

To help understand these issues, it is useful to recognize that quality initiatives—as most business initiatives—follow a natural life cycle.[23] Leonard and McAdam suggest that understanding the life cycle "provides a strategic mechanism to chart and sustain quality while proactively countering shortcomings of its implementation, such as stagnation and limited application, which can ultimately result in failure." The six stages of a quality life cycle are

1. *Adoption*: the implementation stage of a new quality initiative.
2. *Regeneration*: when a new quality initiative is used in conjunction with an existing one to generate new energy and impact.
3. *Energizing*: when an existing quality initiative is refocused and given new resources.
4. *Maturation*: when quality is strategically aligned and deployed across the organization.
5. *Limitation or stagnation*: when quality has not been strategically driven or aligned.
6. *Decline*: When a quality initiative has had a limited impact, is failing and the initiative is awaiting termination.

The following example serves to illustrate the implications of this life-cycle model. One organization began adopting quality by introducing team building and establishing problem-solving teams. However, after four years the quality management initiative failed. Initial training had been limited, and implementation was unfocused and not directly related to the strategic objectives of the organization. As a result, the new teamwork approach came as a culture shock to the organization, and its quality initiative began a decline. The organization was determined to continue with quality management and subsequently adopted a second initiative. This involved new training and teams provided with improvement kits based on problem-solving tools and techniques. In addition, senior management focused on the coordination of improvement efforts with strong links to the organization's strategic goals. Structured performance assessments monitored progress. The quality manager cited "management commitment and leadership from the top" as the key to its successful second quality initiative. The quality life cycle of this second initiative reflects its progress from adoption to maturity. This approach created strong quality dynamics, which achieved strategic alignment and deployment throughout the organization.

From this example, we observe two things:

1. Awareness that separate initiatives create a cumulative impact leads to an appreciation that selection of new quality initiatives must be based on where an organization is in the quality life cycle.
2. Understanding that the quality life-cycle elements enable an organization to apply energizing or regenerating actions proactively to successfully sustain its quality journey.

Understanding such impacts on the dynamics of quality, in particular on the characteristics of the quality life cycle, provides the capability to sustain successful quality management by strategically adopting responses based on energizing and regenerating elements.

In studying Baldrige recipients in the health care sector, a group of former Baldrige examiners and judges proposed a similar model that describes the Baldrige journey, shown in Figure 11.1.[24] At Stage 0, organizations opt to wait for mandates and regulations, and they implement change when required to maintain compliance. While they may experience occasional "random acts of improvement," there is no overarching impetus to drive the organization to higher levels of performance. In Stage 1, organizations commit to a proactive approach to improvement. Initial steps

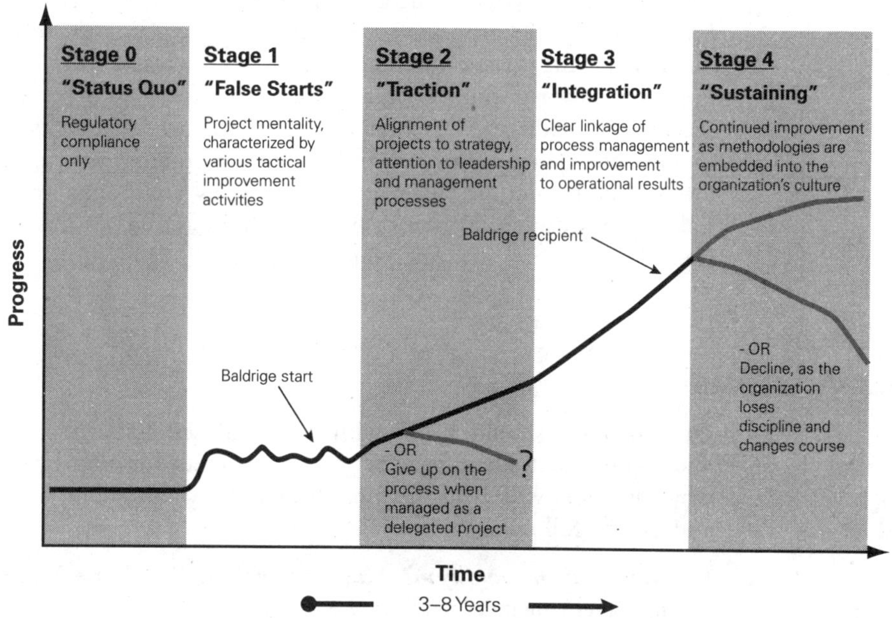

FIGURE 11.1 | BALDRIGE ROADMAP TO PERFORMANCE EXCELLENCE

tend to include learning and implementing quality improvement tools and methods. Often this project-focused phase brings new capabilities to execute initiatives that change routine practices and processes for the better. However, organizations at this stage typically reach a plateau. Leaders became frustrated with the overall impact of their continuous improvement efforts and the pace of change. For most of these organizations, projects succeed often enough, but the overall culture does not change and system-wide performance excellence is elusive. Visionary leaders recognize the inherent limitations of a project-based approach to performance improvement: slow pace of change, incremental gains, and depleted organizational energy. They seek an approach to build system integration across silos and departments in order to create a high-performance, results-oriented culture throughout their organizations.

When senior leaders became personally and actively engaged with the criteria and feedback—whether through simply answering the questions, conducting a self-assessment, or writing an application for a state or national award program—they begin to experience traction on their organizational transformation strategies (Stage 2). This phase marks the transition from the singular focus on change through projects, however well executed, to systematic evaluation and improvement of leadership approaches. Projects become more focused and aligned to organizational strategy, while leadership and management processes receive attention as well, shoring up capability to spread improvements and hardwire sustainability. As organizations become more skillful at these approaches, integration (Stage 3) begins to occur. Approaches and processes of leadership, such as values deployment and culture building, begin to link and align with strategic planning and action planning, scorecards and dashboards, job descriptions and performance review methods, and other operational processes. Nonaligned improvement initiatives are dropped or postponed as focused effort replaces frenetic activity. The Integration phase is characterized by action on the feedback, usually by incorporating it into the strategic planning process.

Finally, the sustaining stage (Stage 4) can result in two outcomes: continued improvement or decline as organizations lose focus or become distracted. Although receiving a Baldrige Award might appear to carry with it the potential for loss of momentum, many organizations renew their commitment to achieving even higher levels of performance. This may occur through continuing annual participation in a Baldrige-based award process, or through internal assessment processes, often as a first step in annual strategic planning.

Self-Assessment

Organizations should begin with a critical self-assessment of where they stand. Such assessment identifies strengths and areas for improvement and determines what practices will yield the most benefit. At a minimum, a self-assessment should address the following:

- *Management involvement and leadership.* To what extent are all levels of management involved?
- *Product and process design.* Do products meet customer needs? Are products designed for easy manufacturability?

- *Product control.* Is a strong product control system in place that concentrates on defect prevention before the fact, rather than defect removal after the product is made?
- *Customer and supplier communications.* Does everyone understand who the customer is? To what extent do customers and suppliers communicate with each other?
- *Quality improvement.* Is a quality improvement plan in place? What results have been achieved?
- *Employee participation.* Are all employees actively involved in quality improvement?
- *Education and training.* What is done to ensure that everyone understands his or her job and has the necessary skills? Are employees trained in quality improvement techniques?
- *Quality information.* How is feedback on quality results collected and used?

Many self-assessment instruments that provide a picture of the state of quality in the organization are available.[25] Most self-administered surveys, however, can provide only a rudimentary assessment of an organization's strengths and weaknesses. The most complete way to assess the level of performance excellence maturity in an organization is to evaluate its practices and results against the Malcolm Baldrige National Quality Award criteria by using trained internal or external examiners, or by actually applying for the Baldrige or a similar state award and receiving comprehensive examiner feedback (see box "Alignment through Assessment"). Understanding one's strengths and opportunities for improvement creates

ALIGNMENT THROUGH ASSESSMENT[26]

Hartford Hospital used a Baldrige assessment to guide its improvement efforts. The hospital needed to align its processes with the rapidly growing managed care environment, leverage internal clinical financial strength, and align employee and department goals with each other and the strategic goals of the organization. Using the Baldrige Health Care criteria, a month-long assessment was completed in 1996. The analysis revealed that the hospital had numerous strengths and many opportunities for improvement. Most areas of the hospital were not aligned with each other, leading to a disconnect between the strategic plan and many of the operational units, processes, and personnel. Major systems, such as human resources, leadership, and planning, were functioning independently of each other. Measures of performance were not trended and did not lead to improvement activities. Performance improvements were ad hoc, lacking priority, and not driven by the strategic plan.

Six initial performance improvement projects involved improving the leadership structure, linking information with the strategic plan, improving deployment of the strategic plan, improving human resource allocation, planning business and programs, and centralizing complaint management processes. The success of the project exceeded all expectations. Despite closing more than 15 percent of its beds, Hartford Hospital has not lost any market share, and it has received numerous recognitions as one of Connecticut's outstanding hospitals.

a basis for evolving toward higher levels of performance. Of course, many companies, especially smaller firms, that are just starting on a quality journey should begin with the basics, for example, a well-documented and consistent quality assurance system such as ISO 9000, which was discussed in Chapter 2.

Although some research suggests a positive relationship between the conduct of self-assessment and performance outcomes, other evidence suggests that many organizations derive little benefit from conducting self-assessment and achieve few of the process improvements suggested by self-study.[27] This lack of follow-through might seem a bit surprising. Why would organizations take the time to conduct a self-assessment and then not follow up on the results? After all, improvement opportunities usually offer significant gains in organizational effectiveness and competitive performance. Some managers may not follow up because they truly do not sense a problem—despite information suggesting otherwise. Often, however, managers get the message but choose not to respond. Many managers react negatively or by denial: "These are wrong," "This is not how it is here," and "These [examiners] missed the boat" are often heard. Such remarks are particularly likely when the report suggested that the organization was a less-than-stellar performer in areas perceived as strengths by senior managers.

Other managers may not know what to do with the information. Managers possessing little understanding of how the organization operates may not know which levers to pull in order to effect change or simply do it to appease their superiors. Typical comments include, "There's some good stuff here, but I have no idea where to go from here," and "It's hard for me to understand how to turn this [assessment report] into action." After reading his copy of the feedback report, the head of one manufacturing company muttered, "Well, we've satisfied [the boss's demand for conducting the self-assessment] for another year. Now we can put this all away and get back to business."

Following up requires senior leaders to engage in two types of activities: action planning and subsequently tracking implementation progress. Managers must take a positive approach to self-assessment findings, no matter how unpleasant they might appear—"Okay, what should we do to improve these areas?" Positive reactions often reinforce long-held but suppressed views about how the organization functioned. For example, at a meeting where results were being presented to the top management team, the chief engineering manager, on hearing of low evaluations related to the organization's communications processes, exclaimed, "I've been telling you guys this for years! Maybe now you'll believe me that we need to do something." The action plan identifies particular activities necessary to address the improvement opportunities. Effective action plans share some common characteristics. First, key actions to address the opportunities must be identified. A meeting to discuss the findings with key employees is often an excellent way to begin. Once identified, action plans should be documented and the who, what, when, where, and how of each action item specified. A draft version of the action plan should be communicated to inform those directly affected and gain their cooperation. Finally, the action plan should be reviewed to ensure that it effectively addresses the key opportunities identified by the self-assessment findings.

Many managers consider their job finished when action plans are set in motion. However, planned changes are rarely implemented as initially intended. Moreover, people responsible for implementing the plans may need to use encouragement or involvement in order to effectively execute their portions of the intended change. Change implementation demands a second component of effective follow-up—tracking the progress of action plan execution—to provide managers with crucial feedback on whether the intervention is effective. To leverage self-assessment findings, managers must do four things:

1. *Prepare to be humbled.* "Humbling" is a word we often hear from managers who have recently digested assessment findings. Many of them have trouble believing that the performance levels of the organization are as low as they appear. Managers can temper their expectations by learning about the self-assessment activities and experiences of other organizations. Hearing it from peers, through phone calls to colleagues, and attending conferences, permit managers to learn firsthand about the self-assessment experiences of others.
2. *Talk though the findings.* Follow-up can be enhanced when the top management team discusses the self-assessment findings. Discussing the issues, concerns, and ideas can generate greater shared perspective among executives and improve consensus.
3. *Recognize institutional influences.* Managers should be sensitive to the institutional forces working on their self-assessment activities, such as pressures from customers. Institutional influence can be covertly transmitted through the literature, presentations, and conversation that managers encounter. During the planning phase of the assessment, frank discussion about the environmental motivators of the project can sensitize managers to these outside influences.
4. *Grind out the follow-up.* Even though follow-up activities may not be as exciting as plotting competitive strategy or entertaining customers, they provide infrastructure for realizing the process improvements possible from self-assessment.

Knowledge Management and Organizational Learning

One Hewlett-Packard manager noted, "The fundamental building material of a modern corporation is knowledge." H. James Harrington observed, "All organizations have it, but most don't know what they know, don't use what they do know, and don't reuse the knowledge they have."[28] Six Sigma efforts build a vast supply of knowledge within an organization, but knowledge is perishable, and if it is not renewed and replenished, it becomes worthless.

Knowledge assets refer to the accumulated intellectual resources that an organization possesses, including information, ideas, learning, understanding, memory, insights, cognitive and technical skills, and capabilities. **Explicit knowledge** includes information stored in documents or other forms of media. **Tacit knowledge** is information that is formed around intangible factors resulting from an individual's experience, and is personal and content-specific. These two aspects represent the "know how" that an organization has available to use, invest, and grow. Employees, software, patents, databases, documents, guides, policies and procedures, and technical drawings are repositories of an organization's knowledge assets. Customers, suppliers, and partners also may hold key knowledge assets. Knowledge assets have become more important than financial and physical assets in many organizations. Process improvement requires new knowledge to result in better processes and procedures. Increasing the knowledge of the organization, both in an individual sense as well as for the organization as a whole, is the essence of learning. Knowledge can easily be lost if information is not documented or when individuals are promoted or leave the organization.

Knowledge management involves the process of identifying, capturing, organizing, and using knowledge assets to create and sustain competitive advantage (see box "Reversing the Brain Drain"). Knowledge management differs from *information management* in that information management is focused on data whereas knowledge management is focused on information. A knowledge management system allows intangible information to be managed as an organizational asset in a manner similar to tangible assets. Skandia, a large Swedish financial services company, internally audits its intellectual capital every year for inclusion in its annual report. An effective knowledge management system should include the following:

- A way of capturing and organizing explicit as well as tacit knowledge of how the business operates, including an understanding of how current business processes function.
- A systems-approach to management that facilitates assimilation of new knowledge into the business system and is oriented toward continuous improvement/innovation.
- A common framework for managing knowledge and some way of validating and synthesizing new knowledge as it is acquired.
- A culture and values that support collaborative sharing of knowledge across functions and encourages full participation of all employees in the process.[29]

The transfer of knowledge within organizations and the identification and sharing of best practices often set high-performing organizations apart from the rest. Many organizations perform similar activities at different locations or by different people. Just consider a large organization with many Six Sigma black and master black belts. What happens when one individual develops an innovative practice? How is this knowledge shared among others performing similar jobs? In most organizations, the answer is that knowledge is probably never shared.

Continuous improvement and organizational change are difficult to achieve without creating a "learning organization," a term popularized by Peter Senge, a professor at the Massachusetts Institute of Technology (MIT). He defines the learning organization as: "... an organization that is continually expanding its capacity to create its future." For such an organization, it is not enough merely to survive. "Survival learning" or what is more often termed "adaptive learning" is important—indeed it is necessary. But for a learning organization, "adaptive

REVERSING THE BRAIN DRAIN[30]

By 2010, 40 percent of the U.S. workforce will be eligible to retire. As employees depart an organization, a wealth of critical knowledge can easily go out the door with them. The Tennessee Valley Authority (TVA) began to tackle this problem in 1999, when it broke down the daunting task of retaining knowledge into manageable parts by asking line managers three questions:

1. What knowledge is likely to be lost when particular employees leave? ("What?")
2. What will be the business consequences of losing that knowledge? ("So what?")
3. What can be done to prevent or minimize the damage? ("Now what?")

To get an idea of who was planning to retire, the TVA sent out a questionnaire to all 13,000 employees asking about their retirement plans ("What?"). Based on those survey results, they gave each employee a score of 1 to 5, with 1 denoting a person who doesn't plan to leave for six years or longer and 5 earmarking someone who will be gone within a year. Managers and supervisors assigned the employees a second score of 1 to 5 ("So what?"), reflecting how essential their knowledge is to the power plants' operations, with a score of 5 being the most critical. For instance, a nuclear engineer who plans to retire in six months and takes with him decades' worth of arcane knowledge would receive a 5 on both dimensions, signifying a big red flag that managers needed to address.

The third part of the process ("Now what?") was getting people to share their knowledge. Some information is easy to capture: say, whom to call at GE when a turbine is acting up.

Harder to replace is "tribal knowledge." For example, the TVA had a steamfitter foreman at one plant who had developed an uncanny knack for detecting corrosion inside feedwater pipes by tapping on them with a wrench and listening for a particular sound. The solution was simple: assign a younger engineer to shadow the older one before he retires. John Deere, Chevron, and the World Bank have benchmarked and adopted TVA's methods.

learning" must be joined by "generative learning," learning that enhances our capacity to create.[31]

Art Schneiderman, who had worked with Senge and spent a long career with Analog Devices, offers the following simple definition of organizational learning: "… the acquisition, application, and mastery of new tools and methods that allow more rapid improvement of those processes whose improvement is critical to the success of the organization."[32]

Senge repeatedly points out, "Over the long run, superior performance depends on superior learning." The concept of organizational learning can be thought of as the process of moving through the four stages of learning that we described at the very beginning of this chapter. Effective learning requires an understanding and integration of many of the concepts and principles that are part of the TQ philosophy. It can help avoid repeating mistakes, build sensitivity, and better adapt to a changing world, and help to improve operations by understanding the weaknesses in the past and how to correct them.[33]

Organizational learning is considered a fundamental practice in the Baldrige criteria, which defines it as "continuous improvement of existing approaches and processes and adaptation to change, leading to new goals and/or approaches."[34] The criteria view learning as having four distinct stages:

1. planning, including the design of processes, selection of measures, and deployment of requirements;
2. execution of plans;
3. assessment of progress, taking into account internal and external results; and
4. revision of plans based on assessment findings, learning, new inputs, and new requirements.

In the Leadership category, for example, the requirement of Organizational Performance Review focuses organizations to provide a picture of their "state of health" and examine how well they are currently performing and also how well they are moving toward the future. This review capitalizes on the information generated from the measurement and analysis of business results and is intended to provide a reliable means to guide both improvement and change at the strategic planning level.

Many companies learn from Baldrige recipients (see box "Organizational Learning at Texas Instruments"). Scott McNealy, CEO of Sun Microsystems, for example, invited three CEOs of Baldrige winners (FedEx, Motorola, and Xerox)

Organizational Learning at Texas Instruments

Many firms use self-assessment against the Baldrige criteria as a means of organizational learning. Thus, it is not surprising that perhaps the best examples of learning organizations are Baldrige recipients. In pursuing their TQ efforts that eventually led to the award, they have continually and systematically translated the examiner feedback into improvements in their management practices.

A vice president at Texas Instruments Defense Systems & Electronics (DS&E) Group noted that "participating in the Baldrige Award process energized improvement efforts."[35] By 1997, just before its purchase by Raytheon, DS&E had reduced the number of in-process defects to one-tenth of what they were at the time it received the Baldrige. Production processes that took four weeks several years before were reduced to one week, with costs 20 to 30 percent less.

DS&E's approach began in 1994, when the Texas Instruments Corporation launched the TI Business Excellence Standard (TI-BEST), an assessment and improvement process that grew out of DS&E's Baldrige Award experience.[36] The process is applied to TI businesses around the world. The four steps of TI-BEST are:

1. define business excellence for your business;
2. assess your progress;
3. identify improvement opportunities; and
4. establish and deploy an action plan.

The TI approach to business excellence is achieved through the core principles of total quality discussed in Chapter 1 and a focus on operational excellence through achieving customer satisfaction with processes and teamwork and empowerment. The approach is implemented by an annual improvement process (Strategic Planning) and measured by a balanced scorecard involving customer, process, HR, and financial measurements and indicators.

TI is one of only two semiconductor companies in the world to have gained market share in each of the four consecutive years prior to 1997, and during that time jumped from last place to first in return on net assets, compared to Intel, Motorola, and National Semiconductor.

to visit his company to discuss their quality processes. From those meetings came the core principles and strategies that Sun uses today. The key lessons that Sun learned were

- Quality must be elevated to the level of a "core management process."
- Quality must be the first agenda item of every executive management and board meeting.
- Quality can be managed only if it is measured.
- Quality starts with the employee.
- Achievement in quality must be a factor in compensation.

In explaining this approach, McNealy noted that "Sun was launched as a company in 1982, just about the time that Xerox was starting its Leadership Through Quality process. We wanted to learn as much as we could about what worked and what didn't work before we started solving problems that had already been solved."[37]

One of the indicators of a true learning organization is the ability to identify and transfer best practices within the organization, sometimes called **internal benchmarking**. This is one area where even the most mature organizations falter, even those that are adept at external benchmarking. The American Productivity and Quality Center (APQC) noted that executives have long been frustrated by their inability to identify or transfer outstanding practices from one location or function to another. They know that some facilities have superior practices and processes, yet operation units continue to reinvent or ignore solutions and repeat mistakes.[38]

APQC suggests that although most people have a natural desire to learn and share their knowledge, organizations have a variety of logistical, structural, and cultural hurdles to overcome. These include:

- organizational structures that promote "silo" thinking in which locations, divisions, and functions focus on maximizing their own accomplishments and rewards, or, as Deming called it, suboptimization;
- a culture that values personal technical expertise and knowledge creation over knowledge sharing;
- the lack of contact, relationships, and common perspectives among people who don't work side by side;
- an overreliance on transmitting "explicit" rather than "tacit" information — the information that people need to implement a practice that cannot be codified or written down; and
- not allowing or rewarding people for taking the time to learn and share and help each other outside of their own small corporate village.

Internal benchmarking requires a process: first, identifying and collecting internal knowledge and best practices; second, sharing and understanding those practices; and third, adapting and applying them to new situations and bringing them up to best practice performance levels. Technology, culture, leadership, and measurement are enablers that can help or hinder the process. Many organizations have created internal databases by which employees can share their practices and knowledge. For example, Texas Instruments has a Best Practices Knowledge Base delivered via Lotus Notes, Intranet, and TI's mainframe systems. Information is often organized around business core and support processes. Cultural issues include how to motivate and reward people for sharing best practices and establish a supportive culture. As with any performance excellence effort, senior leadership has to take an active role. This can be done by tying initiatives to the company's vision and strategy, communicating success stories at executive meetings, removing implementation barriers, reinforcing and rewarding positive behaviors, leading by example, and communicating the importance of best practice sharing with all employees. Finally, measuring the frequency of use and satisfaction with best practices databases, linking practices to financial and customer satisfaction, focusing on cycle time to implement best practices, and measuring the growth of virtual teams that share information are ways in which the organization can monitor the effectiveness of its approaches.

Perhaps a more difficult thing for organizations to do is to accept assistance from outside the organization—the "Not Invented Here" syndrome. General Electric, for instance, suddenly asked Southwest Airlines to allow them to help their business become more efficient and cost-effective. GE offered to send over a Six Sigma black belt to work at no cost on a problem involving a component made by another company. Southwest balked, reluctant to share private information about one supplier with another, and many managers were unwilling to accept the rigid scientific approach of Six Sigma into the freewheeling Southwest culture. Nevertheless, Southwest relented and GE's black belt helped eliminate the failures of the part. Since then, Southwest has let dozens of other GE folks work on projects such as financial analysis and invoice flow.[39]

Although this story focused on organizational learning at Southwest, the underlying reason is a push from GE to share its best practices throughout the supply chain to its customers. Dubbed "At the Customer, For the Customer," or ACFC in GE jargon, this initiative is designed to add more customer value and differentiate the company from its competitors. Continuous improvement can be a unique corporate strategy.

ORGANIZATIONAL CHANGE IN ACTION

Many organizations have made substantial changes in their organizations that reflect continuous improvement, breakthrough improvement, and learning. In this section, we highlight some of their approaches.

BOEING

Many organizations have attempted to change their cultures to become more responsive to customer needs. Boeing is a good example of a company in a difficult competitive situation that has undertaken this task.[40] Boeing has been a fixture in the aerospace industry since Bill Boeing built his first airplane—a single-engine seaplane—in 1916. Boeing's planes were heavily involved in World War II, with almost 7,000 produced by Boeing and another 13,000 produced by other manufacturers using Boeing designs. In modern times, approximately half the commercial jets in the world have been produced by Boeing; the company contributes substantially to the U.S. balance of trade by exporting planes all over the world.

Not content to rest on its corporate laurels, however, Boeing was among the early leaders of the quality movement in the United States, implementing quality circles in 1980. (Quality circles are groups of workers who meet for an hour or so each week to work on quality problems; they were a forerunner of total quality efforts in many companies.) Managers at Boeing quickly recognized, however, that the corporate culture would need to be changed if quality efforts were to be successful, and they began a process to do so. This process consisted of five steps:

1. identify norms that currently guide behaviors and attitudes;
2. identify the behaviors necessary to make the organization successful for tomorrow;
3. develop a list of new norms that will move the organization forward;
4. identify the culture gaps—the difference between the desired norms and actual norms; and
5. develop and put in place an action plan to implement the new cultural norms. These new norms will replace the old ones, and this transition will be monitored and enforced.

Boeing backed up this commitment to cultural change with a great deal of training, surveying of employees and customers, and executive commitment. Today the company faces tremendous challenges, including a decline in demand for military aircraft, competition from Airbus Industries (the European airplane consortium) and a very weak global market for jets. Its quality-oriented culture, however, based on customers, continuous improvement, and teamwork, should help it to stay competitive for years to come.

As Boeing's John Black reflected:

> This process of continuous improvement, to which we are committed, is not one that can suddenly be grafted onto a company. Every organization must make it their own. Top management leadership must be provided, and all management must be brought on board. Only when all the people are committed and the process is locked in for the long term, will it achieve the breakthrough that it is capable of providing for us—the key to economic success in the future.

MOTOROLA

Although Motorola introduced the concept of Six Sigma back in 1986, it is significantly different today, clearly demonstrating the value of organizational change for long-term sustainability. Motorola's "second-generation" Six Sigma is an overall high-performance system that executes business strategy.[41] Its results are evident, as Motorola's Commercial, Government, and Industrial Solutions Sector division received a Baldrige Award in 2002. Their new approach to Six Sigma is based on the following four steps.

1. *Align executives to the right objectives and targets*. This step means creating a balanced scorecard of strategic goals, metrics, and initiatives to identify the improvements that will have the most impact on the bottom line. Projects are not limited to traditional product and service domains but extend to market share improvements, better cash flow, and improved human resource processes.
2. *Mobilize improvement teams around appropriate metrics*. Teams use a structured problem-solving process to drive fact-based decisions; however, the focus on defects and defects per million opportunities (dpmo) sigma levels is less important, particularly in human intensive processes such as marketing and human resources. For example, the

definition of a defect as "employee performance that falls below a certain level" can be controversial and be easily manipulated. Continuous measures such as invoice delivery time or credit approval response time are replacing count-based measures such as the number of overdue invoices or the percentage of dissatisfied customers.

3. *Accelerate results*. Motorola uses an action learning framework methodology that combines formal education with real-time project work and coaching to quickly take employees from learning to doing. Project teams receive support from coaches on a just-in-time basis. Projects are driven to be accomplished quickly, rather than over a long period of time. Finally, a campaign management approach helps integrate various project teams so that the cumulative impact on the organization is, in fact, accelerated.
4. *Govern sustained improvement*. Leaders actively and visibly sponsor the key improvement projects required to execute business strategy and review them in the context of outcome goals. An important step is for leaders to actively share best practices and knowledge about improvements with other parts of the organization that can benefit.

Six Sigma continues to be Motorola's method of choice for driving bottom line improvements. More efforts will be focused on product design that enhances the overall customer experience across the value chain. As such, Six Sigma projects increasingly involve key customers, suppliers, and other business partners.

ORGANIZATIONAL CHANGE AND ORGANIZATION THEORY

A large amount of research and writing in organization theory (OT) focuses on organization change. Some of the more prominent organizational models include: Weisbord's six box model, Nadler and Tushman's congruence model, the McKinsey seven-s model, Tichy's change framework and TPC (technical, political, cultural) matrix, and the Burke-Litwin model. Few change models have been rigorously validated. Rather, the validity of most change models has been tested less formally, usually through consultant-based applications with clients and through comparison to empirical observation. The plethora of change models in use suggests that there are many viewpoints of how organizational change is achieved. However, the success by which a number of these models have been employed by scholars and consultants in empirical situations suggests that a number of these viewpoints are valid.

One commonality among these change models is a teleological perspective of organizational change. Van de Ven and Poole[42] suggested that teleology was one of four categories of change process theory. Teleological change theory posits that organizations change through an iterative process of goal setting, implementation, evaluation, and revision. Unlike other theories of change that suggest the environment as the dominant change force, teleology represents change as a deliberate undertaking by individuals affiliated with the organization.

The organizational learning literature makes a fundamental distinction between single- and double-loop levels of learning. Single-loop learning is the most common level of learning, and encompasses the organization's ability to perceive deviations from perceived performance and "fix" them. Single-loop learning occurs, for example, when managers detect a problem in implementing a specific strategic initiative and then take action to correct the deviation. Most diagnostic management control systems exhibit single-loop learning characteristics. Double-loop learning is more sophisticated, as the organization must review the underlying assumptions that created the problem to be "fixed" in the first place, and adapt a better set of assumptions to support future performance.

Research suggests that organizational learning is enhanced when people gather for "dialog." Dialog is defined as a sustained collective inquiry into the processes, assumptions, and certainties that compose everyday experience. An important consequence of effective organizational dialog is the reduction of "defensive routines," which are policies, practices, or actions that prevent people involved in a group activity from being embarrassed or threatened, and, at the same time, prevent people from learning how to reduce the causes of embarrassment or threat. Defensive routines can adversely impact the organization's ability to implement large-scale strategic change. In one research experiment, executives learned to overcome defensive routines by engaging in dialog that forced the managers to articulate their underlying assumptions and reservations about particular strategic decisions to be implemented in their organizations. After the experiment, most managers reported that their strategies were being implemented more effectively.[43]

Several researchers have attempted to draw close relationships between organizational learning and strategy and leadership.[44] For example, Crossan et al. suggest that organizational learning is a fundamental strategic process and the principal means of achieving strategic renewal. Vera and Crossan examine organizational learning in the context of leadership styles (see Chapter 10) and conclude that during times of stability organizational learning processes thrive under transactional leadership, while during times of change they benefit more from transformational leadership.

Organizational Change and Total Quality

This section compares the perspective of TQ on organization change to the organizational theory literature. Given the amount of work in this area, we can only identify a few of the major ideas in the literature on organization change and show how they relate to total quality. Organizational behavior and organization theory textbooks generally have at least one chapter on organization change, which can be consulted for further details on this research. We compare TQ to organization theory in terms of the reasons for change, the source of change, the nature of change, the difficulty of change, and how to manage change. Our overall conclusion is that, despite some differences in focus, the research on change conducted by organization theorists is a rich source of information for those embarking on the changes required by total quality.

The Reason for Change The reason behind TQ-oriented change is quality improvement for customer satisfaction. This has not been a major focus of the OT literature on change, which has focused primarily on changes intended to improve productivity and/or improve job satisfaction. Of course, many quality-oriented changes may improve productivity or job satisfaction, but that isn't usually their main objective.

The Source of Change The source of most change considered in OT is top management. In general, top management responds to changes in the organizational environment, such as increased competitiveness or declining demand. This parallels the cultural change aspect of TQ. In fact, the OT literature on change is most relevant to cultural change, as opposed to continuous improvement or process redesign.

Types of Change The types of changes considered in OT theories partially overlap with TQ-oriented changes. In particular, OT theories that deal with changes in values and norms are relevant to the transformations associated with cultural change in TQ. Other types of change featured in OT theories, such as the introduction of new technology, are not as directly relevant to TQ. (Reengineering, however, often involves the application of some type of information technology.)

Furthermore, the changes discussed in the OT literature tend to differ in two important ways from TQ-oriented change. First, they tend to be limited in scope, usually to one or two departments, and even to only a few aspects of the work of these departments. Second, they tend to be limited in duration, with the idea being to get the change over with and get on with organizational life. This may apply to cultural change (and to some extent to process redesign), but is very different from continuous improvement. Indeed, the management of continuous change over a long period of time has not been addressed often by OT research and presents a clear opportunity for research.

One of the earliest studies of organization change was conducted by Coch and French in a Virginia factory that produced pajamas.[45] In this study, a change in procedure was made in three different ways. In one group, the workers themselves devised the change. In a second group, workers appointed representatives who devised the change. In a third group, the new system was imposed on the workers by management.

The study found that the change was much more successful in the more participative groups; this study is often cited as support for the need for employee participation in organizational change. What is interesting from a TQ perspective is that it is a study of process redesign and, in the participative groups at least, of process redesign initiated by the people actually doing the work. Thus, it anticipates by 40 years the kinds of changes that have become commonplace among firms practicing total quality. True to the limits in the thinking at the time, however, the improvement was a one-shot deal. Continuous improvement was an idea whose time had not yet come.

TQ and the OT literature agree on the difficulty of successfully changing organizations and on the fact that "resistance to change" is often the underlying problem. OT research has made significant progress in identifying why organization members resist change and even in identifying various methods for dealing with this problem.[46] Resistance is at least as likely to come from managers as from lower-level employees.

The whole idea of resistance, however, flows from a concept of change mandated by top management. Managers or workers are unlikely to resist a process change that they themselves have devised. For such changes, the literature on resistance to change seems off the mark.

Perhaps the literature on population ecology provides a more helpful perspective on the difficulty of organizational change in the TQ context.[47] From this perspective, worker resistance is not to blame for the difficulty of change. Rather, the structures and systems that management has created are at fault. For example, the hierarchical organization structure of most firms makes it difficult for them to adapt effectively to environmental changes such as the evolution in customer demand. This idea is consistent with Deming's theory that problems are more often related to system imperfections than to worker inability or lack of motivation.

Population ecology theorists generally argue that the difficulty of changing structures, authority, reward systems, and so forth, renders most organizations unsuccessful in their change efforts. Writers on TQ often have commented on the major impediments such structures and systems create, but have gone on to identify ways in which such obstacles can be removed. This difference in prognosis should not mask the fundamental agreement between the ecological OT perspective and TQ on the importance of structural and systemic impediments to change.

From the ecological perspective, change in a set of similar organizations often comes about by ineffective organizations going out of business and being replaced by new ones, rather than by changing from ineffective to effective. Clearly both processes occur. Many organizations that did not provide the quality customers demanded are no longer with us, whereas others (Xerox is an excellent example) have managed to transform themselves in order to survive. Needless to say, the battle between transformation and extinction continues to be fought every day in many firms throughout the world.

Many of the principles for managing change derived from the OT literature apply directly to total quality change. Some of these principles are as follows:

1. *It is necessary to "unfreeze" people's attitudes and behavior before they can be changed.*[48] This principle, a staple of the OT understanding of change, relates directly to TQ. Before organizations can change in the direction of practicing TQ, people must see why the current approach is inappropriate or incomplete and what problems of competitiveness and customer dissatisfaction this causes. Cultural change in TQ is often the vehicle for unfreezing behavior.
2. *Change can only succeed with effective leadership.* One early proponent of this view was Thomas Bennett.[49] Bennett identified the need for leaders to deal with the emotional aspects of the change for subordinates, the need for clear goals, and the importance of logical problem-solving processes. These and other aspects of the leader's role identified by OT theorists clearly are relevant to TQ.
3. *Change agents must manage interdependence.* Few things in organizations—for example, jobs or technology—can be changed without affecting other things—structures or processes. Many OT theorists of change recognized this fact and based their theories on the need to identify and manage the interdependence among organizational phenomena.[50] This applies directly to process redesign and is consistent with Deming's emphasis on organizations as systems.
4. *Effective change must involve the people whose jobs are being changed.* This point was noted in reference to the Coch and French study. Although a

variety of rationales for the importance of participation have been advanced, its significance for reducing resistance is an article of faith among organization change theorists.[51] This is probably the point of greatest overlap between OT and TQ. The "participation" and "involvement" championed by OT theorists as much as 50 years ago have become so widely accepted in industry that they have evolved into today's concepts of "empowerment" and "self-management."

5. *Refreezing is needed to make gains permanent.* Research in OT has concluded that steps are needed to lock in the changes that have been made.[52] This point has not been lost upon the TQ community, as many organizations are now becoming concerned about maintaining, as opposed to creating, change. Many of the recommendations of the OT literature, especially the need to monitor and revise change efforts continually, are quite relevant to TQ.

Perhaps it is fitting to conclude this chapter and this book with a quote from Aristotle:

> Excellence is an art won by training and habituation. We do not act rightly because we have virtue or excellence, but we rather have those because we have acted rightly. We are what we repeatedly do. Excellence, then, is not an act but a habit.[53]

We hope that quality and performance excellence becomes a habit in your life and business career.

Review and Discussion Questions

1. Why was it important for Park Place Lexus in the Performance Excellence Profile to benchmark business practices outside of the automobile industry? How difficult would it be for a typical "Big Three" automobile dealership to embrace and implement the types of practices used by Park Place Lexus?
2. Describe some personal experiences in which you traveled through the four stages of learning described in this chapter.
3. Briefly describe the three kinds of organizational change practiced in total quality efforts.
4. You probably have, unfortunately, heard the term "dysfunctional family" in news stories about our society. What might the term "dysfunctional corporate culture" mean?
5. Describe the culture of an organization you have worked in or are familiar with. What is valued in this culture? Do you think this culture provides fertile ground for total quality? Why or why not?
6. Will an organization's culture be the same throughout or will it vary from department to department? Why?
7. Find and examine five Internet Web sites for large corporations. What do these sites tell you about the company's culture?
8. For each of the core values of the Baldrige criteria, describe some practices that you would expect to see high-performing organizations implement.
9. Download the latest version of the Baldrige criteria from the NIST Web site (http://www.baldrige.nist.gov) and discuss how the core values and concepts underlying the Baldrige criteria are reflected in each category of the criteria.
10. Managers can enforce rules about what people do and say at work. But can they enforce a culture? If yes, how can they do it?

If no, what does this say about the limits of managers' ability to ensure quality?

11. A major stumbling block in implementing TQ in the United States has been the traditional adversarial relationship between unions and management. What should be the role of both unions and management in building a TQ culture?
12. Compare the quality life cycle with the Baldrige model in Figure 11.1. How are they similar? How do they differ?
13. What might the "learning organization" concept mean to a college or university?
14. How might internal benchmarking be applied within your college? What types of activities would be appropriate?

CASES

The Yellow Brick Road to Quality[54]

In the film *The Wizard of Oz*, Dorothy learned many lessons. Surprisingly, managers can learn a lot from the *Wizard of Oz* also. For each of the following summaries of scenes in the film, discuss the lessons that organizations can learn in pursuing change and a performance excellence culture.

A. Dorothy was not happy with the world as she knew it. A tornado came along and transported her to the Land of Oz. The tornado dropped Dorothy's house on the Wicked Witch of the East, killing the witch. "Ding, dong, the witch is dead!" rang throughout Munchkinland, but Dorothy had enraged the dead witch's sister. Dorothy only temporarily lost her home support provided by family back in Kansas. All is not good, however, in the Land of Oz. Dorothy's problem is to find her way home to Kansas. Her call to action was precipitated by a crisis—the tornado that transported her to an alien land.

B. In the throes of a Kansas tornado, Dorothy is transported to an unfamiliar land. Immediately, she realizes her world is different and the processes and people she encounters are different, yet bear some similarity to her Kansas existence. She is lost and confused and uncertain about the next steps to take. She realizes she is in a changed state—the Land of Oz—and must devise a plan to get home.

C. Dorothy is a hero for killing the Wicked Witch of the East. Glinda the Good Witch sends Dorothy on her way to meet the Wizard of Oz who will help her get back to Kansas. The Wicked Witch of the West tries to get Dorothy's newly acquired ruby slippers, but to no avail. Dorothy and Toto leave for Oz via the Yellow Brick Road. Along the way, they are joined by the Scarecrow, the Tin Man, and the Lion. Through their teamwork, they provide mutual support to endure the vexing journey. They overcome many risks and barriers on the way to Oz, including a field of poppies that puts them to sleep, flying monkeys, and a haunted forest.

D. Dorothy and her entourage finally reach Oz and meet the Wizard. Rather than instantly granting their wishes, the Wizard gives them an assignment—to obtain the Wicked Witch's broom. They depart for the West.

E. Charged with the task of obtaining the broom, Dorothy and company experience several encounters with near disaster, including Dorothy's incarceration in the witch's castle while an hourglass counts the time to her death. In a struggle to extinguish the Scarecrow's fire (incited by the Wicked Witch), Dorothy tosses a bucket of water, some of which hits the Witch and melts her. Dorothy is rewarded with the broomstick and returns to Oz.

F. Returning to Oz, the group talks with the Wizard, expecting him to help Dorothy return to Kansas. After defrocking the Wizard, they find out he does not know how. The Wizard tries to use a hot air balloon to return and accidentally leaves Dorothy and Toto behind upon takeoff. Glinda arrives and helps Dorothy realize she can return to Kansas on her own with the help of the ruby slippers.

G. Dorothy awakens from her dream and experiences a new understanding and appreciation for her home and family in Kansas. "Oh, Auntie Em, there's no place like home."

The Competitive Construction Companies[55]

Two Midwestern construction companies were vying for market share dominance. Company A embraced total quality, while Company B did not. After an initial transition of whitewater turbulence created by various change initiatives, during which Company A lost some of its employees because of the quality initiative, a period of equilibrium and growth ensued. Customers were surveyed, employees trained, and teams began working on customer value and satisfaction improvements. At first Company B was not too concerned with Company A. Company B actually hired the former employees from Company A and watched as Company A's employees talked to customers and spent their off-season conducting employee training and forming problem and project teams. However, things changed. Company B began losing good customers to its rival, and they were replaced with other customers who had strained credit and multiple grievances. In addition, some of Company B's finest employees left for Company A despite promises of higher salaries and future bonuses. Company B decided to mimic Company A's quality program by hiring an outside consultant. Time was spent advertising for and screening an appropriate consultant. The consultant was empowered to lead the program, with the blessings and support of the owner and president. The consultant met with the executive team and later with the employees and laid out his vision for the new quality program. This included training all employees in the concepts and principles of total quality. Shortly after the training sessions ended, teams were assembled with specific issues to solve. Meanwhile, valuable off-season time was expended, and the new construction season was drawing near. The new season meant employee workloads increased, which in turn required more employee work hours.

Profit opportunities quickly replaced quality meetings, tempers flared, scapegoating developed, and employees were left angry and confused. The initial hope of more involvement with work activities, better contact with customers and increased communications was replaced with frustration and cynicism. Before much could be done, the new construction season was in full swing.

Later, as Company B's construction season came to an end, the consultant had difficulty staffing the quality teams voluntarily. Conscripts were found, and teams resumed their work. Team meetings were plagued with personal attacks, finger pointing, general apathy and conflict. Employees were threatened and sometimes fired before the whole quality program was shelved.

What went wrong? Why couldn't Company B mimic Company A's apparent success with quality? What might you have done differently?

Endnotes

1. 2005 Malcolm Baldrige National Quality Award Profile, U.S. Department of Commerce.
2. Quoted in E. F. Cudworth, "3M's Commitment to Quality as a Way of Life," *Industrial Engineering*, July 1985.
3. Based on *Everyone Knows His First Name* by Levi Strauss & Company.
4. Matthew W. Ford and James R. Evans, "Baldrige Assessment and Organizational Learning: The Need for Change Management," *Quality Management Journal*, Vol. 8, No. 3, 2001, pp. 9–25.
5. See, for example, B. Schneider, *Organizational Climate and Culture*, Jossey-Bass, 1990; and B. Schneider, S.K. Gunnarson, and K. Niles-Jolly, "Creating the Climate and Culture of Success," *Organizational Dynamics*, Vol. 23, Summer 1994.
6. Julia Graham "Performance-Based Culture," *The Journal for Quality & Participation*, Spring 2004, pp. 5–8.
7. For a more detailed look at leadership's role in performance excellence, see Chapter 9.
8. Interview with Richard Garula.
9. Mike Carnell, "Forget Silver Bullets and Instant Pudding," *Quality Progress*, January 2008, pp. 72–73.
10. Gregory P. Smith, "A Change in Culture Brings Dramatic Quality Improvements," *The Quality Observer*, January 1997, pp. 14–15, 37.
11. J. M. Delsanter, "On the Right Track," *TQM Magazine*, March/April 1992, pp. 17–20.
12. Kiron Kasbekar and Namita Devidayal, "Improvement Is Not All Smooth Sailing," *The Times of India*, January 8, 1993.
13. Dan Ciampa, *Total Quality: A User's Guide to Implementation* (Reading, Mass.: Addison-Wesley, 1992); Ciampa cautions about trying to change culture.
14. Several reasons for managerial resistance to change are outlined by J.M. Juran in *Juran on Leadership for Quality*, New York: Free Press, 1989.
15. Michael Beer and Nitin Nohria, "Cracking the Code of Change," *Harvard Business Review*, May–June 2000.
16. Janet Young, "Driving Performance Results at American Express," *Six Sigma Forum Magazine*, Vol. 1, No. 1, November 2001, pp. 19–27.

17. Arthur R. Tenner and Irving J. DeToro, *Total Quality Management: Three Steps to Continuous Improvement*, Reading, Mass.: Addison Wesley, 1992.
18. Mark Samuel, "Catalysts for Change," *TQM Magazine*, 1992.
19. Samuel, "Catalysts for Change."
20. James H. Davis, "Who Owns Your Quality Program? Lessons from the Baldrige Award Winners," College of Business Administration, University of Notre Dame (n.d.).
21. Leadership Steering Committec, *A Report of the Total Quality Leadership Steering Committee and Working Councils*, Procter & Gamble Total Quality Forum, November 1992.
22. Thomas H. Patten, Jr., "Beyond Systems—The Politics of Managing in a TQM Environment," *National Productivity Review*, 1991/1992.
23. This discussion and examples are adapted from Denis Leonard and Rodney McAdam, "Quality's Six Life Cycle Stages," *Quality Progress*, August 2003, 50–55.
24. Kathleen J. Goonan, Joseph Muzikowski, and Patricia K. Stoltz, "Journey to Excellence: Healthcare Baldrige Leaders Speak Out," *Quality in Healthcare*, American Society for Quality publication, January 2009, p. 11–15, www.asq.org/qhc.
25. See, for example, Mark Graham Brown, "Measuring Up Against the 1997 Baldrige Criteria," *Journal for Quality and Participation*, Vol. 20, No. 4, September 1997, pp. 22–28.
26. Mark S. Leggitt and Rhonda Anderson, "Linking Strategic and Quality Plans," *Quality Progress*, October 2001, pp. 61–63.
27. Matthew W. Ford and James R. Evans, "Managing Organizational Self-Assessment: Follow-up and Its Influencing Factors," Working Paper, College of Business, Northern Kentucky University and College of Business, University of Cincinnati. See also Matthew W. Ford, "A Model of Change Process and Its Use in Self Assessment," Doctoral Dissertation, University of Cincinnati, 2000.
28. H. James Harrington, "Creating Organizational Excellence—Part Four," *Quality Digest*, April 2003, p. 14.
29. Chuck Cobb, "Knowledge Management and Quality Systems," *The 54th Annual Quality Congress Proceedings*, 2000, American Society for Quality, pp. 276–287.
30. Anne Fisher, "Retain Your Brains," *Fortune*, July 24, 2006, pp. 49–50.
31. Peter M. Senge, *The Fifth Discipline: The Art and Practice of the Learning Organization*, New York: Doubleday Currency, 1990, p. 14.
32. Arthur M. Schneiderman, "Measuring Organizational Learning," Unpublished note; http://www.schneiderman.com/.
33. Thomas H. Lee, "Learning, What Does It Really Mean?" *Center for Quality of Management Journal*, Vol. 4, No. 4, Winter 1995, pp. 4–14.
34. See Matthew W. Ford and James R. Evans, "Baldrige Assessment and Organizational Learning: The Need for Change Management," *Quality Management Journal* 8, No. 3, 2001, pp. 9–25.
35. Ann B. Rich, "Continuous Improvement: The Key to Success," *Quality Progress*, Vol. 30, No. 6, June 1997.
36. Brad Stratton, "TI Has Eye on Alignment," *Quality Progress*, Vol. 30, No. 10, October 1997, pp. 28–34.
37. Larry Hambly, "Sun Microsystems Embeds Quality into Its DNA," *The Quality Observer*, July 1997, pp. 16–20, 45.
38. Carla O'Dell and C. Jackson Grayson, "Identifying and Transferring Internal Best Practices," APQC White Paper, 2000 (www.apqc.org/free/whitepapers/cmifwp/index.htm).
39. Diane Brady, "Will Jeff Immelt's New Push Pay Off for GE?" *Business Week*, October 13, 2003, pp. 94–98.
40. Based on John R. Black, "Boeing's Quality Strategy: A Continuing Evolution," *The Quest for Competitiveness: Lessons from America's Productivity and Quality Leaders*, Y. Krishna Shetty and Vernon M. Buehler (eds.), New York: Quorum Books, 1991.
41. Matt Barney, "Motorola's Second Generation," *Six Sigma Forum Magazine* 1, No. 3, May 2002, pp. 13–22.
42. A.H. Van de Ven and M.S. Poole, "Explaining Development and Change in Organizations," *Academy of Management Review*, Vol. 20, No. 3, pp. 510–540.
43. C. Argyris, "Strategy Implementation: An Experience in Learning," *Organizational Dynamics*, Vol. 18, No. 2, pp. 5–15.
44. Dusya Vera and Mary Crossan, "Strategic Leadership and Organizational Learning," *Academy of Management Review*, 2004, pp. 29, 2, 222–240.

45. L. Coch and J. P. French, "Overcoming Resistance to Change," *Human Relations*, Vol. 1, 1948, pp. 512–532.
46. For a summary of this material, see J.P. Kotter and L.A. Schlesinger, "Choosing Strategies for Change," in J.J. Gabarro (ed.), *Managing People and Organizations*, Boston: Harvard Business School Publications, 1992, pp. 395–409.
47. See, for example, H.A. Aldrich, *Organizations and Environments*, Englewood Cliffs, N.J.: Prentice Hall, 1979.
48. K. Lewin, "Forces Behind Food Habits and Methods of Change," *Bulletin of the National Research Council* 108, 1947, pp. 35–65. See also E. Schein, "Organizational Socialization and the Profession of Management," *Industrial Management Review*, 1968, pp. 1–16.
49. See Thomas R. Bennett III, *Planning for Change*, Washington, D.C.: Leadership Resources, 1961.
50. See, for example, Harold J. Leavitt, "Applied Organization Change in Industry: Structural, Technical, and Human Approaches," in W.W. Cooper, H.J. Leavitt, and M.W. Shelly (eds.), *New Perspectives in Organizational Research*, New York: Wiley, 1964.
51. For an interesting (and now classic) discussion of this issue, see P.R. Lawrence, "How to Deal with Resistance to Change," *Harvard Business Review*, May/June 1954.
52. See Schein, "Organizational Socialization," *Industrial Management Review*. See also, P.S. Goodman and J.W. Dean, Jr., "Creating Long-Term Change," in P.S. Goodman (ed.), *Change in Organizations*, San Francisco: Jossey-Bass, 1983.
53. QuotationsBook, http://quotationsbook.com/quote/12996.
54. David M. Lyth and Larry A. Mallak, "'We're Not in Kansas Anymore, Toto' or Quality Lessons from the Land of Oz," *Quality Engineering*, Vol. 10, No. 30, 1998, pp. 579–588.
55. This example was described in Gregory S. Shinn, "15 Waste Scenarios," *Quality Progress*, December 2002, pp. 67–73.

INDEX

Absolutes of Quality Management, 57–58
accessibility, 17
accreditation, hospital, 19
accuracy, 17
acquired needs theory, 356–357
ACS (American College of Surgeons), 19
action plans, 206, 409–10
ADAC Laboratories, 254–55
Adamson, Francis, 372
adaptive learning, 411–12
The Adventures of a Self-Managing Team (Kelly), 279
aesthetics, 14
affinity diagrams, 210–11
agency theory, 35–37
agility
- competitive advantage and, 193–5
- defined, 27
- organizational structures and, 284
- process design and, 112

Akers, John, 291
Alaska Airlines, 191
alignment, 224, 408
Allaire, Paul, 269, 390
Allied Signal, 82–83, 370
Amalgamated Clothing & Textile Workers, 390
Amazon.com, 271
American College of Surgeons (ACS), 19
American Express, 146, 390, 402
American National Standards Institute (ANSI), 5–6, 76
American Productivity and Quality Center (APQC), 58, 414
American Red Cross, 21–22
American Society for Quality (ASQ), 5–6, 13—14, 76, 324, 368–369
American Supplier Institute, Inc., 103
Ames Rubber Corporation, 245
AMP, Inc., 246, 278
Analog Devices, 325–26, 412
Anesthesia Circuits, 324
Anheuser-Busch, 186
ANSI (American National Standards Institute), 5–6, 76
Apple Computers, 187, 216, 371
approach, in Baldrige process, 65–66
APQC (American Productivity and Quality Center), 58, 414
Aristotle, 421
Armstrong, 251
arrow diagrams, 216
Artzt, Edwin L., 369–70, 372
Asea Brown Boveri, 374
ASQ (American Society for Quality), 5–6, 13–14, 76, 324, 368–69
assignable causes of variation, 49–51
AT&T, 24, 243, 278
AT&T Consumer Communications Services (CSS), 161
attribute data, 148
attributes, customer, 103

Aune, Asbjorn, 159
Australian business awards, 73–74
autonomous work groups, 309–11, 325–27
availability, product, 56
award programs, international, 70–75. *See also* Malcom Baldrige National Quality Award (MBNQA)

baby boomers, 13
balanced scorecard, 200–1
Baldrige Award. *See* Malcom Baldrige National Quality Award (MBNQA)
Baldrige Roadmap, 406–7
The Bama Companies, Inc. case study, 224
Bank One, 23, 243
banks, 23
Baptist Hospital, 209
bargaining, integrative, 257
Barrett, Colleen, 235
Basecamp, 285
Basic Elements of Improvement, 58
Basil, Thomas, 311
basketball free throws, 152–151
Bass, Bernard, 385
behavior
- employee, 16, 18
- in organizational cultures, 397–98

Bell Telephone Laboratories, 10
benchmarking
- in breakthrough improvement, 155–158
- competitive vs. generic, 157
- example, 375
- internal, 414–15
- process, 157
- purpose and benefits of, 155–156

Bennett, Thomas, 420
Bennis, Warren, 163
Best Buy, 202
best practices, 155–156
bestroute.com, 77
Bethune, Gordon, 347
Big Q, 12
Binney & Smith, 243
Black, John, 416
black belts, in Six-Sigma teams, 312
Blanchard, Ken, 385–87
blogs, 285
Blum, Jonathan, 348
Boeing
- benchmarking, 155
- organizational change, 415–16
- performance measures, 199
- supplier base, 235
- teams, 306

Boeing, Bill, 415
Boeing Aerospace Support (AS), 265–70
Boeing Airlift and Tanker (A&T) Division
- adoption of total quality, 398
- organizational structure, 286–87
- teams, 278, 305, 322

bonuses, 352
boomerang principle, 238
Bose Corporation, 102
Bossidy, Larry, 82, 370
boundaryless learning, 165
Bowen, David E., 22
brainstorming, 101
Branch-Smith Printing Division, 112, 219–22, 376–78
breakthrough improvement, 155–156
British Airways PLC (BAB), 164, 241
Bronson Methodist Hospital, 217–19
Brookhouse, Robert, 281
Buck, Richard, 283–84
bullwhip effect, 119
Burger King, 194
Burke-Litwin model, 417
businesses. *See* manufacturing; service organizations
Business Week, 8, 11

Cadillac, 103
The Campus Food Court case study, 260–61
Canadian awards for business excellence, 73
Carlson, Terry A., 236
Carnell, Mike, 401
Carroll, Dave, 234
Carroll, Jane, 371
case studies
- The Bama Companies, Inc., 224
- Building a Leadership System for Landmark Dining, 391
- The Campus Food Court, 260–61
- Can Six Sigma Work in Health Care? 94–95
- The Case of the Missing Reservation, 259
- The Case of the Rotary Compressor, 226–27
- Child Focus, Inc., 297
- Clifton Metal Works (CMW), 227
- The Competitive Construction Companies, 423–24
- Customer Service Processes at Orbitz, 129–130
- David Kearns and the Transformation of Xerox, 389–390
- The Frustrated Manager, 359
- Golden Plaza Hotel, 329

The HMO Pharmacy Crisis, 130–132
Landmark Dining, 260
Landmark Dining: Employee Engagement and Motivation, 359
Landmark Dining: Team Processes, 330–31
LT, Inc., 172–174
The MBA Candidate, 359–360
National Furniture, 171
Nightingale College of Nursing, 90–93
The Parable of the Green Lawn, 421–22
Pauli's Restaurant and Microbrewery, 259–60
The Power of Leadership Teams, 330–31
The Reservation Nightmare, 41
Santa Cruz Guitar Company, 41–42
Scott's Fitness Center, 130
Situational Leadership in Action, 390–91
Southwest Regional Center, 130
The State University Experience, 295
The Technical Support Clerk, 90
TecSmart Electronics, 93–94
U.S. Water Resource Agency, 40
Walker Auto Sales and Service, 296
Welz Business Machines, 170–171
The Yellow Brick Road to Quality, 421
You Want Us to Work with Marketing??? 295–6
Caterpillar, 100–101
cause-and-effect (fishbone) diagrams, 150–151
CE (concept engineering), 101–102
Center for Quality of Management, 101
certification of suppliers, 251–52
chain reaction, Deming's, 48
Chalmer, David, 227
champions, in Six-Sigma teams, 312
change, cultural
customer expectations and, 395
examples, 415–16
hierarchies and, 282
imitation, 401
importance of, 13, 395–6, 402
for innovation, 162–164
leadership and, 401–2, 419
mistakes in implementing, 404
models, 417
organization theory and, 417–21
people roles in, 402–3
principles for managing, 420–21
as process, 402
process improvement and, 139, 160
reasons to adopt, 418
resistance to, 346–47, 357, 374, 419–21
rewards and, 402
self-assessment and, 407–10
strategic vs. process, 396–97
total quality and, 418–21
change framework, 417
change models, 417
change process theory, 417
Chase, Richard B., 113
check sheets, 147–149
Child Focus, Inc. case study, 297
China, quality awards in, 74–75
Chrysler, 77, 314
Chugach School District, 125–27
CIA (Central Intelligence Agency), 116
Ciampa, Dan, 370
Citibank, 83
Clark, Timothy, 152
Clarke-American Checks, 8, 162, 201
Clear Lake Plant, 279–80
CLEP (Comprehensive Local Education Plan), 20
Clifton Metal Works (CMW) case study, 227
CNH Capital, 86
coaching, 386
Coca-Cola, 115, 164
Coch, Lester, 419
Codman, Ernest, 18–19
cognitive styles, 164
College Works Painting, 247
Collins, Jim, 67
commitment, 34, 52, 372–73. *See also* leadership
common causes of variation, 49–51
communication, 320, 401
Companywide Quality Control (CWQC), 71
compensation, 352–353
competencies, core, 216–17, 252
competitive advantage
agility, 193–195
characteristics of, 181–82
cost leadership, 185–86
defined, 180
differentiation, 186–87
differentiation strategies, 188–199
employees, 187–88
information and knowledge for, 199–202
innovation, 196–7
product design, 188–90
service, 190–193
Six Sigma and, 186
sources of, 185–88
time, 197–199
total quality management and, 183–85
competitive benchmarking, 155

competitive evaluation, 104, 105
complaint resolution, 192, 246
completeness, 17
Comprehensive Local Education Plan (CLEP), 20
compromise, 257
concept engineering (CE), 101–2
concurrent engineering, 107, 190
conformance, 14, 15, 56, 109
congruence model, 417
consensus stage, in Baldrige process, 66
consideration, 383–84
consistency, 17
construction companies case study, 423–24
consumers. *See* customers
contextual factors and total quality, 292–4
Continental Airlines, 347
contingent reward behavior, 385
continuous improvement. *See also* breakthrough improvement
    barriers, 374
    cost leadership and, 185–86
    customer satisfaction and, 140
    data in, 147–148
    Deming's 14 Points and, 52
    examples, 377–78, 380–81
    implementation of, 58
    leadership and, 373–74
    organizational culture and, 139
    processes, 136–137, 139, 141–145
    of products, 26–27
    quality and, 56, 279
    in services sector, 26–27
    seven QC tools for, 146–152
    total quality and, 136, 138
    turnover rate and, 16
continuous quality improvement (CQI), 19
contracts, supplier, 251
control, process. *See* process control
control charts, 121–124, 152
control systems, 115–118
convenience, 17
Convex Computer Corporation, 157
cooperative relationships, 29, 252
coordination mapping, 276–78
Coors, Pete, 339
Coors Brewing, 339, 340–41
Coral Springs, City of, 8, 45–47, 222–23, 275
core competencies, 216–17, 252
core processes, 112, 271–72
core values, 399–400
Corning Glass, 345, 372
Corning Telecommunications Products Division (TPD), 112, 201, 251–52, 305
corrective actions, 385
corrective action teams, 307–9
cost leadership, 185–86
cost of quality, 57
courtesy, 17
Covey, Stephen, 279
CQI (continuous quality improvement), 19
creativity, 160–165. *See also* innovation
Credit Suisse, 240–41
criteria evolution, 66
Criteria for Performance Excellence, 62–64
critical to quality (CTQ), 86
CRM (customer relationship management) software, 247–48
Crosby, Philip B., 57, 58, 182–83, 307
Crossan, Mary, 418
cross-functional processes, 112, 198–199, 273–78
cross-functional teams
    for problem solving, 30, 307–9, 313–14
    quality function deployment and, 107
    supplier relationships and, 251–52
Crownover, Dale, 274, 344
CSRs. See customer-supplier relationships (CSRs)
CTQ (critical to quality), 86
cultural change. *See* change, cultural
cultural organizational model, 37–38
culture. *See also* change, cultural
    continuous improvement in, 139
    defined, 397–99
cultures, acceptance of teamwork concept and, 327–28
Curtis, Pat, 325
customer-contact employees, 246
customer dissatisfaction. *See* customer satisfaction
customer-driven decisions, 23
customer engagement, 23, 234. *See also* customer focus
customer errors, 114
customer expectations
    classes of, 26–27
    as definition of quality, 5–6
    differentiation and, 188, 189
    organizational change and, 395
    perceptions and, 18, 192–193
    process improvement and, 140
    product design and, 15, 99
customer focus. *See also* mass customization
    in Baldrige criteria, 62, 193
    organizational structure and, 268–69, 275–78

principles and practices, 23–24
customer importance ratings, 105
customer information. *See also* customer expectations
collecting, 239–43
disseminating, 243, 244
imprint analysis for, 241–42
using, 243–45
customer needs. *See* customer expectations
customer relationship management (CRM) software, 247–48
customers. *See also* customer expectations; customer- supplier relationships (CSRs)
attributes of, 103
complaint resolution, 192, 246–47
engagement and, 234
environments of, 101
external, 23, 272–73, 275
information about, 239–45
internal, 23, 248, 249, 272–73, 276–78
Japanese notion of, 16
organizational structures and, 268–69, 275–78
practices for dealing with, 239–48
roles for, 254
voice of, 103–107, 241
customer satisfaction
continuous improvement and, 140
employee satisfaction and, 192, 336–37
loyalty and, 233–35
organization size and, 284
service standards and, 246–47
customer-supplier relationships (CSRs) examples, 252–53
importance of, 237–38
managing, 245–46
in organization theory, 254–57
practices for dealing with customers, 239–48
practices for dealing with suppliers, 248–52
principles for, 237–39
software for, 247–48
supply chain management and, 231–32
total quality and, 234–35
trust, 239
win-win situations, 237
customization, 111
custom products, 194–195
Custom Research, Inc., 282, 283, 307, 354, 372
CWQC (Companywide Quality Control), 71
cycle times, 27, 112, 197–199

D.J. Inc., 253
Daimler-Chrysler, 118, 236
data, in continuous improvement, 31, 147–148
David, Colin, 94–95
Dean, James W., Jr., 22
decisional roles, 383
decision making, 23, 31, 250. *See also* empowerment; strategic planning
Deer Valley Resort, 6
defects, 5–6
defensive routines, 418
define, measure, analyze, design, and verify (DMADV), 100
define, measure, analyze, improve, and control (DMAIC), 86, 144–145, 146
define, measure, explore, design, implement (DMEDI), 100–101
DeHont, Chuck, 373
Delco Moraine Division, 249
Delcor Homes, 80
delegating, 387
delighters/exciters, 26–27
Dell
core competencies, 216
customer service, 110
differentiation, 186–87
mass customization, 111
process improvement, 136
work systems, 217
Dell, Michael, 136, 186–87
Deming, W. Edwards
on customer-supplier relationships, 232
on employee fear, 342 influences on, 10
on interdepartmental teams, 270
introduced to American business, 11
on leadership, 385
on motivation, 351
personal background, 47–48
on responsibility for control, 116
Deming Cycle, 142–144
Deming Philosophy
Baldrige Critera and, 69–70
chain reaction, 48
Deming Cycle, 142–144
education, 55, 58, 59
14 Points for Management, 52–54
psychology, 51, 52
System of Profound Knowledge, 48–52
systems, 49, 51–52
theory of knowledge, 51
understanding, 51–52
variation of processes, 49–51, 52
vs. Juran Philosophy, 56
Deming Prize, 11, 71–72
deployment

in Baldrige criteria, 66
policy, 207–09
quality-function, 102–107
design
of products, 15, 99–107, 188–90
for services, 56, 108–110
design, organizational. *See* organizational structures
design, process. *See* process design
design failure mode and effects analysis (DFMEA), 107–108
design for Six Sigma (DFSS), 100–101
design reviews, 190
determination. *See* commitment
Dexler, Brad, 244
DFMEA (design failure mode and effects analysis), 107–108
DFSS (design for Six Sigma), 100–101
dialog, 418
diaper changing, 143
differentiation, 186–87
differentiation strategies, 188–199
discussion groups, 241
Disney, 127–128, 157
dissatisfiers, 26–27
diversity, 305, 317–18, 327–28
DM (DynMcDermott) Petroleum Operations Company, 324, 349–50
DMADV (define, measure, analyze, design, and verify), 100
DMAIC (define, measure, analyze, improve, and control), 86, 144–145, 146
DMEDI (define, measure, explore, design, implement), 100–101
Dodge, Harold, 10
Domino's Pizza, 158, 198, 253, 354
Dooley, Kevin, 143
do the job right the first time, 57
double-loop learning, 418
Dresdner Kleinwork Wasserstein, 285
DuPont, 80, 86, 344–45
durability, 14
DynMcDermott (DM) Petroleum Operations Company, 324, 349–50

Eastman Chemical Company, 141–142, 397
Ecklin, Rob, 365, 366
education. *See also* learning; training in Deming Philosophy, 55, 57, 58
public, 19–21
Edwards, George, 10
efficient layout, 152
EFQM (European Foundation for Quality Management), 72–73
EI (employee involvement), 339–40. *See also* empowerment; engagement, employee elections, 114
EMC Corporation, 253
employee engagement. *See* engagement, employee
employee involvement (EI), 339–40. *See also* empowerment; engagement, employee
employees. *See also* change, cultural; empowerment; engagement, employee
competition *vs.* cooperation among, 29
competitive advantage, 187–88
customer-contact, 246
performance of, 284–86, 321–22
service quality and, 191–192
work environment, 355
empowerment. *See also* employees; engagement, employee
access to information, 344–45
decision making, 340, 342
defined, 340
Deming's 14 Points and, 341
examples, 112, 340–41
failure of, 348
Juran on, 341
in manufacturing *vs.* service sectors, 341
middle management and, 346–47
objectives of, 340
ownership, 403
principles of, 342–43
reward systems, 347–48
self-managed teams, 340–41
sincerity and, 343
systems and, 341–42
training, 345–46
trust and, 28, 343–44
ENBI Corporation, 139
end result system, 18–19
engagement, customer, 23, 234
engagement, employee. *See also* employees; empowerment
benefits of, 337, 338
customer satisfaction and, 192, 336–37
defined, 336
examples, 349–52
involvement and, 140–141, 339–40
motivation and, 28, 338, 355–358
teamwork and, 28–30
total quality and, 28–30, 337, 338, 354–358
Engibous, Tom, 12–13
engineering, quality, 189–90

Enterprise Rent-A-Car, 23
environmental concerns, 13
environments
  customer, 101
  work, 162–164, 354
errors, 17, 113–115
European Excellence Award, 72–73
European Foundation for Quality Management (EFQM), 72–73
evaluation process, Baldrige, 65–66
exciters/delighters, 26–27
executive leadership, 369
experimental design, 190
explicit knowledge, 410–11
external customers, 23, 272–73, 275
extrinsic motivation, 351

FAA (U.S. Federal Aviation Administration), 235
factories, hidden, 86
failure of products, 107–108
fear, 53–54, 164, 342. *See also* change, cultural features
  in manufactured products, 14
  technical, 103–107
FedEx (Federal Express)
  customer and employee satisfaction, 192, 336
  partnership with Jostens, 252
  process design, 111
  rewards, 354
  teams, 278, 305, 309, 310
  vision, 371
feedback report, in evaluation process, 66
Fidelity Wide Processing, 324
field service, 56
fishbone diagrams, 150–151
fitness for use, 5–6, 56, 238
5S's, 152
flexibility, 27, 193
Flores, Fernando, 276
Florida Power and Light (FPL), 11, 72
flowcharts (process maps), 146–7, 276
follow-through, 409–10
Forbes (magazine), 186
Ford, Henry, 157, 195, 216
Ford Motor Company, 11, 77, 250
Ford Taurus, 341
Fortune (magazine), 8, 187, 271, 370
Forum Corporation, 371
14 Points for Management, 52–54
FPL (Florida Power and Light), 11, 72
frameworks for quality, 87–88
Frederick C. Carder Elementary School, 20
French, John R. P., 419
Froedtert Hospital, 166–167
The Frustrated Manager case study, 359
Fujitsu Network Transmissions Systems, 6
Fuji-Xerox, 202
functional structure, 268–70
function *vs.* process, 25

gainsharing, 352
Galvin, Robert, 82, 367
Gantt, Henry, 188
GAO (General Accounting Office) study, 183–85
Garvin, David, 372–73
GE. *See* General Electric (GE)
GE Appliance, 252
Genentech, 187
General Accounting Office (GAO) study, 183–85
General Electric (GE)
  competitive advantage, 226–27
  leadership, 370
  process improvement, 165–166
  reengineering, 158–159
  self-managed teams, 310
  Six Sigma, 82–83
  Southwest Airlines and, 415
  strategic change, 397
  strategic implementation, 209
  vision, 371
General Mills, 158
General Motors (GM), 8, 77, 250, 341
General Systems Company, 182
generative learning, 411–12
generic benchmarking, 157
Gersuny and Rosengren, 254
Gilbreth, Frank and Lillian, 188
Gillette Company, 251
Global Business Communications Systems, 243
globalization, 13, 311–12
GM (General Motors), 8, 77, 250, 341
GOAL/QPC, 103
goals, stretch, 153, 374
goal-setting theory, 357–358
Godfrey, A. Blanton, 271
Godrej Soaps, 402
Golden Plaza Hotel case study, 329
Gold Star Chili, Inc., 273, 274
Google, 338
Gore, Al, 11
government agencies, quality in, 21
Graham, Julia, 399

Graniterock Company, 118, 158, 253, 278, 305
green belts, in Six Sigma teams, 312–13
groups, 327. *See also* teams
GTE Directories Corporation, 161, 280, 369
GTE Supply, 249
guiding principles. *See* values

H&M (Hennes & Mauritz), 112
Haas, Walter, 396
Hackman and Oldham, 359
Harley-Davidson, 373
Harrah's Entertainment, 245
Harrington, H. James, 7, 41, 410
Hartford Hospital, 408
health care industries, 13, 18–19, 121–124
Heinz U.S.A., 372
Hendricks and Singhal, 9
Hennes & Mauritz (H&M), 112
Hersey, Paul, 385–87
Hewitt Associates, 350–51
Hewlett-Packard, 374, 397, 410
hierarchy, reducing, 282
high-performance work, 284–85
Hillerich, Jack, 55
Hillerich & Bradsby Co., 55
histograms, 148–149
Hitachi Corporation, 335
The HMO Pharmacy Crisis case study, 130–132
Hollywood Casino Resort, 6
Home Depot, 233
Honda, 190, 195, 239
Honeywell, 83
horizontal teamwork, 30
hoshin planning (policy deployment), 207–09
hospitals, standardization in, 18–19
Houghton Jamie, 372
house of quality, 103–107
Hubbard, James, 227
human resources, 209–10
Hunter, Richard L., 110
Hutchinson, Ron, 373

IBM
- customer-supplier relationships, 231–32
- job enlargement, 285
- performance measures, 202
- reorganization, 291
- rewards, 353
- team awards, 322
- vision, 371

IBM Credit Corporation, reengineering at, 159
IHI (Institute for Healthcare Improvement), 19
image, in service organizations, 18
Imai Masaaki, 207–08
imitation, 401
implementation, as element of improvement, 58
implementation mistakes, 404
imprint analysis, 242
improvement, continuous. *See* continuous improvement
improvement breakthrough, 155
improvements, small, 137–140
incentives, 351
Industrial Revolution, 10, 187–88
information
- customer, 239–45
- employee access to, 344–45

informational roles, 383
information management, 31–32, 199–202, 411
information technology, service quality and, 192, 246
initiating structure, 383–84
innovation, 160–165, 196–197
In Search of Excellence (Peters and Waterman), 190
inspection, 52, 153
Institute for Healthcare Improvement (IHI), 19
institutional theory, 291–292
integrative bargaining, 257
Intel Corporation, 158
interchangeable parts, 10
interdependence, 256–57, 420
internal benchmarking, 414–15
internal customers, 23, 248, 249, 272–73, 276–78
International award programs, 70–75
International Organization for Standardization, 76
International Team Excellence Award Competition, 306, 324
Internet, 241, 271
interpersonal roles, 382–83
interpersonal skills, 317
interrelationship diagraphs, 211–12
interrelationships, customer and product, 105
intrinsic motivation, 351
involvement, employee, 339–40. *See also* empowerment; engagement, employee
Iredell-Statesville Schools, 134–136
Isdell, E. Neville, 164
ISO 9000:1920 standards
- benefits of, 80
- development of, 77–78
- implementation, 79–80
- objectives, 76
- principles, 78
- process design and, 112
- registration of, 79–80

structure of, 76
total quality and, 77
vs. other frameworks, 87–88

J. D. Power Gold Plant Quality Award, 187
Japan, 10, 16, 308
JCAHO (Joint Commission on Accreditation of Healthcare Organizations), 19, 69, 121
Jefferson, Thomas, 10
Jenks Public Schools, 9, 19–21
job characteristics theory, 356
job enlargement, 285
job enrichment, 285
job loss, 282
job rotation, 285
job satisfaction, 192, 284
Johnson & Johnson, 355
Joiner, Brian, 119
Joint Commission on Accreditation of Healthcare Organizations (JCAHO), 19, 69, 121
Jostens, 252
JPMorgan Chase, 324
Juran, Joseph M.
and Deming Philosophy, 55
on empowerment, 341
on fitness for use, 56
influences on, 10
Juran Philosophy, 56
pattern of collaboration, 239
on problem diagnosis, 319
quality councils, 307
Quality Trilogy, 56, 98
on responsibility for control, 116
on trends, 7–8
Juran Institute, 271
JUSE (Union of Japanese Scientists and Engineers), 70, 308
just-in-time (JIT) tool, 138, 152

kaizen (small improvements), 137–140
kaizen blitz, 140–141
Kano, Noriaki, 26–27
Kansai Electric Power Company, 72
Kaplan, Robert, 200
KARLEE Company, Inc., 36, 303–5
KBkids.com, 271
Kearns, David, 389–390
Kelleher, Herb, 187, 337
Kelly, Jim, 342
Kelly, Mark, 279
KFC (Kentucky Fried Chicken), 348
King, Bob, 207
Kizer, Kenneth W., 287–88
Kmart, 202
Knorr, Robert, 281
knowledge, explicit *vs.* tacit, 410–11
knowledge assets, 410–11
knowledge management, 31–32, 62, 410–15
Knowlton, Troy, 344
Kolind, Lars, 288–89
Kotter, John, 387–388
Kraft Foods, 318

L. L. Bean, 157, 354
Lafley, A. G., 245–46
lagging measures, 200–201
LANB (Los Alamos National Bank), 351–352
Landmark Dining case studies
employee engagement and motivation, 359
leadership system, 391
standards, 260
team processes, 330–31
Landor & Associates, 115
languages within an organization, 56
layout, efficient, 152
leaders. *See also* managers, roles of
as coaches, 54
as role models, 401
roles of, 371–74, 382–83
leadership. *See also* management
activities, 369, 370
in Baldrige criteria, 62, 367
competencies and characteristics, 368–369
consideration and, 383–84
continuous improvement and, 373–74
cultural change and, 401–02, 419
defined, 367
Deming's 14 Points and, 366–367, 385
examples, 374–81
executive, 369
fostering creativity, 163
importance of, 369
initiating structure, 383–84
leadership theory and, 382–388
management and, 387–388
reward systems and, 374
sincerity and, 401
situational, 385–87
styles of, 385–87
transformational leadership theory and, 384–85, 386, 418
values and, 33–34, 372–73
vision and, 33–35, 204–205, 371–72
leadership systems, 381–82

leadership teams, 282–84, 307
leadership teams case study, 330–31
leadership theory, 382–388
leading measures, 200–201
lead time, 197
Lean Six Sigma, 155
lean thinking (waste reduction), 152, 151–153
learning. *See also* training
  adaptive, 411–12
  Baldrige Critera and, 412–13
  boundaryless, 165
  in Deming Philosophy, 54, 57, 58
  double-loop, 418
  four stages of, 394–95
  generative, 411–12
  organizational, 21, 410–15, 418
  single-loop, 417–18
  survival, 411–12
  team-based, 21
learning cycles, 27
learning organizations, 21, 411–12
Le Blanc, Honore, 10
LeBoeuf, Lamb, Greene, & MacRae, LLP, 246
Lehr, Lewis, 395
Lengnick-Hall, 254
Leonard, Denis, 405
Levinson, Harry, 373
Levi Strauss & Co., 242, 396
Levitt, Paul, 227
Lewin, Kurt, 327
Lewis, Clarence Irving, 51
Lexus automobiles, 15, 123–125, 237
life-cycle cost, 250
life-cycle model of sustaining quality, 405–06
Little Q, 12
Lockheed, 308, 320
Los Alamos National Bank (LANB), 351–352
Los Angeles Times, 116
Loveman, Gary, 245
Lowell, Francis, 157
LT, Inc. case study, 172–174

MacArthur, Douglas, 10
Macy's, 242–43
Malcom Baldrige National Quality Award (MBNQA)
  appropriateness for all organizations, 68–69
  core values of, 399–400
  creativity, 160–162
  criteria, 61–64, 67
  Deming Philosophy and, 70–71
  deployment in, 65
  evaluation process, 65–66
  history of, 58–61
  impacts of, 67–69
  innovation, 160–162, 196–197
  as integrated management system, 63–64
  leadership, 367
  organizational learning, 412–13
  performance measures and, 201
  purpose of, 58–61
  recipients of, 59–61
  Resource Dependence Perspective (RDP) and, 255–57
  results in, 63, 65
  strategic planning, 62
  transformational leadership theory and, 385
  values and, 399–400
  vs. other frameworks, 87–88
management. *See also* leadership
  commitment, 34, 52, 372–73
  cultural change and, 346–47, 402, 403
  14 Points for, 52–54
  job loss and, 282
  leadership and, 387–388
  teams and, 321–23
management by exception, 385
management by fact, 30–32
management by objective (MBO), 54, 385
managers, roles of, 382–83. *See also* leaders
managing customer relationships. *See* customer-supplier relationships (CSRs)
manufacturing
  quality dimensions, 14–15
  vs. service organizations, 16–17, 18, 85–86, 108, 113, 341
mapping, process, 146–147, 276
marketing, differentiation and, 189
Marriott, Bill, Jr., 240
Marriott Hotels, 17, 240
Mary Kay Cosmetics, 157
mass customization, 111
master black belts, in Six-Sigma teams, 312
matrix data analysis, 214–15
matrix diagrams, 212–14
Mays & Valentine, 140
Maytag, 236
The MBA Candidate case study, 359–360
MBNQA. *See* Malcom Baldrige National Quality Award (MBNQA)
MBO (management by objective), 54, 385
McAdam, Rodney, 405
McConnell, John, 316

McDonald, Marshall, 72
McDonald's, 109, 194
McGregor, Douglas, 28
McKinsey seven-s model, 417
McNealy, Scott, 413–14
measurement. *See also* tools
  balanced scorecard, 200–201
  benefits of, 30–32
  cost of quality and, 57
  customer information and, 243–44
  operationalizing, 101
  performance excellence and, 62, 200–201
  of service standards, 18
mechanistic organizational model, 37
mechanistic organization structures, 290–291
Medrad, 352–353
Mehne, Patrick, 233
Mercedes-Benz, 139, 310
Mercy Health System, 230–31
MESA Products, Inc., 9
Milliken, 400
Mintzberg, Henry, 223–24
Mintzberg model, 382–83
missing reservation case study, 259
mission, 204–205. *See also* values
mistake-proofing, 112–114
mistrust, costs of, 239
Miura, Takeo, 335
models, change, 417
Moen, Inc., 198
moments of truth, 245–46
Monaghan, Tom, 198
Monsanto Company, 353
motivation. *See also* empowerment; reward systems
  acquired needs theory and, 356–357
  compensation, 352–353
  continuous improvement and, 357–358
  employee engagement, 28, 338, 355–358
  intrinsic vs. extrinsic, 351
  job characteristics theory and, 356
  recognition and rewards, 353–354
  teamwork, 306
  Theory X and Theory Y models of, 28
  work environment, 355
Motorola
  customer-supplier relationships, 236
  empowerment, 341
  goals, 374
  leadership, 367
  process design model, 110–111
  Six Sigma, 83, 416–17
  strategic planning, 209
  supplier relationships, 251
Munoz, Daniel, 306
mutual trust. *See* trust
MySQL, 311

Nadler and Tushman's congruence model, 417
NASCAR pit crews, 158
National Cash Register Company (NCR), 137, 196
National Education Quality Initiative, 11–12
National Furniture case study, 171
National Housing Quality Award (NHQA), 88
National Institute of Standards and Technology, 62
National Performance Review, 11
National Quality Month, 11
National Quality Program, 62
Nationwide Insurance, Trial Division, 67
natural-work teams, 309
NCR (National Cash Register Company), 137, 196
NEC Electronics, 48
Netflix, 111
new philosophies, 52
New York Life Insurance Company, 314
NHQA (National Housing Quality Award), 88
Nightingale College of Nursing case study, 90–93
Nissan Motor Co. Ltd., 138, 195, 246–47
nominal group technique, 327
Nordstrom, 216
North Mississippi Medical Center, 9, 205
Norton, David, 200
not-for-profits, 21–22, 45–47
Nucor Corporation, 353

OB (organizational behavior) theories, 327–28, 355–358
Ohsone, Kozo, 240
operationalizing, 101
option-oriented products, 194–195
Orbitz case study, 129–130
Oregon State University, 279
organic organization structures, 290–291
organismic organizational model, 37–37
organizational behavior (OB) theories, 327–28, 355–358
organizational change. *See* change, cultural
organizational climate, 398. *See also* culture
organizational culture. *See* culture
organizational design. *See* organizational structures
organizational development (OD), 326–27
organizational learning, 21, 410–15, 418. *See also* change, cultural

organizational models, 37–38
organizational profiles, 65
organizational structures
  agility and, 284
  customers and, 268–69, 275–78
  employee performance, 284–85
  examples, 286–290
  external customers, 275
  factors influencing, 267–68
  functional, 268–70
  hierarchy, 282
  institutional theory, 291–2
  internal customers, 276–78
  mechanistic, 290–291
  organic, 290–291
  organizational design theory and, 290–4
  processes and, 270–73
  redesign of, 270–73
  structural contingency theory and, 290–1
  teamwork and, 273–74, 278–84, 323
  total quality and, 268–86, 290–294
  work systems, 216–17, 284–86
organizational sustainability, 32–33
organizations, levels in, 285
organizations, process-based, 273, 274
organizations, service. *See* service organizations
organization size, 284
organization theory (OT)
  customer-supplier relationships (CSRs) in, 254–57
  organizational change and, 417–21
  vs. total quality, 290–294
Oticon, 288–89
out of control, 120
Outpost.com, 271
outsourcing, 217
ownership, 403. *See also* empowerment

Palermo, Richard, 270
Palermo's law, 270
Pal's Sudden Service, 272
The Parable of the Green Lawn case study, 421–22
Pareto diagrams, 149–150
Parker, James F, 344
Park Place Lexus (PPL), 282, 393–94, 395
partnerships, 30, 236, 238, 251–52. *See also* customer-supplier relationships (CSRs)
Paton, Scott, 129
pattern of collaboration, 239
Pauli's Restaurant and Microbrewery case study, 259–60
pay, 353
PDPC (process decision program charts), 215
PDSA (Plan, Do, Study, Act), 20, 134, 135
Peppers, Don, 231
perceived quality, 14, 18, 192–193
performance, employee, 284–86, 321–22
performance, product, 14
performance, supplier, 251–52
performance appraisals, 321–22. *See also* reward systems
performance excellence. *See* total quality (TQ)
performance measures, 31, 200–201
Peters, Tom, 190, 339
Petersen, Donald, 11
Pfeffer, Jeffrey, 255
Philip Crosby Associates, 57
PIMS Associates, Inc., 182
Plan, Do, Study, Act (PDSA), 20, 134, 135
planning, strategic. *See* strategic planning
poka-yoke (mistake-proofing), 112–114
Polaroid, 101
policy deployment, 207–09
Poole, M. S., 417
population ecology, 420
Portman Equipment Company, 140, 283–84
Poudre Valley Health System, 3–5
PPL (Park Place Lexus), 282, 393–94, 395
practices of total quality
  customer focus, 24
  employee engagement and teamwork, 28–29
  leadership, 34–35
  managing information and knowledge, 31–32
  process orientation, 25
  strategic planning, 32–33
Pratt & Whitney, 337
Premier, Inc., 9, 179–80, 204
principles, guiding. *See* values
problem diagnosis, 319
problem selection, 318–19
problem-solving teams, 307–9
process-based organizations, 273, 274
process change, 396–97
process control
  components of, 115–118
  defined, 115
  examples, 123–128
  responsibility for, 116
  service sector and, 124
  statistical, 120–124, 152, 253
  vs. process improvement, 136–137
process decision program charts (PDPC), 215
process design
  agility, 112

examples, 123–132
ISO 9000:1920 standards and, 112
owners of, 271
poka-yoke (mistake-proofing), 112–114
reengineering and, 158–160
standardized, 111, 152
processes. *See also* process improvement; process management
core, 112, 271–72
cross-functional, 112, 198–199, 273–78
defined, 24
Deming Cycle and, 142–144
improvement, 136–137, 139, 141–145
problem-solving, 142
in production, 49
redesigning organizations and, 270–73
in service organizations, 109, 124
Six-Sigma approach, 144–145
standardization of, 111, 152
support, 271–72
team, 318–23
value-creation, 271–72
vs. functions, 25
process improvement
benefits of, 27
continuous improvement and, 136–137, 139, 141–145
cross-functional teams, 313
cultural change and, 139, 164
customer feedback, 140 data, 31, 147–148
employee suggestions, 140–141
examples, 164–168
kaizen (small improvements), 137–139
kaizen blitz, 140–141
organizational structure and, 269–86
vs. process control, 136–137
process management, 62, 98–99
process maps, 146–147, 276
process orientation, 24–27
process owners, 110, 271
process redesign, 158–160
process vs. function, 25
Procter & Gamble (P&G)
core competencies, 216
customer-supplier relationships, 232–33
leadership, 369–370
managing customer relationships, 245–46
reengineering, 158–160
selection processes, 322
values, 372
production processes, variation in, 49
products
design of, 15, 99–107, 188–90
failure of, 107–108
improvement of, 26–27
performance of, 14
types of, 194–195
profitability of quality, 182–84
progress, tracking, 410
project scoping, 144
project teams, 281, 312–13
PRO-TEC Coating Company, 8, 334–35, 336
psychology, in Deming Philosophy, 51, 52
pull production, 138, 154
punishments, contingent, 385
purchasing decisions, 250

QC (quality circles), 307–9
QFD (quality function deployment), 102–107, 243
QS-9000, 78
quality. *See also* quality control; quality improvement; sustaining quality; total quality (TQ)
cost of, 57
defined, 5–6, 48
future of, 12–14
history of, 10–12
importance of, 7
organizational structure and, 270
perceptions of, 14, 18, 192–193
profitability, 182–84
in service processes, 109
quality assurance, 270
quality circles (QC), 307–9
quality control, 10, 56, 270
Quality Control Handbook (Juran), 56
quality councils, 282–84, 307
quality departments, roles of, 57
Quality Digest, 7, 12, 41, 129
quality engineering, 189–90
quality function deployment (QFD), 102–107, 243
quality improvement, 56, 279
quality improvement teams, 307
quality initiatives, life cycle of, 405–06
Quality is Free (Crosby), 57, 182–83
quality planning, 56
quality revolution, 11–12
Quality Trilogy, 56, 98
Quinn, Feargal, 238
quotas, 54

Radius, 310
Rath & Strong, 370

RBC (Royal Bank of Canada), 242–43
RDP (Resource Dependence Perspective), 255–57
recognition. *See* reward systems
redesign, process, 158–160
redesign, product, 15, 99–107, 188–90
reengineering (process redesign), 158–160
relationship-oriented role, 317
relationships, customer-supplier. *See* customer-supplier relationships (CSRs)
reliability, 14
The Reservation Nightmare case study, 41
resistance to change, 346–47, 374, 419–21
Resource Dependence Perspective (RDP), 255–57
responsiveness, in service organizations, 17, 27
results, in Baldrige Award, 62, 66
retirement, redefining, 13
reward systems. *See also* motivation
- contingent, 385
- cultural change and, 402
- empowerment and, 347–48
- impact on teams, 321–23
- leadership and, 374
- motivation and, 353–354

Ritz-Carlton Hotel Company, L.L.C.
- Baldrige leadership practices, 65
- complaint resolution, 247
- on customer satisfaction and loyalty, 234
- employees, 187, 188
- empowerment, 345
- leadership, 34
- process control, 116, 124
- process improvement, 137
- rewards, 353
- strategic planning, 207
- team awards, 322

Rogers, Martha, 231
Rosenbluth, Hal, 337–38
Rosenbluth Travel, 337–38
The Rotary Compressor case study, 226–27
Royal Bank of Canada (RBC), 242–43
Ryan, Mary Jean, 380

Salancik, Gerald, 255
Samuel, Mark, 403
San Diego Zoo, 289–290
Santa Cruz Guitar Company case study, 41–42
satisfiers, 26–27
Saturn Corporation, 240, 348
scatter diagrams, 151–152, 244–45
Schlitz Brewing Company, 186
Schlow, Michael, 310
Schneiderman, Art, 412
Scholtes, Peter, 51–52, 315–16
Schonberger, Richard, 276
Schulmeyer, Gerhard, 374
scientific management, 10, 187–88
SCM (supply chain management), 53, 231–32
Scott's Fitness Center case study, 130
search conference method, 207
Sears, Roebuck and Co., 81
self-assessment, 407–10
self-managed teams, 309–11, 325–27, 340–41
selling points, 105
semiautonomous work groups, 309–11, 325–27, 340–41
Senge, Peter, 345, 411–12
Sentara Norfolk General Hospital, 324–25
service organizations
- competitive advantage and, 190–193
- design in, 56, 108–110
- employees and, 191–192
- errors, 113–114
- improvement, 26–27
- lean thinking, 152
- processes, 109, 124
- quality dimensions of, 15–18, 192–193
- Six Sigma and, 85–87
- standards, 18, 245–46
- three components of, 109
- time, 17
- turnover rate, 16
- *vs.* manufacturing, 16–17, 18, 85–86, 108, 113, 341

service standards, 18, 245–46
Seven Habits of Highly Effective People (Covey), 279
seven management and planning tools, 210–16
seven QC tools, 146–152
seven-s model, 417
Sewell, Carl, 233
Sewell Cadillac, 233
SFF (Sunny Fresh Foods), 286
Sharp Healthcare, 8
Shewhart, Walter, 10, 51, 121, 152
Shewhart Cycle, 142
Shingo, Shigeo, 112, 139
Sierra Semiconductor, 373
single-loop learning, 417–18
single-minute exchange of dies (SMED), 154
situational leadership, 385–87
Situational Leadership in Action case study, 390–91
six-box model, 417
Six Sigma
- competitive advantage, 186
- core philosophy, 82

cost leadership, 186
design for, 100–101
DMAIC methodology, 144–145
evolution of, 82–83
goal of, 81
health care case study, 94–95
lean thinking, 152
origin of name, 81–82
processes in, 144–145
product design and, 100–101
project teams, 281, 312–13
service organizations, 85–87
transactional, 85
vs. other frameworks, 84–85, 87–88
Skandia, 411
Skype, 311
SMED (single-minute exchange of dies), 154
Smith, Bill, 82
social responsibility (SR), 13
socioemotional orientation, 383–84
sociotechnical systems (STS), 327
software, 247–48
Solar Turbines, Inc., 207, 288, 381–82
Solectron Corporation, 280
Solucient, 9
Sony, 50, 111, 240
source inspection, 154
Southern Pacific Lines, 402
Southwest Airlines, 187, 235, 337, 343–44, 415
Southwest Louisiana Regional Medical Center, 94–95
Southwest Regional Center case study, 130
SPC (statistical process control), 120–124, 152, 252
special causes of variation, 49–51
specifications, conformance to, 15
SR (social responsibility), 13
SSM Health Care, 19, 116–118, 378–81
stakeholder focus, 23
standardization of processes, 111, 152
standardization of quality. *See* ISO 9000:2000 standards
standard operating procedures (SOP), 17
standard products, 194–195
Starbucks Coffee, 346
The State University Experience case study, 295
statistical process control (SPC), 120–124, 152, 252
statistical thinking, 118–120
statistics, Six-Sigma training and, 145
Stead, Jerre, 243
Stealth pilots and crews, 158
steering committees, 282–84, 307
Stewart, Douglas M., 113
Stewart, Matt, 247
STMicroelectronics, 251
Stoner Incorporated, 279, 365–366, 382
strategic alliances, 252
strategic challenges, 205–206
strategic change, 396–97
strategic content, 224
strategic management theory, 223–25
strategic objectives, 206
strategic planning
in Baldrige criteria, 62
data, 31
defined, 66, 180–81
development stage, 204–207
as driver of quality, 32–33
examples, 217–23
human resources in, 209–10
implementation stage, 207–09
role of quality in, 202–07
search conference method and, 20
tools, 210–16
values and, 204–205
Strategic Planning Institute, 182
strategy, defined, 180, 206
stretch goals, 155, 374
structural contingency theory, 290–291
STS (sociotechnical systems), 327
suboptimization, 49
Sugiura, Hideo, 239
Sun Microsystems, 80, 413–14
Sunny Fresh Foods (SFF), 286
Superquinn, 239
suppliers. *See also* customer-supplier relationships (CSRs)
certification, 251–52
external, 23, 272–73, 275
importance of, 235–36, 248–49
internal, 23, 248, 249, 272–73, 276–78
long-term contracts, 251
measuring performance, 251–52
number of, 238, 250–51
partnering with, 251–52
practices for dealing with, 248–52
purchasing decisions and, 250
supply chain management (SCM), 53, 231–32
support processes, 271–72
survival learning, 411–12
sustainability, organizational, 32–33
sustaining quality
action plans, 409–10
Baldrige Roadmap, 406–07

knowledge management, 411–15
life-cycle model, 405–06
self-assessment, 407–09, 410
System of Profound Knowledge, 48–52. *See also* Deming Philosophy
systems, in Deming Philosophy, 49, 51–52

tacit knowledge, 410–11
Taco Bell, 158
Tampopo, 375
tangible errors, 113–114
targets, 15
task errors, 113
task orientation, 383–84
task-oriented role, 317
Tavistock Institute, 327
Taylor, Frederick W., 10, 187–88
Taylor, Jack, 23
team-based learning, 21
team-based organizations, 278–81
team-based pay and gainsharing, 352
team charters, 322
team members, in Six Sigma, 313
teams
boundary-spanner role, 320
communication on, 320
coordination on, 320–21
corrective-action, 307–9
cross-functional, 30, 107, 251–52, 307–9, 313–14
defined, 304
Deming's 14 Points and, 270
diversity on, 305, 317–18, 327–28
effectiveness of, 314–23, 323
employee engagement, 28–30
examples, 322–26
importance of, 305–6
leadership, 282–84, 307
membership on, 316–18
motivation and, 306
motives for joining, 316–17
natural-work, 309
Olympic, 316
organizational behavior theories on, 327–28
organizational structures and, 273–74, 278–84, 323
organizational support for, 321–23, 323
problem-solving, 307–9
processes of, 318–23
project, 281, 312–13
quality-improvement, 307
reward systems and, 321–23
roles on, 316–18, 320
self-managed, 309–11, 325–27, 340–41
with suppliers, 251–52
training and, 29–30
types of, 29–30, 306
virtual, 311–12
win-win relationships and, 237
vs. groups, 327
teamwork. *See* teams
technical, political, cultural (TPC) matrix, 417
technical features, 103–107
The Technical Support Clerk case study, 90
technology, 14, 285
TecSmart Electronics case study, 93–94
teleological change theory, 417
Tennessee Valley Authority (TVA), 412
Texas Eastman Chemicals Plant, 345
Texas Instruments (TI)
on continuous improvement, 26
customer information, 243
internal benchmarking, 414–15
measuring supplier performance, 251
on quality, 12–13
Texas Instruments Defense Systems and Electronics Group, 68, 157, 372, 413
Texas Nameplate Company, Inc. (TNC)
quality management, 97–98
supplier relationships, 252
teams, 273–74, 279
trust, 344
vision, 371
Theory of Knowledge, 51
Theory X and Theory Y models, 28
Thiede, Edward, 281
3M
customer information, 239
goals, 374
innovation, 196
organizational change, 395
self-managed teams, 310
TI. *See* Texas Instruments (TI)
Tichy's change framework, 417
time, in service organizations, 17. *See also* cycle times
TNC. *See* Texas Nameplate Company, Inc. (TNC)
tolerances, 15
tools. *See also* measurement
affinity diagrams, 210–11
arrow diagrams, 216
cause-and-effect (fishbone) diagrams, 150–151
check sheets, 147–149

concept engineering, 101–102
control charts, 121–124, 152
customer relationship management (CRM) software, 247–48
DFMEA (design failure mode and effects analysis), 107–108
5S's, 152
flowcharts (process maps), 146–147, 276
histograms, 148–149
interrelationship diagraphs, 211–12
just-in-time, 138, 153, 154
for lean thinking, 152–153
matrix data analysis, 214–15
matrix diagrams, 212–14
Pareto diagrams, 149–150
poka-yoke (mistake-proofing), 112–114
process decision program charts (PDPC), 215
pull production (just-in-time), 138, 154
for quality, 146–152
quality function deployment, 102–107, 243
scatter diagrams, 151–152, 244–45
single-minute exchange of dies, 154
source inspection, 154
statistical process control, 120–124, 152, 252
total productive maintenance, 154
tree diagrams, 212, 213
visual controls, 152
Toshiba, 195
total productive maintenance, 154
total quality (TQ). *See also* quality
agency theory and, 35–37
competitive advantage and, 183–85
contextual factors and, 292–4
continuous improvement, 136, 138
culture of, 399–400
customer and stakeholder focus, 23–24
customer-supplier relationships, 236–37
defined, 22–35
employee engagement, 28–30, 337, 338, 355–358
history of, 12
implementation mistakes, 404
ISO 9000:2000 standards and, 78
leadership, 34–35
leadership theory and, 382–388
management by fact, 30–32
measurement and, 62, 200–201
organizational behavior (OB) theories and, 355–358
organizational change and, 418–21
organizational models and, 37–38
organizational structure and, 268–86
organization theory and, 290–294
performance excellence and, 6–7, 22
principles and practices, 22–35
process orientation, 24–27
resistance to change and, 402–03
Resource Dependence Perspective (RDP) and, 255–57
strategic focus, 32–33
strategic management theory and, 223–25
structural contingency theory and, 290–291
tools, 146–152
visionary leadership, 33–35
win-win relationships, 237, 257
total quality management (TQM). *See* total quality (TQ)
Toyota
core competencies, 216
creativity, 160
employee involvement, 339
just-in-time (JIT) improvement, 138
lean thinking, 152, 151
product design, 15
quality function deployment, 103
supplier partnerships, 236
workforce, 187
TPC (technical, political, cultural) matrix, 417
TPD (Corning Telecommunications Products Division), 112, 201, 251–52, 305
TQ. *See* total quality (TQ)
TQM (total quality management). *See* total quality (TQ)
tracking progress, 410
training. *See also* learning
in Deming Philosophy, 54, 55, 58
empowerment and, 345–46
quality and, 16, 18, 53
teamwork and, 29–30
vs. education, 54
transactional Six Sigma, 85
Transformational Leadership Theory, 384–85, 386, 418
treatment errors, 113
tree diagrams, 212, 213
Tribus, Myron, 269
triple bottom line, 13
Trist, Eric, 327
trust
in customer-supplier relationships, 236–39
empowerment and, 28, 343–44
truth, moments of, 245–46

turnover rates, 16
TVA (Tennessee Valley Authority), 412

U.S. election process, 114
U.S. Federal Aviation Administration (FAA), 235
U.S. Steel's Gary Works, 308
U.S. Water Resource Agency case study, 40
Union of Japanese Scientists and Engineers (JUSE), 71, 308
United Airlines, 234
UPS (United Postal Service), 342
USA Today, 395

VA Hospitals, 287–88
value, defined, 183
value analysis, 190
value-creation processes, 271–72
values
  diversity and, 327–28
  examples, 377, 379–80
  leaders and, 33–34, 372–73
  strategic planning and, 204–205
Van de Ven, A. H., 417
variable data, 148
variation, 10, 49–51, 52, 118–120, 251
variety, 193
Vera, Dusya, 418
Veridian Homes, 88
vertical integration, 217
vertical teamwork, 29–30
Veterans' Affairs Hospitals, 287–88
Virgin Atlantic Airways Ltd., 164
virtual teams, 311–12
vision, 33–35, 204–205, 371–72, 376, 378–79. *See also* values
visual controls, 152
Vogt Gary, 345
voice of the customer, 103–107, 241, 242

Wainwright Industries creativity, 161
  cultural change, 401
  customer information, 243
  employee involvement, 339–40
  empowerment, 28, 140
  performance measures, 201
Wales, Jimmy, 326
Walker Auto Sales and Service case study, 296
Walt Disney Company, 127–128, 157
Washington Mutual, 23
waste reduction, 152, 151–153
Waterman, Bob, 190
Wegner, Art, 337
Weisbord's six box model, 417
Welch, Jack, 82–83, 159, 164–165, 370, 371
Welz Business Machines case study, 170–171
Wendy's, 108–109, 194
Western Electric, 10
Westinghouse, 308, 403
Whitney, Eli, 10
Wikipedia, 326
wikis, 285
William Schiemann & Associates, 200
win-win relationships, 237, 257
Woolpert, Bruce, 253
Woolworth, 202
work allocation, 319–20
work environments, 162–164, 355
Workflow Dynamics, Inc., 277–78
workforce focus, 62. *See also* employees
workmanship, 10, 54
work-out (process improvement), 165
work systems, 216–17, 284–86
World War II, 10
Worthington Industries, 316

Xerox
  benchmarking, 155, 390
  case study, 389–390
  functional structure, 269, 270
  leadership, 389–390
  process organization, 281
  quality, 396
  rewards, 322, 322, 353
  suppliers, 250

Yahoo! 271
Yamaha, 195
The Yellow Brick Road to Quality case study, 421
You Want Us to Work with Marketing??? case study, 295–6
Yum Brands, Inc., 348

zero defects (ZD), 57
Zytec, 69